Lecture Notes in Computer Science 13377

More information about this series at https://link.springer.com/bookseries/558

Osvaldo Gervasi · Beniamino Murgante ·
Sanjay Misra · Ana Maria A. C. Rocha ·
Chiara Garau (Eds.)

Computational Science and Its Applications – ICCSA 2022 Workshops

Malaga, Spain, July 4–7, 2022
Proceedings, Part I

 Springer

Editors
Osvaldo Gervasi ⓘD
University of Perugia
Perugia, Italy

Sanjay Misra ⓘD
Østfold University College
Halden, Norway

Chiara Garau ⓘD
University of Cagliari
Cagliari, Italy

Beniamino Murgante ⓘD
University of Basilicata
Potenza, Potenza, Italy

Ana Maria A. C. Rocha ⓘD
University of Minho
Braga, Portugal

ISSN 0302-9743   ISSN 1611-3349 (electronic)
Lecture Notes in Computer Science
ISBN 978-3-031-10535-7   ISBN 978-3-031-10536-4 (eBook)
https://doi.org/10.1007/978-3-031-10536-4

This Springer imprint is published by the registered company Springer Nature Switzerland AG
The registered company address is: Gewerbestrasse 11, 6330 Cham, Switzerland

Preface

These six volumes (LNCS 13377–13382) consist of the peer-reviewed papers from the workshops at the 22nd International Conference on Computational Science and Its Applications (ICCSA 2022), which took place during July 4–7, 2022. The peer-reviewed papers of the main conference tracks are published in a separate set consisting of two volumes (LNCS 13375–13376).

This year, we again decided to organize a hybrid conference, with some of the delegates attending in person and others taking part online. Despite the enormous benefits achieved by the intensive vaccination campaigns in many countries, at the crucial moment of organizing the event, there was no certainty about the evolution of COVID-19. Fortunately, more and more researchers were able to attend the event in person, foreshadowing a slow but gradual exit from the pandemic and the limitations that have weighed so heavily on the lives of all citizens over the past three years.

ICCSA 2022 was another successful event in the International Conference on Computational Science and Its Applications (ICCSA) series. Last year, the conference was held as a hybrid event in Cagliari, Italy, and in 2020 it was organized as virtual event, whilst earlier editions took place in Saint Petersburg, Russia (2019), Melbourne, Australia (2018), Trieste, Italy (2017), Beijing, China (2016), Banff, Canada (2015), Guimaraes, Portugal (2014), Ho Chi Minh City, Vietnam (2013), Salvador, Brazil (2012), Santander, Spain (2011), Fukuoka, Japan (2010), Suwon, South Korea (2009), Perugia, Italy (2008), Kuala Lumpur, Malaysia (2007), Glasgow, UK (2006), Singapore (2005), Assisi, Italy (2004), Montreal, Canada (2003), and (as ICCS) Amsterdam, The Netherlands (2002) and San Francisco, USA (2001).

Computational science is the main pillar of most of the present research, and industrial and commercial applications, and plays a unique role in exploiting ICT innovative technologies. The ICCSA conference series provides a venue to researchers and industry practitioners to discuss new ideas, to share complex problems and their solutions, and to shape new trends in computational science.

Apart from the 52 workshops, ICCSA 2022 also included six main tracks on topics ranging from computational science technologies and application in many fields to specific areas of computational sciences, such as software engineering, security, machine learning and artificial intelligence, and blockchain technologies. For the 52 workshops we have accepted 285 papers. For the main conference tracks we accepted 57 papers and 24 short papers out of 279 submissions (an acceptance rate of 29%). We would like to express our appreciation to the Workshops chairs and co-chairs for their hard work and dedication.

The success of the ICCSA conference series in general, and of ICCSA 2022 in particular, vitally depends on the support of many people: authors, presenters, participants, keynote speakers, workshop chairs, session chairs, organizing committee members, student volunteers, Program Committee members, advisory committee members, international liaison chairs, reviewers, and others in various roles. We take this opportunity to wholehartedly thank them all.

We also wish to thank our publisher, Springer, for their acceptance to publish the proceedings, for sponsoring some of the best papers awards, and for their kind assistance and cooperation during the editing process.

We cordially invite you to visit the ICCSA website https://iccsa.org where you can find all the relevant information about this interesting and exciting event.

July 2022

Osvaldo Gervasi
Beniamino Murgante
Sanjay Misra

Welcome Message from Organizers

The ICCSA 2021 conference in the Mediterranean city of Cagliari provided us with inspiration to offer the ICCSA 2022 conference in the Mediterranean city of Málaga, Spain. The additional considerations due to the COVID-19 pandemic, which necessitated a hybrid conference, also stimulated the idea to use the School of Informatics of the University of Málaga. It has an open structure where we could take lunch and coffee outdoors and the lecture halls have open windows on two sides providing optimal conditions for meeting more safely.

The school is connected to the center of the old town via a metro system, for which we offered cards to the participants. This provided the opportunity to stay in lodgings in the old town close to the beach because, at the end of the day, that is the place to be to exchange ideas with your fellow scientists. The social program allowed us to enjoy the history of Malaga from its founding by the Phoenicians...

In order to provoke as much scientific interaction as possible we organized online sessions that could easily be followed by all participants from their own devices. We tried to ensure that participants from Asia could participate in morning sessions and those from the Americas in evening sessions. On-site sessions could be followed and debated on-site and discussed online using a chat system. To realize this, we relied on the developed technological infrastructure based on open source software, with the addition of streaming channels on YouTube. The implementation of the software infrastructure and the technical coordination of the volunteers were carried out by Damiano Perri and Marco Simonetti. Nine student volunteers from the universities of Málaga, Minho, Almeria, and Helsinki provided technical support and ensured smooth interaction during the conference.

A big thank you goes to all of the participants willing to exchange their ideas during their daytime. Participants of ICCSA 2022 came from 58 countries scattered over many time zones of the globe. Very interesting keynote talks were provided by well-known international scientists who provided us with more ideas to reflect upon, and we are grateful for their insights.

Eligius M. T. Hendrix

Organization

ICCSA 2022 was organized by the University of Malaga (Spain), the University of Perugia (Italy), the University of Cagliari (Italy), the University of Basilicata (Italy), Monash University (Australia), Kyushu Sangyo University (Japan), and the University of Minho, (Portugal).

Honorary General Chairs

Norio Shiratori	Chuo University, Japan
Kenneth C. J. Tan	Sardina Systems, UK

General Chairs

Osvaldo Gervasi	University of Perugia, Italy
Eligius Hendrix	University of Malaga, Italy
Bernady O. Apduhan	Kyushu Sangyo University, Japan

Program Committee Chairs

Beniamino Murgante	University of Basilicata, Italy
Inmaculada Garcia Fernandez	University of Malaga, Spain
Ana Maria A. C. Rocha	University of Minho, Portugal
David Taniar	Monash University, Australia

International Advisory Committee

Jemal Abawajy	Deakin University, Australia
Dharma P. Agarwal	University of Cincinnati, USA
Rajkumar Buyya	Melbourne University, Australia
Claudia Bauzer Medeiros	University of Campinas, Brazil
Manfred M. Fisher	Vienna University of Economics and Business, Austria
Marina L. Gavrilova	University of Calgary, Canada
Sumi Helal	University of Florida, USA, and University of Lancaster, UK
Yee Leung	Chinese University of Hong Kong, China

International Liaison Chairs

Ivan Blečić	University of Cagliari, Italy
Giuseppe Borruso	University of Trieste, Italy

Elise De Donker	Western Michigan University, USA
Maria Irene Falcão	University of Minho, Portugal
Robert C. H. Hsu	Chung Hua University, Taiwan
Tai-Hoon Kim	Beijing Jiaotong University, China
Vladimir Korkhov	St Petersburg University, Russia
Sanjay Misra	Østfold University College, Norway
Takashi Naka	Kyushu Sangyo University, Japan
Rafael D. C. Santos	National Institute for Space Research, Brazil
Maribel Yasmina Santos	University of Minho, Portugal
Elena Stankova	St Petersburg University, Russia

Workshop and Session Organizing Chairs

Beniamino Murgante	University of Basilicata, Italy
Chiara Garau	University of Cagliari, Italy
Sanjay Misra	Ostfold University College, Norway

Award Chair

Wenny Rahayu	La Trobe University, Australia

Publicity Committee Chairs

Elmer Dadios	De La Salle University, Philippines
Nataliia Kulabukhova	St Petersburg University, Russia
Daisuke Takahashi	Tsukuba University, Japan
Shangwang Wang	Beijing University of Posts and Telecommunications, China

Local Arrangement Chairs

Eligius Hendrix	University of Malaga, Spain
Inmaculada Garcia Fernandez	University of Malaga, Spain
Salvador Merino Cordoba	University of Malaga, Spain
Pablo Guerrero-García	University of Malaga, Spain

Technology Chairs

Damiano Perri	University of Florence, Italy
Marco Simonetti	University of Florence, Italy

Program Committee

Vera Afreixo	University of Aveiro, Portugal
Filipe Alvelos	University of Minho, Portugal

Hartmut Asche	Hasso-Plattner-Institut für Digital Engineering gGmbH, Germany
Ginevra Balletto	University of Cagliari, Italy
Michela Bertolotto	University College Dublin, Ireland
Sandro Bimonte	TSCF, INRAE, France
Rod Blais	University of Calgary, Canada
Ivan Blečić	University of Sassari, Italy
Giuseppe Borruso	University of Trieste, Italy
Ana Cristina Braga	University of Minho, Portugal
Massimo Cafaro	University of Salento, Italy
Yves Caniou	ENS Lyon, France
Ermanno Cardelli	University of Perugia, Italy
José A. Cardoso e Cunha	Universidade Nova de Lisboa, Portugal
Rui Cardoso	University of Beira Interior, Portugal
Leocadio G. Casado	University of Almeria, Spain
Carlo Cattani	University of Salerno, Italy
Mete Celik	Erciyes University, Turkey
Maria Cerreta	University of Naples Federico II, Italy
Hyunseung Choo	Sungkyunkwan University, South Korea
Rachel Chieng-Sing Lee	Sunway University, Malaysia
Min Young Chung	Sungkyunkwan University, South Korea
Florbela Maria da Cruz Domingues Correia	Polytechnic Institute of Viana do Castelo, Portugal
Gilberto Corso Pereira	Federal University of Bahia, Brazil
Alessandro Costantini	INFN, Italy
Carla Dal Sasso Freitas	Universidade Federal do Rio Grande do Sul, Brazil
Pradesh Debba	Council for Scientific and Industrial Research (CSIR), South Africa
Hendrik Decker	Instituto Tecnológico de Informática, Spain
Robertas Damaševičius	Kaunas University of Technology, Lithuania
Frank Devai	London South Bank University, UK
Rodolphe Devillers	Memorial University of Newfoundland, Canada
Joana Matos Dias	University of Coimbra, Portugal
Paolino Di Felice	University of L'Aquila, Italy
Prabu Dorairaj	NetApp, India/USA
M. Noelia Faginas Lago	University of Perugia, Italy
M. Irene Falcao	University of Minho, Portugal
Florbela P. Fernandes	Polytechnic Institute of Bragança, Portugal
Jose-Jesus Fernandez	National Centre for Biotechnology, Spain
Paula Odete Fernandes	Polytechnic Institute of Bragança, Portugal
Adelaide de Fátima Baptista Valente Freitas	University of Aveiro, Portugal
Manuel Carlos Figueiredo	University of Minho, Portugal
Maria Celia Furtado Rocha	Federal University of Bahia, Brazil
Chiara Garau	University of Cagliari, Italy
Paulino Jose Garcia Nieto	University of Oviedo, Spain

Raffaele Garrisi	Polizia di Stato, Italy
Jerome Gensel	LSR-IMAG, France
Maria Giaoutzi	National Technical University of Athens, Greece
Arminda Manuela Andrade Pereira Gonçalves	University of Minho, Portugal
Andrzej M. Goscinski	Deakin University, Australia
Sevin Gümgüm	Izmir University of Economics, Turkey
Alex Hagen-Zanker	University of Cambridge, UK
Shanmugasundaram Hariharan	B.S. Abdur Rahman Crescent Institute of Science and Technology, India
Eligius M. T. Hendrix	University of Malaga, Spain and Wageningen University, The Netherlands
Hisamoto Hiyoshi	Gunma University, Japan
Mustafa Inceoglu	Ege University, Turkey
Peter Jimack	University of Leeds, UK
Qun Jin	Waseda University, Japan
Yeliz Karaca	UMass Chan Medical School, USA
Farid Karimipour	Vienna University of Technology, Austria
Baris Kazar	Oracle Corp., USA
Maulana Adhinugraha Kiki	Telkom University, Indonesia
DongSeong Kim	University of Canterbury, New Zealand
Taihoon Kim	Hannam University, South Korea
Ivana Kolingerova	University of West Bohemia, Czech Republic
Nataliia Kulabukhova	St. Petersburg University, Russia
Vladimir Korkhov	St. Petersburg University, Russia
Rosa Lasaponara	National Research Council, Italy
Maurizio Lazzari	National Research Council, Italy
Cheng Siong Lee	Monash University, Australia
Sangyoun Lee	Yonsei University, South Korea
Jongchan Lee	Kunsan National University, South Korea
Chendong Li	University of Connecticut, USA
Gang Li	Deakin University, Australia
Fang (Cherry) Liu	Ames Laboratory, USA
Xin Liu	University of Calgary, Canada
Andrea Lombardi	University of Perugia, Italy
Savino Longo	University of Bari, Italy
Tinghuai Ma	Nanjing University of Information Science and Technology, China
Ernesto Marcheggiani	Katholieke Universiteit Leuven, Belgium
Antonino Marvuglia	Public Research Centre Henri Tudor, Luxembourg
Nicola Masini	National Research Council, Italy
Ilaria Matteucci	National Research Council, Italy
Nirvana Meratnia	University of Twente, The Netherlands
Fernando Miranda	University of Minho, Portugal
Giuseppe Modica	University of Reggio Calabria, Italy
Josè Luis Montaña	University of Cantabria, Spain

Maria Filipa Mourão	Instituto Politécnico de Viana do Castelo, Portugal
Louiza de Macedo Mourelle	State University of Rio de Janeiro, Brazil
Nadia Nedjah	State University of Rio de Janeiro, Brazil
Laszlo Neumann	University of Girona, Spain
Kok-Leong Ong	Deakin University, Australia
Belen Palop	Universidad de Valladolid, Spain
Marcin Paprzycki	Polish Academy of Sciences, Poland
Eric Pardede	La Trobe University, Australia
Kwangjin Park	Wonkwang University, South Korea
Ana Isabel Pereira	Polytechnic Institute of Bragança, Portugal
Massimiliano Petri	University of Pisa, Italy
Telmo Pinto	University of Coimbra, Portugal
Maurizio Pollino	Italian National Agency for New Technologies, Energy and Sustainable Economic Development, Italy
Alenka Poplin	University of Hamburg, Germany
Vidyasagar Potdar	Curtin University of Technology, Australia
David C. Prosperi	Florida Atlantic University, USA
Wenny Rahayu	La Trobe University, Australia
Jerzy Respondek	Silesian University of Technology, Poland
Humberto Rocha	INESC-Coimbra, Portugal
Jon Rokne	University of Calgary, Canada
Octavio Roncero	CSIC, Spain
Maytham Safar	Kuwait University, Kuwait
Chiara Saracino	A.O. Ospedale Niguarda Ca' Granda, Italy
Marco Paulo Seabra dos Reis	University of Coimbra, Portugal
Jie Shen	University of Michigan, USA
Qi Shi	Liverpool John Moores University, UK
Dale Shires	U.S. Army Research Laboratory, USA
Inês Soares	University of Coimbra, Portugal
Elena Stankova	St Petersburg University, Russia
Takuo Suganuma	Tohoku University, Japan
Eufemia Tarantino	Polytechnic Universiy of Bari, Italy
Sergio Tasso	University of Perugia, Italy
Ana Paula Teixeira	University of Trás-os-Montes and Alto Douro, Portugal
M. Filomena Teodoro	Portuguese Naval Academy and University of Lisbon, Portugal
Parimala Thulasiraman	University of Manitoba, Canada
Carmelo Torre	Polytechnic University of Bari, Italy
Javier Martinez Torres	Centro Universitario de la Defensa Zaragoza, Spain
Giuseppe A. Trunfio	University of Sassari, Italy
Pablo Vanegas	University of Cuenca, Equador
Marco Vizzari	University of Perugia, Italy
Varun Vohra	Merck Inc., USA
Koichi Wada	University of Tsukuba, Japan
Krzysztof Walkowiak	Wroclaw University of Technology, Poland

Zequn Wang	Intelligent Automation Inc, USA
Robert Weibel	University of Zurich, Switzerland
Frank Westad	Norwegian University of Science and Technology, Norway
Roland Wismüller	Universität Siegen, Germany
Mudasser Wyne	National University, USA
Chung-Huang Yang	National Kaohsiung Normal University, Taiwan
Xin-She Yang	National Physical Laboratory, UK
Salim Zabir	France Telecom Japan Co., Japan
Haifeng Zhao	University of California, Davis, USA
Fabiana Zollo	Ca' Foscari University of Venice, Italy
Albert Y. Zomaya	University of Sydney, Australia

Workshop Organizers

International Workshop on Advances in Artificial Intelligence Learning Technologies: Blended Learning, STEM, Computational Thinking and Coding (AAILT 2022)

Alfredo Milani	University of Perugia, Italy
Valentina Franzoni	University of Perugia, Italy
Osvaldo Gervasi	University of Perugia, Italy

International Workshop on Advancements in Applied Machine-Learning and Data Analytics (AAMDA 2022)

Alessandro Costantini	INFN, Italy
Davide Salomoni	INFN, Italy
Doina Cristina Duma	INFN, Italy
Daniele Cesini	INFN, Italy

International Workshop on Advances in Information Systems and Technologies for Emergency Management, Risk Assessment and Mitigation Based on the Resilience (ASTER 2022)

Maurizio Pollino	ENEA, Italy
Marco Vona	University of Basilicata, Italy
Sonia Giovinazzi	ENEA, Italy
Benedetto Manganelli	University of Basilicata, Italy
Beniamino Murgante	University of Basilicata, Italy

International Workshop on Advances in Web Based Learning (AWBL 2022)

Birol Ciloglugil	Ege University, Turkey
Mustafa Inceoglu	Ege University, Turkey

International Workshop on Blockchain and Distributed Ledgers: Technologies and Applications (BDLTA 2022)

Vladimir Korkhov	St Petersburg State University, Russia
Elena Stankova	St Petersburg State University, Russia
Nataliia Kulabukhova	St Petersburg State University, Russia

International Workshop on Bio and Neuro Inspired Computing and Applications (BIONCA 2022)

Nadia Nedjah	State University of Rio De Janeiro, Brazil
Luiza De Macedo Mourelle	State University of Rio De Janeiro, Brazil

International Workshop on Configurational Analysis For Cities (CA CITIES 2022)

Claudia Yamu	Oslo Metropolitan University, Norway
Valerio Cutini	Università di Pisa, Italy
Beniamino Murgante	University of Basilicata, Italy
Chiara Garau	Dicaar, University of Cagliari, Italy

International Workshop on Computational and Applied Mathematics (CAM 2022)

Maria Irene Falcão	University of Minho, Portugal
Fernando Miranda	University of Minho, Portugal

International Workshop on Computational and Applied Statistics (CAS 2022)

Ana Cristina Braga	University of Minho, Portugal

International Workshop on Computational Mathematics, Statistics and Information Management (CMSIM 2022)

Maria Filomena Teodoro	University of Lisbon and Portuguese Naval Academy, Portugal

International Workshop on Computational Optimization and Applications (COA 2022)

Ana Maria A. C. Rocha	University of Minho, Portugal
Humberto Rocha	University of Coimbra, Portugal

International Workshop on Computational Astrochemistry (CompAstro 2022)

Marzio Rosi	University of Perugia, Italy
Nadia Balucani	University of Perugia, Italy
Cecilia Ceccarelli	Université Grenoble Alpes, France
Stefano Falcinelli	University of Perugia, Italy

International Workshop on Computational Methods for Porous Geomaterials (CompPor 2022)

Vadim Lisitsa	Sobolev Institute of Mathematics, Russia
Evgeniy Romenski	Sobolev Institute of Mathematics, Russia

International Workshop on Computational Approaches for Smart, Conscious Cities (CASCC 2022)

Andreas Fricke	University of Potsdam, Germany
Juergen Doellner	University of Potsdam, Germany
Salvador Merino	University of Malaga, Spain
Jürgen Bund	Graphics Vision AI Association, Germany/Portugal
Markus Jobst	Federal Office of Metrology and Surveying, Austria
Francisco Guzman	University of Malaga, Spain

International Workshop on Computational Science and HPC (CSHPC 2022)

Elise De Doncker	Western Michigan University, USA
Fukuko Yuasa	High Energy Accelerator Research Organization (KEK), Japan
Hideo Matsufuru	High Energy Accelerator Research Organization (KEK), Japan

International Workshop on Cities, Technologies and Planning (CTP 2022)

Giuseppe Borruso	University of Trieste, Italy
Malgorzata Hanzl	Lodz University of Technology, Poland
Beniamino Murgante	University of Basilicata, Italy

Anastasia Stratigea   National Technical University of Athens, Grece
Ginevra Balletto   University of Cagliari, Italy
Ljiljana Zivkovic   Republic Geodetic Authority, Serbia

International Workshop on Digital Sustainability and Circular Economy (DiSCE 2022)

Giuseppe Borruso   University of Trieste, Italy
Stefano Epifani   Digital Sustainability Institute, Italy
Ginevra Balletto   University of Cagliari, Italy
Luigi Mundula   University of Cagliari, Italy
Alessandra Milesi   University of Cagliari, Italy
Mara Ladu   University of Cagliari, Italy
Stefano De Nicolai   University of Pavia, Italy
Tu Anh Trinh   University of Economics Ho Chi Minh City, Vietnam

International Workshop on Econometrics and Multidimensional Evaluation in Urban Environment (EMEUE 2022)

Carmelo Maria Torre   Polytechnic University of Bari, Italy
Maria Cerreta   University of Naples Federico II, Italy
Pierluigi Morano   Polytechnic University of Bari, Italy
Giuliano Poli   University of Naples Federico II, Italy
Marco Locurcio   Polytechnic University of Bari, Italy
Francesco Tajani   Sapienza University of Rome, Italy

International Workshop on Ethical AI Applications for a Human-Centered Cyber Society (EthicAI 2022)

Valentina Franzoni   University of Perugia, Italy
Alfredo Milani   University of Perugia, Italy

International Workshop on Future Computing System Technologies and Applications (FiSTA 2022)

Bernady Apduhan   Kyushu Sangyo University, Japan
Rafael Santos   INPE, Brazil

International Workshop on Geodesign in Decision Making: Meta Planning and Collaborative Design for Sustainable and Inclusive Development (GDM 2022)

Francesco Scorza   University of Basilicata, Italy
Michele Campagna   University of Cagliari, Italy
Ana Clara Mourão Moura   Federal University of Minas Gerais, Brazil

International Workshop on Geomatics in Agriculture and Forestry: New Advances and Perspectives (GeoForAgr 2022)

Maurizio Pollino	ENEA, Italy
Giuseppe Modica	University of Reggio Calabria, Italy
Marco Vizzari	University of Perugia, Italy

International Workshop on Geographical Analysis, Urban Modeling, Spatial Statistics (Geog-An-Mod 2022)

Giuseppe Borruso	University of Trieste, Italy
Beniamino Murgante	University of Basilicata, Italy
Harmut Asche	Hasso-Plattner-Institut für Digital Engineering gGmbH, Germany

International Workshop on Geomatics for Resource Monitoring and Management (GRMM 2022)

Alessandra Capolupo	Polytechnic of Bari, Italy
Eufemia Tarantino	Polytechnic of Bari, Italy
Enrico Borgogno Mondino	University of Turin, Italy

International Workshop on Information and Knowledge in the Internet of Things (IKIT 2022)

Teresa Guarda	State University of Santa Elena Peninsula, Ecuador
Filipe Portela	University of Minho, Portugal
Maria Fernanda Augusto	Bitrum Research Center, Spain

13th International Symposium on Software Quality (ISSQ 2022)

Sanjay Misra	Østfold University College, Norway

International Workshop on Machine Learning for Space and Earth Observation Data (MALSEOD 2022)

Rafael Santos	INPE, Brazil
Karine Reis Ferreira Gomes	INPE, Brazil

International Workshop on Building Multi-dimensional Models for Assessing Complex Environmental Systems (MES 2022)

Vanessa Assumma	Politecnico di Torino, Italy
Caterina Caprioli	Politecnico di Torino, Italy
Giulia Datola	Politecnico di Torino, Italy

Federico Dell'Anna   Politecnico di Torino, Italy
Marta Dell'Ovo   Politecnico di Milano, Italy

International Workshop on Models and Indicators for Assessing and Measuring the Urban Settlement Development in the View of ZERO Net Land Take by 2050 (MOVEto0 2022)

Lucia Saganeiti   University of L'Aquila, Italy
Lorena Fiorini   University of L'aquila, Italy
Angela Pilogallo   University of Basilicata, Italy
Alessandro Marucci   University of L'Aquila, Italy
Francesco Zullo   University of L'Aquila, Italy

International Workshop on Modelling Post-Covid Cities (MPCC 2022)

Beniamino Murgante   University of Basilicata, Italy
Ginevra Balletto   University of Cagliari, Italy
Giuseppe Borruso   University of Trieste, Italy
Marco Dettori   Università degli Studi di Sassari, Italy
Lucia Saganeiti   University of L'Aquila, Italy

International Workshop on Ecosystem Services: Nature's Contribution to People in Practice. Assessment Frameworks, Models, Mapping, and Implications (NC2P 2022)

Francesco Scorza   University of Basilicata, Italy
Sabrina Lai   University of Cagliari, Italy
Silvia Ronchi   University of Cagliari, Italy
Dani Broitman   Israel Institute of Technology, Israel
Ana Clara Mourão Moura   Federal University of Minas Gerais, Brazil
Corrado Zoppi   University of Cagliari, Italy

International Workshop on New Mobility Choices for Sustainable and Alternative Scenarios (NEWMOB 2022)

Tiziana Campisi   University of Enna Kore, Italy
Socrates Basbas   Aristotle University of Thessaloniki, Greece
Aleksandra Deluka T.   University of Rijeka, Croatia
Alexandros Nikitas   University of Huddersfield, UK
Ioannis Politis   Aristotle University of Thessaloniki, Greece
Georgios Georgiadis   Aristotle University of Thessaloniki, Greece
Irena Ištoka Otković   University of Osijek, Croatia
Sanja Surdonja   University of Rijeka, Croatia

International Workshop on Privacy in the Cloud/Edge/IoT World (PCEIoT 2022)

Michele Mastroianni	University of Campania Luigi Vanvitelli, Italy
Lelio Campanile	University of Campania Luigi Vanvitelli, Italy
Mauro Iacono	University of Campania Luigi Vanvitelli, Italy

International Workshop on Psycho-Social Analysis of Sustainable Mobility in the Pre- and Post-Pandemic Phase (PSYCHE 2022)

Tiziana Campisi	University of Enna Kore, Italy
Socrates Basbas	Aristotle University of Thessaloniki, Greece
Dilum Dissanayake	Newcastle University, UK
Nurten Akgün Tanbay	Bursa Technical University, Turkey
Elena Cocuzza	University of Catania, Italy
Nazam Ali	University of Management and Technology, Pakistan
Vincenza Torrisi	University of Catania, Italy

International Workshop on Processes, Methods and Tools Towards Resilient Cities and Cultural Heritage Prone to SOD and ROD Disasters (RES 2022)

Elena Cantatore	Polytechnic University of Bari, Italy
Alberico Sonnessa	Polytechnic University of Bari, Italy
Dario Esposito	Polytechnic University of Bari, Italy

International Workshop on Scientific Computing Infrastructure (SCI 2022)

Elena Stankova	St Petersburg University, Russia
Vladimir Korkhov	St Petersburg University, Russia

International Workshop on Socio-Economic and Environmental Models for Land Use Management (SEMLUM 2022)

Debora Anelli	Polytechnic University of Bari, Italy
Pierluigi Morano	Polytechnic University of Bari, Italy
Francesco Tajani	Sapienza University of Rome, Italy
Marco Locurcio	Polytechnic University of Bari, Italy
Paola Amoruso	LUM University, Italy

14th International Symposium on Software Engineering Processes and Applications (SEPA 2022)

Sanjay Misra	Østfold University College, Norway

International Workshop on Ports of the Future – Smartness and Sustainability (SmartPorts 2022)

Giuseppe Borruso	University of Trieste, Italy
Gianfranco Fancello	University of Cagliari, Italy
Ginevra Balletto	University of Cagliari, Italy
Patrizia Serra	University of Cagliari, Italy
Maria del Mar Munoz Leonisio	University of Cadiz, Spain
Marco Mazzarino	University of Venice, Italy
Marcello Tadini	Università del Piemonte Orientale, Italy

International Workshop on Smart Tourism (SmartTourism 2022)

Giuseppe Borruso	University of Trieste, Italy
Silvia Battino	University of Sassari, Italy
Ainhoa Amaro Garcia	Universidad de Alcalà and Universidad de Las Palmas, Spain
Maria del Mar Munoz Leonisio	University of Cadiz, Spain
Carlo Donato	University of Sassari, Italy
Francesca Krasna	University of Trieste, Italy
Ginevra Balletto	University of Cagliari, Italy

International Workshop on Sustainability Performance Assessment: Models, Approaches and Applications Toward Interdisciplinary and Integrated Solutions (SPA 2022)

Francesco Scorza	University of Basilicata, Italy
Sabrina Lai	University of Cagliari, Italy
Jolanta Dvarioniene	Kaunas University of Technology, Lithuania
Iole Cerminara	University of Basilicata, Italy
Georgia Pozoukidou	Aristotle University of Thessaloniki, Greece
Valentin Grecu	Lucian Blaga University of Sibiu, Romania
Corrado Zoppi	University of Cagliari, Italy

International Workshop on Specifics of Smart Cities Development in Europe (SPEED 2022)

Chiara Garau	University of Cagliari, Italy
Katarína Vitálišová	Matej Bel University, Slovakia
Paolo Nesi	University of Florence, Italy
Anna Vanova	Matej Bel University, Slovakia
Kamila Borsekova	Matej Bel University, Slovakia
Paola Zamperlin	University of Pisa, Italy

| Federico Cugurullo | Trinity College Dublin, Ireland |
| Gerardo Carpentieri | University of Naples Federico II, Italy |

International Workshop on Smart and Sustainable Island Communities (SSIC 2022)

Chiara Garau	University of Cagliari, Italy
Anastasia Stratigea	National Technical University of Athens, Greece
Paola Zamperlin	University of Pisa, Italy
Francesco Scorza	University of Basilicata, Italy

International Workshop on Theoretical and Computational Chemistry and Its Applications (TCCMA 2022)

| Noelia Faginas-Lago | University of Perugia, Italy |
| Andrea Lombardi | University of Perugia, Italy |

International Workshop on Transport Infrastructures for Smart Cities (TISC 2022)

Francesca Maltinti	University of Cagliari, Italy
Mauro Coni	University of Cagliari, Italy
Francesco Pinna	University of Cagliari, Italy
Chiara Garau	University of Cagliari, Italy
Nicoletta Rassu	Univesity of Cagliari, Italy
James Rombi	University of Cagliari, Italy
Benedetto Barabino	University of Brescia, Italy

14th International Workshop on Tools and Techniques in Software Development Process (TTSDP 2022)

| Sanjay Misra | Østfold University College, Norway |

International Workshop on Urban Form Studies (UForm 2022)

Malgorzata Hanzl	Lodz University of Technology, Poland
Beniamino Murgante	University of Basilicata, Italy
Alessandro Camiz	Özyeğin University, Turkey
Tomasz Bradecki	Silesian University of Technology, Poland

International Workshop on Urban Regeneration: Innovative Tools and Evaluation Model (URITEM 2022)

Fabrizio Battisti	University of Florence, Italy
Laura Ricci	Sapienza University of Rome, Italy
Orazio Campo	Sapienza University of Rome, Italy

International Workshop on Urban Space Accessibility and Mobilities (USAM 2022)

Chiara Garau	University of Cagliari, Italy
Matteo Ignaccolo	University of Catania, Italy
Enrica Papa	University of Westminster, UK
Francesco Pinna	University of Cagliari, Italy
Silvia Rossetti	University of Parma, Italy
Wendy Tan	Wageningen University and Research, The Netherlands
Michela Tiboni	University of Brescia, Italy
Vincenza Torrisi	University of Catania, Italy

International Workshop on Virtual Reality and Augmented Reality and Applications (VRA 2022)

Osvaldo Gervasi	University of Perugia, Italy
Damiano Perri	University of Florence, Italy
Marco Simonetti	University of Florence, Italy
Sergio Tasso	University of Perugia, Italy

International Workshop on Advanced and Computational Methods for Earth Science Applications (WACM4ES 2022)

Luca Piroddi	University of Cagliari, Italy
Sebastiano Damico	University of Malta, Malta

International Workshop on Advanced Mathematics and Computing Methods in Complex Computational Systems (WAMCM 2022)

Yeliz Karaca	UMass Chan Medical School, USA
Dumitru Baleanu	Cankaya University, Turkey
Osvaldo Gervasi	University of Perugia, Italy
Yudong Zhang	University of Leicester, UK
Majaz Moonis	UMass Chan Medical School, USA

Additional Reviewers

Akshat Agrawal	Amity University, Haryana, India
Waseem Ahmad	National Institute of Technology Karnataka, India
Vladimir Alarcon	Universidad Diego Portales, Chile
Oylum Alatlı	Ege University, Turkey
Raffaele Albano	University of Basilicata, Italy
Abraham Alfa	FUT Minna, Nigeria
Diego Altafini	Università di Pisa, Italy
Filipe Alvelos	Universidade do Minho, Portugal

Marina Alexandra Pedro Andrade	ISCTE-IUL, Portugal
Debora Anelli	Polytechnic University of Bari, Italy
Gennaro Angiello	AlmavivA de Belgique, Belgium
Alfonso Annunziata	Università di Cagliari, Italy
Bernady Apduhan	Kyushu Sangyo University, Japan
Daniela Ascenzi	Università degli Studi di Trento, Italy
Burak Galip Aslan	Izmir Insitute of Technology, Turkey
Vanessa Assumma	Politecnico di Torino, Italy
Daniel Atzberger	Hasso-Plattner-Institute für Digital Engineering gGmbH, Germany
Dominique Aury	École Polytechnique Fédérale de Lausanne, Switzerland
Joseph Awotumde	University of Alcala, Spain
Birim Balci	Celal Bayar University, Turkey
Juliana Balera	INPE, Brazil
Ginevra Balletto	University of Cagliari, Italy
Benedetto Barabino	University of Brescia, Italy
Kaushik Barik	University of Alcala, Spain
Carlo Barletta	Politecnico di Bari, Italy
Socrates Basbas	Aristotle University of Thessaloniki, Greece
Rosaria Battarra	ISMed-CNR, Italy
Silvia Battino	University of Sassari, Italy
Chiara Bedan	University of Trieste, Italy
Ranjan Kumar Behera	National Institute of Technology Rourkela, India
Gulmira Bekmanova	L.N. Gumilyov Eurasian National University, Kazakhstan
Mario Bentivenga	University of Basilicata, Italy
Asrat Mulatu Beyene	Addis Ababa Science and Technology University, Ethiopia
Tiziana Binda	Politecnico di Torino, Italy
Giulio Biondi	University of Firenze, Italy
Alexander Bogdanov	St Petersburg University, Russia
Costanza Borghesi	University of Perugia, Italy
Giuseppe Borruso	University of Trieste, Italy
Marilisa Botte	University of Naples Federico II, Italy
Tomasz Bradecki	Silesian University of Technology, Poland
Ana Cristina Braga	University of Minho, Portugal
Luca Braidotti	University of Trieste, Italy
Bazon Brock	University of Wuppertal, Germany
Dani Broitman	Israel Institute of Technology, Israel
Maria Antonia Brovelli	Politecnico di Milano, Italy
Jorge Buele	Universidad Tecnológica Indoamérica, Ecuador
Isabel Cacao	University of Aveiro, Portugal
Federica Cadamuro Morgante	Politecnico di Milano, Italy

Rogerio Calazan	IEAPM, Brazil
Michele Campagna	University of Cagliari, Italy
Lelio Campanile	Università degli Studi della Campania Luigi Vanvitelli, Italy
Tiziana Campisi	University of Enna Kore, Italy
Antonino Canale	University of Enna Kore, Italy
Elena Cantatore	Polytechnic University of Bari, Italy
Patrizia Capizzi	Univerity of Palermo, Italy
Alessandra Capolupo	Polytechnic University of Bari, Italy
Giacomo Caporusso	Politecnico di Bari, Italy
Caterina Caprioli	Politecnico di Torino, Italy
Gerardo Carpentieri	University of Naples Federico II, Italy
Martina Carra	University of Brescia, Italy
Pedro Carrasqueira	INESC Coimbra, Portugal
Barbara Caselli	Università degli Studi di Parma, Italy
Cecilia Castro	University of Minho, Portugal
Giulio Cavana	Politecnico di Torino, Italy
Iole Cerminara	University of Basilicata, Italy
Maria Cerreta	University of Naples Federico II, Italy
Daniele Cesini	INFN, Italy
Jabed Chowdhury	La Trobe University, Australia
Birol Ciloglugil	Ege University, Turkey
Elena Cocuzza	Univesity of Catania, Italy
Emanuele Colica	University of Malta, Malta
Mauro Coni	University of Cagliari, Italy
Elisete Correia	Universidade de Trás-os-Montes e Alto Douro, Portugal
Florbela Correia	Polytechnic Institute of Viana do Castelo, Portugal
Paulo Cortez	University of Minho, Portugal
Lino Costa	Universidade do Minho, Portugal
Alessandro Costantini	INFN, Italy
Marilena Cozzolino	Università del Molise, Italy
Alfredo Cuzzocrea	University of Calabria, Italy
Sebastiano D'amico	University of Malta, Malta
Gianni D'Angelo	University of Salerno, Italy
Tijana Dabovic	University of Belgrade, Serbia
Hiroshi Daisaka	Hitotsubashi University, Japan
Giulia Datola	Politecnico di Torino, Italy
Regina De Almeida	University of Trás-os-Montes and Alto Douro, Portugal
Maria Stella De Biase	Università della Campania Luigi Vanvitelli, Italy
Elise De Doncker	Western Michigan University, USA
Itamir De Morais Barroca Filho	Federal University of Rio Grande do Norte, Brazil
Samuele De Petris	University of Turin, Italy
Alan De Sá	Marinha do Brasil, Brazil
Alexander Degtyarev	St Petersburg University, Russia

Federico Dell'Anna	Politecnico di Torino, Italy
Marta Dell'Ovo	Politecnico di Milano, Italy
Ahu Dereli Dursun	Istanbul Commerce University, Turkey
Giulia Desogus	University of Cagliari, Italy
Piero Di Bonito	Università degli Studi della Campania, Italia
Paolino Di Felice	University of L'Aquila, Italy
Felicia Di Liddo	Polytechnic University of Bari, Italy
Isabel Dimas	University of Coimbra, Portugal
Doina Cristina Duma	INFN, Italy
Aziz Dursun	Virginia Tech University, USA
Jaroslav Dvořak	Klaipėda University, Lithuania
Dario Esposito	Polytechnic University of Bari, Italy
M. Noelia Faginas-Lago	University of Perugia, Italy
Stefano Falcinelli	University of Perugia, Italy
Falcone Giacomo	University of Reggio Calabria, Italy
Maria Irene Falcão	University of Minho, Portugal
Stefano Federico	CNR-ISAC, Italy
Marcin Feltynowski	University of Lodz, Poland
António Fernandes	Instituto Politécnico de Bragança, Portugal
Florbela Fernandes	Instituto Politecnico de Braganca, Portugal
Paula Odete Fernandes	Instituto Politécnico de Bragança, Portugal
Luis Fernandez-Sanz	University of Alcala, Spain
Luís Ferrás	University of Minho, Portugal
Ângela Ferreira	Instituto Politécnico de Bragança, Portugal
Lorena Fiorini	University of L'Aquila, Italy
Hector Florez	Universidad Distrital Francisco Jose de Caldas, Colombia
Stefano Franco	LUISS Guido Carli, Italy
Valentina Franzoni	Perugia University, Italy
Adelaide Freitas	University of Aveiro, Portugal
Andreas Fricke	Hasso Plattner Institute, Germany
Junpei Fujimoto	KEK, Japan
Federica Gaglione	Università del Sannio, Italy
Andrea Gallo	Università degli Studi di Trieste, Italy
Luciano Galone	University of Malta, Malta
Adam Galuszka	Silesian University of Technology, Poland
Chiara Garau	University of Cagliari, Italy
Ernesto Garcia Para	Universidad del País Vasco, Spain
Aniket A. Gaurav	Østfold University College, Norway
Marina Gavrilova	University of Calgary, Canada
Osvaldo Gervasi	University of Perugia, Italy
Andrea Ghirardi	Università di Brescia, Italy
Andrea Gioia	Politecnico di Bari, Italy
Giacomo Giorgi	Università degli Studi di Perugia, Italy
Stanislav Glubokovskikh	Lawrence Berkeley National Laboratory, USA
A. Manuela Gonçalves	University of Minho, Portugal

Leocadio González Casado	University of Almería, Spain
Angela Gorgoglione	Universidad de la República Uruguay, Uruguay
Yusuke Gotoh	Okayama University, Japan
Daniele Granata	Università degli Studi della Campania, Italy
Christian Grévisse	University of Luxembourg, Luxembourg
Silvana Grillo	University of Cagliari, Italy
Teresa Guarda	State University of Santa Elena Peninsula, Ecuador
Carmen Guida	Università degli Studi di Napoli Federico II, Italy
Kemal Güven Gülen	Namık Kemal University, Turkey
Ipek Guler	Leuven Biostatistics and Statistical Bioinformatics Centre, Belgium
Sevin Gumgum	Izmir University of Economics, Turkey
Martina Halásková	VSB Technical University in Ostrava, Czech Republic
Peter Hegedus	University of Szeged, Hungary
Eligius M. T. Hendrix	Universidad de Málaga, Spain
Mauro Iacono	Università degli Studi della Campania, Italy
Oleg Iakushkin	St Petersburg University, Russia
Matteo Ignaccolo	University of Catania, Italy
Mustafa Inceoglu	Ege University, Turkey
Markus Jobst	Federal Office of Metrology and Surveying, Austria
Issaku Kanamori	RIKEN Center for Computational Science, Japan
Yeliz Karaca	UMass Chan Medical School, USA
Aarti Karande	Sardar Patel Institute of Technology, India
András Kicsi	University of Szeged, Hungary
Vladimir Korkhov	St Petersburg University, Russia
Nataliia Kulabukhova	St Petersburg University, Russia
Claudio Ladisa	Politecnico di Bari, Italy
Mara Ladu	University of Cagliari, Italy
Sabrina Lai	University of Cagliari, Italy
Mark Lajko	University of Szeged, Hungary
Giuseppe Francesco Cesare Lama	University of Napoli Federico II, Italy
Vincenzo Laporta	CNR, Italy
Margherita Lasorella	Politecnico di Bari, Italy
Francesca Leccis	Università di Cagliari, Italy
Federica Leone	University of Cagliari, Italy
Chien-sing Lee	Sunway University, Malaysia
Marco Locurcio	Polytechnic University of Bari, Italy
Francesco Loddo	Henge S.r.l., Italy
Andrea Lombardi	Università di Perugia, Italy
Isabel Lopes	Instituto Politécnico de Bragança, Portugal
Fernando Lopez Gayarre	University of Oviedo, Spain
Vanda Lourenço	Universidade Nova de Lisboa, Portugal
Jing Ma	Luleå University of Technology, Sweden
Helmuth Malonek	University of Aveiro, Portugal
Francesca Maltinti	University of Cagliari, Italy

Fernando Pirani	University of Perugia, Italy
Luca Piroddi	University of Cagliari, Italy
Bojana Pjanović	University of Belgrade, Serbia
Giuliano Poli	University of Naples Federico II, Italy
Maurizio Pollino	ENEA, Italy
Salvatore Praticò	University of Reggio Calabria, Italy
Zbigniew Przygodzki	University of Lodz, Poland
Carlotta Quagliolo	Politecnico di Torino, Italy
Raffaele Garrisi	Polizia Postale e delle Comunicazioni, Italy
Mariapia Raimondo	Università della Campania Luigi Vanvitelli, Italy
Deep Raj	IIIT Naya Raipur, India
Buna Ramos	Universidade Lusíada Norte, Portugal
Nicoletta Rassu	Univesity of Cagliari, Italy
Michela Ravanelli	Sapienza Università di Roma, Italy
Roberta Ravanelli	Sapienza Università di Roma, Italy
Pier Francesco Recchi	University of Naples Federico II, Italy
Stefania Regalbuto	University of Naples Federico II, Italy
Marco Reis	University of Coimbra, Portugal
Maria Reitano	University of Naples Federico II, Italy
Anatoly Resnyansky	Defence Science and Technology Group, Australia
Jerzy Respondek	Silesian University of Technology, Poland
Isabel Ribeiro	Instituto Politécnico Bragança, Portugal
Albert Rimola	Universitat Autònoma de Barcelona, Spain
Corrado Rindone	University of Reggio Calabria, Italy
Ana Maria A. C. Rocha	University of Minho, Portugal
Humberto Rocha	University of Coimbra, Portugal
Maria Clara Rocha	Instituto Politécnico de Coimbra, Portugal
James Rombi	University of Cagliari, Italy
Elisabetta Ronchieri	INFN, Italy
Marzio Rosi	University of Perugia, Italy
Silvia Rossetti	Università degli Studi di Parma, Italy
Marco Rossitti	Politecnico di Milano, Italy
Mária Rostašová	Universtiy of Žilina, Slovakia
Lucia Saganeiti	University of L'Aquila, Italy
Giovanni Salzillo	Università degli Studi della Campania, Italy
Valentina Santarsiero	University of Basilicata, Italy
Luigi Santopietro	University of Basilicata, Italy
Stefania Santoro	Politecnico di Bari, Italy
Rafael Santos	INPE, Brazil
Valentino Santucci	Università per Stranieri di Perugia, Italy
Mirko Saponaro	Polytechnic University of Bari, Italy
Filippo Sarvia	University of Turin, Italy
Andrea Scianna	ICAR-CNR, Italy
Francesco Scorza	University of Basilicata, Italy
Ester Scotto Di Perta	University of Naples Federico II, Italy
Ricardo Severino	University of Minho, Portugal

Jie Shen	University of Michigan, USA
Luneque Silva Junior	Universidade Federal do ABC, Brazil
Carina Silva	Instituto Politécnico de Lisboa, Portugal
Joao Carlos Silva	Polytechnic Institute of Cavado and Ave, Portugal
Ilya Silvestrov	Saudi Aramco, Saudi Arabia
Marco Simonetti	University of Florence, Italy
Maria Joana Soares	University of Minho, Portugal
Michel Soares	Federal University of Sergipe, Brazil
Alberico Sonnessa	Politecnico di Bari, Italy
Lisete Sousa	University of Lisbon, Portugal
Elena Stankova	St Petersburg University, Russia
Jan Stejskal	University of Pardubice, Czech Republic
Silvia Stranieri	University of Naples Federico II, Italy
Anastasia Stratigea	National Technical University of Athens, Greece
Yue Sun	European XFEL GmbH, Germany
Anthony Suppa	Politecnico di Torino, Italy
Kirill Sviatov	Ulyanovsk State Technical University, Russia
David Taniar	Monash University, Australia
Rodrigo Tapia-McClung	Centro de Investigación en Ciencias de Información Geoespacial, Mexico
Eufemia Tarantino	Politecnico di Bari, Italy
Sergio Tasso	University of Perugia, Italy
Vladimir Tcheverda	Institute of Petroleum Geology and Geophysics, SB RAS, Russia
Ana Paula Teixeira	Universidade de Trás-os-Montes e Alto Douro, Portugal
Tengku Adil Tengku Izhar	Universiti Teknologi MARA, Malaysia
Maria Filomena Teodoro	University of Lisbon and Portuguese Naval Academy, Portugal
Yiota Theodora	National Technical University of Athens, Greece
Graça Tomaz	Instituto Politécnico da Guarda, Portugal
Gokchan Tonbul	Atilim University, Turkey
Rosa Claudia Torcasio	CNR-ISAC, Italy
Carmelo Maria Torre	Polytechnic University of Bari, Italy
Vincenza Torrisi	University of Catania, Italy
Vincenzo Totaro	Politecnico di Bari, Italy
Pham Trung	HCMUT, Vietnam
Po-yu Tsai	National Chung Hsing University, Taiwan
Dimitrios Tsoukalas	Centre of Research and Technology Hellas, Greece
Toshihiro Uchibayashi	Kyushu University, Japan
Takahiro Ueda	Seikei University, Japan
Piero Ugliengo	Università degli Studi di Torino, Italy
Gianmarco Vanuzzo	University of Perugia, Italy
Clara Vaz	Instituto Politécnico de Bragança, Portugal
Laura Verde	University of Campania Luigi Vanvitelli, Italy
Katarína Vitálišová	Matej Bel University, Slovakia

Daniel Mark Vitiello	University of Cagliari, Italy
Marco Vizzari	University of Perugia, Italy
Alexander Vodyaho	St. Petersburg State Electrotechnical University "LETI", Russia
Agustinus Borgy Waluyo	Monash University, Australia
Chao Wang	USTC, China
Marcin Wozniak	Silesian University of Technology, Poland
Jitao Yang	Beijing Language and Culture University, China
Fenghui Yao	Tennessee State University, USA
Fukuko Yuasa	KEK, Japan
Paola Zamperlin	University of Pisa, Italy
Michal Žemlička	Charles University, Czech Republic
Nataly Zhukova	ITMO University, Russia
Alcinia Zita Sampaio	University of Lisbon, Portugal
Ljiljana Zivkovic	Republic Geodetic Authority, Serbia
Floriana Zucaro	University of Naples Federico II, Italy
Marco Zucca	Politecnico di Milano, Italy
Camila Zyngier	Ibmec, Belo Horizonte, Brazil

Sponsoring Organizations

ICCSA 2022 would not have been possible without tremendous support of many organizations and institutions, for which all organizers and participants of ICCSA 2022 express their sincere gratitude:

Springer International Publishing AG, Germany (https://www.springer.com)

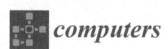

Computers Open Access Journal (https://www.mdpi.com/journal/computers)

Computation Open Access Journal (https://www.mdpi.com/journal/computation)

University of Malaga, Spain (https://www.uma.es/)

University of Perugia, Italy
(https://www.unipg.it)

University of Basilicata, Italy
(http://www.unibas.it)

Monash University, Australia
(https://www.monash.edu/)

Kyushu Sangyo University, Japan
(https://www.kyusan-u.ac.jp/)

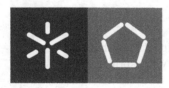

University of Minho, Portugal
(https://www.uminho.pt/)

Universidade do Minho
Escola de Engenharia

Contents – Part I

**International Workshop on Advances in information Systems
and Technologies for Emergency management, risk assessment
and mitigation based on the Resilience (ASTER 2022)**

**International Workshop on Advances in Web Based Learning
(AWBL 2022)**

**International Workshop on Block chain and Distributed Ledgers:
Technologies and Applications (BDLTA 2022)**

International Workshop on Bio and Neuro inspired Computing and Applications (BIONCA 2022)

International Workshop on Configurational Analysis for Cities (CA CITIES 2022)

International Workshop on Advances in Artificial Intelligence Learning Technologies: Blended Learning, STEM, Computational Thinking and Coding (AAILT 2022)

Real-Time Flight Recording via Mobile Devices for Autonomous and Assisted Navigation Tasks

Edison Espinosa[1]([✉]), Víctor H. Andaluz[1], and Víctor Enríquez[2]

[1] Universidad de las Fuerzas Armadas ESPE, Sangolquí, Ecuador
{egespinosa1,vhandaluz1}@espe.edu.ec
[2] Centro de Investigación y Desarrollo de las Fuerza Aérea Ecuatoriana, Ambato, Ecuador
venriquez@fae.mil.ec

Abstract. This article presents the implementation of an application developed under the android operating system to evaluate the actions performed after a flight mission in manned aircrafts. The informatics application will be installed on an Android device that will be transported by a crew member of the aircraft. In order to obtain the required signals for the post-flight analysis, two sensors are used: Global Positioning System (GPS) and Inertial Measurement Unit (IMU), which are immersed in the Android device. The information generated at aircraft corresponding to the attitude and position is stored within a SD memory of the android device. The stored data corresponding to the position are: latitude, length, height, velocity, and hour; while the data corresponding to the attitude are Roll, Pitch, and Yaw.

Keywords: Software development · Mobile applications · Android · Debriefing · Aircraft

1 Introduction

In the military field, flight practices can be real or simulated and are carried out through flight missions that include the planning, briefing, fulfillment and debriefing phases of the mission [1]. The debriefing tasks (post-flight) are routine and mandatory once the flight practice is finished and they bring together the personnel involved in the flight mission in order to analyze everything that happened during the mission, e.g., flight path, flight behavior. the aircraft, emotional states of the pilot, skills and abilities of the pilot. The information collected with the objective that the pilots improve or maintain their performance for future flight missions [2].

In order to carry out the debriefing analysis, data obtained from the flight mission must be available that allow knowing the behavior of the personnel involved in the mission. These data are commonly stored in a file that is generated in two ways: *i) On board the aircraft,* in this case it is necessary to wait for the aircraft to complete the flight mission, in order to download the generated file and analyze the fulfillment of the

O. Gervasi et al. (Eds.): ICCSA 2022 Workshops, LNCS 13377, pp. 3–14, 2022.
https://doi.org/10.1007/978-3-031-10536-4_1

mission; and *ii) Remotely* for this case, a means of communication is considered that allows the monitoring of the flight mission from a remote control station. The aicraft must be permanently linked with the command station, to avoid the risk of losing flight information.

Currently there are several commercial tools, e.g., Commercial Off The Shelf (COTS) developed especially to perform virtual analysis based on military requirements using logs generated in real or simulated missions. The American company AGI has the STK Highlights tool that performs all stages of a flight from planning to debriefing [3–5]. In addition, the company Viasat has the FlightTestAnalyzer tool that allows migrating the trajectory and positioning data of the aircraft stored in a file to the Google Earth platform [3]. Finally, The Universal Flight Analysis Tool allows to simulate the flight of the aircraft by reading data from a file in which the altitude and positioning information of the aircraft is stored.

As described, this paper reports the development and implementation of a Gpsimu apk implemented in the Android PAD IP67 device, which was tested in a hexacopter and in an aircraft. The preliminary results show that the data allows the generation of information to support the Debriefing analysis in real or simulated flight missions and allows the operators to supervise and control the fulfillment of the mission in relation to the trajectory and behavior of the aircraft. In addition, this paper presents the modeling and autonomous control of an unmanned aerial vehicle (UAV). The design of a controller based on the kinematics of the UAV is presented in which the saturation of the maneuverability velocities through trigonometric functions is considered. Finally, the results obtained from the autonomous control of the UAV are presented; and the experimental results obtained from the data acquisition system for which an Aircraft Flight of the Armed Forces of Ecuador (FAE) is considered.

The paper is structured in 4 Sections including the Introduction: In Sect. 2, the developed architecture of the data acquisition system is described. In addition, the modeling and autonomous control of the UAV is presented. The tests performed are detailed in Sect. 3. Meanwhile, Sect. 4 describes the conclusions and future work.

2 Data Acquisition System Architecture

Figure 1 shows the proposed architecture of the data acquisition system that supports the execution of Debriefing tasks, considering the real-time monitoring of data obtained through the GPS (Global Positioning System) and IMU (Inertial Measuring Unit) sensors.). The information collected is analyzed with the android device scale, in order to organize the information and generate a flat file (*.csv) that is commonly stored on the computer disk or in an external device. The stored data will be analyzed with the use of commercially available tools [6].

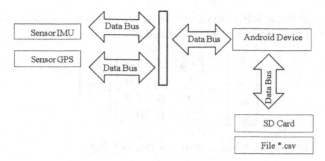

Fig. 1. Android device architecture.

The sensors that are connected to the data acquisition system can be analog or digital, coming from the GPS, IMU, and the physiological characteristics sensor. The data acquired from the GPS are latitude, longitude, height, speed, time. Meanwhile, the data acquired from the IMU are angles of roll (Roll), pitch (Pitch), yaw (Yaw). In aeronautics, three direction axes l, m and n are considered, on the mobile reference system. The l axis is the direction of motion (usually the axis that passes through the nose and tail of the aircraft). The m axis is perpendicular to the direction of movement, always in the same plane of the plane (the axis that passes through the wings). Finally, the n axis is considered the axis perpendicular to the previous ones, and therefore perpendicular to the plane of the plane, see Fig. 2.

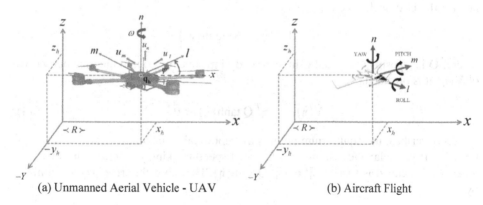

(a) Unmanned Aerial Vehicle - UAV   (b) Aircraft Flight

Fig. 2. Turning axes

2.1 Unmanned Aerial Vehicle Modeling and Control

To obtain the kinematic model of the UAV, the point of interest in the robot center is considered. The kinematic model of the aerial robot contains the four maneuverability velocities to achieve displacement and four velocities that represent the velocities within the frame of reference. Figure 1 represents the kinematic variables of the quadcopter on the fixed reference frame <R>. In other words, the movement of the quadcopter over the fixed frame of the reference <R> is defined as:

$$
\begin{bmatrix} \dot{\eta}_x \\ \dot{\eta}_y \\ \dot{\eta}_z \\ \dot{\eta}_\psi \end{bmatrix} = \begin{bmatrix} C_\psi & -S_\psi & 0 & 0 \\ S_\psi & C_\psi & 0 & 0 \\ 0 & 0 & 1 & 0 \\ 0 & 0 & 0 & 1 \end{bmatrix} \begin{bmatrix} u_l \\ u_m \\ u_n \\ \omega \end{bmatrix} \tag{1}
$$

Equation (1) can be described in matrix form, as follows:

$$
\dot{\eta}(t) = \mathbf{J_Q}(\mathbf{q_Q})\mathbf{u}(t) \tag{2}
$$

where, $\dot{\eta}(t) \in R^n$ represents the velocity vector of the point of interest with respect to the inertial reference system $\{\mathcal{R}\}$; $\mathbf{J_Q}(\mathbf{q_Q}) \in R^{m \times n}$ is the Jacobian matrix of the UAV; and $\mathbf{u}(t) \in \mathfrak{R}^n$ is the maneuverability vector of the UAV with respect to $\{\mathcal{R_Q}\}$ with $m = n = 4$ the $\mathbf{J_Q}(\mathbf{q_Q})$ matrix is of full rank with $|\mathbf{J_Q}| = 1$.

For the UAV autonomous navigation mission $\eta_d = [\, \eta_{xd}\; \eta_{yd}\; \eta_{zd}\,]^T$ of the UAV with a variation $\dot{\eta}_d = [\, \dot{\eta}_{xd}\; \dot{\eta}_{yd}\; \dot{\eta}_{zd}\,]^T$ are obtained; therefore, the control error is defined as $\tilde{\eta}(t) = \eta_d(t) - \eta(t)$ with its variation in time $\dot{\tilde{\eta}} = \dot{\eta}_d - \dot{\eta}$. In order to demonstrate stability, a Lyapunov-based controller is proposed. Proposing a positive candidate function defined as, $\mathbf{V}(\tilde{\eta}) = \frac{1}{2}\tilde{\eta}^T\tilde{\eta} > 0$. Taking the first derivative and replacing $\dot{\tilde{\eta}} = \dot{\eta}_d - \dot{\eta}$ and considering that $\dot{\eta} = \mathbf{J_Q}\mathbf{u}$ is obtained, $\dot{\mathbf{V}}(\tilde{\eta}) = \tilde{\eta}^T(\dot{\eta}_d - \mathbf{J_Q}\mathbf{u})$. The proposed control law for the UAV is defined as,

$$
\mathbf{u} = \mathbf{J_Q}^{-1}\left(\dot{\eta}_d + \mathbf{Q}\tanh(\tilde{\eta})\right) \tag{3}
$$

where, $\mathbf{Q}$ is a positive diagonal gain matrix. By introducing (3) into the time derivative of $\dot{\mathbf{V}}(\tilde{\eta})$ it is obtained.,

$$
\dot{\mathbf{V}}(\tilde{\eta}) = -\tilde{\eta}^T\mathbf{Q}\tanh(\tilde{\eta}) < 0 \tag{4}
$$

As described, the equilibrium point is asymptotically stable, *i.e.* $\tilde{\eta}(t) \to 0$ asymptotically. If you relax the assumption of perfect speed tracking you have to $\tilde{\mathbf{u}} = \mathbf{u}_d - \mathbf{u}$ where (4) is defined as $\dot{\mathbf{V}}(\tilde{\eta}) = \tilde{\eta}^T\tilde{\mathbf{u}} - \tilde{\eta}^T\mathbf{Q}\tanh(\tilde{\eta})$. Therefore, the error $\tilde{\eta}(t)$ is delimited by,

$$
\|\tilde{\eta}\| \leq \frac{\|\tilde{\mathbf{u}}\|}{\zeta\lambda_{\min}(Q)}; \quad \text{with } 0 < \zeta < 1 \tag{5}
$$

Therefore, if $\tilde{\mathbf{u}}(t) \neq 0$ the formation error $\tilde{\mathbf{h}}(t)$ is ultimately bounded by (5).

2.2 Data Acquisition System Algorithm

The algorithm of the acquisition system is implemented in an apk called Gpsimu that must be downloaded to mobile or fixed devices. This algorithm includes three blocks of code in the first lines of code enable permissions to the GPS device to determine that the API use WiFi data or mobile data that establishes the location of the device. The API returns the location through the available location providers, including the GPS global positioning system and WFi data and mobile data cell phone using the android. Permission functions. ACCESS_COARSE_LOCATION and android.permission. ACCESS_FINE_LOCATION. The second block of code allows to establish the trajectory and the behavior of the aircraft based on obtaining the positioning, height, speed, time, attitude, Roll, Pitch, Yaw. Finally, the third block of code allows the information to be stored in a *.cvs file that will then be processed for mission analysis. The operation algorithm of the acquisition system represented in the flow diagram is shown in Fig. 3.

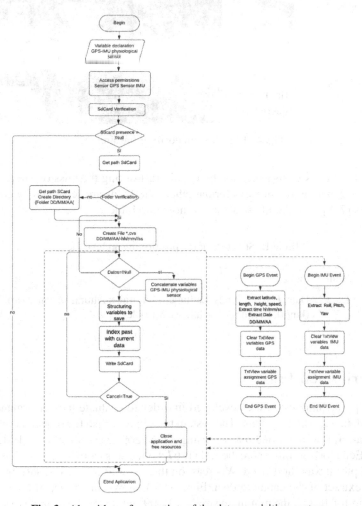

Fig. 3. Algorithm of operation of the data acquisition system.

2.3 Operation of the Data Acquisition System

The Gpsimu APK must be installed on a mobile or fixed processing device. For this work, an IP67 PAD that is placed on board the aircraft was considered, as shown in Fig. 4.

APP for data reading

Data Storage

Handheld
Rugged IP67

Fig. 4. PAD IP67 on board of the aircraft

The data of the signals generated by the aircraft during the mission are recorded in the IP67 PAD in a flat file in *.cvs format where the fields are separated by commas or semicolons [7, 8]. The flat file structure is shown in Table 1.

Table 1. Structure of the positioning archive file

Extension	Name	Fields
CSV	Date	Date, Hour, seconds, Latitude, Longitude, Altura, Distance (m), Velocity (km/h), Roll(deg), Pitch(deg), Yaw(deg)

3 Experimental Tests

Several experimental tests were developed in order to evaluate the performance of the proposed data acquisition system. The system tests to establish the trajectory and behavior of the aircraft were carried out first using a hexacopter and then on an FAE (Armed Forces of Ecuador) aircraft where the PAD IP67 device was placed, see Fig. 5. The test in the hexacopter it was short-lived. Whereas, on the air-craft it was long lasting. Figure 6 shows an extract of the captured data. Figure 6(a) shows an extract of the time-stress relationship for 100[s], the minimum stress is 11,09, while the maximum stress is about 12,8. Figure 6(b) shows the heart rate maintained a minimum average frequency of 65,08 and a maximum frequency of 76,79. Finally, Fig. 6(c) shows temperature during the 100[s].

(a) Unmanned aerial vehicle with six rotating propellers

(b) Aircraft Flight

Fig. 5. Aerial vehicles for experimental tests with the IP67 PAD device

3.1 UAV Autonomous Navigation

For the control of the hexacopter, an autonomous mission is considered, for which the control law proposed in Subsect. 2.1 is considered. Figure 7 presents the results of the experiment, showing the desired task and the task obtained by implementing the autonomous control through the controller proposed in the Eq. (3). Figure 8 shows the control errors, where it can be seen that the errors are finally bounded, as demonstrated in the robustness analysis in Eq. (5).

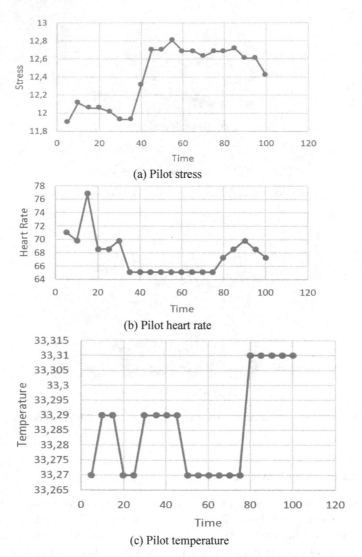

(a) Pilot stress

(b) Pilot heart rate

(c) Pilot temperature

Fig. 6. Extract of data stored in the archive.

3.2 Results of the Roll, Pitch and Yaw Attitude Variables

Aircraft navigation angles are a type of Euler angle that is used to indicate the orientation of an object in three dimensions. The angles as indicated are yaw, pitch, and roll. [9] The device used to store the three angles that give the aircraft attitude has an internally inertial sensor (IMU) which delivers the values of the angles in radians (roll, pitch and yaw). To verify the efficiency of the sensor used to acquire the aircraft's attitude parameters, a comparison pattern was used. The 3DMGX525 sensor [10] was in-stalled on the platform with the data acquisition device and the data obtained was logged and the results generated are shown in Figs. 9, 10 and 11.

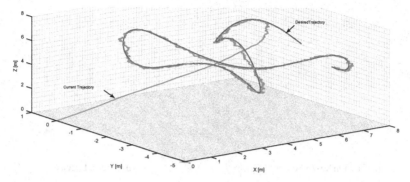

Fig. 7. Stroboscopic movement of the autonomous control of the UAV

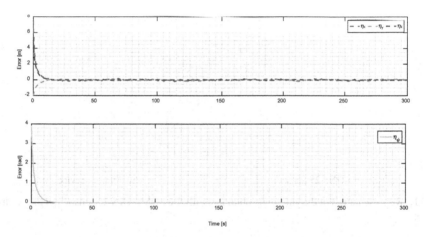

Fig. 8. UAV control errors

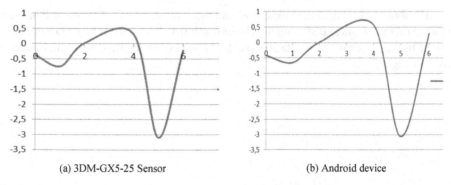

(a) 3DM-GX5-25 Sensor   (b) Android device

Fig. 9. Representation of the roll angle obtained with the 3DM-GX5-25 sensor and the Android

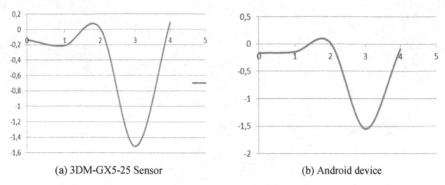

(a) 3DM-GX5-25 Sensor   (b) Android device

Fig. 10. Representation of the pitch angle obtained with the 3DM-GX5-25 sensor and the Android

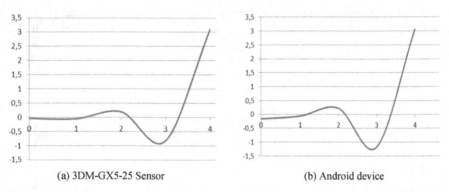

(a) 3DM-GX5-25 Sensor   (b) Android device

Fig. 11. Representation of the yaw angle obtained with the 3DM-GX5-25 sensor and the Android device.

3.3   Results of the Positioning Variables

The data obtained on board the hexacopter and the King Air FAE 1141 manned aircraft that were recorded and stored using the Gpsimu apk installed in the IP67 PAD were used as input in the Tacview flight data analysis tool to generate the trajectory and behavior shown in Fig. 12.

(a) Flight Reconstruction of the Unmanned Aerial Vehicle With Six Rotating Propellers.

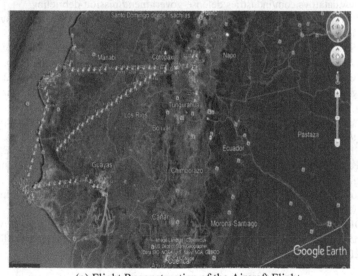

(a) Flight Reconstruction of the Aircraft Flight

Fig. 12. Representation of the data obtained from the log generated from the hexacopter and aircraft file

4 Conclusions

This research was aimed at solving the problem of obtaining data in real time to carry out debriefing analysis based on storing data in real time for subsequent processing and analysis. The Gpsimu apk was developed and installed in an Android PAD IP67 device and the tests were generated in a hexacopter and an aircraft. The results found when analyzing the data stored in the file with the *.csc extension is coherent, practical and very useful to carry out the Debriefing analysis in real or simulated missions and allows the operators to supervise and control the fulfillment of the mission. Finally, as future work, it is proposed to visualize the trajectory and behavior of the aircraft in real time in the same mobile device app.

Acknowledgements. The authors would like to thank the Universidad de las Fuerzas Armadas ESPE for the financing given to research and development of the project "Sistema experto para el análisis y diagnóstico en tiempo real de una misión de vuelo"; also to ESPE Innovativa E.P.; Centro de Investigación Científica y Tecnológica del Ejercito (CICTE); Centro de Investigación y Desarrollo de las Fuerza Aérea Ecuatoriana (CIDFAE); and Grupo de Investigación GITBIO y ARSI, for the support for the development of this work.

References

1. IFIS3 (2018). http://www.ais.aviacioncivil.gob.ec/ifis3/aip/ENR%201.10
2. Mission Debriefing - Datatoys Data & Video Systems by Bad Wolf Technologies (2018). http://www.datatoys.com/industries/defense-government/mission-debriefing/
3. ViaSat Inc. Video/ISR Data Links | ViaSat (1986–2016). https://www.viasat.com/products/isr-data-links
4. Bansal, S.K.: Towards a semantic extract-transform-load (ETL) framework for big data integration. In: 2014 IEEE International Congress on Big Data, Anchorage, AK, pp. 522–529. IEEE Press, New York (2014). https://doi.org/10.1109/BigData.Congress.2014.82
5. AGI Engineering Tools STK Highlights. https://www.agi.com/products/engineeringtools
6. Tacview The Universal Flight Analysis Tool. https://www.tacview.net/
7. Pimienta, P.: Arquitecturas de aplicaciones moviles. ZENVA PTY LTD (2018). https://deidea aapp.org/arquitecturas-de-aplicaciones-moviles/
8. Mahmud, S., Hossin, M., Jahan, H., Noori, S., Bhuiyan, T.: CSV-ANNOTATE: generate annotated tables from CSV file. In: 2018 International Conference On Artificial Intelligence And Big Data (ICAIBD) (2018). https://doi.org/10.1109/icaibd.2018.8396169
9. Shafranovich, Y.: Common Format and MIME Type for Comma-Separated Values (CSV) Files. IETF RFC 4180, October 2005. http://tools.ietf.org/html/rfc4180
10. VECTORNAV, Embedde Navigation Solutions VN-200 GPS-Aided INS. https://www.vector nav.com/products/vn-200?gclid=Cj0KCQjwof3cBRD9ARIsAP8x70PiuHeXjIZ8f0MZQe wQKrseEsjRKlefnnF-Rtey_2A6fHfE9jCoEoMaAleZEALw_wcB

Natural Language Processing and Deep Learning Based Techniques for Evaluation of Companies' Privacy Policies

Saka John[1]($\boxtimes$), Binyamin Adeniyi Ajayi[1], and Samaila Musa Marafa[2]

[1] Department of Computer Science, Nasarawa State University Keffi, Keffi, Nigeria
1johnsaka78@yahoo.com
[2] Department of Computer Science, Federal University Gusau, Gusau, Nigeria

Abstract. Companies' websites are vulnerable to privacy attacks that can compromise the confidentiality of data which, particularly in sensitive use cases like personal data, financial transaction details, medical diagnosis, could be detrimental and unethical. The noncompliance of companies with privacy policies requirements as stipulated by the various Data Protection Regulations has raised lot of concerns for users and other practitioners. To address this issue, previous research developed a model using conventional algorithms such as Neural Network (NN), Logistic Regression (LR) and Support Vector Machine (SVM) to evaluate the levels of compliance of companies to general data protection regulations. However, the research performance shows to be unsatisfactory as the model's performance across the selected core requirements of the legislation attained F1-score of between 0.52–0.71. This paper improved this model's performance by using Natural Language Processing (NLP) and Deep Learning (DL) techniques. This was done by evaluating the same dataset used by the previous researcher to train the proposed model. The overall results show that LSTM outperform both GRU and CNN models in terms of F1-score and accuracy. This research paper is to assist the Supervisory Authority and other practitioners to better determine the state of companies' privacy policies compliance with the relevant data protection regulations.

Keywords: Privacy policies · Natural language processing · Deep Learning · Manual Annotation · Machine Learning · Artificial Intelligent · Crowdsourcing

1 Introduction

Companies' privacy policies are legal document that are generally used to communicate how the personal information or data collected are used or managed. Accepting it means that users have agreed to release their personal information and data to the company as contained in the conditions specified by the company policy (Costante et al. 2012). Today, businesses around the world generally depend on data and other related information that are derived from people's data. Nowadays, data is the world's most important and

O. Gervasi et al. (Eds.): ICCSA 2022 Workshops, LNCS 13377, pp. 15–32, 2022.
https://doi.org/10.1007/978-3-031-10536-4_2

valuable resources, it is no longer oil (Labadie and Legner 2019). Thus, data is of more value than many other assets.

However, due to the widespread breaches and leaks of data and then information, many users are now concerned about its privacy. As a result, they would like to know the privacy control that can be exercised by them in privacy policy (Sathyendra et al. 2017). To comply with provisions of data protection regulations, companies are now being forced to appraise and simplify their privacy policies to make their users or customers aware of how their data are collected, processed and used (Sánchez et al. 2021). Thus, data privacy has become the most significant issues in companies across the globe. There is need for transparency in how companies obtain consent, abide with their policies and effectively manage all data collected from the users. This is vital in building a strong trust and accountability with all customers and other partners who expect data privacy (Chika and Tochukwu 2020).

Many business owners and companies have taken steps to protect their user's data by drafting a concise and clear company's privacy policy that gives user a better understanding of how their data is being processed or used. This is expected to instill faith, trust and protects companies from a number of liability issues. Most countries have adopted or are in the course of adopting an all-inclusive data protection regulation similar to the General Data Protection Regulation (GDPR). In January 2019, Nigeria released a revised legislation called the Nigeria Data Protection Regulation (NDPR), which resemble the current GDPR. The NDPR was designed to completely change the corporate and other personal transactions within the country in order to strengthen data privacy and protection policies.

Table 1. GDPR Requirements (Muller et al. 2019)

No	Category	Required companies privacy policy content
1	DPO	Contact details for the data protection officer or Equivalent
2	Purpose	Disclosure of the purpose for which personal data is or is not used for
3	Acquired Data Disclosure	that personal data is or is not collected, and/or which data is collected
4	Data sharing	Disclosure if 3rd parties can or cannot access a user's personal data
5	Rights	Disclosure of the user's right to rectify or erase personal data

This study evaluates companies' privacy policies using NLP and DL based techniques so as to determine the state of various companies' privacy policies compliance with the data protection and privacy legislation. A study that has developed a similar model in the past is (Muller, Kowatsch, Debus, Mirdita & Böttinger, 2019). The authors created a dataset labelled in accordance to the core GDPR requirements to support practitioners in analysis and detection of policy non-compliance with the provision of GDPR as shown in Table 1.

However, their model's F1-scores performance achieved between 0.52–0.71 across the five core requirements of the data protection regulations. This study aims to improve this model performance by using NLP and DL as well as a more proficient word embedding technique to achieve a better result.

2 Related Works

Most of the existing literature in the area of data protection regulations and privacy policies tackles different issues of compliance, readability and clarity of the privacy policies. Most of the researchers employed the use of NLP, DL, Manual Annotation, Machine Learning, Artificial Intelligent, Crowdsourcing and Automatic Classification techniques.

A study, Connor (2004) analyzed companies' privacy statement and found that in most cases, they failed to comply with globally known standard The study designed an intelligent software to carry out an in-depth structural analysis of privacy policies documents using content analysis techniques on a small data set. Also, to ensure the privacy of children's data Micheti et al. (2010) designed a privacy policies re-written framework and employed comparative analysis using statistical methods. Their framework encouraged teenagers to use personal data and information on company website.

Similarly, Costante et al. (2012) developed a solution to enable users make an informed decision while surfing the internet. The study used shallow machine learning approach to build text classifier. This classifier was tested by simulating a user browsing session and obtained an accuracy of 99.3% and 97.9% precision, but the recall was relatively. In Sadeh et al. (2013), the researcher showed that many users hardly read these policies and those who sometimes does most often struggle to understand its content. The study developed an algorithm that interpret companies' privacy policies using traditional ML and NLP. This approach only allows user to gain a deeper understanding of the privacy policies and to drive the privacy decision making processes.

To provide better understanding of the privacy policies documents, Zimmeck and Bellovin (2014) designed Privee - a software architecture for analyzing essential policy. It combines crowd sourcing with rule and machine learning classifiers to classify privacy policies that are not already rated in the crowd sourcing repository. The classifiers achieved an overall F1-score of 90%. However, this was done before the advent of GDPR.

In Liu et al. (2016), the author developed a DNN for vector representation of textual content in the companies' privacy policies documents. The study designed and analyzed vector representations for each of the word or token in the privacy policies documents. This was fed into the Long Short Term Memory Visualization tools (LSTMV) so as to test it capability to learn semantically and syntactically vague terms.

Due to the fact that the companies' privacy policy is usually very long, (Sathyendra et al. 2017) presented another way to detect text of choices in privacy policy documents. The study used corpus that consists of 115 website privacy policies and annotations created by law students. The authors achieved a F1-score of 0.735 for their classification model. This technique enabled the creation of systems to help internet users to learn about their choices, thereby improving data privacy.

Goltz and Mayo (2018) investigated the issue of non-compliance and proposed a framework to enhance regulatory compliance using Machine Learning (ML) to identify compliance clauses in the regulations. The study obtained an average accuracy of 90% for all approaches. Similarly, an automated framework for Privacy Policy Analysis Polisis, was introduced by Harkous et al. (2018). The study used Convolutional Neural Networks (CNNs) internally within all the classifiers to analyze and examine the depth and breadth of companies' privacy policies. This was done to summarize what Personally Identifiable Information, PII, that the companies' privacy policies documents claim to be requesting for, collecting from their users and sharing with other partners.

Zaeem et al. (2018) designed a browser add-on called Privacy Check that gives graphical and at-a-glance detailed summary of companies' privacy policies textual documents. Privacy Check used data mining tool to analyze textual content of the privacy policies documents and answers the ten (10) basic questions in respect of user's data privacy and data security as well as the information that are being collected from the users and how they are being used.

Another study, Andow et al. (2019) developed Policy Lint with the aid of NLP tool to find potential contradictions in the privacy policies text of various company. The study analysis focused on policies of Android apps. Privacy Guide was developed by Tesfay et al. (2018) to examine the issues of privacy policies readability and other complexities associated with the document. This guide was designed based on ML and NLP techniques. However, due to the problem of extracting companies' privacy policies online using web scrapers, Degeling et al. (2018) developed a system that can automatically scan websites for links to firm's privacy policies documents. The study used NLP tools to perform the analysis on the word-level and check if companies' privacy policies documents stated the phrases that are specifically mentioned in the data protection and privacy regulations.

In all the foregoing related studies, the most closely related work to the proposed study is Müller et al. (2019). The study introduced new labeled dataset of companies' privacy policies to study GDPR compliance. This dataset comprises of 250 companies' privacy policies text of different firms and over 18,390 sentences, labeled across the five (5) major classes of Acquired Data, Rights, DPO, Data Sharing and Purpose, were applied to a set of NLP and ML algorithms to analyze the dataset. The study achieved F1-scores of 0.52–0.71 across these five classes of data protection requirements. However, this result shows there is room to improve their work with respect to word embedding techniques and the classification algorithm. The subsequent sections highlight the procedure employed to obtained the set goals.

3   Methodology and Proposed Architecture

This section focusses on the research designs and techniques that were adopted in this study with the aim of achieving the research objectives. The goal of this study is to improve the performance of the model developed by Müller et al. (2019). Doing this, it developed a model that increase the F1-score and also address observed methodological gaps in their work.

The proposed model was experimented on the same dataset used by Müller et al. (2019). It is informative that the author used NLP tool and ML algorithms such as SVM,

LR and NN. However, the model's performance seems to be unsatisfactory as it only achieved a classification accuracies F1-scores between 0.52 to 0.71 across the five core requirements of data protection regulations. According to Franzoni and Kozak (2021), since performances of classifiers based on LR and SVM were not particularly remarkable, the possibility to improve their precision has been explored, applying different techniques of feature extraction and feature selection.

This research work relies mostly on the secondary data sourced from the first large-scale dataset created by (Müller et al. 2019) for GDPR compliance test. Using mathematical models or deep learning approaches, they result highly efficient on basic models (Baia et al. (2022). Hence, the proposed solution seeks to improve the model using NLP techniques, GloVe Word Embedding techniques and DL algorithms. Thus, DL algorithms availed include Long Short-Term Memory (LSTM), Gated Recurrent Unit (GRU) and Convolutional Neural Network (CNN) were used for classification of companies' privacy policies documents based on core requirements of data protection regulations.

3.1 Proposed Companies' Privacy Policies Analysis Framework

Companies' websites usually disclose new rules, products, information and technologies that are being implemented. Although, this information is generally available to the public, when extracted from the organization's website, it is usually unstructured (Kinne and Axenbeck 2018). Hence, there is need to refine this information with a more reliable methodology for collection or gathering and harmonizing companies' privacy policies text. This is to enable extraction of the core requirements of data protection and privacy regulations done with a view to check the companies' compliance with these legislations, which is the goal of this research work.

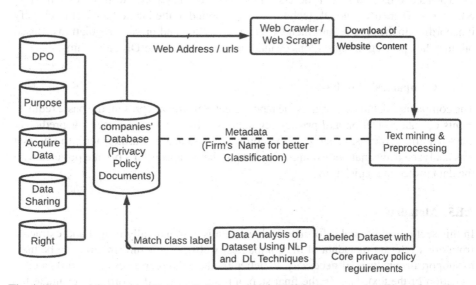

Fig. 1. Proposed Companies' Privacy Policies Analysis (CPPA) Framework. Adapted from Kinne and Axenbeck (2018)

Figure 1 outlined a methodology tagged Companies' Privacy Policies Analysis (CPPA) Framework adapted from Kinne and Axenbeck (2018). The framework is proposed for extracting and classifying the companies' privacy policies based on the identified core requirement of data protection and privacy regulation. The details components of this methodology were discussed in the next sub-section.

3.1.1 Web Crawler or Web Scraper

In the first step, web crawler or web scraper is to download the website content containing the privacy policies of various company. The main data and information that is extracted includes the privacy policy statement, company name and website addresses (URLs). However, since this study is to use the dataset created by Müller et al. (2019) there is no need to repeat this process.

3.1.2 Text Mining and Preprocessing

A text mining is also known as text data mining which is the process of deriving relevant information or information of interest for the classification of privacy policies documents so as to draw meaningful insights and patterns from the unstructured data. At this stage, the textual data that is extracted during the first stage is preprocess so as to clean the text document into a form that is predictable and analyzable for the task at hand. Data preprocessing organize a raw textual data for processing.

3.1.3 Data Analysis Using NLP and DL Techniques

At this point, relevant textual data was analyzed using a combination of NLP tools to extract needed data to match the class label. The top keywords were extracted using NLP tools. Thereafter, the DL techniques was applied to the labeled dataset to classify it according to the core requirements of data protection and privacy regulations. Based on this, data protection regulations evaluation is perform using DL algorithms.

3.1.4 Companies' Database

The companies' database contains the labelled dataset which represent the basic requirements of data protection and privacy regulations. This dataset was used for predictive classification purposes, or store in the companies' database. Furthermore, the dataset was analyzed to evaluate or examine the state of the organization's private policies with the data protection legislations.

3.1.5 Metadata

In this section, additional information about data is automatically mined and extracted from other relevant metadata of the companies' website. This information can be used to support the analysis, if necessary, to better enhance the preprocessing and data classification of the text data. In the final step, a model is trained in order to evaluate the state of companies' privacy policies using the core requirements of data protection and privacy regulations described in Table 1.

3.2 System Architecture

The proposed approach was developed using NLP, DL and sentence embedding pre-training techniques for the analysis and evaluation of companies' privacy policies documents. A deep neural network was trained using textual data which were extracted from websites of organizations for which established privacy policies are obtainable. These policies were used to create the training data set of labelled textual data.

According to Kinne and Axenbeck (2018) recent developments in the NLP gives DL approaches a more potentially and make it most promising when it comes to gathering data and information about processes and activity based on textual document content. In this study, the privacy policies text classification was carried out using NLP techniques and DL algorithms. Figure 2 illustrates the schema of the proposed model system architecture adapted from Kinne and Axenbeck (2018).

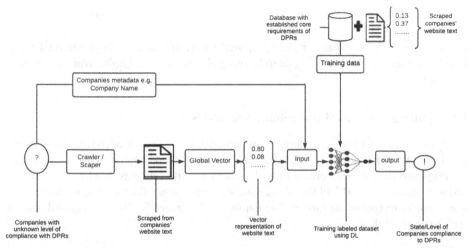

Fig. 2. Proposed Approach for the Evaluation of Companies Privacy Policies using NLP and DL Technique, Adapted from Kinne and Axenbeck (2018)

In Fig. 2, the first step is to extract the dataset from the companies' web data. The dataset contains information about the organization's privacy policy, url, name, location and address of the company. This dataset was used to train the model that checks if the companies' privacy policies contain core requirements of the data protection regulations. However, for the purpose of this study, a secondary dataset that has been extracted from companies with unknown level of data privacy compliance created by Müller et al. (2019) was adopted.

The second step deal with the analysis of the data set mined by the previous study from the companies' privacy policies. Likewise, a number of NLP tools was employed along with word embeddings techniques such as GloVe to map textual data to their respective vector representation. Each instance was mapped into a deep semantic vector representation and used as input to train the proposed model.

Finally, a DL algorithm and training data sets were used to build, develop and train the proposed model. Meanwhile, the information extracted from unseen companies' privacy policies (test data) were used to test the trained model. The model was then analyzed and evaluated to check if it contains the core requirements stipulated by DPR.

3.3 Programming Language

For the implementation of this study, the programming language of choice is Python version 3.6. Other software requirements were TensorFlow and Keras DL frameworks. This software was executed on Window Operating System environment deployed on HP Laptop, Core (TM)i3-5005U CPU with 4 GB of RAM and 2 GHz Processor Speed. All the required libraries were installed on the python note-book and used for the data analysis and models development.

4   System Implementation and Experimental Evaluation

Having reviewed the existing model proposed by Muller el at. (2019), the next thing is to implement the system using deep learning algorithms and GloVe Word Embeding techniques.

4.1   Splitting of Dataset into Training and Test Set

The dataset created by the pervious researchers which was downloaded from their http:// git.aisec.fraunhofer.de/projects/GDPRCOM/repos/on-gdprcompliance was used to train the proposed model. After obtaining a clean data set, the data was divided into training and testing data sets. 70% of the whole data was apportioned for the training while 30% was used for testing of the model. The number of instances for the training and test set are shown in Table 2.

Table 2. Data split

Dataset	Number of sentences
Training	12877
Test	5520
Total	**18397**

4.2   Word Tokenization

Tokenization involves converting text into sequence of integers or numbers. This was applied in this study because statistical techniques such as machine learning can only deal with numbers. Therefore, it is important to convert the textual data into numbers as required. This study applied tokenizer from keras for the tokenization.

4.3 Word Embeddings

A word embeddings technique is a class of approach for the representation of word and document using a vector representation. GloVe was used in this study to obtain a vector representation for words in the textual data set. A word embeddings dimensions 100 vector was used. This means that each of the word was mapped to a 100-dimensioned float numbers. This mapping was adjusted during the training of the model.

4.4 Classification

To resolve the issue of imbalance, this study applied Synthetic Minority Oversampling Technique SMOTE (Bowyer et al. 2011). After performing SMOTE operation on the companies' privacy policies dataset, the training data and its corresponding labels were fed into the classification model. LSTM, CNN and GRU algorithms were used for the classification tasks. This was implemented on Keras framework built on tensorflow (backend) used to design framework. The LSTM, CNN and GRU units takes it parameters as a number of units which is the vector dimension of the output of each network blocks. The next subsection shows details of the learning process.

4.5 Experiments: DL Learning Curves

This subsection discusses the outcome of CNN, GRU and LSTM learning process during training. The plots below show the learning curves (accuracy and loss plot on training and validation sets) for both SMOTE and Non-SMOTE GDPR datasets. This was carried out on each category or parameter. Both accuracy and loss were plotted against 5 epochs. Figure 3 depicts the acquired data class using CNN algorithm.

Figure 3 shows the acquired data class by implementing the CNN algorithm.

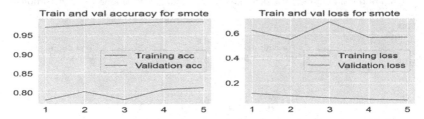

Fig. 3. Train and validation accuracy and loss of SMOTE using CNN

Figure 4 shows the acquired data class by implementing the GRU algorithm.

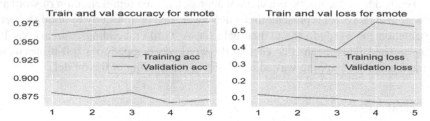

Fig. 4. Train and validation accuracy and loss of SMOTE using GRU

Figure 5 depicts the acquired data class by implementing the LSTM algorithm.

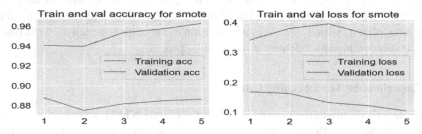

Fig. 5. Training for validation accuracy and loss of SMOTE using LSTM

Figure 6 depicts the DPO class using CNN algorithm.

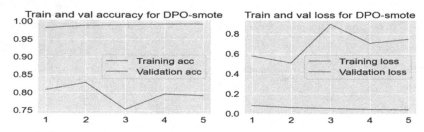

Fig. 6. Training for validation accuracy and loss of SMOTE using CNN

Figure 7 depicts the DPO class using the GRU algorithm.

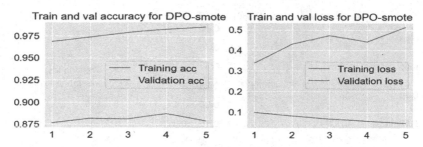

Fig. 7. Training for validation accuracy and loss of SMOTE using GRU

Figure 8 depicts the DPO class using the using LSTM algorithm.

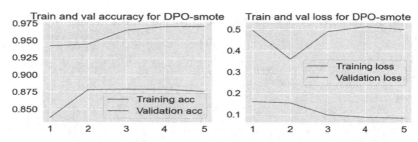

Fig. 8. Training for validation accuracy and loss of SMOTE using LSTM

Figure 9 is the Purpose class using the CNN algorithm.

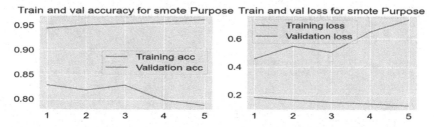

Fig. 9. Training for validation accuracy and loss of SMOTE using CNN

Figure 10 depicts the Purpose class using GRU algorithm.

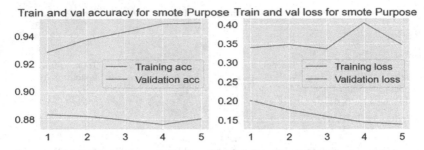

Fig. 10. Training for validation accuracy and loss of SMOTE using GRU

Figure 11 depicts the Purpose class using LSTM algorithm.

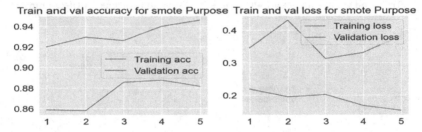

Fig. 11. Training for validation accuracy and loss of SMOTE using LSTM

Figure 12 depicts the Rights Class using CNN algorithm.

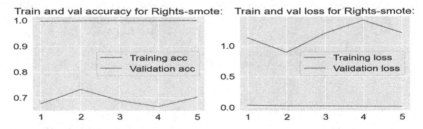

Fig. 12. Training for validation accuracy and loss of SMOTE using CNN

Figure 13 depicts the Rights class using GRU algorithm.

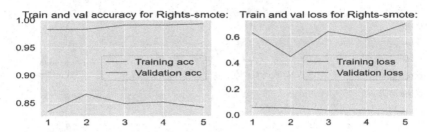

Fig. 13. Training for validation accuracy and loss of SMOTE using GRU

Figure 14 depicts the Rights class using the LSTM algorithm.

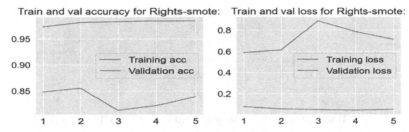

Fig. 14. Training for validation accuracy and loss of SMOTE using GRU

Figure 15 depicts the Data Sharing (DS) class using the CNN algorithm.

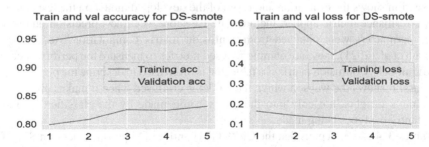

Fig. 15. Training for validation accuracy and loss of SMOTE using CNN

Figure 16 depicts the Data Sharing (DS) class using the GRU algorithm.

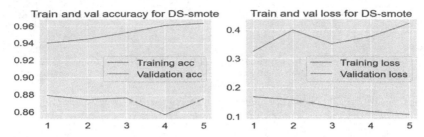

Fig. 16. Training for validation accuracy and loss of SMOTE Using GRU

Figure 17 depicts the Data Sharing (DS) class using the LSTM algorithm.

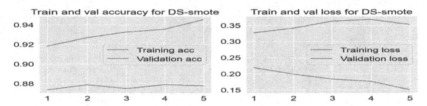

Fig. 17. Training for validation accuracy and loss of SMOTE using LSTM

4.6 Experimental Results and Discussion

This section shows the evaluation and result of the developed model on the test data set. The performance metric applied includes the F1-score, accuracy, precision and recall whose parameters were obtained from confusion matrix computation. According to Ramaiah et al. (2021), these are commonly used metrics to measure the performances of the ML models. Confusion matrix is a table that is often used to describe the performance of a class. It shows the ways in which the model is confused when it makes predictions and depicts insights, not only into the errors being made by the classifier but more importantly the types being made.

Tables 3, 4 and 5, depicts that the CNN, GRU and LSTM performances on SMOTE companies' privacy dataset was very low despite the high accuracy score. The poor recall, precision and F1-score show that the model favoured more of the majority class set than the minority class. However, the model performed better on balanced data using SMOTE with a higher precision, recall, and F1-score. Table 3 shows CNN performances on SMOTE companies' privacy dataset.

Table 3. Performance evaluation of the model on test data using CNN

Categories	CNN			
	Accuracy	Precision	Recall	F1-score
Acquire Data	0.80	0.81	0.66	0.73
DPO	0.78	0.79	0.65	0.71
Purpose	0.75	0.65	0.81	0.73
Data sharing	0.79	0.74	0.77	0.75
Right	0.74	0.90	0.42	0.57

Table 4 shows GRU performances on SMOTE companies' privacy dataset.

Table 4. Performance evaluation of the model on test data using GRU

Categories	GRU			
	Accuracy	Precision	Recall	F1-score
Acquire data	0.87	0.98	0.70	0.82
DPO	0.88	0.97	0.73	0.83
Purpose	0.88	0.94	0.76	0.84
Data Sharing	0.88	0.93	0.76	0.83
Right	0.84	0.97	0.63	0.77

Table 5 shows LSTM performances on SMOTE companies' privacy dataset.

Table 5. Performance evaluation of the model on test data using LSTM

Categories	LSTM			
	Accuracy	Precision	Recall	F1-score
Acquire data	0.86	0.84	0.81	0.83
DPO	0.89	0.93	0.78	0.85
Purpose	0.87	0.99	0.68	0.81
Data sharing	0.88	0.92	0.78	0.84
Right	0.84	0.96	0.63	0.76

The overall results show that LSTM outperform both GRU and CNN models. LSTM achieves F1-scores of 0.76–0.85 and accuracy of 0.84–0.89. Likewise, GRU's F1-scores stood at 0.77–0.84 and accuracy of 0.84–0.88. CNN achieves a F1-scores of 0.57–0.75

and accuracy of 0.74–0.80 which is an improvement over the previous study. Figure 18 shows the F1-scores of the CNN, LSTM and GRU algorithms.

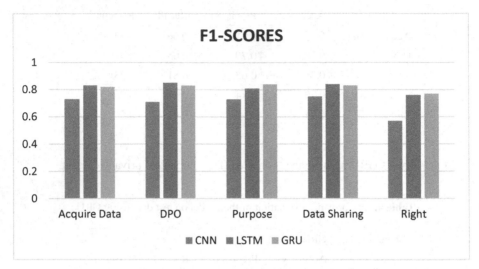

Fig. 18. Comparing F1-Scores of CNN, LSTM and GRU

Figure 19 shows the model accuracy of the CNN, LSTM and GRU algorithms.

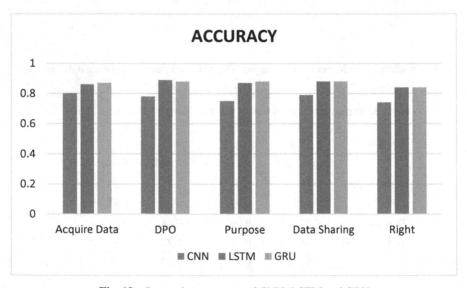

Fig. 19. Comparing accuracy of CNN, LSTM and GRU

5 Conclusion

This research presents a solution to better evaluate companies' privacy policies, using Natural Language Processing and Deep Learning techniques. This study shows that, given the significance and complexity of companies' privacy policies, being able to automatically evaluate their completeness would give significant benefits to the end-users and other key practitioners. This study used CNN, LSTM and GRU algorithms over a corpus of companies' privacy policies dataset, to prove the viability of the proposed model. The overall results across the five selected core requirement of companies' privacy policies shows that LSTM outperform both GRU and CNN models. The LSTM achieves an F1-scores of 0.76–0.85 and accuracy of 0.84–0.89. Likewise, GRU achieves an F1-scores of 0.77–0.84 and accuracy of 0.84–0.88 while CNN achieves an F1-scores of 0.57–0.75 and accuracy of 0.74–0.80 which is an improvement over the previous model using the same dataset.

The outcome of the proposed model shows an accurate classification framework for the analysis of companies' privacy policies. It is expected that this framework will give an effective result whenever Supervisory Regulators and other practitioners want to evaluate the state of compliance of company privacy policy with the core requirement of the data protection and privacy regulations. Such policies and regulations are as enacted by various countries across the globe.

The model testing and performance evaluation results show an excellent improvement than the existing model and classification systems. Therefore, the CPPA model implementation is recommended to overcome the observed methodological gaps and inadequacies inherent in previous model and systems of operation.

References

Andow, B., et al.: Policylint: investigating internal privacy policy contradictions on google play. In: 28th USENIX Security Symposium (USENIX Security 19), pp. 585–602 (2019)

Baia, A.E., Biondi, G., Franzoni, V., Milani, A., Poggioni, V.: Lie to me: shield your emotions from prying software. Sensors **22**(3), 967 (2022)

Bowyer, K.W., Chawla, N.V., Hall, L.O., Kegelmeyer, W.P.: SMOTE: synthetic minority over-sampling technique. CoRR abs/1106.1813 (2011). http://arxiv.org/abs/1106.1813

Costante, E., Sun, Y., Petković, M., Den Hartog, J.: A Machine Learning Solution to Assess Privacy Policy Completeness: (short paper). In: Proceedings of the 2012 ACM Workshop on Privacy in the Electronic Society, pp. 91–96, October 2012

Chika, D.M., Tochukwu, E.S.: An Analysis of Data Protection and Compliance in Nigeria (2020). https://www.rsisinternational.org/journals/ijriss/DigitalLibrary/volume-4-issue-5/377-382.pdf

Degeling, M., Utz, C., Lentzsch, C., Hosseini, H., Schaub, F., Holz, T.: We value your privacy... now take some cookies: Measuring the GDPR's impact on web privacy. arXiv preprint arXiv: 1808.05096 (2018)

Franzoni, V., Kozak, Y.: Yeasts automated classification with extremely randomized forests. In International Conference on Computational Science and Its Applications, pp. 436–447. Springer, Cham, September 2021

Goltz, N., Mayo, M.: Enhancing regulatory compliance by using artificial intelligence text mining to identify penalty clauses in legislation. RAIL 1, 175 (2018)

Harkous, H., Fawaz, K., Lebret, R., Schaub, F., Shin, K. G., Aberer, K.: Polisis: Automated analysis and presentation of privacy policies using deep learning. In: 27th USENIX Security Symposium (USENIX Security 18), pp. 531–548 (2018)

Kinne, J., Axenbeck, J.: Web Mining of Firm Websites: A Framework for Web Scraping and a Pilot Study for Germany. In: ZEW-Centre for European Economic Research Discussion Paper, (18–033) (2018)

Micheti, A., Burkell, J., Steeves, V.: Fixing broken doors: strategies for drafting privacy policies young people can understand. Bull. Sci. Technol. Soc. **30**(2), 130–143 (2010)

Muller, N. M., Kowatsch, D., Debus, P., Mirdita, D., Böttinger, K. (2019, September). On GDPR Compliance of Companies' Privacy Policies. In: International Conference on Text, Speech, and Dialogue, pp. 151–159. Springer, Cham (2019)

Labadie, C., Legner, C.: Understanding data protection regulations from a data management perspective: a capability-based approach to EU-GDPR. In: Proceedings of the 14th International Conference on Wirtschaftsinformatik, February 2019

Liu, F., Fella, N. L., Liao, K.: Modeling Language Vagueness in Privacy Policies Using Deep Neural Networks. In: 2016 AAAI Fall Symposium Series, September 2016

O'Connor, P.: Privacy and the online travel customer: an analysis of privacy policy content, use and compliance by online travel agencies. In: ENTER, pp. 401–412, January 2004

Ramaiah, M., Chandrasekaran, V., Ravi, V., Kumar, N.: An intrusion detection system using optimized deep neural network architecture. Trans. Emerging Telecommun. Technol. **32**(4), e4221 (2021)

Sadeh, N., et al.: The usable privacy policy project: Combining crowdsourcing. Machine Learning and Natural Language Processing to Semi-Automatically Answer Those Privacy Questions Users Care About. Carnegie Mellon University Technical Report CMU-ISR-13–119, 1–24 (2013)

Sathyendra, K.M., Wilson, S., Schaub, F., Zimmeck, S., Sadeh, N.: Identifying the provision of choices in privacy policy text. In: Proceedings of the 2017 Conference on Empirical Methods in Natural Language Processing, pp. 2774–2779, September 2017

Sánchez, D., Viejo, A., Batet, M.: Automatic assessment of privacy policies under the GDPR. Appl. Sci. **11**(4), 1762 (2021)

Tesfay, W.B., Hofmann, P., Nakamura, T., Kiyomoto, S., Serna, J.: PrivacyGuide: Towards an Implementation of the EU GDPR on Internet Privacy Policy Evaluation. In: Proceedings of the Fourth ACM International Workshop on Security and Privacy Analytics, pp. 15–21, March 2018

Zaeem, R.N., German, R.L., Barber, K.S.: Privacycheck: automatic summarization of privacy policies using data mining. ACM Trans. Internet Technol. (TOIT) **18**(4), 1–18 (2018)

Zimmeck, S., Bellovin, S.M.: Privee: an architecture for automatically analyzing web privacy policies. In 23rd Security Symposium (USENIX Security 14), pp. 1–16 (2014)

International Workshop on Advancements in Applied Machine-learning and Data Analytics (AAMDA 2022)

Methodology for Product Recommendation Based on User-System Interaction Data: A Case Study on Computer Systems E-Commerce Web Site

Tahir Enes Adak[1], Yunus Sahin[1], Mounes Zaval[2(✉)], and Mehmet S. Aktas[2]

[1] Research and Development Center, Casper Computer Systems, Istanbul, Turkey
{TahirEnes.Adak,Yunus.Sahin}@casper.com.tr
[2] Computer Engineering Department, Yildiz Technical University, Istanbul, Turkey
mounes.zaval@std.yildiz.edu.tr, aktas@yildiz.edu.tr

Abstract. Within the scope of this study, we developed a product recommendation methodology for customers by analyzing shopping behaviors based on user-system interaction data collected on Casper Computer Systems' website. To achieve the "right product to the right customer" objective, we predict customer interests using a collaborative filtering algorithm on collected data from previous customer activities. In turn, this minimizes prediction errors and enables better-personalized suggestions of computer system configuration. We took advantage of the implicit feedback approach while modeling customer behaviors if they liked or disliked a particular product. After customer behavior data is collected, we form the customer-product matrix and generate personalized product suggestions for each customer with the help of user-item-based collaborating filtering and item-item-based collaborating filtering algorithms. Customer-website interaction is considered a key input variable in creating personalized recommendations. Customers are supposed to use the website and leave interaction data regarding product configurations they're interested in. To prove the efficiency of this methodology, we developed a prototype application. The product suggestion success rate of the application is tested on datasets generated from log data of the Casper website. Performance results prove that the developed methodology is successful.

Keywords: E-Commerce · Machine learning · Collaborative filtering · Recommendation systems

1 Introduction

E-commerce is one of the essential fields today, due to the noticeable increase in the emergence of E-commerce websites, especially during the Covid-19 pandemic, which prompted people to stay at home in order to preserve their lives from danger, so people were forced to buy their needs from the Internet [1,2]. Due to this increase, recommendation systems are an important factor in attracting customers because they try to understand the needs and desires of the customer to suggest the most suitable products specifically for this customer based on the history of interaction between the system and the customer. In the field of the computer industry, there is a tremendous number of computer configurations that make unknowledgeable customers get lost among all these configurations, which leads to the purchase of a product that does not meet their needs, causing a bad experience for the customer. For this reason, companies have had to come up with a reasonable solution to overcome this problem. Casper company has the Easy builder tool _, which consists of simple, non-technical questions so the user can answer them. At the end of this process, this tool suggests the most suitable computer configuration for this user based on his answers. The resulted computer configuration is then to be considered the user's preferences.

The vast majority of technology customers are defined as everyday users who do not have expertise in features or do not want to take the time to research. In this case, there is a possibility that the purchased products are not suitable for their needs. Product vendors present products in different segments and cater to general customer profiles. These profiles group people with similar expectations but do not capture the accuracy of personalized product customization. There are risks such as product dissatisfaction and product return.

Motivation: The KUR/AL project (Easy Builder tool) brings together the products most suitable for the customers' needs by making personalized recommendations. Thus, users get products with the right features at a more affordable price, maximizing product and shopping satisfaction.

We introduce the needs that determine the goal of completing this project as follows:

- The need for decision support systems that will reduce Casper's return risk and increase customer satisfaction.
- The need for the customer to be able to reach the product they need much more easily and with a point shot.
- The need for software that will bring customers to Casper brand and that we can offer the right product to the customer.
- The need for decision support systems that will indirectly increase Casper brand perception and increase Casper's customer satisfaction.
- The need for software in which the customer can define the product he needs even if he does not know the detailed features of the computer.
- The need to provide the customer with the ability to easily access the most suitable computer for their needs with simple questions and answers.

Research Problem: This study proposes a novel methodology for collecting users' preferences from implicit feedback through their interaction with the E-commerce website and applies collaborative filtering algorithms to provide recommendations for active users. Therefore, we are investigating the answer to the following questions:

1. How can we model such interaction data to capture user preferences in computer configuration?
2. After modeling the data, how can we apply recommendation algorithms?
3. What would be the evaluation results of the applied methodology, and how useful is it?

Contribution: Within the scope of this study, we introduce a novel software architecture that produces recommendations by a method based on the customer's tastes, identifying customers with similar tastes and suggesting different product tastes of the identified customers. The developed software offers the optimum product in different configurations according to customers' price and usage preferences. A prototype of this software is implemented and evaluated so we can measure how successful such software could be. The results of the evaluation were promising.

Organization of the Paper: After we have introduced our motivations and the research problem that circulates this research, we move on to present the fundamental concepts and similar works in the literature. Then we explain the methodology that guided the process of implementing this project. Furthermore, we report the used technologies and the evaluation results for the recommendation system software architecture.

2   Fundamental Concepts and Literature Review

2.1   Fundamental Concepts

Collaborative Filtering adopts a methodology that aims to consider the point of view of other users of similar behavior when trying to guess whether an item will appeal to the desired user [3]. This way, CF draws attention to other users' opinions and brings new factors to the recommendation process other than depending solely on the user profile. Let us assume a website with two frequent users that contains three items: $item_X$, $item_Y$, and $item_Z$; since we only have two users, then they are the most similar users of the website; If the first user likes all three items, and the second user only liked $item_X$ and $item_Y$, then we can predict $item_Z$ being desired by the second user as well based on the first user opinion [4]. Designing a successful collaborative filtering system needs an efficient algorithm that can overcome environmental challenges, including:

- **Shilling attacks.** The vulnerability that appears through creating an enormous number of fake profiles in the system anonymously with the purpose of targetting a particular item to increase its popularity [5–7].
- **Synonymy.** Usually, the recommendation system cannot determine the exact similarity of two similar items but with different names in the system. This condition imposes challenges and difficulties in generating item recommendations for the users [8].

– **Cold Start.** When new items or users are added to the system with no prior engagements or ratings, the recommendation system usually cannot predict ratings for such new products. Consequently, it cannot generate recommendations for such new users [8–10].
– **Others.** like Data Sparity, Scalability, etc. [8,11–15].

Choosing the most suitable similarity metric plays a crucial role for the system to succeed; each metric follows a unique formula that deals with the rating matrix differently, so the similarity results will be different. There are many similarity metrics in the literature, such as Tanimoto similarity metric, Pearson correlation similarity metric, and many others [12,16].

The rating matrix represents the user-system interaction information extracted from analyzing e-commerce websites' log files. It could be constructed in two different ways; either the rows represent users and columns represent products/items or the other way around. Hence, two branches of collaborative filtering algorithms emerge based on how we allocate users and items. Both **User-Based CF** and **Item-Based CF** follow the same approach for calculations. Still, UBCF performs the calculation on a user-item rating matrix, and IBCF performs it on an item-user rating matrix which is the transpose matrix of the user-item rating matrix. Therefore UBCF is concerned with calculating similarities between users in contrast to IBCF, which focuses on the similarities between items [16]. Tables 1 and 2 demonstrate the difference between the explained two formations of the rating matrix. On the left-hand side, we have our item-user matrix _computer configurations being the item in our case_, and on the right-hand side, we have the user-item matrix.

Where: CC → Computer Configuration and $x_{i,j}$ → Rating of $item_j$ by $user_i$. Figure 1 concludes the collaborative algorithm approach procedure. So, for a random user U_a, we assign a predicted rating score for each item in the item vector that this specific user did not rate or engage with directly, then we rank this

Table 1. Item-user rating matrix

CCs\Users	user$_1$	user$_2$	user$_3$
CC$_1$	$x_{1,1}$	$x_{2,1}$	
CC$_2$		$x_{2,2}$	$x_{3,2}$
CC$_3$	$x_{1,3}$	$x_{2,3}$	

Table 2. User-item rating matrix

Users\CCs	CC$_1$	CC$_2$	CC$_3$
user$_1$	$x_{1,1}$		$x_{1,3}$
user$_2$	$x_{2,1}$	$x_{2,2}$	$x_{2,3}$
user$_3$		$x_{3,2}$	

vector's elements based on the predicted score. Therefore, we obtain a finalized list of top-N recommendations.

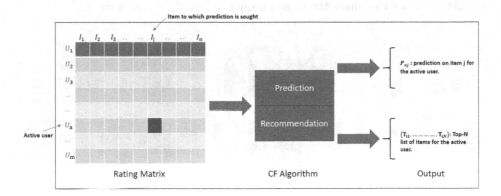

Fig. 1. CF process [17]

2.2   Literature Review

Within the scope of the research, the transactions made by the customers using the Easy Builder application on the Casper site will be monitored, and product suggestions that can be made to the customers will be determined. In the suitable computer configuration mapping to the right customer, the collaborative filtering method will predict what the customers might be interested in based on the customer activity data in the past. This way, it will be possible to offer customers a computer configuration that will match their needs and expectations. Here, the uses of the collaborative filtering method in the literature are examined, and the most successful use of this method in the research is studied [18–24]. This study assumes that the customers have previously used the Easy Builder application at a sufficient level and left information about the configurations they are interested in to make configuration suggestions to the customers. There exist studies that focus on analyzing user's browsing graph data to extract knowledge [25–28]. However, in this study, we focus on user's purchase behaviour on the computer systems e-commerce website.

3   Methodology

Figure 2 illustrates the pipeline of the applied methodology for building a recommendation system for Casper e-commerce website. This system provides recommendations for those users who completed the questions series of the easy builder tool sufficiently; then, we capture their preferences based on the easy builder tool's results. We then construct a preferences vector that concludes user's interactions in the system, and from that, we construct the rating matrix that would be provided to the collaborative filtering algorithms. At the end of this process, we obtain a recommendation engine that captures the users' interests, predicts what might appeal to them, and then recommends the most suitable product to deliver the right product to the right customer.

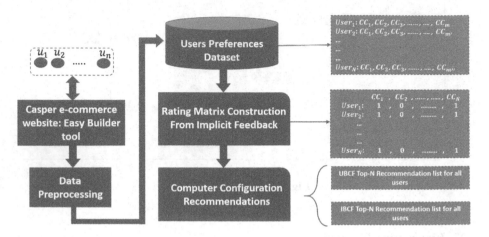

Fig. 2. The proposed software architecture for computer configurations recommendation system

Capturing Users Preferences: Casper's e-commerce website has an overwhelming amount of computer configurations, Which makes eliciting users' preferences difficult. Additionally, regular customers lack the adequate education to build or select their computer, so when they try to do so, there is a high possibility that the purchased product is not what they wanted at first. Casper company introduces the easy builder tool (KUR/AL) as a way to overcome this challenging problem preventing users' dissatisfaction; besides, it captures users' interests. The easy builder tool is a series of multi-choice, easy-to-answer questions related to the user's purpose of using the computer (education, work, daily usage, gaming), desired platform (laptop, desktop), and budget. The system suggests the most suited computer configurations based on the user's answers by completing these questions. Since this is the case, we consider that this user is interested in the final product, which satisfies the user's needs. The more the user interacts with this tool, the more we can understand their needs and interests through analyzing these user-system interaction data later.

Data Pre-processing and Preparing: The outputs and results of the easy builder tool are collected and stored in the websites' log files, so we need to capture this information and convert it into a format that satisfies our goal. Besides, websites' log files have noisy and dirty raw data that needs to be cleaned in order to be useful for data analysis tasks. Subsequently, for each active user of the websites that used the easy builder tool, we make an array that includes all the easy builder tool's computer configuration results and consider that these configurations represent this user's preferences.

Rating Matrix Construction from Implicit Feedback: Based on the easy builder tool results, we constructed a vector array that captures users' preferences for each user. However, we should convert this into numbers to have the rating matrix that can be fed to UBCF and IBCF algorithms. Since the user is not providing any explicit rating for the computer configuration, we follow the implicit feedback methodology by calculating the frequency of a particular product presented to the users at the end of the Q&As series and the user has clicked through the resulted product; then for each user, we normalize these frequencies bringing back the values into the closed interval [1,5]. Hence, We define our rating matrix $Y \in R^{U \times I}$ _Where: U, I → the size of the users, items sets, respectively_ as:

$$y_{ui} = \begin{cases} [1,5] \text{ Normalized CC's View number in the easy builder results;} \\ 0, \quad\quad\quad\quad\quad\quad\quad\quad\quad\quad\quad\quad \text{Otherwise.} \end{cases} \quad (1)$$

Table 3 reveals for us an example of the rating matrix, which will be given to the user-based and item-based collaborative filtering algorithms. The output of this stage is a very similar matrix, with the columns representing the set of all computer configurations and the rows representing the set or the opposite.

Table 3. Rating matrix

Users\CCs	CC_1	CC_2	...	CC_I
$user_1$	1	0	...	3
$user_2$	4	2	...	5
...	...	...	...	...
...	...	...	...	...
$user_U$	3	2	...	0

Applying User-Based and Item-Based Collaborative Filtering Algorithms: After processing and converting the data into the proper format, we can apply both user-based and item-based collaborative filtering algorithms based on the rating matrix that we obtained in the previous section. Pursuing the success of our recommendation system, we followed a simple pipeline to get the best results:

- **Calculating Similarity:** the Log Likelihood similarity metric is applied to calculate both users' and items' similarities. **Log Likelihood similarity** is a statistical test that is independent of the explicit preferences values. Its value expresses how unlikely it is for two customers to have the same interests [12,29].

- **Neighborhood Selection:** we take into account only the most 15 similar users/items that contribute to the process of generating recommendations for computer configurations.
- **UB/IB Recommender:** we provide the calculated similarity and neighborhood information to the generic user/item-based recommender.

4   Prototype and Evaluation

4.1   Prototype and Evaluation Strategy

The prototype implementation of this research was carried out using C# and .Net framework to provide the web API services of this project. For integrating user-based and item-based collaborative filtering algorithms into this project, the NReco library has been utilized. NReco Recommender [30] is .Net implementation of the non-hadoop version of Apache Mahout collaborative filtering engine. Naming the classes and public methods is the same as in Apache Mahout but aligned with C# naming conventions. And with the help of user-based and item-based recommender classes, we implemented our approach on top of the dataset explained in the next section. We chose the root mean squares error as our metric for evaluating the system, and we report the results in the experimental results section. The goal of the developed prototype is to bring the mentioned software architecture in the methodology section to real life so we can observe and test its usefulness and efficiency.

4.2   Dataset

This study's dataset is created by obtaining the user's unique identity, product's unique identity, and viewing rate over the data of the products visited by the users on www.casper.com.tr. On this website, Casper provides corporate services and makes sales. It is stored in CSV and delivered to the collaborative filtering algorithms. The dataset comprises three fields (UserId, AssetId, and Viewing Rate normalized between 1 and 5) with approximately 100K records, as shown below. The dataset was split into two parts for the sake of testing by 80% for training and 20% for testing, which corresponds to around 80,000 and 20,000 records, respectively (Fig. 3).

```
514,163,3
514,172,2
514,175,5
514,176,5
514,180,3
514,190,3
514,194,4
```

Fig. 3. Sample dataset

4.3 Test Design

For the purpose of understanding how successful the developed system is based on the applied methodology explained in this paper, we utilized the root mean squares error (RMSE); RMSE is a statistical metric that is used to evaluate machine learning models by calculating the difference between the model's predictions values and the actual observations values, using the formula:

$$RMSE = \sqrt{\frac{1}{N}\Sigma_{i=1}^{N}\left(o_i - \hat{e}_i\right)^2} \tag{2}$$

where:

- N $\rightarrow$ Number of instances.
- o_i $\rightarrow$ Observation preference value.
- $\hat{e}_i$ $\rightarrow$ Estimated preference value.

RMSE value is interpreted in terms of accuracy so that the smaller its value is, the better the model is performing. Therefore, we seek to accomplish this work by obtaining as low RMSE value as possible [31,32].

4.4 Experimental Results

Table 4 reports the evaluation results of our prototype implementation. These results are positive and promising, prompting us to investigate the designed methodology further and combine more than two collaborative filtering algorithms to increase Casper company's customers' satisfaction.

Table 4. RMSE evaluation results

Algorithm	Item-based CF	User-based CF
RMSE	0.98	1.03

We again observe that the item-based collaborative filtering algorithm performed better than the user-based collaborative filtering algorithm in real-world cases. Even though these two algorithms are theoretically the same, the item-based CF algorithm proves its superiority over the user-based CF algorithm.

5   Conclusion and Future Work

This research introduces a methodology for product recommendation based on user-system interaction data on computer systems E-Commerce Web Site accompanied by an appropriate software architecture that illustrates the necessary stages of implementing such methodology in real life. We have also implemented and tested a prototype with the help of NReco framework to ensure the positive outcomes of this project. The results are promising, with 0.98 and 1.03 RMSE scores for item-based CF recommendation engine and user-based CF recommendation engine, respectively. In future work, we plan on integrating multiple recommendation algorithms into this system, including deep learning algorithms. Also, we will try running these algorithms on more extensive and extended datasets.

Acknowledgement. Thanks to Casper Computer Systems company for supporting this study by providing all the necessary requirements and datasets.

References

1. Bhatti, A., et al.: E-commerce trends during covid-19 pandemic. Int. J. Future Gener. Commun. Netw. **13**(2), 1449–1452 (2020)
2. Hanson, W.A., Kalyanam, K.: Internet Marketing and E-commerce. (Student ed.). Thomson/South-Western (2020)
3. Goldberg, K., et al.: Eigentaste: a constant time collaborative filtering algorithm. Inf. Retrieval **4**, 133–151 (2001)
4. Miller, B., Konstan, J., Riedl, J.: Pocketlens: toward a personal recommender system. ACM Trans. Off. Inf. Syst. **22**(3), 437–476 (2004). Copyright: Copyright 2012 Elsevier B.V., All rights reserved
5. Gunes, I., Kaleli, C., Bilge, A., Polat, H.: Shilling attacks against recommender systems: a comprehensive survey. Artif. Intell. Rev. **42**(4), 767–799 (2012). https://doi.org/10.1007/s10462-012-9364-9
6. Kaur, P., Goel, S.: Shilling attack models in recommender system. In: 2016 International Conference on Inventive Computation Technologies (ICICT), vol. 2, pp. 1–5. IEEE (2016)
7. Lam, S.K., Riedl, J.: Shilling recommender systems for fun and profit. In: Proceedings of the 13th International Conference on World Wide Web, pp. 393–402 (2004)
8. Pandey, A.K., Rajpoot, D.S.: Resolving cold start problem in recommendation system using demographic approach. In: 2016 International Conference on Signal Processing and Communication (ICSC), pp. 213–218. IEEE (2016)
9. Li, X.: Collaborative filtering recommendation algorithm based on cluster. In: Proceedings of 2011 International Conference on Computer Science and Network Technology, vol. 4, pp. 2682–2685. IEEE (2011)
10. Jindal, H., Singh, S.K.: A hybrid recommendation system for coldstart problem using online commercial dataset. Int. J. Comp. Eng. Appl. **7**(1), 100 (2014)
11. Linden, G., Smith, B., York, J.: Amazon.com recommendations: item-to-item collaborative filtering. IEEE Internet Comput. **7**, 76–80 (2003)

12. Bagchi, S.: Performance and quality assessment of similarity measures in collaborative filtering using mahout. Procedia Comp. Sci. **50**, 229–234 (2015). Big Data, Cloud and Computing Challenges

13. Claypool, M., et al.: Combining content-based and collaborative filters in an online newspaper. In: Proceedings of the ACM SIGIR 1999 Workshop on Recommender Systems: Algorithms and Evaluation, Berkeley, California. ACM (1999)

14. Su, X., Khoshgoftaar, T.: A survey of collaborative filtering techniques. Adv. Artif. Intell. **2009**, 2–7 (2009)

15. Sarwar, B.M., et al.: Recommender systems for large-scale e-commerce: Scalable neighborhood formation using clustering. In: Proceedings of the Fifth International Conference on Computer and Information Technology, vol. 1. Citeseer, pp. 291–324 (2002)

16. Papagelis, M., Plexousakis, D.: Qualitative analysis of user-based and item-based prediction algorithms for recommendation agents. Eng. Appl. Artif. Intell. **18**(7), 781–789 (2005)

17. Bokde, D.K., et al.: Role of matrix factorization model in collaborative filtering algorithm: a survey. ArXiv abs/1503.07475 (2015)

18. Duzen, Z., Aktas, M.S.: An approach to hybrid personalized recommender systems. In: 2016 International Symposium on INnovations in Intelligent SysTems and Applications (INISTA), pp. 1–8. IEEE (2016)

19. Arpacı, A., Aktaş, M.: Investigation of different approaches for recommendation system. In: ELECO 2018 (2018)

20. Tas, K., et al.: On the implicit feedback based data modeling approaches for recommendation systems. In: 2021 International Conference on Electrical, Communication, and Computer Engineering (ICECCE), pp. 1–6. IEEE (2021)

21. Uzun-Per, M., et al.: An approach to recommendation systems using scalable association mining algorithms on big data processing platforms: a case study in airline industry. In: 2021 International Conference on INnovations in Intelligent SysTems and Applications (INISTA), pp. 1–6. IEEE (2021)

22. Uzun-Per, M., et al.: Scalable recommendation systems based on finding similar items and sequences. Concurrency Comput. Pract. Exp. e6841 (2022). https://doi.org/10.1002/cpe.6841

23. Uzun-Per, M., et al.: Big data testing framework for recommendation systems in e-science and e-commerce domains. In: 2021 IEEE International Conference on Big Data (Big Data), pp. 2353–2361. IEEE (2021)

24. Aktas, M.S., et al.: A web based conversational case-based recommender system for ontology aided metadata discovery. In: Fifth IEEE/ACM International Workshop on Grid Computing, pp. 69–75. IEEE (2004)

25. Olmezogullari, E., Aktas, M.: Representation of click-stream datasequences for learning user navigational behavior by using embeddings. In: 2020 IEEE International Conference on Big Data (Big Data), pp. 3173–3179. IEEE (2020)

26. Uygun, Y., et al.: On the large-scale graph data processing for user interface testing in big data science projects. In: 2020 IEEE International Conference on Big Data (Big Data), pp. 3173–3179. IEEE (2020)

27. Oz, M., et al.: On the use of generative deep learning approaches for generating hidden test scripts. Int. J. Softw. Eng. Knowl. Eng. **31**(10), 1447–1468 (2021)

28. Olmezogullari, E., Aktas, M.: Pattern2Vec: representation of clickstream data sequences for learning user navigational behavior. Concurrency Comput. Pract. Exp. **34**(9), e6546 (2022)

29. Vivek, M.B., Manju, N., Vijay, M.B.: Machine learning based food recipe recommendation system. In: Guru, D.S., Vasudev, T., Chethan, H.K., Sharath Kumar, Y.H. (eds.) Proceedings of International Conference on Cognition and Recognition. LNNS, vol. 14, pp. 11–19. Springer, Singapore (2018). https://doi.org/10.1007/978-981-10-5146-3_2
30. NReco Recommender: Official library website. https://www.nrecosite.com/recommender_net.aspx
31. Hananto, A.L., Sulaiman, S., Widiyanto, S., Rahman, A.Y.: Evaluation comparison of wave amount measurement results in brass-plated tire steel cord using RMSE and cosine similarity. Indones. J. Electr. Eng. Comput. Sci **22**(1), 207 (2021)
32. Chai, T., Draxler, R.R.: Root mean square error (RMSE) or mean absolute error (MAE)?-Arguments against avoiding RMSE in the literature. Geoscientific Model Develop. **7**(3), 1247–1250 (2014)

A Systematic Literature Review
of Question Answering: Research Trends,
Datasets, Methods

Dilan Bakır[ID] and Mehmet S. Aktas[✉][ID]

Yildiz Technical University, Istanbul, Turkey
dilan.bakir@std.yildiz.edu.tr, aktas@yildiz.edu.tr

Abstract. Answering questions, finding the most appropriate answer to
the question given by the user as input are among the important tasks
of natural language processing. Many studies have been done on question answering and datasets, methods have been published. The aim of
this article is to reveal the studies done in question answering and to
identify the missing research topics. In this literature review, it is tried
to determine the datasets, methods and frameworks used for question
answering between 2000 and 2022. From the articles published between
these years, 91 papers are selected based on inclusion and exclusion criteria. This systematic literature review consists of research analyzes such
as research questions, search strategy, inclusion and exclusion criteria,
data extraction. We see that the selected final study focuses on four
topics. These are Natural Language Processing, Information Retrieval,
Knowledge Base, Hybrid Based.

Keywords: Question answering · Information retrieval · Knowledge
based question answering · NLP based question answering · Systematic
literature review

1 Introduction

In the growing technology world, the importance of data is increasing. Question and answer systems have been developed for the growth of the data, the
extraction of the desired information from the data and the processing of this
information. Question answering (QA) is the system that takes a certain query
input from the user and brings the closest answer to this query over the desired
data.

QA consists of various systems such as search engine, chatbot. These systems
vary according to needs. At first, search engines would only return documents
containing information related to queries created by users in natural language,
but over time, it is desired to return a direct answer to the user's question along
with the documents and the needs are increasing. Question answering systems
consist of research areas such as Information Retrieval (IR), Answer Extraction

O. Gervasi et al. (Eds.): ICCSA 2022 Workshops, LNCS 13377, pp. 47–62, 2022.
https://doi.org/10.1007/978-3-031-10536-4_4

(AE), and Natural Language Processing (NLP). Different studies, methods and datasets have been published in the field of QA. To this end, a comprehensive picture of the current state of QA is requested.

In this study, our purpose is to analyze the studies conducted between 2000 and 2022 in the field of QA. These analyzes are prepared on the methods used, the most used techniques, and datasets. The sections of this article are determined as follows. In Sect. 2, research methods are described. The criteria and results determined for the research questions are given in Sect. 3. In the last section, the summary of this study is given.

2 Methodology

2.1 Review Method

A systematic approach is chosen when conducting a literature search on question answering systems. Systematic literature reviews are well established method of review in question answering. In a systematic literature review, it can be defined as examining all the necessary research in a subject area and drawing conclusions [1]. This systematic literature review was prepared according to the criteria suggested by Kitchenham and Charters (2007). Some of the works and figures in this section have also been adapted by (Radjenović, Heričko, Torkar, Živkovič, 2013) [2], (Unterkalmsteiner et al. 2012) [3] and Wahono [4].

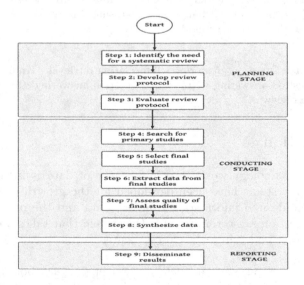

Fig. 1. Systematic literature review steps

As shown in Fig. 1, Srl work consists of certain stages. These stages are planning, executing and reporting. In the planning stage, the needs are determined.

In the introduction part, realization targets are mentioned. Then, existing slr studies on question answering are collected and reviewed. The purpose of this review is designed to reduce researcher bias when conducting the slr study (Step 2). Research questions, search strategy, inclusion and exclusion criteria, study process, data extraction are described in Sects. 2.2, 2.3, 2.4 and 2.5.

2.2 Research Questions

The research questions studied in this review are indicated in Table 1.

Table 1. Identified research questions

ID	Research question
RQ1	Which journal is the most significant Question Answering journal?
RQ2	Who are the most active and influential researchers in the Question Answering field?
RQ3	What kind of research topics are selected by researchers in the Question Answering field?
RQ4	What kind of datasets are the most used for Question Answering?
RQ5	What kind of methods are used for Question Answering?
RQ6	Which method performs best when used for Question Answering?
RQ7	What kind of method improvements are proposed for Question Answering?

The methods and datasets used in the question answering area shown in Table 1 from RQ1 to RQ7 were analyzed. Important methods, datasets are analyzed between RQ4 and RQ7. It gives a summary of the work done in the field of question answering from RQ1 to RQ3.

2.3 Search Strategy

The search process (Step 4) consists of several stages. Determination of digital libraries, determination of search keywords, development of search queries and final studies that match the search query from digital libraries are extracted. In order to select the most relevant articles, first of all, appropriate database sets are determined. The most popular literature database sets are researched and selected in order to keep our field of study wide. Digital databases used: ACM Digital Library, IEEE eXplore, ScienceDirect, Springer, Scopus

The search query is determined according to certain criteria. These criteria are;

1. Search terms were determined from the research questions
2. Searching the generated query in related titles, abstracts and keywords
3. Identifying different spellings, synonyms and opposite meaning of query
4. A comprehensive search string was created using the specified search terms

Boolean AND and OR. The generated search string is as follows.
("question answering" AND "natural language processing") AND ("information retrieval") AND ("Document Retrieval" OR "Passage Retrieval" OR "Answer Extraction")

Digital databases were scanned based on keywords, titles and abstracts. The search limited publications between 2000 and 2022. Within the scope of the research, only journal articles and conference papers published in English were included in the search.

2.4 Study Selection

Inclusion and exclusion criteria specified in Table 2 are shown in order to determine the final studies.

Table 2. Inclusion and exclusion criteria

Inclusion criteria	Studies in academic and industry using large and small scale data sets
	Studies discussing and comparing modeling performance in the area of question answering
	For studies that have both the conference and journal versions, only the journal version will be included
	For duplicate publications of the same study, only the most complete and newest one will be included
Exclusion criteria	Studies without a strong validation or including experimental results of question answering
	Studies discussing question answering datasets, methods, frameworks in a context other than question answering
	Studies not written in English

Figure 2 shows each step of the review process and the number determined. The study selection process was carried out in 2 steps. Title, abstract and full-text studies have been removed. Literature studies and studies that did not include experimental results were also excluded. Other studies were included according to the degree of similarity with question answering from the remaining studies.

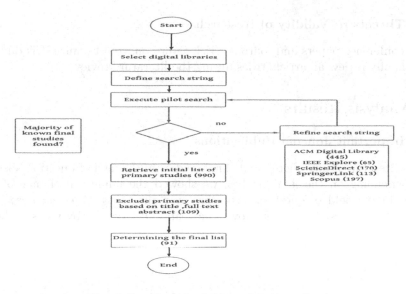

Fig. 2. Search and selection of final studies

In the first stage, the final list was selected. The final list includes 91 final studies. Considering the inclusion and exclusion criteria of 91 final studies, research questions and study similarities were examined.

2.5 Data Extraction

In the final study, our goal is to identify studies that contribute to the research questions. A data extraction form was created for each of the 91 final studies. This form was designed to collect information on studies and to answer research questions. In Table 3, five features were used to analyze the research questions.

Table 3. Data extraction features matched to research questions

Feature	Research questions
Researchers and Publications	RQ1, RQ2
Question Answering Trends and Topics	RQ3
Question Answering Datasets	RQ4
Question Answering Metrics	RQ4
Question Answering Methods	RQ5, RQ6, RQ7

2.6   Threats to Validity of Research

Some conference papers and journal articles were omitted because it is difficult
to manually review all article titles during the literature review.

3   Analysis Results

3.1   Important Journal Publications

In this literature study, there are 91 final studies in the field of question answering. Depending on the final studies, we showed the numerical change of the
studies in the field of question answering over the years. Our aim here is to
see how the interest has changed over the years. Observation by years is shown
in Fig. 3. It is observed that the interest in the field of question answering has
increased more since 2005 and it shows that the studies carried out are more
contemporary.

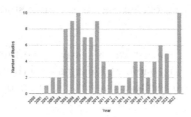

Fig. 3. Distribution of selected studies over the years

The most important journals included in this literature study are shown in
Fig. 4.

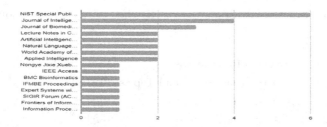

Fig. 4. Journal publications

The Scimago Journal Rank (SJR) values of the most important journals with
final studies are given in Table 4.

Table 4. SJR of journals

Journal Publications	SJR
BMC Bioinformatics	1,567
Expert Systems with Applications	1,368
SIGIR Forum (ACM Special Interest Group on Information Retrieval)	1,337
Information Processing Management	1,061
Journal of Biomedical Informatics	1,057
Artificial Intelligence in Medicine	0,98
Applied Intelligence	0,791
IEEE Access	0,587
Nongye Jixie Xuebao/Transactions of the Chinese Society for Agricultural Machinery	0,461
Journal of Intelligent Information Systems	0,424
Frontiers of Information Technology, Electronic Engineering	0,406
Natural Language Engineering	0,29
Lecture Notes in Computer Science	0,249
NIST Special Publication	0,202
IFMBE Proceedings	0,152
World Academy of Science	0,137

3.2 Most Active Researchers

The researchers who are most active in the field of question answering are shown in Fig. 5 according to the number of studies. Boris Katz, Yuan-ping Nie, Mourad Sarrouti, SaidOuatik El Alaoui, Prodromos Malakasiotis, Ion Androutsopoulos, Paolo Rosso, Stefanie Tellex, Aaron Fernandes, Gregory Marton, Dragomir Radev, Weiguo Fan, Davide Buscaldi, Emilio Sanchis, Dietrich Klakow, Matthew W. Bilottiare are the most active researchers.

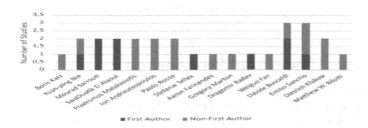

Fig. 5. Influential researchers and number of studies

3.3   Research Topics in the Question Answering Field

To answer this question, we considered Yao's classification paper. When the final studies were examined, it was seen that the studies were carried out on four topics [5].

1. Natural Language Processing based (NLP): Machine learning, NLP techniques are used to extract the answers.
2. Information Retrieval based (IR): It deals with the retrieval or sorting of answers, documents and passages in search engine usage.
3. Knowledge Base based (KB): Finding answers is done through structured data. Standard database queries are used in replacement of word-based searches [6].
4. Hybrid Based: A hybrid approach is the combination of IR, NLP and KB.

Figure 6 shows the total distribution of research topics on question answering from 2000 until 2022. From the 91 studies, 6.72% of the papers implemented a knowledge base, 31.94% implemented a natural language processing, 59.24% implemented an information retrieval and 2.1% implemented a Hybrid. When the final studies are examined, it is seen that there are more studies in the field of NLP. As the reasons why researchers focus on this issue, studies on obtaining information through the search engine are increasing. A lot of text nlp and machine learning techniques have been tried to be applied in order to extract the most correct answer from the unstructured data.

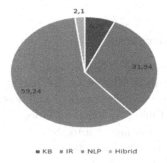

■ KB   ■ IR   ■ NLP   ■ Hibrid

Fig. 6. Ratio of subjects

3.4   Datasets Used for Question Answering

Dataset is a data collection on which machine learning is applied [6]. The training set is the data on which the model is trained by giving it to the learning system. The test set or evaluation set is a dataset used to evaluate the model developed on a training set.

The distribution of datasets by years is presented. 35.95% of the studies are private datasets. Since these datasets are not public, the results of the studies cannot be compared with the results of the proposed models. The distribution of final studies by years is shown in Fig. 7. Looking at the distribution, there is an increasing awareness of the use of public data.

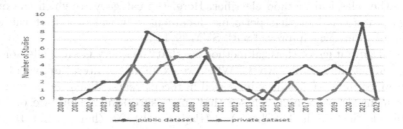

Fig. 7. Number of datasets

3.5   Methods Used in Question Answering

As can be seen in Fig. 8, fourteen methods used and recommended in the field of question answering since 2000 have been determined. These determined methods are shown in Fig. 8.

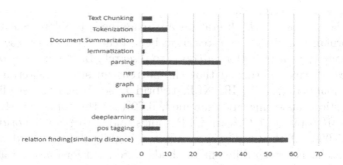

Fig. 8. Methods used in question answering

3.6   Best Method Used for Question Answering

Many studies have been carried out in the field of question answering. When the literature is examined, there is a pipeline process consisting of Natural Language Processing (NLP), Information Retrieval (IR), and Answer Extraction (IE). A question given in natural language first goes through the analysis phase. In other words, search queries are created to facilitate document retrieval, which is the next step. When the literature is examined, it is seen that the first studies used mostly classical methods such as tf-idf, bm25 [8–10] in the retrieval phase. Here, retrieval is provided by searching for words similar to the query received by the user as input.

When we look at other studies, one of the most used methods is the name entity recognition(ner) and post tagging methods. It has been observed that success in the retrieval phase increases thanks to semantic role labeling with these methods [11–13]. It is seen that support vector machine (SVM) is used as the other classical method classifier. Here, the category to which the query belongs is the classifier that performs document retrieval over that category. Semantic capture was improved with SVM [9,14].

The disadvantage of classical methods is that the query is misspelled or fails to find semantically similar words. When we examine the literature, we observe that deep learning studies have increased in recent years. When we examine the studies using deep learning, we see that more successful results are obtained than the classical methods (Chen, Y.,) (Pappas, D.) (X. Zhang,) (Lin, H.) (Nie P.) [15–18]. The advantage of deeplearning is that words are captured in semantic and misspelled words. In this way, most of the studies in the field of question answering in recent years are on deep learning.

4   Conclusion and Future Works

In this systematic literature study, our goal is to analyze and summarize the trends, datasets and methods used in the studies in the field of question answering between 2000–2022. According to the inclusion and exclusion criteria, 91 final studies were determined.

When the studies in the literature are examined, problems such as noisy data, performance and success rates have been dealt with and these problems are still among the subjects that are open to research. In the analysis of selected final studies, it was determined that the current question answering research focused on four topics: KB, IR, NLP, Hybrid Base. When the studies in the field of question answering are examined, 6.72% of the topics are KB topics, 31.94% are IR topics, 59.24% are NLP topics and 2.10% are Hybrid base. In addition, 65.05% of the studies were used as public datasets and 34.95% as private datasets. Fourteen different methods were used for question answering. Among the fourteen methods, seven most applied methods were determined in the field of question answering. These are relation finding(similarity distance), parsing, ner, Tokenize, deep learning, post tagging, graph. Using some of these techniques, the researchers proposed some techniques to improve accuracy in the QA field.

References

1. Kitchenham, B., Charters, S.: Guidelines for performing systematic literature reviews in software engineering. EBSE Technical Report Version 2.3, EBSE (2007)
2. Radjenović, D., Heričko, M., Torkar, R., Živkovič, A.: Software fault prediction metrics: a systematic literature review. Inf. Softw. Technol. 55(8), 1397–1418 (2013). https://doi.org/10.1016/j.infsof.2013.02.009

3. Unterkalmsteiner, M., Gorschek, T., Islam, A., Cheng, C.K., Permadi, R.B., Feldt, R.: Evaluation and measurement of software process improvement-a systematic literature review. IEEE Trans. Softw. Eng. **38**(2), 398–424 (2012). https://doi.org/10.1109/TSE.2011.26

4. Wahono, R.S.: A systematic literature review of software defect prediction: research trends, datasets, methods and frameworks. J. Softw. Eng. **1**(1), 1–16 (2015)

5. Yao, X.: Feature-Driven Question Answering with Natural Language Alignment. John Hopkins University (2014)

6. Sammut, C., Webb, G.I.: Encyclopedia of Machine Learning. Springer, New York (2011). https://doi.org/10.1007/978-0-387-30164-8

7. Yang, M.-C., Lee, D.-G., Park, S.-Y., Rim, II.-C.: Knowledge-based question answering using the semantic embedding space. Expert Syst. Appl. **42**(23), 9086–9104 (2015). https://doi.org/10.1016/j.eswa.2015.07.009

8. Brokos, G.-I., Malakasiotis, P., Androutsopoulos, I.: Using centroids of word embeddings and word mover's distance for biomedical document retrieval in question answering. In: BioNLP 2016 - Proceedings of the 15th Workshop on Biomedical Natural Language, pp. 114–118 (2016). https://doi.org/10.18653/v1/W16-2915

9. Cao, Y., Liu, F., Simpson, P., Ely, J., Yu, H.: AskHERMES, an online question answering system for complex clinical questions. J. Biomed. Inform. **44**(2), 277–288 (2011)

10. Tellex, S., Katz, B., Fernandes, A., Marton, G.: Quantitative evaluation of passage retrieval algorithms for question answering. In: SIGIR 2003, Proceedings of the 26th Annual International ACM SIGIR Conference on Research and Development in Information Retrieval, pp. 41–47 (2003)

11. Bilotti, M.W., Elsas, J., Carbonell, J., Nyberg, E.: Rank learning for factoid question answering with linguistic and semantic constraints. In: International Conference on Information and Knowledge Management, Proceedings, pp. 459–468 (2010)

12. Pardiño, M., Gómez, J.M., Llorens, H., Moreda, P., Palomar, M.: Adapting IBQAS to work with text transcriptions in QAst task. In: IBQAst: CEUR Workshop Proceedings (2008)

13. Roth, B., Conforti, C., Poerner, N., Karn, S.K., Schütze, H.: Neural architectures for open-type relation argument extraction. Nat. Lang. Eng. **25**(2), 219–238 (2019)

14. Niu, Y., Hirst, G.: Identifying cores of semantic classes in unstructured text with a semi-supervised learning approach. In: International Conference Recent Advances in Natural Language Processing, RANLP (2007)

15. Chen, Y., Zhang, X., Chen, A., Zhao, X., Dong, Y.: QA system for food safety events based on information extraction. Nongye Jixie Xuebao/Trans. Chin. Soc. Agric. Mach. **51**, 442–448 (2020)

16. Pappas, D., Androutsopoulos, I.: A neural model for joint document and snippet ranking in question answering for large document collections. In: ACL-IJCNLP 2021–59th Annual Meeting of the Association for Computational Linguistics and the 11th International Joint Conference on Natural Language Processing, Proceedings of the Conference, pp. 3896–3907 (2021)

17. Lin, H.-Y., Lo, T.-H., Chen, B.: Enhanced Bert-based ranking models for spoken document retrieval. In: IEEE Automatic Speech Recognition and Understanding Workshop, ASRU 2019 - Proceedings, vol. 9003890, pp. 601–606 (2019)

18. Zhang, Y., Nie, P., Ramamurthy, A., Song, L.: Answering any-hop open-domain questions with iterative document reranking. In: SIGIR 2021 - Proceedings of the 44th International ACM SIGIR Conference on Research and Development in Information Retrieval, vol. 3462853, pp. 481–490 (2021)

19. Kratzwald, B., Feuerriegel, S.: Adaptive document retrieval for deep question answering. In: Proceedings of the 2018 Conference on Empirical Methods in Natural Language Processing, EMNLP, pp. 576–581 (2018)
20. Cong, Y., Wu, Y., Liang, X., Pei, J., Qin, Z.: PH-model: enhancing multi-passage machine reading comprehension with passage reranking and hierarchical information. Appl. Intell. **51**(8), 5440–5452 (2021). https://doi.org/10.1007/s10489-020-02168-3
21. Nguyen, T.M., Tran, V.-L., Can, D.-C., Vu, L.T., Chng, E.S.: QASA advanced document retriever for open-domain question answering by learning to rank question-aware self-attentive document representations. In: ACM International Conference Proceeding Series, pp. 221–225 (2019)
22. Guo, Q.-L., Zhang, M.: Semantic information integration and question answering based on pervasive agent ontology. Expert Syst. Appl. **36**(6), 10068–10077 (2009)
23. Grau, B.: Finding an answer to a question. In: Proceedings of the International Workshop on Research Issues in Digital Libraries, IWRIDL-2006. In: Association with ACM SIGIR, vol. 1364751 (2007)
24. Radev, D., Fan, W., Qi, H., Wu, H., Grewal, A.: Probabilistic question answering on the web. In: Proceedings of the 11th International Conference on World Wide Web, WWW 2002, pp. 408–419 (2002)
25. Lin, J., et al.: The role of context in question answering systems. In: CHI EA 2003: CHI 2003 Extended Abstracts on Human Factors in Computing Systems (2003)
26. Pérez-Coutiño, M., Solorio, T., Montes-y-Gómez, M., López-López, A., Villaseñor-Pineda, L.: Question answering for Spanish based on lexical and context annotation. In: Lemaître, C., Reyes, C.A., González, J.A. (eds.) IBERAMIA 2004. LNCS (LNAI), vol. 3315, pp. 325–333. Springer, Heidelberg (2004). https://doi.org/10.1007/978-3-540-30498-2_33
27. Zhang, X., Zhan, K., Hu, E., Fu, C., Luo, L., Jiang, H.: Answer complex questions: path ranker is all you need. Artif. Intell. Rev. **55**(1), 207–253 (2021)
28. Fan, Y., , J., Ma, X., Zhang, R., Lan, Y., Cheng, X.: A linguistic study on relevance modeling in information retrieval. In: The Web Conference 2021 - Proceedings of the World Wide Web Conference, WWW 2021, pp. 1053–1064 (2021)
29. Kaiser, M. : Incorporating user feedback in conversational question answering over heterogeneous web sources. In: SIGIR 2020 - Proceedings of the 43rd International ACM SIGIR Conference on Research and Development in Information Retrieval, pp. 28–42 (2020)
30. Lamurias, A., Sousa, D., Couto, F.M.: Generating biomedical question answering corpora from QA forums. IEEE Access **8**(9184044), 161042–161051 (2020). https://doi.org/10.1109/ACCESS.2020.3020868
31. Sarrouti, M., Ouatik El Alaoui, S.: SemBioNLQA a semantic biomedical question answering system for retrieving exact and ideal answers to natural language questions. Artif. Intell. Med. **102**(101767) (2020)
32. Shah, A.A., Ravana, S.D., Hamid, S., Ismail, M.A.: Accuracy evaluation of methods and techniques in Web-based question answering systems. Knowl. Inf. Syst. **58**(3), 611–650 (2019). https://doi.org/10.1016/j.artmed.2019.101767
33. Roth, B., Conforti, C., Poerner, N., Karn, S.K., Schütze, H.: Neural architectures for open-type relation argument extraction. Nat. Lang. Eng. **25**(2), 219–238 (2019)
34. Samarinas, C., Tsoumakas, G.: WamBY: an information retrieval approach to web-based question answering. In: ACM International Conference Proceeding Series (2018)

35. Novotn, V., Sojka, P.: Weighting of passages in question answering. In: Recent Advances in Slavonic Natural Language Processing, December 2018, pp. 31–40 (2018)
36. Sarrouti, M., Ouatik El Alaoui, S.: A passage retrieval method based on probabilistic information retrieval and UMLS concepts in biomedical question answering. J. Biomed. Inform. **68**, 96–103 (2017). https://doi.org/10.1016/j.jbi.2017.03.001
37. Jin, Z.-X., Zhang, B.-W., Fang, F., Zhang, L.-L., Yin, X.-C.: A multi-strategy query processing approach for biomedical question answering. In: BioNLP 2017 - SIGBioMed Workshop on Biomedical Natural Language Processing, Proceedings of the 16th BioNLP Workshop, pp. 373–380 (2017)
38. Aroussi, S.A., Habib, N.E., Beqqali, O.E.: Improving question answering systems by using the explicit semantic analysis method. In: SITA 2016–11th International Conference on Intelligent Systems: Theories and Applications 7772300 (2016)
39. Omari, A., Carmel, D., Rokhlenko, O., Szpektor, I.: Novelty based ranking of human answers for community questions. In: SIGIR 2016 - Proceedings of the 39th International ACM SIGIR Conference on Research and Development in Information Retrieval, pp. 215–224 (2016)
40. Hoque, M.M., Quaresma, P.: An effective approach for relevant paragraph retrieval in Question Answering systems. In: 2015 18th International Conference on Computer and Information Technology, ICCIT 2015 7488040, pp. 44–49 (2016)
41. Brokos, G.-I., Malakasiotis, P., Androutsopoulos, I.: Using centroids of word embeddings and word mover's distance for biomedical document retrieval in question answering. In: BioNLP 2016-Proceedings of the 15th Workshop on Biomedical Natural Language Processing, pp. 114–118 (2016)
42. Tsatsaronis, G., et al.: An overview of the BioASQ large-scale biomedical semantic indexing and question answering competition. BMC Bioinform. **16**(1), 138 (2015)
43. Neves, M.: HPI question answering system in the BioASQ 2015 challenge. In: CEUR Workshop Proceedings, vol. 1391 (2015)
44. Liu, Z.J., Wang, X.L., Chen, Q.C., Zhang, Y.Y., Xiang, Y.: A Chinese question answering system based on web search. In: Proceedings-International Conference on Machine Learning and Cybernetics, vol. 2,7009714, pp. 816–820 (2014)
45. Ageev, M., Lagun, D., Agichtein, E.: The answer is at your fingertips: improving passage retrieval for web question answering with search behavior data. In: EMNLP 2013–2013 Conference on Empirical Methods in Natural Language Processing, Proceedings of the Conference, pp. 1011–1021 (2013)
46. Sun, W., Fu, C., Xiao, Q.: A text inference based answer extraction for Chinese question answering. In: Proceedings-2012 9th International Conference on Fuzzy Systems and Knowledge Discovery, FSKD 2012, vol. 6234145, pp. 2870–2874 (2012)
47. Lu, W., Cheng, J., Yang, Q.: Question answering system based on web. In: Proceedings-2012 5th International Conference on Intelligent Computation Technology and Automation, ICICTA 2012, vol. 6150169, pp. 573–576 (2012)
48. Saias, J., Quaresma, P.: Question answering approach to the multiple choice QA4MRE challenge. In: CEUR Workshop Proceedings, vol. 1178 (2012)
49. Foucault, N., Adda, G., Rosset, S.: Language modeling for document selection in question answering. In: International Conference Recent Advances in Natural Language Processing, RANLP, pp. 716–720 (2011)
50. Monz, C.: Machine learning for query formulation in question answering. Nat. Lang. Eng. **17**(4), 425–454 (2011)

51. Zhang, W., Duan, L., Chen, J.: Reasoning and realization based on ontology model and Jena. In: Proceedings 2010 IEEE 5th International Conference on Bio-Inspired Computing: Theories and Applications, BIC-TA 2010, vol. 5645115, pp. 1057–1060 (2010)
52. Li, F., Kang, H., Zhang, Y., Su, W.: Question intention analysis and entropy-based paragraph extraction for medical question answering. In: ICCASM 2010–2010 International Conference on Computer Application and System Modeling, Proceedings, vol. 3,5620229, pp. V3354–V3357 (2010)
53. Li, X., Chen, E.: Graph-based answer passage ranking for question answering. In: Proceedings-2010 International Conference on Computational Intelligence and Security, vol. 5696360, pp. 634–638 (2010)
54. Lu, W.-H., Tung, C.-M., Lin, C.-W.: Question intention analysis and entropy-based paragraph extraction for medical question answering. In: IFMBE Proceedings 31 IFMBE, pp. 1582–1586 (2010)
55. Nguyen, D.T., Pham, T.N., Phan, Q.T.: A semantic model for building the Vietnamese language query processing framework in e-library searching application. In: ICMLC 2010 - The 2nd International Conference on Machine Learning and Computing, vol. 5460746, pp. 179–183 (2010)
56. Nguyen, D.T., Nguyen, H.V., Phan, Q.T.: Using the Vietnamese language query processing framework to build a courseware searching system. In: 2010 2nd International Conference on Computer Engineering and Applications, ICCEA 2010, vol. 2,5445613, pp. 117–121 (2010)
57. Buscaldi, D., Rosso, P., Gómez-Soriano, J.M., Sanchis, E.: Answering questions with an n-gram based passage retrieval engine. J. Intell. Inf. Syst. 34(2), 113–134 (2010)
58. Momtazi, S., Klakow, D.: A word clustering approach for language model-based sentence retrieval in question answering systems. In: International Conference on Information and Knowledge Management, Proceedings, pp. 1911–1914 (2009)
59. Dang, N.T., Thi, D., Tuyen, T.: Document retrieval based on question answering system. In: 2009 2nd International Conference on Information and Computing Science, ICIC 2009, vol. 1,5169570, pp. 183–186 (2009)
60. Guo, Q.-L., Zhang, M.: Semantic information integration and question answering based on pervasive agent ontology. Expert Syst. Appl. 36(6), 10068–10077 (2009)
61. Dang, N.T., Tuyen, D.T.T.: Natural language question-answering model applied to document retrieval system: world academy of science. Eng. Technol. 39, 36–39 (2009)
62. Dang, N.T., Tuyen, D.T.T.: E-document retrieval by question answering system: world academy of science. Eng. Technol. 38, 395–398 (2009)
63. Abouenour, L., Bouzoubaa, K., Rosso, P.: Structure-based evaluation of an Arabic semantic query expansion using the JIRS passage retrieval system. In: Proceedings of the EACL 2009 Workshop on Computational Approaches to Semitic Languages, SEMITIC@EACL 2009, pp. 62–68 (2009)
64. Ortiz-Arroyo, D.: Flexible question answering system for mobile devices: 3rd International Conference on Digital Information Management, ICDIM 2008, vol. 4746794, pp. 266–271 (2008)
65. Lita, L.V., Carbonell, J.: Cluster-based query expansion for statistical question answering. In: JCNLP 2008–3rd International Joint Conference on Natural Language Processing, Proceedings of the Conference (2008)
66. Kürsten, J., Kundisch, H., Eibl, M.: QA extension for Xtrieval: contribution to the QAst track. In: CEUR Workshop Proceedings, vol. 1174 (2008)

67. Comas, P.R., Turmo, J.: Robust question answering for speech transcripts: UPC experience in QAst. In: CEUR Workshop Proceedings, vol. 1174 (2008)
68. Hu, B.-S., Wang, D.-L., Yu, G., Ma, T.: Answer extraction algorithm based on syntax structure feature parsing and classification. Jisuanji Xuebao/Chin. J. Comput. **31**(4), 662–676 (2008)
69. Yang, Z., Lin, H., Cui, B., Li, Y., Zhang, X.: DUTIR at TREC 2007 genomics track. NIST Special Publication (2007)
70. Schlaefer, N., Ko, J., Betteridge, J., Pathak, M., Nyberg, E.: Semantic extensions of the ephyra QA system for TREC 2007. NIST Special Publication (2007)
71. Hickl, A., Roberts, K., Rink, B., Shi, Y., Williams, J.: Question answering with LCC's CHAUCER-2 at TREC 2007. NIST Special Publication (2007)
72. Pasca, M.: Lightweight web-based fact repositories for textual question answering. In: International Conference on Information and Knowledge Management, Proceedings, pp. 87–96 (2007)
73. Peters, C.: Multilingual information access: the contribution of evaluation. In: Proceedings of the International Workshop on Research Issues in Digital Libraries, IWRIDL-2006, vol. 1364761. Association with ACM SIGIR (2007)
74. Yang, Y., Liu, S., Kuroiwa, S., Ren, F.: Question answering system of confusian analects based on pragmatics information and categories. In: IEEE NLP-KE 2007 - Proceedings of International Conference on Natural Language Processing and Knowledge Engineering, vol. 4368056, pp. 361–366 (2007)
75. Tiedemann, J.: Comparing document segmentation strategies for passage retrieval in question answering. In: International Conference Recent Advances in Natural Language Processing, RANL (2007)
76. Yarmohammadi, M.A., Shamsfard, M., Yarmohammadi, M.A., Rouhizadeh, M.: Using WordNet in extracting the final answer from retrieved documents in a question answering system. In: GWC 2008: 4th Global WordNet Conference, Proceedings, pp. 520–530 (2007)
77. Niu, Y., Hirst, G.: Comparing document segmentation strategies for passage retrieval in question answering. In: International Conference Recent Advances in Natural Language Processing, RANLP 2007-January, pp. 418–424 (2007)
78. Hussain, M., Merkel, A., Klakow, D.: Dedicated backing-off distributions for language model based passage retrieval. Lernen, Wissensentdeckung und Adaptivitat, LWA **2006**, 138–143 (2006)
79. Jinguji, D., Lewis, W., Efthimiadis, E.N., Yu, P., Zhou, Z.: The university of Washington's UWCLMAQA system. NIST Special Publication (2006)
80. Balantrapu, S., Khan, M., Nagubandi, A.: TREC 2006 Q&A factoid TI experience. NIST Special Publication (2006)
81. Ofoghi, B., Yearwood, J., Ghosh, R.: TREC 2006 Q&A factoid: TI experience. In: Conferences in Research and Practice in Information Technology Series, vol. 48, pp. 95–101 (2006)
82. Ferrés, D., Rodríguez, H.: Experiments using JIRS and Lucene with the ADL feature type Thesaurus. In: CEUR Workshop Proceedings, vol. 1172 (2006)
83. García-Cumbreras, M.A., Ureña-Lòpez, L.A., Santiago, F.M., Perea-Ortega, J.M.: BRUJA system. The University of Jaén at the Spanish task of CLEFQA 2006. In: CEUR Workshop Proceedings, vol. 1172 (2006)
84. Blake, C.: A comparison of document, sentence, and term event spaces. In: COLING/ACL 2006-21st International Conference on Computational Linguistics and 44th Annual Meeting of the Association for Computational Linguistics, Proceedings of the Conference, vol. 1, pp. 601–608 (2006)

85. Yu, Z.T., Zheng, Z.Y., Tang, S.P., Guo, J.Y.I.: Query expansion for answer document retrieval in Chinese question answering system. In: 2005 International Conference on Machine Learning and Cybernetics, ICMLC 2005, pp. 72–77 (2005)

86. Jousse, F., Tellier, I., Tommasi, M., Marty, P.: Learning to extract answers in question answering. In: CORIA 2005–2EME Conference en Recherche Informations et Applications (2005)

87. Ferrés, D., Kanaan, S., Dominguez-Sal, D, Surdeanu, M., Turmo, J.: Experiments using a voting scheme among three heterogeneous QA systems. NIST Special Publication (2005)

88. Yang, G.C., Oh, H.U.: ANEX an answer extraction system based on conceptual graphs. In: Proceedings of the 2005 International Conference on Information and Knowledge Engineering, IKE 2005, pp. 17–24 (2005)

89. Tiedemann, J.: Integrating linguistic knowledge in passage retrieval for question answering. In: HLT/EMNLP 2005-Human Language Technology Conference and Conference on Empirical Methods in Natural Language Processing, Proceedings of the Conference, pp. 939–946 (2005)

90. Isozaki, H.: An analysis of a high-performance Japanese question answering system. ACM Trans. Asian Lang. Inf. Process. **4**(3), 263–279 (2005)

91. Tiedemann, J. : Integrating linguistic knowledge in passage retrieval for question answering. In: International Conference Recent Advances in Natural Language Processing, RANLP 2005-January, pp. 540–546 (2005)

92. Amaral, C., Figueira, H., Martins, A., Mendes, P., Pinto, C.: Priberam's question answering system for Portuguese. In: CEUR Workshop Proceedings, vol. 1171 (2005). (Subseries of Lecture Notes in Computer Science), vol. 3315, pp. 325–333 (2004)

93. Banerjee P, Han H.: Incorporation of corpus-specific semantic information into question answering context. In: ONISW 2008 Proceedings of the 2nd International Workshop on Ontologies and Information Systems for the Semantic (2008)

94. Khushhal, S., Majid, A., Abbas, S.A., Nadeem, M.S.A., Shah, S.A.: Question retrieval using combined queries in community question answering. J. Intell. Inf. Syst. **55**(2), 307–327 (2020). https://doi.org/10.1007/s10844-020-00612-x

95. Nie, Y., Han, Y., Huang, J., Jiao, B., Li, A.: Attention-based encoder-decoder model for answer selection in question answering. Front. Inf. Technol. Electron. Eng. **18**, 535–544 (2017)

96. Cao, Y., Wen, Y., Chin, Y., Yong, Y.: A structural support vector method for extracting contexts and answers of questions from online forums. Inf. Process. Manag. **47**(6), 886–898 (2011)

97. Monroy, A., Calvo, H., Gelbukh, A.: Using graphs for shallow question answering on legal documents. In: Gelbukh, A., Morales, E.F. (eds.) MICAI 2008. LNCS (LNAI), vol. 5317, pp. 165–173. Springer, Heidelberg (2008). https://doi.org/10.1007/978-3-540-88636-5_15

98. Ofoghi, B., Yearwood, J., Ghosh, R.: A semantic approach to boost passage retrieval effectiveness for question answering. In: ACSC 2006: Proceedings of the 29th Australasian Computer Science Conference, vol. 48, pp. 95–101 (2006)

Steel Quality Monitoring Using Data-Driven Approaches: ArcelorMittal Case Study

Mohamed Laib[1]([✉])[iD], Riad Aggoune[1][iD], Rafael Crespo[2], and Pierre Hubsch[2]

[1] ITIS Department, Luxembourg Institute for Science and Technology,
Esch-sur-Alzette, Luxembourg
Mohamed.Laib@list.lu
[2] ArcelorMittal Global R&D, Esch-sur-Alzette, Luxembourg

Abstract. Studying manufacturing production process via data-driven approaches needs the collection of all possible parameters that control and influence the quality of the final product. The recorded features usually come from different steps of the manufacturing process. In many cases, recorded data contains a high number of features and is collected from several stages in the production process, which makes the prediction of product quality more difficult. The paper presents a new data-driven approach to deal with such kind of issues. The proposed approach helps not only in predicting the quality, but also in finding to which stage of the production process the quality is most related. The paper proposes a challenging case study from ArcelorMittal steel industry in Luxembourg.

Keywords: Industry 4.0 · Quality monitoring · Predictive modelling · Dimension reduction · Machine learning

1 Introduction

The concept of *Industry 4.0* (also known as the 4th industrial revolution) is gaining great popularity in several sectors. It aims at helping manufacturing industry to be more competitive and efficient by improving their performance. In addition, it gives more flexibility in handling different aspects of business processes [1]. The core asset in going toward Industry 4.0, among others, is to focus on the collection of data, and the good use of the extracted information from this data. Consequently, the digital transformation in manufacturing industry covers many modern research topics in data science such as statistical and machine learning techniques, big data technologies, and the expert knowledge in factories [2–4].

Nowadays, data science research and the advancements in Applied Machine learning and Data Analytics are becoming a very attractive topic in industrial

---

The present work is partly supported by the Luxembourg National Research Fund, FNR (BRIDGES18/IS/13307925).

sectors. In recent years, new methodologies and frameworks are being considered in the literature regarding the use of data-driven approaches for decision-making and quality improvement. The range of applied methods is wide, like, for instance, regularized linear regression in predicting product quality, in the semiconductor manufacturing process [5], or extreme learning machine for predicting heat effected zones of the laser cutting process [6]. Other techniques have been used and investigated, Loyer et al. did a comparison of some machine learning methods to estimate manufacturing cost of jet engine components [7]. A detailed literature review about data analytics in manufacturing is proposed by Sivri and Oztaysi [8]. Cheng et al. emphasized some limitations of the available data mining techniques in dealing with complex and unstructured data issued from manufacturing [9]. Iffat et al. suggested some methodologies and approaches on how to deal with high dimensional unstructured data, containing sequence data. They worked mainly on summarizing the sequences using some time series measures and Variational autoencoders [10].

Furthermore, the technology of collecting data is being continuously improved, and many sectors are paying attention to intelligent ways on how to collect data. Consequently, the volume of data is increasing day by day. Moreover, in several manufacturing sectors, data is collected from different stages of production. Thus, assessing quality of the final product using data-driven approaches becomes more challenging because of (1) the existing redundancy in data; and (2) the fact that there are different stages of the manufacturing process. Depending on the aspect of quality, the deviation can be linked to a specific step of production and detecting that is very important in order to improve the quality.

This paper focuses on how to extract information from manufacturing data in order to understand it and predict product quality. The quality is defined with regard to international standards, depending on the product and regions. In fact, the paper investigates one specific product, and proposes a new methodology of dealing with (1) high dimensional manufacturing data collected from different stages; and (2) finding in which stage of the production the quality can be most improved. The present work uses, as case study, ArcelorMittal (AM) steel data collected with the help of experts domain. Several data-driven studies have been conducted on manufacturing data, Konrad et al. proposed a production control concept based on data mining techniques [11]. Lieber et al. proposed a quality prediction in manufacturing processes in two steps. The first step introduces data preprocessing and feature extraction, and the second one combines several supervised and unsupervised machine learning methods to predict product quality [12]. Bai et al. gave a reinforcement learning framework based on AdaBoost algorithm to predict quality [13]. In the present paper, dimension of data is reduced in order to minimize the redundancy, which is a very important step that helps in the understanding of the data [14, 15]. Then, a predictive model is applied at each stage of the production in order to monitor the quality through the different stages of production. The aim of the proposed methodology is not only to predict the quality of the product, but also to monitor the product quality through the production stages.

The rest of the paper is organized as follows. Section 2 presents data and the exploratory analysis. Section 3 explains the proposed approach and the used techniques. Results and discussions are presented in Sect. 4, with validation and interpretation from AM experts. Finally, conclusions and future challenges are given in the last section.

2 Data and Exploratory Analysis

2.1 Data Description

First, the database contains mainly five tables (datasets): Ebauche (EBCH), Blooming (BLM), Tandem (TDM), Thermal Treatment (TT), and Finishing (FIN), which corresponds to the five main steps of the production. These datasets are extracted from the Manufacturing Execution System (MES) from Arcelor-Mittal Luxembourg and correspond to four years of production. The dataset entails the complete transformation process the steel undergoes from scrap to finished product in order to explore as broad correlations as it is currently possible. Individual products are tracked through the whole production process; each entry in the database can be associated with one individual, identified product. The step resolution grows finer, as do the process parameters linked to each step: initially every entry in the database corresponds to a ladle load of 150 tons, then reduced to semi product entries of 10–25 tons. Furthermore, TT treated beams have the highest resolution of information, with a database entry every 3.2 m.

Before the Continuous Caster Machine (CCM), the scrap is molten into recycled steel. The liquid steel's chemical composition is tested once and then undergoes several selective processes including degassing, killing and finally is brought to the desired grade on the ladle furnace. Such process parameters are recorded in the Database. Grades and mixing zones logged for each individual strand of the CCM, leading to a complete histogram of the material until solidified.

For every bar in EBCH, the exact specification of the semi-product including, amongst other the casting date, the heat number, the grade, the strand number are recorded together with the information on the final product including the rolling campaign as well as the product type and dimensions. Although the Reheating Furnace Model was excluded in this analysis, the impact is indirectly inferred as stay time in the furnace, entry state and temperature of the product are taken into account both before and after the furnace.

Concerning the Blooming Stand, it is structured under multiple passes, in which are included roll position and guiding system position. Added to these are a set of guidelines, corrections as well as sensor measurements to ensure process control. The BLM dataset contains detailed information on temperature and time along with roll geometry, some relevant groove parameters and number, guiding system positioning, rolling speed, feeding speed and bar rotation histogram.

Regarding TDM, the universal rolling mode and grooves are taken into account. The process is similar to BLM, insofar as the bar is hot rolled in back and forth passes, with gap adjustments in the roll positions. At each one of these passes, speed, force as well as temperatures on flanges and selective cooling are recorded. In contrast to BLM, universal rolling and edger stands have only one groove, but the positioning of the rolls and their vertical or horizontal positions are all recorded. Same with calculated strand length and rolling speed.

The bar passes the finishing stand FIN, once. Recorded in that database are, amongst others, rolling speed, roll gaps, roll geometry, forces and a set of temperatures on a number of defined points on the surface of the beam. Not all bars pass through the thermal treatment unit. For the ones that do, speed, flow-rate and ratios as well as temperature of the coolant are recorded alongside with a set of temperature measurements. In TT, bars contain a series of measurements per bar, including a series of cooling parameters specific to the process and cooling models. These include more detailed temperature measurements as well as web and both sides of flanges, in addition to the evolution of temperature lengthwise. Speed variations, and water temperatures, flow rates and rations are also stored to ensure a homogeneous cooling and tailor-made crystallography.

The finished product undergoes multiple checks with regard to its surface quality, its geometry and its mechanical properties. The recorded values are associated to individual pieces and stored in a database. It is through this link that the association between the quality of the final product and the process parameters can be achieved. We aim to improve the predictability of process deviations to ensure the corrections are made before they can have an impact on the product, and instead act proactively to ensure a tight control before process discrepancies occur. This work aims at understanding the origin of deviation using data-driven approaches based on dimension reduction and classification models.

After extracting data from the production steps, a cleaning process has been done to handle missing values and/or outliers. Especially for BLM and TDM where data is structured with multiple passes. These passes have been summarized by taking values corresponding to the finale pass and also some statistics of previous passes (median and standard deviation).

2.2 Exploratory Data Analysis

As in any data-driven study, exploratory data analysis (EDA) is a crucial step. In this part, we investigate and visualize the five datasets used in this paper. The panel of available EDA tools is very large, and since the datasets have a high number of features, we focus first on correlations between them. As mentioned above, features are highly correlated. Figure 1 shows the correlations, each dataset has grouped features.

In order to investigate more the used datasets, and since the features are continuous, principal component analysis (PCA) is applied as dimension reduction method to explore the most important part of each dataset. EBCH dataset is used as example to visualize the existing relationship between feature. The correlation matrices are difficult to inspect due to the large number of features. However, one can already see some grouping among the feature of each dataset.

Figure 2 shows results of the PCA, 75% as information is gathered in the first 7 principal components (PCs), where the elbow (4 PCs) shown in the left panel of Fig. 2 is equivalent to 60% of the total variance. The correlation circle (on the 2 first PCs) highlights the redundancy showed in Fig. 1a. Further, it shows mainly

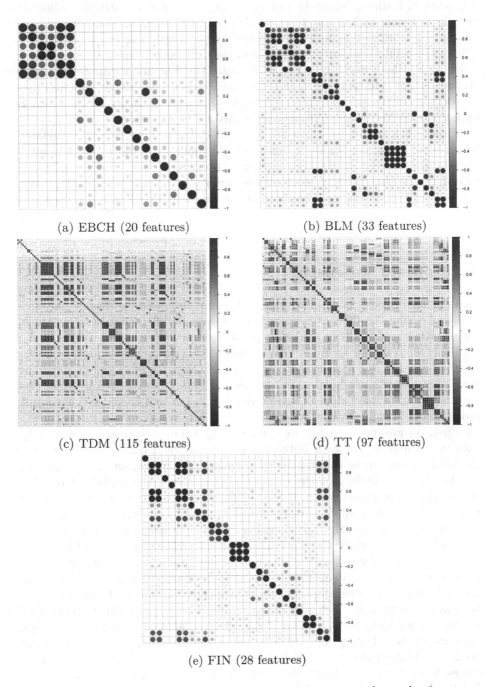

(a) EBCH (20 features)

(b) BLM (33 features)

(c) TDM (115 features)

(d) TT (97 features)

(e) FIN (28 features)

Fig. 1. Correlation matrices for the five datasets, which represent the production steps.

3 groups of features, where two of them are correlated negatively. Following the elbow shown in Fig. 2 and considering only the four first components, one can see the contribution of each input variable on Fig. 3. Further investigations using PCA results against the output show the difference between the two classes (with and without deviation), Fig. 4 visualizes the four first components versus the output. In addition, Fig. 5 shows variables that have higher contributions (according to Fig. 3). The difference between classes is hardly clear, which is expected since the production process is only at its beginning.

From EDA results, one can see that all datasets have several correlated features. Merging all datasets cannot help in monitoring the product quality, because correlated features between production steps could lead the engineer to a database that has less effect on the deviation understudy. Therefore, this merges can lead to wrong conclusions about the important features responsible for the deviation, and it would be difficult to monitor the quality through the production procedure.

3 Proposed Approach

The quality of the final product cannot be modelled with the use of only one dataset because the different datasets corresponds to different production steps, each of which contributes to the final properties of the products.

Using only one dataset is not enough in detecting the deviation in the process, mainly because this deviation may not happen in this step of production and one would need more input features from other datasets. However, before using new features from the next steps of the production, we should consider the existing redundancy. The proposed approach is divided into two part (see Fig. 6):

First, an unsupervised feature selection algorithm is applied to reduce the existing redundancy in each dataset. As in many high dimensional datasets, the information can be summarized in a subset of features, and the remainder can be either redundant or irrelevant. In other words, the useful information that explains the phenomenon, described by the data, is in a smaller subset of features [14,15]. In manufacturing data, it is hard to say which features bring more information and which of them are completely irrelevant. In fact, in the ArcelorMittal case study, the dataset contain many features collected for many reasons, not only for monitoring the quality. Some of these feature are highly correlated (see Fig. 1 for example). These high (linear/nonlinear) correlations (i.e. redundancy) may lead, apart to the mentioned problems on the introduction, to difficulty in finding which step of the production has more effect on the final product. Therefore, in the present paper, this redundancy is reduced by using the coverage-based algorithm [16]. This algorithm was used because it does not need to find hyperparameter, which can help in having an automatic procedure to choose less redundant features. Furthermore, this algorithm showed its efficiency in manufacturing data in [10]. The dimensionality reduction performed in this step consists mainly in reducing the redundancy from each dataset of the process procedures.

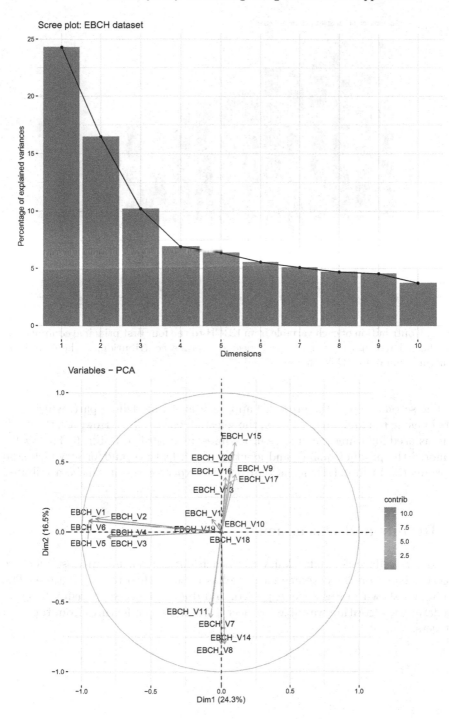

Fig. 2. PCA results applied on EBCH dataset. Top panel: eigenvalues plot representing the percentage of information of each principal component. Bottom panel: correlation circle on the 2 first components.

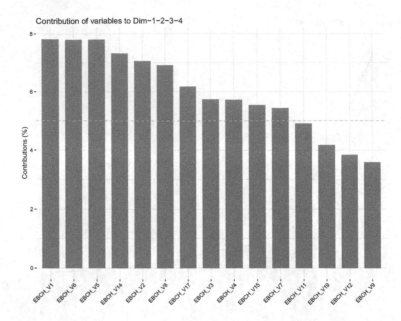

Fig. 3. Contribution of each variable from EBCH to the four first principal components. The dashed red line represents the expected average contribution, if there were no redundancy in data. (Color figure online)

The second step of the proposed approach is the modelling part, which consists in using random forest (RF) on the selected features [17]. However, the modelling is used following the process procedures, as described in Fig. 6. The goal is to model the product quality and identify which feature (and/or at which step of production) can detect deviation from the expected result can be attributed to.

4   Results and Discussions

In order to reduce the redundancy from each dataset, an unsupervised feature selection based on the coverage measure has been applied to each dataset. The results are shown in Fig. 7. As expected, and due to the existing redundancy in the data, the algorithm was able to select a smaller set of features from the used datasets.

In each dataset, the number of selected features is much lower than the original number of features. Table 1 summarizes the results for each stage of the production. Furthermore, one can see already through random forest results, applied on separated dataset, that TDM gives the best performance of classification. Therefore, TDM is responsible for this kind of deviation happened to product. However, to confirm this result, other random forest models have been applied, by adding more feature recorded from other steps of the production process. In fact, we accumulated the datasets following the production process, in order to understand better the data and improve the performance of the classifier. Figure 8 shows the comparison between using only separated dataset and accumulating them.

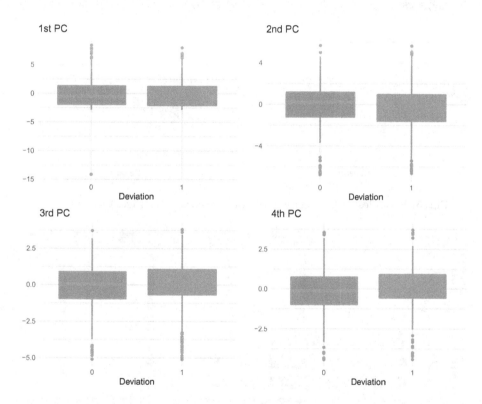

Fig. 4. Four first principal components vs output. PCA components do not a clear distinction between presence and absence of deviation.

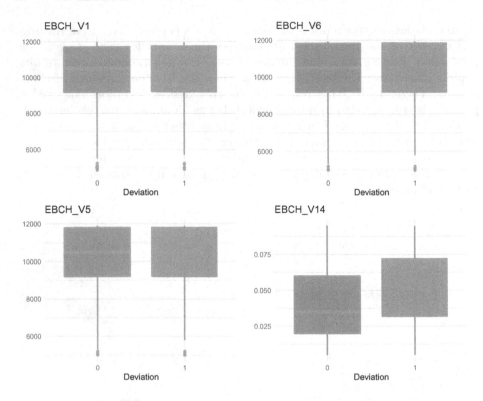

Fig. 5. Variables with higher contribution (according to Fig. 3) vs. output.

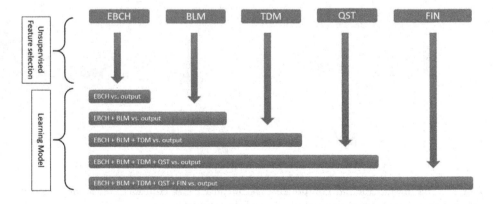

Fig. 6. The proposed approach consisted in reducing the number of features, then apply a learning algorithm at each step of the production by accumulating the features of previous steps.

In Fig. 8 the black line reaches its maximum with accumulating EBCH, BLM, and TDM. After TDM, the performance is slightly lower but stay stable for TT and FIN (mainly because of the presence of variables from TDM). However, the red line, presenting the results of separated dataset, FIN performance drops too low, which means that this stage has less effect on the manufacturing process and does not influence the finale outcome.

As mentioned above, the quality is defined following international standards that depend on the type of product and also the region to which the product is delivered to. In this case study, we have chosen one particular measure of quality, which is adherence to the prescribed geometry (defined by international standards) and we can read from our results that features recorded in TDM have more effect in describing and predicting the final product quality.

Table 1. Summary of feature selection results and random forest classifier for each dataset.

Datasets	# Original feat.	# Selected feat.	Kappa (Separated)
EBCH	20	4	0.26
BLM	33	12	0.28
TDM	115	15	0.31
TT	97	19	0.31
FIN	28	12	0.3

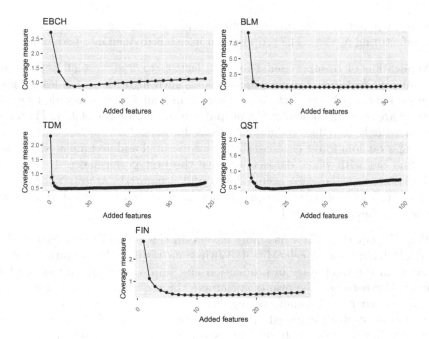

Fig. 7. Unsupervised feature selection applied on each dataset.

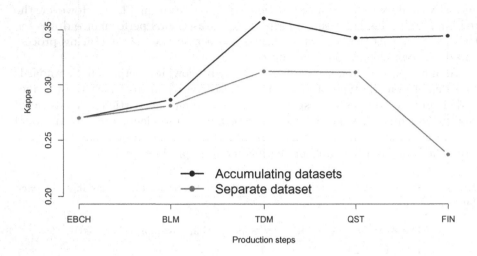

Fig. 8. Random forest results from different datasets. Black line presents the results when the datasets are accumulated following the production process. The red line is the results by using the dataset separately. (Color figure online)

5   Conclusion

This paper presents a data-driven approach for monitoring quality deviation in a manufacturing process. The proposed approach is divided into two main steps:

1. Application of unsupervised feature selection to find a small set of non-redundant features. The purpose of using such algorithm, besides its good performance, is because we know that almost all features recorded for this study are relevant to predict the output but are highly correlated. Therefore, we need only to reduce redundancy from datasets.
2. Using a random forest classifier for both separated and accumulated datasets to find out with which dataset we have the best performance. In addition, the comparison between accumulated and separated datasets allows us to conclude which stage of the production is most sensitive to deviation and must be closely monitored.

Pointing out that TDM has more effects on this deviation was expected by the R&D team from ArcelorMittal. With such results, the deviation will be corrected in the right stage of production and improve the quality of the final product. Furthermore, the results encourage the use of data-driven approaches to explore, understand manufacturing data, and improve the quality.

The present work explored several datasets collected from several stages of the production process. It presents a contribution to the understanding of ArcelorMittal data. Further works could be in using more advanced dimension reduction tools that take into account data collected from different sources, such as integrated principal component [18], which may help in extracting more knowledge and gives more insights that can improve classification models.

Acknowledgment. The authors thank both teams from ArcelorMittal and LIST, who were involved in discussions about the PAX project.

References

1. Kagermann, H., Wahlster, W., Helbig, J.: Recommendations for implementing the strategic initiative industrie 4.0. In: Final report of the Industrie 4.0 Working Group, Federal Ministry of Education and Research, p. 84 (2013). http://forschungsunion.de/pdf/industrie_4_0_final_report.pdf
2. Khan, M., Wu, X., Xu, X., Dou, W.: Big data challenges and opportunities in the hype of industry 4.0. In: 2017 IEEE International Conference on Communications (ICC), pp. 1–6 (2017). https://doi.org/10.1109/ICC.2017.7996801
3. Lu, Y.: Industry 4.0: a survey on technologies, applications and open research issues. J. Ind. Inf. Integr. **6**, 1–10 (2017). https://doi.org/10.1016/j.jii.2017.04.005
4. Rossit, D.A., Tohmé, F., Frutos, M.: A data-driven scheduling approach to smart manufacturing. J. Ind. Inf. Integr. **15**, 69–79 (2019). https://doi.org/10.1016/j.jii.2019.04.003
5. Melhem, M., Ananou, B., Ouladsine, M., Pinaton, J.: Regression methods for predicting the product quality in the semiconductor manufacturing process. IFAC-PapersOnLine **49**(12), 83–88 (2016). 8th IFAC Conference on Manufacturing Modelling, Management and Control MIM 2016. https://doi.org/10.1016/j.ifacol.2016.07.554
6. Anicic, O., Jović, S., Skrijelj, H., Nedić, B.: Prediction of laser cutting heat affected zone by extreme learning machine. Opt. Lasers Eng. **88**, 1–4 (2017). https://doi.org/10.1016/j.optlaseng.2016.07.005
7. Loyer, J.-L., Henriques, E., Fontul, M., Wiseall, S.: Comparison of machine learning methods applied to the estimation of manufacturing cost of jet engine components. Int. J. Prod. Econ. **178**, 109–119 (2016). https://doi.org/10.1016/j.ijpe.2016.05.006
8. Sivri, M.S., Oztaysi, B.: Data Analytics in Manufacturing, pp. 155–172. Springer, Cham (2018). https://doi.org/10.1007/978-3-319-57870-5_9
9. Cheng, Y., Chen, K., Sun, H., Zhang, Y., Tao, F.: Data and knowledge mining with big data towards smart production. J. Ind. Inf. Integr. **9**, 1–13 (2018). https://doi.org/10.1016/j.jii.2017.08.001
10. Iffat, U., Roseren, E., Laib, M.: Dealing with high dimensional sequence data in manufacturing. Procedia CIRP **104**, 1298–1303 (2021). 54th CIRP CMS 2021 - Towards Digitalized Manufacturing 4.0. https://doi.org/10.1016/j.procir.2021.11.218
11. Konrad, B., Lieber, D., Deuse, J.: Striving for zero defect production: intelligent manufacturing control through data mining in continuous rolling mill processes. In: Windt, K. (ed.) Robust Manufacturing Control. LNPE, pp. 215–229. Springer, Berlin Heidelberg, Berlin, Heidelberg (2013). https://doi.org/10.1007/978-3-642-30749-2_16
12. Lieber, D., Stolpe, M., Konrad, B., Deuse, J., Morik, K.: Quality prediction in interlinked manufacturing processes based on supervised & unsupervised machine learning. Procedia CIRP **7**, 193–198 (2013). forty Sixth CIRP Conference on Manufacturing Systems 2013. https://doi.org/10.1016/j.procir.2013.05.033

13. Bai, Y., Xie, J., Wang, D., Zhang, W., Li, C.: A manufacturing quality prediction model based on AdaBoost-LSTM with rough knowledge. Comput. Ind. Eng. **155**, 107227 (2021)
14. Lee, J.A., Verleysen, M. (eds.): Nonlinear Dimensionality Reduction. Springer, New York (2007). https://doi.org/10.1007/978-0-387-39351-3
15. Guyon, I., Elisseeff, A.: An introduction to variable and feature selection. J. Mach. Learn. Res. **3**, 1157–1182 (2003)
16. Laib, M., Kanevski, M.: A new algorithm for redundancy minimisation in geo-environmental data. Comput. Geosci. **133**, 104328 (2019)
17. Breiman, L.: Random forests. Mach. Learn. **45**, 5–32 (2001). https://doi.org/10.1023/A:1010933404324
18. Tang, T.M., Allen, G.I.: Integrated principal components analysis. arXiv:Methodology (2018)

Adding Material Embedding
to the image2mass Problem

Divya Patel[1], Amar Nath[2], and Rajdeep Niyogi[1(✉)]

[1] Indian Institute of Technology Roorkee, Roorkee 247667, India
divya.patel.iitr@gmail.com, rajdeep.niyogi@cs.iitr.ac.in
[2] SLIET Deemed University, Longowal 148106, India
amarnath@sliet.ac.in

Abstract. An agent has to form a team at run-time in a dynamic environment for some tasks that are not completely specified. For instance, the mass of an object may not be given. Estimating the mass of an object helps in determining the team size, which can then be used for team formation. It has recently been shown that the mass of an object can be estimated from its image. In this paper we augment the existing image2mass model with material embedding. The resulting model has been extensively tested. The experimental results indicate that our model has achieved some improvements on the existing state-of-the-art model for some performance metrics.

Keywords: CNN · image2mass · image2material

1 Introduction

There are some situations (e.g., search and rescue [20], space exploration [1]) where complete knowledge of the world (e.g., description of agents and tasks, total number of agents), is not known in advance. The agents are dispersed in the environment and none of them has a global view. The states and locations of agents may change; agents may enter or exit the environment. The arrival times and locations for tasks are not known a priori. So, an agent who has detected a task needs to form a team at run-time autonomously without the assistance of a central agent. Distributed approaches for team formation in such an environment have been suggested recently [14,15]. In these works, the specification of a task has the following components: name of a task (e.g., move glass container B to location l'), the set of skills/ the number of agents required to execute the task, the location where the task arrived, and the time at which the task arrived.

Another type of task specification has the following components: name of a task (e.g., move glass container B of mass 10kg to location l'), the location where the task arrived, and the time at which the task arrived. The number of agents required to execute the task, however, is not specified. This is because the required number of agents can be determined by (i) the agent who is trying to form a team for the task, and (ii) the physical properties of the object (e.g.,

O. Gervasi et al. (Eds.): ICCSA 2022 Workshops, LNCS 13377, pp. 77–90, 2022.
https://doi.org/10.1007/978-3-031-10536-4_6

mass, geometry). In this paper, we consider the situation where the mass of the object is not specified. However, the agent can perceive the object through its sensors. Due to the incomplete information, it may appear that the agent cannot figure out the required number of agents for task execution, and thus task execution by the agent fails. One possible approach to come out of the predicament would be to use the past experience of the agent in executing such tasks. Another somewhat easier approach would be to guess/estimate the mass of the object. We take the latter approach.

Our motivation for the latter approach comes from a recent development where the mass of an object can be estimated from its image, referred to as image2mass problem [18]. Thus, given an incomplete task specification, the required number of agents can be found from the estimation of the mass of the object from its image(s). Another development is the image2material model [4,5]. Taking inspirations from such developments, we suggest an augmented model for the image2mass problem that takes into account the material of an object. We show empirically that the performance of our model outperforms that of the existing model.

The remainder of this paper is structured as follows. Related work is given in Sect. 2. The state-of-the art approaches for estimation of mass and material from image is discussed in Sect. 3. In Sect. 4 we suggest a framework for mass estimation. In Sect. 5 we discuss the experimental setup. The experimental results and analysis are given in Sect. 6. Concluding remarks are given in Sect. 7.

2   Related Work

The work [18] first developed a method to estimate the mass of an object from its 2D image. The authors published image2mass dataset: a large dataset of online product information containing images, sizes and mass, and image2mass model (Shape-aware model): a model that estimates the mass from an object's image.

[2] suggest a technique for mass estimation of unknown objects using active thermography. The authors present a method that makes use of active learning. The classification between samples was done using the thermography and proprietary multi-channel neural networks.

Active thermography is a non-contact, remote technology that can investigate the physical attributes of objects in unfamiliar surroundings, such as material classification or thermal characterization. This method involves shining a laser source at the object's surface, examining the dissipation of thermal heat at the object's surface with a thermal camera, and feeding the thermal stream into a machine learning classifier or regressor to determine the object's material class or estimate its corresponding physical properties [2].

The works [3,6,12] discuss the weight estimation for a specific object or material. Their models are tested and trained with same domain data. In [7], mass of two types of foods, i.e., bananas and bread is estimated. All these model are specific and can be used for limited domain.

The works [17,21,22] proposed a methodology that combines image processing and machine learning for measuring the size and mass of several rice kernels, almonds and pistachio. In all these works mass and size are estimated for a narrow domain like rice, almond, and pistachio. In another work [8], a convolutional neural network (CNN) model was developed to predict the body mass of heifers. This model is also applicable to a specific domain.

3   Mass and Material Estimation from Image

3.1   image2mass: Mass Estimation Using Image

In [18], the authors have addressed the problem of estimating the mass of an object from its image. The work published the image2mass dataset: a large dataset of online product information containing images, sizes and mass. The work suggested the image2mass model: a model that estimates the mass of an object from it's image. Images of ≈3 million products listed with mass and dimensions using the Amazon Marketplace Web Service (MWS) API were collected. A sample of image2mass dataset is shown in Fig. 1 [18], where the dimensions of the images are in inch.

Image	Dimensions	Mass
	(3.75, 1.50, 4.75)	0.1 lbs (0.05 kg)
	(2.88, 2.88, 8.25)	0.35 lbs (0.16 kg)

Fig. 1. Samples from image2mass dataset

image2mass Architecture [18]: The deep architecture, referred to as shape-aware model, is used for estimating the mass of an object using RGB image and its dimensions. The central idea is that an object's mass is the product of its density and volume. Density is determined by the object's material and volume by the object's 3D geometry. Both the density and volume information are captured using different neural networks and then the output of these networks are multiplied to estimate the object's mass. In the architecture there are three main modules: geometry module, volume tower, and density tower.

3.2   image2material: Material Recognition Using Image

Recognizing material in real-world image is a challenging task because real-world materials have rich surface texture, geometry, lighting conditions and clutter. The works [4,5] addressed the problem of estimating the material of an object from its image. A new large-scale material dataset in wild, the Materials in Context Database (MINC) is given in [4,5]. Two approaches for the task of material recognition: (i) to identify the material of a patch of an image, (ii) to segment full images and identify materials in different segments are suggested in [4,5].

Materials in Context Database (MINC) Dataset: This is a collection of images collected from the public, crowd sourced and open surfaces dataset [4]. But this dataset has few limitations such as many categories are not well sampled, and the images come from a single source (Flickr). Therefore, the data from another source of imagery i.e., professional photos on the interior design website Houzz 3 is also gathered. The material annotations using segments, clicks for full scene material recognition, and patches for material classification are gathered.

The MINC-2500 [5] is a subset of MINC for material classification on single patches as shown in Fig. 2. This dataset is balanced with 2500 samples per category, each sample sized 362×362. Five random splits of 2250 training and 250 testing samples per category are provided. Each sample comes from a distinct photo (no photo is sampled twice).

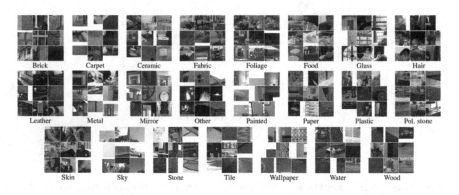

Fig. 2. MINC-2500 dataset [5]

Patch Material Classification: In patch material classification as shown in Fig. 3, classifier predicts for the point at the center of the input patch. The remainder of the input patch may be more of the same material or may be contextual information. The classifier was trained to predict with an input patch which is 23.3% of the smaller image dimension when the image is a full photographic composition. [4,5] trained different CNN classifiers like AlexNet [10], ResNet [16], GoogLeNet [19], etc. The best performing CNN architectures GoogLeNet can achieve 85.2% mean class accuracy.

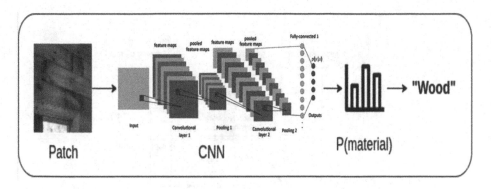

Fig. 3. Architecture of patch material classification [5]

4 Augmented image2mass Model with Material Embedding

In this section we discuss the proposed model obtained by augmenting the state-of-the-art image2mass model with material embedding. In the existing image2mass approach for mass estimation, lack of material information leads to poor performance. So we include explicit material information in the image2mass model. We used the pre-trained image2material model [11,13] to produce a 1024×1 material embedding. Material embedding is an output of average pool layer of the best image2material model (GoogLeNet). It captures the material information of an object in the image. Our model is shown in Fig. 4. We took the estimated mass using the image2mass model, material embedding as input to the fully connected layers, and trained the rest of the network.

5 Experiments

5.1 Material Recognition of image2mass Dataset

We conducted the manual analysis to establish the need of material for estimating mass. An object mass is the product of volume and density. If the volume of the two objects is almost the same, but the object material is different, then the mass will also be different. Different objects have different density. Object with the high density has high mass. Object A is made of metal, and Object B is made of plastic, having the same volume. Metal density is higher than the plastic; therefore, Object A is heavier than Object B. We analyzed the imae2mass dataset for this property. Figure 5 shows that the volume of these two objects is almost the same, but due to different materials their mass are different.

image2material Model: Caffe to PyTorch Conversion:
We used a pre-trained model of image2material to produce the material embedding of objects in the image2mass dataset, using Caffe deep learning

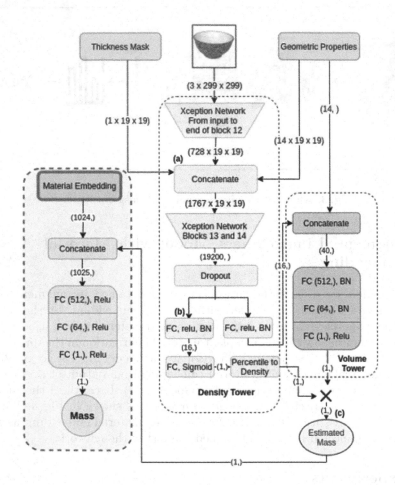

Fig. 4. Augmented shape-aware network model with material embedding

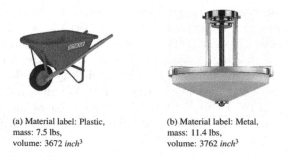

(a) Material label: Plastic,
mass: 7.5 lbs,
volume: 3672 $inch^3$

(b) Material label: Metal,
mass: 11.4 lbs,
volume: 3762 $inch^3$

Fig. 5. Relationship between object mass and material

framework. The proposed model is implemented using PyTorch deep learning framework. Therefore, we converted the Caffe model into the PyTorch using Caffe2PyTorch tool[1].

We tested the correctness of the conversion. For an input image (shown in Fig. 6(a)) we estimated the probability of the image belonging to a category using Caffe and PyTorch model. Figure 6(b) shows the output probabilities are almost same. The true label of the input image is 'Brick'. The label predicted is also 'Brick' using Caffe and PyTorch models with probability 0.784312 and 0.796180 respectively.

(a) Input image

Catergory	Caffe Output	PyTorch Output
brick	0.784312	0.796180
carpet	0.000189	0.000177
ceramic	0.000036	0.000034
fabric	0.000444	0.000416
foliage	0.000076	0.000072
food	0.000019	0.000017
glass	0.000766	0.000737
hair	0.000033	0.000032
leather	0.000100	0.000092
metal	0.001428	0.001351
mirror	0.000229	0.000226
other	0.005335	0.004821
painted	0.002624	0.002434
paper	0.000065	0.000057
plastic	0.000600	0.000522
polishedstone	0.009640	0.009143
skin	0.000015	0.000014
sky	0.000008	0.000007
stone	0.046870	0.048022
tile	0.128572	0.119490
wallpaper	0.001159	0.001192
water	0.000028	0.000025
wood	0.017653	0.014945

(b) Probabilities

Fig. 6. Comparison of Caffe and PyTorch results

Analysis of Material Prediction of image2mass Images: image2material model was trained on the MINC dataset, discussed in Sect. 3. For our task, we are using the image2mass dataset for training, validation, and testing. Therefore, we produced material labels of images from the image2mass dataset. We do not have ground truth material labels for the image2mass dataset. To check the correctness of the prediction, we selected random images. We found that very few of the predicted material labels are incorrect. Figure 7 shows the estimation of material on few images of image2mass dataset.

---

[1] https://github.com/penguinnnnn/Caffe2Pytorch.

(a) label: plastic   (b) lable: metal

(c) label: ceramic

(d) label: wood   (e) label: fabric   (f) label: glass

Fig. 7. Material recognition of image2Mass

t-SNE Analysis of Material Embedding: We used the average pooling layer output of image2material as material embedding. We do not have the ground truth value of material for the image2mass dataset. Therefore, we did the qualitative analysis of material embedding using t-SNE. Figures 8, 9, and 10 show the t-SNE plot of training, validation, and test set of image2mass dataset. t-SNE plots show that similar material vectors are near to each other and make a cluster. Sometimes material predictions are incorrect but their embeddings are near to the true material embedding. Figure 11 shows that predicted material for the object is sky, whereas the true material label is metal. In t-SNE plot of test dataset, these objects are near to the metal material embedding.

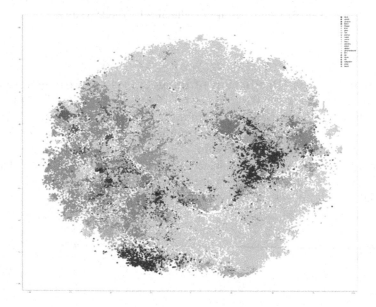

Fig. 8. t-SNE plot of material embedding of the training dataset

5.2   Experimentation Details of Modified Networks

We froze the image2mass model, i.e., weights of that model will not be updated during training, and took the output of the shape-aware model as input to the fully-connected network. The model was trained on an Nvidia DGX-1. We used Pytorch as a deep learning framework. The training was halted after **20** epochs through the data. Validation performance was calculated after each pass, and we used the best model for testing.

A hyper-parameter search was performed. Our model was optimized using Adam [9] with learning rate 0.001. Geometric properties and material embedding were pre-computed for the image2mass dataset. During training, validation and testing, images were randomly rotated by up to 360°, translated by up to 12%, and mirrored 50% of the time.

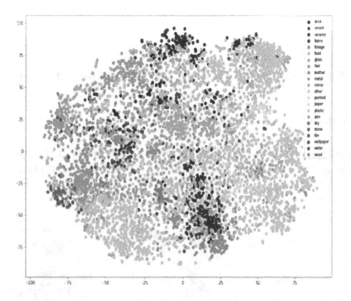

Fig. 9. t-SNE plot of material embedding of the validation dataset

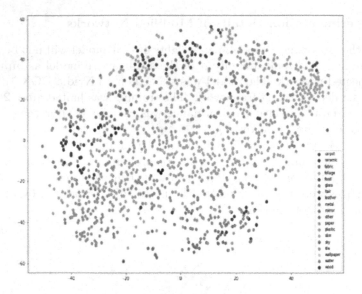

Fig. 10. t-SNE plot of material embedding of the test dataset

6 Results and Analysis

We measured the performance of each model on the basis of the following metrics [18]. Here, the true mass is denoted by t, and the predicted mass by p.

(a) Predicted material: sky
Near to: metal

(b) Predicted material: Sky
Near to: metal

(c) Predicted material: hair
Near to: fabric

Fig. 11. t-SNE analysis on test dataset

- Mean Squared Error (MSE): $\frac{1}{n}\sum_{i=1}^{n}(t_i - p_i)^2$
- Absolute Log Difference Error (ALDE):$|\ln t - \ln p|$, which is our training loss function.
- Absolute Percentage Error (APE): $|\frac{t-p}{t}|$. This metric prefers models that underestimate systematically.

- Coefficient of determination in log space r_{ls}^2 : This metric is a squared correlation between $\ln t$ and $\ln p$.
- Min Ratio Error (MnRE): $min(\frac{p}{t}, \frac{t}{p})$. This is the ideal metric. It has a value of 0 when the model predicts zero or infinity and value 1 when the model makes perfect predictions.
- q: It gives the proportion of the time a model was within a factor of 2 of the true mass.

Figure 12 shows that after adding the material information, we got significant improvement in estimating mass. The three values, for example, 4.95 (**6.23**), [16.91], corresponding to each object in the figure, are to be read as *true value of mass, value obtained using our model, value obtained using the existing image2mass model*; all the values are in *lb*. We considered different types of objects. For instance, when we considered two water bottle containers having similar dimensions (inch) but made of different materials, the estimation of mass by our model is very close to the true value as compared to the image2mass model. This is shown in Fig. 13.

We computed each metric for all models on the image2mass test dataset. Table 1 shows that our model has some improvement over the state-of-the-art image2mass shape-aware model for the metrics MSE, mALDE, and mAPE.

Table 1. Performance of the models on the image2mass test dataset (1435 images)

Model	MSE ($\downarrow$)	mALDE ($\downarrow$)	mAPE ($\downarrow$)	r_{ls}^2	mMnRE ($\uparrow$)	q ($\uparrow$)
[18]	2.266 ± 0.230	0.492 ± 0.011	0.689 ± 0.032	0.761	0.662 ± 0.006	0.758 ± 0.011
This paper	1.943 ± 0.179	0.479 ± 0.011	0.616 ± 0.027	0.770	0.669 ± 0.005	0.755 ± 0.011

(a) Plastic
4.95 (**6.23**) [16.91]

(b) Metal
11.4 (**11.24**) [7.38]

(c) Ceramic
0.75 (**0.66**) [1.27]

(d) Glass
1.5 (**1.51**) [1.72]

(e) Fabric
2.65 (**2.05**) [1.99]

(f) Wood
6 (**5.82**) [7.89]

Fig. 12. Improvement after adding material embedding

(a) Material: Metal
Dimensions: 2.75, 2.75, 10.00
Mass: 0.74 **(0.76)** [0.82]

(b) Material: Plastic
Dimensions: 3.25, 4.25, 9.25
Mass: 0.41 **(0.42)** [0.51]

Fig. 13. Mass estimation of water bottles made of different materials

Failure Cases: Figure 14 shows objects for which the estimations made by our model prediction are far from the true values. Many of these errors seem to be due to incorrect material identification. For example, in Fig. 14(a), the correct material of the object is metal, but estimated material is paper, which leads to negative changes in the mass estimation. Figure 14(b) shows that prediction is too high because the estimated material is metal, but correct material of the object is wood. In Fig. 14(d), the prediction is too high because the correct object material is light metal. In Fig. 14(e) the object material is heavy plastic but it is incorrectly identified as plastic and hence the estimated value is too low. This is because the current labels are relatively coarse grained. In other cases, due to lack of knowledge about real-world objects the prediction by our model is not much accurate. For example, in Fig. 14(f) the predicted value is less than the correct value because the object is filled with other components.

(a) Material: Paper
Mass: 13.01 **(6.57)** [13.00]

(b) Material: Metal
Mass: 2.5 **(7.51)** [5.70]

(c) Material: Metal
Mass: 1.6 **(7.24)** [9.49]

(d) Material: Metal
Mass: 0.2 **(0.70)** [0.70]

(e) Material: Plastic
Mass: 10 **(4.61)** [5.01]

(f) Material: Plastic
Mass: 11 **(4.77)** [4.11]

Fig. 14. Failure cases of our model

7   Conclusion

We considered the problem of filling the knowledge gap in incompletely specified tasks. We developed a model, by augmenting the state-of-the-art image2mass model with explicit material information, to estimate the mass of an object from its image. The experimental results indicate that our model has achieved some improvements on the existing state-of-the-art model for some performance metrics.

As part of future work we would like to explore the hyper-parameter space that may increase the likelihood of better estimation. To overcome the problem of the coarse-grained material label, we can categorize material into different abstract classes based on mass (light, medium, heavy) and use these abstract categories to improve material representations. We can use the segmentation of the image into different patches. We can extract the material representation extracted for each patch and aggregate it for utilization.

Acknowledgements. The third author was in part supported by a research grant from Google.

References

1. Agmon, N., Stone, P.: Leading ad hoc agents in joint action settings with multiple teammates. In: AAMAS, pp. 341–348 (2012)
2. Aujeszky, T., Korres, G., Eid, M., Khorrami, F.: Estimating weight of unknown objects using active thermography. Robotics **8**(4), 1–13 (2019)
3. Balaban, M.O., Ünal Şengör, G.F., Soriano, M.G., Ruiz, E.G.: Using image analysis to predict the weight of Alaskan salmon of different species. J. Food Sci. **75**(3), E157–E162 (2010)
4. Bell, S., Upchurch, P., Snavely, N., Bala, K.: Opensurfaces: a richly annotated catalog of surface appearance. ACM Trans. Graph. **32**(4), 1–17 (2013)
5. Bell, S., Upchurch, P., Snavely, N., Bala, K.: Material recognition in the wild with the materials in context database. In: Proceedings of the IEEE Conference on Computer Vision and Pattern Recognition, pp. 3479–3487 (2015)
6. Bozkurt, Y., Aktan, S., Ozkaya, S.: Body weight prediction using digital image analysis for slaughtered beef cattle. J. Appl. Anim. Res. **32**(2), 195–198 (2007)
7. Chaithanya, C., Priya, S.: Object weight estimation from 2D images. ARPN J. Eng. Appl. Sci. **10**(17) (2015)
8. Dohmen, R., Catal, C., Liu, Q.: Image-based body mass prediction of heifers using deep neural networks. Biosys. Eng. **204**, 283–293 (2021)
9. Kingma, D.P., Ba, J.: Adam: a method for stochastic optimization. arXiv preprint arXiv:1412.6980 (2014)
10. Krizhevsky, A., Sutskever, I., Hinton, G.E.: ImageNet classification with deep convolutional neural networks. Adv. Neural. Inf. Process. Syst. **25**, 1097–1105 (2012)
11. Krotkov, E.: Robotic perception of material. In: IJCAI, pp. 88–95 (1995)
12. Le, S., Lee, M., Fang, A.: Non-linear image-based regression of body segment parameters. In: Lim, C.T., Goh, J.C.H. (eds.) 13th International Conference on Biomedical Engineering. IFMBE Proceedings, vol. 23, pp. 2038–2042. Springer, Heidelberg (2009). https://doi.org/10.1007/978-3-540-92841-6_508

13. Mavrakis, N., Stolkin, R.: Estimation and exploitation of objects' inertial parameters in robotic grasping and manipulation: a survey. Robot. Auton. Syst. **124**, 103374 (2020)
14. Nath, A., AR, A., Niyogi, R.: A distributed approach for road clearance with multi-robot in urban search and rescue environment. Int. J. Intell. Robot. Appl. **3**(4), 392–406 (2019)
15. Nath, A., AR, A., Niyogi, R.: A distributed approach for autonomous cooperative transportation in a dynamic multi-robot environment. In: Proceedings of the 35th Annual ACM Symposium on Applied Computing, pp. 792–799 (2020)
16. Simonyan, K., Zisserman, A.: Very deep convolutional networks for large-scale image recognition. arXiv preprint arXiv:1409.1556 (2014)
17. Singh, S.K., Vidyarthi, S.K., Tiwari, R.: Machine learnt image processing to predict weight and size of rice kernels. J. Food Eng. **274**, 109828 (2020)
18. Standley, T., Sener, O., Chen, D., Savarese, S.: image2mass: estimating the mass of an object from its image. In: Conference on Robot Learning, pp. 324–333 (2017)
19. Szegedy, C., et al.: Going deeper with convolutions. In: Proceedings of the IEEE Conference on Computer Vision and Pattern Recognition, pp. 1–9 (2015)
20. Tadokoro, S., et al.: The robocup-rescue project: a robotic approach to the disaster mitigation problem. In: Proceedings ICRA, vol. 4, pp. 4089–4094. IEEE (2000)
21. Vidyarthi, S.K., Tiwari, R., Singh, S.K.: Size and mass prediction of almond kernels using machine learning image processing. bioRxiv p. 736348 (2020)
22. Vidyarthi, S.K., Tiwari, R., Singh, S.K., Xiao, H.W.: Prediction of size and mass of pistachio kernels using random forest machine learning. J. Food Process Eng. **43**(9), e13473 (2020)

Hyperparameter Optimisation of Artificial Intelligence for Digital REStoration of Cultural Heritages (AIRES-CH) Models

Alessandro Bombini[1]([✉]), Lucio Anderlini[1], Luca dell'Agnello[2],
Francesco Giacomini[2], Chiara Ruberto[1], and Francesco Taccetti[1]

[1] INFN, Florence Section, Via Bruno Rossi 1, 50019 Sesto Fiorentino, FI, Italy
bombini@fi.infn.it
[2] INFN CNAF, Viale Carlo Berti Pichat 6, 40127 Bologna, BO, Italy

Abstract. Artificial Intelligence for digital REStoration of Cultural Heritage (AIRES-CH) aims at building a web-based app for the digital restoration of pictorial artworks through Computer Vision technologies applied to physical imaging raw data.

In previous work [7], it was shown that it is possible to develop a multidimensional deep neural network capable of inferring the RGB image from an X-Ray Fluorescence raw data.

The developed network comprises two branches: a one-dimensional branch, which works pixel-by-pixel, and a two-dimensional branch, capable of performing image segmentation.

In this project, we report the results of the hyperparameter optimisation of both branches.

Keywords: Machine learning · Cultural Heritage · Nuclear physics

1 Introduction

In recent times, the digital technologies for image manipulation are becoming increasingly relevant in the context of physical technologies applied to pictorial artworks imaging. An interesting example is the application of modern artificial intelligence-based image inpainting to physical imaging [14,16,18,32,36][1].

In a previous work [7], we focused on the application of a multidimensional, multi-spectral deep neural network (DNN) to raw data of physical imaging techniques, as a means to digitally reconstruct non-visible pictorial layer; this was

---

[1] For other Machine learning approaches in Cultural Heritage, see [9], and references therein.

This research is part of the project AIRES-CH - Artificial Intelligence for digital REStoration of Cultural Heritage (CUP I95F21001120008) jointly funded by Tuscany Region (Progetto Giovani Sì) and INFN.

O. Gervasi et al. (Eds.): ICCSA 2022 Workshops, LNCS 13377, pp. 91–106, 2022.
https://doi.org/10.1007/978-3-031-10536-4_7

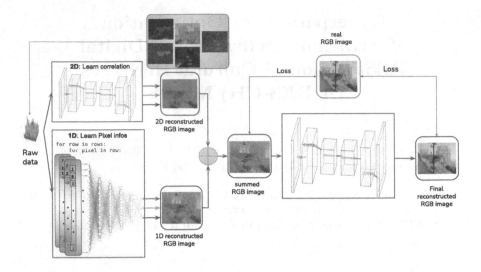

Fig. 1. A sketch of the multidimensional DNN.

done in order to furnish a visual help to restoration professionals through digital technologies.

In [7], we have shown that both branches of the multidimensional DNN we developed were actually capable of inferring an RGB image from a X-Ray Fluorescence raw data. The devised network has two branches: a one-dimensional-branch, trained to infer the colour of each pixel taking the energy spectrum as an input; and a two-dimensional-branch, trained to capture spatial correlations between adjacent pixels.

The results obtained with a custom DNN and several well-known architectures for either the 1D and 2D branches have been compared. The alpha version of the network was also offered in the INFN-CHNet cloud service [8].

In this work, instead, motivated by those results, we employ a different approach: we use *Optuna* [2,3] to actively generate deep neural networks, architecturally similar to the ones developed in [7], and optimise their hyperparameters.

The approach is to use the Optuna capacities of exploring categorical spaces, to let it explore neural networks with different numbers *and* types of layers: either pure Convolutional, Inception [31] and/or (Dilated) Residual blocks [12,35].

After that, we briefly analyse the best model found using *WeightWatcher*, an open-source Python tool for computing quality metrics of trained Deep Neural Networks, based on Random Matrix Theory [20,22,23]; we will show that the two-dimensional branches' layers are either rightly or under-fitted, as expected, leaving room for improvement by enlarging the training dataset. Thus, to increase the size of the dataset, a campaign of new XRF imaging measurements on pictorial artworks of the *Biblioteca Marucelliana* in Florence is scheduled to begin soon, in the context of the joint project AIRES-CH.

Nevertheless, this is just a small step forward. The ultimate goal of the AIRES-CH project, in fact, is to develop a DNN capable of inferring the RGB image from an XRF image. This is per se useful, since it may give already few information to cultural heritage scientists, but the final goal is broader. Such networks, while providing immediate visual support to physicists performing XRF analyses, represent a necessary building block towards the implementation of algorithms designed to digitally restore hidden (or damaged) pictorial layers, by removing from the XRF scan the components describing the most superficial, visible, layer, in order to furnish a visual aid to CH experts, before the application of any invasive restoration process.

2   The AIRES-CH Project so Far

Artificial Intelligence for digital REStoration of Cultural Heritage (AIRES-CH) is an INFN project devoted to the building of a web application for the digital restoration of pictorial artworks through Computer Vision technologies applied to raw data of physical techniques, such as the X-Ray Fluorescence (the one employed in [7], and in this work).

X-Ray Fluorescence (XRF) spectrometry is a technique suitable for a wide range of applications in many disciplinary fields, providing a fast, sensitive, multi-elemental analysis. It is widely employed in Cultural Heritage (CH) applications, since it allows for non-invasive, non-destructive measurements and no sample pre-treatment is required (see [15, 19], and references therein). It is possible to perform a macro mapping, known as Macro X-Ray Fluorescence mapping (MA-XRF), to produce elemental distribution maps of an artwork, proving to be extremely useful for material characterisation, and for understanding the artist's painting and production techniques [5].

Furthermore, and crucially, XRF is able to detect signal coming from hidden pictorial layers; therefore, XRF raw data are suitable to devise a neural network capable of digitally restoring pictorial artworks.

The first step toward such goal, is to develop a neural capable to infer the RGB image from the XRF raw data, seen as a rank-3 tensor $\mathcal{I}_{ij;k}$; the $(i, j) \in$ $[0, \text{width}] \times [0, \text{height}]$ indices refers to pixel's location, while the k index refers to the energy channel in the $(0.5, 38.5)$ KeV portion of the X-Ray spectra (the one explored by our detector)[2].

In order to do so, and prove that is feasible, we developed a *multidimensional* neural network, comprising two branches (Fig. 1):

1. The 1D branch, whose goal is to learn how to associate a 3-vector living in $[0, 1]^3 \subseteq \mathbb{R}^3$, (i.e. the RGB colour) to a vector living in $\mathbb{N}^{500}$ (one for each channels of the detector), the histogram of XRF counts in the energy range;
2. The 2D branch, whose goal is to learn how to associate to 500 grey-scale images a single RGB image.

---

[2] The tensor $\mathcal{I}_{i,j}$ contains, for each pixel (i, j), the histogram of the counts in bins of the X photon energies. It is customary to convert the raw data into elemental maps by integrating the per-pixel energy spectra around the characteristic energy peak associated to each element [15, 19].

2.1   The Training Dataset

The training dataset is the same employed in [7]. It is composed by 62 XRF raw data coming from several XRF analysis on multiple paintings performed both in the LABEC facility in Florence, as well as in situ analysis (the data comes not only from published works, and include some private artworks) [1,4,6,10, 24,26,28,29]; for the training of the one-dimensional models, only a 50% of the pixels where employed and randomly chosen, giving a training dataset of around 2 059 780 [histogram, RGB] pairs, divided into training, test, and validation set. Instead, for the training the 2D models, 45 XRF scans are used, reserving the remaining as 9 for test, and 8 for validation.

The raw data comes from different artwork techniques: multi-layered paintings, drawings without preparatory layers, and illuminated manuscripts, all spanning different periods and epochs, from middle ages to contemporary art.

2.2   The Neural Network Models

We have devised several models for each branch. Following a customary choice in Computer Vision, all the networks inferring an RGB colour code are trained using the *Binary Cross Entropy* (BCE) as loss function, while their performance is assessed through several common Image Quality measures [37]: *Peak Signal-to-Noise Ratio* (PSNR), the *Structural Similarity Index Measure* (SSIM) [34] and its variant, the Multi-Scale SSIM (MS-SSIM) [33].

For the 1D branch, we have seen that a custom multi-input DilResNet network slightly outperformed a FractalNet and a WaveNet model; in particular, we noticed that the custom multi-input model performs slightly better in all visual scores, and has the lowest (averaged) Mean Squared Error on the validation images. Instead, the WaveNet mode, which is also the model who has the lowest Binary Cross Entropy error, i.e. the loss function, is the one whose training was longer and more stable. This seems to suggest that future training should be performed using different losses (or metrics).

The peculiarity of the multi-input network relies in the fact its non-topologically trivial, since another input is fed to the Neural Network. In fact, we additionally pass a set of four element peak histograms to a branch of the network: Tin (Sn) Kα, Potassium (K) Kα, Manganese (Mn) Kα, and Titanium (Ti) Kα. Those elements were selected because are usually relevant in pigments, but appears with very small abundance, and thus fewer counts. So we force the network to look carefully for them, by inserting them into a preliminary network.

2.3   Summary of Results

For the 2D branch, we have tested deeply two model architectures of UNet-like shapes [27]: a VGG-based [30] Encoder-Decoder architecture, and a dilated residual UNet network, loosely based on the *Globally and Locally Consistent Image Completion* (GLCIC) network [13]. The summary of the results found are reported in Tables 1a, b, 2b.

Table 1. Performances of the 1D models in [7]. v5 is the custom multi-input model described in the text, v6 is a FractalNet model [17], while v7 is a WaveNet model [25].

(a) Comparison table of the visual scores performances of the v5, v6, v7 1D models.

	SSIM	MS-SSIM	PSNR
v5	0.38844	0.68032	20.10390
v6	0.37207	0.67664	20.07558
v7	0.35640	0.67343	19.97972

(b) Comparison table of the losses performances of the v5, v6, v7 1D models.

	BCE	MSE
v5	0.63645	0.01280
v6	0.63306	0.01407
v7	0.62872	0.01456

Table 2. Performances of the 2D models in [7].

(a) Comparison table of the visual scores performances of the VGG, DilResNet 2D models.

	SSIM	MS-SSIM	PSNR
VGG	0.73290	0.62626	19.69109
DRN	0.74470	0.66946	21.09683

(b) Comparison table of the losses performances of the VGG, DilResNet 2D models.

	BCE	MSE
VGG	0.48037	0.01589
DRN	0.46043	0.01212

The scores of the 2D models appear to be significantly higher w.r.t. the 1D models' scores, as seen in Table 3, but the visual result is less satisfying; as an example, we refer to Fig. 2, where the two best performing models, one for each branch, i.e. the custom multi-input model and the two-dimensional DilResNet model, were applied on one of the validation set raw data, which is a detail of the painting *Putto*, Unknown author, 18th-century (circa) [1].

Table 3. Comparison table of the visual scores performances of the best 1D and 2D models on the detail of *Putto*, Unknown author, 18th-century (circa).

	SSIM	MS-SSIM	PSNR
1D v5_custom multi-input	0.497	0.840	22.048
2D DilResNet	0.818	0.810	25.529

3   Hyperparameter Optimisation

As said in Sect. 1, in this work we follow a different approach to handle the task at hand: starting from the same dataset employed in [7], we decided to employ the open-source python package *Optuna* to fine-tune the DNN hyperparameters;

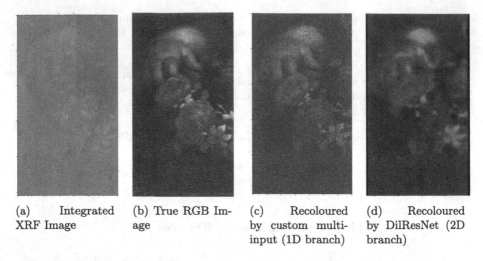

(a)   Integrated XRF Image

(b) True RGB Image

(c)   Recoloured by custom multi-input (1D branch)

(d)   Recoloured by DilResNet (2D branch)

Fig. 2. Comparison on the results of 1D and 2D best models applied to a detail of the painting *Putto*, Unknown author, 18th-century (circa) [1].

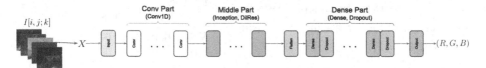

Fig. 3. Generic architecture for 1D models.

in particular, we exploited the Optuna ability of explore categorical parameter space to build different genres of layers (Fig. 3).

Note on the Loss Choice: we use the binary cross-entropy as loss, because is the same loss employed in [7].

3.1 1D Branch

For the 1D branch, we explore a variety of models' composition by join subsequent, different parts, each of which picked by optuna:

1. the first part may comprise various Conv1D networks, with various kernel sizes and number of filters, and may comprise a Batch Normalisation layer;
2. the second part is formed by a series of either Inception block or Dilated Residual block, their kernel size, and their number of filters. For the dilated residual blocks, their dilation rate (with dilation rate = 1 allowed, so we can have standard Residual block);
3. the third part is a series of couples Dense+Dropout; optuna picks the number of dense nodes, the dropout percentage and the activation function, chosen from the list ['RELU', 'SIGMOID', 'TANH', 'SOFTSIGN', 'SELU'].

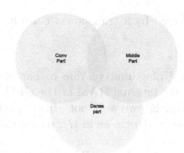

Fig. 4. All the 1D model possibilities explored by Optuna.

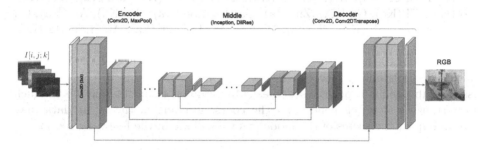

Fig. 5. Generic architecture for 2D models.

Notice that each part may have zero blocks; so, in one go, optuna is capable of explore either pure convolutional, pure dense, pure inception/resnet networks, and each possible 2- and 3-part combinations.

3.2 2D Branch

For the 2D branch, starting from a Encoder-Decoder UNet-shape of the model architecture (see Fig. 5), we let Optuna explore the possibilities, by either picking:

1. The number of Convolutional block layers in the Encoder/Decoder, and each of their kernel sizes and the number of filters;
2. The number of internal blocks;
3. For each internal block, its type (either Inception block or Dilated Residual block), its kernel size, and its number of filters. For the dilated residual block(s), its dilation rate (with dilation rate= 1 allowed, so we can have standard Residual block).

In this case, the Encoder convolutional blocks are based on the VGG-blocks, and can be either formed by 2- or 3- convolutional layers, followed by a $(2, 2)$ Max Pooling layer; similarly, the Decoder convolutional blocks can be either formed by 2- or 3- convolutional layers, preceded by a concatenating layer, merging the output of the previous block with the skip connection output coming from the symmetric block, and followed by a transposed convolutional block for upsampling.

Technical Issue Faced: Unfortunately, due to hardware limitations (in particular, the limited size of the internal RAM of the GPU, and the in-ram initialisation size of the Optuna trials), we were not able to perform the training using the whole 500-channels energy depth, as in [7], where the $\mathcal{I}_{ij;k}$ tensors analysed have $(384, 288, 500)$ shape[3].

To reduce the in-memory size of the XRF tensors, we extracted the (supposedly) most relevant elemental maps:

Al (Ka), Si (Ka), K (Ka), Ca (Ka), Ti (Ka), Cr (Ka), Mn (Ka), Fe (Ka), Co (Ka), Ni (Ka), Cu (Ka), Zn (Ka), Ga (Ka), Se (Ka), Pd (Ka), Ag (Ka), Cd (Ka), Sn (Ka), Sb (Ka), Sb (La), W (La), Ir (La), Pt (La), Au (La), Hg (La), Pb (La).

This reduces the size of the tensor passed to the network to $(384, 288, 26)$, allowing the training. Nevertheless, we did not expect this to come without issues: sub-dominant peaks, as well as sub-dominant elements, may be as much important as those elements, and the coarse-graining of the input data may vastly impact the scores of the model, as we will see in the following section.

Table 4. Performances of the optimised models. The scores where the optimised model over-performs the respective best-models in [7] are written in red.

(a) Comparison table of the visual scores performances of the optimised models.

	SSIM	MS-SSIM	PSNR
1D	0.45916	0.73961	19.52408
2D	0.65938	0.64781	17.41894

(b) Comparison table of the losses performances of the optimised models.

1D	0.65856	0.01191
2D	0.49498	0.02302

4   Results and Discussion

The optimisation procedure was performed over 1000 trials; each training was performed over a 150-epochs, but with the caveat of invoking a callback for imposing an early stopping condition by monitoring the validation loss, to avoid overfitting. On top of that, Optuna imposes its pruning condition to abort unpromising trials.

---

[3] Which means each energy bin is $(38.5 - 0.5)\,\mathrm{KeV}/500 = 0.076\,\mathrm{KeV} = 76\,\mathrm{eV}$ wide.

4.1 1D Branch

The optimised model found by optuna is a model in the intersection of the Venn Fig. 4, since it has all three kinds of blocks:

- Convolutional Part:
  1. Input layer;
  2. Conv1D, $K = 6$ + ReLU activation;
  3. Conv1D, $K = 6$ + BatchNorm + ReLU activation;
  4. Conv1D, $K = 6$ + BatchNorm + ReLU activation;
  5. Conv1D, $K = 5$ + ReLU activation;
- Middle Part:
  1. Inception block;
  2. Inception block;
  3. Inception block;
  4. Inception block;
  5. Inception block;
  6. Inception block;
- Dense part:
  1. Average Pooling 1D, pool size = 6;
  2. Dropout layer, $\alpha = 0.43$;
  3. Flatten layers;
  4. Dense + selu activation;
  5. Dropout layer, $\alpha = 0.39$;
  6. Dense + sigmoid activation;
  7. Dropout layer, $\alpha = 0.23$;
  8. Dense + sigmoid activation;
  9. Output Dense layer;

where K is the (1-dimensional) kernel size, and *alpha* the drop-out rate.

Also, optuna picked a learning rate of 0.001639 for the RMSprop optimiser. The total number of parameters is 15.568.497, and the final binary cross-entropy loss was $\mathcal{L} = 0.5994$.

Once applied to the validation set, the results obtained are reported in Tables 4a, b, first row. We see that it slightly outperforms the best model of [7] in most scores, especially in the one found in that work as the most relevant, the MS-SSIM.

In Fig. 7 we report the visual confront between the best 1D model of [7] and the optimised model described above, applied on a validation set raw data. We can see a small improvement in the average appearance, especially on the dark tones, as the SSIM and MS-SSIM scores (reported in Table 5 tells us; nevertheless, it seems that, even if a little bit noisy, the model of [7] seems to be more capable of detecting rare pigment specimen, as the PSNR score seems to suggest (Fig. 6).

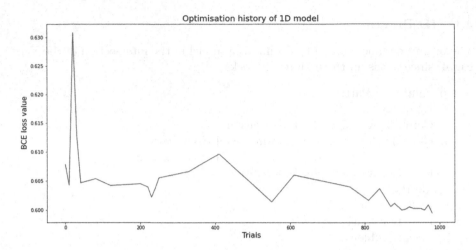

Fig. 6. History of optimisation for the 1D model.

4.2 2D Branch

The model found by optuna is:

- Encoder:
    1. Input layer;
    2. Conv Block, $K = (5, 5)$ + MaxPool $(2, 2)$;
    3. Conv Block, $K = (3, 3)$ + MaxPool $(2, 2)$;
    4. Conv Block, $K = (4, 4)$ + MaxPool $(2, 2)$;
    5. Conv Block, $K = (2, 2)$ + MaxPool $(2, 2)$;
    6. Conv Block, $K = (1, 1)$ + MaxPool $(2, 2)$;
- Middle Part:
    1. Inception block;
    2. Inception block;
    3. DilResNet block, $K = (4, 4)$, $d = 4$;
    4. DilResNet block, $K = (5, 5)$, $d = 2$;
    5. DilResNet block, $K = (5, 5)$, $d = 4$;
    6. DilResNet block, $K = (5, 5)$, $d = 4$;
- Decoder part [symmetric to Encoder) + output layer]:
    1. Conv Block, $K = (1, 1)$ + Conv2DT $(2, 2)$;
    2. Conv Block, $K = (2, 2)$ + Conv2DT $(2, 2)$;
    3. Conv Block, $K = (4, 4)$ + Conv2DT $(2, 2)$;
    4. Conv Block, $K = (3, 3)$ + Conv2DT $(2, 2)$;
    5. Conv Block, $K = (5, 5)$ + Conv2DT $(2, 2)$;
    6. Output Conv2D layer, $K = (3, 3)$;

where K is the (2-dimensional) kernel size, and d the dilation rate. Also, optuna picked a learning rate of 0.0004837 for the RMSprop optimiser. The total number of parameters is as small as 175.451, as somehow expected, due to the smallness

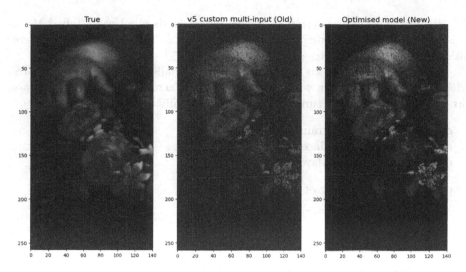

Fig. 7. Visual confront on the results of the 1D models; the true RGB image is shown on the left, the prediction of v5 custom multi-line model of [7] on the middle, and the prediction of the optimised model on the right.

of 2D dataset w.r.t. the 1D one, and the final binary cross-entropy loss was $\mathcal{L} = 0.39555$.

Unfortunately, due to the issues described in Sect. 3.2, the performances of the model, reported in the second row of Tables 4a, b, were slightly lower w.r.t. the ones of the best 2D model of [7]. This clearly implies that we can dramatically improve the hyperparameter optimisation of the 2D models, simply by improving the hardware set up.

Table 5. Comparison table of the visual scores performances of the 1D best old and new models on the detail of *Putto*, Unknown author, 18th-century (circa).

	SSIM	MS-SSIM	PSNR
1D v5_custom multi-input	0.497	0.840	22.048
1D Optimised	0.543	0.858	19.601

4.3   A Brief Weight Analysis

To try to shed light on the training process efficiency, we resort to the Theory of Implicit Heavy-Tailed Self-Regularization (HT-SR), in which a new Universal capacity control metric for Deep Neural Networks, α, is developed [20, 22, 23][4].

---

[4] For more theoretical details, see [21]. Link to paper.

HT-SR indicates that modern deep neural networks show a Heavy-Tailed Mechanistic Universality, meaning the spectral density of the normalised layer correlation matrix[5] can be fit to a power law, $\rho(\lambda) \sim \lambda^{-\alpha}$.

In [20, 22, 23], was shown that, empirically, a smaller value of α is correlated with better generalisation, with $\alpha \simeq 2$ universally across different best-in-class, pre-trained DNN architectures. So, it was empirically suggested that

- $\alpha < 2$: probably over-trained layer;
- $\alpha \simeq 2$: successfully-trained layer;
- $\alpha \gg 2$: poorly-trained layer.

In particular, the training of a layer is said to be

- Over-trained if $\alpha < 2$;
- Successfully trained if $2 \leq \alpha < 6$;
- Under-trained if $\alpha > 6$;

The implementation of these works is offered in the open source python package *WeightWatcher*[6]. The results are:

1. 1D:
    - average α: 2.00172
    - Percentage of over-trained layers: 33.33%
    - Percentage of successfully-trained layers: 66.66%
    - Percentage of under-trained layers: 0%
2. 2D:
    - average α: 6.09428
    - Percentage of over-trained layers: 8.62%
    - Percentage of successfully-trained layers: 51.72%
    - Percentage of under-trained layers: 39.66%

This seems to suggest that, as expected, the 1D network has experienced a more in-depth training (due to the size of its dataset), while the 2D network suffers the low-dimensionality of the dataset, and it was hard to properly train the model, to unleash its full capacity; this fact, joint to the technical issues reported in Sect. 3.2, may explain the non-completely satisfactory performances of the 2D models w.r.t. the 1D model. Nevertheless, it seems to suggest that we are set up for an improvement of the DNN performance by increasing the hardware resources, leaving room for further exploratory works.

---

[5] i.e., if $\mathbb{W}$ indicates the individual layer weight matrix, ρ is the density of the eigenvalues of

$$\mathbb{X} = \frac{1}{N} \mathbb{W}^T \mathbb{W}.$$

[6] GitHub: https://github.com/CalculatedContent/WeightWatcher.

5   Conclusions and Outlook

In this contribution, we outlined the results of hyperparameter optimisation of the model described firstly [7], developed withing the early stages of the AIRES-CH project, whose aim is to build a web-based app for digital restoration of pictorial artworks through Computer Vision technologies applied to physical imaging raw data.

Up to now, a set of 1D and 2D models to perform automatic recolouring were developed, trained, optimised and tested upon a relatively small dataset of X-Ray fluorescence imaging raw data, obtained from different kind of pictorial artworks, such as Flemish and modern multi-layered paintings, medieval illuminated manuscripts, and Renaissance drawings.

We have also employed these models in a web application for on-line analysis of XRF raw data, hosted in the CHNet cloud.

While the main result of [7] was to prove that the 1D and 2D branches are indeed able to provide complementary information to the reconstruction of the acquired image, here we tried to extend that result by means of hyperparameter optimisation, showing that, at least for the 1D branch, some improvement may be found.

Nevertheless, the main takeaway is that the small dimension of the dataset constitutes a limit to the learning capabilities of any network. Thus, to improve the scores of both branches by increasing the size of the dataset, a campaign of new XRF imaging measurements on pictorial artworks of the *Biblioteca Marucelliana* is scheduled to begin soon, in the context of the joint project AIRES-CH. Biblioteca Marucelliana will offer its vast collection of drawings, preparatory drawings, and sketches, all from the Italian *Renaissance*, ranging from the late XIV century to early XVI century; this will account for both an enlargement of the training dataset, as well as a standardisation of it, by having dataset entries of similar pictorial technique and created employing similar pigments; the analysis will also be conducted with the same apparatus (both in-situ as well as in-lab), providing a most valuable dataset for developing statistical analyses.

Furthermore, we have to develop the technique to take into account the presence of hidden pictorial layers and to recolour them, somehow factoring out the contribution from the outermost pictorial layer.

To do so, the full AIRES-CH DNN will comprise a *Generative, Adversarial* part [11]; the goal of this part is to associate a guessed XRF image to the colored image, which is the outermost pictorial layer; this is crucial to "extract" the covered image from the raw data. The generated XRF will have to be removed from the true raw data, to extract the hidden layer contribution to the XRF image.

This will finally allow to fed the generated XRF raw data to the recolouring architecture, to obtain a recoloured version of the *hidden* layers.

References

1. Ahmetovic, M.: Multi-analytical approach for the study of a XVII century Florentine painting: complementarity and data-crossing of the results of non-invasive diagnostics aimed at attribution and conservation. Master's thesis, University of Florence (2020)
2. Akiba, T., Sano, S., Yanase, T., Ohta, T., Koyama, M.: Optuna: a next-generation hyperparameter optimization framework (2019). https://doi.org/10.48550/ARXIV.1907.10902, https://arxiv.org/abs/1907.10902
3. Akiba, T., Sano, S., Yanase, T., Ohta, T., Koyama, M.: Optuna: a next-generation hyperparameter optimization framework. In: Proceedings of the 25rd ACM SIGKDD International Conference on Knowledge Discovery and Data Mining (2019)
4. Albertin, F., et al.: "Ecce Homo" by Antonello da Messina, from non-invasive investigations to data fusion and dissemination. Sci. Rep. **11**(1), 15868 (2021). https://doi.org/10.1038/s41598-021-95212-2
5. Alfeld, M.: MA-XRF for historical paintings: state of the art and perspective. Microscopy Microanalysis **26**(S2), 72–75 (2020)
6. Bochicchio, L., et al.: Chapter 7 "Art is Not Science": a study of materials and techniques in five of Enrico Baj's nuclear paintings. In: Sgamellotti, A. (ed.) Science and Art: The Contemporary Painted Surface, pp. 139–168. The Royal Society of Chemistry (2020). https://doi.org/10.1039/9781788016384-00139
7. Bombini, A., Anderlini, L., dell'Agnello, L., Giacomini, F., Ruberto, C., Taccetti, F.: The AIRES-CH project: artificial Intelligence for digital REStoration of Cultural Heritages using physical imaging and multidimensional adversarial neural networks. Accepted for Publication on the ICIAP2021 Conference Proceedings (2021)
8. Bombini, A., et al.: CHNet cloud: an EOSC-based cloud for physical technologies applied to cultural heritages. In: GARR (ed.) Conferenza GARR 2021 - Sostenibile/Digitale. Dati e tecnologie per il futuro, vol. Selected Papers. Associazione Consortium GARR (2021). https://doi.org/10.26314/GARR-Conf21-proceedings-09
9. Fiorucci, M., Khoroshiltseva, M., Pontil, M., Traviglia, A., Del Bue, A., James, S.: Machine learning for cultural heritage: a survey. Pattern Recogn. Lett. **133**, 102–108 (2020). https://doi.org/10.1016/j.patrec.2020.02.017
10. Gagliani, L.: Multi-technique investigations on a XIX century painting for the non-invasive characterization of visible and hidden materials and pictorial layers. Master's thesis, University of Florence (2020)
11. Goodfellow, I., Bengio, Y., Courville, A.: Deep Learning. MIT Press, Cambridge (2016). http://www.deeplearningbook.org
12. He, K., Zhang, X., Ren, S., Sun, J.: Deep residual learning for image recognition. CoRR abs/1512.03385 (2015)
13. Iizuka, S., Simo-Serra, E., Ishikawa, H.: Globally and locally consistent image completion. ACM Trans. Graph. **36**(4) (2017). https://doi.org/10.1145/3072959.3073659
14. Kleynhans, T., Schmidt Patterson, C.M., Dooley, K.A., Messinger, D.W., Delaney, J.K.: An alternative approach to mapping pigments in paintings with hyperspectral reflectance image cubes using artificial intelligence. Heritage Sci. **8**(1), 1–16 (2020). https://doi.org/10.1186/s40494-020-00427-7
15. Knoll, G.F.: Radiation Detection and Measurement, 4 edn. Wiley, Hoboken (2010)

16. Kogou, S., Lee, L., Shahtahmassebi, G., Liang, H.: A new approach to the interpretation of XRF spectral imaging data using neural networks. X-Ray Spectrometry **50**(4) (2020). https://doi.org/10.1002/xrs.3188

17. Larsson, G., Maire, M., Shakhnarovich, G.: FractalNet: ultra-deep neural networks without residuals. CoRR abs/1605.07648 (2016)

18. Licciardi, G.A., Del Frate, F.: Pixel unmixing in hyperspectral data by means of neural networks. IEEE Trans. Geosci. Remote Sens. **49**(11), 4163–4172 (2011). https://doi.org/10.1109/TGRS.2011.2160950

19. Mandò, P.A., Przybyłowicz, W.J.: Particle-Induced X-Ray Emission (PIXE), pp. 1–48. American Cancer Society (2016). https://doi.org/10.1002/9780470027318. a6210.pub3,   https://onlinelibrary.wiley.com/doi/abs/10.1002/9780470027318. a6210.pub3

20. Martin, C.H., Mahoney, M.W.: Heavy-tailed universality predicts trends in test accuracies for very large pre-trained deep neural networks (2019). https://doi.org/ 10.48550/ARXIV.1901.08278, https://arxiv.org/abs/1901.08278

21. Martin, C.H., Mahoney, M.W.: Universality and Capacity Metrics in Deep Neural Networks (2019)

22. Martin, C.H., Mahoney, M.W.: Implicit self-regularization in deep neural networks: evidence from random matrix theory and implications for learning. J. Mach. Learn. Res. **22**, 165:1–165:73 (2021)

23. Martin, C.H., Peng, T.S., Mahoney, M.W.: Predicting trends in the quality of state-of-the-art neural networks without access to training or testing data. Nat. Commun. **12**(1), 4122 (2021)

24. Mazzinghi, A., et al.: MA-XRF for the characterisation of the painting materials and technique of the entombment of christ by Rogier van der Weyden. Appl. Sci. **11**(13) (2021). https://doi.org/10.3390/app11136151

25. van den Oord, A., et al.: WaveNet: a generative model for raw audio. CoRR abs/1609.03499 (2016)

26. Ricciardi, P., Mazzinghi, A., Legnaioli, S., Ruberto, C., Castelli, L.: The choir books of San Giorgio Maggiore in Venice: results of in depth non-invasive analyses. Heritage **2**(2), 1684–1701 (2019). https://doi.org/10.3390/heritage2020103

27. Ronneberger, O., Fischer, P., Brox, T.: U-Net: convolutional networks for biomedical image segmentation. CoRR abs/1505.04597 (2015)

28. Ruberto, C., et al.: La rete CHNet a servizio di Ottavio Leoni: la diagnostica per la comprensione dei materiali da disegno. In: Leo S. Olschki editore, F. (ed.) Accademia toscana di scienze e lettere la colombaria. atti e memorie, vol. LXXXV (2020)

29. Ruberto, C., et al.: Imaging study of Raffaello's La Muta by a portable XRF spectrometer. Microchem. J. **126**, 63–69 (2016). https://doi.org/10.1016/j.microc. 2015.11.037

30. Simonyan, K., Zisserman, A.: Very deep convolutional networks for large-scale image recognition (2015)

31. Szegedy, C., et al.: Going deeper with convolutions. CoRR abs/1409.4842 (2014), http://arxiv.org/abs/1409.4842

32. Wang, M., Zhao, M., Chen, J., Rahardja, S.: Nonlinear unmixing of hyperspectral data via deep autoencoder networks. IEEE Geosci. Remote Sens. Lett. **16**(9), 1467–1471 (2019). https://doi.org/10.1109/LGRS.2019.2900733

33. Wang, Z., Simoncelli, E., Bovik, A.: Multiscale structural similarity for image quality assessment (2003). https://doi.org/10.1109/ACSSC.2003.1292216

34. Wang, Z., Bovik, A., Sheikh, H., Simoncelli, E.: Image quality assessment: from error visibility to structural similarity. IEEE Trans. Image Process. **13**(4), 600–612 (2004). https://doi.org/10.1109/TIP.2003.819861
35. Yu, F., Koltun, V.: Multi-scale context aggregation by dilated convolutions (2016)
36. Zhang, X., Sun, Y., Zhang, J., Wu, P., Jiao, L.: Hyperspectral unmixing via deep convolutional neural networks. IEEE Geosci. Remote Sens. Lett. **15**(11), 1755–1759 (2018). https://doi.org/10.1109/LGRS.2018.2857804
37. Zhao, H., Gallo, O., Frosio, I., Kautz, J.: Loss functions for neural networks for image processing. CoRR abs/1511.08861 (2015)

A Computational Measure
for the Semantic Readability
of Segmented Texts

Valentino Santucci[1]([✉]) [iD], Umberto Bartoccini[1] [iD], Paolo Mengoni[2] [iD],
and Fabio Zanda[1] [iD]

[1] University for Foreigners of Perugia, Perugia, Italy
{valentino.santucci,umberto.bartoccini,fabio.zanda}@unistrapg.it
[2] School of Communication and Film, Hong Kong Baptist University,
Hong Kong, China
pmengoni@hkbu.edu.hk

Abstract. In this paper we introduce a computational procedure for
measuring the semantic readability of a segmented text. The procedure
mainly consists of three steps. First, natural language processing tools
and unsupervised machine learning techniques are adopted in order to
obtain a vectorized numerical representation for any section or segment
of the inputted text. Hence, similar or semantically related text segments
are modeled by nearby points in a vector space, then the shortest and
longest Hamiltonian paths passing through them are computed. Lastly,
the lengths of these paths and that of the original ordering on the segments are combined into an arithmetic expression in order to derive an
index, which may be used to gauge the semantic difficulty that a reader
is supposed to experience when reading the text. A preliminary experimental study is conducted on seven classic narrative texts written in
English, which were obtained from the well-known Gutenberg project.
The experimental results appear to be in line with our expectations.

Keywords: Semantic readability of texts · Natural Language
Processing · Unsupervised machine learning · Hamiltonian path

1 Introduction

As is widely known, some texts are more difficult to read than others. Books like
Ulysses and *Finnegans Wake*, by the Irish writer James Joyce, or *Infinite Jest*,
by the American author David Foster Wallace, are challenging reads also for the
most voracious and experienced readers.

The readability of a written text is defined as a measure of how easy it is
to understand the content of the text from a reader's point of view. It has been
investigated in various works taking into account different aspects. The richness
of the vocabulary, the syntactic structure of the discourse, and how the text is
presented to the reader (i.e., character, background, material, etc.) are features

O. Gervasi et al. (Eds.): ICCSA 2022 Workshops, LNCS 13377, pp. 107–119, 2022.
https://doi.org/10.1007/978-3-031-10536-4_8

that have an impact on the readability of the texts. Considering these factors, researchers introduced of a set of qualitative and quantitative readability metrics.

Qualitative metrics are usually based on surveys with readers [15,18], where the readability is assessed by interviewing the readers on aspects such as the ease of understanding the content and the text presentation. The results of the surveys are then interpreted and assessed by experts.

Quantitative measures aim to assess the readability using semantic and linguistic features of the texts. This kind of measures can be computed automatically using Natural Language Processing (NLP) techniques [28,31].

Semantic and linguistic measures are computed by using supervised learning approaches. The learning procedure requires an annotated dataset where class labels are assigned to the texts segments by experts or are automatically discovered [12,27]. Various syntactic and lexical features are considered to assign the class labels. Syntactic features include basic attributes and properties of the texts such as word length, word count, and word frequency in sentences and in higher-level text structures (e.g., paragraphs, chapters, etc.). Lexical features are unigrams, bigrams, and the surface form of the target word. Afterwards a NLP classifier using Decision Trees, Random Forest, Support Vector Machines, or Artificial Neural Networks learn to automatically assign a complexity label to the texts [11].

Many readability measures consider the text segments (i.e. the phrases, paragraphs, chapters, etc.) as isolated parts. A few works in literature take in account the sequence of presentation of the various aprts of the text to the readers [5]. However, the structure and organization of the different segments to form high level structures has been proved to improve the readability [10]. Stories that are presented linearly are more readable than stories where the discourse, the plot, and the storylines interleave. Therefore, in this work we will try to fill this gap by defining a readability measure that take in account the sequence of presentation of the various segments that compose a text.

The rest of the paper is organized as follows. The high level description of the readability measure is provided in Sect. 2, while the detailed operational procedures for the computation of the text segment embeddings, Hamiltonian paths and the final arithmetic expression for the readability index are presented in Sects. 3, 4 and 5, respectively. Experiments are described and discussed in Sect. 6, while conclusions are drawn in Sect. 7, where future lines of research are also depicted.

2   The Semantic Readability Index for Segmented Texts

Most of the texts naturally present a shallow structure formed by linearly ordered segments. For instance, this is the case of most of narrative books, film scripts, textbooks, scientific articles and several other kinds of texts.

By denoting $[n] = \{1, 2, \ldots, n\}$, a segmented text T may be formally defined as a sequence of textual segments, i.e., $T = \langle t_1, t_2, \ldots, t_n \rangle$, where n is the total number of segments of T, and t_i, for any $i \in [n]$, denotes the i–th segment of T.

In the case of a narrative text, such segments are naturally identified with the actual chapters of the text.

Informally speaking, one way to define the semantic readability of a segmented text is to measure somehow the semantic jump between two consecutive segments and sum up these measurements for all the pairs of adjacent segments. A formal and procedural definition of this idea allows to define a quantitative semantic readability index which gauges how smooth the reading of the text is.

With the recent growth of Natural Language Processing (NLP) techniques [6], it has now become possible to numerically tackle a considerable number of semantic aspects which, in the past, were only qualitatively approached. In particular, text and word embeddings (see e.g. [7–9, 19, 22, 29]) are among the main NLP methodologies which allow to semantically handle text data.

Given a segmented text $T = \langle t_1, t_2, \ldots, t_n \rangle$, here we define a computational procedure for computing its semantic readability $\mathtt{SemRead}(T) \in [0, 1]$. Therefore, $\mathtt{SemRead}(T)$ represents a semantic readability index which measures the semantic smoothness a hypothetical reader is supposed to experience when reading the text T. At the edge values, we obtain $\mathtt{SemRead}(T) = 0$ when T is very difficult to read, and $\mathtt{SemRead}(T) = 1$ when the reading of T is very smooth.

The procedure $\mathtt{SemRead}$ consists of three main computational stages, as depicted in Fig. 1 and described below.

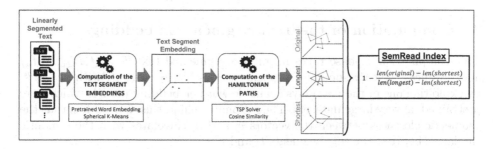

Fig. 1. High level architecture of the computational system

1. **Computation of the text segment embeddings**
   Given the segmented text $T = \langle t_1, t_2, \ldots, t_n \rangle$ in input, the objective of this stage is to compute an embedding $v_i \in \mathbb{R}^m$, for any textual segment $t_i \in T$, in such a way that two segment embeddings v_i and v_j are geometrically close – in the high dimensional embedding space $\mathbb{R}^m$ – when their corresponding text segments t_i and t_j are semantically related. Substantially, v_i is the numerical representation of t_i in the vector space $\mathbb{R}^m$, which may be obtained by exploiting one of the available word embedding models that were pretrained on very large datasets (see e.g. [13, 22, 24]). Further details of this computational phase are provided in Sect. 3.

2. **Computation of the Hamiltonian paths**
   By considering a suitable distance function d, this computational phase starts by computing a distance value $d(v_i, v_j) \geq 0$, for all the pairs of vectorized segments v_i, v_j. Then, these distances are used to compute the shortest and longest Hamiltonian paths [23] passing through all the vectorized segments $v_1, v_2, \ldots, v_n$ (seen as points in the multidimensional space $\mathbb{R}^m$). The rationale is that the shortest (longest) Hamiltonian path represents the smoothest (most rugged) ordering on the segments of T. Further details of this computational phase are provided in Sect. 4.

3. **Computation of the SemRead index**
   Given the shortest and longest Hamiltonian paths, denoted respectively as α and ω, their total lengths $\texttt{len}(\alpha)$ and $\texttt{len}(\omega)$ are computed on the basis of the distance function d. Moreover, the total length $\texttt{len}(T)$ of the actual ordering of segments (i.e., the canonical ordering $v_1, v_2, \ldots, v_n$) is computed as well. Therefore, the semantic readability index of the text T is given by the following arithmetic expression:

$$\texttt{SemRead}(T) = 1 - \frac{\texttt{len}(T) - \texttt{len}(\alpha)}{\texttt{len}(\omega) - \texttt{len}(\alpha)}. \tag{1}$$

A more precise description of this computational phase is provided in Sect. 5.

3   Computation of the Text Segment Embeddings

This computational phase takes in input a segmented text $T = \langle t_1, t_2, \ldots, t_n \rangle$ and produces the corresponding segment vectors $\langle v_1, v_2, \ldots, v_n \rangle$, with $v_i \in \mathbb{R}^m$, by exploiting one of the nowadays available word embedding models which were pretrained on very large datasets. The rationale behind this approach is that the geometric closeness between the vectors v_i and v_j correlates with the semantic similarity between the text segments t_i and t_j.

A word embedding model [21] is a mapping from words to their vector representations, computed starting from a set of text data in a totally unsupervised way. Today, there are a variety of publicly available word embedding models pretrained on very large datasets.

In this work, we considered the `glove-wiki-gigaword-100` model[1] which is formed by 400 000 word vectors trained on a dataset formed by 6 billions of tokens from the full English Wikipedia pages and the English Gigaword corpus [14]. This model is obtained by means of the well-known GloVe algorithm [22], which exploits the probabilities on the observed words co-occurrences and matrix factorization operations in order to transform the one-hot word encodings to their continuous vector representations in the multidimensional space $\mathbb{R}^k$, where k is a user defined parameter. The model `glove-wiki-gigaword-100` is pretrained with $k = 100$.

---

[1] `glove-wiki-gigaword-100` is available with the Python module Gensim [17] at the url https://github.com/RaRe-Technologies/gensim-data.

We now depict a procedure to aggregate the pretrained word vectors of all the words belonging to a text segment in order to obtain a semantically meaningful mathematical representation of the text segment.

Therefore, for each text segment $t_i \in T$, we perform the following steps:

1. for any word $s \in t_i$, which is not a stop word, we obtain its word vector $w \in \mathbb{R}^k$ from the pretrained word embedding model (words not included in the model are discarded);
2. the word vectors $w_1, w_2, \ldots$ are then clustered into c groups through the Spherical K-Means algorithm [3], i.e., a variant of K-Means which considers the cosine distance measure [20] instead of the Euclidean distance, because cosine distance is known to be more appropriate for word embeddings [30];
3. the vectors of the centroids of the c groups are concatenated in order to form the final $(c \cdot k)$-dimensional representation for the text segment t_i.

In this work we have decided to set $c = 10$ and, by also recalling that $k = 100$, we have that any text segment t_i, of the inputted text T, is converted to a vector $v_i \in \mathbb{R}^{1000}$. Note anyway that any other setting for k, c and any other choice of the pretrained word embedding model could potentially be adopted, even for a different language.

For the sake of completeness, the pseudo-code of the segment embedding procedure is provided in Algorithm 1.

Algorithm 1. Computation of the segment embeddings

```
 1: function EMBED(T = ⟨t₁,...,tₙ⟩, WEM)        ▷ WEM is a pretr. word emb. model
 2:     Tᵉᵐᵇ ← ⟨ ⟩                              ▷ The embedding of T, initially empty
 3:     for i ← 1 to n do
 4:         w ← ⟨ ⟩                             ▷ List of word vectors, initially empty
 5:         for each token tok ∈ tᵢ do
 6:             convert tok to lowercase
 7:             if tok is a stop word or tok ∉ WEM then
 8:                 skip tok and continue with the next token
 9:             append the word vector WEM[tok] to w
10:         centroids ← SphericalKMeans(w)
11:         vᵢ ← concatenate the centroids into a vector
12:         append the segment embedding vᵢ to Tᵉᵐᵇ
13:     return Tᵉᵐᵇ
```

---

4   Computation of the Hamiltonian Paths

After the previous computational phase, the n text segments are represented by n vectors $v_1, \ldots, v_n \in \mathbb{R}^m$, with $m = 1000$ for the setting here adopted.

It is now possible to compute a distance matrix D such that $D_{i,j}$ contains a distance measure between v_i and v_j. As previously discussed, the cosine distance is known to be the most suitable distance measure for mathematical text representations [30]. Therefore, we set

$$D_{i,j} = 1 - \frac{v_i \cdot v_j}{||v_i|| \cdot ||v_j||}, \tag{2}$$

where: the numerator $v_i \cdot v_j$ is the dot product between the vectors v_i and v_j, $||v||$ is the Euclidean norm of the vector v, while the second term in Eq. (2) is subtracted to 1 because it is the *cosine similarity* – defined in $[0, 1]$ – which we want to complement in order to have the *cosine distance*. Clearly, $D_{i,j} \in [0, 1]$, $D_{i,j} = D_{j,i}$ and $D_{i,i} = 0$, for $i, j \in \{1, \ldots, n\}$.

Since the distance between the text embeddings correlates with their semantic similarity, we can now measure the semantic smoothness of a sequence of text segments as the total distance traveled by linearly moving through their embeddings.

Formally, an ordering of the n text segments can be represented by a permutation $\pi \in \mathcal{S}_n$ of the set of indices $[n] = \{1, 2, \ldots, n\}$. Hence, $\pi_i \in [n]$ is the index of the i-th segment in the ordering π, while the total semantic length $\texttt{len}(\pi)$ of the ordering π is given by the sum of the distances between all the pairs of segment vectors which are adjacent in π, i.e., more formally:

$$\texttt{len}(\pi) = \sum_{i=1}^{n-1} D_{\pi_i, \pi_{i+1}}. \tag{3}$$

For a segmented text $T = \langle t_1, t_2, \ldots, t_n \rangle$ in input, the actual ordering of segments is represented by the identity permutation $\iota = \langle 1, 2, \ldots, n \rangle$, whose semantic length is $\texttt{len}(\iota)$.

Moreover, for the purposes of this work, it is important to compute the shortest and longest orderings $\alpha, \omega \in \mathcal{S}_n$ such that

$$\alpha = \arg\min_{\pi \in \mathcal{S}_n} \texttt{len}(\pi), \tag{4}$$

$$\omega = \arg\max_{\pi \in \mathcal{S}_n} \texttt{len}(\pi). \tag{5}$$

The orderings α and ω are the shortest and longest Hamiltonian paths passing through the points $v_1, v_2, \ldots, v_n \in \mathbb{R}^m$ and such that their distances are defined as in Eq. (2).

Interestingly, the Hamiltonian Path Problem (HPP) [23], i.e., the problem of computing the shortest Hamiltonian path, can be easily reduced to the Traveling Salesman Problem (TSP) [2,16], i.e., the problem of computing the shortest Hamiltonian cycle (also known as "TSP tour"). This reduction allows to exploit the very efficient TSP solvers nowadays available that, though the NP-hardness of TSP, are often able to exactly solve a TSP instance formed by dozens or hundreds of points in few seconds. In this work, we adopt the well-known exact TSP solver called Concorde[2] [1].

Given an HPP instance, the corresponding TSP instance is obtained by simply adding a fake point with null distance from all the other points. Formally, an HPP instance is defined by the distance matrix $D \in [0,1]^{n \times n}$ of Eq. (2), thus the corresponding TSP instance $D' \in [0,1]^{(n+1) \times (n+1)}$ contains D and has one extra row and one extra column, that we both identify with the index 0, such that

$$D'_{i,j} = \begin{cases} 0 & \text{if } i = 0 \text{ or } j = 0, \\ D_{i,j} & \text{otherwise.} \end{cases} \tag{6}$$

The TSP solver is executed on the TSP instance D' and returns the shortest TSP tour, which is formed by all the indexes in $\{0, 1, \dots, n\}$. Then, the tour is broken and unrolled at the position of the fake index 0 which is removed as well, thus to obtain the permutation $\alpha \in \mathcal{S}_n$, which is guaranteed to be the shortest Hamiltonian path for the HPP instance D, as required by Eq. (4).

Finally, the longest Hamiltonian path is computed in a similar way, but considering an additional reduction step – known as "MAX-TSP to TSP reduction" [4] – which mainly consists in complementing the TSP matrix. Formally, the TSP solver is executed on the TSP instance $D'' \in [0,1]^{(n+1) \times (n+1)}$ defined as follows:

$$D''_{i,j} = \begin{cases} 0 & \text{if } i = 0 \text{ or } j = 0, \\ 1 - D_{i,j} & \text{otherwise.} \end{cases} \tag{7}$$

The shortest TSP tour for D'' is the longest tour for D', therefore removing the fake point from the tour gives rise to the permutation $\omega \in \mathcal{S}_n$, which represents the longest Hamiltonian path for the HPP instance D, as required by Eq. (5).

5   Computation of the Readability Index

By using the notation provided in Sect. 4, it is possible to rewrite Eq. (1) as follows:

$$\texttt{SemRead}(T) = 1 - \frac{\texttt{len}(\iota) - \texttt{len}(\alpha)}{\texttt{len}(\omega) - \texttt{len}(\alpha)} = \frac{\texttt{len}(\omega) - \texttt{len}(\iota)}{\texttt{len}(\omega) - \texttt{len}(\alpha)}. \tag{8}$$

Clearly, since the length of the actual ordering of segments ι cannot be lesser than the length of the shortest segments ordering α and greater than the length of the longest segments ordering ω, i.e., $\texttt{len}(\alpha) \leq \texttt{len}(T) \leq \texttt{len}(\omega)$, we have that $\texttt{SemRead}(T) \in [0,1]$.

Therefore, Eq. (8) states that $\texttt{SemRead}(T)$ is a normalized value representing how close $\texttt{len}(\iota)$ is to $\texttt{len}(\alpha)$ and how far it is from $\texttt{len}(\omega)$. At one extreme, when $\texttt{len}(\iota) = \texttt{len}(\alpha)$, the passing through the text segments results in a very

---

[2] Concorde is available from https://www.math.uwaterloo.ca/tsp/concorde.html.

smooth "semantic walk", thus T is supposed to have a high readability and $\mathrm{SemRead}(T) = 1$. Conversely, when $\mathrm{len}(\iota) = \mathrm{len}(\omega)$, $\mathrm{SemRead}(T) = 0$ and the "semantic walk" through the text segments appears very rugged.

6 Experiments

A series of computational experiments was conducted in order to validate our proposal. The texts considered for this experimental analysis are described in Sect. 6.1. Moreover, for the sake of reproducibility, Sect. 6.2 provides all the details of the algorithmic settings adopted in the experimentation. Finally, the experimental results are presented and discussed in Sect. 6.3.

6.1 Selected Texts

For this first series of experiments, we decided to select seven very popular texts from the classic literature, written by native English authors.

The texts were obtained from the well-known public repository of the Gutenber project [32], which mainly includes the plain text versions of a variety of out-of-copyright books – under the US copyright law (i.e., published 95 or more years ago).

The list of the seven selected texts is presented in Table 1 which includes: the identifier of the text used later on in this paper, the title and the author of the text, and the number of text segments in which it is divided.

Table 1. Texts considered in the experimentation.

Id	Title	Author	Segments
AliceWonderland	Alice's Adventures in Wonderland	L. Carrol	12
SherlockHolmes	The Adventures of Sherlock Holmes	A.C. Doyle	12
GreatGatsby	The Great Gatsby	F.S. Fitzgerald	9
DorianGray	The Picture of Dorian Gray	O. Wilde	20
TimeMachine	The Time Machine	H.G. Wells	16
WizardOz	The Wonderful Wizard of Oz	L.F. Baum	24
Ulysses	Ulysses	J. Joyce	18

These texts are very popular narrative books which are already subdivided into parts, or chapters, by their respective authors, therefore these original chapters are considered as segments in this work. It is worthwhile to note that this choice relieved us of the task of arbitrarily splitting the texts into linear segments.

Finally, the number of segments in the selected texts, as shown in Table 1, goes from 9 ("The Great Gatsby") to 24 ("The Wonderful Wizard of Oz").

6.2   Experimental Setting

For the sake of reproducibility, we provide in Table 2 the algorithmic settings of the computational procedures of SemRead which were adopted in this experimentation.

Table 2. Settings for the algorithmic components used in the experimentation.

Tokenization	Tokenizer from Gensim 4.1.2 every token is converted to lower case English stop words from NLTK 3.7
Word embedding	Gensim model = glove-wiki-gigaword-100 dimensionality = 100
Spherical K-Means	Python module = spherecluster 0.1.7 no. of clusters = 10 no. of executions = 10 max iterations = 300 tolerance = 10^{-4}
Distance measure	Cosine distance
TSP solver	Concorde 3.12.19 precision = 6 digits default settings

The word embedding model and distance measure adopted were already discussed in the previous sections. The widely adopted tokenizer of the Gensim library [17] was considered. An execution of the Spherical K-Means procedure [3] depends on the initial random choice of the clusters' centroids thus, to increase the robustness of the clusterization, ten executions are carried out and the best clusterization is used to build up the segment embeddings. Finally, the Concorde TSP solver [1] is run with its default parameter setting and, since it only accepts an integer distance matrix, the real values in $[0, 1]$ of our distances are multiplied by 10^6 and rounded up to the closest integer.

6.3   Experimental Results

The semantic readability measure SemRead was computed on the seven texts indicated in Table 1 by adopting the algorithmic settings described in Table 2. Therefore, for any text T, the value SemRead(T) is provided in Table 3 together with additional information such as: the number of segments in T and the lengths of the actual, shortest and longest segment orderings, len(ι), len(α) and len(ω), respectively. The results are ordered from the most readable to the less readable text.

The results shown in Table 3 may be commented as follows.

Table 3. Experimental results.

Text	SemRead	len(ι)	len(α)	len(ω)	Segments
GreatGatsby	0.53	4.49	3.78	5.29	9
WizardOz	0.47	13.86	11.06	16.35	24
DorianGray	0.46	11.49	8.84	13.70	20
TimeMachine	0.45	9.14	7.18	10.76	16
SherlockHolmes	0.45	5.92	4.77	6.84	12
Ulysses	0.36	12.51	9.12	14.38	18
AliceWonderland	0.26	7.11	5.61	7.64	12

GreatGatsby appears to be the most readable text in our analysis, while Ulysses and AliceWonderland have the lowest readability scores. This appears to be in line with our expectations. In fact, although a fully objective validation is not inherently possible in this case, it is somehow commonly accepted that the GreatGatsby represents a straightforward reading, while Ulysses and AliceWonderland have a more complex semantic structure.

The highest readability score is 0.53, quite far from the theoretical upper bound of 1. This may indicate that the text genre considered in this work, i.e., classic narrative books, does not represent the most readable kind of texts. However, further experimentation with other text genres is required to corroborate this hypothesis.

Four out of seven texts have a readability score in the very narrow range [0.45, 0.47], thus plausibly indicating that their readability is nearly identical.

Finally. the lengths len(ι), len(α), len(ω) and the number of the segments does not have a significant influence on the readability score. In fact, a quick inspection to Table 3 shows that their respective columns have a low correlation with the SemRead column.

7   Conclusion and Future Work

In this work we introduced a novel readability measure SemRead that take in account the sequence of presentation of the various text segments that compose a text. The readability index computation is based on an unsupervised learning approach [33] that first proceeds with the computation of the text segment's embeddings and subsequently compute the Hamiltonian paths connecting the various segments. Experiments have been performed on a series of very popular texts from the classic literature. The assessment of the measurement performance shows that the results are in line with the expectations. The SemRead measure is able to distinguish between texts that are easy to read from the ones that present more complex storylines and semantic structures.

Although the findings of the present study are very useful, the semantic readability score was computed on books which are not necessarily meant to be read in a different order of chapters than the one that they were given by their authors when completed. It would therefore be of great value to carry out a follow up study considering books which were indeed devised with an increasing semantic - yet not only semantic - complexity in mind, i.e. the so-called *graded readers*. Graded readers are easy-to-read books addressing L2 language learners and are often presented split up into chapters. They can be found addressing different language proficiency level readers and their vocabulary is frequently "limited" to a certain lemma frequency threshold, according to the proficiency of the targeted readership. Furthermore, computing a semantic readability score could be a farther validating element to be taken into account when publishing new graded readers.

Finally, another interesting line of research is to encode the problem as an instance of the well-known Linear Ordering Problem [25, 26], thus to take into account all pairwise relationships among the text segments.

References

1. Applegate, D., Bixby, R., Chvátal, V., Cook, W.: TSP cuts which do not conform to the template paradigm. In: Jünger, M., Naddef, D. (eds.) Computational Combinatorial Optimization. LNCS, vol. 2241, pp. 261–303. Springer, Heidelberg (2001). https://doi.org/10.1007/3-540-45586-8_7
2. Baioletti, M., Milani, A., Santucci, V., Bartoccini, U.: An experimental comparison of algebraic differential evolution using different generating sets. In: Proceedings of the Genetic and Evolutionary Computation Conference Companion, GECCO 2019, pp. 1527–1534. (2019). https://doi.org/10.1145/3319619.3326854
3. Banerjee, A., Dhillon, I.S., Ghosh, J., Sra, S., Ridgeway, G.: Clustering on the unit hypersphere using von Mises-Fisher distributions. J. Mach. Learning Res. 6(9), 1345–1382 (2005)
4. Barvinok, A., Gimadi, E.K., Serdyukov, A.I.: The maximum TSP. In: Gutin, G., Punnen, A.P. (eds.) The Traveling Salesman Problem and Its Variations. Combinatorial Optimization, vol. 12, pp. 585–607. Springer, Boston (2007). https://doi.org/10.1007/0-306-48213-4_12
5. Calfee, R.C., Curley, R.: Structures of prose in content areas. In: Understanding Reading Comprehension, pp. 161–180 (1984)
6. Chowdhary, K.: Natural language processing. Fundamentals of Artificial Intelligence, pp. 603–649 (2020)
7. Church, K.W.: Word2vec. Nat. Lang. Eng. 23(1), 155–162 (2017)
8. Devlin, J., Chang, M.W., Lee, K., Toutanova, K.: BERT: pre-training of deep bidirectional transformers for language understanding. arXiv preprint arXiv:1810.04805 (2018)
9. Dieng, A.B., Ruiz, F.J., Blei, D.M.: Topic modeling in embedding spaces. Trans. Assoc. Comput. Linguis. 8, 439–453 (2020)
10. DuBay, W.H.: The principles of readability. Online Submission (2004)
11. Forti, L., Grego Bolli, G., Santarelli, F., Santucci, V., Spina, S.: MALT-IT2: a new resource to measure text difficulty in light of CEFR levels for Italian L2 learning. In: Proceedings of the 12th Language Resources and Evaluation Conference, Marseille, France, May 2020, pp. 7204–7211. European Language Resources Association (2020). https://aclanthology.org/2020.lrec-1.890

12. Forti, L., Milani, A., Piersanti, L., Santarelli, F., Santucci, V., Spina, S.: Measuring text complexity for Italian as a second language learning purposes. In: Proceedings of the Fourteenth Workshop on Innovative Use of NLP for Building Educational Applications. Florence, Italy, August 2019, pp. 360–368. Association for Computational Linguistics (2019). https://doi.org/10.18653/v1/W19-4438

13. Gourru, A., Guille, A., Velcin, J., Jacques, J.: Document network projection in pretrained word embedding space. In: Jose, J.M., et al. (eds.) ECIR 2020. LNCS, vol. 12036, pp. 150–157. Springer, Cham (2020). https://doi.org/10.1007/978-3-030-45442-5_19

14. Graff, D., Kong, J., Chen, K., Maeda, K.: English Gigaword. Linguis. Data Consortium Philadelphia 4(1), 34 (2003)

15. Jones, M.J., Shoemaker, P.A.: Accounting narratives: a review of empirical studies of content and readability. J. Acc. Lit. 13, 142 (1994)

16. Jünger, M., Reinelt, G., Rinaldi, G.: The traveling salesman problem. In: Handbooks in Operations Research and Management Science, vol. 7, pp. 225–330 (1995)

17. Khosrovian, K., Pfahl, D., Garousi, V.: GENSIM 2.0: a customizable process simulation model for software process evaluation. In: Wang, Q., Pfahl, D., Raffo, D.M. (eds.) ICSP 2008. LNCS, vol. 5007, pp. 294–306. Springer, Heidelberg (2008). https://doi.org/10.1007/978-3-540-79588-9_26

18. Kwolek, W.F.: A readability survey of technical and popular literature. Journalism Q. 50(2), 255–264 (1973). https://doi.org/10.1177/107769907305000206

19. Le, Q., Mikolov, T.: Distributed representations of sentences and documents. In: International Conference on Machine learning, pp. 1188–1196. PMLR (2014)

20. Li, B., Han, L.: Distance weighted cosine similarity measure for text classification. In: Yin, H., et al. (eds.) IDEAL 2013. LNCS, vol. 8206, pp. 611–618. Springer, Heidelberg (2013). https://doi.org/10.1007/978-3-642-41278-3_74

21. Li, Y., Yang, T.: Word embedding for understanding natural language: a survey. In: Srinivasan, S. (ed.) Guide to Big Data Applications. SBD, vol. 26, pp. 83–104. Springer, Cham (2018). https://doi.org/10.1007/978-3-319-53817-4_4

22. Pennington, J., Socher, R., Manning, C.D.: GloVe: global vectors for word representation. In: Proceedings of the 2014 Conference on Empirical Methods in Natural Language Processing (EMNLP), pp. 1532–1543 (2014)

23. Rahman, M.S., Kaykobad, M.: On Hamiltonian cycles and Hamiltonian paths. Inf. Process. Lett. 94(1), 37–41 (2005)

24. Ruder, S., Peters, M.E., Swayamdipta, S., Wolf, T.: Transfer learning in natural language processing. In: Proceedings of the 2019 Conference of the North American Chapter of the Association for Computational Linguistics: Tutorials, pp. 15–18 (2019)

25. Santucci, V., Baioletti, M., Milani, A.: An algebraic differential evolution for the linear ordering problem. In: Companion Material Proceedings of Genetic and Evolutionary Computation Conference, GECCO 2015, pp. 1479–1480 (2015). https://doi.org/10.1145/2739482.2764693

26. Santucci, V., Ceberio, J.: Using pairwise precedences for solving the linear ordering problem. Appl. Soft Comput. 87, 105998 (2020). https://doi.org/10.1016/j.asoc.2019.105998

27. Santucci, V., Forti, L., Santarelli, F., Spina, S., Milani, A.: Learning to classify text complexity for the Italian language using support vector machines. In: Gervasi, O., et al. (eds.) ICCSA 2020. LNCS, vol. 12250, pp. 367–376. Springer, Cham (2020). https://doi.org/10.1007/978-3-030-58802-1_27

28. Santucci, V., Santarelli, F., Forti, L., Spina, S.: Automatic classification of text complexity. Appl. Sci. **10**(20) (2020). https://doi.org/10.3390/app10207285, https://www.mdpi.com/2076-3417/10/20/7285
29. Santucci, V., Spina, S., Milani, A., Biondi, G., Di Bari, G.: Detecting hate speech for Italian language in social media. In: EVALITA 2018, Co-located with the Fifth Italian Conference on Computational Linguistics (CLiC-it 2018), vol. 2263 (2018)
30. Schnabel, T., Labutov, I., Mimno, D., Joachims, T.: Evaluation methods for unsupervised word embeddings. In: Proceedings of the 2015 Conference on Empirical Methods in Natural Language Processing, pp. 298–307 (2015)
31. Smith, E.A., Kincaid, J.P.: Derivation and validation of the automated readability index for use with technical materials. Hum. Factors **12**(5), 457–564 (1970). https://doi.org/10.1177/001872087001200505
32. Stroube, B.: Literary freedom: project Gutenberg. XRDS: Crossroads, ACM Mag. Students **10**(1), 3–3 (2003)
33. Yeoh, J.M., Caraffini, F., Homapour, E., Santucci, V., Milani, A.: A clustering system for dynamic data streams based on metaheuristic optimisation. Mathematics **7**(12), 1229 (2019)

Predictive Maintenance Experiences on Imbalanced Data with Bayesian Optimization Approach

Nicola Ronzoni[1], Andrea De Marco[2], and Elisabetta Ronchieri[1,3(✉)] ⓘD

[1] Department of Statistical Sciences, University of Bologna, Bologna, Italy
nicola.ronzoni@studio.unibo.it
[2] BitBang s.r.l., Bologna, Italy
ademarco@bitbang.com
[3] INFN CNAF, Bologna, Italy
elisabetta.ronchieri@cnaf.infn.it

Abstract. Predictive maintenance solutions have been recently applied in industries for various problems, such as handling the machine status and maintaining the transmission lines. Industrial digital transformation promotes the collection of operational and conditional data generated from different parts of equipment (or power plant) for automatically detecting failures and seeking solutions. Predictive maintenance aims at e.g., minimizing downtime and increasing the whole productivity of manufacturing processes. In this context machine learning techniques have emerged as promising approaches, however it is challenging to select proper methods when data contain imbalanced class labels.

In this paper, we propose a pipeline for constructing machine learning models based on Bayesian optimization approach for imbalanced datasets, in order to improve the classification performance of this model in manufacturing and transmission line applications. In this pipeline, the Bayesian optimization solution is used to suggest the best combination of hyperparameters for model variables. We analyze four multi-output models, such as Adaptive Boosting, Gradient Boosting, Random Forest and MultiLayer Perceptron, to design and develop multi-class and binary imbalanced classifiers.

We have trained each model on two different imbalanced datasets, i.e., AI4I 2020 and electrical power system transmission lines, aiming at constructing a versatile pipeline able to deal with two tasks: failure type and machine (or electrical) status. In the AI4I 2020 case, Random Forest model has performed better than other models for both tasks. In the electrical power system transmission lines case, the MultiLayer Perceptron model has performed better than the others for the failure type task.

Keywords: Failure types · Machine status · Predictive maintenance · Bayesian optimization · Imbalance data · Random Forest · Multilayer Perceptron

1 Introduction

Predictive maintenance (PdM) is a specialization of condition-based maintenance that requires data from sensors (e.g., used to monitor the machine) as
well as other operational data, aiming at detecting and solving performance
equipment issues before they take place. PdM focuses on utilizing predictive info
in order to schedule the future maintenance operations [1]. Through the data
collected with the machine under operation, descriptive, statistical or probabilistic approaches can be used to drive prediction and identify potential problems. With PdM various goals can be achieved, such as reducing the operational
risk of missing-critical equipment; controlling cost of maintenance by enabling
just-in-time maintenance operations; discovering patterns connected to various
maintenance problems; providing key performance indicators. Machine learning
is successfully applied in industrial systems for predictive maintenance [8, 28].
Selecting the most appropriate machine learning methods can be very challenging for the requirements of the predictive maintenance problem. Their perfor
mance can be influenced by the characteristics of the datasets, therefore it is
important to apply machine learning on as many datasets as possible.

In this paper the field of predictive maintenance in manufacturing and transmission line is considered. The aim is to classify failure modes in class-imbalanced
tabular data according to a supervised fashion. These tabular data contain data
points as rows, and regressors and targets as columns. Moreover machine learning models and neural networks, combined with Bayesian optimization approach [26], may open new perspectives in detecting fault configurations. With
this in mind, we have developed a pipeline that satisfies the following requirements on tabular data: supporting versatile applicability in different contexts;
tackling classification problems with imbalanced classes; discriminating among
different failure modes (primary dependent variable); being able to recognize
faulty and healthy status (secondary dependent variable) with the same settings
(i.e., hyperparameters) used for the primary dependent variable. In order to be
versatile, the pipeline supports multiple models under different settings. The
best set of hyperparameters for each model is the result of an informed search
method based on Bayesian optimization solution. Once the best set of hyperparameters has been selected, the model is fitted twice with different tasks. The
multi-output approach fits the same model for each dependent variable: first to
solve a multi-class problem (primary dependent variable), then to figure out a
binary problem (secondary dependent variable). Furthermore, we have considered two different use cases, such as AI4I 2020 predictive maintenance dataset [9]
and electrical power system transmission lines [16] dataset.

The model has been built by considering four machine learning methods:
three techniques belong to the ensemble machine learning methods (where the
model makes predictions based on different decision trees) such as Adaptive
Boosting, Gradient Boosting, Random Forest; and one technique is an artificial
neural network, such as Multilayer Perceptron. Our contribution, beside applying
for a predictive maintenance solution based on Bayesian optimization technique,
aims at replying to the following research question: can a model, whose settings

are tuned on a more complex task (primary dependent variable), perform well also on a relative simple task (secondary dependent variable) connected to the complex one?

2   Background and Related Works

With regards to the related works, our starting point has been focused on maintenance modelling approaches on imbalanced classes. A short literature review has been performed to highlight previous research in the predictive maintenance field. The machine learning-based PdM strategies are usually modeled as a problem of failure prediction. With imbalanced classes, ensemble learning methods as well as neural networks, combined with Bayesian optimization method, can be used to improve model performances. In the following we have summarized some papers related to the machine learning methods, such as Adaptive Boosting, Gradient Boosting, Random Forest and Multilayer Perceptron, adopted in this study showing interesting results in PdM.

Adaptive Boosting is one of the most popular ensamble learning algorithms [30]. I. Martin-Diaz et al. [17] presented a supervised classification approach for induction motors based on the adaptive boosting algorithm with SMOTE - i.e., a method that combined together the oversampling of the unusual minority class with the undersampling of the normal majority class - to deal with imbalanced data. The combined use of SMOTE and Adaptive Boosting presents stable results. Another ensemble method is the Gradient Boosting method. Calabrese et al. [6] used a data-driven approach based on machine learning in woodworking industrial machine predictive maintenance. They achieved an excellent accuracy 98.9%, recall 99.6% and precision 99.1% with the Gradient Boosting model.

Some other studies use the Random Forest classifier [21]. M. Paolanti et al. [22] described a machine learning architecture for predictive maintenance of electric motors and other equipments based on Random Forest approach. They developed their methodology in an industrial group focused on cutting machine, predicting different machine states with high accuracy (95%) on a data set collected in real time from the tested cutting machine. Qin et al. [24] used the Random Forest method to predict the malfunction of wind turbines. The wind turbine data is obtained through the use of the supervisory control and data acquisition (SCADA) approach [24] .

V. Ghate et al. [10] evaluated the performance of the developed MultiLayer Perceptron and self-organizing map neural network based classifier to detect four conditions of the three-phase induction motor. In this work, the authors computed statistical parameters to specify the feature space and performed Principal Component analysis to reduce the input dimension. M. Jamil et al. [16] applied artificial neural networks for the detection and classification of faults on a three-phase transmission lines system. All the artificial neural networks adopted the back-propagation architecture, providing satisfactory performances once the most appropriate configuration has been chosen.

There are many methods for optimizing over hyperparameter settings, ranging from simplistic procedures, like grid or random search [2], to more sophisticated model-based approaches using Random Forests [15] or Gaussian processes [26].

3 Dataset Description

3.1 AI4I 2020 Predictive Maintenance Dataset

The AI4I 2020 predictive maintenance dataset [9] comprises 10000 data points, representing synthetic multivariate time series. It represents a manufacturing machine where variables reflect (simulate) real signals registered from the equipment. The dataset indicates at each timestamp (row) a failure type and the machine status. The failure type consists of six independent classes including a *no failure* class. If at least one of the five failure modes (one of the 5 classes that differ from *no failure* class) is true, the machine stops and the machine status is set to *failure*; while if the failure type belongs to *no failure* class the machine status is set to *working*. At each timestamp we have a set of regressors and two connected targets: the failure type (multi-class) and the machine status (binary class). The set of regressors includes the original variables and the estimation of variables of which there are no measurement, by employing measures on other variables that have been recorded.

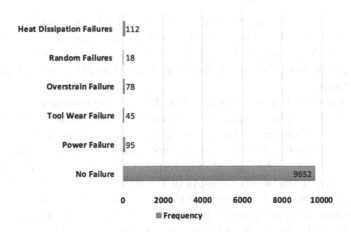

Fig. 1. AI4I 2020 dataset: failure types frequencies

The original variables that represent directly real signals are: type, process temperature in Kelvin [K], rotational speed in revolutions per minute [rpm] and tool wear in minutes [min]. Type is a categorical variable that is composed of three classes, representing the quality variants of the process (i.e., low 50%, medium 30% and high 20%). We have mapped this variable with a label encoding. Process temperature symbolizes the temperature of the machine that is generated by using a random walk process, normalized to a standard deviation of 1 K, and added to the air temperature plus 10 K. The temperature of the environment is generated by using a random walk process, normalized to a standard deviation of 2 K around an average of 300 K. Rotational speed reproduces the rate of rotation in revolution per minute of the cutting tool that is computed from a power of 2860 W with a normal noise distribution. Tool wear returns the minutes of regular operation of the cutting tool in the process.

The estimated variables are defined based on specific failure mode that may occur. Heat dissipation in Kelvin [K] depicts the absolute difference between the air temperature and process temperature. Power in Watt [W] acts as a sample of the power, obtained by the multiplication of the torque (in Newton meter) applied to the cutting tool and the rotational speed (in radians per seconds): the torque is generated from a Gaussian distribution around 40 N meter with a standard deviation of 10 N meter and no negative values. Overstrain in Newton meter per minute [Nm × min] outlines the demand of resilience by the cutting tool, expressed by the product of Tool wear (in minutes) and Torque (in Newton meter). The set of seven regressors reproduces physical conditions responsible of the failure modes. Figure 1 shows the six failure types on the manufacturing machine.

3.2   Electrical Power System Transmission Lines Dataset

The electrical power system transmission lines [16] dataset collects 7861 points of a three-phase power system. The electrical system consists of 4 generators of 11×10^3 Volts [V], each pair located at each end of the transmission line. Data simulates signals from the circuit under no faulty condition as well as different fault conditions.

The measures of line voltages in Volts [V] and line currents in Amperes [A] for each of the three phases (i.e., A, B, C) are collected at the output side of the power system. Each point in the dataset takes values for: the six regressors (line currents and line voltages for each of the three phases), the failure types and the electrical status (connected tasks). The failure type consists of six independent classes including a *no failure* class. As in the AI4I 2020 dataset, if at least one of the five failure modes is true (one of the 5 class that differ from the *no failure* class), the electrical transmission goes down and the electrical status is set to *failure*; while if the failure type belongs to *no failure* class the electrical status is set to *working*. Figure 2 shows the failure types on the electrical system.

4   Exploratory Analysis

The AI4I 2020 and the electrical power system transmission lines datasets share some similarities. They have a small number of regressors and data points. Both

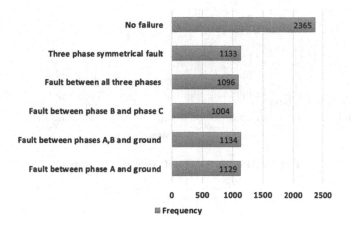

Fig. 2. Electrical power system transmission lines dataset: failure types frequencies

datasets contain 6 classes for the failure type task. The distribution of points across the known classes is biased with different degree of skewness.

Figure 1 demonstrates the severe imbalance of AI4I 2020 dataset. Even when the five failure modes are aggregated together at the machine status level, the distribution of *failure* and *working* labels is uneven by a large amount of data points. The *random failure* class (standing for the chance of 0.2% to fail regardless the value of its regressors) is included in the *no failure* class due to its low frequency and its randomness.

Figure 2 represents the slight imbalance of the electrical power system transmission lines dataset. Failure modes are in the same order of magnitude of the *no failure* class. Furthermore, when these five modes are aggregated together in the electrical status, the *failure* class becomes more frequent than the *working* one.

According to the way machine (or electrical) status is defined in Sect. 3, it is reasonable to consider it connected and correlated to the failure type . The machine (or electrical) status is a binary variable in which one class aggregates together the five failure modes of the failure type. Specifically the *failure* class, in the machine (or electrical) status dependent variable, includes the five failure modes, while the *working* class corresponds to the *no failure* class of the failure type dependent variable.

In the two datasets, faults are defined by a single condition or multiple conditions: for AI4I 2020 dataset the *tool wear failure* consists of randomly selected tool wear time between 200 and 240 min, as showed in Fig. 3; the *heat dissipation failure* occurs when the heat dissipation is below 8.6 Kelvin [K] and the rotational speed is below 1380 revolution per minute [rpm]. For the electrical power system transmission lines dataset, the *fault between phase A and ground* only involves one phase that is shorted to ground; the *three phase symmetrical fault* considers all phases that are shorted to ground, as displayed in Figs. 4, 5.

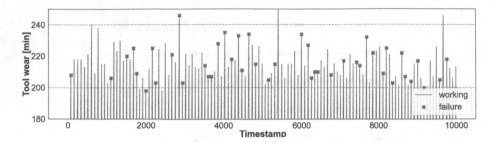

Fig. 3. AI4I 2020 dataset: tool wear failures

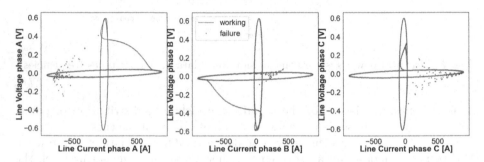

Fig. 4. Electrical power system transmission lines dataset: three phases symmetrical faults.

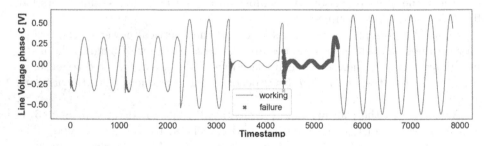

Fig. 5. Line voltage phase C: three phases symmetrical faults.

5 Methodology for Predictive Maintenance

The main objective of this study has been the development and validation of a predictive maintenance model for machine status and fault type detection by using different use cases. A generalized workflow is shown in Fig. 6 that schematizes the actions that have been undertaken to implement predictive maintenance model.

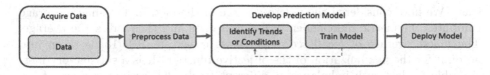

Fig. 6. Methodology overview

Our work has started with the datasets selection. We have continued processing data to prepare them for machine learning (ML) techniques, then we have built our ML-based prediction models and assessed them with respect to machine status and failure type tasks. The acquired data (already introduced in Sect. 3) are from AI4I 2020 predictive maintenance and electrical power system transmission lines. Considering the characteristics of data (such as the imbalance of data and single or multiple-failure conditions), we have decided to build multi-class and binary imbalanced classifiers. Four multi-output models have been analyzed and compared: two boosting ensemble classifiers - i.e., Adaptive Boosting and Gradient Boosting that differ in the way they learn from previous mistakes; one bagging ensemble classifier - i.e., Random Forest that trains a bunch of individual models in a parallel way without depending from previous model; and one neural network method - i.e., Multilayer Perceptron.

For all the classifiers an informed search method based on a Bayesian optimization algorithm has been applied to choose the best set of hyperparameters. Figure 7 shows details to build our models. For each model the pipeline is characterized by two phases: firstly we have found a combination of hyperparameters that best describes train data; and secondly we have deployed the model on unseen data by using the best settings found on the train set.

The first phase takes advantage of: an objective function, a range of values for each model's hyperparameter (i.e. hyperparameters spaces), a conjugate prior distribution for the hyperparameters (prior Knowledge) and an acquisition function, allowing to determine the next set of hyperparameters to be evaluated. At each step the search computes a posterior distribution of functions by fitting a Gaussian process model on the set of hyperparameters candidate and the objective function whose output have tried to maximize. The next set of hyperparameters to be evaluated is determined by the upper confidence bound acquisition function [27]. This function tries to explore regions in the hyperparameter spaces where we have been getting good performance based on previous search, rather than trying all possible combinations of hyperparameters. The optimization process [26] is repeated for a defined number of iterations, then the model is fitted on unseen data with the values of the hyperparameters leading to the global optimum of the objective function.

Despite the multi-output setting, the objective to be maximized in the Bayesian search [19] is only computed on the failure type. This choice wants to test the reliability of the hyperparameters selection computed on multi-class problem, even into binary problem. In extending a binary metric to multi-class problem, the data is covered as a collection of binary problems, one for each class. We have considered the macro average of the metric. The macro average computes the metric independently for each class and then takes the average. The macro average of recall scores per class (macro-recall) [18] is taken into account for the maximization of the objective function. It is a satisfactory metrics able to deal with imbalance at different levels [29], as in our cases of the severe imbalanced AI4I 2020 dataset and the slight imbalanced electrical power system transmission lines dataset.

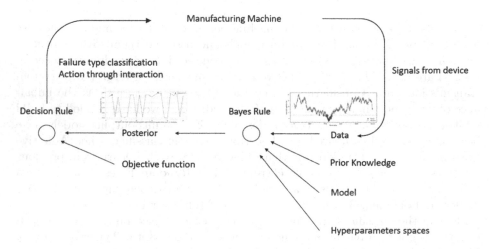

Fig. 7. Model pipeline

5.1   Algorithm Description

Let us summarize the used machine learning techniques together with the already introduced optimization strategy.

The Bayesian optimization approach fits probabilistic models for finding the maximum of the objective function. At each iteration, it exploits the probabilistic model, through the acquisition function, in order to decide where in the hyperparameters spaces next evaluates the objective function. It takes into account uncertainty by balancing exploration (not taking the optimal decision since the sets of hyperparameters explored are not sufficient to correctly identify the best set) and exploitation (taking the best set of hyperparameters with respect to the sets observed so far) during the search. The most commonly used probabilistic model for the Bayesian optimization solution is the Gaussian process due to its simplicity and flexibility in terms of conditions and inference [5].

Adaptive Boosting [11] is an algorithm that combines several classifiers into one superior classifier. This classifier begins by fitting a tree classifier on the original dataset and then fits additional copies of the classifier on the same dataset, where the weights of incorrectly classified instances are adjusted, so that subsequent classifiers focus more on difficult cases.

Gradient Boosting [7] is a family of powerful machine learning techniques that has shown success in a wide range of practical applications. It builds an additive model based on decision trees. The model fits a new decision tree on the residual errors that are made by the previous predictor. For this reason it learns from the residual errors directly, rather than update the weights of data points.

Random Forest (RF) classifier [12] is an ensemble learning algorithm based on bagging method of trees. It fits a number of decision tree classifiers using samples from the dataset and uses averaging to improve the predictive accuracy and control over-fitting. Random Forest uses bootstrap sampling and feature sampling, and it considers different sets of regressors for different decision trees. Furthermore, decision trees, used in all ensemble models, are immune to multicollinearity and perform feature selection by selecting appropriate split points.

Multilayer Perceptron [20] is used as an artificial neural network classification algorithm. It trains using back propagation and supports multi-outputs by changing the output layer activator. The softmax activator is used with multiclass while the logistic activator is used with binary output. In the Bayesian optimization we have considered just one hidden layer. This option prevents overfitting since the small number of data points in the two datasets [14]. In addition, a simple architecture of the neural network can manage changes in the dependent variable from which it learns. We have specified the range for the number of neurons (hidden layer size) used in the Bayes optimization based on the number of regressors of the dataset. Ensamble learning algorithms are not sensible to scaling. However, the MultiLayer Perceptron is sensitive to feature scaling. In order to compare the performances with the same input data, we have applied a scaling on the regressors to obtain all values within the range [0,1].

5.2   Training Phase

Despite data from manufacturing machine and transmission lines, registered at regular cadence, creates multivariate time series, we have not considered the temporal order of observations (data points) in the analysis. Our aim has been to discover configurations of regressors values connected to various maintenance problems. Data points (rows) are randomly located in the train or test set, generating two independent subsets. We have performed the hyperparameter selection, with the Bayesian optimization solution, in the train set by a cross-validation approach as shown in Fig. 8.

The training set is split into five smaller sets, preserving the percentage of samples for each failure type class. A model, with a given set of hyperparameters, is trained using four of the folds as training data and it is validated on the remaining fold. This fold is used to compute the performance measure: the macro-recall of the failure type (primary dependent variable). The performance measure reported by the five-fold cross validation is the average of the macro-recall values computed in the loop. Furthermore, it is the objective function to be maximized in the Bayesian optimization solution. The cross-validation approach

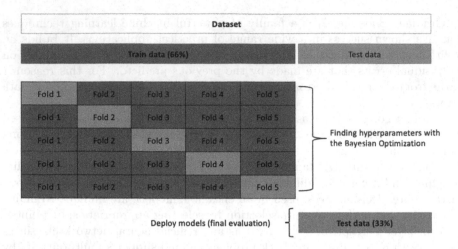

Fig. 8. Training phase description for both datasets.

can be computationally expensive: however, it is used along the Bayesian optimization method that is trustworthy for finding the maximum of an objective function (that is expensive to evaluate).

The 33% of the datasets have been used as test set to deploy our predictive maintenance models on failure type and machine (or electrical) status. Test data have been scaled by using minimum and maximum values of each regressor of the train set to simulate unseen data. In order to do a fair comparison among the models, we have used the Bayesian optimization approach with 20 iterations and 5 random explorations for each model to tune hyperparameters. The hyperparameters for each model are listed in Table 1, while the hyperparameters spaces are available online along with our code [25].

6   Results and Discussions

To evaluate the performances of the models we have taken into account the known threshold metrics for imbalanced datasets [13]. We extend binary metrics to multi-class problem, by taking the macro average of the metrics, as mentioned in Sect. 5. We have also reported confusion matrices for the models that perform better with respect to the failure type and machine (or electrical) status classification tasks in the two datasets.

Table 1. Best hyperparameters suggested by Bayesian optimization

Hyperparameter	Adaptive Boosting	Gradient Boosting	Random Forest	MultiLayer Perceptron
learning_rate	×	×		×
max_depth		×	×	
max_features		×	×	
n_estimators	×	×	×	
subsample		×		
activation				×
momentum				×
validation_fraction				×
batch_size				×
solver				×
early_stopping				×
max_iter				×
alpha				×
hidden_layer_size				×

In Figs. 9, 11 Adaptive Boosting shows poorest quality with respect to Gradient Boosting in the failure type classification. Among boosting ensamble classifier, both Adaptive Boosting and Gradient Boosting use an additive structure of trees. However the lack of previous tree, identified by high-weight data points (Adaptive Boosting), behaves worse than the residuals of each tree that step-by step reduce the error by identifying the negative gradient and moving in the opposite direction (Gradient Boosting).

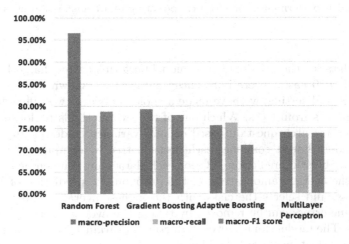

Fig. 9. Models performances on AI4I 2020 test data: failure type task

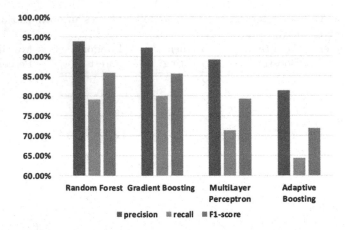

Fig. 10. Models performances on AI4I 2020 test data: machine status task

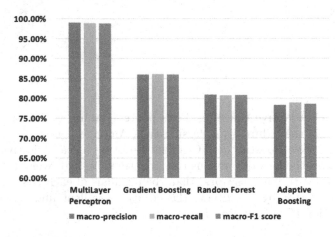

Fig. 11. Models performances on electrical power system transmission lines test data: failure type task

For both tasks, the Random Forest model performs better than other models in the AI4I 2020 case (severe imbalanced dataset), as shown in Figs. 9, 10. In our experimental setting, we have made a choice between two different ways of averaging results from trees. Which one of the two methods performs better is still an open research question based on bias-variance trade off. In our application, Random Forest combines each decision tree by computing the average of their probabilistic prediction [23]: for each data point, the ensemble method computes the average among trees of the probabilistic prediction of belonging in each class, and selects the class with the highest average probabilistic prediction. Some errors can be removed by taking the average of the probabilistic predictions. The model can achieve a reduction in variance by combining diverse trees at the cost of increasing the bias.

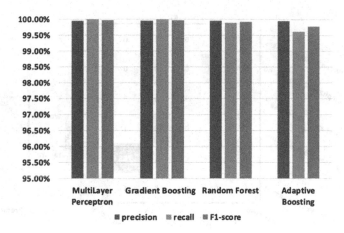

Fig. 12. Models performances on electrical power system transmission lines: electrical status task

Alternatively, each decision tree votes for a single class [4]: for a single data point each tree returns a class, the selected class will be the one with the highest absolute frequency among the trees. Notice that this combination can lead to a reduction in bias at the cost of greater variance.

In the failure type task, the MultiLayer Perceptron model performs better than other models in the electrical power system transmission lines case (slight imbalanced dataset), as shown in Figs. 11, 13. In this work MultiLayer Perceptron model is not superior to tree-based ensemble learning methods in the AI4I 2020 case (severe imbalanced dataset). It is not understood fully why neural network cannot reveal its superiority of predictive quality in presence of severe class-imbalanced tabular data. In this direction a recent work [3] has shown that tree ensemble still outperforms the deep learning models on tabular data. In addition, the MultiLayer Perceptron model has a large amount of hyperparameters, while tree ensemble models have fewer hyperparameters as displayed in Table 1. Therefore, the MultiLayer Perceptron model may need a higher number of iterations in the Bayesian optimization solution to produce predictive quality. Generally, a small number of hyperparameters is more desirable in order to improve the versatility and robustness of the model.

In the AI4I 2020 case, the *tool wear failure* is undetected in the four models with diverse level of evidence. It is unclear why the models is not able to properly recognize this class. We have identified two possible reasons: the number of observed failures in the dataset is quite small (see Fig. 1); this failures are defined as random failures within a large range of tool wear minutes as shown in Fig. 3.

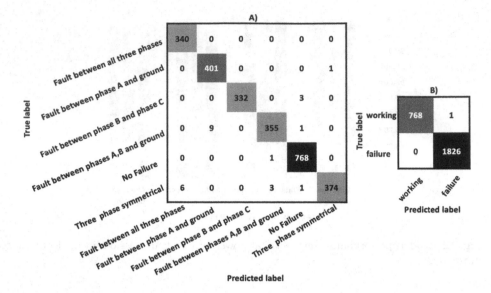

Fig. 13. Electrical power system transmission lines dataset: MultiLayer Perceptron performances, A) failure type task, B) electrical status task.

The proposed models present encouraging results not only for the multi-class problem (primary dependent variable), but also for the binary problem (secondary dependent variable) on imbalanced data, showing good generalization properties. The choice of selecting the best set of hyperparameters with the Bayesian optimization method on the multi-class problem, and fitting the model in the multi-output configuration, has proved to be reliable; firstly solving the failure type problem, secondly recognizing faulty and healthy status related to the first one. The electrical status is detected with outstanding quality in the electrical power system transmission lines case, where all models have excellent performances (see Fig. 12). Random Forest model identifies better the machine status than the other models in the AI4I 2020 case (Fig. 10), however its performance is biased by the *tool wear failures* that remain mainly not perceived (see Fig. 14).

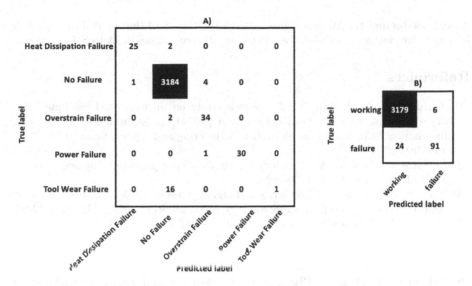

Fig. 14. AI4I 2020 dataset: Random Forest performances, A) failure type task, B) machine status task.

7 Conclusions

In this paper we present a pipeline based on the Bayesian optimization solution for imbalanced datasets in order to design and develop multi-class and binary imbalanced classifiers. We have considered four models, such as Adaptive Boosting, Gradient Boosting, Random Forest and MultiLayer Perceptron. The Bayesian optimization approach has been used to determine the best combination of hyperparameters for model variables to improve machine learning performances. This pipeline has been applied to two different imbalanced datasets, such as AI4I 2020 and electrical power system transmission lines, to classify two connected tasks: failure type and machine (or electrical) status.

Our work includes promising evidence on the ability of models (whose hyperparameters are tuned in the Bayesian optimization method on the failure type variable) to perform well not only on the failure type classification but also on the machine (or electrical) status by using a multi-output configuration.

In the AI4I 2020 case, the Random Forest model performs better than other models for both tasks. In the electrical power system transmission lines case, the MultiLayer Perceptron model performs better than others for the failure type task. Despite the different domain of the datasets, we have observed the tendency of tree ensemble models to succeed on the severe imbalanced dataset, the liability of the MultiLayer Perceptron model to succeed on the slight imbalanced dataset. This work can serve as a valuable starting point for data scientists and practitioners interested in predictive maintenance solutions with imbalanced tabular data.

Acknowledgements. We would like to thank BitBang S.r.l that funded this research; in particular Matteo Casadei, Luca Guerra and the colleagues of Data Science team.

References

1. Amruthnath, N., Gupta, T.: A research study on unsupervised machine learning algorithms for early fault detection in predictive maintenance. In: 2018 5th International Conference on Industrial Engineering and Applications (ICIEA), pp. 355–361 (2018)
2. Bergstra, J., Bengio, Y.: Random search for hyper-parameter optimization. J. Mach. Learn. Res. **13**, 281–305 (2012)
3. Borisov, V., Leemann, T., Seßler, K., Haug, J., Pawelczyk, M., Kasneci, G.: Deep neural networks and tabular data: a survey. arXiv preprint arXiv:2110.01889 (2021)
4. Breiman, L.: Random forests. Mach. Learn. **45**(1), 5–32 (2001)
5. Brochu, E., Cora, V.M., De Freitas, N.: A tutorial on Bayesian optimization of expensive cost functions, with application to active user modeling and hierarchical reinforcement learning. arXiv preprint arXiv:1012.2599 (2010)
6. Calabrese, M., et al.: SOPHIA: an event-based IoT and machine learning architecture for predictive maintenance in Industry 4.0. Information **11**(4), 202 (2020). https://www.mdpi.com/2078-2489/11/4/202
7. Cao, H., Nguyen, M., Phua, C., Krishnaswamy, S., Li, X.: An integrated framework for human activity recognition. In: 2012 ACM Conference on Ubiquitous Computing, pp. 621–622 (2012)
8. Carvalho, T.P., Soares, F.A.A.M.N., Vita, R., P. Francisco, R., Basto, J.P., Alcalá, S.G.S.: A systematic literature review of machine learning methods applied to predictive maintenance. Comput. Ind. Eng. **137**, 106024 (2019)
9. Dua, D., Graff, C.: UCI machine learning repository (2017). http://archive.ics.uci.edu/ml
10. Ghate, V.N., Dudul, S.V.: Optimal MLP neural network classifier for fault detection of three phase induction motor. Expert Syst. Appl. **37**(4), 3468–3481 (2010)
11. Hastie, T., Rosset, S., Zhu, J., Zou, H.: Multi-class AdaBoost. Stat. Interface **2**(3), 349–360 (2009)
12. Hastie, T., Tibshirani, R., Friedman, J.: The Elements of Statistical Learning. SSS, Springer, New York (2009). https://doi.org/10.1007/978-0-387-84858-7
13. He, H., Ma, Y.: Imbalanced Learning: Foundations, Algorithms, and Applications. Wiley-IEEE Press, Hoboken, 216 pages (2013)
14. Heaton, J.: Introduction to Neural Networks with Java. Heaton Research, Inc. Chesterfield (2008)
15. Hutter, F., Hoos, H.H., Leyton-Brown, K.: Sequential model-based optimization for general algorithm configuration. In: Coello, C.A.C. (ed.) LION 2011. LNCS, vol. 6683, pp. 507–523. Springer, Heidelberg (2011). https://doi.org/10.1007/978-3-642-25566-3_40
16. Jamil, M., Sharma, S.K., Singh, R.: Fault detection and classification in electrical power transmission system using artificial neural network. SpringerPlus **4**(1), 1–13 (2015). https://doi.org/10.1186/s40064-015-1080-x
17. Martin-Diaz, I., Morinigo-Sotelo, D., Duque-Perez, O., de J. Romero-Troncoso, R.: Early fault detection in induction motors using AdaBoost with imbalanced small data and optimized sampling. IEEE Trans. Ind. Appl. **53**(3), 3066–3075 (2017)
18. Mosley, L.: A balanced approach to the multi-class imbalance problem. Ph.D. thesis, Iowa State University (2013)

19. Nogueira, F.: Bayesian Optimization: open source constrained global optimization tool for Python (2014). https://github.com/fmfn/BayesianOptimization
20. Orrù, P.F., Zoccheddu, A., Sassu, L., Mattia, C., Cozza, R., Arena, S.: Machine learning approach using MLP and SVM algorithms for the fault prediction of a centrifugal pump in the oil and gas industry. Sustainability **12**, 4776 (2020)
21. Ouadah, A., Leila, Z.-G., Salhi, N.: Selecting an appropriate supervised machine learning algorithm for predictive maintenance. Int. J. Adv. Manufact. Tech. **119**, 4277–4301 (2022)
22. Paolanti, M., Romeo, L., Felicetti, A., Mancini, A., Frontoni, E., Loncarski, J.: Machine learning approach for predictive maintenance in Industry 4.0. In: 2018 14th IEEE/ASME International Conference on Mechatronic and Embedded Systems and Applications (MESA), pp. 1–6. IEEE (2018)
23. Pedregosa, F., et al.: Scikit-learn: machine learning in Python. J. Mach. Learn. Res. **12**, 2825–2830 (2011)
24. Qin, S., Wang, K., Ma, X., Wang, W., Li, M.: Chapter 9: step standard in design and manufacturing ensemble learning-based wind turbine fault prediction method with adaptive feature selection. Communications in Computer and Information Science Data Science, pp. 572–582 (2017)
25. Ronzoni, N.: Predictive maintenance experiences on imbalance data with Bayesian optimization. https://gitlab.com/system_anomaly_detection/predictivemeintenance
26. Snoek, J., Larochelle, H., Adams, R.P.: Practical Bayesian optimization of machine learning algorithms. Adv. Neural Inform. Proc. Syst. **25**, 2951–2959 (2012)
27. Srinivas, N., Krause, A., Kakade, S.M., Seeger, M.: Gaussian process optimization in the bandit setting: no regret and experimental design. arXiv preprint arXiv:0912.3995 (2009)
28. Susto, G., Schirru, A., Pampuri, S., Mcloone, S., Beghi, A.: Machine learning for predictive maintenance: a multiple classifier approach. IEEE Trans. Ind. Inf. **11**, 812–820 (2015)
29. Urbanowicz, R.J., Moore, J.H.: ExSTraCS 2.0: description and evaluation of a scalable learning classifier system. Evol. Intell. **8**(2), 89–116 (2015)
30. Vasilić, P., Vujnović, S., Popović, N., Marjanović, A., Željko Durović: Adaboost algorithm in the frame of predictive maintenance tasks. In: 23rd International Scientific-Professional Conference on Information Technology (IT), IEEE, pp. 1–4 (2018)

Empowering COVID-19 Fact-Checking with Extended Knowledge Graphs

Paolo Mengoni[1]([✉])(iD) and Jinyu Yang[2](iD)

[1] School of Communication and Film, Hong Kong Baptist University,
Hong Kong, China
pmengoni@hkbu.edu.hk
[2] Hong Kong Baptist University, Hong Kong, China
18252591@life.hkbu.edu.hk

Abstract. During the COVID-19 outbreak, fake news regarding the disease have spread at an increasing rate. Let's think, for instance, to face masks wearing related news or various home-made treatments to cure the disease. To contrast this phenomenon, the fact-checking community has intensified its efforts by producing a large number of fact-checking reports. In this work, we focus on empowering knowledge-based approaches for misinformation identification with previous knowledge gathered from existing fact-checking reports. Very few works in literature have exploited the information regarding claims that have been already fact-checked. The main idea that we explore in this work is to exploit the detailed information in the COVID-19 fact check reports in order to create an extended Knowledge Graph. By analysing the graph information about the already checked claims, we can verify newly coming content more effectively. Another gap that we aim to fill is the temporal representation of the facts stored in the knowledge graph. At the best of our knowledge, this is the first attempt to associate the temporal validity to the KG relations. This additional information can be used to further enhance the validation of claims.

Keywords: Fact checking · Knowledge graphs · Natural Language Processing

1 Introduction

During the current COVID-19 outbreak, we are witnessing a new wave of misinformation spreading on different media. Social media, forums and traditional news outlets are evenly affected by the diffusion of fake news, disinformation and misinformation. On the opposite side, the efforts from the scientific community have brought to a wide range of initiatives in fact-checking and veracity assessment.

The common approaches to misinformation identification involve professional fact-checkers or experts to produce reports that assess the veracity (i.e. veracity level) of the rumours. Those fact-checkers rely on their expertise, that can vary from journalism to the medical fields, to annotate the misleading content. On the other hand, computational approaches for misinformation are introduced to tackle the increased volume and speed of fake news creation. These approaches can be categorized in four different categories: (i) knowledge-based methods that classify the veracity of content on the basis of pre-existing knowledge bases; (ii) style-based approaches that analyse the information semantic and syntactic features; (iii) credibility-based techniques that take into account the credibility of the content spreading subjects; (iv) propagation-based approaches that exploit social network analyses to understand the content propagation [10,12]. The first two categories focus on analysing the content of the news, while the latter two rely on the analysis of the medium where the content spreads.

The result of this process - manual or automatic - is usually a fact-check report that contains a classification of claims given a specific assessment label. The veracity assessment can vary from the simple assignment of {True; False} labels, to a more detailed classification using {True, Partially True, False, Unsubstantiated}, to fine-grain classification like in *Snopes* that use an extended set of labels including {True; Mostly true; Mixture; Mostly false; False; Unproven; Outdated; Miscaptioned; Correct attribution; Misattributed; Scam; Legend, Labeled Satire, Lost Legend}. The fact-check reports also contain details about the assessment process and include a wide range of information pertaining to the assessed claim and related facts.

In this work, we focus on a novel knowledge-based approach that will take in account multiple sources to assess the veracity level of a new claim. The knowledge base is then transformed to a Knowledge Graph (KG): a graph structure that represents the facts in a knowledge base as nodes and their relationships as edges. Usually the content of the KG is assumed to be true, while it is not possible to make any assumption on the information that is absent. In our approach we will associate a veracity label to the facts, gathering this information from the existing fact-checking reports. This kind of approach has been rarely explored in literature and will be exploited to create a specialized, thematic KG to support fact-checking.

The research questions that we will try to answer can be summarised as follows: (i) how to transform a fact-checking report into a Knowledge Graph, (ii) how to integrate temporal information into the Knowledge Graph, and (iii) how the Knowledge Graph can be used to support fact-checking.

The rest of the paper is organized as follows. In Sect. 2, we discuss related works using Knowledge Graphs to support fact-checking. In Sect. 3, we introduce in detail the methodology used for this work. Section 4 reports the results of our approach and in Sect. 5 we analyse and discuss them. In Sect. 6, we draw conclusions and introduce future works.

2   Related Works

The knowledge-based approaches to fact-checking, like the one we propose in this work, usually rely on pre-existing knowledge bases that contain general information. The knowledge bases may contain information stored in structured way (e.g. like in DBPedia[1]), semi-structured (e.g. as in Wikipedia[2]), or unstructured like in other open access repositories and ontologies. Some techniques will directly rely on the knowledge base content of one (single-source approaches) or more (open-source approaches) to assess the truthfulness of a claim.

The knowledge base can be transformed into a Knowledge Graph (KG), a graph structure that represents the facts in a knowledge base as nodes and their relationships as edges. Facts in the knowledge base are usually stored as sets of (Subject, Predicate, Object) (SPO) triples. The Subject and Object of the SPO triples will become the nodes of the knowledge graph, while the Predicate will be the label associated with the edges between the nodes. The Predicate will define the relationship between the nodes [1]. Metadata will be associated with the relationship between the nodes and usually will define the relationship type and other additional information deemed needed for the fact-checking task. The metadata annotations can be crowdsourced [6], manually annotated by experts [5], or automatically generated by using Natural Language Processing (NLP) techniques [11].

Some assumptions are made on the content of the KG. In general, the information present in the graph is always considered to be True, while absent SPO triples may take any possible veracity value [12]. Given these assumptions, to support fact-checking there has been an emerging need to add additional information to the knowledge graphs. Recent works associated to the KG metadata the truth values of the statements as assessed by fact-checking organisations (such as *Snopes*[3], AFP Fact Check[4], etc.) [11].

The KG information is then used to support various fact-checking strategies, such as the Entity Location, Relation Verification, and Knowledge Inference [12]. Given a claim, the fact-checking goal is to evaluate the probability (or possibility) that an edge exists or may exist in the KG [8,9].

The ClaimsKG [11] is a similar work that is focusing more on Fact Retrieval, while our approach is focusing more on structuring the KG to empower the Relation Verification and, in future works, Knowledge Inference tasks. The novel approach we here introduce, very less explored in literature until recently [7], is motivated from making good use of the previously fact-checked claims to assess the veracity of new ones.

3   Methodology

In this work we will explore the Relation Verification task. This aspect of the knowledge-based fact checking is using information in the KG to verify newly coming content.

---

[1] https://wiki.dbpedia.org/.
[2] https://www.wikipedia.org/.
[3] https://www.snopes.com/.
[4] https://factcheck.afp.com/.

In the approach introduced in this work, the fact-checking reports are transformed to an extended KG *FactsKG* that can be used to assess claim veracity using various knowledge-based techniques. The approach we are introducing here is general but given the availability of data and the importance of the topic, we focus on COVID-19 related claims and the associated fact-checking reports.

By analysing the fact-checking reports, we will extract facts that have been already assessed by fact-checking organisations. These facts will be stored in the KG in the form of SPO triples. Unlike many other KG, the graph that we are going to generate will include facts with various veracity levels as assessed in the fact-checking reports. This is one of the most innovative aspect of our approach, that will extend the classical KG definition by adding additional information about the facts in the metadata of the SPO triples. The edge metadata will store the relation veracity that has been assessed by the fact checking reports. Additionally, *FactsKG* will also include temporal information as the relationship between Subject and Object may vary during time. Fact-checkers will be able to immediately and effectively assess newly coming claims using directly the *FactsKG* or through automated Relation Verification techniques.

The methodology used in this work includes the fact-checking report dataset creation, SPO generation from the dataset, and finally the transformation of SPO triples into *FactsKG*.

The first step of the process is the creation of a dataset from previously produced fact-checking reports. This task involves the retrieval and collection of public fact-checking reports from fact-checking websites. We implemented a scraper for obtaining automatically the information from the fact-checking websites, using Python and the Beautifulsoup library. After analysing the data scraped from the various fact-checking websites, we implemented the dataset schema including information about the report *retrieved date, url, title, publisher name, publisher website, textual veracity rating, language code, report text, claimant, claim date and time*. During analysis and early testing of the methodology we have found that we should save a permanent copy of the reports. This was needed to keep our dataset consistent as some reports were updated and deleted by the fact-checking organisations. The permanent copy of the reports found by our scraper has been saved online using Internet Archive[5] and PermaCC[6] services and stored in the dataset field *claim permanent url*. An additional offline copy has been saved offline as html file and stored in the dataset field *report permanent html filename*.

Once the fact-checking reports have been collected, we perform the second step of our methodology. By using Natural Language Processing (NLP) techniques we automatically transform the fact-checking reports in (Subject, Predicate, Object) (SPO) triples. The dataset is analysed through the NLP pipeline included in the *spaCy* Python library [2]. The process includes stop word removal, tokenization, token transformation to vector using convolutional neural networks (*tok2vec*), part of speech tagging, sentence segmentation, dependency

---

[5] https://archive.org/.
[6] https://perma.cc/.

parsing, sentence entity recognition, named entity recognition, attribute ruler, and lemmatization. All the NLP steps allow to extract informative SPO triples from the fact checking reports, thus transforming the unstructured textual data in a structured form. Contextually extended metadata will be associated with the SPO triples. This includes the triples' veracity level, temporal information and other features deemed to be useful for future tasks.

The last step of our methodology is the construction of the Knowledge Graph (KG). First we analysed and designed various possible solutions for the KG structure and its storage. For the data storage we selected the Neo4J[7] database management system that supports native graph data storage. In the analysis phase we explored the transformation of the SPOs in the dataset with a 2-nodes and a 3-nodes graph model. The 2-nodes model involves the storage of Subject and Object as nodes of the graph, while the Predicate is the label of the edge between the pair of nodes. In the 3-nodes model each element is stored as a node with Subject/Object nodes and Predicate nodes. The Subject node have outbound connections to Predicate nodes and the Object nodes have inbound connection from the Predicate nodes. The Predicate edges and nodes attributes, for the 2-nodes and 3-nodes respectively, will contain the veracity level, temporal information, and other features.

4   Results

Working with real-life data is always difficult. During the phases of data collection, cleaning, transformation, and knowledge graph creation we faced various challenges.

4.1   Dataset Creation

The structure of the fact-checking reports is different for every website, making difficult to access the information from automated systems. As shown in Fig. 1, AFP Fact check report[8] is a textual report with a simple structure as shown in Fig. 1a, that makes the collection task easy. However, there is no clear textual indication of the claim veracity assessment. AFP is using different colours (i.e., red, orange, etc.) for the cross drawn over the assessed claim to display the veracity of the claim, as shown in Fig. 1b. In this work, we extract the veracity information from the text, but in this case it is more difficult to give a clear classification of AFP reports.

On the other hand, as shown in Fig. 2a, the content of the fact-check report from *Snopes*[9] is more structured, requiring a different scraping strategy. How-

---

[7] https://neo4j.com.

[8] Available at the address:
https://factcheck.afp.com/http%253A%252F%252Fdoc.afp.com%252F9VY4M3-1.

[9] Permanent copy available at the address:
https://web.archive.org/web/20220315225545/https://www.snopes.com/fact-check/pfizer-covid-19-vaccine-fetal-cells/.

ever, the veracity of the claim is clearly displayed in a specific section of the report as shown in Fig. 2b.

During the scraping process we faced also the problem that some reports structure is not consistent, also internally to each source. Moreover, the reports structure is changing during time requiring manual intervention for adjusting the scraping parameters. Moreover, some of the reports are missing some parts requiring specific error management strategies.

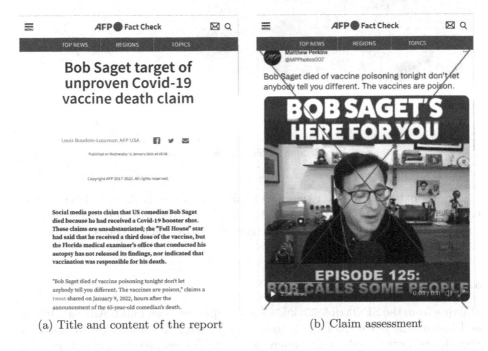

(a) Title and content of the report   (b) Claim assessment

Fig. 1. AFP fact-checking report

4.2 SPO Extraction

After scraping the content, we applied NLP techniques to extract the SPO triples from the reports content. As introduced in Sect. 3, we used Python and *spaCy* library to analysis the content at syntactic and semantic level.

The first challenge we faced came from the library itself. With *spaCy* version 2.x we were able to use *neuralcoref* [4], a very powerful co-reference library that uses artificial neural networks to correctly replace the pronouns with the corresponding subjects. However, the predicate's tense extraction is only available in *spaCy* version 3.x and *neuralcoref* still doesn't support it. As an alternative, we started to use the *corefere* [3] coreference library. This library is available for the latest version of *spaCy* and after evaluation it achieves comparable results to *neuralcoref* but with a more convoluted approach.

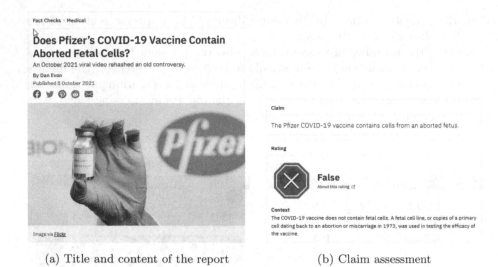

(a) Title and content of the report   (b) Claim assessment

Fig. 2. Snopes fact-checking report

Additional challenges for the SPO triples extraction task are related to the fact-checking reports authors' writing styles. When the phrasing become more complex, the NLP libraries tend to struggle in identifying the correct tokens and complete sentences.

4.3 Knowledge Graph Creation

Starting from the SPO triples, a knowledge graph has been build. After analysing and testing the features of the 2-nodes and 3-nodes KG models, introduced in Sect. 3, the latter model was chosen. After careful evaluation and testing, the 3-nodes model has several advantages over the 2-nodes KG model. Given the characteristics of the Neo4J's Cypher query language, the 3-nodes model has higher computational speed, it allows to store more information in the node's attributes, and makes available the relation information when executing queries.

These characteristics also make the model suitable for the Relation Verification task. In Fig. 3 we show the partial view of the *FactsKG* representing the *AFP* fact-checking report shown in Fig. 1. The red colour nodes are Predicates nodes, in blue are shown the Subject/Object nodes. The links are also labelled with the report id stored in our dataset, as shown in Fig. 4.

5   Discussion

Processing the fact-checking reports with our methodology allows the creation of a knowledge graph. In *FactsKG* we were able to incorporate valuable metadata for the fact-checker that includes the assessed veracity value from multiple sources, the temporal information, original report and claim link, and so on.

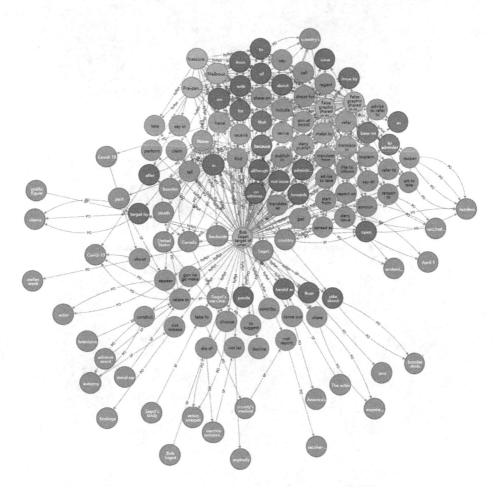

Fig. 3. Knowledge graph representing fact-checking report from AFP. (Color figure online)

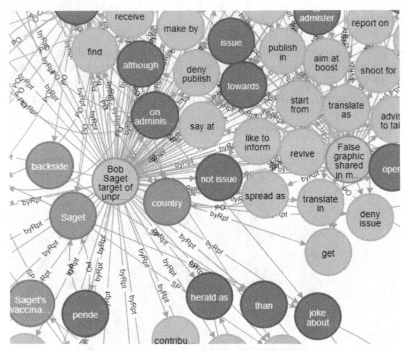

(a) Two reports are connected by relationships on the KG through various nodes.

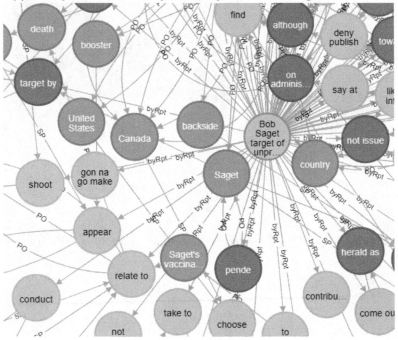

(b) Multiple connections from various predicates connect to the same subject/object.

Fig. 4. Zoom on a section of the KG (Color figure online)

This information has been made accessible for the fact-checkers through a web interface. The process of claim-checking starts with the input of a claim. The claim text will be processed with the same SPO extraction procedure introduced in Sect. 4.2. The SPOs extracted from the claim will be matched with the SPOs in *FactsKG*. Each SPO can be extracted by using a combination of complete or partial matching and with a direct or indirect search. The matching depends on whether we may consider the full SPO triple (complete matching) for the KG query or a part of it such as considering only subject or object as starting nodes (partial strategy). Moreover, the search strategy can be either direct or indirect, depending on whether we may consider only direct edges on the graphs or allow a longer path search. For the scope of this work we limited the number of steps for the partial indirect matching to 3, but the parameter can be freely adjusted.

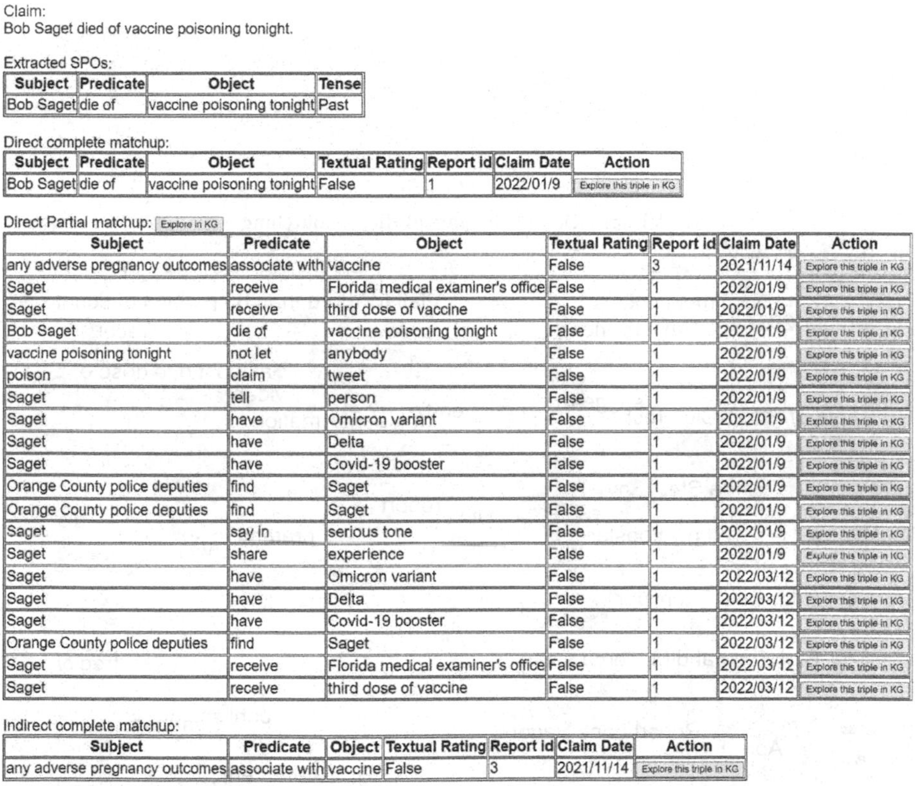

Claim:
Bob Saget died of vaccine poisoning tonight.

Extracted SPOs:

Subject	Predicate	Object	Tense
Bob Saget	die of	vaccine poisoning tonight	Past

Direct complete matchup:

Subject	Predicate	Object	Textual Rating	Report id	Claim Date	Action
Bob Saget	die of	vaccine poisoning tonight	False	1	2022/01/9	Explore this triple in KG

Direct Partial matchup: Explore in KG

Subject	Predicate	Object	Textual Rating	Report id	Claim Date	Action
any adverse pregnancy outcomes	associate with	vaccine	False	3	2021/11/14	Explore this triple in KG
Saget	receive	Florida medical examiner's office	False	1	2022/01/9	Explore this triple in KG
Saget	receive	third dose of vaccine	False	1	2022/01/9	Explore this triple in KG
Bob Saget	die of	vaccine poisoning tonight	False	1	2022/01/9	Explore this triple in KG
vaccine poisoning tonight	not let	anybody	False	1	2022/01/9	Explore this triple in KG
poison	claim	tweet	False	1	2022/01/9	Explore this triple in KG
Saget	tell	person	False	1	2022/01/9	Explore this triple in KG
Saget	have	Omicron variant	False	1	2022/01/9	Explore this triple in KG
Saget	have	Delta	False	1	2022/01/9	Explore this triple in KG
Saget	have	Covid-19 booster	False	1	2022/01/9	Explore this triple in KG
Orange County police deputies	find	Saget	False	1	2022/01/9	Explore this triple in KG
Orange County police deputies	find	Saget	False	1	2022/01/9	Explore this triple in KG
Saget	say in	serious tone	False	1	2022/01/9	Explore this triple in KG
Saget	share	experience	False	1	2022/01/9	Explore this triple in KG
Saget	have	Omicron variant	False	1	2022/03/12	Explore this triple in KG
Saget	have	Delta	False	1	2022/03/12	Explore this triple in KG
Saget	have	Covid-19 booster	False	1	2022/03/12	Explore this triple in KG
Orange County police deputies	find	Saget	False	1	2022/03/12	Explore this triple in KG
Saget	receive	Florida medical examiner's office	False	1	2022/03/12	Explore this triple in KG
Saget	receive	third dose of vaccine	False	1	2022/03/12	Explore this triple in KG

Indirect complete matchup:

Subject	Predicate	Object	Textual Rating	Report id	Claim Date	Action
any adverse pregnancy outcomes	associate with	vaccine	False	3	2021/11/14	Explore this triple in KG

Fig. 5. Screenshot of the tabulated results of the claim matching.

The results of the matching are visualised using tabulated lists and graphical visualisation. In Fig. 5 is shown the tabulated results view, that reports the results for each matching and search combination. The textual list includes also

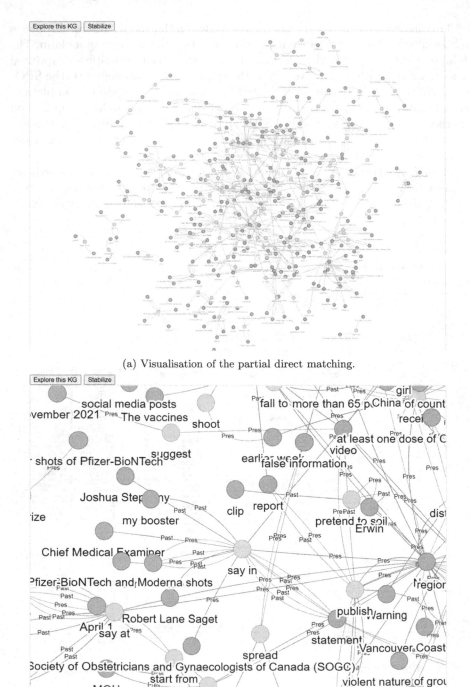

(a) Visualisation of the partial direct matching.

(b) Zoom on a part of the partial direct matching KG.

Fig. 6. Visualisation of the partial direct matching results. (Color figure online)

the option to visualise the results in graphical way. For each section there is also the additional button to show all the results within a single visualisation, as shown in Fig. 6. The graphical visualisation include the nodes and the relations involved in the matching. The blue colour nodes are subjects or objects, the yellow colour nodes are predicates, the blue links connect a subject to a predicates, and the orange links connect the predicates to the objects as stored in the KG. By using this interface it makes easier for fact-checkers to check the path and the reasoning that lead to the veracity assessment on multiple sources combined together in the *FactsKG*.

6   Conclusions and Future Works

In this work, we introduced a novel methodology for extracting a Knowledge Graph from fact-checking reports. The novel knowledge-based approach takes in account fact-checking reports from multiple sources to help the veracity level assessment by fact-checkers. The knowledge base storing the fact-checking reports, is first transformed in Subject-Predicate-Object triples and then integrated into the Knowledge Graph (KG). The *FactsKG* is an extended KG as integrates additional metadata about the facts. The metadata includes the veracity label associated to the facts, temporal information about the facts, and additional information useful for the task. The visual interface developed for matching new claims on *FactsKG*, when integrated in the fact-checking process, may facilitate the work of the fact-checkers.

In future works, we will introduce complex network analysis for the automatic Relation Verification task. The assessment of new claims will be performed on the KG using automated complex network analysis techniques.

Acknowledgements. This work is partly supported by the "AI-Info Communication Study (AIS) Scheme 2021/22 (Ref. AIS 21–22/05)" and "Teaching Development Grant" - School of Communication and Film, Hong Kong Baptist University, Hong Kong, China.

References

1. Hogan, A., et. al.: Knowledge Graphs. Synthesis Lectures on Data, Semantics, and Knowledge, vol. 12, no. 2, pp. 1–257 (2021). https://doi.org/10.2200/S01125ED1V01Y202109DSK022
2. Honnibal, M., Montani, I., Van Landeghem, S., Boyd, A.: SpaCy: Industrial-Strength Natural Language Processing in Python (2020). https://doi.org/10.5281/zenodo.1212303
3. Hudson, R.P., msg systems ag: coreferee: coreference resolution for multiple languages. https://github.com/msg-systems/coreferee
4. Huggingface: neuralcoref: fast coreference resolution in spaCy with neural networks. https://github.com/huggingface/neuralcoref
5. Mihaylova, T., et. al.: Fact checking in community forums. In: Thirty-Second AAAI Conference on Artificial Intelligence (2018)

6. Pérez-Rosas, V., Mihalcea, R.: Experiments in open domain deception detection. In: Proceedings of the 2015 Conference on Empirical Methods in Natural Language Processing, pp. 1120–1125 (2015)
7. Shaar, S., Martino, G.D.S., Babulkov, N., Nakov, P.: That is a known lie: detecting previously fact-checked claims. arXiv preprint arXiv:2005.06058 (2020)
8. Shi, B., Weninger, T.: Discriminative predicate path mining for fact checking in knowledge graphs. Knowl. Based Syst. **104**, 123–133 (2016)
9. Shiralkar, P., Flammini, A., Menczer, F., Ciampaglia, G.L.: Finding streams in knowledge graphs to support fact checking. In: 2017 IEEE International Conference on Data Mining (ICDM), pp. 859–864. IEEE (2017)
10. Shu, K., Sliva, A., Wang, S., Tang, J., Liu, H.: Fake news detection on social media: a data mining perspective. ACM SIGKDD Explor. Newsl. **19**(1), 22–36 (2017)
11. Tchechmedjiev, A., et al.: ClaimsKG: a knowledge graph of fact-checked claims. In: Ghidini, C., et al. (eds.) ISWC 2019. LNCS, vol. 11779, pp. 309–324. Springer, Cham (2019). https://doi.org/10.1007/978-3-030-30796-7_20
12. Zhou, X., Zafarani, R.: A survey of fake news: fundamental theories, detection methods, and opportunities. ACM Comput. Surv. (CSUR) **53**(5), 1–40 (2020)

International Workshop on Advances in information Systems and Technologies for Emergency management, risk assessment and mitigation based on the Resilience (ASTER 2022)

Multi-hazard Analysis and Mapping of Infrastructure Systems at National Level Using GIS Techniques: Preliminary Results

Maurizio Pollino[1]([✉]) [iD], Sergio Cappucci[1] [iD], Cristiano Pesaresi[2] [iD], Maria Giuseppina Farrace[3], Lorenzo Della Morte[2], and Giulio Vegliante[2]

[1] ENEA - Italian National Agency for New Technologies, Energy and Sustainable Economic Development, Casaccia Research Centre, Via Anguillarese, 301-00123 Rome, Italy
maurizio.pollino@enea.it
[2] University of Rome "Sapienza", Rome, Italy
[3] Civil Protection Department, Rome, Italy

Abstract. Preliminary results of the multi-hazard (seismic, landslide, floods) analysis, conducted on some Critical Infrastructures (CI), are presented. Lifelines an CI such as roads, railways, gas and power networks are essential for the Country's economy, but also to ensure the overcoming of emergencies in those territories in case of natural disasters. ENEA CIPCast platform, an innovative Decision Support System (DSS), has been used for the GIS-based analysis of physical impacts induced by natural hazards on CI. It has been exploited in several projects, including RAFAEL that, by means of analytical and geoprocessing tools, was focus on the extensive assessment and mapping of CI hazard. Geospatial layers, describing and classifying the different hazards in Italy, has allowed to produce a set of specific hazard maps for each CI considered. Multi-hazard values were assigned by using a suitable matrix having four classes. Preliminary results are discussed focusing on the impact on CI exposed to different level of seismic, flood and landslide hazard.

Keywords: Hazard analysis · Hazard mapping · Critical Infrastructures · Lifelines · Geoprocessing

1 Introduction

1.1 The Italian Territorial Context

Italy is among the countries at greatest geological risk in the Mediterranean area, where seismicity is strongly gathered [1] and with some seismically active zones particularly worthy of note [2]. The position of the Italian territory in the convergence zone between the African and Eurasian plates causes strong compressive forces, which have allowed the formation of mountain belts of Alps and Apennines during Mesozoic. From Neogene, a distensive tectonic phase was activated, resulting in numerous high-intensity and long-lasting seismic events. The frequency of earthquakes that have affected our

© The Author(s), under exclusive license to Springer Nature Switzerland AG 2022
O. Gervasi et al. (Eds.): ICCSA 2022 Workshops, LNCS 13377, pp. 153–168, 2022.
https://doi.org/10.1007/978-3-031-10536-4_11

country throughout history, as well as the energy that some events have reached, have a considerable impact on infrastructures [3]. Landslides and floods can expose lifelines and infrastructures to hazard [4, 5].

Risk is a measure of the expected damage over a period of time, based on the type of catastrophic event, building resistance and level of anthropization. Risks related to flooding, landslides and earthquake in Italy are correlated to the high vulnerability of Critical Infrastructures (CI) and their exposure to different catastrophic events [6]. The dangerousness is given by the frequency and strength of the catastrophic event that affects an area: it will be higher in case of high intensity and high probability of occurrence in a given time interval. The susceptibility of structures or infrastructures to being damaged is called vulnerability. Finally, exposure is determined by the possibility to have economic damages, injuries or loss of life and damage to assets in due to the presence of structures or infrastructures (e.g., lifelines) exposed to the event.

In case of calamitous event, depending on its extent and on the territorial ability to respond, the decision-makers (according to the reference legislation, deriving from EU Directives) are appointed to manage the emergency and to provide support to the population affected, by activating the national civil protection system (Italian Civil Protection Code [7]. This system regulates all the expertise involved and the activities to be carried out, aiming at the protection and physical integrity of citizens, assets, settlements, livestock and, more in general, the environment from hazards or damages caused by calamitous events of natural origin or resulting from human activity [8].

The knowledge and awareness of the territorial hazard and vulnerability, allow to identify, before an event occurs, the most suitable guidelines to be adopted at National level for the subsequent definition at local level of emergency planning to be implemented when the event actually occurs.

Therefore, Italian territory has been classified into different hazard zones in order to prevent the effects of earthquakes, floods, landslides and other natural disasters. Intensity and frequency of past earthquakes, for example, are considered in the definition and application of specific standards for buildings. To this end, Italian anti-seismic legislation prescribes technical standards on the basis of which to design structures and infrastructures. The census of areas prone to landslides or flooding is also carried out and the entire territory has Hydrogeological Master Plan (called PAI, *"Piano di Assetto Idrogeologico"*; [9].

In this framework, a crucial issue is related to the Critical Infrastructure Protection (CIP). This aspect is at the heart of the European and International Agenda since several years. Natural disasters affecting CI are able to cause huge damages and consequences, both from social and economic points of view [10]. Thus, the use of effective tools and approaches should be pursued to support Public Administration and Operators in their tasks concerning the hazard and risk assessment, especially to carry out an effective protection of their assets from impacts arising from natural disasters, which can harm the infrastructures and reduce the continuity of services delivered.

In particular, for the aims of the activities described in the present paper, we focused on the hazard analysis and mapping of CI systems represented by energy, gas and transportation (road and railway) networks.

The study carried-out represents a fundamental step to develop an extensive approach aiming at the reduction of the vulnerabilities and the mitigation of the risks, facing the threats to which these complex systems, essential for the everyday life, are exposed.

There is a large number of studies that illustrates the effects of natural phenomena on CI systems. Many researchers have proved that an integrated and multi-hazard approach can support effective measures in both prevention and quantitative analysis of risk assessment enhancing the capacity for disaster risk reduction [11–14]. The aim is to support the risk analysis related to the CI of interest and provide a quantitative analysis based on overlapping of seismic, floods, landslide hazard with essential infrastructure systems.

1.2 The CIPCast Platform

To perform the study described in the present paper, the ENEA CIPCast platform has been employed. It is an innovative Decision Support System (DSS) and interoperable platform for the operational 24/7 monitoring of CI and for the prediction of physical and functional impacts induced by natural events on CI. It can also support risk analysis and mapping [15]. The CIPCast platform has been developed as a combination of free/open-source software (FOSS) environments including GIS features, which play a major role in the construction of a Spatial DSS. In order to store and share all data and information available, a PostGIS-based [16] GeoDatabase for data storage and management has been implemented. The Geodatabase can be directly accessed by means of different desktop GIS software suites (e.g., QGIS). In addition, by means of the server stratum, represented by the GeoServer suite [17], data can be accessed via web by using OGC standards (WMS, WFS and WCS) [18]. Thus, in the GeoDatabase numerous (more then 400) maps and information layers are stored and constantly updated:

- Basic data and maps describing the territory;
- Environmental hazard maps (floods, landslides, earthquakes);
- Data about the location and topology of the main National CI systems and networks (i.e., High Voltage, gas, transportation networks, etc.)
- Outputs from forecast models (weather, nowcasting, flooding);
- Real time seismic data (INGV National Earthquake Observatory) and meteorological data (National Civil Protection);
- Data from distributed sensors (ground sensing) located on specific CI.

The geospatial data used to carry out the activities described in the present paper will be specifically listed and detailed in Sect. 3.1.

CIPCast can run in operational mode (on a 24/7 basis, as an alert system) [19] and in offline mode by performing hazard/risk assessments and/or simulating events [20]. In the first case, CIPCast gets external data from many different sources (e.g., seismic network, meteo/hydrological models), to establish the current conditions and elaborate an expected "damage scenario" for the area in which is located the CI of interest. In the second case, CIPCast can be employed as a GIS tool enabling risk mapping and assessment for each element of the CI considered, depending on the type of event expected (hazard) and the specific vulnerabilities [21]. A specific WebGIS application has been implemented in order to be used as geographical interface of data and information provided and/or produced within CIPCast.

1.3 The RAFAEL Project

The study and the related applicative cases presented in this paper have been carried out in the framework of the RAFAEL Project ("system for Risk Analysis and Forecast for critical infrastructure in ApenninEs dorsaL regions", PNR 2015–2020, co-funded by the Italian Ministry of University and Research, Grant no. ARS01_00305, ended in November 2021, https://www.progetto-rafael.it/). The Project aimed at integrating different approaches and technologies, developed within its activities, into the CIPCast platform [21]. RAFAEL was focused on the risk assessment and monitoring of numerous infrastructural systems, by evaluating the impacts and the damages deriving from natural disastrous events. Among its objectives, the RAFAEL project has implemented new capabilities in CIPCast, by means of analytical and geoprocessing tools able to assess and map the hazard for CI as described in the present paper.

2 Study Area Characteristics

Hazard analyses and researches can be considered as a set of studies that quantitatively determine how the territory in which we live is subject to the effects of various natural disasters. The starting point to implement such approach is to describe and map the hazards, by distinguishing the various phenomena to which a portion of territory may be exposed (i.e., earthquakes, hydrogeological disruptions, etc.) and to characterise them into different levels by using a proper classification.

2.1 Hazards

In this Section, the three main hazard typologies considered in the present study (flood, landslide and seismic hazards) are described, with a specific focus on the Italian situation.

Flood Hazard. In Italy there are several areas prone to hydraulic hazard, due to flooding caused by rivers, streams, canals, lakes and, for coastal areas, by the sea. In Italy, the Legislative Decree 49/2010 has implemented the Directive 2007/60/EC (Floods Directive - FD), aiming at the definition of a framework for the assessment and management of flood risks.

The Italian territory is particularly exposed to flood events due to its geographical, morphological and geological characteristics. These include, for example, flash floods, which are triggered by rainfall phenomena of short duration but of considerable intensity. Although these natural phenomena are impossible to be predicted, a series of human activities have contributed to increasing the probability of occurrence of floods and have also amplified their impact on structures/infrastructures and consequently on the population. Destructive flood events, such as those that have affected several areas of Italy [22] in recent years, are paradigmatic of floods with similar characteristics.

Firstly, the destructive consequences of floods are intensified by the expansion of urban settlements and production sites. Such anthropic interventions resulted in an increase of impervious surface areas (roads, buildings, etc.), causing detrimental hydro-logic changes, stream channel erosion and habitat degradation. Secondly, the probability of occurrence of extreme flood events has increased due to the combined effect of the climate change (which alters the thermo-pluviometric regime) and the increasing land consumption [22].

In 2017, ISPRA released the new National Mosaic (v. 4.0 - December 2017) [23] of the flood hazard zones mapped by the River Basin District Authorities according to the following three scenarios defined by Legislative Decree 49/2010 (implementation of the Flood Directive 2007/60/EC) as follows:

– high probability scenario (P3) with a return period of 20–50 years (frequent floods);
– medium probability scenario (P2) with a return period of 100–200 years;
– low probability or extreme event scenario (P1).

Since flood hazard refers to the probability of occurrence of an event of a given intensity in a given period of time and over a given area, the cited hazard maps show the delimitation of the areas that could be affected by floods according to the three probabilities (i.e., hazard) scenarios listed above [24].

Landslide Hazard. Considering the landslides, Italy is one of most affected Countries in Europe [14, 25]. On the basis of the data surveyed and archived by the Italian Land-slide Inventory (IFFI Project), there are about 621,000 landslides affecting an area of 23,700 km^2, equal to about 8% of the entire National territory [22]. About one third of these landslides is represented by rapid phenomena (falls/topples, mud flows and debris flows), having a high speed and able to produce destructive consequences on structures/infrastructures as well as to cause loss of human life. On the other hand, landslides characterised by moderate or slow speed (e.g., complex landslides, rota-tional/translational slides, slow earth flows), not only are able to damage structures in built-up areas, but can also cause significant damages to linear lifelines, such as - for example - roads, or other infrastructures such as railways, buried pipelines, etc.

Among the most important factors for triggering landslides [26–28] can be consid-ered: short and intense rainfall, continuous and persistent rainfall, earthquakes (ground shaking caused by earthquakes can destabilize the slope directly (e.g., by inducing soil liquefaction) or can weaken the material and cause cracks that could eventually produce a landslide).

In this framework, the reference dataset is the National mosaic (v. 3.0 – December 2017) of landslide hazard zones of the River Basin Plans (PAI), mapped by the River Basin District Authorities and released by ISPRA in 2017 [23, 24]. Such mapping is based on the landslides already occurred, the areas of possible evolution of the existing landslide phenomena, and the areas potentially susceptible to new events.

According to this approach, the National territory has been classified into five hazard classes:

– very high H4;
– high H3;
– medium H2;

- moderate H1;
- attention zones AA.

Seismic Hazard. As stated in the Introduction Section, seismicity in Italy is distributed in the entire territory [1]. Due to the rich historical documentation in Italy, several databases have been compiled to integrate all the available data about historical seismicity [29, 30]. One of the last compilations is represented by the Parametric Catalogue of Italian Earthquakes of INGV (CPTI15 [31], which covers the entire Italian territory. It includes 4,894 earthquakes in the time interval 1000–2020, characterized by maximum intensity equal or greater than 5 (and instrumental magnitude greater or equivalent to Mw = 4.0). In the last twenty years, 49 seismic events with Mw greater than 5 have been recorded in Italy: among these, is worth to mention the 2009 L'Aquila earthquake and the 2016–2017 Central Italy seismic sequence [32–35].

A new hazard map of the national territory was released in 2004, based on the most up-to-date information, for which periodic revisions are required by law. An assessment of the most dangerous areas of the National territory is provided by the seismic hazard map [36].

Peak horizontal acceleration (PGA) is a parameter traditionally used in the design of the elastic response of buildings. The PGA value refer to a hypothetical homogeneous soil foundation of the infrastructure with good characteristics. Designers apply appropriate corrections to consider the different nature of the soil on a local basis, if necessary. A design of an infrastructure must consider zonation of the National territory.

Four seismic zones are defined [38], based on ground acceleration values g (acceleration of gravity is equal to 9.81 m/s^2):

- Zone 4 (0.25–0.3 g) has the strongest shaking values and is expected throughout the central-southern Apennines (with maximum peaks in Calabria and south-eastern Sicily, and in Friuli Venezia Giulia);
- Zone 3 (0.15–0.25 g) has moderate values as reported on the Salento Peninsula, along the Tyrrhenian coast between Tuscany and Latium, in Liguria, within the Po Valley, and along the entire Alpine arc;
- Zone 2 (0.05–0.15 g) has low value of ground acceleration and is expected along western Alpine Arch and all-around Zone 3 in Central Apennine;
- Zone 1 (< 0.025–0.05 g) is located in Sardinia that, among the Italian regions is the least dangerous, and statistically very low shaking values are statistically expected.

3 Materials and Methods

In this Section the datasets used and the methodological steps implemented in CIPCast in order to evaluate the multi-hazard (hydrogeological and seismic) in Italy are presented.

3.1 Datasets

To carry out the multi-hazard (flood hazard; landslide hazard; seismic hazard) analysis and mapping, a series of geo-referenced information layers were integrated in the

CIPCast GeoDatabase. Those data were acquired from open/public sources or gathered within the RAFAEL Project activities. Thus, data stored into the CIPCast GeoDatabase and used for the purposed of the present study can be subdivided according to their typology, as follows (Table 1 and Table 2):

Table 1. Data describing and characterizing the Italian territory in terms of hazards

#	Description	Source
A-1	National mosaic of flood hazard - PAI 2017	ISPRA Idrogeo [24]
A-2	National mosaic of landslide hazard - PAI 2017	ISPRA Idrogeo [24]
A-3	Italian Seismic Hazard Maps - 2004	INGV [37]
A-3	National seismic classification of municipalities - 2021	Civil protection Dpt. [38]

Table 2. Geographic location, topology and characteristics of the CI of interest within the Italian territory

#	Description	Source
B-1	Road network, containing information on main roads (topology, length, hierarchy and corresponding management authority	ANAS -DBPrior10k
B-2	Railway network, containing topology and main characteristics (track length, type, etc.)	DBPrior10k
B-3	Location and topology of the elements of the Italian national transmission grid: lines, substations and plants	S&P Global Platts
B-4	Location and topology of the elements of the Italian national gas transmission network: pipelines, facilities and storages	S&P Global Platts

3.2 Hazard Mapping

To map and evaluate the specific hazard of the CI systems considered, the related geospatial data describing them (Table 2) were spatially processed (by means of GIS intersection and join) along with the geospatial layers describing and classifying the different hazards in Italy (Table 1). In this way, it has been possible to produce a new set of hazard maps for each CI considered, according the processing steps reported in Fig. 1 and described the following.

In the present study QGIS Desktop and Esri ArcGIS software suites have been used in order to generate:

1. single-hazard maps describing and classifying the different hazard values for each part/element of the CI considered;
2. multi-hazard map, synthesising and combining the three hazard typologies analysed for each part/element of the CI considered.

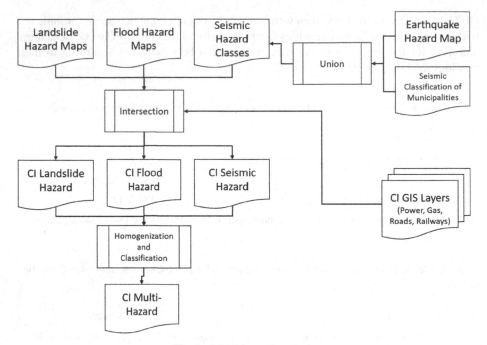

Fig. 1. Multi-hazard analysis.

Firstly, the single-hazard maps (flood, landslide and earthquake separately) and the geospatial layers about CI have been selected (see Sect. 3.1) and pre-processed in order to be used in the subsequent steps. In particular, all the layers have been homogenised in the same geographic reference system: UTM-32 coordinates on the WGS84 Datum (EPSG:32632).

Additional pre-processing steps were needed for the flood hazard maps coming from PAI and for the seismic hazard map. In the first case, the three different original GIS layers (one for each specific probability scenario P_x) were merged (by using Esri ArcGIS geoprocessing tools) in a synthetic GIS layer, in which the hazard classes are jointly mapped and hierarchically organised. In the second case, the geoprocessing was used to join and homogenise the seismic hazard map in terms of PGA [37] with the GIS layer containing the Seismic Classification of Municipalities [38], in order to have an extensive description of the seismic hazard for the entire Italian territory (including the Sardinia Region and the Northern part of Italy), subdivided into the four zones listed in Sect. 2.1. Another pre-processing task was devoted to exclude specific areas (e.g., marine ones or zone with missing data) from the computation. In particular, to deal with the lack of data regarding the flood hazard (PAI [24]) in the Marche Region and the related border areas (especially with the Emilia-Romagna Region) it was decided to remove from the multi-hazard GIS layer the segments of the road network falling into the Marche Region. Such assumption was also justified by the need to process reliable statistical data, not affected by a miscalculation of multi-hazard values deriving from inaccurate and/or missing data.

The next task has regarded the organisation and harmonisation of the attribute tables associated to each GIS layer processed. Attributes titles were (if necessary) cleaned/renamed and redundancies deriving from the multiple geoprocessing steps were eliminated. Such procedure has the scope to allow the comparison of the three different hazards scales and to classify the results according a synthetic multi-hazard value. Moreover, a specific attribute related to the code of each Administrative Region in which Italy is subdivided has been inserted, to make possible performing statistics both at National and Regional level.

Once the pre-processing steps have been accomplished, the next geoprocessing step performed was the spatial intersection between each of the above-described single-hazard maps with each GIS layer related to the CI considered (roads, railways, power and gas networks) within the entire National territory.

4 Results

The single-hazard maps obtained as intermediate result have been merged in new synthetic GIS layers, combining and classifying the three hazards with the CI of interest. In such a way, the final results are represented by four multi-hazard maps, one for each of the four CI systems analysed.

In order to assign the multi-hazard values in a coherent way, a specific matrix was created (Table 3) with four overall classes, spanning from 1 to 4 (where 1 is the minimum value that can be assigned and 4 is the maximum). In particular, flood hazard is described by means of its three increasing-probability classes (P1, P2 and P3) and with a 0 value for the areas not prone to flood. In the case of the landslide hazard, it has been assumed to merge into a unique class the attention zones (AA, for which, by definition, a precise zoning is still not clearly defined) and the H1 zones (moderate hazard). Similarly, the H3 and H4 zones (High and Very High hazard) were merged in the same class. Areas not prone to landslide phenomena have been classified with 0 value. For seismic hazard the four classes defined in the matrix fully reflect the national 4-zones subdivision.

The multi-hazard matrix allows to assign to each element/part of the CI considered an overall hazard value, which can account for each specific single-hazard value in a synthetic and extensive way.

Table 3. Multi-hazard matrix

Flood hazard values	Landslide hazard values	Seismic hazard zones	Multi-hazard index values	Hazard levels
0	0	Zone 4	1	Low
P1 (300–500y)	AA + H1	Zone 3	2	Moderate
P2 (100–200y)	H2	Zone 2	3	High
P3 (20–50y)	H3 + H4	Zone 1	4	Very high

All the GIS layers produced according the above-described processing steps (see Sect. 3.2) have been uploaded into the CIPCast GeoDatabase (PostGIS). Thanks to such data organisation, a statistical analysis has been carried out in order to calculate, both at National and Regional level, the length of each CI network classified according the different classes of hazard.

Subsequently, all the layers were loaded to GeoServer in order to be published within the CIPCast WebGIS application and made available to the users via WMS. In particular, geospatial data were styled (colour, thickness and other visible attributes) to properly render them into the WebGIS.

The following images show some examples of the results of the analysis and mapping: the elements and/or parts of CI classified at different hazard levels are suitably thematised. As an example of the results obtained for a lifeline system, in Fig. 2 the National Road network exposed to flood hazard is reported.

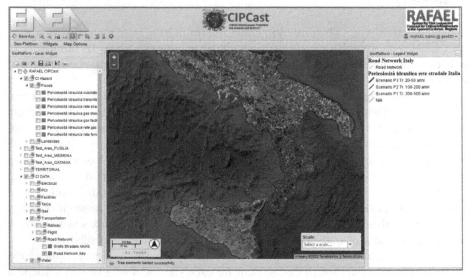

Fig. 2. Flood hazard mapping for the main Italian road network (colour scale indicates the severity of the expected flood scenario regarding the affected portion of road network).

In addition, for the road network the relative statistics were also calculated (i.e., the kilometres classified in each hazard class), according to the following percentage values of total length (Fig. 3): 79.5% not at risk, 6.5% Scenario P1, 6.8% Scenario P2, 3.5 Scenario P3, 3.7% data not available (Marche Region).

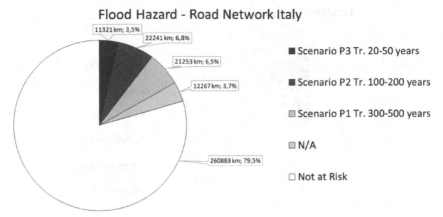

Fig. 3. Statistical analysis of the kilometres of road network falling in areas classified at different levels of flood hazard

In Fig. 4 the map of the National Road network exposed to landslide hazard is reported. In Fig. 5 a chart with the kilometres and the percentage values of total length classified for each hazard level is depicted.

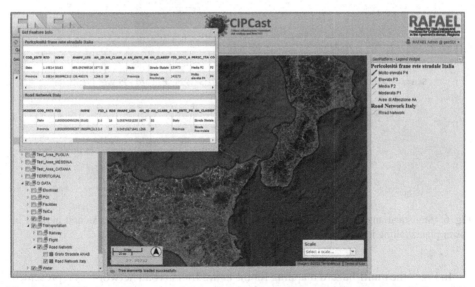

Fig. 4. Landslide hazard mapping for the main Italian road network (colour scale indicates the hazard level regarding the affected portion of road network)

Another example of the results obtained is depicted in Fig. 6, where different charts with the values (kilometres or total number) and percentages of the corresponding infrastructures exposed to seismic hazard are reported.

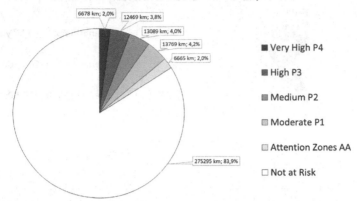

Fig. 5. Statistical analysis of the kilometres of road network falling in areas classified at different levels of landslide hazard

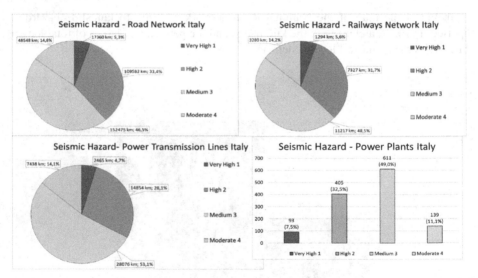

Fig. 6. Statistical analysis of the kilometres of road, gas and railway networks and number of power plants falling in areas classified at different levels of seismic hazard

In Fig. 7 the multi-hazard mapping for the entire Italian road network, as represented within the CIPCast WebGIS interface is reported. In Table 4 the kilometres of road network classified according the 4-classes multi-hazard defined (Low, Moderate, Medium, High) are reported.

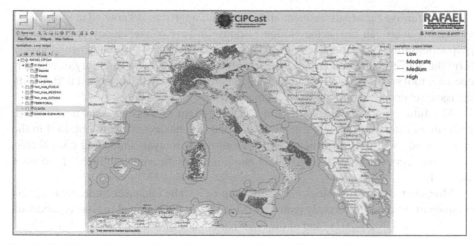

Fig. 7. Multi-hazard mapping for Italian road network: visualization within the CIPCast Web-GIS interface

Table 4. Kilometres of Italian Road Network subdivided for multi-hazard classes

Multi-hazard index	Km
Low	39,716
Moderate	232,876
Medium	42,825
High	489

5 Discussion and Conclusions

Critical Infrastructures play a fundamental role for the economy and development of a Country. Among the different CI, road and power networks are certainly the strategic ones, especially considering the essential and fundamental services provided to the citizens.

For example, the analyses carried out in the present study show that the National Road network (which has a linear extension of about 328,000 km) is exposed to seismic hazard for about 5.3% of its length, 3.5% to flood hazard and 2% to landslide hazard. Thus, considering the multi-hazard (Fig. 7 and Table 4), the majority of National Road network is exposed to moderate-medium values, about 40,000 km are exposed to low values and about 490 km are exposed to high values of multi-hazard.

It is important to observe that the interruption of the road network caused by calamitous events also leads to the production of waste, sludge and debris in the case of floods and landslides, rubble in the case of earthquakes. Those issues can interfere with a prompt response by the operational structures of the Civil Protection System, which relies on such lifeline in order to help the affected population.

An extensive hazard assessment and, above all, a territorial knowledge of the most vulnerable areas can favour the prompt response in case of emergency or support the proper definition of contingency plans. GIS-based approaches are fundamental to perform the above-mentioned hazard assessments. In addition, the availability of an interoperable tool such as the CIPCast platform can provide an effective support to deal with the issue related to hazard analysis and mapping.

The future work should implement the subsequent processing steps necessary to perform an extensive risk assessment: to this end, the hazard mapping obtained in the present study will represent the basis for a multi-risk analysis, including coastal risk, taking into account also the information about the specific vulnerabilities of the asset exposed.

Moreover, the hydrogeological hazard mapping will be update considering the latest versions of the datasets recently issued by ISPRA [24]: the National mosaic of landslide hazard (v. 4.0 – 2020–2021) and of the National mosaic of flood hazard (v. 5.0 – 2020).

Acknowledgments. The research activities described in the present paper have been carried out in the framework of the RAFAEL project, co-funded by Italian Ministry of University and Research, MUR, Grant no. ARS01_00305. The authors acknowledge the support of Flavia Cianfanelli and Valerio Mannelli in GIS-related issues, carried-out in the framework of the internship programme set-up by ENEA and University of Rome "Sapienza", Master Degree in "Territory's management and enhancement" [39].

The present study was also supported by CoCLiCO (Coastal ClimateCOre Services) funded by European Union's Horizon 2020 (H2020-EU.3.5. - SOCIETAL CHALLENGES - Climate action, Environment, Resource Efficiency and Raw Materials and H2020-EU.3.5.1. - Fighting and adapting to climate change programme).

References

1. Scrocca, D., Doglioni, C., Innocenti, F.: Contraints for an interpretation of the italian geodynamics: a review. Mem. Descr. Carta Geol. d'It. LXII, 15–46 (2003)
2. Doglioni, C., Ligi, M., Scrocca, D., et al.: The tectonic puzzle of the Messina area (Southern Italy): insights from new seismic reflection data. Sci. Rep. **2**, 970 (2012)
3. Coltorti, M., Farabollini, P.: Quaternary evolution of the Castelluccio di Norcia Basin (Umbria-Marchean Apennines, Italy). Il Quaternario **8**, 149–166 (1995)
4. Martino, S., Fiorucci, M., Marmoni, G.M. et al.: Increase in landslide activity after a low-magnitude earthquake as inferred from DInSAR interferometry. Sci. Rep. **12**, 2686 (2022). https://doi.org/10.1038/s41598-022-06508-w
5. Guzzetti, F., Stark, C.P., Salvati, P.: Evaluation of flood and landslide risk to the population of Italy. Environ. Manag. **36**, 15–36 (2005)
6. Santoro, S., Totaro, S., Lovreglio R., Camarda, D., Iacobelli, Vito, Fratino, U.: Risk perception and knowledge of protective measures for flood risk planning. The case study of Brindisi (Puglia region). Safety Sci. **153**, 105791 (2022)
7. Legislative D.lgs n.1 del 2 gennaio 2018: Codice della protezione civile- Pubblicato nella Gazzetta Ufficiale n. 17 del 22 gennaio (2018)
8. Legislative Decree of 152/2006: Norme in Materia Ambientale. Pubblicato Nella Gazzetta ciale n. 88 del 14 Aprile 2006—Supplemento Ordinario n. 96; MATTM: Rome, Italy, (2006)

9. Legislative Directive of 30.4.2021: Indirizzi di predisposizione dei piani di Protezione Civile, Dipartimento della protezione civile, Pubblicata nella Gazzetta Ufficiale n. 160 del 6 luglio 2021, (2021)

10. Ritchie, H., Roser, M.: "Natural Disasters". Published online at OurWorldInData.org. https://ourworldindata.org/natural-disasters. Accessed 2022/05/10

11. Gill, J.C., Malamud, B.D.: Reviewing and visualizing the interactions of natural hazards. Rev. Geophys. **52**, 680–722 (2014)

12. Eskandari, M., Omidvar, B., Modiri, M., Nekooie, M.A., Alesheikh, A.A.: Geospatial analysis of earthquake damage probability of water pipelines due to multi-hazard failure. Int. J. Geo-Inform. **6**, 169 (2017)

13. Tilloy, A., Malamud, B.D., Hugo Winter, H., Joly-Laugel, A.: A review of quantification methodologies for multi-hazard interrelationships. Earth-Sc. Rev. **196** (2019)

14. Skilodimou, H.D., Bathrellos, G.D., Chousianitis, K., Youssef, A.M., Pradhan, B.: Multi-hazard assessment modeling via multi-criteria analysis and GIS: a case study. Environ. Earth Sci. **78**(2), 1–21 (2019). https://doi.org/10.1007/s12665-018-8003-4

15. Di Pietro A., Lavalle, L., La Porta, L., Pollino, M., Tofani, A., Rosato, V.: Design of DSS for supporting preparedness to and management of anomalous situations in complex scenario. Managing the complexity of critical infrastructures. Studies in systems, decision and control. Springer International Publishing, Cham, vol. 90, p. 195–232 (2016)

16. PostGIS https://postgis.net/. Accessed 13 May 2022

17. GeoServer https://geoserver.org/. Accessed 13 May 2022

18. OGC Standards and Resources https://www.ogc.org/standards. Accessed 13 May 2022

19. Taraglio, S. et al.: Decision support system for smart urban management: resilience against natural phenomena and aerial environmental assessment. Int. J. Sustain. Energ. Plann. Manag. **24** (2019)

20. Matassoni, L., Giovinazzi, S., Pollino, M., Fiaschi, A., La Porta, L., Rosato, V.: A geospatial decision support tool for seismic risk management: Florence (Italy) case study. In: Gervasi, O., et al. (eds.) ICCSA 2017. LNCS, vol. 10405, pp. 278–293. Springer, Cham (2017). https://doi.org/10.1007/978-3-319-62395-5_20

21. Pollino, M., Di Pietro, A., La Porta, L., Fattoruso, G., Giovinazzi, S., Longobardi, A.: Seismic risk simulations of a water distribution network in Southern Italy. In: Gervasi, O., et al. (eds.) ICCSA 2021. LNCS, vol. 12951, pp. 655–664. Springer, Cham (2021). https://doi.org/10.1007/978-3-030-86970-0_45

22. Trigila, A., Ladanza, C., Bussettini, M., Lastoria, B.: Dissesto idrogeologico in Italia: pericolosità e indicatori di rischio. Rapporto 2018. ISPRA, Rapporti 287/2018 (2018)

23. Ladanza, C., Trigila, A., Starace, P., Dragoni, A., Roccisano, M., Biondo, T.: IdroGEO: a collaborative web mapping application based on REST API services and open data on landslides and floods in Italy. ISPRS Int. J. Geo Inf. **10**(2), 89 (2021)

24. ISPRA – IdroGEO: The Italian web platform on landslides and floods. https://idrogeo.isprambiente.it/. Accessed 13 May 2022

25. Herrera, G., et al.: Landslide databases in the geological surveys of Europe. Landslides **15**(2), 359–379 (2017). https://doi.org/10.1007/s10346-017-0902-z

26. Ladanza, C., Trigila, A., Napolitano, F.: Identification and characterization of rainfall events responsible for triggering of debris flows and shallow landslides. J. Hydrol. **541**, Part A, 230–245 (2016)

27. Trigila, A., Ladanza, C., Esposito, C., Scarascia Mugnozza G.: Comparison of logistic regression and random forests techniques for shallow landslide susceptibility assessment in Giampilieri (NE Sicily, Italy). Geomorphology **249**, 119–136, ISSN: 0169–555X (2015)

28. Falconi, L., Campolo, D., Leoni, G., Lumaca, S., Puglisi, C.: Geomorphology hazard assess-ment of Giampilieri and Briga river basins after the rainfall event on the October 1, 2009 (Sicily, Italy). Landslide science and practice, Volume 1: Landslide inventory and susceptibility and hazard Zoning. Springer, Berlin, pp. 533–540 (2013)
29. Baratta, M.: I terremoti d'Italia : saggio di storia, geografia e bibliografia sismica italiana. Fratelli Bocca, Torin (1901)
30. Boschi, E., Guidoboni, E., Ferrari, G., Valensise, G. & Gasperini, P. Catalogo dei Forti Terremoti in Italia dal 461 a.C. al 1990. p. 644, ING Roma-SGA, Bologna. (1997)
31. Rovida, A., Locati, M., Camassi, R., Lolli, B., Gasperini, P.: The Italian earthquake catalogue CPTI15. Bull. Earthq. Eng. **18**(7), 2953–2984 (2020). https://doi.org/10.1007/s10518-020-00818-y
32. Cappucci, S., et al.: Earthquake's Rubble Heaps volume evaluation: Expeditious approach through Earth observation and geomatics techniques. In: Gervasi, O., et al. (eds.) ICCSA 2017. LNCS, vol. 10405, pp. 261–277. Springer, Cham (2017). https://doi.org/10.1007/978-3-319-62395-5_19
33. Pesaresi, C., Gallinelli, D.: GIS procedure to evaluate the relationship between the period of construction and the outcomes of compliance with building safety standards. The case of the earthquake in L'Aquila (2009). J-READING (Journal of Research and Didactics in Geography)", 2, 7, pp. 41–58 (2018)
34. Pesaresi, C. (Ed.), L'Aquila e il cratere sismico. Le cause e le conseguenze del terremoto (6 aprile 2009) in chiave applicativa e interdisciplinare, "Semestrale di Studi e Ricerche di Geografia", 1 (2012)
35. Pollino, M., et al.: Assessing earthquake-Induced urban rubble by means of multiplatform remotely sensed data. ISPRS Int. J. Geo Inf. **9**(4), 262 (2020)
36. Stucchi, M., Meletti, C., Montaldo, V., Akinci, A., Faccioli, E., Gasperini, P., Malagnini, L., Valensise, G.: Pericolosità sismica di riferimento per il territorio nazionale MPS04 . Istituto Nazionale di Geofisica e Vulcanologia (INGV), (2004)
37. Seismic Hazard Maps, INGV http://zonesismiche.mi.ingv.it/. Accessed 2022/05/13
38. Seismic Classification, Civil protection department. https://rischi.protezionecivile.gov.it/en/seismic/activities/emergency-planning-and-damage-scenarios/seismic-classification. Accessed 2022/05/13
39. Villari, P., Scandone, R., Giacomelli, L., Pollino, M.: Geographical perspectives in research and didactics from other perspectives. Inputs from J-READING. J-Reading (Journal of research and didactics in geography) **2**(10), 73–79 (2021)

International Workshop on Advances in Web Based Learning (AWBL 2022)

Use of Metaverse in Education

Mustafa Murat Inceoglu[1] and Birol Ciloglugil[2(✉)]

[1] Department of Computer Education and Instructional Technology, Ege University,
35100, Bornova Izmir, Turkey
mustafa.inceoglu@ege.edu.tr

[2] Department of Computer Engineering, Ege University,
35100, Bornova Izmir, Turkey
birol.ciloglugil@ege.edu.tr

Abstract. With the introduction of Metaverse, its use is increasing day by day. In this study, the factors affecting the historical development of Metaverse, the Metaverse architecture and the use of Metaverse in the field of education are discussed. The strengths and weaknesses of the use of Metaverse in the field of education are emphasized; the opportunities it will offer and the problems and threats that may be encountered are examined. Since Metaverse is a new concept, a resource for the use of Metaverse in the field of education has been tried to put forward by using the limited number of sources currently available in the literature. In this study, it is emphasized that the Metaverse environment can add a new dimension to the field of educational technologies. However, it should be taken into account that the necessary technologies and architectures in this field are not mature enough yet. Therefore, it is considered a necessity to determine appropriate strategies for the use of Metaverse in the educational field and to start determining its widespread effect until the infrastructure of Metaverse matures.

Keywords: e-learning · Educational technology · Metaverse · Metaverse in education

1 Introduction

Many historical steps have taken place from the centralized mainframe computers to the decentralized Metaverse environment that works connected to the Internet. In this section, the history of the Internet until the emergence of Metaverse is briefly summarized.

1.1 Web 1.0

The Web, later called Web 1.0, was introduced with the advent of the first browsers. It all started when Tim Berners-Lee wrote the first World Wide Web browser in 1990 by using a Next computer [1]. This was followed in 1992 by the Mosaic browser that was implemented by the National Center for Supercomputer Applications (NCSA) [2]. With Web 1.0, many individuals and institutions

O. Gervasi et al. (Eds.): ICCSA 2022 Workshops, LNCS 13377, pp. 171–184, 2022.
https://doi.org/10.1007/978-3-031-10536-4_12

started to transfer their information to the web. Web 1.0, also referred as the business card web, attracted great attention, especially when it started to be used extensively by e-commerce companies. Many companies that used to sell remotely over the phone easily adapted to this situation and thus, the first seeds of a large e-commerce market were planted.

Web 1.0 was called the read-only web and consisted of static, read-only web pages shared by individuals or companies. Since the web pages were kept on the servers, the interaction between the users and the company websites was either asynchronous with the use of e-mail or synchronous via the telephone. In addition, although the search engines searching the web were very fast, they were far from giving the desired results. The structure of Web 1.0 can be shown as in Fig. 1. The guestbook presented in Fig. 1 is an Internet application with one-way communication where users can only send their comments.

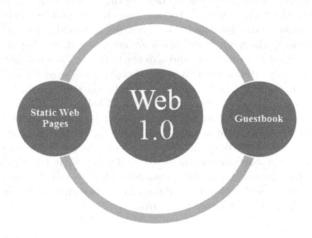

Fig. 1. Schematic illustration for Web 1.0

From an educational standpoint, like Web 1.0, e-learning was largely a one-way process during its early period. Students tried to learn through lecture notes, text-books, videos, animations and websites shared by their teachers [3,4].

1.2   Web 2.0

The concept of Web 2.0 was first introduced in 2004 in the web conference organized by Dale Dougherty, Tim O'Reilly and MediaLive International, in which the leading companies of the Web such as Google, Yahoo, MSN, Amazon, and EBay attended [5]. The Web 2.0 concept emerged during the discussions of the developments in the web field and the future of the web. Web 2.0 can be evaluated as an enhanced version of Web 1.0. With Web 2.0, users began to produce and share their own content. For this reason, Web 2.0 is also referred as a participatory social network [5]. The most important technologies in Web 2.0 systems are AJAX and JavaScript. The most important components in the booming of Web 2.0 were mobile devices and social media. Especially, with the use of social media tools as applications on mobile devices, large user groups have started to see social media as a sharing platform. The Social Web includes a set of online tools and platforms where people can share their perspectives, thoughts, views and experiences. Web 2.0 applications are developed with much more interaction possibilities with the end users than traditional applications. Therefore, the end users are not only the users but also the participants of the application. The most widely used Web 2.0 tools can be grouped as podcasting, blogging, tagging, curating with RSS, social bookmarking, social networking, social media, and web content voting. The structure of Web 2.0 and its relationship with Web 1.0 is shown in Fig. 2.

Fig. 2. Schematic illustration for Web 2.0

Web 2.0 technologies and especially social networking sites like MySpace and Facebook, affect the lives of millions of students in a powerful way. Researchers investigated the extent of this effect in various studies, and they agree that social networks should be included in education if it is to have a significant impact [6]. The Horizon Report, prepared by the New Media Consortium and EDUCAUSE in 2008, points out that it is necessary to develop strategies to take advantage of social networks for educational purposes [7].

1.3   Web 3.0

Web 3.0, defined as the future of the Internet, is also known as the read, write and run web [8]. Web 3.0 is also named as the Semantic Web by Tim Berners-Lee, and is designed as a more autonomous, intelligent and open Internet [9]. However, it is anticipated that a new definition will be needed, especially with the development of artificial intelligence, wearable technologies, Internet of Things technologies and 5G communication technologies. In addition, technologies such as decentralized blockchain, NFTs (Non-Fungible Tokens) and AR (Augmented Reality) Cloud that have emerged in the last few years also mean a move towards decentralization of data and a transparent, secure Internet. The schematic representation of Web 3.0 and its relationship with its predecessors Web 1.0 and Web 2.0 is shown in Fig. 3.

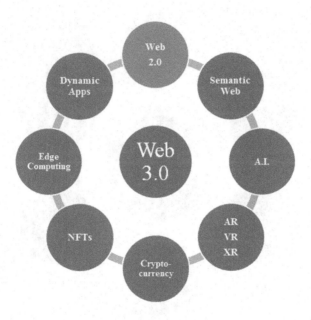

Fig. 3. Schematic illustration for Web 3.0

The following results were obtained by [10] on the effects of Web 3.0 technologies on education: with social semantic networks, openness and interoperability processes, the diversity of information will increase, so learning will take place at a more effective level. With technologies such as big data, linked data, cloud computing and mobile computing, information resources in the learning process will be connected, thus the connections in the relevant learning area will also improve [11]. Thanks to artificial intelligence, machine learning and 3D environments, learning will be more permanent.

2   Metaverse Environment

One of the environments that is built on Web 3.0 technologies and covers all Web 3.0 technologies emerges as Metaverse (Fig. 4). Although there are many different definitions, if a comprehensive definition is required, Metaverse can be defined as worlds in the digital environment where you have a digital copy and can perform some actions using recent technologies [12–14]. Here, the digital copy can be your digital twin made by preserving your physical features, or an avatar designed by you.

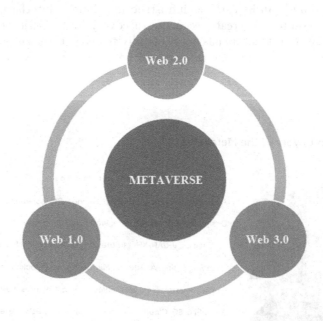

Fig. 4. Metaverse structure supported by Web 1.0, Web 2.0 and Web 3.0

The concept of Metaverse is one of the concepts that have become popular recently. The trend graph of this concept is presented in Fig. 5.

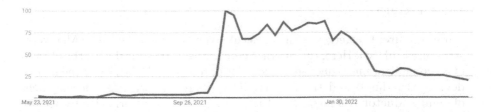

Fig. 5. Google trend of the word "Metaverse" worldwide [15]

Looking at the last year's Google trends, it is seen that the concept of Metaverse was searched a little before, but it peaked after November 2021 and its popularity decreased over time (Fig. 5). It is observed that the top 5 countries contributing to these trends by searching on Google are Turkey, China, Singapore, Cyprus and Hong Kong [15].

3   Metaverse Architecture

Metaverse architecture consists of seven proposed layers [16]. These layers are shown in Fig. 6 and can be listed as infrastructure, human interface, decentralization, spatial computing, creator economy, discovery, and experience. Although the proposed layered structure has not been fully tested yet, the subject of which layers will work best in the coming years will be a separate research infrastructure.

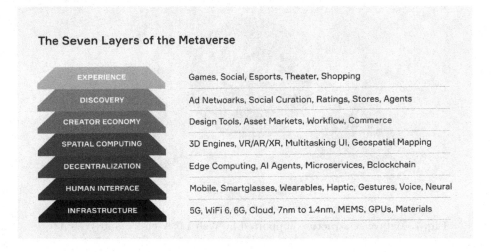

Fig. 6. Seven layers of Metaverse [16]

The seven layers of Metaverse can be briefly explained as follows, starting from the innermost.

– Infrastructure: It emerges as the physical layer on which the entire Metaverse structure is placed. Here, the Internet bandwidth is increased with the 5G and 6G communication technologies, the delays are reduced, the size of the mobile devices is reduced and the battery life is increased with the development of semiconductor technology, and the sensors are transformed into a more sensitive and smaller form with microelectromechanical systems (MEMS).

– Human Interface: As semiconductor manufacturing technologies are getting closer to support design structures approaching 3 nm, the produced hardware will be used more frequently in and on the human body. Thus, with the use of biosensors and neural interfaces, the sense of touch and feeling will be activated in addition to the senses of sight and hearing. With the support of haptic technologies, it will be possible to control devices without any physical interface.

– Decentralization: It is one of the most important features of Metaverse. Metaverse is designed for users and content producers to own the system, and it is anticipated that it will not develop under the leadership of any company or institution. In particular, edge computing and blockchain technologies will provide significant support in this direction.

– Spatial Computing: The environment that comes to mind for many people about Metaverse is the 3D environment. However, Metaverse offers more than just a 3D environment. Objects can be digitized by using spatial computing and combining virtual/augmented/extended reality (VR/AR/XR), sensors can be developed to react with motors, and the physical world can be digitized by utilizing spatial mapping.

– Creator Economy: In the earlier versions of the Internet, creators were required to have at least some degree of programming knowledge in order to design and build tools, applications or asset markets. Nowadays, it is possible to develop web applications without coding thanks to web application frameworks. As a result of this, the number of content creators and designers on the web is growing exponentially. It is expected that anyone will be able to be create web contents in the near future without even learning how to program. The increase in the number of web content creators is a defining component of the Web 3.0 economy, which can be referred as the age of content creators.

– Discovery: It is the layer which introduces users to brand new experiences on Metaverse. With the widespread use of Metaverse, assets in this layer will be able to be marketed and advertised by companies. In Metaverse environment, where information sharing is very important, users will be able to create their own content and freely publish it to communities. Nowadays, the most important example of this experience is observed as NFTs.

– Experience: It is the most emphasized layer of Metaverse. With this layer, it is thought that people can have different and new experiences (such as multi-user games, shopping, etc.). The most important of these experiences will be live events (such as concerts, fairs, trainings, excursions, etc.). In this way, Metaverse users will be able to access events that they may never be able to access in real life.

4   A Brief History of Metaverse

Although the concept of Metaverse became popular in October 2021, when Mark Zuckerberg announced that Facebook would change its name to Meta [17] and make significant investments in Metaverse, it is not a new concept. In their extensive work on Metaverse, Lee et al. [18, p. 4] take the history of Metaverse back to the book/game Dungeons & Dragons published in 1974. Then, Neuromancer, a cyber frenzy science fiction novel by William Gibson, which was released in 1984, is considered as another critical milestone for the development of Metaverse. The novel Neuromancer has also been the subject of films such as The Matrix and Ghost [19]. The word Metaverse was first used in 1992 in the science fiction novel Snow Crash which was written by Neal Stephenson [20].

The years between 1992 and 2016 are referred as the period of virtual worlds and multiplayer online gaming platforms. Some of the milestones for multiplayer virtual world concept can be expressed as Active World released in 1995, Online Traveler realized in 1996, Second Life launched in 2003 and Minecraft launched in 2011. Pokemen Go, which was released in 2016, VR Chat, which was released in 2017, Super Mario AR, which appeared in the same year, CryptoKitties in 2017 and Alien Worlds in 2020 can be listed as more recent cornerstones of this period. The announcement of Facebook founder Mark Zuckerberg in 2021 that Facebook would change its name to Meta [17], and South Korea's statement that it would make Metaverse a state policy, and sharing of important strategic plans and policies in this direction with the public [21, 22] clearly reveals why a new era has begun for Metaverse structure. The movie Ready Player One (released in 2018) was adapted from the 2011 novel of the same name by Ernest Cline. The movie is about people who are bored with their lives in cities, and spend a lot of time in the virtual world called OASIS by using their avatars in 2045 [23].

5   Use of Metaverse in Education

When academic studies scanned in Web of Science and Scopus databases were searched using the word "Metaverse", 128 publications have been identified. However, only 7 of these publications are related to the field of education. Common publications in both databases are counted only once in the Web of Science database. 5 studies and 2 studies are detected in the Web of Science and Scopus databases, respectively [24, 25]. Brief summaries of these pioneering publications are detailed below:

In a study which was conducted to determine how closely Metaverse is related to the daily lives of primary school students, it was aimed to analyze Metaverse experiences and attitudes of students in a student-centered education setting by using a constructivist perspective [26]. This study also examines how students become the focus of new educational technologies. A survey was conducted with 336 primary school students in Korea by using 18 items to measure different factors of actions performed in Metaverse (such as studying, attending class, playing games, etc.). Then, statistical analyzes, including the difference of means and an independent sample t-test, were performed. The findings showed that 97.9% of primary school students have experience with Metaverse and 95.5% consider it closely related to their daily lives [26].

A system that utilizes virtual reality and Metaverse in a classroom setting is proposed by [27] to overcome the limitations and deficiencies of the existing distance applied education methods. An aircraft maintenance simulation was developed based on the VR and Metaverse oriented approach and an experiment was conducted to compare the proposed system with a traditional video training based approach. In order to measure the effectiveness of both approaches, knowledge acquisition and retention tests were applied. The findings of the experiment revealed that the group that followed the VR and Metaverse oriented approach scored higher on both knowledge tests than the group that followed the video training based approach. Besides, the answers to the questionnaires indicated that the participants felt a sense of spatial presence, and it was concluded that the usability of the proposed approach was higher than the video training based approach [27].

In a study conducted in dentistry education, [28] presents different ways to use virtual environments that simulate operating room environments and focuses on teaching students various stages of surgeries. The use of different scenarios during the training of dentists provides a crucial advantage on their education.

The study proposed by [29] introduces a training course in Metaverse that was held in Korea and illustrates the prospects for how this technology can be used in the medical field in the future with a lung cancer surgery example. The utilization of different surgery scenarios and different solutions by using of the information about the patients registered in the hospital databases plays an important role in increasing the knowledge levels of students.

It is emphasized by [30] that providing interaction between participants in virtual worlds with Metaverse technology can also be valuable in language education. This study examines the application examples of Metaverse technology in Korean language education and presents a classroom model for task-based teaching methods. Consequently, it is anticipated that this will be used as data to guide Metaverse-based Korean language education [30].

It is shown in [31] that VR production experience for developing instructional content is conducive to improving pre-service teachers' technological preparation, critical thinking, creativity, collaboration, communication and pedagogical perception on digital citizenship. Findings of this study show that such studies can be used for sustainable education.

In a study based on developing measurement tools, [32] determined that the main variables affecting confidence in the future use of Metaverse in education are the lack of understanding of Metaverse, the lack of belief in the current technology, and the lack of awareness about the application of Metaverse in education. As a result of this study, it was concluded that the dissemination of the current technological level and the current speed of technological development can significantly increase people's trust in Metaverse.

6 Advantages and Disadvantages of Using Metaverse in Education

As every new technology gets used in education after a while, 3D virtual worlds, which were used mostly for games and entertainment before Metaverse, were also used in education [33]. Bringing education together with entertainment makes educational environments more attractive and this way more active participation of learners can be achieved [34]. Therefore, Metaverse has started to be used in educational processes as a 3D virtual environment. However, it is gradually emerging that the concept of Metaverse has some problems and limitations as well.

Based on the limited number of resources available for Metaverse, the advantages of using Metaverse in educational environments can be explained as follows:

- By providing realistic and rich educational experiences for learning, it facilitates the relationship between the real world and the virtual world for learning by doing and living [28,30,31].
- It enables the acquisition, sharing and discussion of information provided by visual, audio and touching inputs [27,29,30].
- By appealing to students' visual, auditory and tactile senses, it can contribute greatly to the realization of concrete learning which is one of the most desired functions in teaching environments [28,29,31].
- By providing access to students from different geographies, it enables students to study in the same environment [30].
- By enabling the engagement with time-consuming, difficult, risky, and complex learning experiences in real life, it facilitates learning in these areas [27–29].
- For skill-based learning, it provides the opportunity to practice different skill types and repeat these practices as much as desired [28,29].
- It helps to eliminate the problems experienced in collaborative working due to disability, time, cost, physical distance and geographical limitations [28].
- It enables learners to socialize with their gestures, mimics and movements, by establishing multi-channel communication in written, oral and both written and oral forms, and thus, facilitates social learning [30].
- By developing serious game and gamification opportunities in Metaverse, it provides a fun learning environment [26].

Besides the positive contributions that Metaverse can bring to learning environments, there are also negative aspects [35–37]. These are presented below:

- It is necessary to analyze the knowledge levels of the learning stakeholders on Metaverse and their the beliefs about the use of Metaverse in education, and to eliminate the lack of knowledge and misunderstandings [32].
- From a technical point of view, developing Metaverse environments is a time-consuming, expensive and extensive process. When examined from this aspect, a large team of pedagogues, teachers, 3D designers, software developers, and graphic designers should work together in harmony.
- Instead of completing the learning tasks assigned to them, the learners using Metaverse may start to spend time with more fun and interesting elements and the problem of time wasting may arise.
- Problems may arise regarding learners' level of knowledge on information technologies, especially due to lack of computer usage knowledge and intrinsic motivation.

- Problems related to cultural and social differences may arise in the socialization and cooperation processes of learners from different cultures and geographies using Metaverse.
- Ethical problems such as using slang expressions, insulting, bullying and humiliating each other may occur in the communication between learners. In addition, it seems likely that companies in Metaverse may experience ethical problems with each other and with learners.
- Learners using poorly designed Metaverse interfaces may experience usability and accessibility problems, and additionally, the cognitive load of the learners may increase due to the limitations caused by inadequate interface designs.

In addition to the items mentioned above, it is possible to add new items that may indirectly affect the limitations of Metaverse in the field of education. These are listed below:

- Since Metaverse is a new concept, Metaverse environment is currently followed as an anomalous environment. There are no national or international legal regulations in this area. As a result, it is necessary to make legal arrangements for this situation, which may be of interest to both national and international educational communities.
- Since Metaverse environment is a decentralized Internet environment, it seems weak in terms of computer security. In particular, some or all of Metaverse can be neutralized, for example, by DDOS attacks [36, 38].
- In order to use Metaverse (also chat software, virtual reality, computer games, mobile applications, and social media) in the field of education, especially teachers and parents should approach very carefully and be cautious.
- Because, especially young children and adolescents moving away from reality and staying in Metaverse with content that will only make them happy, will negatively affect their mental state [39].

7 Conclusion

With its intriguing, interesting and entertaining features, Metaverse environment will have many contributions to distance education, learning by doing and experiencing, educational simulations, social learning environments, and guided and unguided learning processes. In addition, it is clear that new opportunities can be provided to learners with disabilities and/or those who have problems in accessing learning resources, in terms of providing equal opportunities in education with Metaverse environment where physical boundaries have been removed.

However, the use of every new technology in education may cause some problems in terms of instructional technologies. In particular, there are some problems such as how to make effective instructional designs for Metaverse environment, how the learning will take place, how to conduct effective assessment and evaluation studies in this field. It does not seem possible to achieve effective learning by using the opportunities provided by Metaverse environment with classical learning approaches. Therefore, a new pedagogy, which can be called Metaverse pedagogy, needs to be introduced.

Since Metaverse is a new technology body, this technological structure needs to be accepted by learners, instructors, school administrators and all stakeholders involved in teaching. Factors such as psychological and social norms and cultural differences will affect the acceptance process of Metaverse technologies. Therefore, it is necessary to approach the use of Metaverse carefully in learning processes.

Since Metaverse is a new concept, its components and architecture have not been fully realized and adopted yet. Since it is not certain exactly which levels of the architecture will be accepted in the coming years, it is open to radical changes. Therefore, it is necessary not to rush to move learning environments to Metaverse.

The design and full implementation of Metaverse will be an extensive process that will take a long time. Therefore, before moving the learning environments to Metaverse, it should be analyzed in sufficient detail whether the use of Metaverse for learning purposes is appropriate for the learning to be carried out.

The most important feature of Metaverse is the experience offered in the top layer of its architecture. However, in order to be able to live and let live this experience fully and satisfactorily in learning environments, the equipment that will involve the sense organs in the process will need to be more usable and cheaper. The development and widespread use of these hardware will take time.

In order for Metaverse to take place effectively in learning environments and to use the resources allocated for it correctly, national and international collaborations should be developed. In this regard, academic and non-academic stakeholders need to come together and carefully plan the process in order to produce the necessary hardware, software, content and human resources.

References

1. Berners-Lee, T.: The WorldWideWeb browser. https://www.w3.org/People/Berners-Lee/WorldWideWeb.html. Accessed 19 Apr 2022
2. Stewart, W.: Mosaic - The First Global Web Browser. http://www.livinginternet.com/w/wi_mosaic.htm. Accessed 19 Apr 2022
3. Ciloglugil, B., Inceoglu, M.M.: Exploring the state of the art in adaptive distributed learning environments. In: Taniar, D., Gervasi, O., Murgante, B., Pardede, E., Apduhan, B.O. (eds.) ICCSA 2010. LNCS, vol. 6017, pp. 556–569. Springer, Heidelberg (2010). https://doi.org/10.1007/978-3-642-12165-4_44
4. Ciloglugil, B., Inceoglu, M.M.: User modeling for adaptive e-learning systems. In: Murgante, B., et al. (eds.) ICCSA 2012. LNCS, vol. 7335, pp. 550–561. Springer, Heidelberg (2012). https://doi.org/10.1007/978-3-642-31137-6_42
5. Morkoç, D.K., Erdönmez, C.: Web 2.0 Uygulamalarının Eğitim Süreçlerine Etkisi: Çanakkale Sosyal Bilimler Meslek Yüksekokul Örneği. AJIT-e Online Acad. J. Inform. Technol. 5(15) (2014) https://doi.org/10.5824/1309-1581.2014.2.002.x
6. Perikos, I., Grivokostopoulou, F., Kovas, K., Hatzilygeroudis, I.: Utilizing social networks and Web 2.0 technologies in education. In: 2015 IEEE Seventh International Conference on Technology for Education (T4E), pp. 118–119 (2015)

7. Genç Z.: Web 2.0 Yeniliklerinin Eğitimde Kullanımı: Bir Facebook Eğtim Uygulama Örneğ. In: XII. Akademik Bilişim Konferansı Bildirileri, Muğla, Türkiye, pp. 287–292 (2010)
8. What Is Web 3.0? The Future of the Internet. https://www.singlegrain.com/web3/web-3-0/. Accessed 22 May 2022
9. The 8 Defining Features of Web 3.0. https://www.expert.ai/blog/web-3-0/. Accessed 29 Apr 2022
10. Hussain, F.: E-Learning 3.0= E-Learning 2.0+ Web 3.0?. International Association for Development of the Information Society (2012)
11. Inceoglu, M.M., Ciloglugil, B.: Industry 4.0 briefcase: an innovative engineering outreach project for professions of the future. In: Gervasi, O., et al. (eds.) ICCSA 2020. LNCS, vol. 12250, pp. 979–988. Springer, Cham (2020). https://doi.org/10.1007/978-3-030-58802-1_70
12. Newton, C.: Mark Zuckerberg is betting Facebook's future on the metaverse. https://www.theverge.com/22588022/mark-zuckerberg-facebook-ceo-metaverse-interview. Accessed 01 Apr 2022
13. Robertson, A.: What is the metaverse, and do I have to care?. https://www.theverge.com/22701104/metaverse-explained-fortnite-roblox-facebook-horizon. Accessed 01 Apr 2022
14. Clark, P.A.: What Is the Metaverse and Why Should I Care?. https://time.com/6116826/what-is-the-metaverse/. Accessed 01 Apr 2022
15. Google Trends. https://trends.google.com/trends/explore?q=metaverse. Accessed 19 Apr 2022
16. Radof J.: Building the Metaverse. https://medium.com/building-the-metaverse/building-the-metaverse-megadeck-7fc052cfe748. Accessed 01 Apr 2022
17. Nesbo, E.: The Metaverse vs. Virtual Reality: 6 Key Differences. https://www.makeuseof.com/metaverse-vs-virtualreality/. Accessed 01 Apr 2022
18. Lee, L.H., et al.: All one needs to know about metaverse: a complete survey on technological singularity, virtual ecosystem, and research agenda. arXiv preprint arXiv: 2110.05352 (2021)
19. Neuromancer. https://tr.wikipedia.org/wiki/Neuromancer. Accessed 01 Apr 2022
20. Joshua, J.: Information bodies: computational anxiety in Neal Stephenson's snow crash. Interdisciplinary Literary Stud. **19**(1), 17–47 (2017)
21. Kim, S.: South Korea's Approach to the Metaverse. https://thediplomat.com/2021/11/south-koreas-approach-to-the-metaverse/. Accessed 01 Apr 2022
22. Newar, B. South Korea embraces the proto-metaverse. https://cointelegraph.com/news/south-korea-embraces-theproto-metaverse. Accessed 01 Apr 2022
23. Ready Player One (2018). https://www.imdb.com/title/tt1677720/. Accessed 22 May 2022
24. WebofScience.   https://www.webofscience.com/wos/woscc/summary/c22e6aa9-b7e9-420e-a536-3bd211f2da99-344e1878/relevance/1. Accessed 19 Apr 2022
25. Scopus.   https://www.scopus.com/results/results.uri?sort=plf-f&src=s&st1=metaverse&st2=education&sid=45c88a66cddc8408444c0a7c29eb8c06&sot=b&sdt=b&sl=39&s=%28TITLE%28metaverse%29+AND+TITLE%28education%29%29&origin=searchbasic&editSaveSearch=&yearFrom=Before+1960&yearTo=Present. Accessed 11 May 2022
26. Suh, W., Ahn, S.: Utilizing the metaverse for learner-centered constructivist education in the post-pandemic era: an analysis of elementary school students. J. Intell. **10**(1) (2022). https://doi.org/10.3390/jintelligence10010017

27. Lee, H., Woo, D., Yu, S.: Virtual reality metaverse system supplementing remote education methods: based on aircraft maintenance simulation. Appl. Sci. **12**(5) (2022). https://doi.org/10.3390/app12052667
28. Locurcio, L.L.: Dental education in the metaverse. Br. Dent. J. **232**(4), 191 (2022)
29. Koo H.: Training in lung cancer surgery through the metaverse, including extended reality, in the smart operating room of Seoul National University Bundang Hospital, Korea. J. Educ. Eval. Health Prof. **18**, 33 (2021)
30. Park, J.: Exploring the possibility of using metaverse in Korean language education. J. Int. Netw. Korean Lang. Cult. **18**(3), 117–146 (2021)
31. Lee, H., Hwang, Y.: Technology-enhanced education through VR-making and metaverse-linking to foster teacher readiness and sustainable learning. Sustainability **14**(8), 4786 (2022)
32. Yue, K.: Breaking down the barrier between teachers and students by using metaverse technology in education: based on a survey and analysis of Shenzhen City, China. In: 2022 13th International Conference on E-Education, E-Business, E-Management, and E-Learning (IC4E), pp. 40–44, January 2022
33. Bulu, S.T.: Place presence, social presence, co-presence, and satisfaction in virtual worlds. Comput. Educ. **58**(1), 154–161 (2012)
34. Minocha, S., Reeves, A.J.: Design of learning spaces in 3D virtual worlds: an empirical investigation of second life. Learn. Media Technol. **35**(2), 111–137 (2010)
35. SWOT Analysis of the Metaverse for Businesses. https://quantilus.com/swot-analysis-of-the-metaverse-for-businesses/. Accessed 29 Apr 2022
36. The 7 Biggest Threats To Metaverse. https://discover.hubpages.com/technology/The-7-Biggest-Threats-To-Metaverse. Accessed 29 Apr 2022
37. Marr, B.: 7 Important Problems & Disadvantages of the Metaverse. https://bernardmarr.com/7-important-problems-disadvantages-of-the-metaverse/. Accessed 11 May 2022
38. Security Trends to Address Now, on Our Way to the Metaverse. https://www.akamai.com/blog/trends/security-trends-to-address-now-on-our-way-to-the-metaverse. Accessed 29 Apr 2022
39. Baltaş, A.: Metaverse'ün Hayatımıza Getirecekleri. https://www.acarbaltas.com/metaverseun-hayatimiza-getirecekleri-v/. Accessed 11 May 2022

Peculiarities of Formation and Implementation of State Policy in the Field of Continuous Education in Ukraine

Ljudmyla Ivashova[1] , Alina Kyrpale[1] , Volodymyr Baibakov[2] , Huba Mariia[1] ,
George Abuselidze[3] (✉) , and Andrii Romin[4]

[1] University of Customs and Finance, Vladimir Vernadsky, 2/4, Dnipro 49000, Ukraine
[2] Dnipro Medical Institute of Traditional and Alternative Medicine, Sevastopolska, 17, Dnipro 49000, Ukraine
[3] Batumi Shota Rustaveli State University, Ninoshvili 35, Batumi 6010, Georgia
george.abuselidze@gmail.com
[4] National University of Civil Defence of Ukraine, Chernyshevska, 94, Kharkiv 61023, Ukraine

Abstract. The main purpose of the article is to highlight the peculiarities of the formation of the system of continuing education in Ukraine. The evolution of the views of scientists of different periods on the need for continuing education is analyzed. The influence of government institutions on the creation of regulatory and legal and organizational support for the implementation of state policy for the development of continuing education in modern Ukraine. The role of the state in the implementation of primary and secondary school reforms for the formation of quality knowledge as a basis for the development of the individual and his need to learn throughout life. The article analyzes the effect of legal and organizational mechanisms of public management of the system of continuing education in the conditions of innovative development of society and implementation of educational reforms. The main problems of legal and organizational nature regarding the formation of a single educational space as a favorable environment for the development of continuing education are identified. On the example of educational institutions of Ukraine the efficiency of mechanisms of public management of the system of continuous education and quality assurance of education in the conditions of application of innovative technologies of education is estimated.

Keywords: Education policy · Lifelong learning · Public education management · Educational service · Consumer of educational services · Satisfaction with the quality of education

1 Introduction

In the modern world there is a tendency to actively implement the concept of continuing education - lifelong learning. Continuing education is becoming an integral part of the education system as it helps to increase competition, reduce unemployment and attract social and economic innovation. It is continuing education that unites the entire educational space of the country. We are in solidarity with Sychenko and other scientists [1], that due to this education the following features and characteristics: responsibility for the level of national intelligence; compliance of continuing education with European and world trends in economic and social development; advanced development compared to the dynamics of society; systemicity, continuity, problems and compatibility at the global, state and regional levels. However, the issues of forming public policy in the field of continuing education in Ukraine, especially from the standpoint of the science of public administration, are still insufficiently studied. Most scientific papers cover the practical aspects of the development of the educational system, but there are no works on a comprehensive analysis of the formation and development of public policy in the field of continuing education.

Some ideas about the need and continuity of education, which should take care of the state, some researchers in philosophical [2], historical [3] and pedagogical sciences [4–7] are found in the scholars of antiquity - Herodotus, Aristotle, Socrates, Plato, Confucius, Seneca. It was the ancient philosophers who formed the idea and doctrine of the constant spiritual improvement of man and his need and ability to learn throughout life.

The forerunner of modern views on continuing education is the Czech scientist J.A. Comenius [2, 8], who noted that every age is suitable for learning and a person in life has no purpose other than learning.

Among domestic contemporaries, the apologist for the need for continuing education is Nychkalo [9], who noted in his work that in modern conditions have developed different approaches to defining the essence of the concept of "continuing education", at the same time as a philosophical and pedagogical concept, according to which education is interpreted as a process covering all human life and as an important aspect of educational practice at various levels of the education system, and as a principle of organization of education at the national and regional levels, and as a principle of implementation of state policy in the field of education. At the same time, the author is convinced that due to its content and unlimited time, continuing professional education has opportunities to perform socio-cultural, developmental, general education, compensatory, adaptive and economic functions that are interconnected and complementary. Along with this, new functions appear, due to the specifics and dynamics of changes in socio-cultural development in each state at different historical stages [10], so it is the state that should take care of the development of continuing education. In addition, some countries have regional, national and international centers that develop issues and coordinate programs and information exchange on continuing education (mainly on adult education).

In the works of Lugovyy [11] the problems of formation of continuous education in the countries of organization of economic cooperation and development and the value of their experience for Ukraine are highlighted. And in the works of Russian scientist Wolfson [12] notes that in each country the process of development of the theory and practice of continuing education has its own specific features. At the same time, there are general principles: flexibility and variability of the education system; improving the organization and operation of the general education system, restructuring vocational education systems and coordinating the activities of vocational schools with the broad interests of production, meeting the non-professional needs of people, developing so-called third age education, using the latest technology, which greatly expands learning opportunities and information at all stages of human life. Problems of organization of lifelong learning for adults are covered in the works of Oliynyk (2010) [13].

Other scholars are investigating various aspects of the development of continuing education. In particular, the article by Teteruk (2020) [14] highlights the peculiarities of the formation of human capital in the implementation of the concept of "lifelong learning". The work of Zastrozhnikova (2021) [15] reveals the problems of financial and economic autonomy in the field of higher education. Thus, the problem of implementing educational policy in Ukraine is relevant and widely covered in the scientific literature.

However, most scientific papers investigate the problems of continuing education for adults. At the same time, there are almost no studies of the initial stage of the organization of the educational process, starting with preschool education, as well as school education as a foundation for further education. It is from preschool and school education that personality formation begins. Therefore, the formation of public policy in the field of continuing education should start from the lowest level. This article is devoted to these issues.

2   Materials and Methods

To achieve the goal of the study, the authors used a systematic approach and methods of comparative, functional-legal and organizational-functional analysis, mathematical and statistical methods and techniques and techniques of sociological surveys. The theoretical and methodological bases of the study were the scientific works of Ukrainian and foreign scientists. Processing and systematization of data from the survey of participants in the educational process and consumers of educational services allowed to make a comprehensive analysis of students and their parents' satisfaction with the quality of educational services provided in secondary schools and specialized lyceums in higher education. Structural and functional analysis determined the elements of the institutional and legal framework for the development of public education management. The use of a systematic approach to the formation and implementation of public policy in the field of continuing education made it possible to identify problems and provide recommendations for improving the system of public administration in the field of continuing education.

3   Results and Discussion

3.1   Theoretical Approaches to the Formation of State Policy in the Field of Continuing Education

External and internal socio-economic conditions significantly affect the modern educational environment and society's requirements for the formation of new professional and social knowledge, skills and abilities. The formation of a personality that develops constantly and continuously from birth and throughout life is a requirement of the modern world. Therefore, one of the leading educational ideas today is the idea of continuing education, which is closely related to the desire to constantly enrich the potential of the individual, professional opportunities in accordance with the ideals of culture, morality, professionalism, full self-realization in life [1].

These ideas in the form of principles, rights and freedoms are enshrined in a number of fundamental international legal instruments and norms of the European Community.

In general, as noted in his works [10, 16, 17], the continuity of vocational education, as a global trend, is formed in the second half of XX century. It was during this period that the trend towards international cooperation in the field of vocational education intensified. First of all, we are talking about the broad activities of the UN, UNESCO, and the International Labor Organization (ILO), which have adopted documents on the problems of continuing vocational training for various categories of the population (Table 1):

Table 1. The main international legal instruments governing lifelong learning

Document: year of adoption, title	Level of document approval
1962 recommendation on vocational training)	46th session of the general conference of the international labor organization
1974 recommendations on vocational and technical training	UN general conference on education, science and culture
1975 convention on vocational guidance and training in human resources development; recommendations for career guidance and training in the field of human resources	General conference of the international labor organization
1976 recommendations on the development of adult education UN	General conference on science, education and culture, 19th conference
1989 convention on technical and vocational education UN	General conference on science, education and culture
1997 resolutions on two programs: "Education for All Lifelong Learning"	"Educational Reform for Lifelong Learning" UNBSCO General conference
1999 Recommendations to the director-general of UNESCO "Technical and Vocational Education and Training: A Look for the 21st Century"	Second UNESCO international congress on technical and vocational education "Education and Lifelong Learning: A Roadmap to the Future"

Source: compiled by the authors

These documents clearly substantiate the need for continuity of vocational training, which is enshrined in specially formulated postulates and corresponds to the principle: training is a process that lasts throughout a person's working life in accordance with his needs as an individual and a member of society;

The same approaches are stated in the basic EU documents regulating the social rights of people in the field of education. Some documents state that everyone has the right to quality and inclusive education, basic and lifelong learning to acquire and maintain skills that enable them to participate fully in society and successfully adapt to changes in the labor market [18].

The same principles were declared in the Community Charter of the Fundamental Social Rights of Workers, adopted by the Heads of State or Government of the Member States of the European Community at a meeting in Strasbourg on 9 December 1989. In particular, paragraph 15 of this Charter states that every employee of the European Community must have access to and use of vocational training throughout his or her employment. These principles were ratified by the Verkhovna Rada of Ukraine in 2005 [19]. It is also clearly stated in this document that the competent public authorities and enterprises, as two social partners, each within its own sphere of competence, must introduce continuous and continuous training systems that enable each person to undergo re-training, especially by granting study leave, in order to improve her professional skills or acquire new professional skills, in particular in the light of technical development (ibid.).

Later, on 7 December 2000, the Charter of Fundamental Rights of the European Union was adopted by EU member states in Nice, which enshrines in Article 14 the right of everyone to education and to have access to vocational training and retraining. And on 17 January 2018, the European Parliament and the Council of the European Union approved a Framework Program on renewed key competences for lifelong learning (Council of the European Union, 2018) [20], which was adopted in the framework of Recommendation 2006/962 / EU of the European Parliament and of the Council (EU) of 18.12.2006 and ratified in Ukraine [21].

The main objectives of the European Union Framework Program are:

1. Identify the key competencies needed for employment, personal capacity building, active citizenship and social inclusion.
2. Create a handbook for developers of educational policies, providers of educational and training services, managers of educational institutions, employers, as well as directly those who study.
3. Support efforts at European, national, regional and local levels to promote the development of lifelong learning competencies.

Competences are defined as a combination of knowledge, skills and attitudes, where:

• knowledge consists of facts and figures, concepts, ideas and theories that are already established and support the understanding of a particular area or subject;
• skills are defined as the ability and capacity to perform processes and use existing knowledge to achieve results;
• Attitudes describe the dispositions of perception and attitude towards ideas, people or situations and encourage appropriate reactions or actions.

However, it should be noted that both in the world and in most domestic scientific and practical approaches, the concept of continuing education is seen as a process consisting of basic and further education and involves the second stage of sequential alternation of training in specially created educational institutions with professional activities. The process of personality formation in the system of continuing education consists of two main stages: 1) basic education - preparatory training and education, which chronologically precedes the activities of the individual in the professional sphere; 2) post-basic (postgraduate) education - further training and education, combined with practical activities in the field of social production. At the same time, the period of preschool and school education is practically ignored, which in our opinion is the main thing in a person's life, because it shapes him as a person.

However, it is worth noting another foreign experience. In particular, in the United States there are Pre-School classes, which are located directly in the primary school, where children study from 4 years until the end of primary school with a gradual transition to learning and learning about the world. After graduating from primary school, children move to the senior adolescent school (secondary school) where they study until the 9 th grade with a gradual transition to graduating classes, which are considered from 10 to 12. According to the results of education, graduates enter universities or colleges.

An attempt to consider the field of education as a systemic phenomenon that combines all types of educational activities and the provision of educational services and really provides continuing education throughout life is carried out in Ukraine. Thus, at the legislative level, such an approach is enshrined in Art. 10 of the Law of Ukraine "On Education" [22] where it is determined that the integral components of the education system are: preschool education; complete secondary education; extracurricular education; specialized education; professional (vocational) education; professional higher education; Higher Education; adult education, including postgraduate education. This is the approach we consider systemic and one that meets the needs of society.

However, the implementation of this approach is determined by a number of other pieces of legislation and various public administration bodies, which raises a number of different problems and inconsistencies. In the course of this study, we will focus in more detail on the organization and legal regulation of the system of continuing education in Ukraine with an emphasis on school and extracurricular education as a defining component of this system. It should be noted that in practice for continuing education, educational institutions use mainly the following mechanisms of public administration: administrative and managerial; socio-economic; institutional and design-analytical.

Marchak (2007) [23] in his research emphasizes the role of civil society in the system of public education management, on the example of a secondary school. She notes that community-based management of an educational institution is a type of flexible management that involves public involvement in management decisions at various levels of management (from the Ministry of Education and Science to the student), establishing a moving balance between community demands and providing educational services. Achieving maximum results in teaching and educating students, local community development.

Analyzing the scientific experience of Onats and Kalinina (2015) [24] it can be concluded that public administration and public administration in education provide for coordinated interaction between the state and the community in the implementation of continuing education, to effectively influence educational policy, management decisions, gaining equal access to quality education.

3.2 Analysis of the Current State of Implementation of State Policy in the Field of Continuing Education

In Ukraine, preschools, secondary schools and higher education institutions operate on separate subsystems.

Preschool institutions are separate institutions that have their own structure and systemic subordination, which is focused on the implementation of goals, objectives, principles and functions of state policy in the field of preschool education.

Secondary schools in Ukraine are currently in the process of reform until 2024 and should have certain levels and distinctions:

- Primary school for students of grades 1–4;
- Gymnasium for students of 5–9 grades;
- Gymnasium, which may include a separate unit of primary school, as an exception for demographics for students in grades 1–9;
- Lyceum for students of 10–12 grades;
- Lyceum, which may include a separate unit of primary school and gymnasium, as an exception under an international agreement, or private ownership, for students in grades 1–12.

If the Lyceum has a scientific status, the Lyceum may include a Gymnasium, but such lyceums have the opportunity to teach children from 8 to 12 classes, subject to close cooperation with higher education and must contain in its teaching staff at least 5% teachers with a degree.

Higher education institutions are also in the process of reformation, but a clear legal framework has not yet been formed, which will have a certain course for its implementation.

During the study we made an author's comparison of the features of public management systems: preschool education, general secondary education, higher education, continuing education and the differences between them (Table 2).

Table 2. Matrix of expectations of customers of educational services from educational institutions of different levels.

Society's orders	Preschool education	General secondary education	Higher education	Continuing education
Mandatory presence of the control object in the system	Yes	Yes	Yes	Selectively

(*continued*)

Table 2. (*continued*)

Society's orders	Preschool education	General secondary education	Higher education	Continuing education
Mandatory regulatory support (rules and regulations)	Yes	Yes	Yes	It is recommended
Strategic goals, objectives, principles and functions of management	Yes	Yes	Yes	It is recommended
Performance evaluation	Yes	Yes	Yes	Selectively
Adapted transition from learning to learning	No	No	No	No

Source: compiled by the authors

That is, such subsystems of the education system as: preschool, general secondary and higher education have clear economic, political, social and organizational mechanisms of public administration, while the system of continuing education does not have clear regulatory influences to ensure sustainable development of society (recommended nature).

In addition, each stage of transition now becomes a psychological aspect of the impact on each individual through a sharp change in educational space and constant changes in learning conditions, which mostly negatively affects the education of each individual, as the process of personality development depends on team change and management. At the same time, it is important that the functions and tasks facing the subjects of management of educational institutions and the educational sector as a whole are correlated with each other and do not contradict, but are subordinated to the tasks that ensure the implementation of state policy in education.

Unfortunately, there is currently no clear sequence in the formation of a holistic education management system. The peculiarities of the provision of educational services at different levels of education are not taken into account, taking into account the needs of society for the formation of a holistic system of lifelong learning. This leads to some differences and chaotic actions in the implementation of educational reform. Government bodies are not able to develop common approaches and set clear tasks for all participants in the educational process to implement reforms, and performers at different levels cannot set a clear task in the internal system for implementing public education policy in educational institutions at different levels (Fig. 1).

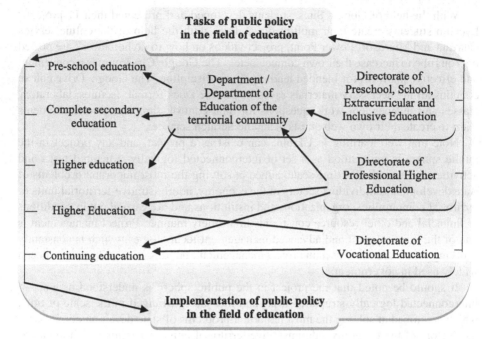

Fig. 1. The current education management system

In our opinion, there is an urgent need to introduce radical changes in the context of continuing education and education in general, with the aim of innovative integration into the international educational space. To form areas of non-traditional types and forms of educational activities, to determine their effectiveness and the possibility of explication and extrapolation in educational institutions of different levels in Ukraine is possible through project management using web learning methods.

Today, such changes can be made through web-based learning. Project management is one of the most relevant and advanced management technologies, which is constantly evolving. Due to project management, the application of technologies and methods for web-learning is relevant for the development of education in Ukraine, but this concept has not yet been widely used in government.

Researchers understand the web as an information component of a local or wide area network, through which the use of web resources (text, graphics, audio, video resources), which are interconnected by hypertext links. When it comes to the use of educational web resources, then the term "web learning" is used.

Analyzing scientific and methodological research and achievements of online learning in the lyceum as a structural unit of the university, we will reveal our own experience of using various web technologies (Google services (Google Classroom, Google Docs, Google Sites, YouTube), cloud services Canva, Piktochart, Scratch and etc.) in the process of preparing students for grades 8–10 of the lyceum, as well as describe the main ways in the educational process.

With the help of Google Sites, students developed and presented their IT projects. Lyceum students create their multimedia abilities with the help of the online service Canvata and Microsoft Power Point, project videos on how to do homework are posted on YouTube to increase their own competencies. The Google Classroom is a convenient and effective platform for blended learning in the discipline. The Google Drive course contains all the necessary materials saved in Google Docs format: lectures, laboratory classes and independent work, questions for final control, samples of work. Students learn to create their own web quests using the Scratch service.

Note that web-learning in Ukraine can exist as a project, and any project in the public sphere is understood as a set of interconnected logically-structured tasks and activities, organized on a time scale, aimed at solving the most important problems of state development, individual sectors of the economy, administrative-territorial units or territorial communities, organizations and institutions and are carried out in conditions of financial and other resource constraints in a timely manner. Project management is one of the most relevant and advanced management technologies, which is constantly evolving. Many areas are used in project management, but this concept has not yet been widely used in government.

It should be noted that the project in the public sphere is understood as a set of interconnected logically-structured tasks and measures, arranged in the scale of time, which are aimed at solving the most important problems of state development, individual sectors of the economy, administrative-territorial units or territorial communities, organizations and institutions and are carried out in conditions of financial and other resource constraints in due time.

Project management in the public sphere is a process of institutionalization in a program-targeted format of ways of intervention of state authorities or local self- government bodies in social reality in order to solve a public problem. At the same time, as noted by A. Chemeryz (2012) [25], in conditions of limited time and resources, unique products or services are created that have not been developed before and differ from existing analogues. Therefore, we believe that the application of modern methods of project management is the best, proven way to quickly and effectively implement change with the involvement in the management process of society or a group of people who are considered leaders of public opinion.

And we support the position of Azarenkova and Piskunov (2015) [26], who note that based on the methodology of project management can develop projects in any area of public administration, including in the field of continuing education.

In the political sphere, these are draft legislation and legal regulation, improvement of the institution of power, and so on.

In economic - reforming and creating new enterprises; fuel and energy systems development projects; creation of ecological systems of regions; projects of demonopolization, development of the private sector; financial system rehabilitation projects, etc.

In the social sphere - insurance and social security projects, housing projects, pension projects.

Equally important are educational projects, health and health care projects, projects to overcome technological backwardness and many others [27].

John Pfiffner [28], a professor at the University of Southern California et al., noted in his paper "Public Administration" that it is "paradoxical because it reflects, among other things, the proper balance between the flexible decision-making mechanism needed in management and certain rules." provided by law".

Therefore, for the formation of knowledge, skills, rational behavior, ways of critical thinking and the acquisition of other competencies necessary for a competitive individual, it is important to explore the forms, methods and consequences of public administration mechanisms in modern educational activities.

The Concept of the new Ukrainian school defines the following key competencies of student youth:

- the ability of students by means of the Ukrainian language to successfully interact in the process of solving age-old life problems;
- the ability and inner need to independently acquire knowledge and develop skills in accordance with the goals for self-improvement and self-realization;
- the ability of an individual to apply mathematical skills in real life, to work with numerical information;
- ability to navigate in the information space, to own and operate information according to needs, to use ICT in education and everyday life, to find, process and systematize information;
- ability to be open to innovations, to realize oneself in the changing technological, life, educational and work environment;
- the ability to understand the information environment, critically analyze the necessary information, transform, store and broadcast it and act in accordance with their goals and accepted in society communication ethics;
- ability to plan, self-organize and organize entrepreneurial activity, to implement ideas in the sphere of economic life, to resolve conflict situations, to make decisions, to take responsibility, to form models of behavior necessary for successful solution of urgent production problems;
- ability to take an active position in life in matters of environmental protection and to adhere to a healthy lifestyle and promote it;
- awareness of civic duty and responsibility, ability to exercise civil rights and responsibilities;
- ability to consciously perceive cultural heritage as a value, analyze and evaluate the achievements of national and world culture, navigate in the cultural and spiritual context of modern society, apply traditional methods of self-education for the culture of the Ukrainian people.

Based on the above, the study initiated the project in the context of improving the mechanisms of public administration of continuing education, in particular, with the formation of key competencies in future students with adaptation to higher education, as well as improving the competencies of high school students using web methods -learning, in various subjects and profiles of study to choose a future profession to improve the mechanisms of public administration of continuing education in terms of innovative development of society.

Guided by the Laws of Ukraine: "On Education", "On Higher Education", "On Complete General Secondary Education", Resolution of the Cabinet of Ministers of Ukraine of May 22, 2019 № 438 "On Approval of the Regulations on the Scientific Lyceum" and Concepts: "New Ukrainian School", "Development of pedagogical education" and "Profile education in high school", a separate structural subdivision "Scientific Lyceum of International Relations of II-III degrees" of the University of Customs and Finance "indicating changes in the structure of the University of Customs and Finance.

During the project implementation, licenses were obtained to conduct educational activities at the level of basic secondary education with a licensed volume of 210 people and to conduct educational activities at the level of specialized secondary education with a licensed volume of 210 people.

To determine public satisfaction with the quality of education in the senior classes, due to admission to higher education and higher education institutions, as well as to obtain comparative results on the implemented project "separate structural unit" Scientific Lyceum of International Relations II-III degrees "University of Customs and Finance" interviewed 10768 people in Ukraine who study and work in traditional educational institutions from 8th to 11th grade and separately people who study and work in the newly formed structural unit of the University to get quality results of the implemented project which used web technologies as teaching methods. The survey was conducted in the form of a questionnaire for students, parents, teachers and public figures in the field of education. The results of assessing the level of satisfaction of society have reached different indicators.

Given the results of the survey of parents, students and public figures in the field of education, we have a level of satisfaction with the quality of education in grades 8–11 among respondents by 76.97% from 100%, which on a 5-point scale corresponds to a score of 3.85 points (Fig. 2).

The survey also covered students studying in the newly formed structural unit - the Lyceum of the University of Customs and Finance, which used web technologies as methods of the educational process to obtain results of satisfaction with the quality of education in grades 8–11. They are satisfied with the quality of education by 87.27% out of 100%, which on a 5-point scale corresponds to a score of 4.36 points (Fig. 3).

Analyzing the answers of respondents, we have a significant discrepancy of 10.3%. Thus, we can assume that the relevance of lyceums in the structure of higher education should be studied, start such institutions and analyze their quality of education.

This necessitates further research and development of recommendations for improving the mechanisms of public administration of the continuing education system based on the results of the study.

Education is a priority of state policy of Ukraine, a strategic resource of socio-economic, cultural and spiritual development, guaranteeing the national interests of the state, strengthening its international prestige and image, ensuring the personal development of each person in accordance with the requirements of innovative development.

The design and implementation of public administration mechanisms are divided according to goals and results based on the needs and interests of society, taking into account the management process, monitoring and adjustment, design and modeling.

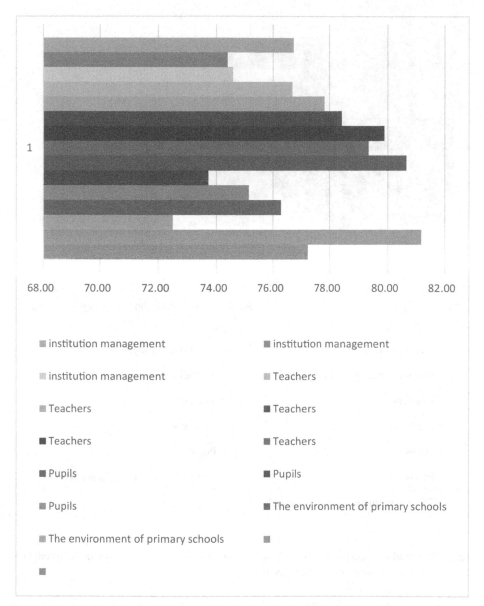

Fig. 2. Results of satisfaction with the quality of education in grades 8–11 among parents, students and public figures (Notation in %).

In the conditions of innovative development of society, any educational institution on educational reform must have close cooperation with public organizations, entrepreneurs, local governments and other educational institutions of the highest level of accreditation. So you can build a constructive partnership and real interaction to solve

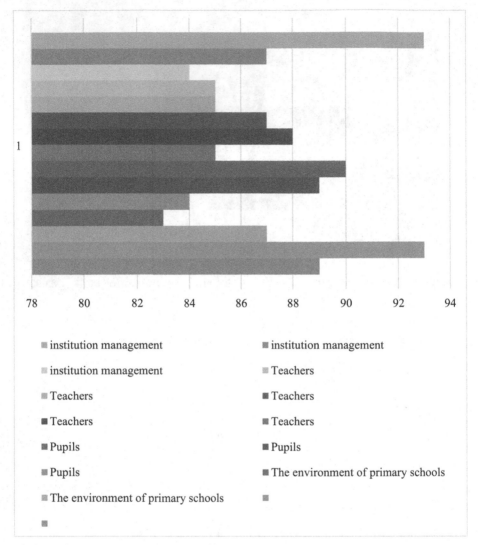

Fig. 3. The results of satisfaction with the quality of education in grades 8–11 in the lyceum of the University of Customs and Finance (Notation in %).

problems in modern education. All participants in the educational process, representatives of government agencies in the field of education and members of the public should be prepared for this. That is possible through scientifically substantiated tested organizational mechanisms that will contribute to the transformation of the school into a social institution in the interests of the individual, society and the state.

Therefore, we can conclude that the development and implementation of projects and programs at the state level in the field of non-traditional types and forms of educational activities of the continuing education system is today one of the most effective vectors of public administration. Project management in educational institutions of different levels will increase the effectiveness of combating such problematic aspects of state project implementation as blurred project implementation deadlines, revision of project implementation estimates, terms of reference, etc. Thus, project management in the system of continuing education should ensure a clear process of implementation of project implementation plans in order to achieve the strategic goals of the state in a timely manner and taking into account limited resources.

4 Conclusion

According to the results of the study, it can be concluded that the approbation of the project "Separate structural unit" Scientific Lyceum of International Relations II-III degrees "of the University of Customs and Finance" gives positive indicators of satisfaction with the quality of education. For greater analysis of the result it is necessary to discuss the data obtained, refine and improve the results obtained. For the implementation and dissemination of the results of the implemented project are practically significant.

The importance of the implementation of the submitted projects is necessary for a qualitative scientific analysis not only of Ukrainian scientists, but also of foreign scientists who see the importance of integrating the senior classes of secondary school into the structure of higher education. It should be noted that higher education institutions are those institutions that are engaged in science and research of web technologies, services, methods, etc. It is taking into account the speed of development of society, it is necessary to consider the possibility of teaching high school students in a more scientific environment, i.e. in higher education.

For a quality organization of the system of continuing education in Ukraine at the national level and the formation of an effective state policy in the field of continuing education requires an integrated approach taking into account various aspects of development and their relationship in the education system. and improving public administration mechanisms.

References

1. Sychenko, V.V., Martynenko, O.M., Rybkina, S.O.: State policy of Ukraine in the field of continuing education. Public Adm. customs Adm. 1(18), 134–140 (2018). http://customs-admin.umsf.in.ua/archive/2018/1/21.pdf
2. Shynkaruk, V., [ed.].: Philosophical encyclopedic dictionary. Hryhoriy Skovoroda Institute of Philosophy of the National Academy of Sciences of Ukraine. Abris. Kyiv (2002)
3. Uzbek, K.: Fragments of the construction of ancient science, philosophy and culture. Eastern Publishing House, Donetsk (2010)
4. Bonner, S.: Education in Ancient Rome. University of California Press, Berkeley (2020). https://doi.org/10.1525/9780520347762
5. Clarke, M.: Higher education in the ancient world. Routledge (2011). https://doi.org/10.4324/9780203181317
6. La Bua, G.: Cicero and Roman education: the reception of the speeches and ancient scholarship. Cambridge University Press (2019)

7. Abuselidze, G., Radzivilova, I., Mohylevska, O.: Psychological-pedagogical problems and prospects of distance learning of students during the Covid-19 pandemics. E3S Web of Conferences. **258**, 10016 (2021). https://doi.org/10.1051/e3sconf/202125810016
8. Kovalenko, Y.: Comenius Jan Amos. Encyclopedia of Education. Academy of Ped. Sciences of Ukraine. Unikom Inter. Kyiv. (2008)
9. Nychkalo, N.: Continuing professional education as a philosophical and pedagogical category. Continuing professional education: theory and practice. Kyiv. vip 1, 13–15 (2001)
10. Nychkalo, N. [ed.].: Continuing education in socio-cultural dimensions: collective monograph. Drahomanov University; Department of Adult Education. Helvetica Publishing House (2018)
11. Lugovyy, V.: Formation of continuing education in the countries of organization of economic cooperation and development (experience for Ukraine). Higher education in Ukraine. Theor. Sci.-methodical J. **4**(1), 7–9 (2008)
12. Vulfson, B.V.: Strategy for the development of education in the West on the threshold of the XXI century. URAO, Moscow (1999)
13. Oliynyk, V.: Lifelong learning: how and why to teach adults? Education management. **1**(229), 4–7 (2010). http://www.apsu.org.ua/en/information/press/956784/
14. Teteruk, K., Datsii, N., Kartashov, E., Ivashova, L., Ortina, G.: Specificity of forming human capital at It-enterprises in conditions of concept lifelong learning. Int. J. Innov. Technol. Exploring Eng. **3**(9), 1379–1387 (2020). https://doi.org/10.35940/ijitee.C8183.019320
15. Zastrozhnikova, I.V., Datsii, N.V., Filyanina, N.M., Lytvyn, L., Bielialov, T.E., Martynets, L.A.: Development of financial and economic autonomy in the field of higher education. Laplage Em Revista. **7**(1), 327–340 (2021). https://doi.org/10.24115/S2446-622020217 1728p.327-340
16. Abuselidze, G., Beridze, L.: Financing models of vocational education and its impact on the economy: Problems and perspectives. SHS Web of Conferences. **66**, 01001 (2019). https://doi.org/10.1051/shsconf/20196601001
17. Abuselidze, G., Davitadze, L.: Analysis of the necessity and efficiency of the HEI diploma holder professional retraining needs in Adjara Autonomous Republic. E3S Web of Conferences. 224, 03015 (2020). https://doi.org/10.1051/e3sconf/202022403015
18. European Commission. European Pillar of Social Rights (2017). https://ec.europa.eu/com mission/priorities/deeper-and-fairer-economicand-monetary-union/european-pillar-social-rights/european-pillar-social-rights-20-principles_en
19. Verkhovna Rada of Ukraine. Community charter of the fundamental social rights of workers acts of European law on social matters. Parliamentary Publishing House, Kyiv (2005). https://zakon.rada.gov.ua/laws/show/994_044#Text
20. Council of the European Union. Commission staff working document accompanying the document proposal for a council recommendation on key competences for lifeLong learning SWD/2018/014 final – 2018/08 (NLE) (2018). https://eur-lex.europa.eu/legal-content/EN/TXT/?uri=SWD:2018:0014:FIN
21. Verkhovna Rada of Ukraine. On core competences for lifelong learning: Recommendation 2006/962 / EU of the European Parliament and of the Council (EU) of 18.12.2006 (2006). https://zakon.rada.gov.ua/laws/show/994_975
22. Verkhovna Rada of Ukraine. On Education: Law of Ukraine of September 5, 2017 № 2145-VIII (2017). https://zakon.rada.gov.ua/laws/show/2145-19#Text
23. Marchak, O.: Development of socially-directed management of general educational institutions in the education system. Adaptive management in education. Style Izdat, Kharkiv. pp. 159–165 (2007). http://umo.edu.ua/images/content/nashi_vydanya/metod_upr_osvit/v_1/8.pdf

24. Onats' O., Kalinina, L.: Conceptual principles of organizational mechanisms and technologies of public-state management of general educational institutions: manual. Kyiv. (2015). https://core.ac.uk/download/pdf/154284069.pdf
25. Chemeryz, A.: Development and management of projects in the public sphere: the European dimension for Ukraine: practice. Way / Swiss-Ukrainian project "Support to decentralization in Ukraine - DESPRO". LLC "Sofia-A", Kyiv (2012). https://despro.org.ua/media/articles/10_book_chemeric__17_12_do_druku.pdf
26. Azarenkova, G., Piskunov, R.: Project analysis (in schemes and examples): textbook. Way. Kyiv. (2015)
27. Ministry of education and science of Ukraine. New Ukrainian school concept (2016). https://mon.gov.ua/storage/app/media/zagalna%20serednya/nova-ukrainska-shkola-compressed.pdf
28. Pfifener, J. M. Presthus, R. V.: Public administration. The Ronald press company, New York (1967). https://catalog.hathitrust.org/Record/001156277

International Workshop on Block chain and Distributed Ledgers: Technologies and Applications (BDLTA 2022)

A Multilayer Approach to the Security of Blockchain Networks of the Future

Alexander Bogdanov[1,2], Alexander Degtyarev[1], Nadezhda Shchegoleva[1,2], Vladimir Korkhov[1], Valery Khvatov[3], Nodir Zaynalov[4], Jasur Kiyamov[1(✉)], and Aleksandr Dik[1]

[1] Saint Petersburg State University, St. Petersburg, Russia
{a.v.bogdanov,a.degtyarev,n.shchegoleva,v.korkhov}@spbu.ru,
{st080634,st087383}@student.spbu.ru
[2] St. Petersburg State Marine Technical University, Saint Petersburg, Russia
[3] DGT Technologies AG, Toronto, Canada
[4] Samarkand Branch Tashkent University of Information Technologies named after Muhammad al-Khwarizmi, Samarkand, Uzbekistan

Abstract. Decentralized computing and blockchain technology play a significant role in the implementation of modern digital economy business models. The most noticeable trends in this economy are the diversification and convergence of platforms and services, which is often achieved through undesirable fragmentation of the overall IT landscape. Business solutions represented by different blockchain networks turn out to be poorly connected, data exchange between them is difficult. The search for ways to overcome barriers between different decentralized networks leads to an increase in the importance of cross-platform integration solutions, providing the necessary level of interoperability. Such solutions must be secure both in terms of confidentiality and fault tolerance. Below is a vision of the architecture of integration gateways using the ODAP-2PC protocol, which provides crash fault-tolerance for the integration of various networks. This architecture provides transparency of interaction, reliability and continuity of audit in digital asset exchange systems or payment systems with increased requirements for interoperability.

Keywords: Blockchain · Distributed recovery · ODAP

1 Introduction

There is a growing interest in digital currencies and virtual assets as the foundation of the next generation digital economy. Blockchain technology has established itself as a reliable tool due to its properties such as immutability, transparency and controllability [1–3]. Private organizations, governments are actively researching and investing in blockchain-based digital assets, for example, by promoting new platforms for digital transactions [4]. The key task on the way to creating a digital economy is the secure connection of various networks, providing network effects between them [5–7]. Thus, the interaction of blockchains is a

© The Author(s), under exclusive license to Springer Nature Switzerland AG 2022
O. Gervasi et al. (Eds.): ICCSA 2022 Workshops, LNCS 13377, pp. 205–216, 2022.
https://doi.org/10.1007/978-3-031-10536-4_14

key moment in this area [2,8–10]. Although significant progress has been made in the interoperability of public and private blockchains, legacy systems cannot yet seamlessly interoperate with each other [11]. Moreover, current solutions are not standardized and do not offer the possibility of seamless blockchain interaction across the enterprise, and the need for adaptability is a motivating factor for combining different blockchains to a heterogeneous ecosystem. The choice of new blockchains allows you to explore new scenarios and keep up with the times. However, each blockchain comes with its own security risks as the technology is still evolving. Therefore, developers have to choose between novelty and stability, which leads to a huge variety of options. This diversity leads to fragmentation: there are many immature solutions for blockchains (for example, without extensive testing). Until recently, blockchains did not take into account the need for interoperability, since each of them was focused on solving specific problems, which led to disparate stores of data and values.

2   Future Developments of Blockchain in 6G Network

Blockchain is one of the most famous technologies unlocking the potential of 6G systems. This section explores the possibilities and strengths of blockchain technology to address potential issues. As 5G connects users, services and applications, security and privacy are paramount. However, data management in 5G is more difficult than in earlier wireless networks, because the connected devices can be more diverse in type, they are expected to be very large in number, and the data they generate will be larger and more distributed (Table 1).

Table 1. Comparison of the new generation network.

	5G	6G
Transmission speed	0.1 Gb/s–20Gb/s	1 Gb/s–1 Tb/s
Reliability (error rate)	$(\leq 10^{-5})$	$(\leq 10^{-5})$
Solidity	$(10^6/km^2)$	$(10^7/km^2)$
Localization accuracy	10 sm in 2D	10 sm in 3D
Mobility	500 km/h	1000 km/h
Throughput	$(10\,mb/s/m^2)$	$(10\,gb/s/m^3)$
Delay	1–5 ms	10–100 ns

Transaction privacy leak: The blockchain relies in part on transparent transactions. Consequently, in blockchain-based systems, user privacy is at risk. Finally, blockchain-based smart contracts have significantly reduced the risk of de-anonymization, thanks to a closed transaction between contract participants [13].

However, as flexible as smart contracts are, they introduce a number of new attack surfaces into the system. The three main attack vectors for blockchain-based smart contracts are vulnerabilities in the blockchain itself, in the smart contract, and in the code-executing virtual machine [14].

The network layer transmits messages related to transactions and system management. Scaling requires each node to select only raw transactions for newly mined blocks; this will effectively halve the number of transactions required. In addition, the network plane topology can be modified to improve broadcast protocols [15].

The storage layer is a ledger - a global memory that stores member state changes resulting from write and read operations mutually agreed upon by all members at the consensus level, as well as smart contracts or other state-related entities. Storage tier performance improvement methods are divided into:

– Storage sharding;
– Distributed hash tables.

6G is expected to dramatically increase the performance and number of wireless network services, resulting in a significant increase in ubiquitous computing resources.

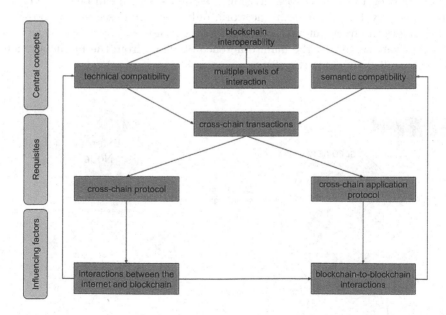

Fig. 1. Illustration of the relationship between different blockchain concepts.

The following types of blockchain network interaction can be distinguished [17]:

– Full state replication between blockchains;

- Blockchain cross-application support;
- Blockchain compatibility with other technologies.

Figure 1 shows the relationship between different blockchain interoperability concepts. This approach can provide interoperability at the semantic level (that is, related to the transfer of a data value that corresponds to the interaction) mapped to the application level. Based on the foregoing, let's take a closer look at multi-level protection, using the DGT platform as an example.

3   Layered Data Protection Approach

Most optimization algorithms require synchronization of local peer-to-peer access to WAN information. This is a separate problem, known as the aggregation problem [7], and refers to a set of functions that provide access to such components of a distributed system as network size, load average and uptime. Consider the solutions of the DGT platform, which considers the problem of fault tolerance with a multi-level data processing approach. This approach is based on the deployment of a virtual network for solving problems or when developing applications. Servers or nodes may also be located on different physical networks. Node clusters are part of a larger network division - segments, which can be of two types: public and private. In a separate network, only one public segment is possible, joining nodes can freely interact with other segment nodes. The network can have several private segments, the main difference of which from the public segment is the controlled topology (Fig. 2).

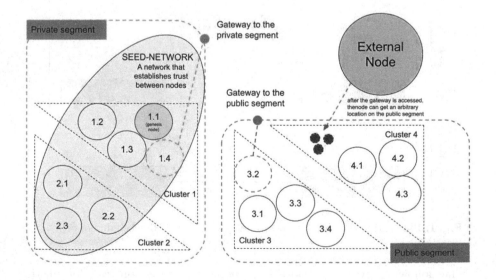

Fig. 2. DGT network topology and node attaching

The initial implementation of the network, also called the "static core", which is a group of nodes that form special trust relationships (the public keys of such nodes are known in advance and are registered at the time of the core deployment). Joining other nodes requires the processing of node certificates for private shards, or a dynamic connection for public shards.

DGT is positioned as a platform for distributed and decentralized computing, where the system processes data regardless of the specific application task. To solve a specific task, it is required to set up a family of transactions, as well as an add-on of the applied client part [19,20]. In fact, the DGT software is the set of typical nodes, which provide interaction with other nodes, data validation and insertion of new data into the storage (registry), also called DAG or State. It is aimed at supporting consortium-based networks. This means that a node can join the network if certain conditions are met. In the simplest terms, this could be checking the host for a certificate. Depending on the implementation of the anchor mechanism, the degree of openness of the network varies - from completely open (public) to completely closed (private). Nodes are combined into groups called clusters. The initial interaction is carried out through connections between nodes with one dedicated node in the cluster - Leader. The leader collects data from transaction checks at each node. Such checks are called "votes". If the number of votes exceeds a certain threshold, then the transaction is considered approved in the cluster and awaits arbitration - performed outside the cluster (additional verification). Within a cluster, nodes interact with each other via dedicated channels, also called permalinks.

Following Sawtooth, DGT is a multi-transactional system in which several families of transactions can be addressed. Each family is processed by a separate transaction processor. Transaction families complement the technology of smart contracts, and also allow you to set the boundaries of the availability of different types of transactions for different network segments. But this approach cannot provide complete system protection, as server components or the server itself may fail.

4   Failure Recovery

To ensure a fair exchange of assets, blockchain gateways must work reliably and be able to withstand various attacks. Thus, a disaster recovery strategy should be a major factor in the design of blockchain gateways, where specific recovery protocols can be developed as part of the digital asset transaction protocol between gateways. The recovery protocol associated with the failover strategy ensures that the source and target DLTs are changed sequentially, i.e. that assets taken from the source DLT are preserved in the destination DLT and no double spending can occur.

Gateways allow the seamless transfer of digital currencies and virtual assets between these systems. The Internet Engineering Task Force is currently working on an asset transfer protocol that works between two gateway devices. In a layered approach, when increasing throughput, communication failure may occur, to solve this problem, you can use the ODAP protocol.

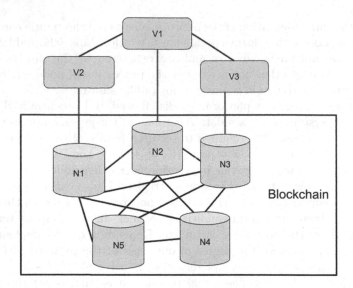

Fig. 3. The structure of a multi-level network. V1, V2 and V3 are the validator nodes, N1, N2, N3, N4 and N5 are the nodes of the blockchain network

5 Open Digital Asset Protocol (ODAP)

ODAP is an internetworking protocol that handles multiple cross-border digital asset transactions using asset profiles (asset schema) and the concept of gateways. The most common layered network architecture is the client-server architecture. It includes two ranks of communication participants, the rank of the client and the rank of the server, while the rank of the server is dominant in the network. This model is the basis for the centralized exchange and storage of information, and the most common network architecture in the modern Internet. The structure of this network is shown in Fig. 3. It can be seen from the figure that "Node 1" is a server and all network clients access it with requests. It can also be seen that the other nodes do not communicate directly with each other, they do not imply such a possibility. All inter-client interactions occur either through the mediation of the server, or do not occur at all. In this case, when the server fails, in fact, the entire network fails and the client nodes absolutely lose the opportunity to receive the service provided by the server node.

Crash fault-tolerant (CFT) systems can fail on $n/2$ nodes, where n is the number of nodes. As long as there are most nodes with the latest state, failures are tolerable [18]. The primary backup model defines a set of n hosts (or nodes) that, as a group, provide fault tolerance for the service, thereby increasing availability. In this model, the application client sends messages to the primary node P. The primary nodes forward message updates to the backup set $B = B_1, ..., B_n$ when it receives a message. Backup server k propagates a new incoming message to backup server $k + 1, k \leq n, k \in R$. Node P is notified of the update when n-node failover is reached. The message has been replicated to at least n nodes.

If such an acknowledgment cannot be received P, the message update request is resubmitted. If P fails, then a new leader $P_{new} \in B$ is chosen. If the standby node receives a request from an application client, it forwards it to P, accepting it only when the latter sends an update request. When an update is received, P sends a message update to its right neighbor, sending back an acknowledgment.

Another recovery mechanism is self-healing [16]. It is assumed that during self-healing, when nodes fail, they sooner or later recover. Although this mode is cheaper than primary backup because it uses fewer nodes, less messages exchanged, and less storage requirements.

6   Distributed Recovery Procedure

One of the key requirements for deploying asset transfer gateways is the high availability of the gateways. The distributed recovery procedure then improves the fault tolerance of the layered nodes through fault tolerance. Next, we present an overview of the ODAP-2PC. ODAP-2PC supports two alternative fault tolerance strategies:

- Self-healing mode: after a failure, the gateway eventually informs other parties about its recovery and continues the protocol execution;
- Primary backup mode: if a node goes down indefinitely, a backup is created using the log storage API to retrieve the most recent version of the log.

We assume that the gateway does not lose its long-term keys (public/private key pair) and can re-establish all TLS connections. In the main-backup mode, we assume that after a period δ_t of failure of the main gateway, the backup gateway unambiguously detects this failure and assumes the role of the main one. Failure is detected using a conservative value of δ_t. To do this, a backup gateway essentially does the same thing as a gateway in self-healing mode:

- reads the log and continues the process. In this mode, the log must be shared between the primary and backup gateways. If there is more than one backup, a leader election protocol must be run to decide which backup will take the lead role.
- In both modes, logs are written before operations to ensure the atomicity and consistency of the protocol used to exchange assets. The log data is considered as a resource that may be internal to the DLT system.

There are several situations where a failure can occur [18]. On Fig. 4 shows the GS (source gatway) failing before it performs the verification operation for the GR (recipient gateway) steps 1 and 2. Both gateways retain their storage APIs. In self-healing mode, the gateway eventually recovers (step 3) by creating a recovered message in the form (step 4). The unbroken gateway requests the log entries that the failover gateway needs (steps 5, 6). In particular, the GS obtains the required log entries in step 7 and compares them with its current log. The GS then attempts to reconcile the changes with its current state (step 8). After processing, if both versions of the log match, the log is updated and

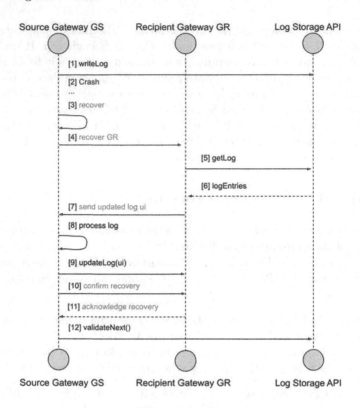

Fig. 4. GS failure before issuing initialization-validation GR

the process can continue. If the logs differ, then the GS calls the updateLog primitive, updating its log (step 9) and thereby allowing the failed gateway to recover the current moment.

In this particular example, step 9 will not occur because the exec-validate, done-validate, and ack-validate operations were not performed by GR. If the Log Storage API is in Shared mode, no additional synchronization steps are required. After that confirms successful recovery (steps 10, 11).

A set of experiments was carried out with a two-rank processing system as shown with fault tolerance on the DGT platform. Initially tested on a stable with 24 presti nodes over 1000 transactions and it resulted in an average throughput of (Fig. 5) 0.009 s per transaction.

In Fig. 6 simulated forced failure of 6 out of 24 nodes while processing 1000 transactions, in this scenario, the node leader started to process voting rounds among 18 nodes and continued to process data. This processing position took an average of 0.0077 s (Fig. 6) of time.

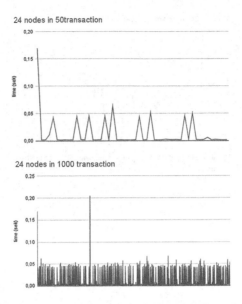

Fig. 5. Transaction processing graph with 24 nodes deployed.

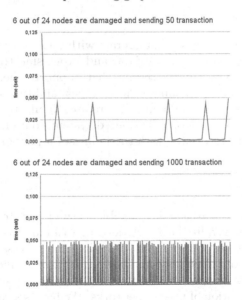

Fig. 6. Graph of transaction processing with 24 deployed nodes which forced a system failure on 6 nodes.

In the third scenario, it was decided to run on 12 nodes to simulate fault tolerance at 24 nodes. Despite such a failure in the number of nodes, the PBFT consensus round of voting was stable, processing one transaction in 0.0073 s on average (Fig. 7).

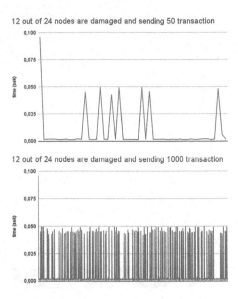

Fig. 7. Graph of transaction processing with 24 deployed nodes which forced a system failure on 12 nodes.

Each node is a set of services that interact with each other and are responsible for organizing the network, storing data, and processing transactions. Even a single node delivers a significant service that supports client applications via APIs. At the same time, a number of network capabilities of the platform can be used only if there are several nodes. Therefore, thanks to this technology, we eliminate the main drawback of a distributed system - data failure, which allows us to reduce the risks associated with the failure of a part of the system.

7   Conclusion

In this article, we have presented a possible view of how to overcome barriers between different decentralized networks leading to an increase in the importance of cross-platform integration solutions, providing the necessary level of interoperability. Such solutions must be secure both in terms of confidentiality and fault tolerance. Integration gateways using the ODAP protocol, which provides crash fault-tolerance integration of various networks. We have shown that our solution is fault tolerant by using a multi-rank distributed recovery mechanism approach.

The research is partially funded by the Ministry of Science and Higher Education of the Russian Federation as part of World-class Research Center program: Advanced Digital Technologies (contract No. 075-15-2020-903 dated 16.11.2020).

References

1. Catalini, C., Gans, J.S.: Some simple economics of the blockchain. Working Paper 22952, National Bureau of Economic Research, December 2016. http://www.nber.org/papers/w22952. https://doi.org/10.3386/w22952
2. Hargreaves, M., Hardjono, T., Belchior, R.: Open Digital Asset Protocol draft 02, Internet-Draft draft-hargreaves-odap-02, Internet Engineering Task Force (2021). https://datatracker.ietf.org/doc/html/draft-hargreaves-odap-02
3. Viriyasitavat, W., Da Xu, L., Bi, Z., Pungpapong, V.: Blockchain and Internet of Things for modern business process in digital economy-the state of the art. IEEE Trans. Comput. Soc. Syst. **6**(6), 1420–1432 (2019)
4. Pentland, A., Lipton, A., Hardjono, T.: Time for a new, digital Bretton Woods, Barron's, June 2021. https://rb.gy/yj31vq
5. Pawczuk, L., Gogh, M., Hewett, N.: Inclusive deployment of blockchain for supply chains: a framework for blockchain interoperability. Technical report, World Economic Forum (2020). https://www.weforum.org
6. Hardjono, T., Lipton, A., Pentland, A.: Towards an interoperability architecture blockchain autonomous systems. IEEE Trans. Eng. Manag. **67**(4), 1298–1309 (2019). https://doi.org/10.1109/TEM.2019.2920154
7. Tam Vo, H., Wang, Z., Karunamoorthy, D., Wagner, J., Abebe, E., Mohania, M.: Internet of blockchains: techniques and challenges ahead. In: 2018 IEEE International Conference on Internet of Things (iThings) and IEEE Green Computing and Communications (GreenCom) and IEEE Cyber, Physical and Social Computing (CPSCom) and IEEE Smart Data (Smart-Data), pp. 1574–1581 (2018)
8. Pillai, B., Biswas, K.: Blockchain Interoperable Digital Objects Innovative Applications of Blockchain Technology View project Blockchain Interoperable Asset Classes View project (2019)
9. Borkowski, M., Sigwart, M., Frauenthaler, P., Hukkinen, T., Schulte, S.: DeXTT: deterministic cross-blockchain token transfers. IEEE Access **7**, 111030–111042 (2019). arXiv
10. Schulte, S., Sigwart, M., Frauenthaler, P., Borkowski, M.: Towards blockchain interoperability. In: Di Ciccio, C., et al. (eds.) BPM 2019. LNBIP, vol. 361, pp. 3–10. Springer, Cham (2019). https://doi.org/10.1007/978-3-030-30429-4_1
11. Belchior, R., Vasconcelos, A., Guerreiro, S., Correia, M.: A survey on blockchain interoperability: past, present, and future trends. ACM Comput. Surv. (2021). arXiv:2005.14282. http://arxiv.org/abs/2005.14282
12. Li, X., Jiang, P., Chen, T., Luo, X., Wen, Q.: A survey on the security of blockchain systems. Future Gener. Comput. Syst. (2017)
13. Wood, G., et al.: Ethereum: a secure decentralised generalised transaction ledger. Ethereum Project Yellow Paper **151**(2014), 1–32 (2014)
14. Atzei, N., Bartoletti, M., Cimoli, T.: A survey of attacks on Ethereum smart contracts (SoK). In: Maffei, M., Ryan, M. (eds.) POST 2017. LNCS, vol. 10204, pp. 164–186. Springer, Heidelberg (2017). https://doi.org/10.1007/978-3-662-54455-6_8
15. Croman, K., et al.: On scaling decentralized blockchains. In: Clark, J., Meiklejohn, S., Ryan, P.Y.A., Wallach, D., Brenner, M., Rohloff, K. (eds.) FC 2016. LNCS, vol. 9604, pp. 106–125. Springer, Heidelberg (2016). https://doi.org/10.1007/978-3-662-53357-4_8
16. Bernstein, P.A., Hadzilacos, V., Goodman, N.: Concurrency Control and Recovery in Database Systems. Addison-Wesley, Boston (1987)

17. Belchior, R., et al.: A survey on blockchain interoperability: past, present, and future trends. ACM Comput. Surv. **54**(8), 168 (2021)
18. Belchior, R., Vasconcelos, A., Correia, M., Hardjono, T.: HERMES: fault-tolerant middleware for blockchain interoperability. Future Gener. Comput. Syst. (2021)
19. DGT One Pager, official and short DGT Platform Description
20. DGT. The Blockchain Handbook

NFT Performance and Security Review

Anastasiya Lavrova[1,2] and Oleg Iakushkin[1,2](✉)

[1] Lanit-Tercom Italia SRL, Bari, Italy
[2] Saint-Petersburg University, Saint Petersburg, Russia
o.yakushkin@spbu.ru

Abstract. In this article we review NFT token architecture and metadata storage options. We show the main disadvantages and risks of the existing NFT architecture and infrastructure. NFT minting performance was analysed on various distributed ledger technologies. The main problem of NFT technology that we highlight is its associated metadata storage options. Since in-secure Web2 based servers are allowed as a storage solution data that is associated with the NFT tokens can be corrupted, modified and lost. Thus harming the end user. We see the main solution for such issues in data blockchains proliferation as they would provide data immutability.

Keywords: NFT · Metadata storage · Architectural risks · Performance

1 Intro

NFT, a non-fungible token is a transferable digital asset. The key difference between an NFT and FT (fungible token), is its uniqueness, which makes it suitable for identifying a certain item. Thus, NFT encodes a unique digital artefact, while FT encodes a type of digital currency [1,3].

In other words, the feature of the NFT token is to create a single digital representation of some object. In turn, FTs are standard coins that are equivalent to each other.

From the point of view of smart contracts, NFT is encoded by a unique identifier [4]. The user accessing the smart contract is returned a link to the JSON file based on this identifier. The file can technically store any information and links to data that is not verifiable at the time of creation and release of the NFT token. At the moment, the most popular uses of NFT are representations in the format of tokens of objects of various spheres:

– digital art, music;
– virtual real estate;
– game assets;
– event tickets, attendance receipts;
– domain names [8];

O. Gervasi et al. (Eds.): ICCSA 2022 Workshops, LNCS 13377, pp. 217–228, 2022.
https://doi.org/10.1007/978-3-031-10536-4_15

– tokenized insurance policies and obligations [9].

Attempts are being made to link NFT to physical objects, for example, the NIKE CryptoKicks technology, patented in 2019 [7].

2   Life of an NFT

2.1   Artist Creates NFT - Minting

The artist calls the function, passing there two types of data:

– (Name, description, link to the picture, other metadata) - used to generate a JSON token file
– The royalties are a commission to the author for each resale of the token (depending on smart-contract it can be stored as in JSON, so in blockchain storage)

After payment of the commission to the platform the token is generated. The main properties of the token used in the process of its life:

– Holder - the smart contract based on which the token was created.
– Author - the creator of the token.
– Owner - the current owner of the token (is the only address that will change "during the life of the token").
– Metadata - link to appropriate JSON file.
– Royalties - percentage after each token resale.

2.2   Selling

By default, the sale function is not included in the token standards. Developers of decentralized applications that require the sale function are forced to independently implement the auction logic in their smart contract. Users who mint the NFT independently using third-party services, such as OpenSea, can use the provided functions of the platform, if such exist, or use AMM.

2.3   Automated Market Maker (AMM)

On traditional exchange platforms, buyers and sellers offer different prices for an asset. When users consider the specified price acceptable, they make a deal, and this price becomes the market price of the asset. Stocks, gold, real estate, and most other assets rely on this traditional market structure to trade. However, with the help of blockchain technology, the usual exchanges were decentralized and transformed into AMM. Instead of using the producer's and recipient's order book, AMMS relies on liquidity pools. For example, ETH-USDT is a pair where users can share their ETH and USDT liquidity to receive trading fees. The main feature of an automated market maker is how anyone can become a market maker due to the simplicity of the operation of adding funds to the pool. AMM is based on a simple mathematical formula that takes different forms. The most common of them are $aTokenBalance(p) * bTokenBalance(p) = k$, where k characterizes a constant balance of assets that determines the price of tokens in the liquidity pool. For example, if AMM has ether (ETH) and bitcoin (BTC), every time ETH is bought, the price of ETH rises because there is less ETH in the pool than before the purchase. Conversely, the price of BTC decreases as there is more BTC in the pool. The pool remains in a constant balance, while the total value of ETH in the pool will always be equal to the total value of BTC in the pool. Only when new liquidity providers join them will the pool size increase. Visually, the token prices in the AMM pool follow the curve defined by this formula. dAMM is a scaled analog of AMM developed by StarkEx, see Fig. 1, with an off-chain operator processing transactions on L2, which is the only person trading under the AMM contract on L2 on L1. It simulates the logic of the contract and offers trading quotes based on the state of AMM at the beginning of the batch and subsequent L2 transactions included in the batch. At the end of the package, the Operator calculates all transactions by performing the net difference under the L2-based AMM contract. The operator must simulate the logic of the contract and apply it to the correct state of the accounts to ensure that the L1 contract can act as a counterparty to L2 transactions.

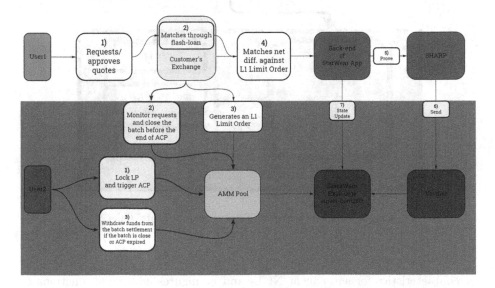

Fig. 1. AMM scheme for StarkEx ZK rollup. On blue background part that happens on Etherium main net, actions on taken by StarkEx apps. (Color figure online)

3   NFT Structure

Currently, many non-fungible tokens operate on the ERC-1155 and ERC721 Ethereum blockchain standards. In this article, we will mostly discuss the

Ethereum approach to NFTs. Yet most of the issues and solutions are similar across various blockchain networks. Thus recommendations of this article are broadly applicable. Services for demonstration, exchange, and creation of new NFT tokens are formed around the interfaces defined in these standards. The interface here implies a smart contract with a predefined minimum set of functions that are necessary for the correct operation of third-party applications, such as exchanges and crypto-wallets, see Fig. 2. The universal algorithm for creating an NFT looks like this:

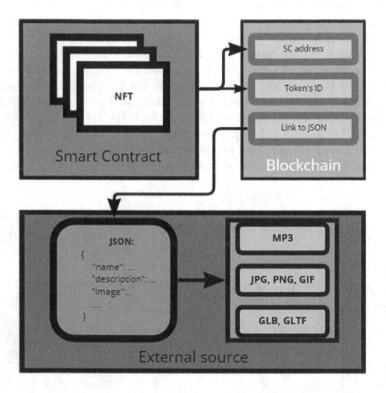

Fig. 2. Architecture of NFT token components' links

1. Creating a smart contract in which the project founder sets a set of basic characteristics for subsequent NFTs and configures additional functions to the basic template.
2. Minting is the process of creating a unique token.
3. Trading – token exchange between users.

Whenever an NFT is created or sold it is required to send a new transaction in the form of a request to the corresponding smart contract. After the transaction is confirmed, ownership information is added to the blockchain, thereby ensuring that the history of the NFT will remain unchanged and ownership will be preserved.

4   NFT Architecture Review

4.1   JSON Files

The problem of creating a universal NFT is to construct universal JSON files that will be supported by the main decentralized applications of any blockchain, see Fig. 3.

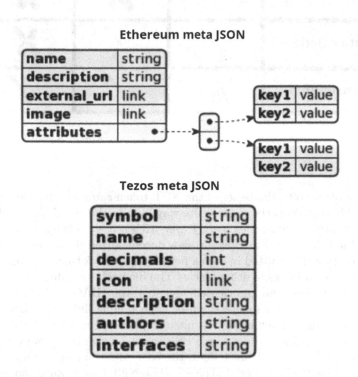

Fig. 3. Metadata format in different blockchains

4.2   Storage of Meta-Information and Media Data Options

The distributed registry itself contains the identifiers of unique tokens created by smart contracts and their owners. All characteristics of objects identified by tokens are stored as JSON files on third-party resources. In addition, each such JSON file contains links to media files that characterize the object "encoded" by tokens.

Currently, there are three different ways of storing characterizing information (JSON and media files) (Fig. 4):

	Personal Server	IPFS	Blockchain
Data changing	✓	✗	✗
Data deletion	✓	✓	✗
Distribution	✗	✓	✓

Fig. 4. Information storage methods (green - better, red - worse) (Color figure online)

1. Personal file server - the issuer of the NFT token can store files on its HTTP server. This option is the least secure way, due to the possibility of changing or deleting the relevant files by any user with access to the server.
2. IPFS (Interplanetary File System) is a decentralized data storage network. A unit of data transmitted in such a network is a block that can contain both parts of a file and links to other blocks. The file itself (or a directory of several files) is assembled from an oriented acyclic graph (DAG), which is based on certain blocks. IPFS provides the user with unique links containing a hash of data, making it much more difficult to replace them. The NFT containing links to meta and media data in IPFS cannot be changed, however, if there are no nodes left storing block data, the user will also receive an error when trying to view the contents of his NFT. The NFT issuer can manage its own IPS node, ensuring the availability of exactly those files that are associated with the NFT tokens issued by it. At the same time, the user is guaranteed that the content of meta and media files will not change.
3. File storage blockchain is a decentralized network that stores fragments from several old files when each new file appears. This approach is more reliable than IPFS, thanks to the consensus algorithms [5] and the replication of data from the past: data stored in a distributed registry cannot be deleted or replaced. However, storing large files in such systems can be very expensive. Currently, blockchains optimized for storing large files, such as Arweave, are emerging, but they are just beginning to gain popularity and are supported by fewer crypto wallets. If the number of users of these newly emerging blockchains for storing files is greatly reduced, data loss is inevitable, which the NFT issuer will not be able to control.

It is important to note that links to metadata and media files are carried out over HTTPS, which means that the files receive a domain name as part of the links. This means that when the domain is blocked, access to metadata is no longer available.

4.3   Options for Interacting with NFT Content

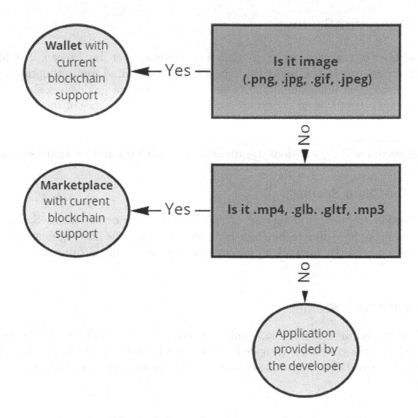

Fig. 5. Information storage methods

As it was shown on Fig. 5, the main components of NFT are records in the blockchain, meta-information, and media data, i.e., the ownership of NFT is fixed in the blockchain, but in a form unsuitable for viewing by the user. Therefore, despite the variety of metadata storage options, the unique token number will be displayed the same in all NFT-compatible crypto wallets of the user. However, it is worth noting that the methods of managing and viewing the token will be different in each case.

NFT digital creativity, such as visual files, music files, and 3D files, the user can view and manage using NFT-compatible crypto wallets supporting the corresponding blockchain or on specialized NFT markets. However, for example, Metamask will allow the user to view only two-dimensional images, while OpenSea will correctly display three-dimensional and audio files in addition to images. Thus, differences in presentation systems and the lack of consistent, open storage rules lead to inadequate support for data stored in NFT.

5 Ethereum Scaling

The number of transactions of the Ethereum network per day exceeds 1 million [10]. However, due to this popularity, the demand for limited computing resources of the network is increasing. The increase in the cost of gas causes significant transaction costs for users. In order to increase the performance of the Ethereum network without compromising security and decentralization, it was decided to scale Ethereum.

Ethereum scaling solutions are divided into on-chain and off-chain scaling.

5.1 On-Chain Scaling

This option implies modification of the main Ethereum network. Scaling is achieved using Sharding technology. It divides transactions into segments, allowing each node of the network to process not the entire block, but only its components.

5.2 Off-Chain Scaling

This option implies the development of a separate solution from the Mainnet. Security in such systems is provided either directly from the Ethereum Mainnet consensus algorithms (Optimistic Rollups, zkRollups), or independently (sidechains, plasma).

Optimistic Rollups. The main idea of the solution is that by default transactions on L2 are considered legitimate. Calculations will be made only in case of suspected fraud.

Zero Knowledge Rollups. Such a solution combines off-chain transactions and generates a specialized cryptographic proof with zero-disclosure SNARK. It allows the proving party to confirm the truth of the possession of information, without the need to disclose it.

Plasma. This solution is a separate blockchain tied to the main network. It allows you to create chains within the main networks, thereby ensuring scalability. The main Ethereum network is connected to the subsidiary "root contracts", which are Ethereum smart contracts, which contain the basic rules for managing each subsidiary chain.

Side-Chains. This solution is an independent blockchain. It is functionally compatible with the Mainnet Ethereum, that is, it allows assets to move between networks. As soon as the assets are in another blockchain, they are frozen in the original one.

6   Main Technological Issues We See in NFT Technology

We have tested several networks providing NFT minting capabilities and have detected the following disadvantages:

1. slow processing of operations,
2. high gas cost,
3. blockchain compatibility,
4. unavailability of NFT data.

6.1   Slow Processing of Operations

Since operations related to NFT are processed by sending transactions through smart contracts and are validated through a single blockchain network for all users, the confirmation time of operations is extremely slow. This problem is solved by scaling the Ethereum network using extensions (for example, L2 and Rollups). Such a solution will greatly increase the complexity of application development and the difficulty of logging in for users.

For comparison, we conducted an analysis in the official testnets of the Ethereum and Tezos blockchain, as well as on scalable Ethereum using ZKSync.

The speed of NFT generation on various blockchain test networks can be found on Fig. 6.

It can be noted that the time for generating tokens in the scaled Ethereum network significantly exceeds the time in conventional test networks. This is because initially the token is generated on L2, however, to perform operations on it, it is necessary to wait for generation, which takes a considerable time. Similarly with the output to L1 - despite the fast speed of operation, confirmation of the operation takes a long time. Speed of creating and displaying NFT in ZkSync testnet for 1 token can be found in Appendix C.

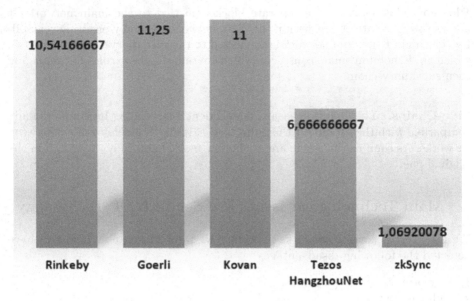

Fig. 6. Proportional minting time difference between 10 and 100 NFT tokens on different blockchain platforms (Testnets)

6.2 High Gas Cost

Each NFT-related transaction is more expensive than a simple transfer transaction because smart contracts require computing resources and storage to process. To avoid paying gas, you can use alternative platforms for creating tokens, such as Open Sea, or by switching to a less popular blockchain, such as BNB Smart Chain, Polygon, Solana, and others. We compared some of them, on Fig. 7.

6.3 Blockchain Compatibility

Existing blockchain systems are isolated from each other, i.e. by purchasing a picture on the Ethereum network and deciding to reduce the gas fee, it will be hard to transfer your picture to another blockchain. The inability to transfer your gaming equipment between two identical games based on different blockchains is also a significant obstacle to the introduction of the NFT ecosystem into crypto games [6]. However, many NFT-related projects use Ethereum as the base platform due to its liquidity capacity. Another solution that is gaining popularity is cross-chain bridges that transfer user assets between wallets of different blockchains shown on Fig. 8.

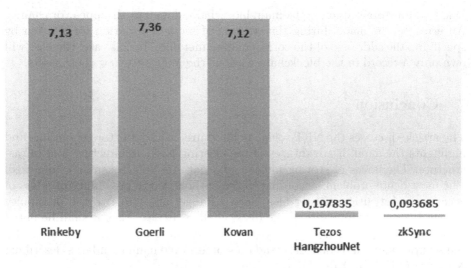

Fig. 7. Price of minting on testnets in USD

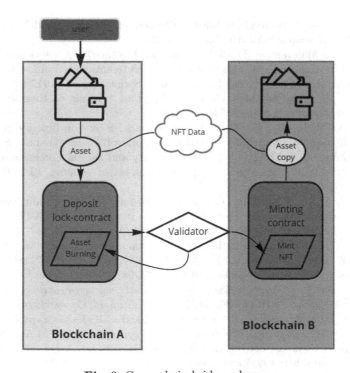

Fig. 8. Cross-chain bridge scheme.

6.4   Unavailability of NFT Data

Due to data storage outside the main blockchain, data may disappear or change. An error can be made during the creation of meta-information for a token by specifying the addresses of the corresponding metafiles. In this case, the user will own only a record in the blockchain without the ability to view their assets.

7   Conclusion

The article discusses the NFT token architecture, metadata storage options and highlights the main disadvantages of the existing NFT architecture and infrastructure. The issues of storing multi-media data of NFT tokens are analyzed. The most acute problem, according to the authors, is the possibility of a loss of access or substitution of user files. Such a danger arises due to the possibility of media files stored outside of the distributed registries. Also, it shall be noted that there is a persistent lack of requirements, rules, and guidelines to ensure the security and uniformity of metadata stored in the main standards describing NFT (ERC-721 and ERC-1155).

References

1. Chohan, U.W.: Non-Fungible Tokens: Blockchains, Scarcity, and Value. Critical Blockchain Research Initiative, Sidney (2021)
2. Shurov, A., Malevanniy, D., Iakushkin, O., Korkhov, V.: Blockchain network threats: the case of PoW and ethereum. In: International Conference on Computational Science and Its Applications 2019, Sydney, pp. 606–617 (2019)
3. Mieszko, M.: Non-Fungible Tokens (NFT). The Analysis of Risk and Return. ESSCA school of management, Paris (2021)
4. Akash, A., Shailender, K.: Smart contracts and NFTs: non-fungible tokens as a core component of blockchain to be used as collectibles. In: Khanna, K., Estrela, V.V., Rodrigues, J.J.P.C. (eds.) Cyber Security and Digital Forensics. LNDECT, vol. 73, pp. 401–422. Springer, Singapore (2021). https://doi.org/10.1007/978-981-16-3961-6_34
5. Rehmani, M.H.: Blockchain consensus algorithms. In: Blockchain Systems and Communication Networks: From Concepts to Implementation. TTE, pp. 61–78. Springer, Cham (2021). https://doi.org/10.1007/978-3-030-71788-9_4
6. Chen, J.-T.: Blockchain and the feature of game development. In: Hung, J.C., Yen, N.Y., Chang, J.-W. (eds.) FC 2019. LNEE, vol. 551, pp. 1797–1802. Springer, Singapore (2020). https://doi.org/10.1007/978-981-15-3250-4_239
7. Patent   NIKE   CryptoKickss.   https://patft.uspto.gov/netacgi/nph-Parser? Sect1=PTO2&Sect2=HITOFF&p=1&u=/netahtml/PTO/search-bool. html&r=1&f=G&l=50&col=AND&d=PTXT&s1=Nike&s2=Crypto& OS=Nike+AND+Crypto&RS=Nike+AND+Crypto. Accessed 26 Apr 2022
8. Unstoppable domains. https://unstoppabledomains.com/. Accessed 26 Apr 2022
9. Yinsure.finance. https://yinsure.finance/. Accessed 26 Apr 2022
10. Ethereum Daily Transactions Chart. https://etherscan.io/chart/tx. Accessed 26 Apr 2022

Building an Example of the DeFi Presale Cross-chain Application

Rita Tsepeleva and Vladimir Korkhov(✉)

Saint Petersburg State University, St. Petersburg, Russia
st062153@student.spbu.ru, v.korkhov@spbu.ru

Abstract. Decentralized finance (DeFi) is now a massive aggregator of many financial blockchain protocols. The overall value locked in them is currently valued at around 80 billion USD. Every day, a growing number of new users bring their investments to DeFi. Decentralized finance entails the creation of a single ecosystem of many blockchains that interact with one another. To enable DeFi, the problem of combining and interacting blockchains becomes critical. In this paper we describe the concept of a DeFi protocol, which employs cross-blockchain interface technologies, and show how a prototype pre-sale application based on the proposed concept can be created.

Keywords: Blockchain · Distributed ledger technologies · Solidity · Smart-contracts · Decentralized finances · Cross-chain

1 Introduction

Blockchain is a promising data storing technology that is still in its infancy. Unlike a traditional backend, this system may provide complete transaction transparency to its users. This means that every user is able to witness every action that takes place within a certain protocol. Furthermore, unlike a traditional backend, the blockchain distributes data storage. It prevents data loss and corruption in the event of a node failure. Furthermore, each user's data is completely secure on the blockchain which is especially important for financial data, mainly cryptocurrencies. All of these benefits make blockchain a reliable technology. Users are no longer frightened to invest in various blockchain systems thanks to them.

Consequently, we now have a massive collection of protocols, each of which is part of a larger ecosystem. The question is how to find a space for your own idea in all of these projects and how to make your crypto-product a huge success. In this paper, we'll look at a DeFi protocol that can be used as a launchpad, providing users a platform to place their own-developed tokens for presale. To expand the project's user base, we propose creating a multichain platform with a cross-chain interacting protocol rather than limiting ourselves to one blockchain network; this issue was considered in our previous work [1].

O. Gervasi et al. (Eds.): ICCSA 2022 Workshops, LNCS 13377, pp. 229–241, 2022.
https://doi.org/10.1007/978-3-031-10536-4_16

2   Related Work

The issue of integrating and interacting blockchains is a hot topic right now. The article [2] explains the fundamentals of cross-chain transactions and divides existing research into three categories: public connectors, blockchains of blockchains, and hybrid connectors. Based on established criteria, each category is further broken into sub-categories. The authors show that cross-blockchain transactions are impossible to carry out in practice without the involvement of a trusted third party. They offer the Blockchain Interoperability Methodology (BIF), a framework for evaluating blockchain interoperability solutions that defines criteria. The authors focus on the cross-chain communication protocol (CCCP), which describes how a pair of homogenous blockchains interact to appropriately synchronize cross-chain transactions.

The cross-chain transaction processing based on version control is proposed by W. Wang et al. [3]. In contrast to conventional locking-based cross-chain transaction systems, the authors suggest optimistic approaches in which modified data can be used instantly with a rolling back procedure that ensures atomicity.

The article [4] provides a variety of solutions and approaches for dealing with this issue. The authors provide a theoretical cross-communication model and compare it to the so-called mother blockchain model in order to handle cross communication across blockchain-based systems without the use of an intermediate.

Li et al. suggest a blockchain architecture to suit industrial norms that frequently require interoperability in their paper [5]. To increase the system's scalability, they introduce the concept of satellite chains, which can privately run several consensus algorithms in parallel. This approach also includes a regulator that oversees the entire network and uses smart contracts to enforce certain policies. Hyperledger Fabric is used in the prototype implementation.

H. Wang et al. present a blockchain router that allows blockchains to communicate and link [6]. To enable different blockchains in the network to communicate with each other in a similar way to the Internet, a special economic model is established. One of the blockchains in the system acts as a router, analyzing and transmitting communication requests while dynamically preserving the blockchain network's topology structure according to the communication protocol.

Zamyatin et al. present a systematic overview of cross-chain communication protocols and formalize the research topic to demonstrate that cross-chain communication is impossible without the assistance of a trusted third party [7]. The authors create a methodology for developing new CCC protocols and evaluating existing ones, focusing on the inherent trust assumptions. A centralized or decentralized trusted third party is possible. The Hyperledger Cactus proposes trustworthy validatorscitemontgomery as an example of centralized trusted parties. Another blockchain can serve as a decentralized trusted party, with members agreeing on the global ledger state via a consensus process.

The Cosmos [8] project is a fast growing ecosystem of interconnected, autonomous blockchains constructed with specific application components (the Cosmos SDK) and connected via the Inter-Blockchain Communication (IBC) protocol. The Tendermint Byzantine Fault Tolerance (BFT) consensus method [9], which ensures finality, order consistency, and optional availability, is at the heart of Cosmos. The shared Cosmos Hub, which is powered by the Tendermint consensus and keeps track of the number of tokens in each connected chain and manages transfers between them, allows for interoperability. The transport layer (TAO), which provides the infrastructure for establishing secure connections and authenticating data packets between chains, and the application layer, which specifies how these data packets should be packaged and interpreted by the sending and receiving chains, are the two layers that make up IBC. The IBC application layer can be used to build a wide range of cross-chain applications, including token transfers, interchain accounts (delegate calls between two chains), non-fungible token transfers and oracle data feeds [10].

3   The Launchpad Application

A presale app is one of the most popular sorts of DeFi apps nowadays. A launchpad platform is another name for this type. The essence of this project type is to provide a platform on which users can pre-sell their own tokens.

There are reasons why such platforms are so popular:

– The advantage for investment users is that a large number of various assets are gathered in one place.
– The platform community is an advantage for token creators. Token holders are no longer required to find their own audience.
– Additionally, token owners are relieved of the necessity to complete numerous complex transactions on their own (token sale transfers, liquidity allocation, etc.)
– The benefit to future token holders is transparency and confidence. Each investor can view the public price of the token, the percentage of tokens guaranteed to go to the liquidity pool, the period of liquidity lock (the creator has no capacity to withdraw liquidity and collapse the liquidity pool), and other information by opening the contract code.
– The ability to collect fees from customers for various sorts of services is a benefit for the platform owner.

Problem to Solve
A platform of this type can be built within a single blockchain. However, the number of supported assets and users will be limited to the network chosen. The target platform is capable of combining assets from various blockchains. The more blockchains the platform owner adds, the more likely the platform's success and earnings will be.

However, keep in mind that when developing such a platform, you must consider the architecture, scalability, security, performance, and other important factors.

3.1   The Components of the Presale Platform

First and foremost, it is critical to distinguish platform users from other cryptocurrency wallet owners. It will assist the platform's owners in protecting their community and users from malicious spam and other information. For example, preventing the publication of a "bad" token for sale, which may be unsecure or cost nothing.

It is proposed to create the platform's own token and introduce a staking smart contract into the system to differentiate platform users from the rest of the network participants. Staking is a generic term for one type of decentralized financial protocol. In general, it works by users sending a certain amount of assets to a smart contract in order to increase them (to get rewards for it). It functions similarly to a bank deposit.

All of these protocols differ in their reward accrual systems for deposits. There are numerous staking protocols, ranging from simple annual interest rates (APR, APY) to a "share" system (in which the smart contract calculates each participant's share of the total deposit and awards him a reward based on the calculated share).

As a result, users will invest the created platform token in the staking protocol in order to participate in all of the other events and receive even more platform tokens. It validates users' intentions toward the platform and encourages them to behave appropriately in the platform community.

On the platform, a ranking system will be created. The more money a user deposits, the higher his rank will be. A high rank indicates that a specific user has some advantages (guaranteed token allocation, a high pool weight, an ability to buy tokens earlier than the other participants, etc.). A system like this will encourage users to invest and participate in presales more and more. Users will also receive rewards for their deposits, allowing their rank to rise in the future. All of these logic details can boost the platform's profit.

After making a minimum deposit and becoming a full-rights member of the platform, the user gains the ability to create presales and participate in existing presales.

If the user owns a new token and wishes to conduct an IDO, he can fill out the form and create a presale contract. What kind of information does the creator provide as a result of completing the form?

- the token contract's address
- amount of tokens for the presale
- the price per one token

That is one of the most important factors to consider when starting a sale. A soft-cap and a hard-cap are also important parameters. These parameters denote a soft-minimum and a hard-maximum of funds raised. So, a soft-cap border is the presale's minimum goal, and a hard-cap border is the maximum amount of funds raised (the presale creator can not earn more funds than the hard-cap value). For instance, suppose the creator decides to sell one million tokens. The cost of one token is 0.0001ETH. As a result, the maximum amount raised will be 1.000.000

* 0.0001ETH = 100ETH (a hard-cap). A soft-cap value should be less than or equal to the hard-cap value. This position is provided by the presale's creator and reflects the success of the presale campaign. If no funds in the amount of a soft-cap or more were collected during the sale process, the presale is usually deemed a failure. As a result, the soft cap is known as the minimum boundary. In this case, it is critical to maintain the integrity and transparency of the contract logic: users must be able to withdraw their investments if the outcome is unsuccessful, and token owners must be able to return all of their tokens.

DEX parameters are also required for carrying out an IDO-process. We will conduct a small educational program to avoid incomprehensible locations. The initial placement of liquidity on the exchange is implied by the IDO process. It means that the owner of a newly created token has decided to begin selling his token. The owner should select a decentralized exchange, which serves as a platform for token sales. In the crypto-community, there are numerous such platforms. There are platforms that are very similar to one another, which allows developers to easily interact with them all. However, there are platforms that are ideologically opposed. It's intriguing, but for a basic understanding, only the standard approach will suffice.

3.2   The Principle of Operation of a Decentralized Exchange (DEX)

To begin, we will only consider two assets: token-1 and token-2. Assume that user-1 is the creator of token-1. He wishes to begin selling token-1. Standard exchanges work on the basis of pools and reserves. The price between pool assets is defined by the reserves (or, more precisely, the reserve ratio) of the current liquidity pool. So, in order to begin selling token-1, user-1 must first create a pool on DEX with such token and some other asset. For example, user-1 is the owner of token-2. As a result, user-1 can create a pool using tokens 1 and 2. Assume that user-1 decides to provide x token-1 and y token-2 (token-1 reserve of liquidity pool equals x, token-2 reserve of liquidity pool equals y. As a result, in order to purchase one token-1 from this pool, the buyer must pay y/x token-2.

However, what happens to the liquidity pool in an exchange transaction? At the start, we have x amount of token-1 and y amount of token-2. Assume we want to purchase 1 token-1. As previously discussed, we should provide y/x token-2. And how will the reserves change? Because we only purchased one token, the reserve of token-1 will become $x-1$ and the reserve of token-2 will become $y+y/x$ (because we have provided such payment amount according to the price). It is easy to see that the reserve ratio has shifted. This implies that the price has shifted as well. The token-1 is now more expensive than before, with the price per token-1 equaling $(x(y+1)+y)/x2$. That is a significant disadvantage of such a system. Everything is dependent on the willingness of both sellers and buyers. It is assumed that demand will fluctuate around the initial price from time to time, but no one is immune from a critical situation in which one of the reserves runs out and the second becomes worthless.

But what are the benefits of using such platforms? Previously, order books were used to exchange one cryptocurrency for another. The principle of order book operation is the creation of an order for the sale or purchase of a specific amount of an asset. When someone finds your offer appealing, he accepts it and the transaction is completed. However, it should be noted that such a person had to be waited for a very long time. Furthermore, there may not be anyone who would agree to the deal at all. In this instance, your offer has "burned out." Thus, the main advantage of decentralized exchanges is that they allow for quick transactions. Users can bring one asset and exchange it for another at any time. Furthermore, if there is no pool on the exchange with the two assets you are interested in, but there are other pools with these assets, the exchange will still find a way to exchange the tokens you are interested in. For example, user-2 owns token-3 and wishes to purchase token-2. However, there is no token-2 – token-3 pool on the DEX. However, token-1 – token-2, and token-1 – token-3 exist. As a result, the DEX will exchange token-3 for token-1 (based on the price in the 1–3 pool), and then token-1 for token-2 (according the 1–2 pool price). Token-1 serves as a connecting link in this case. Such chains can be much longer, but they all work on the same principle as described above.

These are not the only benefits of decentralized exchanges. After all, we were able to consider only the user's perspective, but we have not yet seen everything from the liquidity provider's perspective. What is the advantage of a user investing his funds in a liquidity pool? Decentralized exchanges are designed in such a way that a commission is naturally charged for each exchange transaction (otherwise, why create such a platform?) This fee is shared by all liquidity providers whose funds are currently in the pool. Furthermore, the commission is proportional to the pool's ownership share. So, simply by owning two crypto-assets, you can profit from them by investing in a liquidity pool.

At this point, we will conclude a brief overview of the work of decentralized exchanges, as we have already determined how useful it is and why people use it. Returning to the question of what parameters are required to carry out the IDO process on the launchpad.

DEX parameters fields include:

- the current DEX-platform that will be used in the liquidity allocation process;
- the listing price - from this price, token sales on the exchange will begin in the future;
- liquidity percentage allocation - the percentage of earned funds that will go to the liquidity pool in the specified ratio. For example, the presale raised funds equivalent to 0.01ETH. The creator of this presale specified a percentage value of 30% and a listing price of 0,0008ETH per token. This means that we should subtract 30% from 0.01ETH (resulting in 0.03ETH going to the liquidity pool) and divide the result by the price (0,03ETH/0,0008ETH = 37,5 tokens going to the liquidity pool). This enables the token owner to conduct the initial placement of his token on the exchange automatically by specifying only a few parameters;
- liquidity lock duration - the period of time for which the provided liquidity is "frozen." This procedure protects token buyers from falling prices (the token

owner cannot withdraw liquidity from the pool and collapse the price during this time period);
- liquidity allocation time - the timestamp after which the function of adding liquidity becomes available;

Rather than researching the entire issue and conducting a large number of transactions, the token owner can simply enter these 5 values and the launchpad platform will handle the rest.

The vesting parameters are another interesting set of parameters. The vesting process enables the presale creator to send tokens to buyers in equal parts over time. As a result, the vesting parameters are as follows:

- the percentage of purchased tokens that is available immediately after the completion of sales;
- the percentage of tokens that will be released gradually during the vesting process;
- vesting period – the period of time, each time after which the percentage of tokens is released;

Consider the following example of a simple mechanism: Assume user-1 invested 0.01ETH in token-1 during the presale period (propose that the price equals 0,0005ETH per one token). It means that user-1 should take 20 tokens. However, the creator determines the vesting percentages (suppose 20 percent the first one and 15 percent the second one). As a result, user-1 has the right to take 20 * 20% = 4 tokens at once, and the remaining 16 tokens during the vesting process. If the vesting period is one month, then user-1 will receive his funds for six months (for five months user-1 will take 3 tokens per month, and for the sixth he will receive the remaining one token from the entire amount allotted to him). Such a token release system will assist the creator in smoothly distributing the asset in order to avoid rash transactions by token holders.

3.3   The Crosschain-Part of the Application

As previously stated, it is necessary to enable interaction with various blockchains on the platform in order to increase the number of potential users and investments in the project. Everyone understands that each blockchain network is an autonomous, independent unit that has no idea how to communicate with other blockchain networks. We will use the method described in the article to make this possible on our platform [1].

But where will the cross-chain methods be used in the application? Remember that in order to participate in presales and create your own, you must first make a deposit of project tokens on the staking smart contract. This deposit confirms that you are a full platform member. To make it easier to track platform users, it is suggested that staking contracts be published only on the most popular blockchain networks. These are an Ethereum blockchain [11] and the Binance Smart Chain [12].

We use a cross-chain backend and a signature system to transfer data on the size of user deposits from these networks to other networks to the platform contracts. The signature system implies that the backend role is added to the contract (the smart contract remembers an address of our backend), which will transmit valid information received from outside to the contract (in our case from another network). The backend encrypts this information, formats it so that the contract can recognize it, and signs it with its private key. In turn, when the contract receives a message, it can determine whether the backend truly owns the private key used to sign the message. The message is accepted if the answer is correct. However, if the answer is incorrect, the transaction fails.

The most important piece of information in our staking contract to compile signatures is the deposit size of a specific user. Second, the user's wallet address associated with this deposit. We must require that the information be up to date in addition to the address and the amount of tokens deposited to the contract. As a result, the third parameter will be the time the data was read by the backend. An example is shown in Fig. 1.

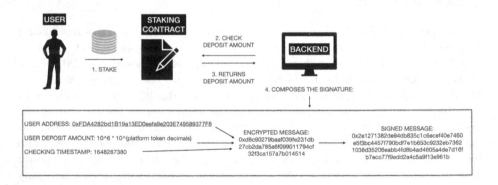

Fig. 1. Signature composing.

The figure depicts how the backend generates the signature. First, the backend receives a request from the frontend to create it, which provides it with the user's address. For this user, the backend polls the staking contract and receives the amount of his deposit at the time, as well as a timestamp of when he received this data. The three parameters are then combined into a single hash, which is used to sign the backend with its private key.

A system like this was developed to provide valid data received from outside (in our case, from another blockchain network) to smart contracts. The contract is assumed to receive the same three parameters and the final signature for the transaction input. The contract then hashes the parameters in the same way, receives a hash message, and sends the message and signature to the recover-function. The output of this function is the public address of the account that signed this message. Because the contract remembers all public addresses that can provide valid information to the contract, it will be easy for the contract to compare the received address from the recover-function with all available ones and determine whether this information is truly from a reliable source. This type of operation allows users to prevent the contract from processing incorrect data from the outside.

3.4 Project Architecture

The architecture of the project is shown in Fig. 2.

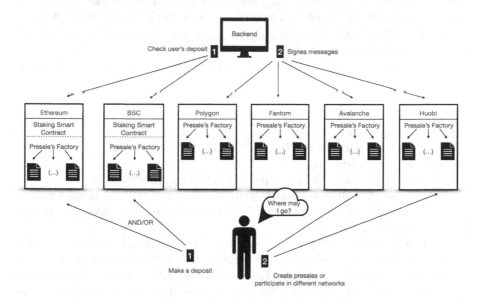

Fig. 2. Project architecture.

The following is provided in different networks:

- Staking smart contracts only available on the Ethereum and Binance Smart Chain networks. Contracts accept user deposits and send corresponding messages to the backend;
- Presale factories - smart contracts that receive messages from the backend and deploy presale contracts with the parameters listed in Sect. 3.1;
- The backend that checks information in the Ethereum and Binance Smart Chain networks and sends messages to other networks.

The backend sends messages to the "main networks" as well. The backend extends its actions to absolutely all networks of the project. Likewise, the user can connect to any network. The most important thing is to make a small deposit in one (or both) of the major networks.

3.5 The Presale's Lifecycle

Further in this section we will go through the entire presale lifecycle to better understand each step of the user on the platform:

- The user must own the platform token (for example, the token can be purchased on a DEX) and approve a staking contract on the Ethereum/BSC blockchain to use his tokens;
- To be able to create presales and participate in others, the user should submit a minimum deposit to the staking contract on the major blockchains.
- If the user wishes to build own presale, he need do the following steps:
  - fill the form with all general necessary presale's parameters:
    1. the presale token address
    2. a hardcap and a softcap (max/min boundaries for the earning funds process)
    3. an open timestamp and a close timestamp (time boundaries for the earning funds process)
    4. a token price
  - fill the form with all DEX presale's parameters:
    1. the DEX address
    2. a listing price (the price per one token on current DEX)
    3. a liquidity allocation timestamp (the time after which adding liquidity function will be available; it is necessary to be lower than close presale timestamp)
    4. a liquidity percentage allocation (a percent from raised funds that will be allocated on current DEX in pair with presale token)
  - make an approve to presales factory contract (allows smart-contract send current amount of user's tokens). The amount of approved tokens is calculated according to the following formula:

$$\frac{hardcap}{price_t} + \frac{hardcap * \frac{listing\_percent}{100}}{price_l},$$

  where $price_t$ is a token price, and $price_l$ is a listing price
  - sign a transaction with these parameters for creating own presale contract;
  - waiting for investment's time passed;
  - Sign a transaction with a function that will provide liquidity to the exchange in the previously defined proportion if the investment procedure ends with "Success" (presale did not collect a soft cap payment amount);
  - If the investment process finishes with a "Fail" (presale did not collect a soft cap payment amount), sign a transaction with a function that returns presale-tokens (it is required to consider multiple scenarios of investment stage completion). In a worst-case scenario, the creator must return the tokens, and investors must return their funds;

- When the investment collection status is "Success" and liquidity is added to the DEX, the presale creator opens the option to withdraw earned cash, and investors open vesting (investors can take the acquired tokens in portions, according to the conditions provided by the campaign creator);
- among other things, when adding liquidity, as mentioned earlier, liquidity is blocked on the presale contract for the period specified by the creator. When this deadline is reached, the owner can take this liquidity back;

- if the user wants to participate in a presale-campaign, he should follow these steps:
  - Select a current presale contract to investigate the price per token and the amount of payment tokens already earned;
  - Decide on the investment amount and the value of the token you will receive at the end;
  - If these values appeal to the user, he can sign an investment transaction (but first, send an approve transaction to authorize the presale contract to receive your payment tokens);
  - As a result, you can make many investment transactions until the presale campaign ends or the hardcap is reached;
  - Vesting begins when the investing process is completed: Every investor can claim tokens only once during each vesting period, and the number of tokens claimed equals the total amount of his investment multiplied by the price and multiplied by the vesting percentage;
  - if the presale status is "Fail" after the presale campaign ends, every investor can withdraw his investments, and vesting does not open in this situation;

User action strategies may differ from each other. Only the main stages of user activity are presented above.

3.6   Analysis of the Results Obtained

Comparing the resulting solution with similar projects

	Our solution	Starter	PinkSale
Verified contracts (security)	Yes	No	No
Crosschain	Yes	No	No
Different strategies	Yes	Yes	Yes
Scalability	Yes	Yes	Yes
Fees	10% from investment	Not found	1BNB/0.2ETH

For greater clarity, Fig. 3 shows histograms that display quantitative estimates of the performance of the compared services.

According to the histograms it is clear that our solution meets the security requirements, and also has prospects for development when adding new blockchains, such as, for example, Tron, HuobiChain, PulseChain, Waves, and adding new DEXes in different networks.

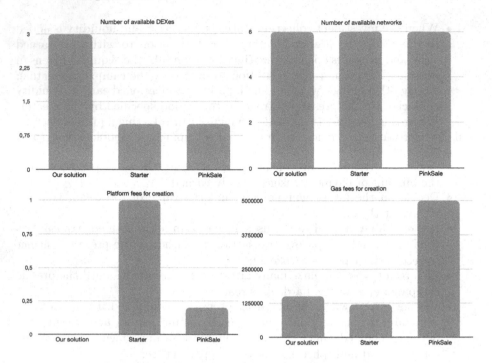

Fig. 3. Comparison of our solution with another ones.

4   Conclusions

Transferring tokens or any other information from one blockchain network to another was impossible just a few years ago. However, we have demonstrated through our experience that it is possible and necessary to develop useful and absolutely secure solutions in this area in order to give users with as much freedom as possible and eliminate all possible barriers to the adoption of blockchain technology.

We've constructed one of the most popular types of decentralized applications, the launchpad, based on the cross-chain asset transfer protocol that we proposed earlier. We've demonstrated that such apps may be scalable, simple to use, and, most significantly, not limited to a single network. DApps with these features will be able to get a lot more out of their blockchain platforms.

References

1. Tsepeleva, R., Korkhov, V.: Implementation of the cross-blockchain interacting protocol. In: Gervasi, O., et al. (eds.) ICCSA 2021. LNCS, vol. 12952, pp. 42–55. Springer, Cham (2021). https://doi.org/10.1007/978-3-030-86973-1_4
2. Belchior, R., Vasconcelos, A., Guerreiro, S., Correia, M.: A survey on blockchain interoperability: past, present, and future trends. ACM Comput. Surv. **54**(8) (2022). https://doi.org/10.1145/3471140. Article no. 168

3. Wang, W., Zhang, Z., Wang, G., Yuan, Y.: Efficient cross-chain transaction processing on blockchains. Appl. Sci. **12**(9), 4434 (2022). https://doi.org/10.3390/app12094434
4. Pillai, B., Biswas, K., Muthukkumarasamy, V.: Cross-chain interoperability among blockchain-based systems using transactions. Knowl. Eng. Rev. (2020). https://doi.org/10.1017/S0269888920000314. Article no. e23
5. Li, W., Sforzin, A., Fedorov, S., Karame, G.O.: Towards scalable and private industrial blockchains. In: Proceedings of the ACM Workshop on Blockchain, Cryptocurrencies and Contracts, April 2017, pp. 9–14 (2017). https://doi.org/10.1145/3055518.3055531
6. Wang, H., Cen, Y., Li, X.: Blockchain router: a cross-chain communication protocol. In: Proceedings of the 6th International Conference on Informatics, Environment, Energy and Applications (2017)
7. Zamyatin, A., et al.: SoK: communication across distributed ledgers. Technical report (2019). https://eprint.iacr.org/2019/1128.pdf
8. Cosmos. https://cosmos.network
9. Kwon, J.: Draft v. fall. Tendermint: Consensus without mining (2014). https://tendermint.com/static/docs/tendermint.pdf
10. IBC Protocol. https://ibcprotocol.org/
11. Ethereum [Electronic resource]. https://ethereum.org
12. Binance Chain Documentation [Electronic resource]. https://docs.binance.org

Decomposition, Depositing and Committing of Digital Footprint of Complex Composite Objects

Viktor Uglev$^{(\boxtimes)}$ and Kirill Zakharin

Siberian Federal University, Krasnoyarsk, Russia
vauglev@sfu-kras.ru

Abstract. The article presents the issue of describing complex composite objects of intellectual activity (OIA), which are placed and maintained in information systems using distributed ledger technology (blockchain). The essence of fragmentation is described, a classification of the stages of maturity of deposited OIAs and their structural configurations is introduced. An approach to decomposition and internal markup of composite objects is described. Examples of depositing such objects on the IPUniversity platform (a composite OIA markup module) are given, as well as recommendations on organizing the work of registries operating with complex objects of intellectual activity.

Keywords: Objects of intellectual activity · Composite object · Distributed ledger technology · Digital footprint · Depositing · IPUniversity platform

1 Introduction and Related Works

The implementation of scientific, educational, and industrial activities today is linked with the creation of various digital objects. Managing the processes of creating and using such objects usually involves committing data about objects in special registries, as well as monitoring their digital footprint. As a rule, such objects have a complex structure and heterogeneous composition. Heterogeneity can manifest itself through the imposition of markup on the integral image of the object, reflecting different points of view during the analysis [1,3]. This is also true for results of intellectual activity obtained by one author or a whole team. The value of such objects is determined not only by the content of the object, but also by the history of its formation, as well as the events above it. Thus, when forming the value (utility) of such an object, it is necessary to take into account both the results of intellectual activity and the volume and features of the formation of its digital footprint. It is often very important to fix, consider and use such objects not only at the technological level, but also at

A part of the reported study was supported by the Ministry of Science and of Higher Education the Russian Federation (research theme code FSRZ-2020-0011).

The original version of this chapter was revised: an error in the names of the authors. The correction to this chapter is available at
https://doi.org/10.1007/978-3-031-10536-4_47

the level of copyright management. In a number of cases, the distribution speed and the commercialization potential depend on the formation completeness of the objects of intellectual activity (OIA) digital footprint and guarantees of its fidelity [9,21]. Therefore, the commit and maintenance of complex composite objects requires a qualitative approach to organizing their structure within the framework of specialized information systems (for example, based on distributed ledger technology).

Digital objects play a special role among OIAs, because the information space in which they are formed is able to commit those changes that increase the potential value of the OIA instance for the end user. For this reason, it is interesting to look at a digital OIA in conjunction with its digital footprint as a composite entity in dynamics [20].

OIAs are subject to copyright or patent law and are effectively protected by law only when copyright priority can be proven. For these purposes, there are various patent organizations and special registries that involve carrying out the object through the deposit procedure. If this procedure is supplemented with the mechanisms of distributed registries (blockchain), it is possible to guarantee the tracking of all changes and operations on the object as well as the agreement of all parties to the terms of smart contracts as confirmed by special certificates [10].

Meanwhile, the description of objects in such registries is very standardized and it is not possible to produce a qualitative description of heterogeneity. Let us consider the characteristics of information systems operating in the Russian Federation, aimed at depositing digital OIAs, as an example: estimates are given by experts, where V is the capability realized, and $\sim$V - the capability is partially realized (see Table 1). The table shows that the digital footprint of an object of intellectual activity (OIA) and the structural heterogeneity of objects are not committed or are only partially committed. For this reason, it is important to consider the fragmentation issue not only from a conceptual and technological point of view, but also taking into account legal specifics.

An analysis of the technology of depositing and patenting in various countries and industries (for example, the works of [12,14,17,21]) showed a similar situation: composite OIAs are described and registered either as a single object, or each independently. At best, authorship is described by the CRediT [15] model, which does not involve decomposition of OIAs. If industry platforms with mechanisms based on distributed ledger technology are used to manage OIAs, then we agree with the conclusion made in the [21] study about the need for "extensive research" mechanisms for depositing and maintaining objects.

The purpose of our study is to describe an approach to formalizing the decomposition of data on complex composite objects for their commit and further maintenance in systems based on distributed ledger technology. For this, we define the essence of composite objects and introduce their maturity stages within the concept of distributed registries; present a typology of variants of structural fragmentation; briefly describe the approach to decomposition and formalization of data on composite objects; provide examples of the decomposition of composite

244 V. Uglev and K. Zakharin

Table 1. Capabilities of information systems depositing OIAs in the Russian Federation.

Deposit systems for objects of intellectual activity	Number of specifications for OIA types	Digital footprint commit	Additional files	Application of blockchain technology	External fragmentation	Internal fragmentation	Description of fragments
– Federal Institute of Industrial Property (www.fips.ru)	4	–	V	∼V	–	–	–
– Unified Depository of Intellectual Activity Results (www.edrid.ru)	5	–	–	V	–	–	–
– National Intellectual Property Registry (www.nris.ru)	5	–	V	V	V	–	V
– Russian Science Citation Index (www.elibrary.ru)	1	∼V	–	–	–	–	–
– (C)opyright.ru (www.copyright.ru)	10	–	V	–	–	–	–
– Digital Platform of Knowledge Sharing and Copyright Management (www.ipuniversity.ru)	15	V	V	V	V	∼V	V

OIAs for the IPUniversity system (https://ipuniversity.ru) [5]; give recommendations on the organization of registries that support the deposit of composite OIAs.

2 Method

2.1 Composite Object and Maturity Stages of Its Commit

According to Aristotelian logic [7], the whole and the part form a dialectical unity and demonstrate a systemic effect, which is also called emergence. Therefore, a composite (or fragmented) OIA is an entity that can be decomposed into parts without losing the integrity of its perception. Based on the methodology of the system approach [2,13], the description of the object can be carried out from various points of view. For us, within the framework of this work, the structural, semantic, authorial and external (borrowing) aspects will be of interest.

Digital objects of intellectual activity are characterized not only by the possibility of their exact copying, but also by the possibility of observing the actions that were performed on them during operations in a digital environment. These actions (operations) form a digital footprint that accompanies an OIA in the form of additional information (metadata) stored jointly or separately from the object (provided they are unambiguously correlated). These metadata appear gradually, expanding the useful amount of information about an OIA itself. Consequently, the genesis of a digital OIA should take place in a certain information environment aimed at increasing the intensity of the OIA turnover. From this position, a number of stages of the objects formation (maturity) can be distinguished:

- a zero stage (creation) - when an object has received a digital form and is not fixed within that information environment/platform (it is a file or a group of them on a data medium).
- the first stage (initialization) - when an object is entered into the system and is completed with a minimum set of identification data (as a rule, it is an identification number, affiliation with the author and date), it may have an incomplete appearance both in description and in structural elements.
- the second stage (description) - when an author commits a description (metadata) for an object that allows it to be effectively represented, searched and evaluated, and the description of its constituent elements is detailed and changes are made (editing).
- the third stage (deposit) - when a public identifier (registration number) is assigned to metadata, and the forms corresponding to the deposit procedure are committed (there may not be public access to an object), and an object itself is placed in a certain register of objects and becomes a full-fledged object of copyright.
- the fourth stage (patenting) - when a number of forms for patenting are committed and an object gets into the register of patents (there may not be public access to an object).
- the fifth stage (turnover) - when an object becomes the subject of property or non-property transactions (for example, through smart contracts), recorded in the information environment as independent events.
- the sixth stage (embedding) - when inclusion/citation events are recorded for the object, allowing to establish the facts of its use by consumers (this stage is characterized by the presence of metrics, for example, [18]).
- an additional stage (rating, "+") - when the metadata of an object is supplemented with external ratings (likes, comments, reviews, inclusion in reviews, etc.), which allows you to determine the range of potential consumers and determine consumer qualities (this stage is characterized by the assessment of altmetrics, for example, [16]).

The maturity stages stated above depend on the purpose for which the information environment is created, in which OIAs should be placed (from a simple file storage to a full-fledged industry-wide distributed registry). Some objects will stop at the first stage and immediately "acquire" operations, citations and/or external evaluations. Others will consistently reach the fourth stage and only after that will form the elements of the footprint responsible for interacting with consumers.

The connection of the formation processes of internal (author's)/external (consumer's) elements of the digital footprint by stages is presented in Fig. 1, conditionally divided into three zones - legal, descriptive and operation. All these data become inseparable from a digital OIA and are stored in the registry. Such an approach allows us to conclude that the totality of aspects, entities and processes that define a digital OIA with a heterogeneous structure needs to identify typical structures.

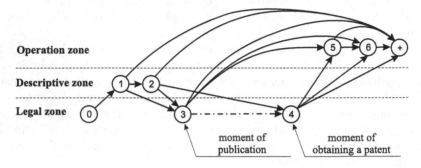

Fig. 1. Formation paths of the digital footprint elements of a composite object relative to the maturity stages.

2.2 Structures of Composite Objects

The methodology of the system engineering approach [13] suggests that the manifestation of fragmentation (decomposition) of an object must be considered from various points of view (aspects). As the basic aspects, we choose the structural, semantic, authorial and external (borrowing) aspect.

The first, and the most obvious, approach is the decomposition of the internal structure into blocks that are heterogeneous in nature. For example, for objects of a textual nature, these are blocks of text, images, tables, and formulas; for audiovisual objects, this is the separation of text/music, audio and video series. For databases - tables and data schemas. For information systems - program listings, flowcharts, and window interfaces. For log reports of automated training systems, this is the path of movements between didactic units, answers to control and measuring materials and questions of questionnaires, etc. The specificity of this type of fragmentation is that blocks can be specified explicitly, relying on the obvious isolation of each of them.

The second approach, i.e. semantic, takes semantic fragments as the basis for division, which an author decided to subjectively isolate into a separate block, for one reason or another. For example, for a text, it can be entire chapters or sections that carry semantic and logical isolation; for a piece of music - parts; for an information system - functions, etc.

The decomposition by author's contribution (the third approach) is based on the degree of each co-author's participation in the formation of one or another structural element of an OIA. For some objects, you can specify the contribution ratio as a whole (transferred to any fragment), while for others, this ratio is so individualized that it records the contribution of each in an explicit form. But there is a case when there is a role division of the contribution [22]: for example, one was the author of the idea, the other supervised the work, and the third and fourth performed it. Then, the author's contribution is indicated subjectively, noting the role of each performer or their groups (for example, relying on the CRediT approach [1]).

The fourth approach (highlighting borrowings) reflects the relations of external OIAs with the deposited ones. An author has the opportunity to highlight those blocks that are borrowed from other sources (directly or indirectly). Then, the knowledge representation about the author's contribution A will be a tuple of (1) type:

$$A = < S \times F \mid L, H >, \tag{1}$$

where S is a selected set of structural fragments of an object (nodes), F is a set of groups of co-authors' activities (for example, in accordance with the CRediT approach), L is a set of structural links between nodes, H is a set of co-authors and copyright holders. This makes it possible to take into account direct citations, references and even creative processing (modification) [23].

Any of the approaches stated above can be taken as a basis for decomposition, and in some cases, they should be combined. Furthermore, internal fragmentation can be combined with external fragmentation. Let us consider the variants of internal and external relations between fragments and objects forming composite OIAs (see Table 2). One should draw attention to that committing an OIA within the registry requires a unique ID that allows you to associate events with an object and include them in the digital footprint.

The table shows that OIAs in the registry can be represented in the form of entities describing a specific object file in metadata, as well as an assembly of objects (Fig. 2), contains graphic images of each OIA decomposition variant (where M is a metadata block, P is a fragment description, F is an associated file, and the "*" sign indicates pointers (links) to external entities). The uppercase and lowercase designation of metadata refers whether a corresponding block has its own (M) or secondary (m) identification number. The presence of its own metadata in a fragment does not guarantee its isolation as an independent OIA. The latter kind of arrangement assumes hybrid relations and/or more than two levels in the object inclusion hierarchy.

2.3   Approach to the Description of External and Internal Fragmentation

Let us move from theoretical issues of the process of describing composite objects to practical ones by illustrating the implementation of these capabilities within the framework of a digital platform for committing composite OIAs. Fragmentation (selection of component parts) presupposes the answer to two questions: "What characterizes a fragment?" and "Where are its boundaries?". The answer to the first question corresponds to the metadata that an author enters into the information system during the deposit process. They are stored in a special database and/or registry and are descriptive of the OIA files themselves. The answer to the second question is not quite obvious and leads to the need to separate the external and internal fragmentation of an OIA.

Table 2. Characteristics of composite OIAs.

Composite type	Deposited entity	Links to external files	Structural blocks (more than one)	ID holder	Examples
1) Single-level simple	One main simple file	No	No	Main OIA file	– block diagram of the algorithm; – DNA sequence file
2) Single-level composite	One main file with fragments	No	Yes	Main OIA file	– preprint of a scientific article
3) Single-level detailed	One main file with a complex structure and external supporting files	Yes	Yes	Main OIA file	– monograph preprint
4) Two-level simple	Virtual object with a description of files as a single collection	Yes	No	Aggregate entity	– atlas; – many images as data-set for AI algorithms (archived)
5) Two-level composite	Virtual object with a description of each file	Yes	Yes	Aggregate entity	– library of design objects as an independent OIA, consisting of a set of OIAs
6) Two-level detailed	Virtual object with a description of each fragment as an OIA	Yes	Yes	Aggregate entity and each fragment	– preprint of a collection of scientific articles published in the registry as independent OIAs
7) Multi-level	Virtual object as an aggregator of a set of nested OIAs	Yes	Yes	Aggregate entity and individual fragments	– e-learning course

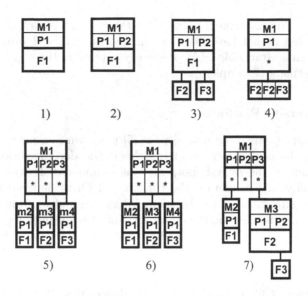

Fig. 2. Conditional graphic sample for OIAs decomposition.

Internal fragmentation, as a process of describing parts of an OIA in the form of separate blocks, implies the presence of a mandatory and variable part of metadata. The mandatory part will include such data about an OIA as the title, authors, date of deposit, identification number, link to the file with the object and several others. The variable part of the metadata depends on the nature of the object and its consumer qualities, which set the accents in the description. If the object has a predominantly textual nature (preprints of scientific articles, digital collections, patents texts, scientific reports, dissertations, etc.), then they can be described in accordance with any (even the most complex) graphical decomposition pattern (see variants in Fig. 2). This implies that each fragment contains a link not only to an OIA file or an supporting file, but also the inclusion of block boundaries in the structure of the file (more precisely, its copy). Markup can be used as a mechanism, i.e. embedding service information (tags) into the OIA structure, which allows to describe all aspects of decomposition at the same time: sequential selection of fragments of a composite OIA and their description [24]. It is convenient to implement the fragment boundary selection mechanism in the form of a WYSIWYG editor, and mark the blocks using the mouse pointer.

External fragmentation is primarily determined by the specifics of the associated OIA objects, which are independent files (up to entire archives). They are presented as images, block diagrams, log reports of scientific equipment, etc. Examples 4–6 and Example 7, with some restrictions, from Fig. 2 correspond to this case. Data about fragments will b independent identifier in the object registry. The component parts will either be just attached files, i.e. have a description, but do not have their own unique identifiers (Examples 4 and 5); or will be external attachable OIAs previously entered in the registry and having their own identifiers (Example 6).

2.4   IPUniversity Platform

The IPUniversity (https://ipuniversity.ru) [5] platform became the information system on the basis of which the research on the decomposition, depositing and committing of the digital footprint was conducted. It was developed in order to simplify and accelerate the turnover of OIAs between scientific and educational organizations of the Russian Federation and interested consumers. The platform work is based on the organization of the business logic of the OIAs turnover with their deposit, storage and commit of transactions using distributed ledger technology. The deposit module allows you to commit a digital OIA by performing the following sequence of actions: Federation

- initialize a new OIA and enter a primary description;
- attach a file with a digital version of the object, or get it from previously placed in the registry;
- describe the OIA fragments using the markup module [24];
- formalize links with external objects;
- send an OIA for registration in the registry, having previously agreed with all co-authors, using the digital signature mechanism.

The result of the work of the platform internal mechanisms are the created copies of an OIA in the repository, as well as the corresponding entry in the registry (including all metadata reflected in an object card). An example of an object card [25] is shown in Fig. 3.

The platform supports 5 types of licenses for managing access to OIAs through the mechanism of smart contracts based on PoS consensus. Each OIA, after its successful placement in the registry (see Fig. 4a), is assigned a special registration number (IPC identifier). According to the object certificate, you can both verify the object itself and get access to the chain of its smart contracts and its digital footprint (see Fig. 4b).

3   Case Study

Let us consider the correlation of OIAs with structural types in two examples. To begin with, let us take the OIA, presented as a RAW file with the results of mass spectrometry (Fig. 5), obtained using the Waters Acquity I CLASS Xevo TQD equipment for the substance $C_{30}H_{26}BrN_3O_4$ [8]. Here, primary data sets combined in the form of an archive are considered as a single object that has common identification data in the registry (corresponds to decomposition Example 3). In this case, the author's layer includes scientists, researchers, as well as

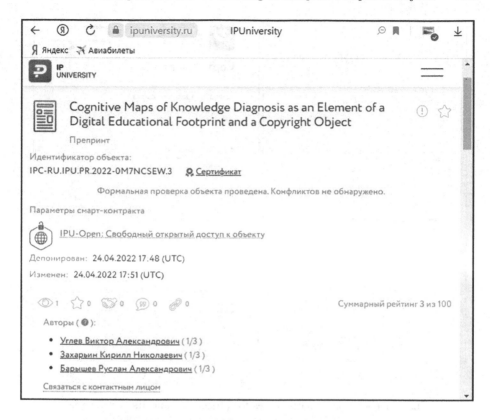

Fig. 3. Object card [25] in the IPUniversity registry.

a laboratory assistant and a head of the laboratory of the organization on the basis of which the spectrogram is obtained.

The second example is the OIA as a result of the work of an intelligent training system for a specific student (part of the educational digital footprint recorded by the LMS [19]). Structurally, this configuration of a composite object corresponds to the decomposition Example 7 and is shown in Fig. 6 in a simplified way. The basic e-course model in the LMS Model itself is a composite object with a rather complex internal structure (mbz format), therefore, within the digital footprint, it has the character of external borrowing. Internal links, for example, include an atlas of Cognitive Maps of Knowledge Diagnosis [22], which play the role of a knowledge base relative to the digital footprint. Thus, the OIA turnes out to have both internal heterogeneity and references to external objects.

Now, let us consider another example typical for describing the internal fragmentation of composite objects using the markup module [24] integrated with the IPUniversity platform. As an object, we choose a scientific article [22], which has structural, semantic and authorial heterogeneity, as well as borrowings.

Let us dwell in more detail on the process of describing the internal fragmentation of this OIA, using a special markup module [24], made in the form of

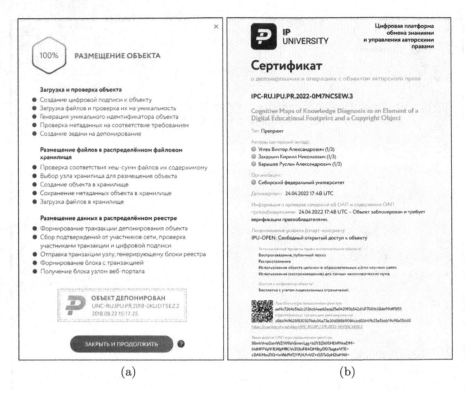

Fig. 4. Depositing process stages for object [25] and its certificate.

a WYSIWYG editor (markup is carried out using a computer mouse pointer). Figure 7 shows a fragment of a window that allows you to formalize the position of structural and semantic blocks:

- metadata (green colour);
- meaningful fragments of the work (light brown colour);
- a list of sources from which the borrowing is carried out (gray colour).

Each fragment has its own metadata, including the ability to specify external links both to other OIAs from the registry (by IPC identifier) and to objects from the Internet (by DOI or link to an Internet page). In the example, this corresponds to Example 3 of Fig. 2. Then the author's contribution for each fragment is indicated.

In the following screen form (see Fig. 8) the markup of borrowings from internal sources is shown (here from the list of references). To do this, the depositing author selects fragments that relate to one of the following types of borrowing:

- direct citation (red colours of the selection from Fig. 8);
- citation with addition;
- mention (not direct citation, blue colours of the selection).

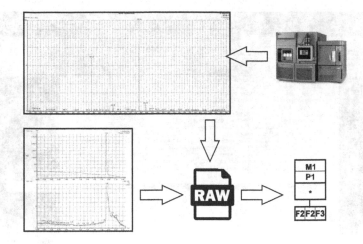

Fig. 5. Mass spectrogram as an inhomogeneous OIA.

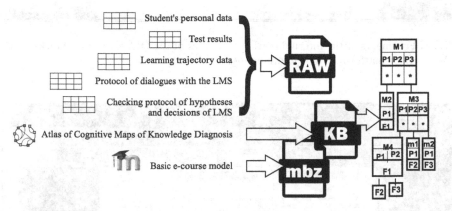

Fig. 6. Educational digital footprint as an OIA.

These types of borrowing allow, during subsequent analysis, to automatically evaluate the contribution of each co-author and evaluate a number of parameters of an OIA itself (for example, the indicator of "author's purity"), as well as introduce original metrics for a fractional assessment of the citation of an object/author (for more details, see [23]). By analogy, it is possible to formalize the internal heterogeneity of an OIA free text by highlighting and describing each fragment in the markup module.

4   Results and Discussion

The practice of depositing OIAs as composite objects was applied on the IPUniversity platform, focused on the scientific and educational content of educational organizations in Russia. Of the 15952 objects placed, 65% were text OIAs

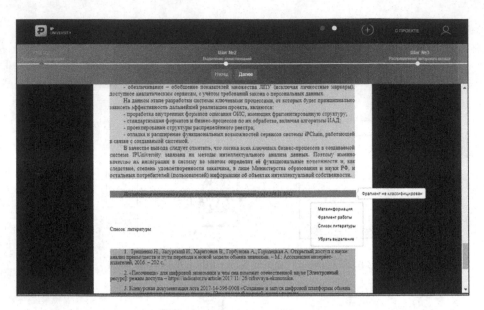

Fig. 7. Fragments of the internal markup windows of the OIA structural blocks on the IPUniversity platform (Color figure online)

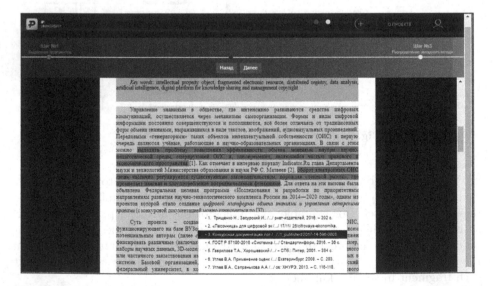

Fig. 8. Fragments of the internal markup windows of the OIA reference fragmentation on the IPUniversity platform (Color figure online)

(preprints), the authors of which had access to the internal fragmentation module. Feedback from the objects authors allowed us to summarize the experience gained and formulate a number of recommendations for developers of registries with composite objects:

- the purpose of the fragmented description of an OIA and its advantages should be practically useful and become in demand at higher stages of object maturity;
- metric estimates of fragmented OIAs should be understandable to a wide range of authors and have a clear practical significance, motivating to a conscious description of the objects structure;
- fragment description fields should be completed with tips and examples, and the process itself should be organized step by step;
- entering data on fragments should be carried out by the authors of an OIA personally, since the third-party performers involved do not have information about the semantic aspect of fragmentation and the specifics of the borrowings made;
- fixing the digital footprint for an OIA should have address links to the relevant fragments to which certain events relate (including smart contracts that meet the requirements of the fourth generation of blockchain technology [6]).

The practical implementation of the registry, which supports the possibility of describing composite objects, had a number of difficulties. In particular, many authors carried out the markup formally, without delving into the specifics of the approach. In addition, the analytical services of the platform at the time of the study were not yet equipped with advanced analytics tools to get the maximum benefit from the availability of data on the internal and external heterogeneities of deposited objects.

As prospects for the development of this approach, the following can be distinguished:

- the ability to create new metrics for evaluating individual OIAs, portfolios of digital assets, individual authors, author teams and departments by analyzing knowledge about external relations between fragments of various OIAs (rating tasks, selection, forecasting, etc.);
- - the ability for a decision-maker to visualize the OIA profile in much greater detail than similar services, such as citation maps in Scopus and Web of Science [4], allow;
- the ability to operate with large arrays of data on the OIA portfolio as Big-Data (tasks of finding patterns, identifying trends [11]);
- the ability to more flexibly maintain objects and their digital footprints in case of their migration between registries throughout their life cycle;
- the ability to use the markup module in combination with other services (primarily analytical) of the digital ecosystem of the organization where fragmented OIAs are the norm (for example, in scientific and educational institutions, as a service https://prometheus.sfu-kras.ru).

Thus, the introduction of composite objects into practical

5   Conclusion

Composite objects recorded as digital OIAs have a number of advantages in relation to OIAs that do not have fragments. Firstly, these are a more flexible description and, as a result, expanded prospects for turnover. Secondly, such objects can be claimed in parts, which makes it possible to more fairly take into account the interests of co-authors when distributing rewards. Thirdly, this is taking into account the genesis and turnover of fragments (especially in the presence of links and fixing borrowings), which allows more adequate assessment of metric and altmetric indicators, i.e. the significance of the result and the author's priority. In addition to this, it becomes possible to separate primary (protocols, RAW files, questionnaires, Data Sets, etc.) and secondary (reports, articles, monographs, and even entire projects) results of intellectual activity during decomposition.

Using the example of the IPUniversity platform, based on the mechanism of distributed registries, we see that it becomes possible not only to fix the right to a non-standard OIA object, but also to form it from heterogeneous data, without missing the contribution of each co-author to the corresponding fragment. This certainly expands the boundaries of the use of digital objects of intellectual property in legal, economic, scientific and applied aspects.

References

1. Contributor roles taxonomy. https://casrai.org/credit/. Accessed 30 Apr 2022
2. ISO/IEC/IEEE 42010:2011 systems and software engineering - architecture description. https://www.iso.org/standard/50508.html. Accessed 30 Apr 2022
3. Using Dublin core - the official usage guide. https://www.dublincore.org/specifications/dublin-core/usageguide/. Accessed 30 Apr 2022
4. AlRyalat, S., Malkawi, L., Momani, S.: Comparing bibliometric analysis using PubMed, Scopus, and web of science databases. JoVE (J. Vis. Exp.) (152), e58494 (2019)
5. Baryshev, R., Barchatov, A., Danilin, M., Zakharin, K., Uglev, V., et al.: Digital platform of knowledge sharing and copyright management (2020). Patent No RU 2020667020
6. Bogdanov, A., Degtyarev, A., Korkhov, V., Kamande, M., Iakushkin, O., Khvatov, V.: About some of the blockchain problems. Advisory committee p. 81 (2018)
7. Charlton, W., Hussey, E., et al.: Aristotle Physics Book VIII, vol. 3. Oxford University Press, Oxford (1999)
8. Dmitriev, M.: Methyl 2-(4-bromophenyl)-4,4-diphenyl-8-pivaloyl-4h-pyrazolo[5,1-b][1,3,5]oxadiazine-7-carboxylate (2018). iPUniversity: IPC-RU.IPU.SP.2018-01XK4RXO.2. (in Russian)
9. Ghimire, T., Joshi, A., Sen, S., Kapruan, C., Chadha, U., Selvaraj, S.K.: Blockchain in additive manufacturing processes: recent trends & its future possibilities. In: 2nd International Conference on Functional Material, Manufacturing and Performances, vol. 50, pp. 2170–2180 (2022). https://doi.org/10.1016/j.matpr.2021.09.444
10. Gürkaynak, G., Yılmaz, I., Yeşilaltay, B., Bengi, B.: Intellectual property law and practice in the blockchain realm. Comput. Law Secur. Rev. **34**(4), 847–862 (2018)

11. Han, J., Kamber, M., Pei, J.: Data Mining: Concepts and Techniques, 3rd edn. The Morgan Kaufmann Series in Data Management Systems, vol. 5, no. 4, pp. 83–124 (2011)
12. Holgersson, M., Aaboen, L.: A literature review of intellectual property management in technology transfer offices: from appropriation to utilization. Technol. Soc. **59**, 101132 (2019)
13. Kossiakoff, A., Sweet, W., Seymour, S., Biemer, S.: Systems Engineering Principles and Practice. Wiley-Interscience (2011)
14. Lage, O., Saiz-Santos, M., Zarzuelo, J.M.: The value and applications of blockchain technology in business: a systematic review of real use cases. In: Prieto, J., Partida, A., Leitão, P., Pinto, A. (eds.) BLOCKCHAIN 2021. LNNS, vol. 320, pp. 149–160. Springer, Cham (2022). https://doi.org/10.1007/978-3-030-86162-9_15
15. Larivière, V., Pontille, D., Sugimoto, C.R.: Investigating the division of scientific labor using the contributor roles taxonomy (credit). Quant. Sci. Stud. **2**(1), 111–128 (2021)
16. Maricato, J.d.M., Vilan Filho, J.L.: The potential for altmetrics to measure other types of impact in scientific production: academic and social impact dynamics in social media and networks. Inf. Res. **23**(1) (2018)
17. McNutt, M.K., et al.: Transparency in authors' contributions and responsibilities to promote integrity in scientific publication. Proc. Natl. Acad. Sci. **115**(11), 2557–2560 (2018)
18. Nielsen, M.W., Andersen, J.P.: Global citation inequality is on the rise. Proc. Natl. Acad. Sci. **118**(7), e2012208118 (2021)
19. Pozdeeva, E., et al.: Assessment of online environment and digital footprint functions in higher education analytics. Educ. Sci. **11**(6) (2021). https://doi.org/10.3390/educsci11060256
20. Savelyev, A.: Copyright in the blockchain era: promises and challenges. Comput. Law Secur. Rev. **34**(3), 550–561 (2018)
21. Sekerin, V.D., Slepov, V.A., Gayduk, V.I., Bank, S.V., Kravets, E.V.: Blockchain technology development as tool for enhancing security in management and protection of intellectual property rights in additive manufacturing. Revista Geintec-Gestao Inovacao E Tecnologias **11**(2), 1184–1200 (2021)
22. Uglev, V.: A model of functional-structural knowledge representation about the author's contribution when depositing objects of law in distributed registries. In: Robotics and Artificial Intelligence: Proceedings of the XIII All-Russian Scientific and Technical Conference, pp. 98–104. LITERA-print (2021). (in Russian)
23. Uglev, V., Feodorov, Y.: Evaluation of the percentage of authorś contribution purity of the authorś text and citation of fragmented resources. In: Neuroinformatics, Its Applications and Data Analysis: XXVI All-Russian Seminar, pp. 133–137. IVM SO RAN (2018). (in Russian)
24. Uglev, V., Frolov, N.: Technology of automated markup of fragmented electronic resources. In: Omsk Scientific Readings: Proceedings of the II All-Russian Scientific Conference, pp. 161–163. Omsk State University Press (2018). (in Russian)
25. Uglev, V., Zakharin, K., Baryshev, R.: Cognitive Maps of Knowledge Diagnosis as an element of a digital educational footprint and a copyright object. In: Software Engineering Perspectives in Intelligent Systems, pp. 349–357. Springer, Cham (2020). https://doi.org/10.1007/978-3-030-63319-6_31

International Workshop on Bio and Neuro inspired Computing and Applications (BIONCA 2022)

PSO Performance for Solving Nonlinear Systems of Equations: Comparing Segmentation of Search Space and Increase of Number of Particles

Sérgio Ribeiro[1]($\boxtimes$) and Luiz Guerreiro Lopes[2]

[1] Postgraduate Programme in Informatics Engineering, University of Madeira,
Funchal, Madeira Is., Portugal
sergioribeiro_91@hotmail.com
[2] Faculty of Exact Sciences and Engineering, University of Madeira,
9020-105 Funchal, Madeira Is., Portugal
lopes@uma.pt

Abstract. Metaheuristic algorithms have been used for different optimization problems and many modifications and hybridizations of these algorithms have been proposed. One such algorithm, Particle Swarm Optimization (PSO), has been proposed and modified for many distinct problems. Solving systems of nonlinear equations is one of its many applications, but as these systems grow, the effectiveness of PSO and PSO-based algorithms decrease. As such, there need to be modifications that impact the performance of the algorithm, such as increasing the number of particles or the number of iterations. However, there are problems where the combined use of both of these strategies does not solve all the drawbacks associated with the use of these algorithms, so a possibility would be to reduce the search space of the problems considered. In this article, the effect of the search space segmentation for solving nonlinear systems of equations using PSO is explored, and an experimental comparison is made between a simple segmentation of the search space to an increase of the number of particles.

Keywords: Computational intelligence · Particle Swarm Optimization · PSO · Space segmentation

1 Introduction

Finding accurate numerical approximations to the solutions of problems involving large systems of nonlinear equations remains a challenging problem [4], not only due to the inherent complexity of obtaining good initial guesses to the solutions so that the algorithm used can converge, but also because these problems can reach considerable proportions, which makes them even more difficult to solve. Nonlinear equation systems are present in most simulations of physical processes, which makes them relevant in many areas, including e.g. Physics, Chemistry and different Engineering fields.

© The Author(s), under exclusive license to Springer Nature Switzerland AG 2022
O. Gervasi et al. (Eds.): ICCSA 2022 Workshops, LNCS 13377, pp. 261–272, 2022.
https://doi.org/10.1007/978-3-031-10536-4_18

An alternative to traditional iterative numerical algorithms are metaheuristic algorithms, which trade high accuracy for robustness and good estimates on a reasonable time. One of these algorithms is the so-called Particle Swarm Optimization (PSO) algorithm, introduced by Eberhart and Kennedy [1] and inspired on the movement of cooperative groups of birds, fishes and other social animals.

In the PSO algorithm, a fixed number of potential or candidate solutions, called particles, move around the search space, trying to find an adequate solution to the problem considered. While larger problems need a bigger number of particles to find good approximations to the solution, adding particles also adds to the computational cost of finding the solution, so blindly adding a large number of particles is not a computationally efficient approach.

A proposed alternative is to reduce the search space into more manageable space sections, and run the algorithm with a smaller number of particles on each smaller section.

The two approaches mentioned above (i.e., increase of number of particles and segmentation of search space) are compared on a set of test problems arising from the literature on systems of nonlinear equations, most of them scalable, and the results are described and analysed in the following sections.

2   Particle Swarm Optimization

Particle Swarm Optimization (PSO), as mentioned above, is a metaheuristic algorithm inspired by the movement of cooperative groups of animals, such as schools of fish and flocks of birds. A number of particles is randomly spread throughout the search space, where each particles position x is a potential solution to the problem, and information is shared between them on the best positions. Then, the particles move towards the more promising regions with velocity v, hopefully converging to a solution of the problem under consideration. Each particle knows the best position it has visited, denoted as $pbest$, as well as the best candidate solution found by all particles in the swarm, called $gbest$.

At each iteration, the velocity and position of each particle i in the swarm is updated as follows (see, e.g., [2]):

$$v_i^{t+1} = w \cdot v_i^t + r_{1i}^t \cdot c_1 \cdot (pbest_i^t - x_i^t) + r_{2i}^t \cdot c_2 \cdot (gbest^t - x_i^t) \tag{1}$$

$$x_i^{t+1} = x_i^t + v_i^{t+1} \tag{2}$$

where c_1 and c_2 are called the cognitive factor and social factor, respectively, which determine the attraction of each particle towards its own best position, $pbest$, and the global best position, $gbest$, while r_1 and r_2 are uniformly distributed random numbers between 0 and 1. Therefore, in order to guarantee that at each iteration a particle does not move further away than it was before, but is also able to explore the space adequately, c_1 and c_2 should have values between 1 and 2. The factor w is the inertia weight, introduced by Shi and Eberhart [12] in order to limit the effect of the velocity of the particle. This modification of the original algorithm is now known as the standard PSO.

The standard PSO (SPSO) algorithm can be used for general optimization and several other modifications have been made to improve its performance, from modifications to the fundamental equations that determine the velocity and position of the particles or different swarm topologies, to hybridization with other optimization algorithms, both traditional and metaheuristic [6,9].

3   Evolution of Search Space

There are a few parameters that have a predictable effect on the performance of the PSO algorithms. While many attempts have been made to select and adjust the parameters in the velocity and position equations, ultimately, these are often problem dependent. On the other hand, adding more particles, more iterations always improves the performance of the algorithms, at a computational cost.

The time complexity of PSO is $\mathcal{O}(n{\cdot}i)$, for a number of particles n and a maximum number of iterations i. Both the number of particles and the maximum number of iterations linearly increase the computation time. However, these are not equivalent. After the particles converge, they will not further explore the search space, so adding more iterations does not have a significant effect. However, adding more particles increases the probability that at least one particle will either be initialized or pass through a good position while the algorithm is running.

The problem function also has some parameters that affect the performance of the algorithm, by making the correct solution harder to find. In a nonlinear system of equations, the higher the number of variables, the more complex and more difficult to solve the system is.

Some research has been done on the dimensionality reduction for optimization using PSO, e.g. in feature selection for classification problems [5] and for the distribution system reconfiguration problem [13]. However, these solutions are not adequate for solving systems of nonlinear equations. These solutions involve alternating variables, which is not possible for solving nonlinear systems of equations, since the system would be underdetermined.

The solution cannot be found by solving for different variables, one at a time, so simplifying the problem in this way is not possible. The search space of the problem is the region where the solution resides. The larger this space, the less likely it is that a particle will find the optimal region of the search space.

Some tests were done on known optimization problems, in order to evaluate the effect of an increase of the search space. The optimization problems chosen are indicated in Table 1. For each of these optimization problems, PSO was run with the following parameters: $w = 0.7$, $c_1 = 1.5$, and $c_2 = 1.8$.

The algorithm was run 50 times for the following combination of parameters:

- number of variables: 1 to 10 with step 1;
- number of iterations: 100 to 400 with step 100;
- number of particles: 30 to 100 with step 10;
- search space dimension: 10 to 100, with step 10.

Table 1. Optimization problems

Name	Expression
Sphere	$f(\boldsymbol{x}) = \sum x_i^2$
Rastigrin	$f(\boldsymbol{x}) = 10d + \sum x_i^2 - 10\cos(2\pi x_i)$
Schwefel	$f(\boldsymbol{x}) = \sum x_i \sin(\sqrt{|x_i|})$
Salomon	$f(\boldsymbol{x}) = -\cos 2\pi \sum x_i^2 + 0.1 \sum x_i^2 + 1$
Griewank	$f(\boldsymbol{x}) = \sum \frac{x_i^2}{4000} - \prod \cos \frac{x_i}{\sqrt{i}} + 1$
Rosenbrock	$f(\boldsymbol{x}) = \sum 100(x_{i+1} - x_i^2)^2 + (x_i - 1)^2$

The results from the simulation, when averaged for all the parameters except for the search space and problem, were plotted as shown on Fig. 1.

Collectively, the data in Fig. 1 indicate that as the search space increases, the worse the average value found by PSO. It seems reasonable to assume that reducing the search space will increase the probability of finding the solution to a large nonlinear system of equations.

4   Segmented PSO

If the search space is separated into two equal sides for each variable, then the number of spaces to be searched is 2^n, where n is the number of variables in the nonlinear system of equations.

The space could be separated into more sections per variable, but since the number of sections grows exponentially with the number of variables, the cost of increasing the number of separations per variable is very high.

As can be seen from Fig. 2, for two variables the search space is segmented into four sections, and for three variables into eight sections. For very large real-world problems where the solution needs to be found only once, it might be more efficient segment the space, even if the time complexity if very large, rather than using a very large number of particles. There is also the advantage that running the algorithm for each section can easily be done in a distributed manner.

Running PSO in this segmented way was done and compared with running PSO with a large number of particles. The parameter values for PSO were the same used in Sect. 3, and 1,000 iterations were performed.

With regard to the number of particles, each segment was run on 50 particles and 400 iterations were performed. Normally, these parameters would not result in convergence for large problems, but only a small portion of the solution space is being searched. In the experiment with a large number of particles, the number of particles was 2^n, which for the problems considered resulted in a very large number of particles that escalates with the number of variables in the same proportion as the number of segments.

Overall, in terms of raw evaluations of the objective function, in the segmented version they were evaluated $400 \times 50 \times 2^n$ times. So, for most of the

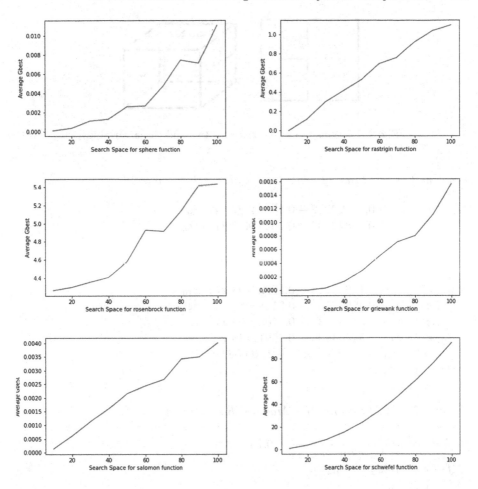

Fig. 1. Effect of increasing the search space

problems, with an n of 12, they were evaluated 81,920,000 times. In comparison with SPSO with an increased number of particles, the evaluations were $2^n \times 1,000$, which for an n of 12 is 4,096,000 evaluations.

In unimodal problems, the number of particles does not need to be so large, provided the number of iterations is enough for convergence. For multimodal problems, the number of particles necessary for convergence is higher, thus requiring a much larger number of particles [11].

5   Test Problems

The following nonlinear systems of equations were chosen as test problems for the comparison performed in this study:

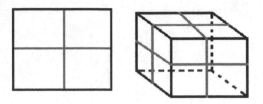

Fig. 2. Sections of search space for two and three variables

Problem 1. ([14], *Interval arithmetic benchmark i1*), $n = 10$.

$$f_1(\boldsymbol{x}) = x_1 - 0.25428722 - 0.18324757\ x_4x_3x_9$$
$$f_2(\boldsymbol{x}) = x_2 - 0.37842197 - 0.16275449\ x_1x_{10}x_6$$
$$f_3(\boldsymbol{x}) = x_3 - 0.27162577 - 0.16955071\ x_1x_2x_{10}$$
$$f_4(\boldsymbol{x}) = x_4 - 0.19807914 - 0.15585316\ x_7x_1x_6$$
$$f_5(\boldsymbol{x}) = x_5 - 0.44166728 - 0.19950920\ x_7x_6x_3$$
$$f_6(\boldsymbol{x}) = x_6 - 0.14654113 - 0.18922793\ x_8x_5x_{10}$$
$$f_7(\boldsymbol{x}) = x_7 - 0.42937161 - 0.21180486\ x_2x_5x_8$$
$$f_8(\boldsymbol{x}) = x_8 - 0.07056438 - 0.17081208\ x_1x_7x_6$$
$$f_9(\boldsymbol{x}) = x_9 - 0.34504906 - 0.19612740\ x_{10}x_6x_8$$
$$f_{10}(\boldsymbol{x}) = x_{10} - 0.42651102 - 0.21466544\ x_4x_8x_1$$
$$D = ([-2, 2], \ldots, [-2, 2])^T$$

Problem 2. ([3], *Problem D1 – Modified Rosenbrock*), $n = 12$.

$$f_{2i-1}(\boldsymbol{x}) = \frac{1}{1 + \exp(-x_{2i-1})} - 0.73$$
$$f_{2i}(\boldsymbol{x}) = 10(x_{2i} - x_{2i-1}^2),$$
$$i = 1, \ldots, \tfrac{n}{2}$$
$$\boldsymbol{x}^{(0)} = (-1.8, -1, \ldots, -1.8, -1)^T$$
$$D = ([-10, 10], \ldots, [-10, 10])^T$$

Problem 3. ([3], *Problem D2 – Augmented Rosenbrock*), $n = 12$.

$$f_{4i-3}(\boldsymbol{x}) = 10(x_{4i-2} - x_{4i-3}^2)$$
$$f_{4i-2}(\boldsymbol{x}) = 1 - x_{4i-3}$$
$$f_{4i-1}(\boldsymbol{x}) = 1.25x_{4i-1} - 0.25x_{4i-1}^3$$
$$f_{4i}(\boldsymbol{x}) = x_{4i},$$
$$i = 1, \ldots, \tfrac{n}{4}$$
$$\boldsymbol{x}^{(0)} = (-1.2, 1, -1, 20, \ldots, -1.2, 1, -1, 20)^T$$
$$D = ([-10, 10], \ldots, [-10, 10])^T$$

Problem 4. ([3], *Problem D3 – Powell badly scaled*), $n = 12$.

$$f_{2i-1}(\boldsymbol{x}) = 10^4 x_{2i-1}x_{2i} - 1$$
$$f_{2i}(\boldsymbol{x}) = \exp(-x_{2i-1}) + \exp(-x_{2i}) - 1.0001, \quad i = 1, \ldots, \tfrac{n}{2}$$

$$\boldsymbol{x}^{(0)} = (0, 100, \ldots, 0, 100)^T$$
$$D = ([0, 100], \ldots, [0, 100])^T$$

Problem 5. ([3], *Problem D4 – Augmented Powell badly scaled*), $n = 12$.

$$f_{3i-2}(\boldsymbol{x}) = 10^4 x_{3i-2} x_{3i-1} - 1$$
$$f_{3i-1}(\boldsymbol{x}) = \exp(-x_{3i-2}) + \exp(-x_{3i-1}) - 1.0001$$
$$f_{3i}(\boldsymbol{x}) = \varphi(x_{3i}),$$
$$i = 1, \ldots, \tfrac{n}{3}, \text{ where:}$$
$$\varphi(t) = \begin{cases} \frac{t}{2} - 2, & \text{if } t \le -1 \\ \frac{1}{1998}(-1924 + 4551t + 888t^2 - 592t^3), & \text{if } t \in [-1, 2] \\ \frac{t}{2} + 2, & \text{if } t \ge 2 \end{cases}$$
$$\boldsymbol{x}^{(0)} = (0, 1, -4, \ldots, 0, 1, -4)^T$$
$$D = ([-5, 5], \ldots, [-5, 5])^T$$

Problem 6. ([3], *Problem D5 – Tridimensional valley*), $n = 12$.

$$f_{3i-2}(\boldsymbol{x}) = (c_2 x_{3i-2}^3 + c_1 x_{3i-1}) \exp\left(-\frac{x_{3i-2}^2}{100}\right) - 1,$$
$$f_{3i-1}(\boldsymbol{x}) = 10 \left(\sin(x_{3i-2}) - x_{3i-1}\right)$$
$$f_{3i}(\boldsymbol{x}) = 10 \left(\cos(x_{3i-2}) - x_{3i}\right),$$
$$i = 1, \ldots, \frac{n}{3},$$

where:

$$c_1 = 1.003344481605351$$
$$c_2 = -3.344481605351171 \times 10^{-3}$$
$$\boldsymbol{x}^{(0)} = (-4, 1, 2, 1, 2, 1, 2, \ldots)^T$$
$$D = ([-10, 10], \ldots, [-10, 10])^T$$

Problem 7. ([3], *Problem D6 – Shifted and augmented trigonometric function with an Euclidean sphere*), $n = 12$.

$$f_i(\boldsymbol{x}) = n - 1 - \sum_{j=1}^{n-1} \cos(x_j - 1) + i(1 - \cos(x_i - 1)) - \sin(x_i - 1),$$
$$i = 1, \ldots, n - 1$$
$$f_n(\boldsymbol{x}) = \sum_{j=1}^{n} x_j^2 - 10000$$
$$\boldsymbol{x}^{(0)} = (0, \ldots, 0)^T$$
$$D = ([-200, 200], \ldots, [-200, 200])^T$$

Problem 8. ([3], *Problem D7 – Diagonal of three variables premultiplied by a quasi-orthogonal matrix*), $n = 12$.

$$f_{3i-2}(\boldsymbol{x}) = 0.6 x_{3i-2} + 1.6 x_{3i-1}^3 - 7.2 x_{3i-1}^2 + 9.6 x_{3i-1} - 4.8$$
$$f_{3i-1}(\boldsymbol{x}) = 0.48 x_{3i-2} - 0.72 x_{3i-1}^3 + 3.24 x_{3i-1}^2 - 4.32 x_{3i-1} - x_{3i} + 0.2 x_{3i}^3 + 2.16$$
$$f_{3i}(\boldsymbol{x}) = 1.25 x_{3i} - 0.25 x_{3i}^3,$$

$i = 1, \ldots, \frac{n}{3}$

$\boldsymbol{x}^{(0)} = (50, 0.5, -1, 50, 0.5, -1, \ldots)^T$

$D = ([-5, 5], \ldots, [-5, 5])^T$

Problem 9. ([3], *Problem D8 – Diagonal of three variables premultiplied by an orthogonal matrix, combined with inverse trigonometric function*), $n = 12$.

$f_{3i-2}(\boldsymbol{x}) = 64(x_{3i-2} + x_{3i-1} + x_{3i}) - 0.64 + 0.48 \arctan(x_{3i}) +$
$0.60(c_1 + c_2 x_{3i-1} + c_3 x_{3i-1}^2 + c_4 x_{3i-1}^3)$
$f_{3i-1}(\boldsymbol{x}) = 0.48 - 48(x_{3i-2} + x_{3i-1} + x_{3i}) + 0.36 \arctan(x_{3i}) +$
$0.80(c_1 + c_2 x_{3i-1} + c_3 x_{3i-1}^2 + c_4 x_{3i-1}^3)$
$f_{3i}(\boldsymbol{x}) = 0.60 - 60(x_{3i-2} + x_{3i-1} + x_{3i}) + 0.80 \arctan(x_{3i}),$
$i = 1, \ldots, \frac{n}{3}$
$c_1 = 13.9010204081632700000$
$c_2 = -1.40561224489796000000$
$c_3 = -2.21836734693877600000$
$c_4 = -0.277040816326530600000$
$\boldsymbol{x}^{(0)} = (10, -5.223, -1.393, 10, -5.223, -1.393, \ldots)^T$
$D = ([-200, 200], \ldots, [-200, 200])^T$

Problem 10. ([10], *22 – Extended Powell singular function*), $n = 12$.

$f_{4i-3}(\boldsymbol{x}) = x_{4i-3} + 10 x_{4i-2}$
$f_{4i-2}(\boldsymbol{x}) = \sqrt{5}(x_{4i-1} - x_{4i})$
$f_{4i-1}(\boldsymbol{x}) = (x_{4i-2} - 2 x_{4i-1})^2$
$f_{4i}(\boldsymbol{x}) = \sqrt{10}(x_{4i-3} - x_{4i})^2,$
$i = 1, \ldots, 5$
$\boldsymbol{x}^{(0)} = (3, -1, 0, 1, \ldots, 3, -1, 0, 1)^T$
$D = ([-100, 100], \ldots, [-100, 100])^T$

Problem 11. ([10], *25 – Variable dimensioned function*), $n = 12$.

$f_i(\boldsymbol{x}) = x_i - 1, \quad i = 1, \ldots, n$
$f_{n+1}(\boldsymbol{x}) = \sum_{j=1}^{n} j(x_j - 1)$

$f_{n+2}(\boldsymbol{x}) = \left(\sum_{j=1}^{n} j(x_j - 1) \right)^2$

$\boldsymbol{x}^{(0)} = (1 - \frac{1}{n}, 1 - \frac{2}{n}, \ldots, 0)^T$
$D = ([-100, 100], \ldots, [-100, 100])^T$

Problem 12. ([10], *28 – Discrete boundary value function*), $n = 12$.

$$f_1(\boldsymbol{x}) = 2x_1 - x_2 + h^2(x_1 + h + 1)^3/2$$
$$f_n(\boldsymbol{x}) = 2x_n - x_{n-1} + h^2(x_n + nh + 1)^3/2$$
$$f_i(\boldsymbol{x}) = 2x_i - x_{i-1} - x_{i+1} + h^2(x_i + t_i + 1)^3/2, \quad i = 2, \dots, n-1,$$

where $\quad h = \frac{1}{n+1} \quad$ e $\quad t_i = ih$.

$$\boldsymbol{x}^{(0)} = (\varphi_j), \quad \varphi_j = t_j(t_j - 1), \quad j = 1, \dots, n$$
$$D = ([0, 5], \dots, [0, 5])^T$$

Problem 13. ([15], *Example 4.2*), $n = 12$.

$$f_i(\boldsymbol{x}) = x_i - \frac{1}{2n}\left(\sum_{j=1}^{n} x_j^3 + i\right), \quad i = 1, \dots, n$$
$$D = ([-10, 10], \dots, [-10, 10])^T$$

6 Results Obtained

The problem functions were tested with two segments. The average and minimum values found are presented in Table 2.

Table 2. Results for PSO with Gbest topology

Problem	Average		Minimum	
	SPSO	Segmented	SPSO	Segmented
Problem 1	1.037663071	0.698486804	0.421814871	0.408340722
Problem 2	1.62	1.608352444	1.62	1.360405712
Problem 3	3	2.903333419	3	2.373871397
Problem 4	6.637033787	6.326612765	6.282627128	6.112016672
Problem 5	5.192528753	4.62293342	4.477480166	3.882171641
Problem 6	15.53367649	10.14796265	10.07173459	7.302318603
Problem 7	17.75618911	10.94764561	12.13551478	6.732026598
Problem 8	6.405438188	4.674562396	4.725153885	3.249000098
Problem 9	77.85882864	72.15770647	72.40134433	47.19050689
Problem 10	9.5408E−15	1.86324E−14	3.38E−15	4.55E−15
Problem 11	4.517171951	3.027601273	3.111794099	1.820649757
Problem 12	0.190782092	0.175340087	0.159467829	0.163692495
Problem 13	9.202443211	6.399087192	6.05988822	4.466427714

From the results, it is possible to observe that, especially for the problems where PSO has a tendency to get stuck in a local minimum, such as the Problems 2 and 3, the segmented alternative does not get stuck, but at the cost of not being able to explore much further, due to the smaller number of particles and iterations.

The premature convergence of PSO is widely acknowledged. Therefore, it is relevant to understand whether a modification to suppress this convergence would yield better results. For this, the same test problems were run, on the same conditions, with the exception of the swarm topology. Instead of using the gbest topology, where every particle communicates with every other particle, the von Neumann topology was chosen. The results obtained are presented in Table 3.

In the comparison of topologies for PSO, the von Neumann with rank 4 has often been found to be better performing than the alternatives [8]. In the von Neumann topology, each particle does not communicate with every other particle, but only with n particles (see Fig. 3), with n being the rank of the topology. So, in this experiment, each particle was connected with four other particles, which delays the convergence of the algorithm, allowing for better exploration of the search space of the problems.

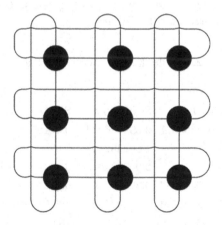

Fig. 3. Diagram of von Neumann topology with rank 4 (extracted from [7])

Table 3. Results for segmented PSO with von Neumann topology

Problem	Average		Minimum	
	SPSO	Segmented	SPSO	Segmented
Problem 1	1.43115E−16	0.000440838	1.43115E−16	5.74899E−05
Problem 2	2.37131E−07	0.841533489	1.66395E−13	0.484539158
Problem 3	1.1831E−08	0.985771992	3.81643E−14	0.420933694
Problem 4	0.000549438	0.000611278	0.000479778	0.000485759
Problem 5	0.038483924	0.024097009	0.002670834	0.000711316
Problem 6	0.077170719	0.225986715	0.059364707	0.078127327
Problem 7	4.273857164	1.420858728	0.684416557	0.55435223
Problem 8	3.11286E−07	0.033136903	8.40785E−08	0.001336032
Problem 9	1.263340747	4.164705179	4.77684E−08	2.778112461
Problem 10	6.69532E−18	4.017634796	1.91271E−18	0.176367453
Problem 11	7.42295E−15	8.570062293	3.55271E−15	2.720638905
Problem 12	1.48766E−15	0.223516272	3.60822E−16	0.048649465
Problem 13	2.8702E−15	0.624939653	9.57567E−16	0.084652142

7 Conclusion

The effects of adding many particles and of reducing the search space, and iteratively running PSO, has been compared on a set of large nonlinear systems of equations. While segmenting the search space does prevent PSO from suffering from premature converge to local minima, the computational cost of this operation is very large, and increases exponentially with the number of variables in the system. A better alternative is to increase the number of particles with a topology that makes PSO more resistant to premature convergence.

The benefit of this decision comes not only from better results, but also from a lower computational cost, because the time complexity of PSO increases linearly with the number of particles used.

References

1. Eberhart, R., Kennedy, J.: A new optimizer using particle swarm theory. In: 6th International Symposium on Micro Machine and Human Science, Nagoya, Japan, 4–6 October 1995, pp. 39–43. IEEE (1995). https://doi.org/10.1109/MHS.1995.494215
2. Freitas, D., Lopes, L., Morgado-Dias, F.: Particle swarm optimisation: a historical review up to the current developments. Energy **22**(3), 362 (2020). https://doi.org/10.3390/e22030362
3. Friedlander, A., Gomes-Ruggiero, M., Kozakevich, D., Martínez, J., Santos, S.: Solving nonlinear systems of equations by means of quasi-Newton methods with a nonmonotone strategy. Optim. Methods Softw. **8**(1), 25–51 (1997). https://doi.org/10.1080/10556789708805664

4. Gong, W., Liao, Z., Mi, X., Wang, L., Guo, Y.: Nonlinear equations solving with intelligent optimization algorithms: a survey. Complex Syst. Model. Simul. **1**(1), 15–32 (2021). https://doi.org/10.23919/CSMS.2021.0002
5. Li, A.D., Xue, B., Zhang, M.: Improved binary particle swarm optimization for feature selection with new initialization and search space reduction strategies. Appl. Soft Comput. **106**, 107302 (2021). https://doi.org/10.1016/j.asoc.2021.107302
6. Li, Y., Wei, Y., Chu, Y.: Research on solving systems of nonlinear equations based on improved PSO. Math. Probl. Eng. **2015**, 727218 (2015). https://doi.org/10.1155/2015/727218
7. Lima, A., Medeiros, Y., Silva, L., Araújo, W.: Estudo comparativo sobre a convergência e o custo computacional das estruturas topológicas aplicadas à otimização por enxame de partículas (PSO). Revista Científica Semana Acadêmica **1**, 1–18 (2016)
8. Liu, Q., Wei, W., Yuan, H., Zhan, Z.H., Li, Y.: Topology selection for particle swarm optimization. Inf. Sci. **363**, 154–173 (2016). https://doi.org/10.1016/j.ins.2016.04.050
9. Mai, X., Li, L.: Bacterial foraging algorithm based on PSO with adaptive inertia weigh for solving nonlinear equations systems. In: Advanced Materials Research, vol. 655–657, pp. 940–947. Trans Tech Publishers (2013). https://doi.org/10.4028/www.scientific.net/AMR.655-657.940
10. Moré, J., Garbow, B., Hillstrom, K.: Testing unconstrained optimization software. ACM Trans. Math. Softw. **7**(1), 17–41 (1981). https://doi.org/10.1145/355934.355936
11. Piotrowski, A.P., Napiorkowski, J.J., Piotrowska, A.E.: Population size in particle swarm optimization. Swarm Evol. Comput. **58**, 100718 (2020). https://doi.org/10.1016/j.swevo.2020.100718
12. Shi, Y., Eberhart, R.: A modified particle swarm optimizer. In: 1998 IEEE International Conference on Evolutionary Computation Proceedings. IEEE World Congress on Computational Intelligence (Cat. No. 98TH8360) 1998, pp. 69–73. IEEE (1998). https://doi.org/10.1109/ICEC.1998.699146
13. Silva, L.I., Belati, E.A., Gerez, C., Silva Junior, I.C.: Reduced search space combined with particle swarm optimization for distribution system reconfiguration. Electr. Eng. **103**(2), 1127–1139 (2020). https://doi.org/10.1007/s00202-020-01150-z
14. van Hentenryck, P., McAllester, D., Kapur, D.: Solving polynomial systems using a branch and prune approach. SIAM J. Numer. Anal. **34**(2), 797–827 (1997). https://doi.org/10.1137/S0036142995281504
15. Yamamura, K., Kawata, H., Tokue, A.: Interval solution of nonlinear equations using linear programming. BIT Numer. Math. **38**(1), 186–199 (1998). https://doi.org/10.1007/BF02510924

Mathematical Modeling of Chiller-Based Refrigeration Systems for Energy Efficiency Optimization

Nadia Nedjah[1]($\boxtimes$), Luiza de Macedo Mourelle[2],
and Marcelo Silveira Dantas Lizarazu[1]

[1] Department of Electronics Engineering and Telecommunications,
State University of Rio de Janeiro, Rio de Janeiro, Brazil
{nadia,lizarazu}@eng.uerj.br
[2] Department of Systems Engineering and Computation,
State University of Rio de Janeiro, Rio de Janeiro, Brazil
ldmm@eng.uerj.br

Abstract. Chillers are the basis of modern refrigeration systems of large facilities, such as oil refineries, power plants and large commercial buildings. The increasing concerns about the scarcity of water and energy resources require careful optimization processes to achieve energy efficiency in industrial buildings. Optimization require mathematical models of real equipment. In this paper, we present two models for a compression chillers, which are one the main equipment in industrial refrigeration systems. We prove that proposed models are precise and faithful to the real compression chiller used in modern refrigeration system. Moreover, we prove that the model's values model accurately the actual values of the global requirements in terms of power consumption of the whole refrigeration system composed of cooling towers, fans and chillers. The models of the cooling tower and corresponding fans are presented in [5].

Keywords: Energy efficiency · Cooling tower · Chiller · Optimization

1 Introduction

Industrial processes usually generate heat. This heat often must dealt with to be eliminated. In general, water is employed to reduce the generated heat effect. Thus, water is used as a cooling element. However, the used water returns from such cooling process hot. So, it must be cooled down to be reused or discarded. The reuse of water is always the preferred solution because nowadays there is always lack of water and water consumption became absurdly expensive.

A refrigeration system based on cooling towers require a set of equipment that operate interdependently, such as chillers. An undue modification of a certain parameter or operational adjustment in one of these equipment can cause either a positive or negative cascading effects on the operation of the others parts of the system. This can consequently trigger a series of effects that are not necessarily

O. Gervasi et al. (Eds.): ICCSA 2022 Workshops, LNCS 13377, pp. 273–288, 2022.
https://doi.org/10.1007/978-3-031-10536-4_19

satisfactory to the overall system, which includes the reduction of its energy efficiency.

Modern industrial refrigeration systems are based on cooling towers, ventilators and chillers. These kind of refrigeration system are expected to deal with application wherein a large cooling demands is expected. These kind of cooling systems offer a clean and economical approaches to cool down the returning water so it can be reused in the cooling process.

In energy efficiency oriented application regarding modern industrial refrigeration system, models of the composing equipment are required so as simulation van be done *a priori* to find out the setpoint of system that provides such energy efficiency. For this purpose, mathematical models of the included complex equipment are needed.

As a first part, in [5], we propose an accurate model for the tower cell, which composed of a cooling tower and corresponding ventilators. As a second part, this work aims at providing a complete model of modern compression chillers to serve as the basis of optimization of many objectives, such as maximizing the thermal exchange efficiency of the cooling tower and minimizing the energy requirement of the refrigeration system, considering all its composing equipment. For the former, a model for the cooling towers is required. Due to lack of space the model of the cooling tower and underlying processes in the refrigeration system is presented in separate paper [5].

This paper is structured into five sections. First, in Sect. 2, we give a brief description of the structure of the modeled compression chillers. After that, in Sect. 3, we present the two proposed model of the chiller. Later, in Sect. 4, we present, discuss and compare the results obtained from the application of the proposed model to those collected from a real operating refrigeration system. Subsequently, in Sect. 5, we show how the chiller's proposed models as well as the model for the cooling tower and corresponding fans, proposed in [5], to obtain a model of the global required power consumption of the whole refrigeration system. Last but not least, in Sect. 6, the conclusions are drawn together with future work.

2   Chillers in Refrigeration System

Figure 1 illustrates the configuration of a refrigeration system composed of a compression chiller and a cooling tower. Therein, the components that composes the chiller can be verified, as well as its interconnections with the cooling tower and the system as fed with chilled water.

It is noteworthy that the heated water that leaves the chiller's condenser is the one that will be pumped to the cooling tower, and that the water cooled by the tower returns to the chiller's condenser. This is the water condensation circuit, which is also called the primary circuit. Furthermore, note that the chilled water that leaves the chiller's evaporator feeds the fan-coils, which use the chilled water to obtain cooled air and distribute it to the rooms of the installation. After passing through the fan-coils, the initially cold water returns

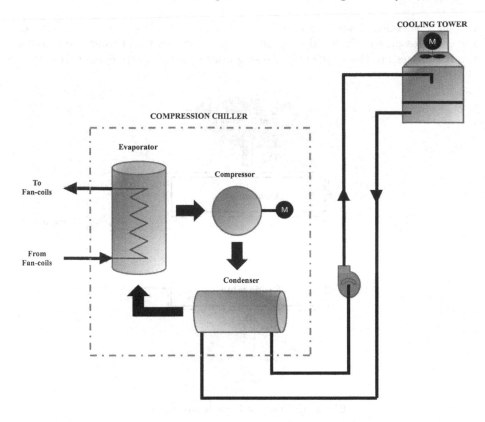

Fig. 1. Cooling system based on compression chiller and cooling tower

to the evaporator with a higher temperature. This is the chilled water circuit, also called the secondary circuit. The fan-coils and other equipment that compose the secondary circuit, such as the water circulation pumps, are not part of the scope of this work. In the fan-coils, the chilled water coming from the evaporator goes to a coil. Therein, the heat exchange is carried out with an induced air flow through forced ventilation occasioned by the fans of the fan-coils. The cooled air resulting from this heat exchange is then distributed.

A water chiller is an equipment whose function is to cool water through a thermodynamic cycle. The two main types of chiller are: compression or electric chiller and absorption chiller. The former uses a physical process, while the latter uses a physical-chemical principle. The system to be optimized in this work uses only compression chillers. Therefore, only this type of chiller will be presented thereafter.

The compression chillers use a mechanical compressor, generally driven by an electric motor, which is used to compress the refrigerant gas that circulates internally to the chiller. The compression of the refrigerant gas is just one of the stages of the thermodynamic cycle necessary for the chiller's operation. The

complete thermodynamic cycle of is shown in Fig. 2. Note that in addition to
the compressor, the chiller also includes other equipment and constituent parts,
the main ones are the condenser, the evaporator and the expansion valve [1].

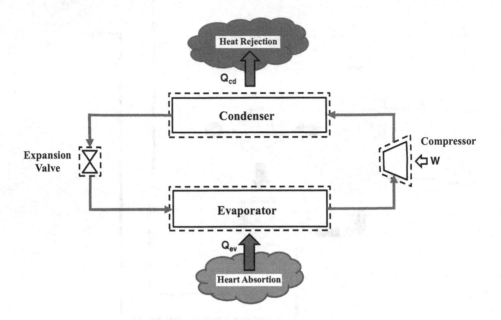

Fig. 2. Chilling cycle by compression

The evaporator, also called cooler, is a heat exchanger composed of finned
tubes where, on one side, there is the passage of the refrigerant fluid, and on the
other, the circulation of water to be refrigerated. Therefore, the evaporator has
the function of cooling the water that circulates through the use of pumps, called
pumps of circulation. It is in this equipment that the evaporation of the refrigerant fluid occurs, a phenomenon that occurs after the thermal exchange with
the hot water coming from the process, which also circulates in the evaporator,
raising the temperature of the refrigerant fluid. Ideally, this process should be
isobaric. However, in practice, there is a small pressure reduction in the refrigerant fluid after its passage through the evaporator. The compressor, which can
be electric or of combustion, compensates for this reduction in pressure of the
refrigerant fluid, sending it to the condenser.

The condenser is a heat exchanger whose function is to condense the refrigerant fluid, which is in a vapor state. This state reached after its passage through
the evaporator. The condenser can be of two types: air-cooled or liquid-cooled.
In the former, fans are used to carry out the thermal exchange between the
forced air and the refrigerant fluid in vapor state, through the circulation of the
refrigerant fluid through finned tubes. In the latter, cooling towers are used, so
that the water circulating through the tower exchanges heat with the refrigerant

fluid in vapor state. This exchange is carried out through coils located inside the condenser, causing the refrigerant fluid to condense. The heated water resulting from this process is raised by means of lifting pumps to the cooling tower. This reduces the temperature of the condensation water, then returns it to the chiller's condenser, in order to allow a continuous thermal exchange with the refrigerant fluid in vapor state coming from the evaporator.

The chilling process also make use of an expansion valve, also called thermostatic valve. This is a direct expansion refrigeration device. So, the expansion of the fluid takes place in the environment to be cooled. Therefore, the thermodynamic cycle of the chiller based on compression occurs as follows: initially, the refrigerant fluid is compressed by the compressor in the super-rheated vapor state, increasing its pressure and temperature. Then, the refrigerant fluid is sent to the condenser, where the heat gained in the compression process is rejected to the outside environment, thus causing the refrigerant fluid to cool down and changing from vapor to liquid. When leaving the condenser in the sub-cooled liquid state, the refrigerant fluid flows through the expansion valve, which causes a pressure drop and consequent temperature drop. Finally, the refrigerant fluid passes through the evaporator, where it absorbs heat from the water to be cooled down, causing the refrigeration effect. Thus, the refrigerant fluid then changes from liquid to vapor, leaving the evaporator as super-heated vapor, returning to the compressor, and the cycle starts again.

3 Proposed Model for the Compression Chiller

In this section, we present the modeling of the process performed by the compression chiller. For the supply of chilled water, the model of a compression chiller can be presented according to Eq. 1:

$$Q_{chiller} = \dot{m}_{water_{evap}} c_{water} (T_{ae_{evap}} - T_{as_{evap}}),$$ (1)

where $Q_{chiller}$ represents the instantaneous capacity of the chiller, $T_{ae_{evap}}$ represents the temperature of the water entering the evaporator of the chiller, i.e. the temperature of the chilled water that returns from the process to be cooled, $T_{as_{evap}}$ represents the temperature of the water leaving the evaporator, i.e. the temperature of the water leaving the chiller and serving the process, c_{water} represents the specific temperature of the water and $\dot{m}_{water_{evap}}$ represents the flow rate of water in the evaporator of the chiller.

The electrical power demanded by the chiller, $P_{chiller}$, can be determined from non-linear regression models as a function of partial load conditions and as a function of temperature values $T_{ae_{evap}}$ and $T_{ae_{cond}}$. The latter represents the temperature of the water that reaches the chiller condenser. According to [6] and [2], the electrical power demanded by the chiller can be determined as indicated in Eq. 2:

$$P_{chiller} = Q_{chiller_{nom}} EIR_{nom} Z_{CAP}(T_{ae_{cond}}, T_{as_{evap}})$$
$$\times Z_{EIR}(T_{ae_{cond}}, T_{as_{evap}}) Z_{EIR}(PLR),$$ (2)

where $Q_{chiller_{nom}}$ represents the nominal capacity of the chiller, EIR_{nom} represents the nominal value of the Energy Input Ratio, which is the ratio between the electrical power and the nominal thermal capacity informed by the chiller manufacturer, function $Z_{CAP}(T_{ae_{cond}}, T_{as_{evap}})$ represents the correction factor for the capacity of the chiller, which depends on the temperatures input to the condenser and output to the evaporator and function $Z_{EIR}(T_{ae_{cond}}, T_{as_{chiller}})$ stands for the correction factor of EIR, which also depends on the temperature of condenser input and evaporator output, and function $Z_{EIR}(PLR)$ represents the correction factor of EIR, which depends on the thermal load factor of the chiller. The PLR stands for the Part Load Ratio, and in this case, represents the partial load condition of the chiller.

In this modeling, two optimization scenarios are considered. This requires providing two different models for the chillers used in the refrigeration system. The considered scenarios are defined as:

- Scenario 1: we consider that the evaporator outlet temperature of the chiller is fixed, and the optimization can be achieved by varying the speed of the cooling tower fans, $i.e.$ by varying the temperature of the condensation water.
- Scenario 2: we consider that the optimization can be achieved by varying the temperature of the evaporator leaving water from the chiller and also by varying the speed of the tower fans.

Regarding the first scenario, based on Eq. 2, obtaining $P_{chiller}$ depends on $T_{as_{evap}}$, which is fixed and previously adjusted in the chillers. Therefore, this variable must be disregarded in the calculation of factors Z_{CAP} and Z_{EIR} employed in Eq. 2. However, by keeping $T_{as_{evap}}$ fixed in Eq. 2, it is assumed that the factors Z_{CAP} and Z_{EIR} are defined only as a function of $T_{ae_{cond}}$, which is not true. IT also requires other information about the evaporator of the chiller to be applied in the modeling of its consumption, since the inlet and outlet temperatures of the evaporator influence the determination of their energy consumption. In this case, the higher the temperature of the water entering the evaporator is, the greater the consumption, and the lower the temperature of the water leaving the evaporator is, the greater the consumption. Thus, for the first scenario, the use of $T_{ae_{evap}}$ is considered instead of $T_{as_{evap}}$ in the consumption model of the chiller through factors Z_{CAP} and Z_{EIR}. The substitution is valid and the motivation is based on the fact that $T_{ae_{evap}}$ represents the thermal load condition of the system, since it is the temperature of the water that returns from the process. As $T_{as_{evap}}$ is fixed, $T_{ae_{evap}}$ becomes the reference for estimating the thermal load of the chiller.

So, to model the electric power demand by chillers considering the first scenario, an approximation of the approach presented by [6] and [2] is used, where factors Z_{CAP} and Z_{EIR} are obtained as a function of $T_{ae_{cond}}$ and $T_{ae_{evap}}$. After the introduction of the aforementioned modifications, we found out that the use of factor $Z_{EIR}(PLR)$ affects the results of the modeling of $P_{chiller}$, which is hence disregarded in the adjusted modeling. Therefore, the model of $P_{chiller}$ for the first scenario is defined by Eq. 3:

$$P_{chiller} = Q_{chiller_{nom}} EIR_{nom} Z_{CAP_1}(T_{ae_{evap}}, T_{ae_{cond}}) Z_{EIR}(T_{ae_{cond}}, T_{ae_{evap}}).$$
(3)

Regarding the second scenario, unlike the first one, the evaporator outlet temperature, $T_{as_{evap}}$, must be used to determine the power demanded by the chiller, since in this scenario it will be allowed to vary $T_{as_{evap}}$ in order to obtain energy efficiency for the refrigeration system. Although the model for $P_{chiller}$ as presented in Eq. 2 considers the use of this variable to evaluate factors Z_{CAP} and Z_{EIR}, we decide to include variable $T_{ae_{evap}}$, since the database obtained in the field presents a more significant range of values for $T_{ae_{evap}}$ compared to $T_{as_{evap}}$. The latter remains constant for long periods of time. So it is safe to conclude that in this case, variable $T_{ae_{evap}}$ has a greater influence on the estimate of consumption of the chiller. Thus, variable $T_{ae_{evap}}$ is included in the model of the electric power demanded by the chiller indicated in Eq. 2. Then, we reach the model defined in Eq. 4:

$$P_{chiller} = Q_{chiller_{nom}} EIR_{nom} Z_{CAP_2}(\Delta T_{ag}, T_{ae_{cond}}) Z_{EIR}(T_{ae_{cond}}, T_{ae_{evap}}). \quad (4)$$

wherein, factor Z_{EIR}, differently from the one indicated in Eq. 2, is obtained as a function of $T_{ae_{cond}}$ and $T_{ae_{evap}}$, in order to maintain the similarity to the model adopted for the first scenario. After the implementation of the aforementioned modifications, similarly to what is verified in the modeling of the first scenario, we found out that the use of factor $Z_{EIR}(PLR)$ hindered the results of the modeling of $P_{chiller}$, so we decided to disregarding the use of this factor in the modeling adopted for the second scenario. Thus, the modeling of $P_{chiller}$ for the second scenario is defined in Eq. 4: Note that factor Z_{CAP} is obtained as a function of $T_{ae_{evap}}$ and $T_{as_{evap}}$ using the variable ΔT_{ag}, which represents the temperature variation in the chilled water circuit, and is defined in Eq. 5:

$$\Delta T_{ag} = T_{ae_{evap}} - T_{as_{evap}}. \quad (5)$$

The analysis of the Eqs. 3 and 4 shows that they basically differ as a function of the factors Z_{CAP}. For this reason, this factor is defined in Eq. 3 as Z_{CAP_1}, and in Eq. 4 as Z_{CAP_2}. As the modeling adopted for the chiller did not follow precisely what is described in [6] and [2], it is necessary to define new equations for factors Z_{CAP_1} and Z_{CAP_2}. In this case, it is established that a quadratic approximation involving variables $T_{ae_{cond}}$ and $T_{ae_{evap}}$ for the modeling of Z_{CAP_1}, and variables ΔT_{ag} and $T_{ae_{evap}}$ for Z_{CAP_2} would be enough. This is later verified with the results obtained after implementing the modeling of these factors. In the same way, we proceed to model factor Z_{EIR}, in this case, involving variables $T_{ae_{cond}}$ and $T_{ae_{evap}}$, similarly to the modeling of the factor Z_{CAP_1}. Equations 6, 7 and 8 describe the models adopted for factors Z_{CAP_1}, Z_{CAP_2} and Z_{EIR}, respectively. In this case, coefficients a_0-a_5 and b_0-b_5 must be obtained from nonlinear regression methods considering the models indicated in Eqs. 6, 7 and 8:

$$Z_{CAP_1} = b_0 + b_1 T_{ae_{evap}} + b_2 T^2_{ae_{evap}} + b_3 T_{ae_{cond}} + b_4 T^2_{ae_{cond}}$$
$$+ b_5 T_{ae_{evap}} T_{ae_{cond}},$$
(6)

$$Z_{CAP_2} = b_0 + b_1 \Delta T_{ag} + b_2 \Delta T_{ag}^2 + b_3 T_{ae_{cond}} + b_4 T_{ae_{cond}}^2$$

$$+ b_5 \Delta T_{ag}^2 T_{ae_{cond}} + b_6 \Delta T_{ag} T_{ae_{cond}}^2, \tag{7}$$

$$Z_{EIR} = a_0 + a_1 T_{ae_{evap}} + a_2 T_{ae_{evap}}^2 + a_3 T_{ae_{cond}} + a_4 T_{ae_{cond}}^2 + a_5 T_{ae_{evap}} T_{ae_{cond}}. \tag{8}$$

In addition to the modeling of the electrical power demanded by the chiller, $P_{chiller}$, it is necessary to obtain a model to estimate the temperature of the water leaving the condenser. This is due to the fact that the temperature of the water leaving the chiller's condenser corresponds to the new temperature of the water that will enter the cooling tower, disregarding the heat loss of the system in the stretch between chiller and the tower [5].

In the operation of the evaporator, the heat transferred to the chiller is defined by Eq. 1. Once the values of $Q_{chiller}$ and $P_{chiller}$ are obtained, applying the first law of thermodynamics to the chiller as a whole, which includes the heat exchanges occurring in the evaporator, in the condenser and in the electric motor that drives the compressor of the chiller, Q_{cond} is obtained. It mainly represent the portion of heat or thermal load to be transferred in the condenser, as indicated in Eq. 9:

$$Q_{cond} = Q_{chiller} - P_{chiller}. \tag{9}$$

In this way, it is possible to estimate the value of the outlet water temperature of the chiller's condenser, $T_{as_{cond}}$, as indicated in Eq. 10:

$$T_{as_{cond}} = \frac{Q_{cond} + \dot{m}_{water} C_{water} T_{ae_{cond}}}{\dot{m}_{water_{cond}} C_{water}}. \tag{10}$$

The value obtained for $T_{as_{cond}}$ is used in the optimization constraint, in order to meet the operational limits of the cooling tower, and also to determine the new effectiveness of the cooling tower [5].

4   Model Validation Results

In order to validate proposed model for the compression chillers, we collect data from the refrigeration system. The database considered for carrying out the modeling is composed of data representing different situations of thermal load, as these are observed during different operational days. These days are selected in way so that to obtain representative data of various thermal load conditions present throughout the day and for different climatic conditions, contemplating hot and cool days. Note that these conditions impact the performance of the cooling system considered in this modeling. We collected 21,385 operating points of the refrigeration system, corresponding to 29 h and 42 min of operation.

To obtain the coefficients of the adopted models, 50% of the points belonging to the database are used, and these coefficients are then applied to the totality of points in the database. The evaluation of the final result using this procedure is performed based on the values of the Mean Square Error (MSE) and the obtained determination coefficient (R^2). The coefficient of determination varies between 0 and 1, and allows assessing how much the adopted model is capable of approximating the actual data. In this case, the closer the value of R^2 to unity is, the better the assessment of the model [4].

In order to obtain the full model of the compression chiller, we first need to determine of the coefficients b_0–b_5, referring to the modeling of the factors Z_{CAP_1} and Z_{CAP_2}, as indicated in Eqs. 6 and 7, respectively. Likewise, the coefficients a_0-a_5 need to be obtained, referring to the modeling of the factor Z_{EIR}, as indicated in Eq. 8. In this case, the Levemberg-Marquardt method is used as a non-linear regression technique to obtain these coefficients [3]. Table 1 indicates the coefficients obtained for the factor Z_{CAP_1}, based on Eq. 6.

Table 1. Obtained values for the coefficient required to model factor Z_{CAP_1}.

Coefficient	Value
b_0	−0.8108
b_1	−0.0838
b_2	+0.0133
b_3	+0.0997
b_4	−0.0012
b_5	−0.0032

Table 2 indicates the coefficients obtained for factor Z_{CAP_2}, based on the use of Eq. 7.

Table 2. Obtained values for the coefficient required to model factor Z_{CAP_2}.

Coefficient	Value
b_0	−0.1177
b_1	+0.3381
b_2	−0.0513
b_3	−0.0276
b_4	+0.0022
b_5	+0.0030
b_6	−0.0006479

Table 3 indicates the coefficients obtained for the factor Z_{EIR} based on the use of the modeling indicated in Eq. 8.

Table 3. Obtained values for the coefficient required to model factor Z_{EIR}.

Coefficient	Value
a_0	−1.0405
a_1	+0.1379
a_2	−0.0090
a_3	+0.0840
a_4	−0.0022
a_5	+0.0033

Figures 3(a), 3(b) and 3(c) depict the modeling of factors Z_{CAP_1}, Z_{CAP_2} and Z_{EIR} when applied to the collected data. All indicate the influence of the temperatures of the condensation water, $T_{ae_{cond}}$, and the return water of the secondary circuit, $T_{ae_{evap}}$, on the consumption of chillers. Recall that these factors are used for their calculation in Eqs. 3 and 4.

Modeling Z_{CAP_1} obtained an MSE of 1.25×10^{-3} and an R^2 of 0.9977 for the value of $Q_{chiller}/Q_{chiller_{nom}}$, i.e. the instantaneous load factor of the chiller. The modeling of Z_{EIR} occasioned an MSE of 1.54×10^{-4} and an R^2 of 0.9999 for the value of EIR/EIR_{nom} of chiller. Both results are excellent, presenting values of R^2 very close to 1, hence validating the models adopted to estimate these factors.

In Fig. 3(a), we can observe that as $T_{ae_{cond}}$ is reduced, the load factor of the chiller is also reduced, as expected. The result of the modeling factor Z_{EIR} can be seen in Fig. 3(c), where we observe that, as $T_{ae_{cond}}$ and $T_{ae_{evap}}$ decrease, the factor EIR/EIR_{nom} also decrease. This represents a condition of lower electrical consumption of the chiller. Analyzing the curve presented in Fig. 3(a) together with the one presented in Fig. 3(c), we can note that the return temperature of the ice water, $T_{ae_{evap}}$, exerts a greater influence on the load factor of the chiller.

The modeling of Z_{CAP_2} provides an MSE of 1.24×10^{-3} and an R^2 of 0.9965 for the estimated value of $Q_{chiller}/Q_{chiller_{nom}}$. This an excellent result as the value for R^2 is very close to 1, validating thus the adopted model. We can observe in Fig. 3(b) that, as ΔT_{ag} increases, the load factor of the chiller also increases. This is correct, since for a given fixed condition of heat load and inlet and outlet temperatures of the water in the cooling tower, an increase in ΔT_{ag} is only possible by reducing the temperature of chiller water output, represented by $T_{as_{evap}}$, which leads to an increase in the chiller load factor.

The models obtained for factors Z_{CAP_1} and Z_{CAP_2} are considered to have comparable performance, since the first presents a slightly higher R^2, while the second presents a larger MSE. Note that factor Z_{CAP_1} is obtained based on two variables, while the factor Z_{CAP_2} needs three variables. Form this point of view, the model using Z_{CAP_1} is a less complex than that is based on Z_{CAP_2}. However, both Z_{CAP_1} and Z_{CAP_2} based models can be implemented and their impact on the optimization algorithms behavior investigated. So, the best model can be selected based on time and precision requirements of the application at hand.

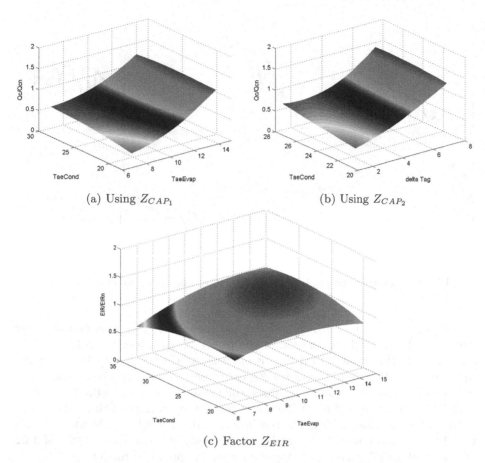

(a) Using Z_{CAP_1} (b) Using Z_{CAP_2}

(c) Factor Z_{EIR}

Fig. 3. Model's results for Q_c/Q_{cn} in terms of ΔT_{ag} and $T_{ae_{cond}}$ as well as EIR/EIR_n in terms of $T_{ae_{cond}}$ e $T_{ae_{evap}}$ for a chiller of 1000 TR.

Figure 4 compares the real values collected in the field with the values obtained from the adopted model. This result is obtained using the factor Z_{CAP_1}. The values of the instantaneous total electrical power of the chillers, in MW, obtained from the model defined by Eq. 3, show a faithful representation in relation to the real values collected in the field. We obtained an MSE of 1.102×10^{-3} and an R^2 of 0.9835. Thus, the values of MSE and R^2 obtained validate the model adopted for the consumption of chillers using factor Z_{CAP_1}.

In the same way, Fig. 5 compares the real values of instantaneous total electrical power of chillers, in MW, with the values obtained from the obtained modeling proposed in Eq. 4, which uses the factor Z_{CAP_2}. The results obtained for the modeling also showed a good representation in relation to the real values collected in the field, providing an MSE of 1.633×10^{-3} and a R^2 of 0.9755. The values of MSE and R^2 obtained validate the modeling adopted for the consumption of chillers using the factor Z_{CAP_2}.

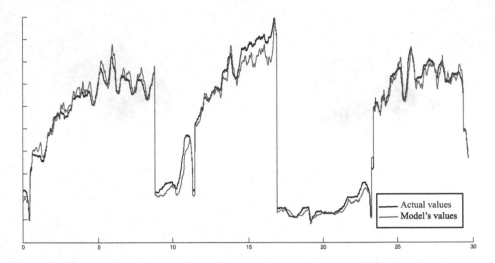

Fig. 4. Actual consumption of chillers *vs.* modeling using the factor Z_{CAP_1}.

We observe that, in terms of modeling the instantaneous total electrical power demanded by the chillers, the use of the factor Z_{CAP_1} presented a lower MSE and a higher R^2 compared to the modeling using the factor Z_{CAP_2}. We conclude, therefore, that the use of the factor Z_{CAP_1} presented more precise results.

Figure 6 compares the real values collected in the field with the values obtained from the modeling of the outlet water temperature of the chillers condenser, obtained from Eq. 10. The result obtained, although a little inferior compared to the other models, showed good representation, with an MSE of 1.51 and a R^2 of 0.8237, thus validating the use of the proposed model.

Recall that the curves represented in Figs. 4, 5 and 6 are the result of applying the models obtained from a database corresponding to 29 h and 42 min of operation of the cooling system, with readings performed every 5 s, corresponding to 21,385 points.

5   Global Energy Demand

The global energy consumption of the considered refrigeration system involves the consumption of the following equipment: cooling tower fans, chillers, condensation water circulation pumps and chilled water circulation pumps. In this case, as the condensed water and chilled water circulation pumps operate at a fixed speed, their energy consumption is therefore constant, regardless of any adjustment in the speed of the cooling tower fans or variation in the temperature of the outlet water of the chiller evaporator. Thus, the inclusion of the consumption of these equipment in the computation of the global consumption is unnecessary. With the modeling of the cooling tower and fans presented in [5] and the compression chillers, presented herein, it is possible to estimate the

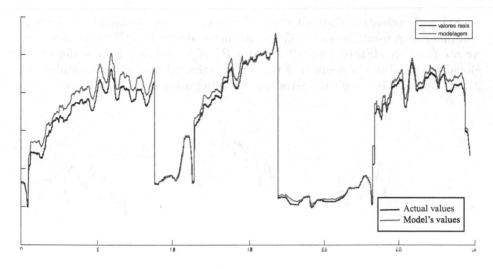

Fig. 5. Actual consumption of chillers *vs.* modeling using the factor Z_{CAP_2}.

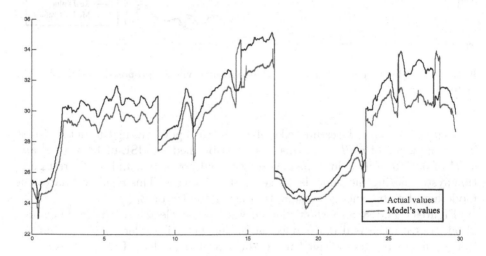

Fig. 6. Actual temperature of the water leaving the chiller condenser *vs.* modeling.

global electric energy savings obtained for the refrigeration system to be used in the energy efficiency oriented optimizations. Therefore, only the consumption of fans and chillers will be included in the modeling of global energy consumption. The instantaneous global power demanded by the cooling system obtained from Eq. 11:

$$P_{global} = n_c P_{chiller} + n_v P_v, \tag{11}$$

where n_c represents the number of chillers that are in operation, and n_v, the number of fans that are in operation. Variable $P_{chiller}$ can be obtained from Eqs. 3 and 4, and P_v is obtained via the model presented in [5].

Figure 7 presents the estimated global electrical power demand for the refrigeration system using the factor Z_{CAP_1} in the modeling of *chillers*. In this case, we obtained an MSE of 1.1×10^{-3} and a R^2 of 0.9830 in the modeling of the global electrical power demand of the refrigeration system, using a database of 21,385 points. This result validates the modeling using the factor Z_{CAP_1}.

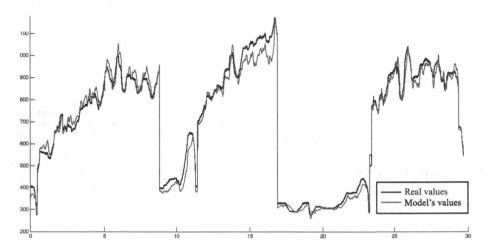

Fig. 7. Real global energy demand *vs.* that obtained via the proposed model using the factor Z_{CAP_1}.

Figure 8 presents the estimated global electrical power using the factor Z_{CAP_2} in the modeling of *chillers*. In this case, we obtained an MSE of 1.6×10^{-3} and a R^2 of 0.9756 in modeling the global electrical power demand of the refrigeration system, using the same database of 21,385 points. This result validates the modeling of global energy consumption using the factor Z_{CAP_2}.

Figures 7 and 8 also show the curves of the electrical power demanded obtained with the real data collected in the field, in order to allow comparison with the results obtained using the adopted models. The total electrical energy consumption of the refrigeration system is numerically equal to the area under each curve shown.

It is clear from the curves and the occasioned error that modeling of the global consumption of the refrigeration system using the factor Z_{CAP_1} presents a more accurate result than the one using factor Z_{CAP_2}. In the former, the actual values are closer to the model's values, as can be noted when comparing the results presented in Figs. 7 and 8.

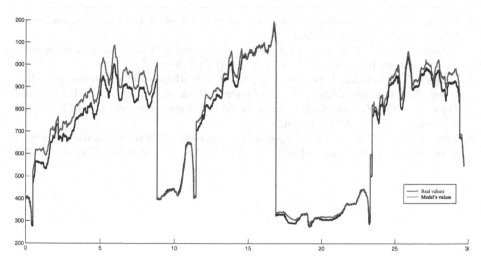

Fig. 8. Real global energy demand *vs.* that obtained via the proposed model using the factor Z_{CAP_2}.

6   Conclusions

In this paper, two models of the compression chiller, which is a main equipment in any industrial refrigeration system based on cooling towers, is presented. Due to lack of space, the proposed model for the cooling tower and the corresponding fans has been be presented in [5]. Both chiller proposed models are validated comparing the model's values to real data, collected from an existing refrigeration system. The models of the chillers show satisfactory results. Moreover, we show that the usage of the proposed model for the whole refrigeration system, which includes several tower cells and several chillers, allows us to model the global demand in terms of energy of the system. We prove that the model's results are accurate and faithful enough to the actual values. This allows their use in successful multi-objective optimization, aiming at energy efficiency.

Acknowledgments. This work is supported by Conselho Nacional de Desenvolvimento Científico e Tecnológico (CNPq - Brazil) and by Fundação Carlos Chagas Filho de Amparo à Pesquisa do Estado do Rio de Janeiro (FAPERJ - Brazil 203.111/2018). We are most grateful for their continuous financial support.

References

1. ASHRAE: Handbook - HVAC Systems and Equipment, SI edition. American Society of Heating, Refrigerating and Air Conditioning Engineers (2012)
2. Brandemuel, M.J., Gabel, S., Andersen, I.A.: Toolkit for secondary HVAC system energy calculation (1993)

3. Gavin, H.P.: The Levenberg-Marquardt method for nonlinear least squares curve-fitting problems, pp. 1–19 (2020)
4. Leontaritis, I.J., Billings, S.A.: Model selection and validation methods for nonlinear systems. Int. J. Control **45**(1), 311–341 (1987)
5. Nedjah, N., Mourelle, L.M., Lizarazu, M.S.D.: Mathematical modeling of cooling towers-based refrigeration systems for energy efficiency optimization. In: Gervasi, O., et al., (eds.) International Conference on Computational Science and Its Applications, pp. 19–27 (2022). accepted
6. Zmeureanu, R., Zelaya, E.M., Giguere, D.: Simulation de la consommation d'énergie d'un aréna à l'aide du logiciel doe-2.1e. In: ESIM2002 Conference, Canada (2002)

Mathematical Modeling of Cooling Towers-Based Refrigeration Systems for Energy Efficiency Optimization

Nadia Nedjah[1]([✉]), Luiza de Macedo Mourelle[2],
and Marcelo Silveira Dantas Lizarazu[1]

[1] Department of Electronics Engineering and Telecommunications,
State University of Rio de Janeiro, Rio de Janeiro, Brazil
{nadia,lizarazu}@eng.uerj.br
[2] Department of Systems Engineering and Computation,
State University of Rio de Janeiro, Rio de Janeiro, Brazil
ldmm@eng.uerj.br

Abstract. Cooling towers and chillers are the basis of modern refrigeration systems of large facilities, such as oil refineries, power plants and large commercial buildings. The increasing concerns about the scarcity of water and energy resources require careful optimization processes to achieve energy efficiency in industrial buildings. Energy efficiency oriented optimizations require mathematical models of real equipment that compose the refrigeration systems. In this paper, we present a complete model cooling towers and corresponding fans based on Merkel's and Braun's methods. We prove that proposed model is accurate and faithful to the real cooling cells in modern refrigeration systems. The obtained value of mean square error when applying the model and comparing the obtained results to the actual ones is minimal, hence validated the proposed model.

Keywords: Energy efficiency · Cooling tower · Chiller · Optimization

1 Introduction

In many industrial processes, heat is generated, and this heat often must be extracted and dissipated. Water is generally used as a cooling element, as can be usually seen in the petrochemical industry and in electricity generating plants. The water used in cooling systems always returns from the process at higher temperatures, which can be discarded or cooled for reuse. The latter is used whenever there is a lack of water for the application, or in cases where water consumption would be absurdly expensive in economic terms.

Cooling towers are equipment intended for application in large cooling demands, as these offer a clean and very economical way to cool the water to be reused in the cooling process. For this reason, its usage is verified in building installations, such as large shopping centers, hotels and large buildings.

O. Gervasi et al. (Eds.): ICCSA 2022 Workshops, LNCS 13377, pp. 289–307, 2022.
https://doi.org/10.1007/978-3-031-10536-4_20

A refrigeration system based on cooling towers does not only involve the cooling towers themselves, but also a set of equipment that operate interdependently, such as chillers. An undue modification of a certain parameter or operational adjustment in one of these equipment can cause either a positive or negative cascading effects on the operation of the others parts of the system. This can consequently trigger a series of effects that are not necessarily satisfactory to the overall system, which includes the reduction of its energy efficiency.

As a first part, this work aims at providing a complete model of modern cooling towers to serve as the basis of optimization of many objectives, such as maximizing the thermal exchange efficiency of the cooling tower and minimizing the energy requirement of the refrigeration system, considering all its composing equipment. For the latter, a model for the chillers is required. Due to lack of space, the model of chillers and underlying processes in the refrigeration system is presented in separate paper [11].

This paper is structured into five sections. First, in Sect. 2, we give a brief description of the structure of the modeled equipment of a modern refrigeration system. Then, in Sect. 3, we review the main methods used to elaborate the proposed models. After that, in Sect. 4.1, we present the model of the cooling tower as well as that of the tower fans. Later, in Sect. 5, we present, discuss and compare the results obtained from the application of the proposed models to those collected from a real operating refrigeration system. Last but not least, in Sect. 6, the conclusions are drawn together with future work.

2   Cooling Tower in Refrigeration System

Cooling towers are a widely used equipment in oil refineries, power plants and large commercial buildings. The role of cooling tower is to recover the heat rejected by the equipment responsible for the refrigeration of the environment and/or processes. A cooling tower operates in conjunction with other equipment such as chillers and pumps to circulate and lift the water in the system. In addition, mechanical draft-type cooling towers have internal fans that operate in order to impose proper air circulation internally. Among these equipment, the chillers are responsible for the largest portion of the power consumption of the system [15]. Figure 1 illustrates the composition and operation of a typical cooling tower as modeled in this work. The function of the cooling tower is to reduce the temperature of the incoming hot water to acceptable levels for the proper functioning of the other process equipment that make up the cooling system.

As for the heat transfer method, cooling towers can be classified as dry, wet or mixed. Another way of classifying cooling towers is the type of relative flow between water and air streams. In this case, they can be classified into towers of counter-current flow or of cross-flow. Moreover, as for the type of draft, the cooling towers can be classified into: natural draft towers, also known as hyperbolic, or mechanical draft towers.

In the natural draft towers, there are no fans at the top, and the air flow occurs naturally through the tower due to the gradual increase in air temperature

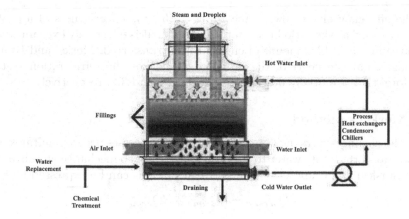

Fig. 1. Typical cooling tower operation, as modeled in this work

as it exchanges heat with the hot water (convection mechanism), and also due to their hyperbolic shape. In contrast, mechanical draft towers use fans to cause air circulation. These can be of the induced draft or forced draft type. In the proposed modeling, we consider cooling towers with mechanical air draft. More details on the cooling system's structure and operation can be found in [1].

3   Modeling Methods

The modeling of the cooling tower is necessary for any optimization simulations to be carried out, allowing the validation of the results obtained by the proposed optimization method. For this purpose, it is necessary to obtain an equation that relates the effectiveness of the tower with the speed of the fans and the temperatures of inlet and outlet of water.

In [10], a theory for evaluating the performance of cooling towers is presented, and this method has been used since then by manufacturers of cooling towers to evaluate the achieved performance. However, Merkel's method relies on several approximations in order to simplify the necessary computations. For instance, water loss by evaporation is not considered, and the *Lewis factor*, which is related to heat and mass transfer in the tower, is set to 1 [4].

In [12], Poppe presented a more precise method without resorting to the approximations made in [10]. The performance comparison between the two methods is studied in [6] and in [7]. The analysis indicated that Merkel's approximations do not compromise the results, proving their effectiveness.

In [14], a model based on a more rigorous analysis of Merkel's model is also proposed. In [2], the effectiveness method is developed, which is also known as e-NTU (Number of Transfer Units). It uses some simplifications based on in Merkel's model. The model proposed therein considers the linearization of the enthalpy of saturated air and a modification in the definition of NTU.

In the literature on cooling towers, two terminologies are commonly found for the parameter of evaluation of cooling towers' performance: the effectiveness and the efficiency of the tower. According to [5], the effectiveness of a cooling tower is defined as the ratio between the energy that is effectively exchanged and the maximum possible amount of energy to be transferred. Merkel and Braun's methods are at the heart of the proposed model for the refrigeration system. Therefore, they are briefly described in Sects. 3.1 and 3.2, respectively.

3.1 Merkel's Method

Inside the cooling towers, heat and mass transfer processes occur simultaneously. Heat is transferred from water to the atmosphere by two mechanisms: convection (heat transfer) and evaporation (mass transfer). This can be expressed by Eq. 1

$$dQ_{overall} = dQ_{conv} + dQ_{evap}, \tag{1}$$

wherein $dQ_{overall}$ is the total heat exchanged, dQ_{conv} is the heat exchanged by convection, and dQ_{evap} is the amount of heat exchanged by evaporation. In convective heat transfer, heat is transferred from water to air through the temperature gradient established with the flow of air in contact with water. Therefore, we have Eq. 2:

$$dQ_{conv} = h_{conv}(T_{water} - T_{air}dA), \tag{2}$$

where h_{conv} is the convection heat transfer coefficient in $W/m^2.°C$, T_{water} is the temperature of the water, T_{air} is the air temperature and dA is the heat exchange area.

Figure 2 illustrates the heat and mass transfer process considered by in [10]. The indicated variables will be defined in the modeling presented in the sequel. Here we consider that the temperature of the drop or water film is constant from its center to its surface.

The process of heat exchange by evaporation occurs due to mass transfer between water and air. In this case, the energy necessary for the state change is taken from the water itself, thus causing its temperature to decrease. Note that thermal exchange by evaporation is responsible for most of the heat exchanged in the cooling tower.

The mass of water that evaporates is transferred to the air through two basic mechanisms: the first is the diffusion of water molecules into the air, along the interface formed between water and air, during contact; the second is the dragging of water molecules by the air current, which is mechanically induced through the use of a fan in the cooling tower. Therefore, we can establish Eq. 3:

$$dQ_{evap} = h_m L_c(UE_2 - UE_1)dA, \tag{3}$$

wherein h_m is the mass transfer coefficient, in kg/m^2.s, L_c is the latent heat of vaporization of water, in kcal/kg, UE_2 and UE_1 represents the specific humidity of saturated air and the specific humidity of the air before contact with water, respectively in $kg\ steam/kg\ ar$, and dA is the heat exchange area, in m^2. The heat received by the air can be expressed through Eq. 4:

$$dQ = \dot{m}_{air}dh_{air}, \tag{4}$$

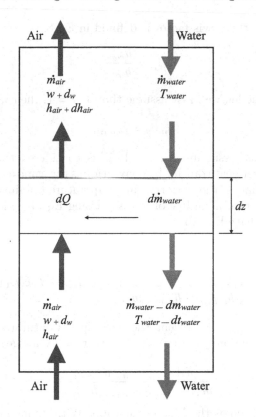

Fig. 2. Energy balance in Merkel's model.

wherein $\dot{m}_{air}$ is the mass flow rate of air, in kg/s, and dh_{air} is the enthalpy change of air, in kcal/kg. The enthalpy variation of the air occurs due to the portions of sensible heat and latent heat received through the heat exchange with water. Therefore, the value of h_{ar} can be approximated as in Eq. 5:

$$h_{air} = c_p T_{air} + L_c U E_{air}, \tag{5}$$

where c_p is the specific heat of air at constant pressure, T_{air} is the temperature of the air, and $U E_{air}$ is the specific humidity of the air. It is also known that the sensible heat transferred from water to air is given by Eq. 6:

$$dQ = \dot{m}_{water} c_{water} dT_{water}, \tag{6}$$

where c_{water} is the specific heat of water, $\dot{m}_{water}$ is the mass flow rate of water, and dT_{water} is the temperature variation of the water. Considering that there is no loss of water mass by evaporation, that is, that $\dot{m}_{water}$ is constant in the cooling tower, and using the equations defined above, we have Eq. 7:

$$dQ = \dot{m}_{water} c_{water} dT_{water} = h_{conv}(T_{water} - T_{air})dA + h_m L_c(U E_2 - U E_1)dA. \tag{7}$$

On the other hand, the Lewis factor is defined in Eq. 8:

$$L_{ef} = \frac{h_{conv}}{h_m c_p}.$$ (8)

As in the Merkel model, we must assume that $L_{ef} = 1$, then we have Eq. 9:

$$h_m c_p = h_{conv}.$$ (9)

In general terms, assuming $L_{ef} = 1$, it is considered that the degree of difficulty (or ease) for heat transfer by convection is the same as for mass transfer by evaporation. That is, the variation in temperature obtained is equal to the variation in the specific humidity of the air. Using Eqs. 7 and 9 and after that applying Eq. 5, we have Eq. 10:

$$
\begin{aligned}
dQ &= \dot{m}_{water} c_{water} dT_{water} \\
&= h_m c_p (T_{water} - T_{air}) dA + h_m L_c (UE_2 - UE_1) dA \\
&= h_m \left[(c_p T_{water} + L_c UE_2) - (c_p T_{air} + L_c UE_1) \right] dA \\
&= h_m (h_{air_{sat}} - h_{air_{dry}}) dA,
\end{aligned}
$$ (10)

where $h_{air_{sat}}$ and $h_{air_{dry}}$ represent the enthalpy of saturated air (after heat exchange) and the enthalpy of dry air (before heat exchange), from Eq. 10 we get Eq. 11:

$$\frac{h_m dA}{\dot{m}_{water}} = \frac{c_{water} dT_{water}}{h_{air_{sat}} - h_{air_{dry}}}.$$ (11)

This equation is known as the Merkel equation. With its integration, we obtain Eq. 12:

$$\frac{KaV}{L} = \frac{h_m a_p A_p z}{\dot{m}_{water}} = \int_{T_1}^{T_2} \frac{c_{water} \, dT_{water}}{h_{air_{sat}} - h_{air_{dry}}},$$ (12)

wherein a_p represents the specific area of the tower infill, in m^2/m^3, A_p represents the frontal cross-sectional area of the infill, in m^2, and z represents the height of the cooling tower, in meters.

It is noteworthy that in Eq. 12, the term $\frac{KaV}{L}$ is dimensionless and represents the overall coefficient of performance of the tower. The term Ka, in $kgs^{-1} \, m^{-3}$, is the result of the product of the total heat coefficient K, in $kgs^{-1} \, m^{-2}$, and the heat transfer area per unit volume a, in $m^2 \, m^{-3}$. The term L represents the mass flow rate of water in the tower, in $kg \, s^{-1}$. The term $\frac{KaV}{L}$ is also found in the literature as Me_M, Merkel's number or NTU (Number of Transfer Units) [3,7]. The term NTU is the most used, and represents the number of times the enthalpy difference between saturated and dry air indicated in the equation is transferred to water.

3.2   Effectiveness Method

The effectiveness method has been introduced in [2], where heat and mass transfers are considered to occur inside the cooling tower as indicated in Fig. 3.

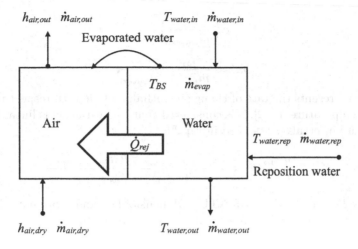

Fig. 3. Energy balance with the effectiveness method.

The energy balance of the control volume considered in Fig. 3 can be analyzed through the Eqs. 13–16, which represent the conservation of air mass, heat of air, mass of water and heat of water, respectively.

$$\dot{m}_{air_{dry}} + \dot{m}_{evap} = \dot{m}_{air_{sat}}, \tag{13}$$

$$\dot{m}_{air_{dry}} h_{air_{dry}} + Q_{rej} - Q_{evap} = \dot{m}_{air_{sat}} h_{air_{sat}}, \tag{14}$$

$$\dot{m}_{water_{in}} - \dot{m}_{evap} = \dot{m}_{water_{out}}, \tag{15}$$

$$\dot{m}_{water_{in}} T_{water_{in}} c_{water} - Q_{rej} + \dot{m}_{water_{rep}} T_{water_{rep}} c_{water} = \dot{m}_{water_{out}} T_{water_{out}} c_{water}, \tag{16}$$

where $\dot{m}_{air_{dry}}$ represents the mass flow rate of dry air entering the tower, $\dot{m}_{air_{sat}}$ is the mass flow rate of saturated air leaving the tower, $\dot{m}_{evap}$ is the mass flow rate of the air leaving the tower due to evaporation, $\dot{m}_{water_{rep}}$ is the flow reposition water mass required due to the volume of water leaving the tower due to evaporation, $T_{water_{rep}}$ is the reposition water temperature, $\dot{m}_{water_{in}}$ is the mass flow rate of hot water entering the tower, $T_{water_{in}}$ is the temperature of hot water entering the tower, $\dot{m}_{water_{out}}$ is the mass flow rate of the cold water leaving the tower, $T_{water_{out}}$ is the temperature of the cold water leaving the tower, T_{BS} is the dry bulb temperature of the air, and Q_{rej} represents the amount of heat that is transferred from water to dry air, making it saturated, and Q_{evap} represents the amount of heat that is removed from the water by the process of evaporation. Note that Fig. 3 illustrates the processes described by Eqs. 13–16.

According to this method, the effectiveness of the tower is given by Eq. 17:

$$\epsilon_a = \frac{1 - e^{-NTU(1-m^*)}}{1 - m^* e^{-NTU(1-m^*)}}, \quad \text{with} \tag{17}$$

$$NTU = c \left(\frac{\dot{m}_{air}}{\dot{m}_{water}} \right)^{-(1+n)} \quad \text{and} \tag{18}$$

$$m^* = \frac{\dot{m}_{air}}{\dot{m}_{water}} \cdot \frac{C_S}{c_{water}}, \tag{19}$$

where C_S represents the rate of change in enthalpy of air with respect to change in water temperature. In [2], it is considered that this variation is linear for small temperature intervals, as defined in Eq. 20:

$$C_S = \frac{dh_{air_{sat}}}{dT_{water}} \approx \frac{h_{air_{sat},T_{water_{in}}} - h_{air_{sat},T_{water_{out}}}}{T_{water_{in}} - T_{water_{out}}}. \tag{20}$$

In Eqs. 17 and 18, the term NTU is dimensionless and represents the global performance of the cooling tower. This term is similar to the $\frac{KaV}{L}$ indicated in Eq. (12).

In Eq. 18, c and n are empirical constants associated with each particular cooling tower. These constants are obtained by the cooling tower manufacturers after performing the performance tests, before starting the tower operation, for a given wet bulb temperature. In Eq. 20, the terms $h_{air_{sat},T_{water_{in}}}$ and $h_{ar_{sat},T_{water_{out}}}$ represent the enthalpy of saturated air, respectively, at the temperatures of the inlet water and the water leaving the tower.

Moreover, from the effectiveness, one can obtain the heat rejected by the cooling tower, Q_{rej}, which is given by Eq. 21:

$$Q_{rej} = \epsilon_a \dot{m}_{air} (h_{air_{sat},T_{water_{in}}} - h_{air_{dry},T_{BS}}). \tag{21}$$

Note that in the effectiveness method, obtaining C_S depends on the conditions at the exit of the tower (cold water temperature and saturated air enthalpy), which requires the use of recursive techniques to solve Eqs. 17–20, from the definition of approximate initial values for the output variables.

4   Cooling Tower's Proposed Model

In this section, we present the modeling of the process performed by the cooling tower and the ventilators. Based on Merkel's and Braun's methods, in Sect. 4.1, we provide a precise and faithful model of the cooling tower and in Sect. 4.2, we do so for the used fans.

4.1   Tower

The modeling adopted for the cooling tower is available in [9]. This defines that the effectiveness of a cooling tower can be approximated by a second order function, from the Merkel's and Braun's models, based on the fundamental laws of heat and mass transfer.

In Braun's model, according to Eq. 20, a linear approximation is performed for the variation of the enthalpy of saturated air with respect to temperature.

In this case, the variation of the enthalpy of saturation is obtained based on the difference in temperature between the hot water that arrives at the tower and the cold water that leaves it [2]. This is the premise adopted by Braun for the calculation of C_S, as indicated in Eq. 20.

From a control and optimization point of view, the leaving water temperature $T_{water_{out}}$ and the enthalpy of saturated air leaving the tower $h_{air_{sat},T_{water_{out}}}$, both used in Eq. 20, are output variables. Therefore, they are variables that need to be controlled and should not be used as input variables, as indicated in Eqs. 17–20. Let us consider the illustration presented in Fig. 4.

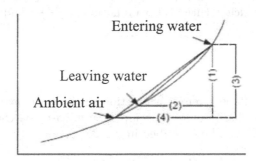

Fig. 4. Enthalpy of saturated air versus temperature.

Based on Fig. 4, Eq. 20 can be approximated as in Eq. 22:

$$C_S = \frac{dh_{air_{sat}}}{dT_{water}} \approx \frac{(h_{air_{sat},T_{water_{in}}} - h_{air_{sat},T_{BU}}) + f_1(\Delta h)}{(T_{water_{in}} - T_{BU}) + f_2(\Delta T)}, \tag{22}$$

where ΔT is defined as the *approach* of the cooling tower. Graphically, this is represented in Fig. 4 as the difference between the length of lines (4) and (2), that is, between the temperature of the water leaving the tower and the local wet bulb temperature. Variable Δh is the enthalpy change of saturated air related to the approach ΔT. Note, as indicated in Fig. 4, that the enthalpy of air saturation varies with approach, ΔT, so that the higher ΔT is, the higher the variation of the enthalpy of saturation.

The term C_S, as indicated in Eq. (20), is defined in Braun's modeling as a linear approximation of the curve that relates the inlet and outlet temperatures of water with the enthalpy of saturation. It is represented in Fig. 4 as the ratio between the lengths of lines (1) and (2), which represent, respectively, the variation of the enthalpy of saturation of the air, $h_{air_{sat},T_{water_{in}}} - h_{air_{sat},T_{water_{out}}}$, and the change in water temperature, $T_{water_{in}} - T_{water_{out}}$. Therefore, Fig. 4 illustrates the behavior of the tower with regard to the variation in enthalpy of air saturation as a function of variations in water and air temperatures. Observe that the approximation of the value of C_S based on the wet bulb temperature, T_{BU}, instead of the leaving water temperature of the tower, $T_{water_{out}}$, unlike the approach adopted in Braun's model (as indicated in Eq. 20), requires a correction, which is obtained by using $f_1(\Delta h)$ and $f_2(\Delta T)$ in Eq. 22.

Thus, based on the laws of conservation of mass and energy, the approach, ΔT, can be approximated as a function of $\frac{\dot{m}_{air}}{\dot{m}_{water}}$ and $(T_{water_{in}} - T_{BU})$. Therefore, we have Eq. 23:

$$f_1(\Delta T) = f_1\left(\frac{\dot{m}_{air}}{\dot{m}_{water}}, (T_{water_{in}} - T_{BU})\right). \tag{23}$$

Still based on the laws of conservation of mass and energy, Δh can be defined as a function of ΔT, which in turn is also a function of $\frac{\dot{m}_{air}}{\dot{m}_{water}}$ and $(T_{water_{in}} - T_{BU})$. So we have Eq. 24:

$$f_2(\Delta h) = f_2\left(\frac{\dot{m}_{air}}{\dot{m}_{water}}, (T_{water_{in}} - T_{BU})\right). \tag{24}$$

Thus, as C_S in Eq. 22 is given as a function of the enthalpy change of the air with respect to the change of water temperature, based on the Eqs. 23 and 24, we conclude that C_S can be described in Eq. 25:

$$C_S = f_3\left(\frac{\dot{m}_{air}}{\dot{m}_{water}}, (T_{water_{in}} - T_{BU})\right). \tag{25}$$

Through Eqs. 17–19, we can deduce that the effectiveness ϵ_a is a function of NTU and m^*, where NTU is a function of $\frac{\dot{m}_{air}}{\dot{m}_{water}}$ and C_S. Therefore, applying Eq. 25 to Eqs. 17–19, we obtain a general expression for the effectiveness ϵ_a as presented in Eq. 26:

$$\epsilon_a = f\left(\frac{\dot{m}_{air}}{\dot{m}_{water}}, (T_{water_{in}} - T_{BU})\right) = f(x, y), \tag{26}$$

where variables x and y are be used, respectively, to represent $\frac{\dot{m}_{air}}{\dot{m}_{water}}$ and $(T_{water_{in}} - T_{BU})$, in order to simplify the following equations. So we have $x = \frac{\dot{m}_{air}}{\dot{m}_{water}}$ and $y = T_{water_{in}} - T_{BU}$.

Note that Eq. 26 can be viewed as a function in which the effectiveness of the heat exchange of the cooling tower ϵ_a can be modeled as a function depending only of input variables, differently from what occurs in Merkel's and Braun's methods. So, considering that the effectiveness ϵ_a is a continuous function under normal operating conditions of the cooling tower, it can be considered derivable. Therefore, one can use the Taylor series as an approximation to solve Eq. 26. Due to the non-linearity characteristic of the cooling tower response, the Taylor series will be used up to the second order, to represent it correctly and precisely.

$$f(x, y) = f(x_0, y_0) + \left[\frac{\partial f(x_0, y_0)}{\partial x}(x - x_0) + \frac{\partial f(x_0, y_0)}{\partial y}(y - y_0) \right]$$
$$+ \frac{1}{2!} \left[\left(\frac{\partial^2 f(x_0, y_0)}{\partial x^2} \right) \cdot (x - x_0)^2 + \left(\frac{\partial^2 f(x_0, y_0)}{\partial y^2} \right) \cdot (y - y_0)^2 \right.$$
$$\left. + \left(\frac{\partial^2 f(x_0, y_0)}{\partial y^2} \right) \cdot (y - y_0)^2 + 2 \left(\frac{\partial^2 f(x_0, y_0)}{\partial x \partial y} \right) \cdot (x - x_0)(y - y_0) \right],$$

$$\tag{27}$$

wherein the point (x_0, y_0) represents any cooling tower operating point close to a hypothetical condition (x, y). The point (x_0, y_0) can be determined experimentally, allowing to consider the terms $f(x_0, y_0)$, $\frac{\partial f(x_0, y_0)}{\partial x}$, $\frac{\partial f(x_0, y_0)}{\partial y}$, $\frac{\partial^2 f(x_0, y_0)}{\partial x^2}$, $\frac{\partial^2 f(x_0, y_0)}{\partial y^2}$ and $\frac{\partial^2 f(x_0, y_0)}{\partial x \partial y}$ as constants. These will be represented by coefficients c_0, c_1, c_2, c_3, c_4 and c_5, respectively. So, replacing $\frac{\dot{m}_{air}}{\dot{m}_{water}}$ and $(T_{water_{in}} - T_{BU})$, respectively, by the variables x and y in Eq. 27, we obtain Eq. 28:

$$\epsilon_a = c_0 + c_1 x + c_2 y + c_3 x^2 + c_4 y^2 + c_5 xy, \tag{28}$$

where coefficients c_0 to c_5 are constants to be determined according to the behavior of the refrigeration process via collected data.

The actual performance curve of a cooling tower is usually provided by manufacturers or surveyed in the field during performance tests. It is then possible, from the data collected in the field, and with the use of the Eq. 29:

$$min \sum_{i=1}^{N} \frac{1}{2} (\epsilon_a - F_{data_i})^2, \tag{29}$$

to determine the coefficients c_0 to c_5 through the minimization of the difference between the surveyed curve and the proposed model, using any optimization algorithm. So, for each point of a total of surveyed points, the coefficients of Eq. 28 must be obtained in order to minimize the error between the surveyed curve and the proposed model, as indicated in Eq. 29. Note that F_{data_i} represents a point on the real curve obtained through field surveys, and N is the number of points used to obtain F_{data}.

In order to obtain good results, the number of points acquired must be greater than the number of coefficients, that is, $N \geq 6$. In addition, the points surveyed must have the widest possible distribution within the operating range of the cooling tower. Gauss-Newton and Levemberg-Marquardt methods are used to obtain the coefficients c_0 to c_5 [9]. In practice, the measurement of air mass flows at the inlet and outlet of the tower is difficult to perform, as this type of instrumentation is generally not available in these locations. However, this problem can be solved considering the principle of conservation of energy, replacing $\dot{m}_{air}(h_{air_{sat}, T_{water_{in}}} - h_{air_{in}})$ by $c_p(T_{water_{in}} - T_{BU})$ and applying to Eqs. 21 and 16. So to obtain ϵ_a, we have Eq. 30:

$$\epsilon_a = \frac{\dot{m}_{water_{in}} T_{water_{in}} + \dot{m}_{water_{rep}} T_{water_{rep}} - \dot{m}_{water_{out}} T_{water_{out}}}{\dot{m}_{water_{out}} (T_{water_{in}} - T_{BU})}. \tag{30}$$

Using Eqs. 28 and 30, we can obtain the temperature of the water leaving the cooling tower, as defined by Eq. 31:

$$T_{water_{out}} = \left(\frac{\dot{m}_{water_{in}}}{\dot{m}_{water_{out}}} \right) T_{water_{in}} + \left(\frac{\dot{m}_{water_{rep}}}{\dot{m}_{water_{out}}} \right) T_{water_{rep}} \\ - y(c_0 + c_1 x + c_2 y + c_3 x^2 + c_4 y^2 + c_5 xy). \tag{31}$$

From Eq. 31, it is possible to estimate how the temperature of the water leaving the cooling tower varies as a function of the mass flow of air induced in the tower, i.e., as a function of the fan speed. Equation 31 takes into account the outlet temperature of the chiller condenser, $T_{water_{in}}$, which is a function of the thermal load of the system.

Still referring to Eq. 31, the wet bulb temperature, T_{BU}, is extremely important to obtain the optimal fan speed, as it represents the minimum theoretical temperature value that can be reached by the water leaving the tower, $T_{water_{out}}$. The temperature of this water can never be lower than the wet bulb temperature, due to the saturation of the air molecules during the mass transfer process that takes place between the hot water and the dry air induced in the tower. The wet bulb temperature can be calculated as a function of ambient temperature and relative humidity, both of which are measured at the cooling tower installation site.

Moreover, the water that leaves the cooling tower corresponds to the water that enters the chiller condenser. Disregarding the thermal losses in the section between the outlet of the cooling tower and the inlet of the condenser, it can be concluded that the temperature of the water leaving the tower is equal to the temperature of the water entering the chiller condenser. The latter directly influences the performance of the chiller itself, and consequently, its energy consumption. Thus, the tower outlet temperature defined by Eq. 31 must be evaluated in relation to its influence on the energy consumption of the chiller, in order to obtain the best operational condition of the chiller and of the cooling tower, aiming at energy efficiency with the least detriment to the tower's effectiveness.

This modeling, in comparison with the Merkel's and Braun's models, offers the advantage that all variables are measurable and correspond to the input variables of the cooling tower. Therefore, there is no need to use recursive techniques. In terms of computational implementation, this modeling is more convenient, as ϵ_a is described as a polynomial function, unlike in Braun's model, where NTU and ϵ_a are described as exponential functions, which substantially increases the computational effort.

4.2   Tower's Fans

Among the equipment that compose the refrigeration system considered in this work, only the tower fans allow the speed variation, through the use of frequency converters. Therefore, condensed water and chilled water circulation pumps, as well as chillers, operate at their fixed speed.

The electrical power demanded by each of the cooling tower fans depends on their speed setting. It is known that the air moved by the fan represents a load with resistant torque, quadratic C_{res} i.e. $C_{res} = kn^2$ wherein n represents the fan speed and k a proportionality constant. The electrical power required to drive the fan, at a given speed, is defined by $P(n) = C_{res} \cdot n = kn^3$. Thus, when reducing the engine speed from speed n_1 to n_2, we get Eq. 32:

$$P_2 = P_1 \cdot \left(\frac{n_2}{n_1}\right)^3, \tag{32}$$

where it is possible to verify that the demanded power drops with the cubic power of the reduction of the engine speed. Therefore, reducing the fan speed of the cooling tower cells should significantly reduce their energy consumption.

Thus, the electrical power demanded by each cooling tower fan, P_v, in kW, for a given speed, can be defined as in Eq. 33:

$$P_v = \sqrt{3}V_n I_n \cdot FP(n) \cdot \left(\frac{\dot{m}_{air}}{\dot{m}_{air_n}}\right)^3, \tag{33}$$

where V_n and I_n represent, respectively, the rated voltage and current of the fan motors, $FP(n)$ represents the motor power factor, which is a function of its rotation speed n, $\dot{m}_{air}$ represents the mass flow rate of air induced by the fan, and $\dot{m}_{air_n}$, the mass flow rate of air induced by the fan.

The speed set for the fan is proportional to the air flow obtained. Therefore, the Eq. 33 can also be defined as a function of the fan speed. The optimal speed value to be adopted for the cooling tower fans will be defined by the optimization system, aiming to obtain the best compromise between minimizing the global energy consumption of the cooling system and maximizing the effectiveness of the cooling tower.

The power factor of an electric motor, as well as its efficiency, are non-linear regarding the motor's rotation n. This is mainly due to the increase in internal heating for speeds below the rated speed. Therefore, in order to estimate the energy consumption of the fan motors for a given speed, taking into account these non-linearities, we adopt the model of Eq. 34:

$$P_v = \sqrt{3}V_n I_n (d_0 n^3 + d_1 n^2 + d_2 n + d_3), \tag{34}$$

where the coefficients $d_i, 0 \geq i \leq 5$ can be obtained using non-linear regression techniques.

The fans' consumption is small when compared to the value of consumption of chillers. However, the operation of the fans at low speed provides considerable energy savings, since it is an equipment that must operate continuously. For instance, running at 50% of the rated speed provides energy savings of around 87.5%, since the motor consumes around 1/8 of the nominal power.

5 Model Validation Results

In order to complete and validate the cooling tower proposed model, it is necessary to collect data from the cooling system and used them to obtain the proper values of the required coefficients c_i and d_i as required in Eq. 31 regarding the cooling tower and Eq. 34 regarding the tower's fans, respectively. The dataset considered for carrying out this operation is composed of points that represent different situations of thermal load. These were collected on different days of operation. The choice of days for the collection of operational data was carried out in order to obtain data that represent the various thermal load conditions present throughout the day and for different climatic conditions. We contemplated both sunny and rainy days, as these conditions influence the performance of the cooling system considered in this work.

Overall, 21,385 operating points of the cooling system were collected, corresponding to 29 h and 42 min of operation. The points were collected on four different days, in order to represent the operation in daytime and nighttime hours. These represent, respectively, conditions of high and low thermal load. The dataset represented by the collected data is divided into two subsets, both equally distributed *i.e.* balanced and corresponding to 50% of the total points collected, The first subset is called the estimation dataset and the second the validation dataset.

The coefficients of the adopted models are obtained using the estimation dataset. Then, the validation dataset is applied to the obtained models. All obtained models for the refrigeration system equipment are evaluated using the same estimation and validation datasets. The evaluation of the final result is performed based on the values of Mean Square Error (MSE) and the Coefficient of Determination, called R^2, computed. The coefficient of determination varies between 0 and 1, and allows assessing how much the adopted model is capable of estimating the actual collected data. Note that the closer the value of R^2 to 1 is, the better the evaluation of the obtained modeling [8].

The modeling of the cooling tower consists of obtaining the coefficients c_0–c_5 indicated in Eq. 31, which estimate the effectiveness of the cooling tower as a function of the terms x and y, which represent, respectively, $\frac{\dot{m}_{air}}{\dot{m}_{water}}$ and $(T_{water_{ent}} - T_{BU})$, thus allowing to obtain the effectiveness of the tower as a function of the speed of its fans. To obtain the coefficients, the Levemberg-Marquardt optimization method is used, based on the use of data collected in the field, as defined in Eq. 29. The use of the Levemberg-Marquardt method is due to the wide application of this regression technique to applications involving nonlinear systems [13]. Table 1 shows the values obtained.

Table 1. Obtained values for the coefficient required by the cooling tower's model.

Coefficient	Value
c_0	+0.0262
c_1	+0.4935
c_2	+0.14350
c_3	−0.0289
c_4	−0.0129
c_5	−0.0533

The tower effectiveness modeling occasioned an MSE of 3.5×10^{-3} and a R^2 of 0.9924. The values presented are quite satisfactory and validate the model adopted. Figure 5(a) indicates the effectiveness curve in terms of G, obtained from Eq. 28, where G is the ratio between the air and water flows inside of the cooling tower. In this case, the air flow varies with the speed of the tower fans. This curve depends on the temperature values of the water entering the tower and the wet bulb temperature. Here, a tower inlet temperature of 25.9 °C and a wet bulb temperature of 22.2 °C is considered. Moreover, Fig. 5(b) indicates the variation in the temperature of the water leaving the cooling tower as a function of the variation in the ratio between the air and water flows, G, obtained from the Eq. 31, considering the application of the coefficients c_0–c_5 from Table 1. In modeling the temperature of the water leaving the tower, an MSE of 1.95×10^{-2} and R^2 of 0.9546 was obtained, a result that validates the adopted model.

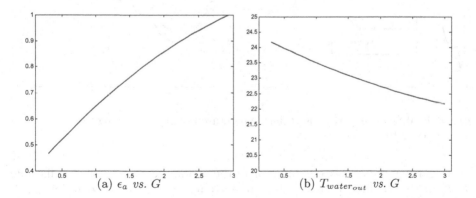

(a) ϵ_a *vs.* G (b) $T_{water_{out}}$ *vs.* G

Fig. 5. Performance results of the cooling tower's model for $T_{water_{in}} = 25.9$ °C and $T_{BU} = 22.2$ °C.

Analyzing the curves in Fig. 5, it can be seen that as the ratio between the mass flow rates of air and water increases, there is a reduction in the water temperature of condensation that leaves the cooling tower. This causes an increase in its effectiveness, as indicated in Eq. 30.

Figure 6 illustrates the comparison between the real values and the values obtained from the proposed model to estimate the temperature of the water leaving the cooling tower, $T_{water_{out}}$, using the Eq. 31. In this case, the model is applied to a dataset obtained during 29 h and 42 min of operation of the cooling system, with readings every 5 s. Hence, it includes a total of 21,385 points. The oscillations shown in Fig. 6 indicate the temperature variation of the water leaving the cooling tower during field data collection. Note that during the considered time period, values are recorded for $T_{water_{out}}$ between 21.5 °C and 27 °C. Moreover, in Fig. 6, points can be observed where the modeling curve presents slight peaks compared to the curve of the real values. However, the recorded peaks represent a maximum deviation of 1.75 °C for the modeling with respect to the actual values, which represents a maximum relative deviation, in modulus, of 7.20%. This deviation is acceptable, since it occurs for a small range of the curve. Furthermore, the average relative deviation obtained for the 21,385 points is, in modulus, 0.005%.

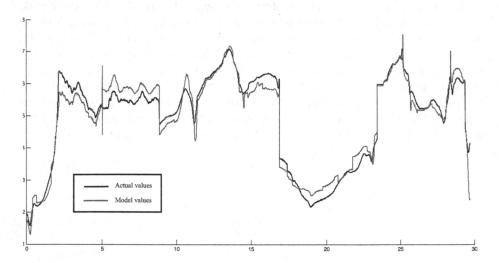

Fig. 6. Real *vs.* estimated value of the temperature leaving the cooling tower, $T_{water_{out}}$ during 30 h interval.

Regarding the energy consumption of the cooling tower fans, the coefficients d_0–d_3 indicated in Eq. 34 are also obtained using the Levemberg-Marquardt method. The values obtained are shown in Table 2. In this case, the points of the used dataset for the modeling were obtained by varying the fan speed, followed by reading the respective demanded electrical power. Overall, 12 operating points are obtained, including the nominal speed, with all other speeds being lower. Figure 7 presents the result of the modeling obtained for the demanded power by one of the cooling tower fans, using the Eq. 34 and the coefficients given in Table 2. An MSE of 2.6505×10^{-4} is occasioned by the model, which is an excellent result.

Table 2. Obtained values for the coefficient required by the fans' model.

Coefficient	Value
d_0	+0.7931
d_1	+0.0330
d_2	+0.0557
d_3	+0.0039

The obtained coefficients are applied to the dataset composed of 21,835 points, obtaining the result shown in Fig. 8. Differently from that indicated in Fig. 7, it illustrates the application of the modeling to the set of fans that are in operation during field data collection. In Fig. 8 it is possible to compare the real values with those obtained via the proposed model. In this case, an MSE of 1.1609 and a R^2 of 0.9947 are obtained. This result validates the model. Note in Fig. 8 that the values obtained using the proposed model follow the real curve of required power by the fans in all the points. Also, it can be observed in the points where there is a sudden reduction or increase in the demanded power. These points indicate the turning off and restarting of the fans, as well as their operation with speeds below the nominal.

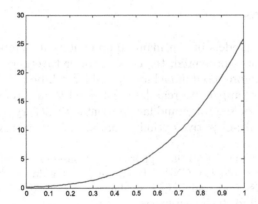

Fig. 7. Result of modeling the power consumption of cooling tower fans in terms of fractions of the nominal rotation speed.

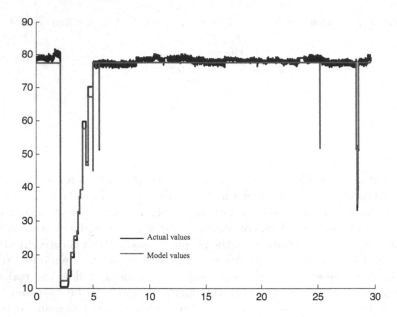

Fig. 8. Actual consumption of cooling tower fans *vs.* values obtained using the proposed model.

6   Conclusions

In this paper, the models of the main equipment that compose an industrial refrigeration system is presented: the cooling tower together with its fans. Due to lack of space, the proposed model for the chiller will be presented in [11]. The models obtained are applied to real data, collected from a refrigeration system. The models of the cooling tower and fans present satisfactory results. This allows their use in any multi-objective optimization, aiming at energy efficiency.

Acknowledgments. This work is supported by Conselho Nacional de Desenvolvimento Científico e Tecnológico (CNPq - Brazil) and by Fundação Carlos Chagas Filho de Amparo à Pesquisa do Estado do Rio de Janeiro (FAPERJ - Brazil 203.111/2018). We are most grateful for their continuous financial support.

References

1. Alpina: Torres de resfriamento de água. Tech. rep., Alpina S/A Indústria e Comércio, São Bernardo do Campo, SP (1978)
2. Braun, J.E., Klein, S.A., Mitchel, J.W.: Effectiveness models cooling towers cooling coils. ASHRAE Trans. **95**(2), 164–174 (1989)
3. Fahmy, A.A., Shouman, L.A.: Deterministic study on the optimum performance of counter flow cooling tower. Int. J. Sci. Eng. Res. **3**(6), 1–5 (2012)
4. Kern, D.Q.: Process Heat Transfer. McGraw-Hill Book Company Inc., Tokyo (1983)

5. Khan, J.R., Zubair, S.M.: An improved design and rating analyses of counter flow wet cooling towers. J. Heat Trans. **123**, 770–778 (2001)
6. Kloppers, J.C., Kroger, D.G.: A critical cooling tower performance evaluation. In: 12th IAHR Symposium in Cooling Towers and Heat Exchangers, UTS, pp. 108–115 (2001)
7. Kloppers, J.C., Kroger, D.G.: Cooling tower performance: a critical evaluation of the Merkel assumptions. Res. Dev. J. Incorporated SA Mech. Eng. **20**(1), 24–29 (2004)
8. Leontaritis, I.J., Billings, S.A.: Model selection and validation methods for non-linear systems. Int. J. Control **45**(1), 311–341 (1987)
9. Lu, L., Cai, W.: A universal engineering model for cooling towers. In: International Refrigeration and Air Conditioning Conference, Indiana, USA (2002)
10. Merkel, F.: Verdunstungskuhlung, pp. 576–583. VDI Forschungsarbeiten, Berlin (1925)
11. Nedjah, N., Mourelle, L.M., Lizarazu, M.S.D.: Mathematical modeling of chiller-based refrigeration systems for energy efficiency optimization. In: Gervasi, O., et al., B.M. (eds.) International Conference on Computational Science and Its Applications, pp. 1–18 (2022, accepted)
12. Poppe, M., Rogener, H.: Berechnung von ruckkuhlwerken, VDI-Warmeatlas (1991). pp. 1001–1015
13. Seber, G.A.F., Wild, C.J.: Nonlinear Regression. Willey-Interscience, Hoboken (2003)
14. Sutherland, J.W.: Analysis of mechanical draught counter flow air water cooling tower. J. Heat Trans. **105**, 576–583 (1983)
15. Yu, K., Hung, Y., Hsieh, S., Hung, S.: Chiller energy saving optimization using artificial neural networks. J. Appl. Sci. **16**(11), 3008–3014 (2011). https://doi.org/10.3923/jas.2011.3008.3014

The Influence of Amyloid-Beta on Calcium Dynamics in Alzheimer's Disease: A Spatio-Temporal Study

Swadesh Pal[1] , Hina Shaheen[1(✉)] , and Roderick Melnik[1,2]

[1] M3AI Laboratory, MS2Discovery Interdisciplinary Research Institute, Wilfrid Laurier University, Waterloo, ON N2L 3C5, Canada
shah8322@mylaurier.ca,
rmelnik@wlu.ca
[2] BCAM - Basque Center for Applied Mathematics, 48009 Bilbao, Spain
http://m3ai.wlu.ca

Abstract. One of the keys to understanding and treating Alzheimer's disease (AD) and dementia is believed to be calcium (Ca^{2+}) in the cytoplasm. Researchers have discovered how an imbalance of Ca^{2+} ions in the cytoplasm can lead to cell death and, more particularly, neurodegeneration in brain cells in Alzheimer's and dementia patients. Many substances are present in brain cells, but Ca^{2+} is the most tractable and is employed for experimental validations. In this study, we employ a spatio-temporal computational model to investigate AD development using Ca^{2+} dynamics in the cytoplasm. We study the spatio-temporal dynamics of biochemical processes via a new coupled model and analyze the sensitivity of this model to some of the critical parameters. As a result of this study, several important contributions have been made. Firstly, we have demonstrated that the SERCA pump flux parameter has a significant impact on the frequency of intracellular calcium concentrations. Furthermore, we studied Ca^{2+} dynamics with diffusion in the presence of different amyloid-beta levels. We found that how amyloid-beta affects various fluxes contributions through voltage-gated calcium channels, amyloid-beta-formed channels and ryanodine receptors. This work contributes to a better understanding of the spatio-temporal action of Ca^{2+} dysregulation in the cytoplasm, and through this, it can offer further insight into AD developments and progression.

Keywords: Alzheimer's disease · Ca^{2+} dysregulation · Cellular excitability · Neurons and astrocytes · Amyloid-beta · SERCA pump · Spatio-temporal coupled models

1 Introduction

Prion-like proliferation and aggregation of harmful proteins are linked to neurodegenerative diseases including Alzheimer's and Parkinson's disease [1].

© The Author(s), under exclusive license to Springer Nature Switzerland AG 2022
O. Gervasi et al. (Eds.): ICCSA 2022 Workshops, LNCS 13377, pp. 308–322, 2022.
https://doi.org/10.1007/978-3-031-10536-4_21

Amyloid- beta (Aβ) oligomers linked with Alzheimer's disease (AD) might cause adverse intracellular calcium Ca^{2+} levels by affecting the intrinsic Ca^{2+} regulation system within cells. These disturbances can result in alterations in homeostasis levels and can have a negative impact on cell functions and survival. Although research has revealed that Aβ can interfere with diverse Ca^{2+} fluxes, the complexities of these interactions largely remain a mystery [2,3]. Due to the widespread involvement of Ca^{2+} disruption in AD development, it's likely that concentrating on Ca^{2+} dysregulation might assist in the development of a possible therapeutic strategy for preventing or treating AD, despite the fact that existing hypotheses about AD have yet to offer curative medicines [4].

Meanwhile, the term "cellular excitability" has been recently introduced to characterise variations in cytosolic Ca^{2+} concentration in response to chemical or mechanical stimulations in astrocytes [5]. Earlier, De Pittà et al. [6], for example, found that they encode synaptic information by modulating intracellular calcium dynamics in response to synaptic activity. This kind of Ca^{2+} homeostasis, whether in neurons or astrocytes, may be disturbed by Aβ, particularly by its soluble oligomeric form, which is more damaging [7]. Aβ has been shown to disrupt several calcium fluxes in astrocytes. Deposition of Aβ oligomers not only creates holes in the lipid bilayer that are permeable to cationic ions, but also activates L-type CaV, increasing intracellular Ca^{2+} concentration [4]. Furthermore, exposure to Aβ increases the expression of astroglial mGluR5 [8]. Aβ can activate ryanodine receptors (RyRs) and inositol triphosphate receptors (IP3Rs) in astrocytes, causing Ca^{2+} release from the endoplasmic reticulum (ER) [4].

Previously, we developed a mathematical model that replicates Alzheimer's Aβ accumulation based on Ca^{2+}-dependent exosome release from neurons and astrocytes [3]. The components for calcium-induced calcium release (CICR) and sarco-endoplasmic Ca^{2+} ATPase pump (SERCA) are used in the majority of the computational investigations presented in this paper. Our model design emphasizes a well-documented pathway for Aβ regulation of intracellular calcium movements, that is amyloid-induced Ca^{2+} permeability through endogenous cation channels such as L- and N-type voltage-gated calcium channels (VGCCs) in the presence of diffusion. Our aim in this paper is to construct a spatio-temporal multiscale mathematical model of brain and to examine computationally astrocytic intracellular Ca^{2+} patterns under the influence of Aβ. In analyzing different scenarios with this model, we consider the initial conditions in such a way that they mimic the injection effect in some parts of the spatial domain [9]. Through voltage-gated calcium channels, Aβ-formed channels, and ryanodine receptors, our model explains how Aβ influences diverse flux contributions. The increasing Ca^{2+} and frequency of calcium oscillations were significantly induced by Aβ, according to bifurcation analysis of Aβ levels, which reflected the corresponding disease progression.

It is not an easy task to develop the complete model of Aβ mediated by calcium dynamics in the brain. However, numerous studies are going on to understand the exact Aβ impacts on astrocytes for AD [4,10]. In this paper, we use Aβ regulation of intracellular calcium regulatory fluxes as it is advantageous in analyzing a variety of cell types with spatial components. Several important contributions have been made as a result of our studies. One of them has been to propose a novel computational spatio-temporal network and corresponding simulations for better understanding the underlying complicated biochemical interactions between $A\beta$ and Ca^{2+}. Our extensive simulations have revealed that the model's excitability in spatio-temporal domain interact to produce calcium signals. Another important feature of our studies has been that the model reproduces the most common calcium signals and shows that their frequency is highly dependent on spontaneously active thalamic astrocytes spatial arrangement. We have also showed that depending on the spatial structure of calcium channels, parallel processes expressing the same calcium channels can exhibit various forms of calcium signals. In some areas of the spatial domain, we have considered the initial conditions in such a way that they approximate the injection effect. It is important to note that since the most terms included in the model change due to their dependency on the cytosolic Ca^{2+} concentrations (details are given in Sect. 3), a series of computational challenges have had to be overcome. Regardless of these challenges, our modeling approach that targets numerous pathways at the same time has shown to be successful to have a better understanding of $A\beta$ impact. It is noteworthy that computational modelling is a strong tool that allows researchers to explore complicated systems because it is crucial to isolate each component for separate investigations experimentally. The effect of amyloid-beta on different pathways can change the calcium flux in the cytoplasm and ER. Therefore, studying the variations of the parameters is important in practical examples too because these parameters can capture such pathways, and their combinations help us to control the disease progression, as we demonstrate it in the next sections on the example of AD.

The remainder of this paper is organized as follows. In Sect. 2, we describe a spatio-temporal mathematical model for astrocytic Ca^{2+} mediated by $A\beta$ in AD. In Sect. 3, we discuss results and present numerical simulations based on the developed model. Finally, we summarize results and outline future directions in Sect. 4.

2   Mathematical Model

In this section, we construct a spatio-temporal multiscale mathematical model that simulates Ca^{2+} patterns under the influence of $A\beta$. We devise our computational model based on the previous studies [3,4,9]. We begin by investigating how $A\beta$ impacts each source of Ca^{2+} via several paths using this computational model. Intracellular Ca^{2+} levels are regulated by external Ca^{2+} influx and controlled release from intracellular Ca^{2+} stores like the ER. Ca^{2+} entrance into astrocytes is characterised by active transport via several kinds of VGCCs scattered across the membrane, as well as passive leakage. However, in astrocytes, IP_3-dependent CICR from the ER is thought to be the major mechanism governing intracellular Ca^{2+} dynamics [11]. CICR is primarily regulated by efflux from the ER to the cytoplasm, which is mediated by IP_3R and RyR, as well as by the influx into the ER, which, in its turn, is mediated by SERCA pumps. The model is derived by following the flux in (J_{in}) and out (J_{out}) of the cytoplasm. The change in intracellular Ca^{2+} is then governed by:

$$\frac{\partial C_c}{\partial t} = \beta_c \left[(D_{Ca}^c + \gamma_m^c D_m^c + \gamma_e^c D_e^c)\nabla^2 C_c - 2\left(\frac{\gamma_m^c D_m^c}{K_m^c + C_c} + \frac{\gamma_e^c D_e^c}{K_e^c + C_c} \right) \nabla C_c \cdot \nabla C_c \right]$$

$$+ J_{VGCC} + J_{in} - J_{out} + J_{CICR} - J_{SERCA} + J_{RyR} + J_{leak}, \tag{1a}$$

$$\frac{\partial C_e}{\partial t} = \beta_e \left[(D_{Ca}^e + \gamma_m^e D_m^e)\nabla^2 C_e - 2\frac{\gamma_m^e D_m^e}{K_m^e + C_e} \nabla C_e \cdot \nabla C_e \right]$$

$$+ \frac{1}{c_1}(J_{SERCA} - J_{CICR} - J_{RyR} - J_{leak}), \tag{1b}$$

where C_c and C_e denote the concentration of Ca^{2+} in the cytoplasm and ER, respectively, and

$$\beta_c = \left(1 + \frac{B_s^c K_s^c}{(K_s^c + C_c)^2} + \frac{B_m^c K_m^c}{(K_m^c + C_c)^2} + \frac{B_e^c K_c^c}{(K_e^c + C_c)^2} \right)^{-1}, \quad \gamma_l^c = \frac{B_l^c K_l^c}{(K_l^c + C_c)^2},$$

$$\beta_e = \left(1 + \frac{B_s^e K_s^e}{(K_s^e + C_e)^2} + \frac{B_m^e K_m^e}{(K_m^e + C_e)^2} \right)^{-1}, \quad \gamma_m^e = \frac{B_m^e K_m^e}{(K_m^e + C_e)^2}$$

with $l = m$ and e. The term J_{VGCC} represents the Ca^{2+} influx through the four types of VGCCs, and it is given by

$$J_{VGCC} = \frac{-I_{VGCC}}{zFV_{ast}}, \tag{2}$$

where

$$I_{VGCC} = I_{Ca,T} + I_{Ca,L} + I_{Ca,N} + I_{Ca,R} \tag{3}$$

is the VGCC-conducted Ca^{2+} current, z is the valence of Ca^{2+}, F is the Faraday constant and V_{ast} is the volume of the astrocyte. $I_{Ca,l}$ ($l = T, L, N$ and R) denote the four types of channels. The term c_1 is the ratio of ER volume to the cytoplasmic volume.

The other terms contributed in the Eq. (1) are given as follows [3, 4, 12]:

$$J_{in} = \nu_5, \tag{4a}$$

$$J_{out} = k_1 C_c, \tag{4b}$$

$$J_{CICR} = \nu_1 m_\infty^3 n_\infty^3 h^3 (C_e - C_c), \tag{4c}$$

$$J_{SERCA} = \frac{\nu_3 C_c^2}{C_c^2 + k_3^2}, \tag{4d}$$

$$J_{RyR} = \left(k_0 + \frac{k_2 C_c^3}{k_d^3 + C_c^3} \right) (C_e - C_c), \tag{4e}$$

$$J_{leak} = \nu_2 (C_e - C_c), \tag{4f}$$

with the gating variable h that satisfies the Hodgkin-Huxley formalism as

$$\frac{dh}{dt} = a_2 d_2 \frac{C_i + d_1}{C_i + d_3}(1 - h) - a_2 C_c h. \tag{5}$$

The relevant parameters are given in Table 1 and $\bar{m}$, $\bar{h}$ are defined as follows [3]:

$$\frac{dy}{dt} = \frac{\bar{y} - y}{\tau_y}, \tag{6}$$

where $y = (m, h)$. As a result, we model V_m as follows:

$$V_m = \frac{RT}{z_K F} \ln \frac{[K_o^+]}{[K_i^+]} + \epsilon, \tag{7}$$

where R is the ideal gas constant, T is the absolute temperature, z_K is the valence of K^+, and F is the Faraday constant. $K_o = [K_o^+]$ and $[K_i^+]$ are the extracellular and intracellular K^+ concentrations, respectively. ϵ is a modulation factor [4].

IP$_3$ is the second messenger involved in signal transduction via G protein-coupled receptors. Phosphatidylinositol 4,5-bisphosphate is hydrolyzed by two phosphoinositide - specific phospholipase C (PLC) isoenzymes, $PLC\beta$ and $PLC\delta$ in astrocytes to generate IP$_3$ [4]. As a consequence, the concentration of IP$_3$ dynamic (C_i) is defined as

$$\frac{\partial C_i}{\partial t} = D_i \nabla^2 C_i + J_{PLC\beta} + J_{PLC\delta} - k_{deg} C_i, \tag{8}$$

where

$$J_{PLC\beta} = \nu_\beta \frac{g^{0.7}}{g^{0.7} + \left(k_R + k_P \frac{C_c}{C_c + k_\pi}\right)^{0.7}}, \quad J_{PLC\delta} = \nu_4 \frac{C_c + (1 - \alpha k_4)}{C_c + k_4}.$$

Experimental results suggested that the Aβ peptide triggers the intracellular calcium oscillations [13]. Alves et al. demonstrated in [14] that the activated Aβ contributes to an additional current in the L-type channel. Taking this into account, $I_{Ca,L}$ can be written as

$$I_{Ca,L} = (g_L + A_\beta a) m_L h_L (V_m - V_{Ca}), \tag{9}$$

where A_β controls the strength of the effect of Aβ on the channel.

Therefore, the Aβ-formed channels supply an additional Ca^{2+} influx into the cytoplasm (see also [7]). It increases the channel open probability and also affects the IP$_3$ levels. Combining all these, we modify the influxes as follows:

$$J_{in} = \nu_5 + k_{in} a^k, \tag{10a}$$

$$J_{RyR} = \left(k_0 + \frac{k_2 C_c^3}{(k_d + k_{RyR} a)^3 + C_c^3}\right)(C_e - C_c), \tag{10b}$$

$$J_{PLC\beta} = (\nu_\beta + k_{PCL\beta} a) \frac{g^{0.7}}{g^{0.7} + \left(k_R + k_P \frac{C_c}{C_c + k_\pi}\right)^{0.7}}, \tag{10c}$$

$$J_{PLC\delta} = (\nu_4 + k_{PCL\delta} a) \frac{C_c + (1 - \alpha k_4)}{C_c + k_4}. \tag{10d}$$

Table 1. Details of the voltage-gated calcium channels [3].

Channel type	Equation of channel kinetics
T – type	$I_{Ca,T} = g_T \bar{m}_T (h_{Tf} + 0.04 h_{Ts})(V_m - V_{Ca})$
	$\bar{m}_T = 1/(1 + \exp(-(V_m + 63.5)/1.5))$
	$h_{Tf} = 1/(1 + \exp((V_m + 76.2)/3))$
	$h_{Ts} = 1/(1 + \exp((V_m + 76.2)/3))$
	$\tau_{h_{Tf}} = 50 * \exp(-((V_m + 72)/10)^2) + 10$
	$\tau_{h_{Ts}} = 400 * \exp(-((V_m + 100)/10)^2) + 400$
	$\tau_{m_T} = 65 * exp(-((V_m + 68)/6)^2) + 12$
L – type	$I_{Ca,L} = g_L \bar{m}_L h_L (V_m - V_{Ca})$
	$\bar{m}_L = 1/(1 + \exp(-(V_m + 50)/3))$
	$h_L = 0.00045/(0.00045 + C_c/1000)$
	$\tau_{m_L} = 18 * \exp(-((V_m + 45)/20)^2) + 1.5$
N – type	$I_{Ca,N} = g_N \bar{m}_N h_N (V_m - V_{Ca})$
	$\bar{m}_N = 1/(1 + \exp(-(V_m + 45)/7))$
	$h_N = 0.0001/(0.0001 + C_c/1000)$
	$\tau_{m_N} = 18 * \exp(-((V_m + 70)/25)^2) + 0.3$
R – type	$I_{Ca,R} = g_R \bar{m}_R h_R (V_m - V_{Ca})$
	$\bar{m}_R = 1/(1 + \exp(-(V_m + 10)/10))$
	$h_R = 1/(1 + \exp((V_m + 48)/5))$
	$\tau_{h_R} = 0.5 * \exp(-((V_m + 55.6)/18)^2) + 0.5$
	$\tau_{m_R} = 0.1 * \exp(-((V_m + 62)/13)^2) + 0.05$

This proposed spatio-temporal model has multiple Aβ-affected Ca^{2+} pathways. Simulations based on our mathematical model have proven to be an essential resource for investigating underlying complex biochemical interactions. This model portrays Ca^{2+} signals as discrete Ca^{2+} transport routes, rather than a macroscopic flow of Ca^{2+} that includes both intracellular release and external inflow.

The model has several computational challenges as maximum terms involved in the model are changing due to the dependence of such terms (e.g., β_c, γ_c, J_{RyR}, etc.) on the cytosolic Ca^{2+} concentration. Hence, the terms are not only time-dependent as it was the case in earlier developed models (e.g., [4]); they are space-dependent also. We have used all the parameter values from Table 2 and [8] unless specified otherwise in the figure caption or the text.

Table 2. Parameter values [4].

Parameter	Value	Parameter	Value	Parameter	Value
B_s^c	225 μM	B_m^e	250 μM	B_m^c	75 μM
B_e^c	0 μM	K_s^e	10 μM	K_s^c	1 mM
K_m^e	6 μM	K_m^c	6 μM	B_s^e	100 mM
K_e^c	0.16 μM	D_{Ca}^c	223.0	D_{Ca}^e	223.0
D_m^c	75.0	D_e^c	75.0	D_m^e	75.0
D_i	283.0	k_1	0.5 s^{-1}	ν_1	6 s^{-1}
d_1	0.13 μM	ν_3	2.2 $\mu M/s$	d_5	0.08234 μM
k_3	0.05 μM	k_0	0.013 s^{-1}	k_2	0.18 s^{-1}
k_d	0.13 μM	ν_2	0.11 s^{-1}	a_2	0.2 s^{-1}
d_2	1.049 μM	d_1	0.13 μM	d_3	0.9434 μM
ν_β	0.05 μM	g	1 μM	k_R	1.3 μM
k_P	10 μM	k_π	0.6 μM	ν_4	0.5 $\mu M/s$
α	0.8	k_4	1.1 μM	A_β	10
k_{in}	1	k_{RyR}	0.2	F	96485 $C/mole$
$k_{PCL\delta}$	0.5	$k_{PCL\beta}$	0.05	V_{ast}	3.49×10^{-13} L
z	2	g_T	0.06	g_L	3.5
g_N	0.39	g_R	0.2225	ν_5	0.36 $\mu M/s$

3   Computational Framework and Numerical Results

Liu et al. [4] has shown that, with an increase in the Aβ levels in the purely temporal model (based on ODEs only), a rapid increase is observed in the oscillation frequency of the intracellular Ca^{2+} concentrations and then C_c converges to its steady-state. At a low level of Aβ, the disease state is mild, but the disease becomes severe with higher Aβ. The dynamics of Aβ is studied here with model (1)–(9).

In this section, we find the numerical solution to the complete model (1)–(9). No-flux boundary conditions and a particular type of initial conditions have been used for the simulations. With the introduction of Ca^{2+} or IP$_3$ in the cytoplasm, calcium waves were experimentally verified in earlier works (e.g., [15]). Typically, Ca^{2+} or IP$_3$ are introduced by injecting them in the living cells. We consider the initial conditions in such a way that they mimic the injection effect in some parts of the spatial domain. A pulse-like initial condition in the specified domain can capture such a phenomenon. With the help of pulse structure, we consider the initial conditions as follows [9]:

$$C_c(x,0) = \begin{cases} 0.2 \ \mu M & 0 \leq x \leq L_c \\ 0.1 \ \mu M & L_c < x \leq 500 \end{cases}, \ C_e(x,0) = \begin{cases} 0.2 \ \mu M & 0 \leq x \leq L_e \\ 1.5 \ \mu M & L_e < x \leq 500 \end{cases},$$

$$C_i(x,0) = \begin{cases} 1.0 \ \mu M & 0 \leq x \leq L_i \\ 0.1 \ \mu M & L_i < x \leq 500 \end{cases}, \ \text{and} \ h(x,0) = 0.78, 0 \leq x \leq 500,$$

where $L_c = 30$, $L_e = 30$ and $L_i = 5$. For the numerical simulations, we have considered spatial dependence of all terms containing calcium concentrations, because of the spatial heterogeneity in calcium concentrations. Unless mentioned otherwise in the text, we use the above pulse initial conditions for all simulation results reported in the remainder of this paper. To our best knowledge, this is one of the very few computational spatio-temporal models that allows the analysis of the contribution of multiple Ca^{2+} fluxes to Ca^{2+} dynamics, including entry and release, under the impact of Aβ.

The required spatio-temporal resolution brings about the computational challenges. The time step has been chosen to be very small due to the diffusion parameter, otherwise the numerical solution diverges to infinity (we have selected $dx = 0.5$ and $dt = 0.0001$). In the numerical computation, forward Euler's method is used for the time derivative, and the central difference is used for the spatial derivatives. The considered model has many terms involving different parameters. So, to find the effect corresponding to one parameter, we need to solve the model (1)–(9) many times by changing its value. In each fixed choice of the parameter values, several million time-steps are typically needed to reach the required total time, and each such time step involves thousands of spatial grid points for each parameter setting. This takes a lot of computational time if we solve the system using standard serial programming. Parallel programming is used in C-language with the help of open MPI, allowing us to save computational time. For each time-iteration, we distribute the sequential jobs involving the spatial points into free processors and compute them in a parallel way. The data have been post-processed, and all figures have been visualized and plotted in Matlab. We have used the SHARCNET supercomputer facilities (64-cores) to minimize the time to obtain results for the parallel computation.

Intracellular Ca^{2+} signals regulate many cell activities. These signals occur not only in a single cell, but also between adjacent cells in the form of calcium waves. As proof-of-concept, we have considered a one-dimensional spatial domain to capture such scenarios. In this case, the diffusion term plays a crucial role in propagating the wave initiated by a pulse of Ca^{2+} or IP_3, mentioned earlier in the initial conditions. The spatio-temporal model also follows the temporal dynamics obtainable with the model developed in [4], but accounting for spatio-temporal interactions brings about distinct advantages. Due to the given pulse on one side of the domain, the waves propagate from that side to the opposite side in the spatial domain [see Fig. 1]. These solutions are action-potential-like spikes of intracellular Ca^{2+} signals, not wave-trains. Here, the spikes appear in different time points in the spatial domain, due to the pulse type initial conditions. This is more realistic because two different cells may produce spikes at different time points.

In Fig. 1, we plot the solutions for the intracellular Ca^{2+} concentrations for three values of Aβ levels, $a = 0, 0.2$ and 0.34. The first appearance of heterogeneous spikes over the entire spatial domain corresponding to $a = 0.2$ takes less time than in the case of $a = 0$. However, with an increment in Aβ level, e.g., $a = 0.34$, the first appearance of heterogeneous spikes takes more time than in the case of $a = 0.2$. Further increase in a causes a longer time for the spikes to appear. Moreover, all spikes fully disappear for $a > a_c$, and the solution converges to a homogeneous solution in the spatial domain, following the purely temporal dynamics of the ODE-based model [4]. It is the advanced stage of the disease, and this critical threshold a_c depends on the parameter values as well as on the initial conditions.

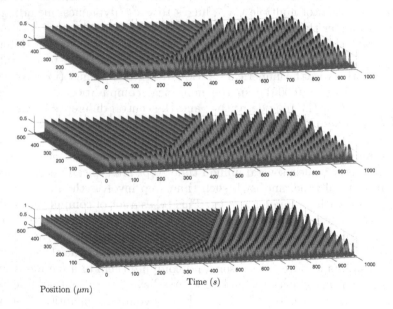

Position (μm)   Time (s)

Fig. 1. Solutions corresponding to C_c for the model: $a = 0$ (top), $a = 0.2$ (middle) and $a = 0.34$ (bottom). (Color figure online)

Recall that the critical threshold of Aβ level for the model without spatial terms is $a_c = 0.6$ [4]. In this case, we can not choose the pulse type initial conditions. But, the critical threshold of Aβ level for the spatio-temporal model presented in Sect. 2, corresponding to the above initial condition, is $a_c = 0.62$. Furthermore, if we take the initial density of C_c in the pulse range $0 \leq x \leq L_c$ as $0.8 \ \mu M$, then the critical threshold is shifted to $a_c = 0.63$. A wave-train solution is observed for $a < 0.63$. It seems that extra calcium concentrations injected in some parts of the cytosol cause oscillations in the system in the presence of higher Aβ levels.

These observations are also valid for a different range in the pulse structure, e.g., $L_c = 60$, $L_e = 60$ and $L_i = 5$. The shifting of the heterogeneous spikes indicates the disease building inside the cytoplasm. Therefore, the spatio-temporal extension of the earlier model helps us to predict the disease state much earlier compared to the predictions based on a purely temporal model. Note that the magnitudes of the oscillations at all spatial points are the same, but of course, they occur at different time instances as shown in Fig. 1.

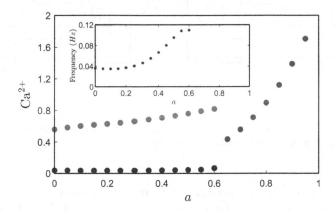

Fig. 2. Bifurcation diagram of C_c against Aβ levels: steady state (blue-dot), maximum amplitude (magenta-dot), minimum amplitude (red-dot), frequencies of the oscillations (black-star). (Color figure online)

Many processes of Ca^{2+} dyshomeostasis are difficult to explore experimentally [2,19], such as the limits of Ca^{2+} indicators and imaging methods. Aβ has been shown to cause C_c transients and C_c oscillations in astrocytes [20]. Such effects might be caused by multiple Ca^{2+} entry mechanisms as well as Ca^{2+} release from the ER [4]. These experimental results have offered us useful information in making our Aβ assumption. However, in the actual world, Aβ accumulation might take months, years, or even decades, which does not correspond to the brief timescale of Ca^{2+} fluctuations. In order to address this issue, we assumed a constant amount of Aβ in our model. We plot the amplitudes and the frequencies of intracellular Ca^{2+} for different Aβ levels in Fig. 2. In this context, we should mention that the oscillations of intracellular calcium concentration (C_c) in glial cells have a peak with an amplitude of 0.6–0.8 μM that have been reported in [17]. Here, for $a = 0$, we obtain a peak with amplitude of 0.71 μM, inside the mentioned range. On the other hand, a subset of spontaneously active thalamic astrocytes exhibits C_c oscillations with an average frequency of 0.019 Hz has been found in [18]. The model considered in this paper produces 0.036 Hz, a spatial average of frequencies in the whole domain without Aβ (i.e., $a = 0$). A similar type of frequency increase is observed in the astrocytic Ca^{2+} experimentally after the Aβ injection [21]. Therefore, the spatio-temporal model is consistent with the experimental data reported earlier in the literature.

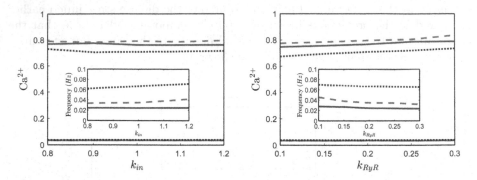

Fig. 3. Effect of bifurcation parameters on C_c and its frequencies for different $A\beta$ levels with other fixed parameters given in Table 2: $a = 0.2$ (solid-blue), $a = 0.3$ (dashed-magenta) and $a = 0.4$ (dotted-red). (Color figure online)

Now, we turn our attention to the effect of the parameters k_{in} and k_{RyR} [see formulas in (10)] on the resulting intracellular Ca^{2+} signals and the frequencies. For each of the bifurcation parameters, the range of the oscillations of the intracellular calcium concentrations and corresponding frequencies is plotted in Fig. 3. In the plot, solid (blue), dashed (magenta) and dotted (red) curves are corresponding to $a = 0.2, 0.3$ and 0.4, respectively. For the case of the parameter k_{in}, the amplitudes of the oscillations are not changing significantly in the considered range $k_{in} \in [0.8, 1.2]$, but the frequency increases with k_{in}. On the other hand, with an increase in the bifurcation parameter $k_{RyR} \in [0.1, 0.3]$, the amplitudes of the oscillations increase, and the frequencies decrease. These results are similar to the results that were obtained based on the purely temporal model, but now the spikes are heterogeneously distributed over the spatial domain.

For a fixed $A\beta$ level, the first appearance of the heterogeneous spikes corresponding to a lower value of k_{in} takes less time compared to a higher value of k_{in}. The opposite case happens when we analyze the bifurcation parameter k_{RyR}. These bifurcation parameters k_{in} and k_{RyR} are correlated with the $A\beta$ levels.

Based on experimental results reported earlier in [16], it was suggested that the calcium increases its frequency at the lower affinity of SERCA1 enzyme. In our spatio-temporal model, the parameter ν_3 is the maximum SERCA pump flux, and we choose ν_3 as a controlling parameter. According to the model (1)–(9), an increase in the removal rate parameter (ν_3) in the cytosol decreases Ca^{2+} concentration in the cytosol but increases Ca^{2+} in the endoplasmic reticulum. We have carried out the simulation and plotted the magnitudes and the frequencies of the oscillations of intracellular calcium densities for the bifurcation parameter ν_3 in Fig. 4. The amplitude of the oscillations of Ca^{2+} in cytosol increases with ν_3.

However, the parameter ν_3 is anti-correlated with the frequency. An increase in ν_3 causes a slow rise of Ca^{2+} in the cytosol to a threshold where the endoplasmic reticulum takes over the autocatalytic release of Ca^{2+} and hence it decreases the frequency of the oscillations.

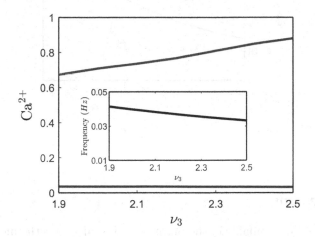

Fig. 4. Bifurcation diagram of C_c and the corresponding frequency against the parameter ν_3 with a fixed Aβ level ($a = 0.2$). (Color figure online)

Due to the differences in extracellular K^+ concentrations from cell to cell, the resulting resting membrane potential may also vary [22]. This resting membrane potential affects the open probability of VGCC, and hence it affects J_{VGCC} and the intracellular calcium dynamics [23]. Figure 5 represents the frequencies of C_c oscillations depending on the extracellular K^+ concentrations for different Aβ levels. With an increase in the resting membrane potentials, the frequency of intracellular Ca^{2+} oscillations increases, and further gain converges to the steady-state solutions. Recall that our studies have demonstrated that the frequency increases with Aβ levels [see Fig. 2], and the same happens for different resting membrane potentials. Therefore, a higher resting membrane potential indicates a further progression of the disease state. Overall, the developed model and our results suggest that we should expect a smaller contribution to the dysregulation of cytosolic Ca^{2+} levels from VGCCs compared to Aβ. This happens because of the robustness of cytosolic Ca^{2+} under Aβ [8].

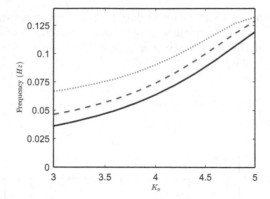

Fig. 5. Bifurcation diagram of the frequencies of C_c against the parameter K_o for different Aβ levels: $a = 0$ (solid-black), $a = 0.3$ (dashed-blue) and $a = 0.4$ (dotted-magenta). (Color figure online)

4   Conclusions

Many chemicals are available in the brain cell, and calcium is the most tractable, used for experimental validations. The calcium concentration oscillates in the living brain cell, but remains steady in the dead cell. Alzheimer's disease (AD) causes neuronal death in the brain, and hence the calcium dynamics of a cell reflects the disease state. In this work, we have studied the AD progression in a heterogeneous environment in the cytoplasm with the help of calcium dynamics. The amyloid-beta peptide plays an essential role in the oscillating dynamics of intracellular and extracellular calcium concentrations. A pulse type of initial conditions has been chosen for the simulations in order to better reflect heterogeneity in the cytoplasm.

The amplitude of intracellular calcium oscillations increases with the amyloid-beta levels. The same happens for the frequencies. But, after a critical threshold of amyloid-beta level, the calcium concentration stops its oscillations and remains in a homogeneous steady-state over the domain. This critical threshold depends on additional calcium concentrations injected in the cytosol but not much on the range of injected domain, dictated by the pulse type initial conditions. We have studied the dynamics of biochemical processes with models by varying different parameters. The parameter ν_3 involved in the SERCA pump flux has a pronounced effect on the frequency of intracellular calcium concentrations. Also, an increase in the resting membrane potential increases the frequency for a fixed amyloid-beta level. The additional influx negatively impacts the astrocytic homeostasis irrespective of the other parameters. We note that several computational models are available in the literature based on Ca^{2+} mechanisms [2–4]. They are presented in a single framework and contain VGCCs and RyRs in astrocytes, but all of them are ODE models. The novelty of our work is that it goes beyond this conventional approach. This work has also important practical significance since our parametric study can provide a guidance to the development of different therapies targeting different Aβ levels, signals, or channels.

In general, it is quite challenging to establish a complete model of Aβ-mediated multi-pathway calcium dynamics in the disease progression, and simulation-based mathematical models help study the dynamics with different parameters. We have accounted for some of the key parameters to capture different pathways, while others have been left out for further studies. As a result, different pathways simultaneously suggest being more effective in targeting combination therapies to provide new insight into the treatment of AD. Furthermore, along with the amyloid-beta, the tau protein also plays an essential role in AD progression [24,25]. Therefore, following those recent works and introducing the tau dynamics into the calcium model would be a natural generalization of the model presented here. Finally, an extension of the presented spatio-temporal model to account for more realistic brain topologies would lead to further insights into the disease progression.

Acknowledgements. Authors are grateful to the NSERC and the CRC Program for their support. RM is also acknowledging support of the BERC 2022–2025 program and Spanish Ministry of Science, Innovation and Universities through the Agencia Estatal de Investigacion (AEI) BCAM Severo Ochoa excellence accreditation SEV-2017–0718 and the Basque Government fund AI in BCAM EXP. 2019/00432. This research was enabled in part by support provided by SHARCNET (www.sharcnet.ca) and Digital Research Alliance of Canada (www.alliancecan.ca).

References

1. Schäfer, A., et al.: Predicting brain atrophy from tau pathology: a summary of clinical findings and their translation into personalized models. J Brain Multiphys. **2**, 100039 (2021)
2. Latulippe, J., Lotito, D., Murby, D.: A mathematical model for the effects of amyloid beta on intracellular calcium. PLoS ONE **13**, e0202503 (2018)
3. Shaheen, H., Singh, S., Melnik, R.: A neuron-glial model of exosomal release in the onset and progression of Alzheimer's disease. Front. Comput. Neurosci. **15**, 79 (2021)
4. Liu, L., Gao, H., Zaikin, A., Chen, S.: Unraveling Aβ-mediated multi-pathway calcium dynamics in astrocytes: implications for Alzheimer's Disease treatment from simulations. Front. Physiol. **12**, 767892 (2021)
5. Verkhratsky, A., et al.: Astroglial atrophy in Alzheimer's disease. Pflügers Archiv-Eur. J. Physiol. **471**(10), 1247–1261 (2019)
6. De Pittà, M., et al.: Glutamate regulation of calcium and IP3 oscillating and pulsating dynamics in astrocytes. J. Biol. Phys. **35**(4), 383–411 (2009)
7. Demuro, A., Parker, I., Stutzmann, G.E.: Calcium signaling and amyloid toxicity in Alzheimer disease. J. Biol. Chem. **285**(17), 12463–12468 (2010)
8. Lim, D., et al.: Amyloid beta deregulates astroglial mGluR5-mediated calcium signaling via calcineurin and Nf-kB. Glia **61**, 1134–1145 (2013)
9. Jafri, M.S., Keizer, J.: On the Roles of Ca^{2+} Diffusion, Ca^{2+} Buffers, and the Endoplasmic Reticulum in IP$_3$-Induced Ca^{2+} Waves. Biophys. J . **69**, 2139–2153 (1995)

10. Semyanov, A., Henneberger, C., Agarwal, A.: Making sense of astrocytic calcium signals-from acquisition to interpretation. Nat. Rev. Neurosci. **21**, 551–564 (2020)
11. Agulhon, C., et al.: What is the role of astrocyte calcium in neurophysiology? Neuron **59**(6), 932–946 (2008)
12. Ullah, G., Jung, P., Cornell-Bell, A.H.: Anti-phase calcium oscillations in astrocytes via inositol (1, 4, 5)-trisphosphate regeneration. Cell Calcium **39**(3), 197–208 (2006)
13. Alberdi, E., et al.: Ca^{2+}-dependent endoplasmic reticulum stress correlates with astrogliosis in oligomeric amyloid β-treated astrocytes and in a model of Alzheimer's disease. Aging Cell **12**, 292–302 (2013)
14. Alves, V.S., et al.: Calcium signaling in neurons and glial cells: role of Cav1 channels. Neuroscience **421**, 95–111 (2019)
15. Atri, A., et al.: A single-pool model for intracellular calcium oscillations and waves in the Xenopus Laevis oocyte. Biophys. J . **65**, 1727–1739 (1993)
16. Camacho, P., Lechleiter, J.D.: Increased frequency of calcium waves in Xenopus Laevis oocytes that express a calcium-ATPase. Science **260**, 226–229 (1993)
17. Charles, A.C., Merrill, J.E., Dirksen, E.R., Sanderson, M.J.: Intercellular signalling in glial cells: calcium waves and oscillations in response to mechanical stimulation and glutamate. Neuron **6**, 983–992 (1991)
18. Parri, H.R., Crunelli, V.: Pacemaker calcium oscillations in thalamic astrocytes in situ. NeuroReport **12**, 3897–3900 (2001)
19. Vassilis, C., Moustafa, A.A.: Neurocomputational models of Alzheimer's disease. Scholarpedia (2017)
20. Alberdi, E., Wyssenbach, A., Alberdi, M., Sánchez-Gómez, M.V., Cavaliere, F., Rodríguez, J.J., Verkhratsky, A., Matute, C.: Ca^{2+}-dependent endoplasmic reticulum stress correlates with astrogliosis in oligomeric amyloid β-treated astrocytes and in a model of Alzheimer's disease. Aging Cell **12**(2), 292–302 (2013)
21. Takano, T., et al.: Two-photon imaging of astrocytic Ca2+ signaling and the microvasculature in experimental mice models of Alzheimer's disease. Ann. N. Y. Acad. Sci. **1097**, 40–50 (2007)
22. Anderson, S., Brismar, T., Hansson, E.: Effect of external K^+, Ca^{2+}, and Ba^{2+} on membrane potential and ionic conductance in rat astrocytes. Cell. Mol. Neurobiol. **15**, 439–450 (1995)
23. Bellot-Saez, A., Kekesi, O., Morley, J.W., Buskila, Y.: Astrocytic modulation of neuronal excitability through K^+ spatial buffering. Neurosci. Biobehav. Rev. **77**, 87–97 (2017)
24. Pal, S., Melnik, R.: Pathology dynamics in healthy-toxic protein interaction and the multiscale analysis of neurodegenerative diseases. In: Paszynski, M., Kranzlmüller, D., Krzhizhanovskaya, V.V., Dongarra, J.J., Sloot, P.M.A. (eds.) ICCS 2021. LNCS, vol. 12746, pp. 528–540. Springer, Cham (2021). https://doi.org/10.1007/978-3-030-77977-1_42
25. Pal, S., Melnik, R.: Nonlocal models in the analysis of brain neurodegenerative protein dynamics with application to Alzheimer's disease. Sci. Rep. **12**, 7328 (2022)

International Workshop
on Configurational Analysis for Cities
(CA CITIES 2022)

Driver Factors, Wildcards and Spatial External Effects of Urban Sprawl in Poland (2016–2022)

Veranika Kaleyeva$^{(\boxtimes)}$ ⓘ, Piotr A. Werner ⓘ, and Mariusz Porczek ⓘ

University of Warsaw, Faculty of Geography and Regional Studies,
Krak.Przedm. 30, Warsaw 00-927, Poland
`v.kaleyeva@gmail.com`

Abstract. The recent years were rich in new and unexpected social and political factors for Poland, such as the COVID-19 lockdown in 2020–2021 and the refugee crisis in 2021–2022. These 'wildcards' will definitely have serious consequences for people and cities, directly and through the impact of so-called externalities. The paper identifies trends in the geographical development of urban areas in Poland during the last five years (2016–2021), particularly in terms of residential suburbanization and urban sprawl. The study aims to explore the driver factors that determine the spatial scale of suburbanization and reveal 'wildcards' that may indirectly affect this process but are hard to be quantified and embedded into spatial analysis. Both wildcards and externalities of suburbanization seem to be underexplored, and this paper's goal is to bring progress on this pass. The spatial analysis applying location quotients (LQ) metrics creates the possibility for comparisons of locations with intensified urbanization for different time moments, thus fulfilling a function similar to the standardization of features considering time and space perspectives. The results makes the evidence to progressive suburbanization around the main Polish cities during the years 2016–2021, revealing, at the same time, distinguishing features of spatial development for the period associated with social and political stresses (2021).

Keywords: Urban sprawl · Residential suburbanization · Driver factors · Wildcards · Poland

1 Introduction

In 2020, the Polish construction industry showed more than just impressive growth, especially against the past twelve years, starting from the 2007–2008 Global Financial Crisis (Fig. 1). Furthermore, 2020 became the first year in which the communist era's indicators were exceeded in terms of construction. It's even more interesting because nowadays, a population decline is observed in Poland, while in the communist era, the high demand for new housing was conditioned, to a large extent, by the post-war (WWII) baby-boomer generation that started entering the labor market [1].

© The Author(s), under exclusive license to Springer Nature Switzerland AG 2022
O. Gervasi et al. (Eds.): ICCSA 2022 Workshops, LNCS 13377, pp. 325–337, 2022.
https://doi.org/10.1007/978-3-031-10536-4_22

This communication paper aims to reveal trends in the geographical development of the urban areas in Poland over the last five years (2016–2021), particularly in terms of suburban sprawl, identify the driver factors that directly determine the spatial extent of suburbanization and look for other phenomena that may indirectly affect the urban sprawl but are hard to be quantified and imbedded into spatial analysis such as COVID-19 lockdown and the war in Ukraine in 2022.

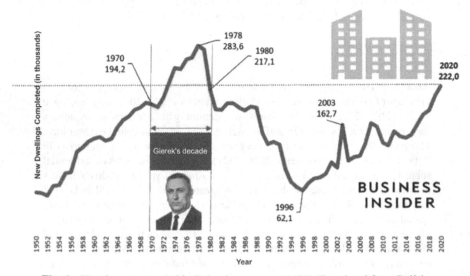

Fig. 1. Housing constructed in Poland, year-on-year [1]. Translated from Polish.

The continuous global trend of urbanization as well as both internal and external (international) migration are apparent factors that empower the development of cities and urban functional areas around them. At the same time, in some cases, the geographical location may imply specific conditions for city development, too.

Among the main dimensions of urban expansion are suburban sprawl [2] and inner-city processes such as gentrification and re-urbanization. At the same time, the recent years have been bringing a disruption impact, with the COVID-19 outbreak (since 2020) and the war in Ukraine (since February 2022). These 'wildcards' will definitely affect - directly and indirectly - all people, especially those living in urban areas, and cities as they are.

Within the COVID-19 lockdown periods (2020/2021), substantially more people were looking for houses outside of the cities (Fig. 2) to relocate from the downtowns.

Another enormous wildcard that may affect the housing market and geographical development was the unanticipated war outbreak in (neighboring to Poland) Ukraine in 2022.

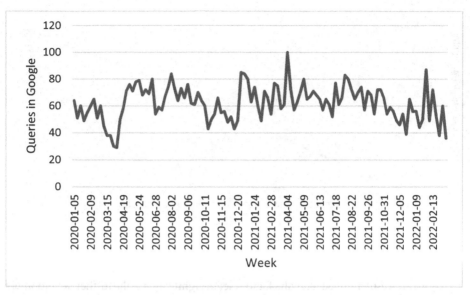

Fig. 2. Google trends data, Poland: 'House to buy'; queries per week: 01.01.2020–20.03.2022

According to the Polish Central Statistical Office data, at the end of February 2020, the last month before the COVID-19 outbreak, there were 1.39 million Ukrainian citizens in Poland inhabiting cities. Later, some of them returned to Ukraine, but at the end of 2021, the Centre of Migration Research of the University of Warsaw estimated this population in about 1 million [3]. The situation has radically changed with the beginning of war outbreak in break in Ukraine on Feb. 24th, 2022, and the colossal (additional) influx of refugees from Ukraine – mainly women, children, and the elderly (Fig. 3).

Not all of the refugees are planning to stay in Poland. Some of them are going farther, but some, especially men who earlier worked in Poland, intend to return or have already returned to Ukraine to fight. Relocation and accommodation of the refugees are temporary for the moment. But, the housing rental market reacted immediately. Rental prices skyrocketed contrary to the pandemic and the lockdown a year ago when there was a bear market. During the two years of the COVID-19 pandemic (2020–2021), apartment rentals ceased to be a profitable business. Remote learning for students, closed borders for foreigners, working from home, uncertainty about one's finances - all these have caused renters to leave the previously thriving market.

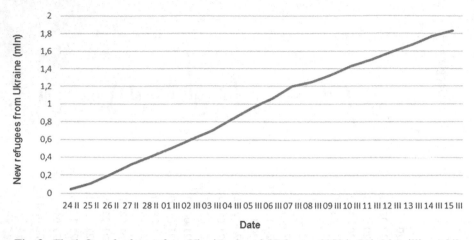

Fig. 3. The influx of refugees from Ukraine since 24 February 2022 in Poland (millions) [4].

Those above-mentioned inter alia factors seem significant for the further development of urbanization in Poland at the moment. However, it would be worth examining the suburban sprawl during the last five years, aimed to check if the global trends sustained in Poland before, during the pandemic period, and nowadays in completely different international and national circumstances.

However, the central hypothesis of the recent study concern confirmation of stability and persistence of global trends concerning suburban sprawl observed since 2016 in Poland despite different impacts of stimulants, de stimulants, and nominates factors taken into account or suspected to affect the observed phenomenon.

2   Factors of Suburban Sprawl, Wildcards, and Externalities

2.1   Urban Sprawl, Suburbanization

Suburbanization refers to population migration to suburbs, resulting in the rapid development of peripheral areas of cities and urban sprawl. While both of the above-mentioned terms are commonly used interchangeably, urban sprawl is generally associated with a spontaneous and uncontrolled dimension of suburbanization and its numerous negative impacts, i.e. poor accessibility, lack of functional open spaces, and huge environmental costs. "A variety of definitions for sprawl have been put forth that describe sprawl as a specific form of urban development with low-density, dispersed, auto-dependent, and environmentally and socially impacting characteristics" [5, p. 160].

The last decade offered a wide range of simple and synthetic indicators, attempting to capture urban sprawl [6–8]. Notwithstanding hot discussions, almost all these multiple indicators are fundamentally-based on land uptake and population variables; wherein there is a strong tendency to consider population density within built-up areas rather than within the whole territory of a unit [2].

Although urban sprawl refers to the urbanization of suburbs, quantification of urban sprawl requires a comparison of relevant indicators for both urban areas (that are losing their functions) and urbanizing peripheral areas (that are gaining new inhabitants) in a time perspective, i.e. estimated at least at the beginning and the end of the analyzed period.

Urban sprawl is conditioned by people's individual decisions about where to live and work for a better quality of life. It can be accelerated by numerous socioeconomic and demographic factors, including the price of land and apartments, transportation availability, rising living standards, and inner-city problems (Fig. 4).

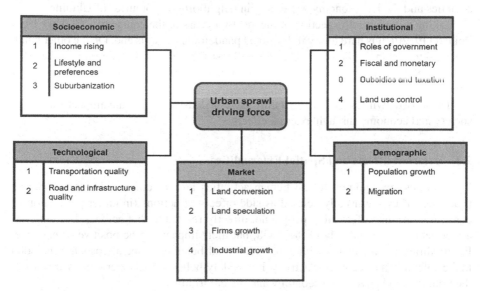

Fig. 4. Urban sprawl driving force [9].

The recent evidence established that in 1990–2014, urbanization in general and urban sprawl specifically are increasingly decoupled from demographic dynamics (such as population growth) and are likely the result of households relocation from city centers to peripheries [10]. It is worth noting that some comprehensive predictive models consider the ethnic composition of the population as a factor of suburbanization [11]. In the American context, it is assumed that increases in the percentage of ethnic minority populations within cities led to a growth in urban sprawl [12]. In a European context, the opposite impact on ethnic minority populations was observed [13].

Evaluation of the existing definitions for urban sprawl reveals that most of them involve three spatial aspects: the expansion of the urban space, the increase of dispersion of the build-up area, and low-density development in suburbia with a high land take per person [14, 15].

Residential suburbanization may be related not only to permanent housing. While seasonal population shifts to "second homes" in some cities have been registered [16], the hypothetical wildcards of suburbanization stay unexplored [17].

2.2 Wildcards (Black Swans)

The 'wildcards' or, according to Taleb [18], 'Black Swans' represent those unexpected (astonishing and shocking) events that are generally considered unlikely but the occurrence of which could fundamentally affect the condition of people (societies). The triplet characteristics summarizing wildcards are rarity outlier, extreme impact, and retrospective (though not prospective) predictability of the event [18].

Two such wildcards are happening during the last years, overlapping in time: the global COVID-19 pandemic since the beginning of 2020 and the outbreak of war in Ukraine in February 2022. Both will have a giant impact on different aspects of European societies and the EU economy, especially in neighborhood countries of Ukraine.

Taking a look at retrospection of the last two years of the course of a COVID-19 in Poland [19, 20], it is hard to say if the global pandemic is near its end. On the other hand, it is hard to assume if the war in Ukraine will last for a longer time (similar to the 2014 invasion of Russia on Crimea, Donetsk, and Lugansk in Ukraine) or there is a solution coming shortly.

These two 'wildcards' will certainly have at least a significant impact on Polish society and economy through external effects.

2.3 External Effects and Spatial Externalities

Externalities are common for all human activities and, of course, also for economic processes. They are usually defined as side effects of actions (in either production or consumption) that affect other people not directly related to that activity. Externalities affect people independently of their will, but their impact can be positive or negative. Externalities are associated with either additional benefits or social costs not included in the calculation of economic activity. It is widely believed that externalities arise from the relationship between the economy and the environment.

Negative externalities are seen in terms of environmental pollution, location of landfills, vandalism, social pathologies, and crime. Positive spillovers in the economy are associated with economies of scale in services, the benefits of agglomeration - location and urbanization, and, more recently, the benefits of globalization. In economics, they are treated as unexpectedly occurring gains from spillover effects [21].

"Broadly defined, spillovers, or other economic neighborhood effects, refer to unanticipated changes in the well-being of the population, i.e., the actions of individuals or third parties, and sometimes events that indirectly affect other people's standard of living. The costs or rewards of externality effects are not included in the direct account of economic activity" [22, p. 167]. Marshall [23] defined spillover effects as market externalities of economic activity, Pigou [24] - as differences between social and private costs and benefits. A more detailed and slightly different definition of externalities was formulated by Mishan [25], who viewed them as expected (anticipated) or unanticipated spillover effects of third-party activities that directly or indirectly affect changes in people's living standards.

Externalities are viewed, through the lens of the growth pole theory, as differences in the action of centripetal and centripetal forces, concentration and dispersion, or attraction and repulsion [26], explaining the spatial order and spatial patterns of urbanization [27–29]. The classification of externalities includes the distinction between financial and technological, sectoral and urbanization, positive and negative, and productivity (labor) or development (regional) effects. In spite of the classification, a detailed description of externalities is most often done through a case-by-case analysis [30].

Spatial Externalities. Tracing the suburban sprawl is one aspect of land-use change research, which is the consideration of spatial externalities [31]. Spatial externalities are defined similarly as unexpected and indirect effects of human actions that cause a decrease (additional cost) or an increase in value (additional gain) for others [25]. Thereby, the pandemic outbreak and the war-related refugee crisis may influence the residential preferences of the population in many ways and result, inter alia, in a considerable population shift and, consequently, involve changes in residential density. The externalities of land-use change are generally revealed by their intensity (rate) and spatial extent. A distinction can be made between both negative and positive spatial effects. It's believed that the higher the level of externalities at a given land-use class (e.g. built-up areas), the higher the probability of land-use change at a given location [32].

3   Data and Methodology of Research

The index chosen as the independent variable, representing suburban sprawl up to 2021, was new Dwellings Completed per 10,000 of population (per 10K) within counties in Poland from 2016 to 2021 per year due to the need to acquire the relative recent spatial and statistical data. It's proposed that geographical location and volume of new investments in given years show the spatial extent of the frontline of urban growth, particularly suburban sprawl. official data were acquired from Statistics Poland (CSO) [33].

Both absolute values of Dwellings completed per 10K and their location quotients (LQ) by counties were detected. The defining reference value for estimating particular LQ in counties was the average LQ for the whole of Poland for a particular year.

Location quotient (LQ_i), or regional index, for a spatial unit (region) is the ratio of the value of an indicator of a specific economic or social activity S_i in spatial unit i (region i) to the value of that indicator A in a higher spatial unit (country, Eq. 1) [34]:

$$LQ_i = \frac{S_i}{A} \tag{1}$$

Thus, location quotient (LQ) may be used to quantify how actively the construction industry performs (per capita) in a particular region as compared to the national level.

LQ also creates the possibility of comparisons for different time moments, thus fulfilling a function similar to the standardization of features. LQ < 1 indicates a 'shortage' of residential construction in the county compared to the national value. LQ > 1 reveal 'overrepresentation' i.e. spatial concentration of residential construction [4].

The study is based on the lastly acquired and recently available data. A deeper insight into the changes in the spatial, social, and economic structure of functional urban areas will be needed when new datasets are released, e.g. detailed data of the functional urban areas in Poland (as well as for other EU countries) and Global Human Settlement Layer data (that currently concern only the year 2018). The just-completed national population census (2021) detailed data results are expected to reveal since Spring 2022, but they will also be outdated due to new factors modifying the economic and market situation.

4   Results. Urban Sprawl in Poland in Light of Dwellings Completed Per 10K Population

The general trend of building industry in Poland was continuous growth of dwellings completed per 10K since 2016. The number of dwellings completed per 10K differed depending on size of county and geographical location, but consequently grew over the past years (Fig. 5).

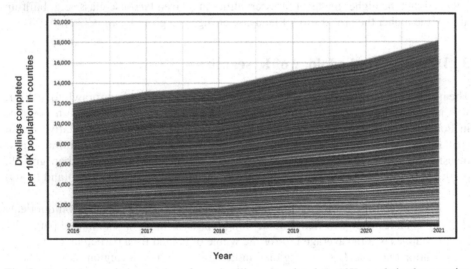

Fig. 5. Stacked, cumulative number of new dwellings completed per 10K population by counties by year in Poland (2016–2021). Counties identified by four-digit statistical number (TERYT).

The spatial diversity of absolute values of dwellings completed per 10K population by counties in starting year of study (2016) is not worth showing. It is better to present LQs because they reveal specific 'bagels' – counties surrounding the main cities in Poland (Fig. 6).

During the observed years before the COVID-19 outbreak (2016–2019), only some minor details of the spatial diversity of the studied phenomenon were changed. Both the absolute values and LQs were similar (Fig. 7).

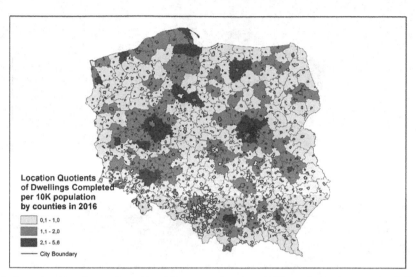

Fig. 6. Location Quotients of new Dwellings completed per 10K population by counties in Poland (2016).

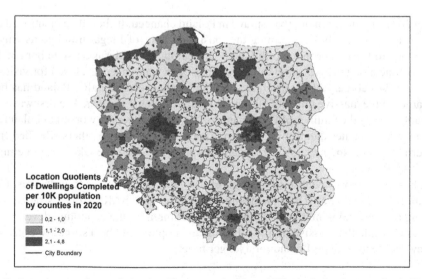

Fig. 7. Location quotients of new dwellings completed per 10K population by counties in Poland (2020).

It seems that after the first year of the COVID-19 pandemic outbreak in Poland, some *'bagels'* have tightened (Fig. 8). However, the Western parts of Poland stayed unchanged. The Eastern part (along the EU border) clearly diminished the spatial extent of new residential constructions. The span of dwellings completed per 10K also dropped and was closer to the national average.

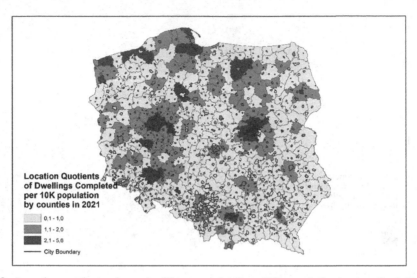

Fig. 8. Location quotients of new dwellings completed per 10K population by counties in Poland (2021).

In 2021, the situation of urban sprawl in Poland changed. It should be mentioned that from August the clashes concerning the 'push and pull' of illegal immigrants tension took place to December in a North East Poland along the Belarusian state border. The special zone along the EU – Belarus border has been announced as closed for visitors.

From 24 February 2022, external conditions changed drastically. Poland has been the target of the massive influx of Ukrainian refugees fleeing the war. The first wave was probably mostly the families of Ukrainian citizens who previously worked in Poland and had a place to shelter themselves. After a few weeks, there were others who fled from Eastern Ukraine. No one knows how many people will yet escape Ukraine, targeting or transiting Poland.

These two above-mentioned external effects will create opposite processes. Continuation of global COVID-19 pandemic waves (e.g. new SARS-COV2 strains in the coming autumn and winter seasons) make another threat to the economic development in Poland, while the massive influx of Ukrainian people could be a stimulus, especially if they decide to settle in Poland for a longer time.

5 Discussion and Conclusions

The paper identifies trends in the geographical development of urban areas in Poland during the last five years (2016–2021), particularly in terms of residential suburbanization and urban sprawl. It's proposed that geographical location and volume of new housing investments in given years show the spatial extent of the frontline of urban sprawl, particularly residential suburbanization. The location quotients (LQ) of new dwellings were used to quantify how actively the construction industry performed in counties in 2016, 2020 and 2021 as compared to the national average.

The results testify to progressive suburbanization around the main Polish cities during the years 2016–2021, revealing, at the same time, distinguishing features of spatial development for the period associated with social and political stresses (2021).

Despite the tendency for a strong development of residential construction in Poland, it is hard to scope out if intensive urbanization processes, especially suburban sprawl, will keep the previous pattern of spatial development and further demonstrate inadequate critical spatial infrastructure investments outside of the cities' boundaries in a longer time perspective.

New releases of (more recent, detailed, and accurate) data can make possible a more comprehensive study which seems to be a natural objective of future research from a long-time perspective. Another opportunity for the possible developments involves replication of estimations of Location quotients of new Dwellings by applying other types of study units, e.g. using data at the municipality level and/or considering the Functional Urban Area classification.

The impact of combinations of different factors shapes synergetic (potentiating) effects and feedback specific to distinct geographic areas. For instance, urbanization in Ukraine is estimated at 69.6% as of the end of 2021 against 60% in Poland as of the end of 2020 [35]. Most refugees from Ukraine seem to be the people from Ukrainian cities. The urban areas were their milieu, and they are migrating to the largest cities of Poland looking for, at least, temporarily or targeting accommodation similar to Ukrainian. It means that Polish cities will note the super high pressure.

The cumulative impact of factors influencing the spatial development of cities is not a simple sum of them but acts in a compound way, but the synergy of the influence of a different number of factors in various geographical areas may not be the same. Then one can expect different ways and different spatial extent of urban sprawl in Polish cities.

References

1. Frączyk, J.: Nowych mieszkań więcej niż "za Gierka". Pobity wynik z 1980 roku. Business Insider Polska (2021). https://businessinsider.com.pl/finanse/makroekonomia/budownictwo-mieszkaniowe-pobilo-wynik-czasow-gierka-nowy-rekord-iii-rp/46q5l5v. Accessed 20 Mar 2022
2. Ottensmann, J.R.: An alternative approach to the measurement of urban sprawl (2018). https://doi.org/10.13140/RG.2.2.10237.46562
3. Olender, L.: Górny: Liczba Ukraińców w Polsce wróciła do poziomu sprzed pandemii; statystyki mogą być zaburzone. , https://www.bankier.pl/wiadomosc/Gorny-Liczba-Ukrain cow-w-Polsce-wrocila-do-poziomu-sprzed-pandemii-statystyki-moga-byc-zaburzone-823 9097.html. Accessed 20 Mar 2022

4. Duszczyk, M.: Ukrainian refugees in Poland: Current situation and what to expect. FREE Network. FREE Policy Briefs Series (2022)
5. Hasse, J.E., Lathrop, R.G.: Land resource impact indicators of urban sprawl. Appl. Geogr. **23**, 159–175 (2003). https://doi.org/10.1016/j.apgeog.2003.08.002
6. Jaeger, J.A., Schwick, C.: Improving the measurement of urban sprawl: Weighted Urban Proliferation (WUP) and its application to Switzerland. Ecol. Ind. **38**, 294–308 (2014)
7. European Environment Agency. Swiss Federal Office for the Environment (FOEN): Urban Sprawl in Europe: Joint EEA FOEN Report.; Publications Office (2016)
8. OECD: Rethinking urban sprawl: Moving towards sustainable cities; OECD (2018)
9. Yasin, M.Y., Yusoff, M.M., Abdullah, J., Noor, N.M., Noor, M.N.: Urban sprawl literature review: definition and driving force. Malaysian J. Soc. Space **17**(2), 116–128 (2021)
10. Guastella, G., Oueslati, W., Pareglio, S.: Patterns of urban spatial expansion in European cities. Sustainability **11**(8), 22–47 (2019). https://doi.org/10.3390/su11082247
11. Selod, H., Zenou, Y.: City structure, job search and labour discrimination: theory and policy implications. Econ. J. **116**, 1057–1087 (2006). https://doi.org/10.1111/j.1468-0297.2006.011 23.x
12. Oueslati, W., Alvanides, S., Garrod, G.: Determinants of urban sprawl in European cities. Urban Stud. **52**, 1594–1614 (2015). https://doi.org/10.1177/0042098015577773
13. Patacchini, E., Zenou, Y., Henderson, J.V., Epple, D.: Urban sprawl in Europe. Brookings-Wharton Papers on Urban Affairs 125–149 (2009)
14. Chin, N.: Unearthing the roots of urban sprawl: a critical analysis of form, function and methodology. CASA Working Papers 47 (2002)
15. Jaeger, J.A.G., Bertiller, R., Schwick, C., Kienast, F.: Suitability criteria for measures of urban sprawl. Ecol. Ind. **10**, 397–406 (2010). https://doi.org/10.1016/j.ecolind.2009.07.007
16. Sheludkov, A., Starikova, A.: Summer suburbanization in Moscow region: investigation with nighttime lights satellite imagery. Environ. Plann. A: Econ. Space **54**, 446–448 (2022). https://doi.org/10.1177/0308518X221076502
17. Hlaváček, P., Kopáček, M., Horáčková, L.: Impact of suburbanisation on sustainable development of settlements in suburban spaces: smart and new solutions. Sustainability **11**, 71–82 (2019). https://doi.org/10.3390/su11247182
18. Taleb, N.N.: The Black Swan: the impact of the highly improbable, 1st edn. Random House, New York (2007)
19. Werner, P.A. et al.: Modeling the spatial and temporal spread of COVID-19 in Poland based on a spatial interaction model. ISPRS Int. J. Geo-Inform. **11** (2022). https://doi.org/10.3390/ijgi11030195
20. Werner, P.A., Skrynyk, O., Porczek, M., Szczepankowska-Bednarek, U., Olszewski, R., Kęsik-Brodacka, M.: The effects of climate and bioclimate on COVID-19 cases in Poland. Remote Sensing **13**, 4946 (2021). https://doi.org/10.3390/rs13234946
21. Spillovers - definition of spillovers by the free dictionary. http://www.thefreedictionary.com/spillovers. Accessed 14 Jul 2016
22. Warf, B. (ed): Encyclopedia of human geography. Sage, Thousand Oaks (2006)
23. Marshall, A.: Principles of economics. Unabridged 8th edn. Cosimo Inc. (2009)
24. Pigou, A.: The economics of welfare. Routledge (2017)
25. Mishan, E.J.: The postwar literature on externalities: An interpretative essay. J. Econ. Lit. **9**, 1–28 (1971)
26. Hoover, Edgar, M., Giarratani, F.: An Introduction to regional economics (1999)
27. Hagoort, M., Geertman, S., Ottens, H.: Spatial externalities, neighbourhood rules and CA land-use modelling. Ann. Reg. Sci. **42**, 39–56 (2008). https://doi.org/10.1007/s00168-007-0140-8
28. Harrop, K.J.: Nuisances and their externality fields. University of Newcastle upon Tyne (1973)

29. Krugman, P.: The role of geography in development. Int. Reg. Sci. Rev. **22**, 142–161 (1999)
30. Maier, G., Sedlacek, S.: Spillovers and innovations. Interdisciplinary studies in economics and management (2005)
31. Hagoort, M.J.: The neighbourhood rules: land-use interactions, urban dynamics and cellular automata modelling. Koninklijk Nederlands Aardrijkskundig Genootschap (2006)
32. Tobler, W.R.: Cellular geography. In Philosophy in Geography. Springer, Dordrecht (1979)
33. Statistics Poland. https://stat.gov.pl/en/. Accessed 20 Mar 2022
34. Czyż, T.: Metoda wskaźnikowa w geografii społeczno-ekonomicznej. Rozwój Regionalny i Polityka Regionalna **34**, 9–19 (2016)
35. Statista - The Statistics Portal. https://www.statista.com/. Accessed 26 Mar 2022

Accessibility and Mobility in the Small Mountain Municipality of Zafferana Etnea (Sicily): Coupling of Walkability Assessment and Space Syntax

Antonio Russo[1] , Tiziana Campisi[1][(✉)] , Giovanni Tesoriere[1] ,
Alfonso Annunziata[2], and Chiara Garau[1]

[1] Faculty of Engineering and Architecture, University of Enna Kore, 94100 Enna, Italy
`tiziana.campisi@unikore.it`
[2] Department of Civil and Environmental Engineering and Architecture, University of Cagliari,
09129 Cagliari, Italy

Abstract. The new mobility paradigm, the spread of new city models and the recent pandemic have highlighted the variability and complexity of people's mobility. There is a widespread need for dynamic urban planning strategies to adapt to circumstances and mitigate the risk of dangerous events such as natural disasters and pandemics. The last decade has been characterised by urban transformation processes that have often led to inequalities in spatial and infrastructural distribution and services. To reduce this criticality, it is necessary to investigate the reciprocal influence between the spatial configuration of the built environment and the way everyday mobility is implemented and becomes habitual, and its relationship with the inequalities mentioned above (e.g. suburbs, degraded areas, urban voids). This research focuses on studying the evolution of the accessibility of the small mountainous urban centre of Zafferana Etnea, which seismic phenomena have hit several times. In the first instance, the work identified and characterised the case study by estimating the mobility demand based on access and the analysis of the spatial configuration (buildings, infrastructures and services). Similarly, the research proposes the definition of the primary attractive nodes of the city, zoning and the purpose of key factors for the definition of mobility indicators that allow the realisation of a quantitative analysis of transport demand and supply based on indicators rather than on the configuration of the urban fabric, which will be addressed with theoretical and methodological tools provided by the spatial syntax.

Keywords: Urban mobility · Walkability · Spatial analysis · Space syntax

This paper is the result of the joint work of the authors. 'Abstract', 'Literature review: Accessibility and mobility and the combination of walkability and Space Syntax', 'Results' and 'Discussion and Conclusions' were written jointly by the authors. Antonio Russo wrote 'The case study of Zafferana Etnea in Sicily'. Tiziana Campisi wrote 'The development of the correlation between mobility and urban spaces in the post-pandemic phase'. Alfonso Annunziata wrote 'Space Syntax analysis'. Chiara Garau wrote the 'Introduction'. Chiara Garau and Tiziana Campisi coordinated and supervised the paper.

1 Introduction

The worldwide pandemic problem triggered by Covid19 has led to reassessing cities' development, especially how modern cities are created and constructed. A reflection on the principles of understanding these issues with cities and the construction of spaces for human living, as well as fields such as social sciences and civil and transport engineering [1].

UN-Habitat report [2] notes that in the pandemic around 120 million people would become impoverished and their standard of living will fall by 23%. In cities, a new reality might develop if housing, services and security are prioritised. Since Covid-19, urban areas have been at the forefront of the crisis. Governments and local communities have been compelled to take swift and decisive action to prevent the virus's spread.

Most countries and cities were unprepared for the spread of SARS-CoV-2, officially declared a pandemic in March 2020. During the second phase, governments attempted to adapt to Covid-19 and started studying ways to mitigate its negative social and economic consequences. The second phase is rebuilding and recovery, which some governments started working on right away in the first months of the pandemic, but others (mostly low-income countries with less resources) have yet to start as they continue to suffer the effects of the virus.

Several literature studies highlighted the need of acquiring higher knowledge of road users' changing travel habits, their attitudes toward public transport, and their perceptions of sustainable urban mobility modes in order to enhance post-pandemic urban and transport planning [3–5].

Political leaders need to reorganise cities by emphasising neighbourhood planning, how people move in urban centres, and ensuring multifunctional and inclusive settlements. Well-planned cities combine residential, commercial, public spaces and affordable housing to foster a sense of community [6–8].

Indeed, cities capable of ensuring the health, housing and safety of the most vulnerable populations may contribute to the "new reality". Local governments must prioritise measures that safeguard land rights, increase access to water, sanitation, public transport, electricity, health, education, and ensure inclusive digital connectivity.

The four key pillars for reviving cities are as follows:

- rethink the shape and function of the city;
- tackle poverty and inequalities;
- rebuild an urban economy;
- clarify urban legislation and urban governance.

New, more sustainable and productive urban systems characterised by compact form, accessible mobility and diversified land use may help create safer and more liveable urban environments [9, 10]. Several actions have been undertaken on a worldwide scale in recent months, from metropolitan cities to small towns.

For instance, Montréal established a network of accessible corridors for pedestrians and cyclists in response to the pandemic, consisting of 112 km of bike and walking lines that connect city residents to parks, schools, essential services and businesses. Additionally, cities around Europe are restructuring their highways to support a larger reliance on non-motorised transport. Milan's city centre will be renovated to offer approximately 35km of road space for bikes and pedestrians. In Brussels, where an extensive pedestrianisation plan was already underway prior the pandemic, the whole city centre was changed into a priority pedestrian and cycling zone. London recognised the need of providing secure accommodation for the city's vast homeless population in order to protect them from illness and prevent viral spread. Vacant hotels and workplaces were swiftly turned into safe spaces.

Following an analysis of the literature related to the concept of accessibility [11, 12], the need to investigate the mutual influence of the built environment's spatial configuration and mobility emerged. This was accomplished by defining the network graphs of a city and estimating access-based mobility demand, both through the analysis of spatial configuration (buildings, infrastructures and services).

The next paragraphs provide an overview of the literature on the notion of city accessibility at different sizes and emphasise crucial challenges pertaining to small mountain urban centres. Subsequently, the case study's features are detailed, emphasising the rationale for selecting the city for analysis and outlining the city's major centroid nodes, zoning, and network graphs, with a special emphasis on pedestrian mobility. Finally, components of the spaces are identified via the use of space syntax analysis through maps and images that depict the relative connectedness and integration of those spaces.

2 Literature Review: Accessibility and Mobility and the Combination of Walkability and Space Syntax

Making the city more inclusive is a worthwhile, achievable, and productive goal. It is vital for everyone's quality of life, but particularly for the most vulnerable people because it improves access to communities, services, and public places by providing safer and more accessible roadways and sidewalks [13–17]. Additionally, it benefits everyone's health by reducing pollution and accidents and enabling better lives. It is beneficial for encouraging social participation [18–20] and increasing the autonomy of disabled individuals [21, 22]. It is also practicable because it may be accomplished with low-cost treatments that have instant results. It is successful since it entails additional advantages for the city's growth.

Moreover, the vitality potential of public space is determined by the spaces' intrinsic qualities, most notably its configurational properties. Configuration may be described as the relationship of access and visibility between interdependent spatial elements that compose an overall structure.

Spatial relations define conditions of the centrality of spatial elements and influence the distribution of natural movement and, consequently, the patterns of co-presence across spaces. Natural movement patterns have an effect on land use patterns, favouring the concentration of functions in integrated and central places and dictating the creation of lively local and supralocal centres as well as quieter monofunctional zones. This, in turn, activates local adaptations of the spatial structure, resulting in the intensification of the urban grid and the densification of built-up areas, resulting in a multiplier effect on the distribution of movements and space use, as well as the location of land uses, resulting in a recursive socio-spatial process denominated as movement economy. As a consequence, the interaction between space and social activities, as well as the effect of space configurations on people's structures, are understood at the configuration level. Indeed, it is centrality that is emerging as the spatial characteristic that reflects and reproduces social norms, connections, and behaviours.

3 Methodology

3.1 Space Syntax Analysis

Space syntax refers to approaches, theories and techniques for analysing spatial configurations. Bill Hillier and colleagues from The Bartlett, University College London devised it in the late 1970s to assist urban planners in simulating the likely social implications of their projects [23].

The underlying concept is that spatial structures can be formalised as a set of spatial components and characterised in terms of topological relations among elements interdependent in a global network. Recent studies on urban spaces, in particular, are focused on lines of movement, and formalised spatial structures as segment maps; segment maps represent spatial structures as a set of segments delimited by consecutive intersections. Afterwards, maps are turned into graphs in which nodes represent spatial components and arcs indicate intersections among spaces. Segment map analysis is characterised by three distinct aspects of centrality of spaces: degree centrality, closeness centrality, and betweenness centrality. Degree centrality is a local configurational property that refers to the number of spatial elements that are contiguously related to a space. Closeness centrality is determined by the distance between a space and all other elements in a spatial layout. As a result, the importance of a space as a destination is defined by its closeness centrality. Finally, betweenness centrality is a configurational attribute that is determined by the likelihood that a space is included inside the shortest paths connecting any origin space to any destination space contained within a spatial layout. As a result, betweenness centrality refers to the through-movement potential of a spatial element. These centrality properties are influenced by the distance among spaces. Distance is conceptualised in three ways in space syntactic theory: metric, topological, and geometric ones.

Geometric distance is defined as the sum of angular deviations along a route from an origin space to a destination space. The proposed research considers the geometric conceptualisation of distance and measures the aspects of centrality via the indicators Normalised Segment angular Integration (NAIN) and Normalised segment angular Choice (NACH). Normalisation of measures of integration and choice aims to enable the comparison of spatial structures of different sizes, and in the case of normalised angular choice, to solve the paradox that segregated structures determine an increase in total and average choice values compared to integrated structures [24]. Moreover, NAIN and NACH are computed at the global scale, and within a radius of 800 m and 300 m of each origin space, respectively, to identify global and local centers and to account for the influence of the configuration of the spatial layout on the distribution local scale pedestrian movements and global motorised travel. Lastly, values of Normalised Choice at the local (at radius 300 m) and global scale are compared to identify spaces intersected by main itineraries and local itineraries that emerge as suitable locations for diversified services and urban functions. Thus, configurational metrics are used to assess the extrinsic properties of the urban structure that connect the system of mobility and circulation to the distribution of natural movement and co-presence, consequently impacting the intensity of individual and social practices across public spaces. This configurational description of the urban structure is central for generating the knowledge base needed for urban regeneration interventions aimed at promoting the vitality and inclusivity of urban spaces [14, 25].

3.2 The Development of the Correlation Between Mobility and Urban Spaces in the Post-pandemic Phase

Mobility is crucial to a region's attractiveness. In particular, the development of infrastructures and transport services facilitates travel, work and leisure activities.

The recent pandemic has highlighted these gaps but has also shown potential opportunities in mountain areas and villages [26]. However, it also stimulated the transport of goods as a result of the growth in e-commerce purchases [27]. In many rural and mountain areas, a traditional dependence on cars prevails, and the lack of adequate collective transport alternatives forces some typologies of rural residents to live in social and geographical exclusion. In such contexts, accessibility is crucial to the success of development initiatives, and the lack of adequate accessibility affects any development strategy implemented in rural areas [28–30].

International and local research demonstrates that such mountainous areas are interchangeable with low demand transport areas, which may reflect negatively on the economic feasibility of public transport lines. Furthermore, they are often characterised by a high number of elderly people, sometimes a high poverty rate and a relative remoteness from the main airports/railways /road connections.

Mountain locations also have specific topographical characteristics, such as slopes, altitude and protected areas, which complicate and increase the cost of road and railway development [31]. The literature highlights the need of considering complementary solutions of transport beyond traditional urban and extra-urban public transport, such as micro-mobility and pedal-assisted bike solutions for short-distance travel, and DRT services for medium and long-distance travel [32, 33]. The evaluation of strategies for optimizing mobility will also have to start from the simplest form, namely walkability.

From these considerations, this paper establishes the framework for a research project aimed at identifying how space syntax analyses at various levels of scale can be used to identify and describe the spatial characteristics of a mountain city and improve its walkability, starting from the case study of Zafferana Etnea in Sicily, Italy.

3.3 The Case Study of Zafferana Etnea in Sicily

This case study was chosen because in mountain areas, the limits imposed by the morphology of the territory, the slow but widespread ageing of the population and the contraction of resources pose the problem of accessibility to basic services. Schools, as well as local health services and community centres (associations, theatres, squares, etc..), are the main sectors with which those who live in areas far from the main urban centres are confronted on a daily basis. Zafferana Etnea, situated on the south-eastern side of

Etna, has 9,262 inhabitants (ISTAT, 2021) and covers an area of 76.67 square kilometres, making it the largest municipality on the south-eastern side. Around 80% of the territory is covered by Etna Park, which is subject to naturalistic restrictions. The territory has a high level of tourism, for the volcano's proximity and the food and wine events (Fig. 1).

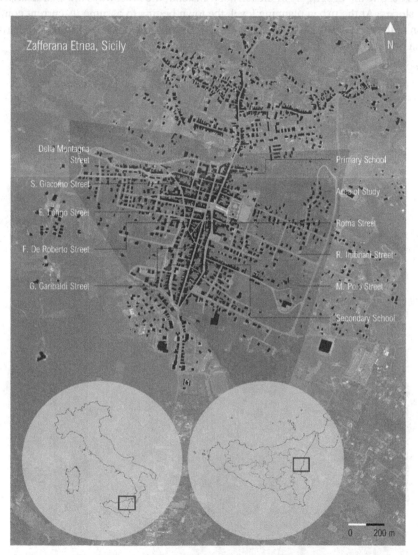

Fig. 1. Zafferana Etnea in Sicily (authors' elaboration).

Zafferana Etnea is located in a highly critical setting, both volcanically and seismically, because it is perched on the slopes of Mount Etna and is susceptible to the danger of periodic volcanic eruptions. The historic centre of the city is characterised by a strong concentration of inhabited areas and hence resident population, as well as characterised by the location of most of the public services (schools, town hall) and private ones. The main road axes are parallel to the contour lines in the NE-SW direction, with a system of crossways in the NW-SE direction acting as linkages. This has resulted in a significant pedestrianisation of the Zafferana's principal axes, which do not have extremely steep slopes despite the orography of the territory. Instead, the crossways are characterised by high slopes. At the urban planning level, the town begins to assume its current configuration in the early 1900s, with the formation of the historic centre's original core around Roma Street (Fig. 2).

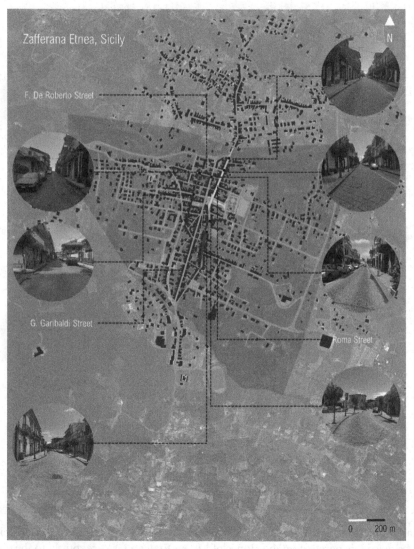

Fig. 2. The significant major routes across Zafferana (authors' elaboration).

The later-created perpendicular "Della Montagna" Street, together with "San Giacomo" Street form a triangle marking the town's original urban core. The expansions to the south and east, which began in the 1970s, represent a continuation of this period. The current urban configuration is bounded to the west by the Etna Park limited by the landscape constraint to the West, due to the presence of the Etna Park; new residential areas are mostly located east of the urban core. The triangle formed by Roma Street, Della Montagna Street and S. Giacomo Street is the historical urban area of Zafferana Etnea, with the surrounding territories mostly used for agricultural, residential, and productive purposes. Its primary attractions include the schools positioned on each side of the major road axis, as well as the offices and banks located around the main square.

4 Results

The segment angular analysis of Zafferana (Table 1) underlines the emerging spatial structures, at distinct levels of scale. In particular, the analysis of configurational properties, at the local scale ($r = 300$ m), describes the structure of the most relevant destination spaces and routes in relation to pedestrian movements.

Table 1. Results of the angular segment analysis of the system of roads and public spaces in Zafferana

Zafferana	NACH 300	NACH 800	NACH N	NAIN 300	NAIN 800	NAIN N
Min	0.301	0.301	0.301	0.793	1.056	1.604
Max	2.501	3.537	3.814	1.756	2.016	2.057
Mean	1.482	2.367	2.498	1.329	1.745	1.902
Standard deviation	0.642	0.862	0.989	0.239	0.221	0.098
Variation Coefficient	0.433	0.364	0.395	0.180	0.126	0.051

The distribution of normalised angular integration, in a 300 m radius, underlines the emergence of a reticular structure of integrated spaces (Fig. 3), comprising part of the centre of the ancient formation and the segments, contiguous to the Cardinal Pappalardo Square, of the system of longitudinal streets, including G. Garibaldi Street, F. De Roberto Street, and Roma Street. A set of segregated spaces are located along the edges of the area of study (Fig. 3). The distribution of choice, at the local scale, underlines a centripetal structure of spaces relevant for pedestrian trips, that intersect the central compact area and includes segments of the longitudinal streets F. de Roberto, San Giacomo and G. Garibaldi streets. Moreover, the distribution of integration and centrality in an 800 m radius, identifies a grid structure of accessible spaces for pedestrians and cyclists, relevant as destination spaces and a radio-centric structure of circulation spaces (Fig. 4).

Lastly, at the global scale, the distribution of centrality underlines the emergence of distinct sub-systems of routes relevant for urban-scale movements: the ring route comprising Marco Polo, R. Imbriani and A. De Gasperi streets; a reticular sub-system

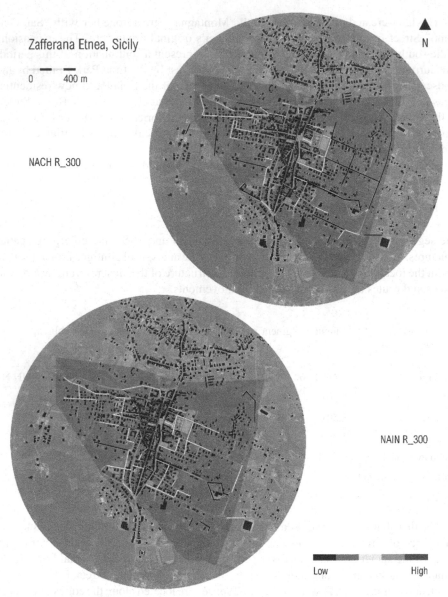

Fig. 3. Distribution of NACH and NAIN at radius 300 m (authors' elaboration).

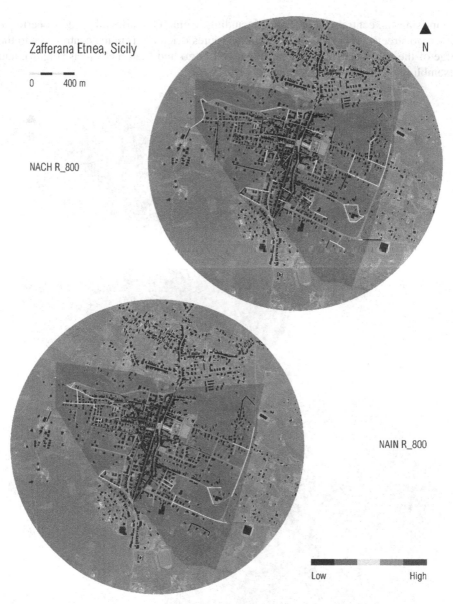

Fig. 4. Distribution of NACH and NAIN at a radius 800 m (authors' elaboration).

comprising the central compact area, including Roma, G. Garibaldi, F. de Roberto, S. Giacomo streets, and a sub-system of radial routes oriented from the central area to the edge of the urbanised area, and including E. Longo and Cassone Streets (Fig. 5), and resembling a deformed wheel structure [23].

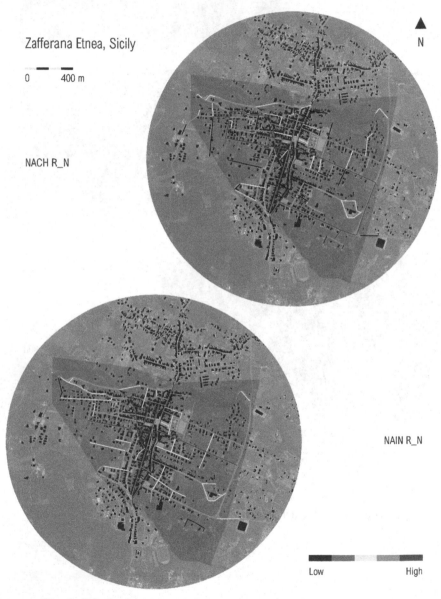

Fig. 5. Distribution of NACH and NAIN at radius n (authors' elaboration).

Moreover, the distribution of integration underlines a reticular structure of routes intersecting the central compact area and a radial structure of routes, including Roma, G. Garibaldi and S. Giacomo streets, connecting the central compact area to the edge of the urbanised area.

Lastly, the comparison of NACH at the local scale, calculated in a 300 m radius, and global scale underlines a centripetal structure of main routes at the local and urban

Fig. 6. Segments constituting a potential vibrant urban centre (authors' elaboration).

scale (Fig. 6) that present a significant spatial pre-condition for the emergence of vibrant central areas.

5 Discussion and Conclusions

Considering the territory's conditions and the exposure to seismic and volcanic activity. Zafferana Etnea requires particular attention in terms of urban planning and mobility. This small mountain municipality is an area to be re-evaluated in light of the recent Sustainable Development Goals of Agenda 2030, but especially in light of the organic measures aimed at promoting economic development and the recovery of territories for reversing the depopulation of the Italian mountain regions.

The urban layout, which twists down the slopes near the woodlands surrounding the volcano Etna, has been subjected to multiple powerful seismic events (1952, 1984, 2002) some of which caused irreversible damage, particularly in the city's hamlets. Despite this, the historical centre attracts many visitors from all over Italy also for a variety of religious and gastronomic events. These peculiarities motivate the spatial syntax analysis of this small urban centre, ensuring the understanding of the organisation's socio-spatial of built environments.

By assuming that space syntax is a theory of space and a set of analytical, quantitative and descriptive tools to analyse the arrangement of space in buildings and cities, the authors highlight its significant utility for the urban areas at risk, such as Zafferana Etnea. Not only does this enable the spatial configuration to be defined as relationships between spaces that take other relationships into account, and thus as relationships between all the various spaces in a system, but it also contributes to a more comprehensive vision for urban planning, mobility, and emergency planning.

This first step of research identifies the urban structure's features, namely finding a "vibrant historical centre" and a radial structure linking to the surrounding areas.

The normalised angular integration and normalised angular choice measures allow the recognition of a deformed wheel structure with central spaces for circulation and co-presence. Moreover, the emerging centripetal structure of central spaces at the local and global scale presents the spatial conditions favourable to the location of services and functions. Thus, these spaces become the focus of future studies, which will examine the underlying geometric and spatial conditions that influence pedestrian activities, and the interactions among the public open space and the enclosed private space of buildings.

Acknowledgements. This work started and developed as a result of a project proposal within the doctoral course "Smart and Sustainable Cities (2nd edition)" (https://dottorati.unica.it/dot ticar/smart-and-sustainable-cities-2- Edizione/). This study was supported by the MIUR through the project "WEAKI TRANSIT: WEAK-demand areas Innovative TRANsport Shared services for Italian Towns (Project code: 20174ARRHT /CUP Code: J74I19000320008), financed with the PRIN 2017 (Research Projects of National Relevance) programme. We authorise the MIUR to reproduce and distribute reprints for Governmental purposes, notwithstanding any copyright notations thereon. Any opinions, findings and conclusions or recommendations expressed in this material are those of the authors, and do not necessarily reflect the views of the MIUR. This paper is also supported by Cagliari Accessibility Lab, an interdepartmental centre at the University of Cagliari (Rector's Decree of 4 March 2020. https://www.unica.it/unica/it/cagliari_accessibi lity_lab.page).

References

1. Campisi, T., et al.: A new vision on smart and resilient urban mobility in the aftermath of the pandemic: key factors on European transport policies. In: Gervasi, O., et al. (eds.) ICCSA 2021. LNCS, vol. 12958, pp. 603–618. Springer, Cham (2021). https://doi.org/10.1007/978-3-030-87016-4_43

2. UN-Habitat report Cties and Pandemics: Towards a more just, green and healthy future, Available at the following link (2021). https://unhabitat.org/un-habitat-report-calls-for-cities-post-pandemic-to-lead-the-way-to-a-fairer-greener-healthier

3. Campisi, T., et al.: The impact of COVID-19 pandemic on the resilience of sustainable mobility in Sicily. Sustainability **12**(21), 8829 (2020)

4. Campisi, T., Caselli, B., Rossetti, S., Torrisi, V.: The evolution of sustainable mobility and urban space planning: exploring the factors contributing to the regeneration of car parking in living spaces. Transp. Res. Procedia **60**, 76–83 (2022)

5. Nahiduzzaman, K.M.: COVID-19 and change dynamics in the transformational cities. J. Urban Manag. (2021)

6. Zhongming, Z., Linong, L., Xiaona, Y., Wangqiang, Z., Wei, L.: Cities and pandemics: towards a more just, green and healthy future (2021)

7. Moraci, F., et al.: Cities under pressure: strategies and tools to face climate change and pandemic. Sustainability **12**(18), 7743 (2020)

8. Mistretta, P., Garau, C.: Città e sfide. Conflitti e Utopie. Strategie di impresa e Politiche del territorio. Successi e criticità dei modelli di governance (2013)

9. Nadeem, M., Aziz, A., Al-Rashid, M.A., Tesoriere, G., Asim, M., Campisi, T.: Scaling the potential of compact city development: the case of Lahore. Pak. Sustain. **13**(9), 5257 (2021)

10. Peiser, R., Forsyth, A. (Eds.). New towns for the Twenty-First Century: a Guide to Planned Communities Worldwide. University of Pennsylvania Press (2021)

11. Nicoletta, R., et al.: Accessibility to Local Public Transport in Cagliari with Focus on the Elderly. In: Gervasi, O., et al. (eds.) ICCSA 2020. LNCS, vol. 12255, pp. 690–705. Springer, Cham (2020). https://doi.org/10.1007/978-3-030-58820-5_50

12. Coni, M., Garau, C., Maltinti, F., Pinna, F.: Accessibility improvements and place-based organization in the Island of Sardinia (Italy). In: Gervasi, O., et al. (eds.) ICCSA 2020. LNCS, vol. 12255, pp. 337–352. Springer, Cham (2020). https://doi.org/10.1007/978-3-030-58820-5_26

13. Garau, C., Pavan, V.M.: Evaluating urban quality: indicators and assessment tools for smart sustainable cities. Sustainability **10**(3), 575 (2018)

14. Garau, C., Annunziata, A., Yamu, C.: A walkability assessment tool coupling multi-criteria analysis and space syntax: the case study of Iglesias, Italy. Europ. Plann. Stud. 1–23 (2020). https://doi.org/10.1080/09654313.2020.1761947

15. Garau, C., Annunziata, A.: A method for assessing the vitality potential of urban areas. the case study of the metropolitan City of Cagliari, Italy. City, Territory Archit. **9**(7), 1–23 (2022). https://doi.org/10.1186/s40410-022-00153-6

16. Annunziata, A., Garau, C.: A literature review on the assessment of vitality and its theoretical framework. emerging perspectives for geodesign in the urban context. In: Gervasi, O., et al. (eds.) ICCSA 2021. LNCS, vol. 12958, pp. 305–322. Springer, Cham (2021). https://doi.org/10.1007/978-3-030-87016-4_23

17. Garau C., Annunziata A.: Public open spaces: connecting people, squares and streets by measuring the usability through the Villanova district in Cagliari, Italy. In: Tira M., Maternini G., Tiboni M., (Eds.). New scenarios for safe mobility in urban areas. Proceedings of the XXV International Conference Living and Walking in Cities (LWC 2021), 9–10 September 2021, Brescia, Italy. Transportation Research Procedia, vol. 60, pp. 314–321 (2022).https://doi.org/10.1016/j.trpro.2021.12.041. ISSN 2352–1465

18. Garau, C.: Focus on citizens: Public engagement with online and face-to-face participation—a case study. Future Internet **4**(2), 592–606 (2012)
19. Garau, C.: Citizen participation in public planning: a literature review. Int. J. Sci. **1**(12), 21–44 (2012)
20. Garau, C.: Processi di piano e partecipazione. Gangemi Editore Spa (2013)
21. Pinna, F., Garau, C., Annunziata, A.: A literature review on urban usability and accessibility to investigate the related criteria for equality in the city. In: Gervasi, O., et al. (eds.) ICCSA 2021. LNCS, vol. 12958, pp. 525–541. Springer, Cham (2021). https://doi.org/10.1007/978-3-030-87016-4_38
22. Garau, C., Annunziata, A.: Supporting children's independent activities in smart and playable public places. Sustainability, **12**, 8352 (2020).https://doi.org/10.3390/su12208352. EISSN 2071–1050
23. Yamu, C., van Nes, A., Garau, C.: Bill Hillier's legacy: space syntax—a synopsis of basic concepts, measures, and empirical application. Sustainability **13**, 1–25 (2021)
24. Hillier, W.R.G., Yang, T., Turner, A.: Normalising least angle choice in Depthmap - and how it opens up new perspectives on the global and local analysis of city space. J. Space Syntax , **3**(2), 155–193 (2012)
25. Garau, C., Annunziata, A.: A method for assessing the vitality potential of urban areas. the case study of the metropolitan city of Cagliari, Italy. City Territory Archit. **9**(7) 1-23 (2022). https://doi.org/10.1186/s40410-022-00153-6
26. Pinto, M.R., Viola, S., Fabbricatti, K., Pacifico, M.G.: Adaptive reuse process of the historic urban landscape post-Covid-19. the potential of the inner areas for a new normal. VITRUVIO-Int. J. Arch.Technol. Sustain. **5**(2), 87–105 (2020)
27. Campisi, T., Russo, A., Tesoriere, G., Bouhouras, E., Basbas, S.: COVID-19's effects over e-commerce: a preliminary statistical assessment for some European countries. In: Gervasi, O., et al. (eds.) ICCSA 2021. LNCS, vol. 12954, pp. 370–385. Springer, Cham (2021). https://doi.org/10.1007/978-3-030-86979-3_27
28. Mikou, M., Rozenberg, J., Koks, E.E., Fox, C.J.E., Peralta Quiros, T.: Assessing rural accessibility and rural roads investment needs using open source data. World Bank Policy Res. Work. Pap. (8746) (2019)
29. Heldt, T., Tydén, T., Waleghwa, B., Brandt, D.: Planning for mobility and accessibility in rural touristic areas: A report on the Swedish case in InterReg MARA project (2021)
30. Tesoriere, G., Campisi, T.: The benefit of engage the "crowd" encouraging a bottom-up approach for shared mobility rating. In: Gervasi, O., et al. (eds.) ICCSA 2020. LNCS, vol. 12250, pp. 836–850. Springer, Cham (2020). https://doi.org/10.1007/978-3-030-58802-1_60
31. Laurence, R.: The Roads of Roman Italy: Mobility and Cultural Change. Routledge (2002)
32. Campisi, T., Canale, A., Ticali, D., Tesoriere, G.: Innovative solutions for sustainable mobility in areas of weak demand. some factors influencing the implementation of the DRT system in Enna (Italy). In: AIP Conference Proceedings, vol. 2343, no. 1, p. 090005. AIP Publishing LLC, March 2021
33. Campisi, T., Garau, C., Acampa, G., Maltinti, F., Canale, A., Coni, M.: Developing flexible mobility on-demand in the era of mobility as a service: an overview of the italian context before and after pandemic. In: Gervasi, O., et al. (eds.) ICCSA 2021. LNCS, vol. 12954, pp. 323–338. Springer, Cham (2021). https://doi.org/10.1007/978-3-030-86979-3_24

Digital City-Surveillance Models and Urban Security: Integrating Isovist and Space Syntax in Realising Adaptive Decision Support Systems

Federico Mara[✉] and Valerio Cutini

University of Pisa, Pisa, Italy
federico.mara@phd.unipi.it, valerio.cutini@unipi.it

Abstract. Urban security plays a fundamental role in achieving sustainable cities. The environmental approach to security proved crucial, with its inner multidisciplinarity, in fighting crime and in promoting crime prevention through environmental design, urban management and situational-oriented strategies, where the importance of surveillance emerges. Among the research fields involved, digital technology has a primary role in the research progress both through the development of advanced analysis and decision support systems (DSS), and through the elaboration of high-tech interconnected devices in a smart-safe city logic. In this vein, the paper first reviews the IT and ICT role in urban security progress, and then it traces the development and the importance of surveillance by focusing on the isovist and the space syntax theory until their last findings. Finally, the paper suggests a schematic proposal of a digital surveillance-city model based on the integration of those concepts, which could be used for analytic, decision support and predictive purposes. The strength of this model resides in its adaptability to different contexts and its potential independence from sensitive data, which permits overcoming privacy issues. Moreover – being surveillance and visibility features that impact different urban life aspects – this model could represent an urban planning DSS for strategies that goes beyond the mere crime-fighting. Furthermore, this model constitutes a first step in the development of a surveillance-oriented Agent-Based Model.

Keywords: Urban security · Crime prevention · Environmental approach · Surveillance · Digital technology · Isovist · Space syntax · Decision support system

1 Introduction

Urban security is a fundamental factor that affects citizens' quality of life [1, 2]. Since the '90s the impact of crime on citizens' well-being has been recognised and has thus become one of the main objectives of the world's leading organisations, also becoming part of the EU SDGs [3]. Even though crimes in urbanized cities are constantly decreasing [4], the perception of insecurity is still very high [5]. Sometimes the fear of crime, which is a fundamental aspect in determining citizens' behaviour and city-life [6, 7], is even

O. Gervasi et al. (Eds.): ICCSA 2022 Workshops, LNCS 13377, pp. 353–369, 2022.
https://doi.org/10.1007/978-3-031-10536-4_24

increasing due to the growing size and complexity of cities, some collateral phenomena and the so-called urban-fear paradoxes. It is therefore necessary to continue investigating how to intervene to reduce both crime and fear of crime to achieve safe and sustainable cities. The topic is inherently complex, being generated by the combination of two complex systems such as the urban dynamics and the criminal logic, which determines the unavoidable need for multidisciplinary studies. Thus, much research has addressed the issue from different perspectives, greatly enhancing the knowledge of crime dynamics and, as a consequence, crime prevention. However, such studies were often developed with a 'tunnel vision', without deep collaboration and integration between different fields. This lack of collaboration generated problems of oversimplification, overlapping, inconsistent language and chaotic development [1, 8, 9].

The main fields involved in this research were sociology, criminology, psychology, architecture and urban planning, which between the '70s and '80s gave birth to the social approach and environmental approach to security, in addition to the traditional one that was already existing [10]. In particular, the environmental approach to security in the last decades is getting new lifeblood from the digital technology evolution: on the one hand, the technology progress allowed analysis and modelling progress, useful to confirm and validate or refute existing theories, thus allowing the scientific evolution and at the same time being used as decision support tool. On the other hand, from the operative point of view, it generated tools and devices aiming at quality-of-life improvement and citizens' safety in a smart-safe city logic. The connection between the theoretical and practical development produced advanced security systems aimed at safer cities. However, these security interconnected systems still leave many shadows and open questions about privacy concerns and data retention issues, psychological perception of citizens and social effects.

Over time, for example, the concepts of smart and safe cities have developed, based on the resource's optimization logic and the use of technology aimed at citizens' quality of life improvement. Whit this aim much progress in developing advanced systems and devices has been done. In particular, concerning safe cities and crime prevention techniques, surveillance plays a fundamental role [9]. For this reason, the theme of visual surveillance is explored in this paper. In fact, many studies show how the spaces that surround us affect our behaviour and, in particular, how the visual scenarios that open up to us, step by step, condition our subsequent choices, for example, in determining a path [11] or deciding whether or not commit a crime [12, 13]. Therefore, the integration of spatial, urban planning and criminological knowledge, with the support of digital technology development can open new scenarios in fighting crime in a surveillance and crime-reduction logic. Moreover, this joint collaboration could play a decisive role in decision support tools development for urban planning processes, for example by fostering rational choices between alternatives. In particular, this paper aims to illustrate the potential of integrating environmental criminology, isovist analysis and configurational analysis (namely the Space Syntax theory) in the development of a digital city-surveillance model as crime-fighting decision support tool. The process is here presented conceptually, and it will be the subject of subsequent applications and in-depth studies.

2 Concepts and Methods

The investigation methodology is developed in two stages (par. 3.1 to 3.4) preceding the presentation of the proposed schematic model (par. 3.5). These two sections consist of brief literature reviews of the topic on which the model is based. The first deals with the importance of the environmental approach to security (par. 3.1) and the fundamental role of digital progress in urban security theoretical and practical advancement (par. 3.2), shown through the reconstruction of the emblematic crime patterns investigation strand. The second one deals with the importance of surveillance, first through an analysis of the current situation in terms of digital surveillance tools and technologies (par. 3.3), and then through a theoretical reconstruction of the visual surveillance foundations (par. 3.4). Finally, as already said, an adaptive digital city-surveillance model aimed at elaborating crime prevention and urban planning strategies is presented.

3 Results and Discussion

Digital technology development has allowed great progress in the elaboration of tools and devices able to promote urban security from multiple points of view: in the theoretical advancement through the experimental verification of crime theories and their consequent modification and integration; in the elaboration of new models to aid planning and urban design; and eventually, from the operative point of view, with the elaboration of technological tools aimed at increasing security in cities through prevention, control and finally repression. These paths seem to be parallel and disjointed, but they are instead closely related, and their boundaries are very blurred, as this review shows.

3.1 Environmental Approach to Security: Origins and Development

The security issue is very ancient, linked to the primordial needs of the human being [8, 14] and closely connected to the primordial need that brought the formation of human settlements first and cities then [15]. However, the city has lost over time its original securitarian image, even reaching today the appellations of 'crime generator' and 'place of insecurity'. Based on these premises and driven by the citizen's growing demand for security, studies on the origins of criminal behaviour from the environmental point of view spread. Environmental criminology then developed, starting from the systematic study of the relations between urban configuration and security. The original contributions date back to the '60s [16–18] and '70s [12, 19], whose roots lie in the maps of Guerry [20] and Quetelet [21], and in the ecology school of Chicago [22, 23]. These original studies opened up a whole new scenario. The first criminological studies were mainly based on psychological and biological investigations, seeking, for example, correlations between criminal behaviour and physical characteristics. Environmental criminology shifts the focus and integrates a new element: the environment, intended in both its physical and situational interpretation. This led to the development of the not obvious idea that the modelling, organisation and management of space can influence criminal behaviour. On this basis, the so-called crime theories were developed: theories that seek to analyse the spatial and situational components that favour crime occurrences [24]. To mention some of the main ones, there are the Situational Crime Prevention (SCP), Routine Activities Approach (RAA), Crime Pattern Theory (CPT), Broken Windows theory (BWT) and Rational Choice Perspective (RCP). These theories are complementary, with blurred boundaries and multiscalar. They have developed over time through modifications, integrations and experiments, and offer interpretative models for understanding the criminal phenomenon. In their theoretical development, IT and technological progress had a role and, in particular, ICT has proved fundamental. Analysing, for example, the so-called crime patterns investigation strand [24], the role of IT and ICT in allowing progress in research could be easily understood.

3.2 The Role of IT and ICT in Urban Security Progress

The crime patterns investigation strand consists of the Routine Activity Approach (RAA) and Crime Pattern Theory (CPT), where the latter actually integrates the geometry of crime, the RAA and RCP. Rather than a deep theoretical discussion of this strand, this paragraph focuses on the role that ICT has played in its development.

Crime pattern investigations developed from the maps of Guerry and Quetelet, which investigated socio-demographic and transport infrastructures' impact on crime distribution [25]. The crime pattern investigations try to reconstruct the logic according to which the patterns of crime develop, organise and branch out within an urban agglomerate, within a social fabric. This is done to understand the spatial logic that guides the distribution of crimes - considered by typology in order to avoid erroneous evaluations [26] - and subsequently to elaborate specific intervention strategies. From a methodological point of view, crime patterns investigation is based on crime mapping. Digital technology progress had a decisive impact on this line: it has considerably increased the possibilities of calculation (data collection, spreadsheets, statistical elaborations…) and opened up new scenarios, still today with unpredictable and intriguing possible developments. Leaving aside the obvious contribution of ICT in the field of data analysis, the scope is here to analyse the contribution provided in the field of representation, spatialisation and prediction. In this development, a decisive step was the diffusion of Geographic Information System (GIS) software, which took place since the '90s and allowed the realisation of visual representations of spatial and temporal crime occurrences distribution [24].

On this basis, with this new digital support, the so-called crime hotspot mapping has developed and has quickly become a widely employed tool for crime prevention and policing resources [27]. In particular, crime mapping has proved to be a fundamental tool in two fields. From the theoretical point of view, it allows evaluating, discussing and testing the assumptions and the logic of crime theories. From a practical point of view instead, once it has been assumed that crime is not uniformly distributed [28], it has proved to be an embryonic predictive tool useful for understanding dynamics, situations and environmental recurrences to be addressed in urban planning. Over time, several hotspot mapping techniques have been developed, although the most widespread and least critical is *Kernel Density Estimation* (KDE), although not being able to consider the crime occurrences timing [28].

However, further technological and IT advancement has allowed – moving from the embryonic predictive character of crime hotspot mapping – more refined tools, which have gradually led to models that take into account the concept of risk. In particular, since the 2000s, predictive tools and risk assessment tools have been developed, often tested in cooperation with government agencies and in many cases being adopted by police forces offices. Examples of these tools are *Promap*, proposed in 2004 [29], which introduced the time variable in predicting crime; *Predpol* (originally called self-exciting point process (SEPP)), introduced by Mohler et al. [30], which is based on the concept of risk and it is able to estimate the possibility that a crime occurrence will occur in spatial-temporal terms; the *Risk Terrain Modeling*, introduced by Caplan et al. [31], which is a forecasting technique – based on the overlapping of multiple risk factors – aimed at determining the micro places where future crime will occur; the *Vulnerable Localities Index and Harm Mapping*, structured on the risk, vulnerability and harm variables; the *Security Rating Index* by Shach-Pinsly [32] that proposes a method to elaborate risk maps without the need for data about past crime occurrences. Finally, *Agent-Based Models* (ABM) represent a very intriguing scenario. Those models have developed considerably in the last 10 years, and they consist of models of interacting agents able to emulate human behaviour taking individual decisions based on a few initial hypotheses [33]. This permits the realisation of tests that would be unethical in society, evaluating and forecasting situational behaviour and group behaviour dynamics [33].

From this quick summary two fundamental aspects emerge. First, it can be seen how technological evolution allowed instruments originally employed exclusively in the theoretical field to evolve into new applications useful for operative tasks, passing from the simple geographical representation of criminal distribution instruments to predictive ones, also able to provide support to police forces and institutional decision-makers. This development has in fact provided tools that, whether combined with criminological and urban planning knowledge, have made possible the investigation of the future rather than the analysis of the past, broadening the focus of environmental criminology to crime prevention rather than post-event investigation or repression. This development, moreover, considering its last and further steps, may become increasingly decisive in the daily live fight against crime in a safe-smart interconnected cities logic. Secondly, an aspect strictly connected to the first one: it clearly emerges what impact digital technology and computer progress may have in the future on the security issue. Just considering the reconstruction of the crime pattern investigations, examined here, it emerges how, in just over 30 years of research, very powerful and unpredictable instruments have been elaborated. On this basis, it is expectable that IT and ICT progress will give crime science and urban crime prevention the necessary support in creating advanced tools for promoting safer cities. In this sense, the joint development of new technologies with tools for reading urban space and environment dynamics, such as Isovist analysis and Space Syntax, represent a fascinating aspect, especially concerning the analysis of human behaviour in urban contexts, the distribution of people flows in the city and the impact of surveillance, as described below (par. 3.4).

Moreover, technological development has also strongly influenced the conception of the city. In fact, over time, increasingly sophisticated systems capable of interconnecting the city have been developed. This with the aim of making them smarter, more connected and well-organised in response to its ever-increasing size and complexity [34]. The concept of smart city has developed and it is now widely used, promoted by many urban programs and incorporated into many government strategies [35]. It has not achieved a final unique definition, being discussed by many fields. However, taking up the various formulations made over time [36], it emerges its aspiration in promoting well-being, inclusion and citizens development. This is achieved through ICT-based solutions aimed at optimising existing networks (real and virtual), innovation and development policies that involve the macro-themes of economy, environment, governance, living, mobility and people [37].

The concept of safe city is associated with the concept of smart city. It develops ICT and IoT systems in order to increase real and perceived security, by recognising the negative impact of crime and lack of security on people's wellbeing. These concepts usually define smart safe cities. However, as Lacinák and Ristvej [38] point out, the field of security is still underestimated and marginal in most smart city studies. This paper intends to fuel interest in investigations on this topic, focusing in particular on the role of surveillance and the possible developments guaranteed by AI.

3.3 The Role of Surveillance in Promoting Urban Security

The fundamental role of surveillance in the promotion of security clearly emerges. Jacobs [17], Angel [18] and Newman [12] first pointed out the importance of this aspect in designing the urban environment. Subsequently, crime theories examined in detail the role of surveillance - whether formal (police patrol, CCTV, sensor systems) or informal (referring to the eyes on the street of the actors living in the city) - highlighting the deterrent power against criminals in a benefit-cost analysis and rational choice logic [13, 39, 40]. Today, surveillance is still a primary tool in the development of security policies, which is also confirmed in the recent guidelines for CPTED (BS ISO 22341:2021). For this reason, ICT science is constantly looking for new systems and technological solutions in this sector, already widely used by governments around the world to increase security [41]. In particular, many systems designed and implemented in cities as part of smart and safe city programs include surveillance as a fundamental tool to tackle crime and, according to much research, even insecurity. The relationship between surveillance and perception of safety is indeed a focal aspect: the debate lies between the ability to reduce the fear of crime through the increasing certainty of punishment, the psychological impact of a sort of 'ipercontrolling society' and the issue of privacy and transparency of data use. However, this complex discussion is left out here and deferred to further studies. Instead, this paper provides a general overview, without claim of completeness, of the AI surveillance techniques, the related enabling technologies and a general surveillance device categories list.

Technological development and ICT research are leading to a considerable growth in artificial intelligence (AI), which is being used increasingly in the creation of smart and safe cities. One of the aspects in which it is being increasingly used is surveillance. In fact, it turns out that at least 75 out of 176 countries in the world are using AI technologies for surveillance purposes (Fig. 1) [41].

Fig. 1. Countries using AI technologies for surveillance aims. Adapted from Feldstein 2019.

From a technological point of view, three key AI surveillance techniques can be described, referring to the classification of Feldstein [41] where the AI Global Surveillance (AIGS) index is introduced. First, the *smart/safe cities*, i.e. the use of sensors that transmit real-time data for, among other things, public safety, which may include facial recognition cameras or police body cameras connected to a central station to prevent crime and respond to emergencies. Second, the *facial recognition systems*, namely the use of biometric technology to recognize individuals and match them with existing databases or evaluate demographic trends or detect feelings via facial recognition (see [42]). Third, the *smart policing*, that is a data-driven analytic technology usually incorporating predicting systems and algorithmic analysis to improve police response. A schematic visualization of the AI surveillance techniques adopted by different countries around the globe is proposed in Fig. 2. Then, the main enabling technologies responsible for realising the aforementioned techniques are the Automated Border Control (ABC) Systems, Cloud Computing and Internet of Things (IoT).

The types of surveillance devices are numerous and constantly evolving. Listing the main ones that come to the authors' mind, there are: surveillance cameras, aerial surveillance or satellite imagery, radio frequency identification and geolocation devices (Radio Frequency Identification tagging, GPS, mobile phones). Moreover, computer surveillance, telephone tracing, social network analysis, biometric surveillance, data mining and profiling. However, the authors suggest the realization of a periodically updated systematic review of all technologies in the field of security - whether instruments, software and systems in general – to provide an exhaustive and comprehensive view of all the existing tools, filling in this way an existing gap.

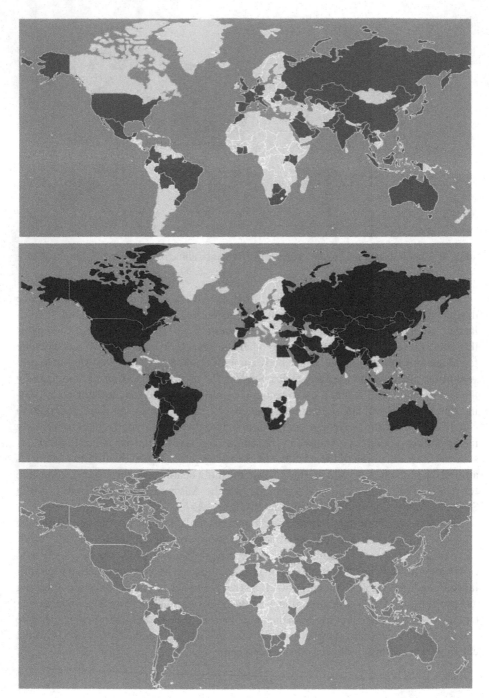

Fig. 2. AI surveillance techniques adopted around the globe: smart/safe cities (a), facial recognition systems (b), smart policing (c). Adapted from Feldstein 2019.

3.4 Exploring the Roots of Surveillance: Isovist, Viewfield and Visibility Graph Analysis

What is surveillance from a conceptual point of view? Although the surveillance construct can refer to a very wide range of meanings, we would like to focus here on visual surveillance. It has always been the leitmotif associated with security and has found a utopian but emblematic declination in Jeremy Bentham's panopticon [43], then becoming central in theoretical crime prevention studies from Jacobs onwards. Visual surveillance in urban contexts refers to the viewfields that the urban configuration allows human beings and any electronic devices placed on the territory, thus creating more or less controlled areas affecting the probability of crime to occur [39]. In fact, just as in the graph theory (for example, referring to the emblematic Königsberg bridge problem) the possibility to find a specific path depends on the inner properties of the graph, and in the configurational theory the properties of an environment depend on the urban form, in the same way, visibility is a characteristic mainly dependent on the spatial configuration and capable of affecting people behaviour. Therefore, urban-visibility characteristics should be taken into account in urban planning and environmental design. It should be stressed that only the manifest presence of people and electronic surveillance devices have a direct effect on crime prevention, being otherwise, through their hidden presence, useful only for possible punitive and repressive purposes. Tandy [44] appears to be the first to have used the term 'isovist', when in parallel the terms 'viewshed' and 'intervisibility' were spreading respectively in the field of landscape architecture [45, 46] and in computer topographic modelling [11]. An isovist is defined as "the set of all points visible from a given vantage point in space and with respect to an environment" [47]. Benedikt [47] contextually introduced a set of measures of isovist properties able to allow quantitative analysis of spatial environments, and he suggested that the way we experience the space is connected to the interplay of isovists. Gibson [48] in particular introduced the concept of perceptual quality of the isovist field. Then Turner et al. [11] integrated the isovist concepts with the graph-based representations – namely the Space Syntax theory and its set of techniques – to interpret networks of social behaviour, obtaining in this way the visibility graph of the environment, which is defined as the "graph of mutually visible locations" [11]. This was done to overcome the hitherto existing limitations, i.e. the absence of studies of relations between viewsheds. In this vein the Visibility Graph Analysis (VGA) develop, representing a technique for analysing the intervisibility connections of the urban grid [11, 49], which evolved over the years through the definition of specific environment-reading measures (for a summary see [50]). Much research, both from the urban planning and criminological fields, highlight the primary role of visibility and surveillance. However, as Turner himself pointed out [51], it is fundamental to overcome the assessment of visibility in vacuo and in 'stationary terms' by referring to fixed positions. For example, Lee and Stucky [52] already faced the isovist variation along a pathway, discussing the path's visual characteristics in terms of pleasantness. Penn et al. [53], Batty and Jiang [54] and Conroy [55] investigate virtual reality (VR) environments in terms of visual paths. In this regard, the study of Turner [51] is noteworthy, from which important aspects emerge. The first is that visual integration is not related to pedestrian movement, while the agents in its Agent-Based Model are, although transition probability is directional. The second is the acknowledged importance of the agents as samplers of the visual configuration, and the suggestion to go back to simpler models of the environment in determining the agent logic of movement: axial lines [56] or sparse visibility graphs between topological nodes [57]. More specifically, Turner himself proposed the use of ABM to correlate human 'individual' movement paths and configurational properties, which is, as argued in this paper, a further development to be achieved. Recently, Benedikt and Mcelhinney [58] have emphasised the importance of studying the pathways within the environment, for example to carry out analysis in terms of privacy or for the CCTV and security guards positioning. By analysing these aspects, they focus on the importance of the concept of occlusive surfaces, which are permeable boundaries "that lie between what can and what cannot be seen and yet through/across which movement is possible" [58]. These surfaces obstruct the view of something new, and only by getting past them it's possible to depart old things in favour of new ones. The focal aspect is that as humans we continuously relate with isovists and we make decisions based on isovists even without realising it: where we sit at a table, where we wait for a friend, what route we choose when taking a walk. We reason by 'good views'. Similarly, a criminal looking for the right opportunity to commit a crime [59, 60] will carefully assess the level of surveillance of places [13, 39, 40]. This is why the study of isovists and the development of surveillance maps as risk indicators can be decisive. Indeed, as Benedikt and Mcelhinney [58] point out, isovists have a great advantage in analytical terms in comparison with social studies, namely their being objective entities in shape and size. However, as Turner suggests [51], from the postpositivist point of view the people's background could impact the visual and space perception, thus being an aspect to be further addressed. Recently, the ISOVIST programme was introduced by Benedikt and Mcelhinney [58], as proof of the growing interest in investigating visibility aspects.

3.5   A Digital Surveillance-City Model: A DSS Integrating Isovist and Space Syntax Logic

We now propose a possible development – here presented in its conceptual idea, which will be the subject of future in-depth studies – aimed at studying the urban environment from a surveillance perspective, aimed primarily at urban security but also extendable to other types of urban analysis. Therefore, considering: the studies carried out over the years on the subject of isovist, Visual Graph Analysis (VGA), and in particular on the aforementioned works of Benedikt and Turner; the whole configurational theory and in particular Space Syntax with its ability to interpret the human behaviour in space (for more details see [49, 61]); and, finally, considering the importance of surveillance in environmental criminology, the study was then developed.

If we consider an environment and a person located there, it is possible to define and represent (e.g. through the ISOVIST application illustrated by Benedikt and McElhinney [58]) the isovist of that individual (Fig. 3a). It is also possible, in general, to study the viewfields of an agent moving according to a certain path in space, and therefore how the isovists vary in time. In particular, it is possible to define the agent 'visual field properties' on the basis of the agent inner characteristics or the type of analysis to be carried out. It could be set, for example, the width of the visual field, hypothesising the behaviour of the agent (more or less interested in visually exploring the surrounding environment), depending on the relationship that links it with the environment (Fig. 3b). In fact, Van Nes and Yamu [49] point out how in the urban context, for example, a local, a tourist or an average person have different behave, thus affecting the path and, as a consequence, the isovists over time. In addition, considerations could be made on the part of the environment that although not being part of the visual field, could be considered under the 'partial control' of the agent [58], thus evaluating 'grey zones' representations. Similarly, it could be considered the reduction of the agent's visual field extension by making appropriate considerations about the human capacity to visualise things at a certain distance, in relation to a specific type of crime, for example. Ultimately, it will be possible to represent, for each instant, the isovists of the agent living the environment (Fig. 3c), with the designed 'visual field properties'.

According to similar reasoning, the isovists of digital surveillance devices can be represented (Fig. 4a), and they could easily be integrated with the previous representation (Fig. 4b). Moreover, by integrating in a single representation the isovists of digital surveillance devices (e.g. CCTV) and the isovists of people experiencing that space, it is possible to represent the hypothetical surveillance map of that environment for a given instant t (Fig. 4c).

This is technically feasible with today's existing tools, and it would allow – if data on the exact position of all the people at different times and the 'visual field properties' of each of them were available – to represent the dynamic surveillance map of that environment. This could permit the identification of the more fragile areas in terms of visibility and surveillance, and it could guide interventions aimed at security improve-ment – by taking into consideration the crime theories logic – at different scales and in different areas: mobility planning, requalification and rehabilitation, urban planning and urban design, lighting, CCTV and police patrols disposal optimization. However, as already mentioned, here the sensitive issue of privacy strongly emerges. How to over-come this problem? This paper tries to overcome the problem by proposing a solution that minimize the data needed in input, still creating a useful decision support tool.

Then, in further studies, the limits and variants that can ensure the optimal develop-ment of the model will be discussed, considering both the goal of a safer community and the personal right to privacy, also considering different existing regulations thorough the world [41].

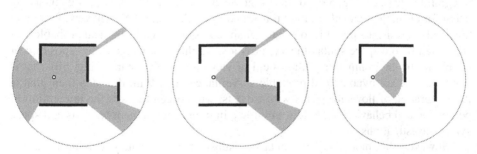

Fig. 3. Scheme of one-agent isovist with 360° and infinite extension (a), 90° and infinite extension (b), 90° and finite extension (c) visual fields within the environment.

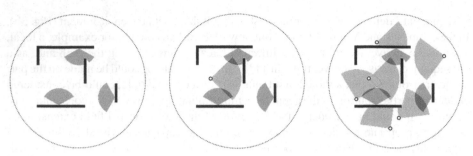

Fig. 4. Scheme of CCTV viewfields (a), CCTV viewfields and one-agent isovist with 90° and finite extension visual field (b), CCTV viewfields and random-positioned agents isovists with 90° and finite extension visual field (c) within the environment. The scheme 4c thus represents a momentary hypothetical surveillance map at a given instant t.

Therefore, considering the general impossibility in tracking the precise agents movement and their visual fields while experiencing the space (situations possibly allowed in maximum security areas requiring anti-terrorist measures, such as airports), the real surveillance map of a given area is not feasible. Here, however, the space syntax comes into play with its ability to interpret the human attitude in terms of flow and movement. In fact, referring to Hillier's theories [62], it is possible to interpret the movement and the human behaviour within a space through the analysis of the space itself ("Space is the machine" [62]), and therefore, as far as we are concerned, it is possible to establish which are the flows in a space through the configurational analysis. In particular, through the axial analysis and the integration, connectivity and choice measures it is possible to assess which routes are most travelled. Moreover, according to the interpretations made by Summers and Johnson [63], it is possible to hypothesise different attitudes – and therefore isovists according to van Nes and Yamu [49] – of the users of the areas. In particular Summers and Johnson [63] hypothesise that the connectivity measure, being a local indicator of accessibility, may represent the movement of locals, which have a higher sense of belonging to their living areas [12, 17]. On the contrary, following this interpretation, integration and choice measures could represent average person patterns. So, we could conduct an axial analysis of the environment and consider, for example, the integration measure (Fig. 5a). At this point we could decide to spatialize this measure, using for example the methodology illustrated by Berhie Haq [64]. Anyway, following the axial analysis, it's possible to create a map representing a hypothetical probable – as supported by the space syntax theory measures (in this case integration) – position of people in the environment and their field of view at a given instant t (Fig. 5b), that is what we can call hypothetical probable surveillance map. With this step then, that is the integration of flows measures with isovists, we proceed towards the integration of perceptive and behavioural aspects, key-issue in urban environment analysis and space syntax investigations.

However, this model still presents two substantial criticalities, leaving aside the needed further investigations aimed at correlating Space Syntax measures and agent visual field properties as well as a more detailed description of the methodology that goes beyond the schematic conceptualisation. The first concerns the distribution of people in the space - proportional to the Space Syntax measures but randomly positioned - and the orientation of the isovists, which are randomly decided. In fact, although the number of people could be decided proportionally to the Space Syntax measures and the visual fields properties can be modelled according to the type of investigation to be performed, the random positioning represents a weakness of this model. The second concerns the model's limitation in terms of time variable analysis. In fact, this model allows the representation of fixed instants t, while, as Turner [51] suggests, it is necessary to overcome the idea of a static, immobile visualisation in favour of a dynamic one, since it is precisely the variation of isovists over time that defines, more or less consciously, the path the agents undertake while experiencing the space and, from an external perspective, that defines more or less surveilled areas.

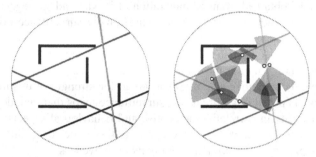

Fig. 5. Scheme of an Axial Analysis (integration) of the environment (a). Scheme of CCTV viewfields and Axial-Integration-related agents isovists with 90° and finite extension visual fields within the environment (b). The scheme 5b thus represents a hypothetical probable surveillance map at a given instant t.

In order to address these weaknesses, which can be summarised as positioning-orientation randomness and isovists stationarity, ICT can be decisive. In fact, referring to what has been said in the previous paragraphs and referring to Turner's studies [51], ABMs could be the ideal tool to integrate the concepts of isovist and configurational analysis, at the same time overcoming the aforementioned criticalities. This integration could push towards the realisation of reliable predictive tools in terms of surveillance. In fact, considering the characteristics of the ABMs, it would be possible to insert additional information to increase the adherence of the model to reality, thus obtaining realistic simulations of surveillance in public spaces. Many types of information could be included: the social behaviour of agents, the land use, the type of activities within the environment and their working hours, the time of day (e.g. night and day could produce very different situations in terms of surveillance). Moreover, this tool could be used not only for crime prevention but also to test in advance the effects on surveillance of hypothetical urban transformations, thus being able to evaluate different alternatives, just as space syntax is already being used. For example, in organising a city event that temporarily modifies the road network and provides for the installation of temporary structures, it would be possible to evaluate different options from multiple perspectives: the impact from the visual point of view, the areas that would be most affected by weak surveillance, the dynamics that could be generated in terms of flows, in addition to all the evaluations that the space syntax already allows. And again, as a decision-support tool for urban planners, it could allow assessments of the establishment of new activities, their location and the visual impact they might have, as well as acting as a decision-making tool for private companies to evaluate the optimal location and arrangement of their activities. Furthermore, and this aspect is truly crucial, this model would be, at least in its basic formulation, independent of the availability of sensitive and aggregated input data that could undermine its effective use, particularly in certain contexts [41].

4 Concluding Remarks

This paper presented the very preliminary results of the elaboration of a digital city-surveillance model obtained from the integration of isovist and space syntax concepts, with a further development consisting of the realisation of a surveillance-oriented Agent-Based model. The potentialities of the model have emerged both from the theoretical and operative perspectives. It can represent a tool to fuel the theoretical debates on environmental criminology and, at the same time, it can be employed as urban planning DSS considering its predictive nature. In particular, the strength of this model consists of three aspects: its possibility of realising surveillance maps that include the temporal component; its ability in correlating perceptive and behavioural aspects; its adaptability in terms of sensitive input data, which permits the model to fit different contexts overcoming the privacy issue still maintaining its effectiveness.

As discussed in the core of the paper, further investigations are required to develop this model: first, it's necessary to deeply explore the Space Syntax measures and refine their interpretations in terms of inhabitants 'characterisation', behaviour, movement – which directly affect the isovist 'dynamics' – and consequently visual field properties. Second, the validity of the methodology has to be confirmed with the elaboration of case studies and through the critical comparison with alternative methodological steps, which can include for example VGA. Third, a technical investigation on how to integrate movement and visual components into an ABM is required.

Moreover, additional intriguing research gaps have been identified; namely the investigation, as Turner [51] suggests, of how different cultures, memories and experiences impact space perception, following the postpositivist logic, as well as the psycho-physiological impact of the environment on the people who are experiencing it. These aspects, if properly addressed, could improve the ABM model and make it increasingly refined. Additionally, taking Turner's [51] cue not to limit studies of isovists in vacuum, the possibility to investigate the effects of people concentration on isovists and human perception, as well as the threshold level whereby the presence of additional "eyes on the streets" produces negative effects emerges. Furthermore, an updated systematic review of all the technological security-aimed tools, software, systems and models, as well as an extensive review of all the ABM models implemented in a surveillance-visibility logic or anyway adaptable to it are interesting research insights.

More in general, this paper had the aim to foster the collaboration between criminologists, urban planners and computer scientists and to feed the interest in visibility and surveillance as fundamental aspects in the elaboration of urban planning strategies, both from the urban security and environmental management perspectives.

References

1. Cozens, P.: Urban Planning and environmental criminology: towards a new perspective for safer cities. Plan. Pract. Res. **26**(4), 481–508 (2011)
2. Mihinjac, M., Saville, G.: Third-generation crime prevention through environmental design (CPTED). Soc. Sci. **8**(182), 1–20 (2019)
3. United Nations: Transforming Our World - The 2030 Agenda for Sustainable Development (2015)
4. Eurostat.   https://ec.europa.eu/eurostat/databrowser/view/SDG_16_20/bookmark/table?lang=en&bookmarkId=3c6f7f93-110e-4888-a3a4-bcc9c0ad2088. Accessed 10 Apr 2022
5. Fasolino, I., Coppola, F., Grimaldi, M.: La sicurezza urbana degli insediamenti. Franco Angeli, Milano (2018)
6. Wilson, J.Q., Kelling, G.L.: The police and neighbourhood safety: broken windows. Atlantic Mon. **3**(2), 29–38 (1982)
7. Chiodi, S.I.: Crime prevention through urban design and planning in the smart city era. J. Place Manag. Dev. **9**(2), 137–152 (2016)
8. Cozens, P., Love, T.: A review and current status of crime prevention through environmental design (CPTED). J. Plan. Lit. **30**(4), 393–412 (2015)
9. Armitage, C.J., Ekblom, P.: Rebuilding Crime Prevention Through Environmental Design: Strengthening the Links with Crime Science. 1st Edition Crime Science Series, Routledge, Abingdon (2019)
10. Morgan, A., Homel, P.: Evaluating crime prevention: lessons from large-scale community crime prevention programs. Trends Issues Crime Criminal Just. **458**, 1–12. Australian Institute of Criminology, Camberra (2013)
11. Turner, A., Doxa, M., O'Sullivan, D., Penn, A.: From isovists to visibility graphs: a methodology for the analysis of architectural space. Environ. Plann. Plann. Des. **28**(1), 103–121 (2001)
12. Newman, O.: Defensible Space: Crime Prevention through Urban Design. Macmillan, New York (1972)
13. Clarke, R.V., Cornish, D.B.: Modeling offender's decisions: a framework for research and policy. In: Tonry, M., Morris, N., (Eds.). Crime and Justice: an Annual Review of Research, vol. 6, pp. 23–42, University of Chicago Press, Chicago (1985)
14. Maslow, A.H.: A theory of human motivation. Psychol. Rev. **50**(4), 370–396 (1943)
15. Ellin, N.: Thresholds of fear: embracing the urban shadow. Urban Stud. **38**, 869–883 (2001)
16. Wood, E.: Housing Design: A Social Theory. Citizens, Housing and Planning Council of New York, New York (1961)
17. Jacobs, J.: The Death and Life of Great American Cities. Jonathon Cope, London (1961)
18. Angel, S.: Discouraging Crime through City Planning. Working paper No. 75, University of California Press, Berkeley (1968)
19. Jeffery, C.: Crime Prevention through Environmental Design. Sage, Beverly Hills (1971)
20. Guerry, A.: Essai sur la Statistique Morale de la France avec Cartes. Crochard, Paris (1833)
21. Quetelet, A.: Sur L'homme et le Development de ses Facultes: Essai de Physique Sociale. Bachelier, Paris (1835)
22. Park, R., Burgess, E., McKenzie, D.: The city. University of Chicago Press, Chicago (1925)
23. Shaw, C., McKay, H.: Juvenile Delinquency and Urban Areas. University of Chicago Press, Chicago (1942)
24. Wortley, R., Townsley, M.: Environmental criminology and crime analysis. In: 2nd ed., eds. Richard Wortley and Michael Townsley. Routledge, Abingdon (2017)
25. Boba Santos, R.: Crime Analysis with Crime Mapping. Sage Publications, London (2017)

26. Mara, F., Altafini, D., Cutini, V.: Urban design, space syntax and crime: an evidence-based approach to evaluate urban crime geographical displacement and surveillance efficiency. In: Proceedings of the 13th International Space Syntax Symposium, forthcoming (2022)

27. Johnson, S.D.: Crime mapping and spatial analysis. In: 2nd ed., Wortley, R., Townsley, M., (eds.) Environmental criminology and crime analysis, pp. 98–115. Routledge, New York (2017)

28. Rosser, G., Davies, T., Bowers, K.J., Johnson, S.D., Cheng, T.: Predictive crime mapping: arbitrary grids or street networks? J. Quant. Criminol. **33**, 569–594 (2016)

29. Bowers, K.J., Johnson, S., Pease, K.: Prospective hotspotting: the future of crime mapping? Br. J. Criminol. **44**(5), 641–658 (2004)

30. Mohler, G.O., Short, M.B., Brantingham, P.J., Schoenberg, F.P., Tita, G.E.: Self-exciting point process modeling of crime. J. Am. Stat. Assoc. **106**(493), 100–108 (2011)

31. Caplan, J.M., Kennedy, L.W.: Risk Terrain Modeling Manual. Rutgers Center on Public Security, Newark (2010)

32. Shach-Pinsly, D.: Measuring security in the built environment: Evaluating urban vulnerability in a human-scale urban form. Landscape Urban Plann. **191**, 10341 (2019)

33. Groff, E.R., Johnson, S.D., Thornton, A.: State of the art in agent-based modeling of urban crime: an overview. J. Quant. Criminol. **35**(1), 155–193 (2018). https://doi.org/10.1007/s10 940-018-9376-y

34. Zhang, C., Ni, B., Song, L., Zhai, G., Yang, X., Zhang, W.: BEST: benchmark and evaluation of surveillance task. In: Chen, C.-S., Lu, J., Ma, K.-K. (eds.) ACCV 2016. LNCS, vol. 10118, pp. 393–407. Springer, Cham (2017). https://doi.org/10.1007/978-3-319-54526-4_29

35. Berry, M.: Technology and organised crime in the smart city: an ethnographic study of the illicit drug trade. City Territory Archit. **5**(1), 16 (2018)

36. Laufs, J.; Borrion, H.; Bradford, B.: Security and the smart city: a systematic review. Sustain. Cities Soc. **55**, 102023 (2020)

37. Camero, A., Alba, E.: Smart city and information technology: a review. Cities **93**, 84–94 (2019)

38. Lacinák, M., Ristvej, J.: Smart city safety and security. Procedia Eng. **192**, 522 (2017)

39. Cohen, L.E., Felson, M.: Social change and crime rate trends: a routine activity approach. Am. Sociol. Rev. **44**, 588–608 (1979)

40. Eck, J.E., Weisburd, D.: Crime places in crime theory. In: John, E., Eck, D., (eds.) Weisburd Crime Prevention Studies. Criminal Justice Press, Monsey NY (1995)

41. Feldstein, S.: The global expansion of AI surveillance. Carnegie Endowment (2019)

42. Vimeo Superflux, https://vimeo.com/124292043. Accessed 10 Apr 2022

43. Bentham, J.: Panopticon, ovvero la casa di ispezione. Marsilio, Padova (1983)

44. Tandy, C.R.V.: The isovist method of landscape survey, in Symposium: Methods of Landscape Analysis Ed. H C Murray, Landscape Research Group, London (1967)

45. Amidon, E.L, Elsner, G.H.: Delineating landscape view areas: a computer approach. Forest Research Note PSW-180, US Department of Agriculture, Washington DC (1968)

46. Lynch, K.: Managing the Sense of Region. MIT Press, Cambridge MA (1976)

47. Benedikt, M.L.: To take hold of space: isovists and isovist fields. Environ. Plann. **6**, 47–65 (1979)

48. Gibson, J.J.: The Ecological Approach to Visual Perception. Houghton Mifflin, Boston MA (1979)

49. Van Nes, A., Yamu, C.: Introduction to Space Syntax in Urban Studies. Springer Nature (2021)

50. Koutsolampros, P., Sailer, K., Varoudis T., Haslem R.: Dissecting visibility graph analysis: the metrics and their role in understanding workplace human behaviour. In: Proceedings of the 12th International Space Syntax Symposium, pp. 1–24 (2019)

51. Turner, A.: Analysing the visual dynamics of spatial morphology. Environ. Plann. Plann. Des. **30**(5), 657–676 (2003)

52. Lee, J., Stucky, D.: On applying viewshed analysis for determining least-cost paths on digital elevation models. Int. J. Geogr. Inf. Syst. **12**, 891–905 (1998)

53. Penn, A., Conroy, R., Dalton, N., Dekker, L., Mottram, C., Turner, A.: Intelligent architecture: new tools for the three dimensional analysis of space and built form. In: Proceedings of the 1st International Symposium on Space Syntax, 30.1- 30.19. University College London, London (1997)

54. Batty, M., Jiang, B.: Multi-agent simulation: new approaches to exploring space time dynamics within GIS, WP 10. University College London, London, Centre for Advanced Spatial Analysis (1999)

55. Conroy, R.A: Spatial Navigation in Immersive Virtual Environments. PhD thesis, Bartlett School of Graduate Studies, University College London, London (2001)

56. Penn, A., Dalton, N.: The architecture of society: stochastic simulation of urban movement. In: Gilbert, J., Doran, N., (eds.) Simulating Societies: The Computer Simulation of Social Phenomena. UCL Press, London, pp. 85–125 (1994)

57. Thomas, G., Donikian, S.: Modelling virtual cities dedicated to behavioural animation. Comput. Graph. Forum **19**(3), C71–C80 (2000)

58. Benedikt, M.L., McElhinney, S.: Isovists and the metrics of architectural space. Conference: ACSA 2019: BLACK BOX: Articulating Architecture's Core in the Post-Digital Era, Pittsburgh (2019)

59. Mayhew, P., Clarke, R.V., Sturman, A., Hough, J.M.: Crime as Opportunity. Home Office Research Study. No. 34. London: Home Office (1976)

60. Wortley, R.: Situational precipitators of crime. In: Wortley, R., Mazerolle, L., (eds.), Environmental Criminology and Crime Analysis, pp. 48–69. Willan Publishing, Cullompton (2008)

61. Yamu, C., van Nes, A., Garau, C.: Bill hillier's legacy: space syntax—a synopsis of basic concepts, measures, and empirical application. Sustainability **13**(6), 1–25 (2021)

62. Hillier, B.: Space is the Machine. Cambridge University Press, Cambridge (1996)

63. Summers, L., Johnson S.D.: Does the configuration of the street network influence where outdoor serious violence takes place? using space syntax to test crime pattern theory. J. Quan. Criminol. 1–24 (2017)

64. Berhie, G., Haq, S.: The effect of spatial configuration on propensity for non-motorised journey to work. In: The 10th International Space Syntax Symposium, vol. 62, pp. 1–17. London, UK (2015)

Towards a Spatial Approach to Territorialize Economic Data in Urban Areas' Industrial Agglomerations

Diego Altafini[✉] and Valerio Cutini

Dipartimento Di Ingegneria Dell'Energia, Dei Sistemi, Università Di Pisa, del Territorio E Delle Costruzioni, Largo Lucio Lazzarino, 56122 Pisa (PI), Italy
diego.altafini@phd.unipi.it

Abstract. The space matters: beyond a mere background for economic activities placement, it constitutes a crucial element for their overall dynamism. This rationale, however, contravenes more traditional urban and regional economics approaches that interpret space as intangible within their spatial models. In that vein, notable constraints can be found in economic-based methods and spatial units oriented to spatialize the territorial endowments and interpret their role within the urban structure. While economics' methods are limited in their spatial representation, urban and regional planning has otherwise focused in providing instruments that address spatial characteristics of areas where urbanization is predominant. Methods that highlight the configurational properties and the organization of the cityscape structure, could aid economics in its methodological issues. Still, a divide persists between these two fields of research, as neither consistently incorporates the methods and variables considered by the other. In this paper we showcase a method used to create a spatial unit oriented to territorialize economic-based datasets represented at a regional scale within the confines of urban areas' industrial agglomerations. In this proof of concept, variables related to labour – average number of firms, employees, and firm-size; and to installed capital – average real estate prices – are spatialized to outline their patterns distribution across Tuscany's cities. Organized in a GIS-based environment, the representation of such variables within a computerized space and with a proper spatial unit provides a basis that can be associated to the configurational aspects of the territory, being a complementary analysis for urban and regional planning.

Keywords: Spatial models · Territorialization · Economic data

1 Introduction

Since the initial rationales on locational theories [1, 2] and through their development into Urban-Regional Economics [3, 4], space has been regarded as a somewhat intractable notion by economists [5]. From a framework standpoint, it is undeniable that Spatial

Economics consider space and its organization as an important factor for economic dynamism: for them, the *space matters*. At the same time, however, the overall role and level of detail that spatial representation and territorialization have in economic models recurrently contravene this assumption. It is well-noticed in contemporary economic-based approaches, be in Urban-Regional Economics [6] or in Economic Geography [7], that space, and the territorial endowments that constitute it, tend to be interpreted as "abstracted" and often "intangible" factors [5] – parameters that have influence but are mainly set as a background for more important economic interactions. Thisse [5] states that technical and conceptual issues inherent to analysing the qualities of space led to such "abstracted" interpretation, as few economic models have an approximation with geography – therefore, are not tailored to address in-detail data about territorial organization, while also maintaining a concision in its economic variables and parameters.

While spatial methods used in economics have limitations regarding their accuracy in territorialization, Urban and Regional Planning has been, otherwise, focused on developing instruments to analyse the spatial characteristics of urbanized areas [8, 9]. Methods that integrate datasets and models with different scopes – such as structural [10], morphological [11], and configurational [12] – in computerized environment such as *Geographic Information Systems* (GIS) [13] have become norm on the field. More recently, those methods have taken a step into Spatial Economics – and have been combined with economic variables and datasets to construct multidimensional analyses that prove to address the amount of support given from territorial endowments towards economic activities placement [14, 15]. Still, the same problems regarding economic datasets territorialization that are faced in Spatial Economics also constitute an important limitation for Urban and Regional Planning's integrated analyses. Economic variables – which are mostly available at regionalized scales, and oftentimes, only as numerical data – prevent direct spatialization and territorialization and limit the accuracy and level of detail of spatial information. Even though Urban and Regional Planning have the spatial instruments to address it, the absence of established spatial units and a more tangible dialogue between the fields of research hampers the development of methods that consider their individual requirements.

Awareness of these limitations and issues that pertain Spatial Economics and Urban and Regional Planning current approaches ought to conduce to the development of novel spatial-economic models. Those must be able to address complex spatial behaviours and interactions that may have influence on territorial disparities within urban-regional settings, therefore, diminishing the scales towards the urban. Nevertheless, this outbound step depends first on a transformation on how economics visualize and understand space, as well as create and interpret spatial knowledge; it depends of an integration with methods currently used in Geography and Urban Planning.

With those points in consideration, this paper proposes a method to spatialize economic data, integrating it to a spatial unit – the *macroarea* – that is based on territorial endowments – the built-structures location. The objective is to establish a process to territorialize economic variables available only at regionalized scales and associate them into the areas that pertain to the urban settlements, hence, providing an in-detail notion of where this data is set on urban space. In this proof-of-concept, made for the Tuscany region territory, we use data from industrial built-structures, to establish spatial units that represent the industrial agglomerations. Those are merged to economic variables related to *labour (average firm-size)* and *installed capital (average real-estate value)* to establish their actual position within the territory. The method showcased in this proof-of concept provides a concise procedure to establish and create spatialized economic information which can be reproduced, not only for other urban economic functions such as retail and services, but also for other regionalized economic variables.

2 Datasets and Variables Used in the Proof of Concept

2.1 Datasets for the Construction of a Spatial Unit – the Macroarea

As a manner to territorialize the industrial activities' location and distribution in Tuscany, we conceived a spatial unit defined as a *macroarea* – or a contiguous aggregation of productive spaces *(industrial spaces)*. This territorialization of economic activities was conceived, tested, and refined throughout three different publications: in Altafini et al., [16, 17] where *industrial spaces* and macroareas were constructed from the land-use data (manufacture and large retail included); and in Altafini & Cutini [15], where, instead, these spatial units were constructed upon volumetric units that represented the built-structures dedicated to industrial-manufacture uses *(industrial assets)*. Both methods resulted in similar territorializations, yet the method using the *industrial assets* provides a greater positional detail. In the present assessment, the same spatial unit constructed in [15] is used, based on data extracted from the Tuscany region built-structures dataset *(Edificato 2k, 10k – 1988–2013)*, obtained from the *Sistema Informativo Territoriale ed Ambientale* (SITA) repository [18].

The *industrial spaces* construction procedure draws a 30 m buffer radius – equivalent to the plot plus the street areas – from each *industrial asset* volumetric unit. Buffered areas are then dissolved into a continuous area. The result, a sole spatial unit (Fig. 1), is then submitted to a negative buffer (30 m), that reduces the excess area created through the positive buffer into the original *industrial assets'* dimensions, while, maintaining the area boundaries and contiguities created in-between them. The resulting *industrial spaces* are then individualized, through their conversion into single parts from the sole territorial unit. A size categorization is then applied in accordance with each *industrial space* area, as well as a corresponding multi-distance buffer radius (Fig. 2, Table 1, p.4) to establish an *area of influence* for each *space*.

Areas created through the multi-distance buffer are then dissolved into a single continuous *macroarea*. The resulting sole spatial unit is then, once again, divided into several single parts based on the presence of spatial contiguities. This results in different-sized *macroareas* that are then categorized in accordance with their size, their *industrial spaces* and their *industrial assets* counts (Table 2).

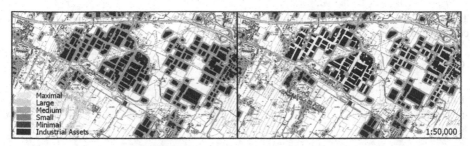

Fig.1. *Industrial assets* conversion in *industrial spaces*: positive (gray) and negative (coloured) buffer results and area categorization

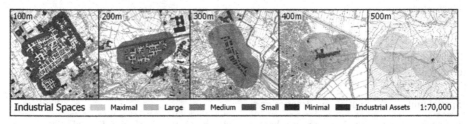

Fig.2. Examples of *industrial spaces* with *categorization* buffer distances applied.

Table 1. *Industrial spaces* classification regarding count, total area, relative multi-distance buffer and total surface after buffer

Classification	Industrial assets count	Industrial spaces count	Total Area [km²]	Buffer radius [m]	Buffered surface [km²]
Maximal (>= 0.6 km²)	2,118	4	4.73	100	9.44
Large (>= 0.2 – <0.6 km²)	6,914	38	11.98	200	47.29
Medium (>= 0.075–<0.2 km²)	9,062	128	15.33	300	131.71
Small (>= 0.02–<0.075 km²)	16,780	623	23.34	400	591.33
Minimal (<0.02 km²)	45,319	14,901	27.60	500	12,741.37
Total	80,193	15,694	82.98	–	13,521.14

Table 2. *Macroareas* size classification according to industrial spaces count, industrial assets count and area ranges' values

Classification	Industrial assets count	Industrial spaces count	Area range [km^2]	No of macroareas
Isolated macroarea	1	1	<5.00	435
Small macroarea	>1	>1	<5.00	862
Medium macroarea	>1	>1	>= 5.00–<100.00	87
Large macroarea	>1	>1	>= 100.00	3

Table 3. Summary of the different spatial units that compose the industrial agglomerates territorialization

Spatial unit	Spatial unit description	Unit count
Industrial assets	A volumetric unit that represents the total area of an industrial building	80,193
Industrial spaces	Spatial unit that describes the contiguous area occupied by groups of *industrial assets* set in proximity or in the same plots/parcels of land	15,694
Macroareas	Spatial unit that territorializes *industrial assets* based on the overall reach of their contiguous *industrial spaces;* denotes the general occupation, distribution, size, as well as the industrialization degree of an urban area, while also indicating the internal and external displacement logics	1,387

Macroareas are conceptualized to establish a visual representation of the Tuscany's industrial territorial occupation, cohesion, and distribution, informing the industrialization patterns and the dynamics of placement for the *industrial assets* across the territory, above all, in those that are located within urbanized areas (Fig. 3, p. 5).

In the same manner, since the *macroareas* establish the displacement reach through *areas of influence* for the collective *industrial assets* and *spaces*, these spatial units can be used to ascertain spatial correlations of proximity with road-circulation network configurational properties, as performed in the Territorial Exposure Index [15].

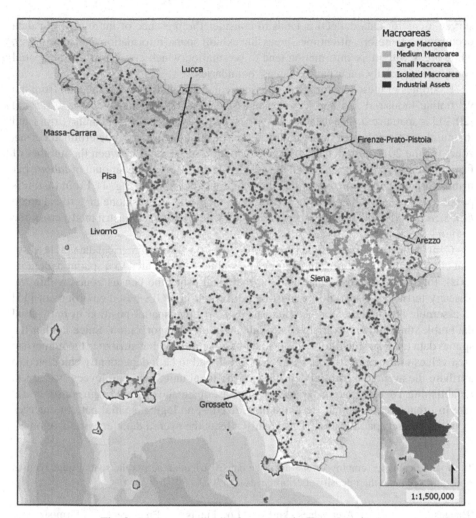

Fig. 3. Macroareas distribution across the Tuscan territory

2.2   Economic Variables and Their Issues of Territorialization

In his firm theory, Robert Lucas Jr. [19] proposes *capital* and *labour* as important economic indicators of firms' overall conditions of operation size and internal dynamism, as the amount of *installed capital* (i.e., buildings and assets) has influence in the allocation of *labour* (i.e., employees). However, by nature, those economic variables tend to be rather intangible when their spatial distribution is considered.

In general, information about *labour* and *capital* is available in a scale of aggregation that is often too extensive to allow a proper territorialization at micro-scales – above all when open data is considered. Moreover, in regionalized assessments even when the smallest spatial units of aggregation are used – as, for example, survey areas or census zones – a distinctiveness persist between the strata of data. The size determination of survey areas for data collection tends to consider the presence of more or fewer data occurrences, therefore, oftentimes, areas that exhibit sparse information tend to be larger, while areas with more information tend to be smaller, which create misleading spatial contrasts, especially, on urbanized areas' boundaries.

Examples of these territorialization issues can be visualized when the data from the 9th Italian Industrial and Services Census (*Censimenti ISTAT dell'industria e servizi*) [20, 21] is spatialized. The database describes the total number of local units (firms) and the number of employees in the industrial and service sectors for a determined census zone, for the 2011 period. Through the calculation of the ratio between the number of firms and employees we can obtain the average *Firm-Size* – or the amount of *labour* per firm – variable territorialized for this proof of concept (Table 4, Fig. 4). From that, it is possible to spatialize the variable according to their total census zone area to calculate *firm-size density* and provide an overview of where *labour* is distributed across the territory.

Census data are organized in a dual-table system, where a numerical data table (.csv) that contains the local units' and employees' values is associated to a spatial data table (.xls), that possess a locational notation that establishes the census zones within the Tuscany territory. A spatial join must be performed in a GIS-based environment [13] to assemble the numerical table datum to its respective spatial position in the spatial data table, thus allowing variables' spatialization and categorization. Since neither the spatial data table nor the information table possess an entry that attributes the numerical area values to the respective census zones, those had to be independently calculated to attribute the average territorial densities for the local units' and employees' variables. Establishing a density parameter is imperative as, due to the differences in census zones size in urban areas – which are not standardized –, no logical spatial pattern emerges from the dataset spatialization. This greatly affects the overall data territorialization.

Table 4. Local units, employees and firm-size data distribution across the spatial units (census zones) according to their density of occurrences (km^2)

Ranges	Area values - km^2	Local units	Employees	Firm-size
Formulae	–	$\dfrac{N_{localunits}}{A_{censuszone}}$	$\dfrac{N_{employees}}{A_{censuszone}}$	$\dfrac{D_{employees}}{D_{localunits}}$
Very high density	>1,000	3,566	6,724	7,000
High density	<= 1,000 > 500	2,484	2,755	3,516
Medium density	<= 500 > 100	7,488	5,983	6,601
Low density	<= 100 > 20	4,188	2,739	1,039
Very low density	<= 20 > 0	3,730	3,255	3,300
No data	0 or Null	7,378	7,378	7,378
Total census zones	-	28,834	28,834	28,834

Table 5. Definition of the OMI values and OMI zones datum.

Datum	File type	Definition
OMI values	.csv	Real-estate surveyed information for rent and square-meter prices
OMI zones	.kmz	Continuous spatial areas that allocate the OMI values within the territory

Table 6. OMI values ranges, categorization, number of OMI zones and total area

Ranges [€/m^2]	Categorization	Number of OMI Zones	(%)	Total Area [km^2]	(%)
0−200	Very low real-estate value	462	33.55%	11534.06	50.22%
200−400	Low real-estate value	232	16.85%	5737.36	24.98%
400−600	Medium real-estate value	237	17.21%	2224.08	9.68%
600−800	High real-estate value	209	15.18%	1816.85	7.91%
800 - inf	Very high real-estate value	237	17.21%	1656.89	7.21%
Total	−	1377	−	22969.23	−

Even with this spatialization, the *Industrial Census* spatialization does not provide a sufficient differentiation – nor an exact positional information – that indicates the differences in distribution on the boundaries and outside the urbanized areas (Fig. 4). When paired with the *industrial assets* dataset, the *Industrial and Services Census* can provide an overview of the actual number of structures set in each census zone, thus providing a positional information that is absent on the original database (Fig. 4). Nevertheless, it does not solve the issues regarding data territorialization.

Similar spatialization issues can be observed in OMI real-estate quotations *(Quotazioni dell'Osservatorio del Mercato Immobiliare)* [22], a dataset that describes average real-estate prices surveyed within a certain area of the territory for the period between 2002 to 2021. These economic variables can be associated to the amount of *installed capital*, as they convey information about the real-estate prices (€/m^2) across a determined region, important for understanding the dynamics of value within the cities. Its territorialization, even if conceived with the idea to differentiate urban areas according to their position and placement within the cityscape [22, 23], still faces the same problems found in the *Industrial and Services Census* regarding data aggregation, as its regionalized territorial division results in areas with significative differences in size and datum quantity.

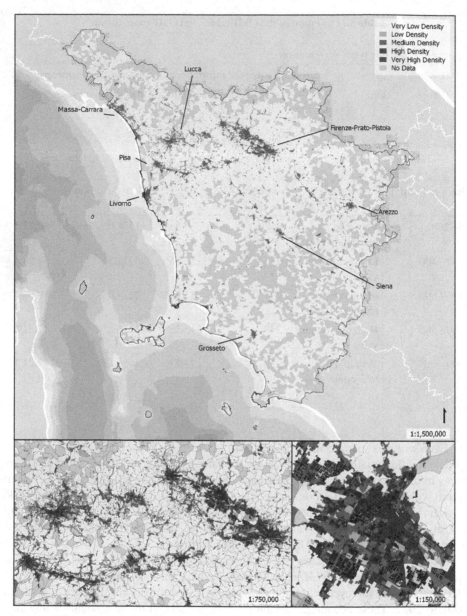

Fig. 4. Spatial distribution of average *firm-size* density in Tuscany

From the methodological standpoint, the OMI datasets spatialization process within a GIS-based environment [13] functions in the same manner as the *Industrial and Services Census*, as data is provided using a dual-table system, where one table represents the OMI values – economic information –, and the other, the OMI zones – surveyed spatial units As in the census dataset, several adaptations in a GIS-based environment were needed to allow the construction of the average real-estate values.

Spatialized OMI values correspond to a measure of *average installed capital* for a determined OMI zone within Tuscany. OMI values must be joined to OMI zones through a common variable for zone [21]. Since the variable possess sub-categories to differentiate structures' urban functions (24 categories) and their state of conservation (3 categories), the dataset had to organized in columns defined from V1 to V72. "V

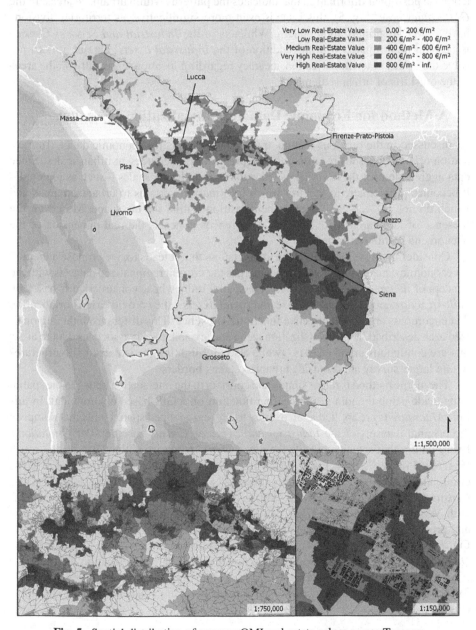

Fig. 5. Spatial distribution of average OMI real-estate values across Tuscany

columns" that corresponded to the industrial urban functions (Warehouses, Industrial Buildings and Laboratories) in all states of conservation were used to calculate the average real-estate values for each OMI zone by considering the minimum and maximum values for prices by square-metre. The results for the OMI dataset are then spatialized and categorized in accordance with their square-meter price range (€/m^2):

Likewise in the *Industrial Census* spatialization, *OMI real-estate values* territorialization provides a limited spatial differentiation, as the data distribution does not provide a precise positional information that indicates the patterns within urbanized areas. In the *OMI values* case (Fig. 5), this issue is even more significant, as territorial divisions have a larger regionalization pattern. While, as in the *Industrial and Services Census*, issues can be mitigated with the addition of the *industrial assets'* dataset, it does not solve the issues in territorialization accuracy regarding location, especially on the areas in the outskirts of urban settlements.

3   A Method for Economic Data Territorialization - Results

As discussed in the previous section, traditional methods for economic data territorialization often face issues regarding their representation accuracy at urban scales. Since data aggregation for those variables tends to be set at larger scales – such as regional – it becomes problematic to identify which information pertains to urbanized areas and which do not, as well as to precise their position within the cityscape. Moreover, the presence of large areas with few data occurrences conceals the real dimension of the phenomena within territories.

Considering these issues, and the imprecisions that it leads to, we propose a method for economic data territorialization that merges the current regionalized datasets with the concept of *macroarea*. As *macroareas* are spatial units whose construction is based on *built-structures* position – in this case, *industrial assets* – they provide a territorialization that encompass areas with effective functional presence. This differs from the regionalized area described in the spatialization using survey zones, as it associates data to areas that are contiguous urban extents – while also highlighting the isolated built-structures within larger survey areas outside urbanized areas borders.

The merge method is rather simple and consists in the intersection between the spatial units made using the join geoprocessing function on a GIS-based environment. In this join, *Macroareas* are applied as an overlay to thr regionalized spatial units that compose the original datasets of the *Industrial and Services Census* and the *OMI Quotations*. Every datum that remains outside the *macroareas'* reach is subtracted from the result (Fig. 6; p.11, Fig. 7., p.11, Fig. 8, p.12, Fig. 9, p.12). This intersection process led to the elimination of most areas within the category "No Data" in the *Industrial and Services Census*, (which were reduced by 92,15%) as well as an overall reduction of the total areas with Very Low Density (80,27%), while preserving the spots where data was present and precising the location of the data where *industrial assets* are placed (Fig. 6 p, 11, Fig. 7, p.11). These differences in terms of area coverage grow in importance in the *OMI Quotations* dataset, as restrictions tend to better reflect the value/location relationships (Fig. 8, p.12), In this case, total areas for each category are extensively reduced (Table 7) and the spatialization now cover only the areas that are adjacent the built-structures (Fig. 9, p.12).

Table 7. OMI values comparison after macroarea reduction

OMI quotations - area (km^2)	Original dataset	Macroarea reduction	Δ%
Very high avg. real-estate value	1656.89	368.46	−77.76%
High avg. real-estate value	1816.85	561.39	−69.10%
Medium avg. real-estate value	2224.08	684.11	−69.24%
Low avg. real-estate value	5737.36	1270.54	−77.85%
Very low avg. real-estate value	11534.06	1562.81	−86.45%

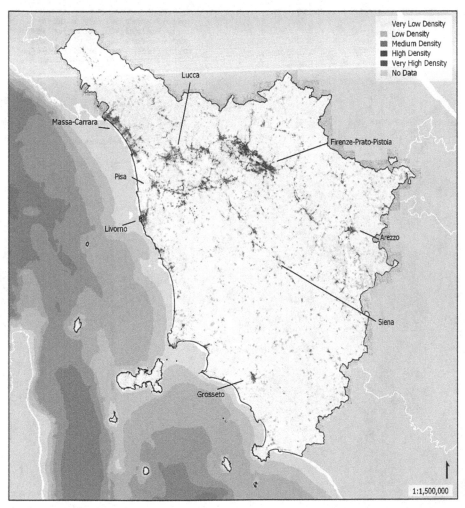

Fig. 6. Spatial distribution of average *firm-size (labour)* combined with macroareas restriction in Tuscany

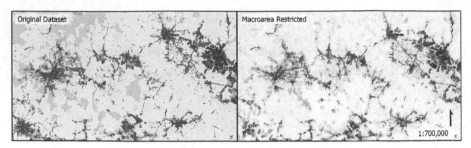

Fig. 7. Comparison between the methods of spatialization for average *Firm Size* in Tuscany

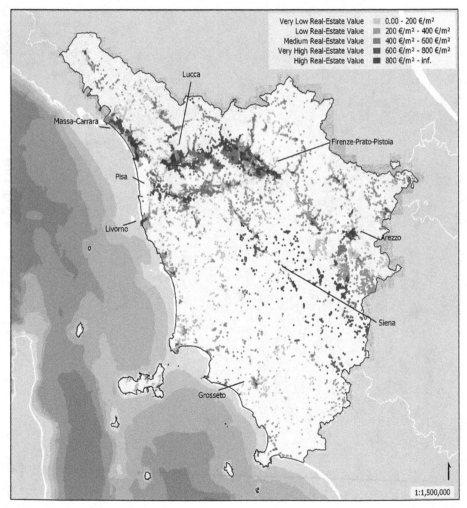

Fig. 8. Spatial distribution of average *OMI real-estate values (installed capital)* combined with macroareas restriction in Tuscany

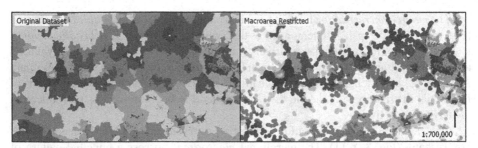

Fig. 9. Comparison between the methods of spatialization for average *OMI real-estate values* in Tuscany

4 Discussion of the *Macroarea-Based* Territorialization Results

Results attained through the *macroarea* restricted territorialization reflect a distinctive concentration pattern for the *average firm-size (labour)*, within septentrional and, to a lesser degree, central Tuscany (Fig. 6, p.11). Those areas correspond to the location of the major urban settlements - the provincial capitals of *Firenze, Livorno, Lucca, Massa-Carrara, Pisa, Prato, Pistoia* – as well as the main conurbations within the region. Moreover, as stated in Altafini & Cutini [15] Northern Tuscany has most of its larger industrial agglomerates under *Low* and *Very Low* Spatial Territorial Exposure, which denotes an adequate territorial support for economic activities there placed.

Although higher ranges of *average firm-size* are predominant within the *macroareas* set on Northern and Central Tuscany, those spaces also possess significative numbers of census zones set under *Low* and *Very Low* ranges, above all, on their hinterlands (Fig. 6, p.11). When compared to the original dataset spatialization method (Fig. 4, p.7) results evidence that most *industrial assets* set on the lower *firm-size* ranges within the Northern and Central *macroareas* are in the boundaries of the large urban settlements. Therefore, located around the census zones within the higher ranges of *average firm-size*, being associated to cityscape continuities (Fig. 7, p.11).

A contrast can be established with Southern Tuscany *macroareas*, where industrial agglomerations effectively follow a hinterland-based spatial distribution. *Industrial assets* tend to be located far from urban centres – as observed in the area between the provincial capitals of *Arezzo* and *Siena* (Fig. 4, p.7, Fig. 7, p.11), and overall *average firm-size* densities tend to be lower. Individuating those territorial patterns is unattainable through the regionalized methods used to spatialize the original datasets (Fig. 7, p.11), which demonstrates the usefulness of the *macroarea* as a spatial unit to improve the overall degree of accuracy in economic variables territorialization.

Concentration patterns for *OMI real-estate values* (Fig. 8 p12) follow similar spatial distributions when compared to the *average firm-size* (Fig. 6, p.11), as areas with higher average prices by square metre (600–800 €/m² and above 800 €/m²) are mostly concentrated in around the provincial capitals in Northern and Central Tuscany. Nevertheless, differences exist as several *macroareas* in Southeast Tuscany hinterlands – between the provincial capitals of *Arezzo* and *Siena* also possess high average prices, as observed in the original dataset spatialization (Fig. 5, p.9).

The *macroarea restriction* reveals a detailed pattern for *real-estate values* distribution (Fig. 8, p.12, Fig. 9, p.12). It demonstrates that, while areas with higher *installed capital* tend to be in proximity to the larger urban centres, the *industrial assets* are mostly placed at the urban settlements' boundaries. Such result can be interpreted as a nod to William Alonso's [3] and Richard Muth's [4] locational theories of urban rent, since patterns of functional distribution assumed in their models tend to be, more-or-less reproduced in the territorial analysis.

Once again, a spatial distribution contrast is observed between Northern and Southern Tuscany (Fig. 8, p.11). The meridional *macroareas* possess a punctual pattern of distribution of *installed capital*, due to its hinterland-based characteristics of industrial placement. Small-localized *macroareas* with high *real-estate values* can be found in smaller and medium settlements, which demonstrate that, as in the North, urban settlements still guide the dynamics of placement to some extent. Southeast Tuscany, however, present a particular characteristic when compared to the Southmost part of the region. While permeated by small *macroareas* with *Low* and *Very Low average firm-size densities* (Fig. 6, p.11), *average real-estate values* are high, which demonstrates that while *industrial assets* tend to be smaller and less contiguous, their *installed capital* and positional value are important (Fig. 8, p.12). In the same manner, ascertain those detailed spatial logics without the use of the *macroarea* is unfeasible, and justifies its usage (Fig. 9, p.12).

5 Concluding Remarks

The territorialization of economic variables is an issue that matters for both Spatial Economics and Urban and Regional Planning. Integrated spatial-economic analysis at urban-regional scales requires a level of detail in spatialization that is unattainable through the sole usage of the traditional regionalized economic variables such as those available through census and surveys. While this kind of territorialization can be reasonably accurate on cities' urban cores, it tends to greatly lose in precisions near the cities' boundaries, due to the increment of the surveyed areas associated to the decrement of the data occurrences. In that aspect, regionalized data can often lead to misjudgements in the assumptions of *what is where* and *why?* In urban settlements.

Acknowledging these issues in territorialization is a first step to solve the problem. In this paper we discussed the characteristics of two regionalized databases, the *Industrial and Service Census* [20] – to describe the distribution of *labour* – and the *OMI Quotations* [22] – to describe the distribution of *installed capital* –, addressing their characteristics of spatialization. Based on that, we proposed a step to merge these datasets to a spatial unit that has been in continuous methodological development – the *macroarea* [15]. The proof-of-concept, made on GIS using data for the Tuscany region, demonstrated the use of a restricted spatial unit based on the built-structures position – the *macroarea* – can mitigate the spatialization problems of regionalized databased, diminishing the overall imprecisions in location. As *macroareas* also establish the reach of each census datum, positioning it within the urbanized spaces, it is a useful variable to analyse dynamics associated to *value*, as well as to establish correlations with other spatial analyses, such as the configurational and morphological. In the same manner, while we establish this proof-of-concept using *industrial assets*, the same method can be applied to other urban functions such as retail and services, or even to analyse real-estate values evolution for the housing market. Hence, while a simple method, merging the *macroarea* spatial units with the economic datasets can very well increase the level of detail for the analysis and well aid in the explanation and of economic phenomena that pertains the urban environments. Further studies are planned to improve the spatial unit and the methods to associate it to other economic variables Nevertheless, we still believe that a shift on how economic data is made available is also due, given the novel requirements of spatial research.

References

1. von Thünen, J.H.: Der isolirte Staat in Beziehung auf Landwirthschaft und Nationalökonomie, oder Untersuchungen über den Einfluss, den die Getreidepreise, der Reichthum des Bodens und die Abgaben auf den Ackerbau ausüben. Hamburg, Friedrich Perthes (1826)
2. Weber, A.: Theory of the Location of Industries. The University of Chicago Press, Chicago, 1929 (1909). https://doi.org/10.1086/254099
3. Alonso, W.: Location and Land Use. Harvard University Press, Cambridge (1964)
4. Muth, R.: Cities and Housing. University of Chicago Press, Chicago (1969)
5. Thisse, J. Walliser, B.: Is space a neglected topic in mainstream economics? Recherches Economiques de Louvain **64**(1), 11-22 (1998)
6. Duranton, G., Henderson, J.V., Strange, W. (eds.) Handbook of Regional and Urban Economics: Regional and Urban Economics, vol. 5A. Amsterdam. Elsevier – North-Holland (2015a)
7. Henderson, J.V., Thisse, J.F., (eds). Handbook of Regional and Urban Economics: Cities and Geography, vol. 4. Amsterdam. Elsevier – North-Holland (2004)
8. Hillier, B.: Spatial sustainability in cities: organic patterns and sustainable forms. In: Koch, D., Marcus, L., Steen, J., (eds.) Proceedings of the 7th International Space Syntax Symposium. Royal Institute of Technology (KTH): Stockholm, Sweden. pp. K01:3 (2009)
9. Hillier, B.: The genetic code for cities: Is it simpler than we think? In: Portugali, J., Meyer, H., Stolk, E., Tan, E. (eds.) Complexity Theories of Cities Have Come of Age: An Overview with Implications to Urban Planning and Design. London: Springer, pp. 67–89 (2012). https://doi.org/10.1007/978-3-642-24544-2_8
10. Garau, C., Annunziata, A.: A method for assessing the vitality potential of urban areas. the case study of the metropolitan City of Cagliari, Italy. City Territ Archit **9**, 7 (2022). https://doi.org/10.1186/s40410-022-00153-6
11. Araldi, A., Fusco, G.: Retail fabric assessment: describing retail patterns within urban space. Cities **85**, 51–62 (2018)
12. Van Nes, A.: Road Building and Urban Change. The Effect of Ring Roads on the Dispersal of Shop and Retail in Western European Towns and Cities. Ph.D. Thesis, Department of Land Use and Landscape Planning, Agricultural University of Norway, Ås, Norway, 27 September (2002)
13. QGIS, Białowieża, version 3.22 (2022). http://www.qgis.org/en/site/index.html
14. Gervasi, O., et al. (eds.): ICCSA 2021. LNCS, vol. 12949. Springer, Cham (2021). https://doi.org/10.1007/978-3-030-86653-2
15. Altafini, D., Cutini, V.: Territorial disparities in Tuscan industrial assets: a model to assess agglomeration and exposure patterns. TeMA – J. Land Use, Mob. Environ. **14**(2), 161–176 (2021b). https://doi.org/10.6092/1970-9870/7976

16. Altafini, D., Pozzobon, E., Rusci, S., Cutini, V.: Lo spazio nella contrazione industriale: specificità e risposte del patrimonio immobiliare produttivo toscano. In: Giaimo, C., Tosi, M.C., Voghera, A., (eds.) Tecniche urbanistiche per una fase di decrescita – Atti della XXIII Conferenza Nazionale SIU. Planum Publisher, pp. 12–19 (2021a)

17. Altafini, D., Pozzobon, E., Rusci, S., Cutini, V.: Computational planning support systems for regional analysis: real-estate values dynamics and road-networks configuration. In: La Rosa, D., Privitera, R. (eds.) INPUT 2021. LNCE, vol. 146, pp. 291–299. Springer, Cham (2021). https://doi.org/10.1007/978-3-030-68824-0_32

18. Toscana, R.: Direzione Urbanistica e Politiche Abitative - Sistema Informativo Territoriale e Ambientale – SITA.: Edificato 2k, 10k 1988–2013. (2019b). http://www502.regione.toscana.it/geoscopio/cartoteca.html

19. Lucas, R.: On the size distribution of business firms. Bell J. Econ. **9**, 508–523 (1978)

20. ISTAT, 9° Censimento ISTAT dell'industria e servizi. Istituto Nazionale di Statistica, Roma (2011). https://www.istat.it/it/archivio/104317

21. ISTAT, Descrizione dei dati geografici e delle variabili censuarie delle Basi territoriali per i censimenti: anni 1991, 2001, 2011. Istituto Nazionale di Statistica, Roma (2016)

22. Agenzia Entrate. Banca Dati Quotazioni dell'Osservatorio del Mercato Immobiliare Direzione Centrale Osservatorio Mercato Immobiliare e Servizi Estimativi, Roma (2021)

23. Entrate, A.: Manuale della Banca Dati Quotazioni dell'Osservatorio del Mercato Immobiliare Istruzioni tecniche per la formazione della Banca Dati Quotazioni OMI. In: Guerrieri, G., Festa, M., Longhi, S., Cantone, G., Papa, F. (eds.). Direzione Centrale Osservatorio Mercato Immobiliare e Servizi Estimativi, Roma (2018)

The 15-Min City: A Configurational Approach for Understanding the Spatial, Economic, and Cognitive Context of Walkability in Vienna

Claudia Yamu[1] and Chiara Garau[2(✉)]

[1] Department of Civil Engineering and Energy Technology, Oslo Metropolitan University, 0166 Oslo, Norway
[2] Department of Civil and Environmental Engineering and Architecture, University of Cagliari, 09129 Cagliari, Italy
cgarau@unica.it

Abstract. This paper focuses on how a city's configurational patterns impact the city-wide and neighbourhood spatial, economic, and cognitive context through the case study of Vienna. The authors investigate Vienna by applying the space syntax method to get a better grasp of the city-wide and local to-movement, through-movement potentials, and intelligibility. This approach allows the authors to determine the degree of street life and liveliness of Vienna in relation to walkability potential, which includes social and economic factors. The case study of Vienna is performed using quantitative analyses, with a mathematical street network modelling approach and statistical analyses. Additionally, this quantitative approach is enriched with a qualitative photographic survey. The data imply that Vienna, as a historically developed city, has a high potential for walkability. This is also confirmed by the balance between the foreground network for long-distance movement via motorised public transport, trams, and cars and the background network for walkability in neighbourhoods. The paper concludes by juxtaposing socio-spatial potentials with realised walkability and influencing factors that support or hinder walkability, and by considering how a sustainable urban future can be achieved through well-functioning strategic planning guidelines.

Keywords: City of short distances · Configurative analysis · Walkable neighbourhoods

1 Introduction

Cities at short distances that are accessible to all urban services within 15 min provide a promising way for redesigning the urban system (temporal, spatial and activity-related) to address contemporary challenges, including not only the most recent COVID-19 pandemic but also the different initiatives related to the evolution of sustainable urban mobility policies [1, 2]. The 15-min city model integrates several urban approaches and is vital for post-COVID-19 recovery and for developing sustainable cities. Walking improves mental and physical health [3] but was restricted for many people during the

© The Author(s), under exclusive license to Springer Nature Switzerland AG 2022
O. Gervasi et al. (Eds.): ICCSA 2022 Workshops, LNCS 13377, pp. 387–404, 2022.
https://doi.org/10.1007/978-3-031-10536-4_26

pandemic period [4], in some cases causing severe threats to public health [5]. Walking can reduce inequities among urban residents as it is not dependent on social status and affordability. Creating inclusive access for all also demands that cities enable walkability through social-spatial integration and by avoiding segregation. However, the 15-min city model is not new; it evolved from the 'neighbourhood unit' concept, which was conceived in 1923 in a national context in Chicago [6]. The concept sought to define compact residential neighbourhoods where the proximity of services and homes is centred on satisfying all the needs of an individual within a 15-min radius with minimal travel. The 15-min concept has been refined by new urbanist ideas. Urban theorists, such as Jane Jacobs, Jahn Gehl, Christopher Alexander, and Leon Krier, have included the pedestrian-friendly city in their work as a key foundation of the 15-min city. The current strategy to remodel cities is in line with the United Nations Sustainable Development Goals (UN SDGs) which aim to promote global development towards universal wellbeing, and the move away from the unsustainable way of life in cities. Applying the "15-min city" model can improve urban planning and policies to create a post-COVID-19 sustainable and healthy community, addressing the city's efficiency and resilience, and contributing to climate change mitigation. It is argued, therefore, that Vienna should follow the example of other global cities and implement the 15-min neighbourhood strategy for creating sustainable, equitable, and socio-economically prosperous communities.

Starting from these assumptions, the purpose of the paper is to determine the degree of street life and the vitality of Vienna in relation to the potential for walkability. It adopts a targeted approach to the 15-min city integrated with the space syntax method through the case study of Vienna. To accomplish this, the paper begins with Hillier's theoretical framework that focuses on the natural movement economic process, the dual network, and the spatial centrality of neighbourhoods (Sect. 2). This is followed by the case study of Vienna (Sect. 3), applying a mixed-methods approach combining qualitative and quantitative analysis, through (1) configurational analysis using the space syntax approach, (2) statistical analysis, and (3) a photographic survey (Sect. 4). Section 5 provides the results and discussion. The final section concludes this paper, providing reflections on the results and the future direction of research in this area.

2   Theoretical Framework

2.1   The Theory of the Natural Movement Economic Process

This theory states that the spatial configuration of the street network influences the flow of human movement and the location of shops in the built environment. There is a causal link between space, movement, and economic activity [7–9]. The more the spatial integration of streets, the greater the flow of movement and the more the land along the street network becomes attractive for economic use [10–12]. However, socio-economic processes are intertwined with spatial processes. Changes in the urban configuration influence the socio-economic context. This theory has shown that over time and when it comes to the location patterns of economic activities, the built environment optimises itself in this regard independently of planning processes. In line with Van Nes and Yamu [12] (p. 179) this theory can be summarised as follows:

(1) The spatial configuration or urban space affects the flow of the human network.
(2) The spatial configuration of the urban space influences the location pattern of economic activities.
(3) The amount of human movement determines the location pattern of economic activities in the built environment.
(4) The location pattern of economic activities has an effect on the amount of human movement in the built environment.

2.2 The Dual Network

According to Hillier, cities have the dual nature of a foreground and a background network. At all scales and levels, the foreground network links urban centres [10]. The citywide through-movement analysis shows the foreground network and is constituted through main routes. In traditional European cities, this foreground network entails a deformed wheel structure with radials and orbitals. The background network is the local network of residential areas. Hillier explains that the foreground network is composed of metrically long roads that connect with each other whereas the background network consists of metrically shorter lines that intersect with each other [12]. Van Nes and Yamu's [12] findings from several space syntax analyses show that the five following spatial conditions exist for generating vital urban areas with a high diversity of active land uses:

- a well-integrated topological and geometric street network exists on a local to global scale;
- primary routes with a high centrality ratio (indicating accessibility) for through-movement and citywide analysis;
- major routes that run through neighbourhoods rather than around them;
- a foreground network that is directly connected to the background network; and
- main routes that run through, or are strongly connected to, a town or city's locally integrated centre.

2.3 Spatial Centrality for Neighbourhoods

According to Hillier (1999), a city or neighbourhood's city centre is a concentrated and mixed-use of land and social activities in a prominent place. Centrality often implies a high degree of movement and flow of people. Thus, the urban configuration plays a vital role in determining the centrality of street segments and, therefore, the generation of movement patterns that affect land use. In line with Hillier's ideas, a cascade of more and less intensive movement and land uses emerges as a result of people's movement patterns, thus generating an urban hierarchy of the centrality and periphery. Centrality becomes diffuse across a city through proximity to smaller and much larger centres. For movement around centres, it is important to differentiate between pedestrian movement and individual motorised movement [9] (p. 517). Whereas often planned centres with their twentieth-century attractions emphasised accessibility by car, historic local centres emphasise the long-standing tradition of pedestrian accessibility. These walkable local centres appear with spatial qualities that include a walkable environment, mixed land use, and urban density. Often, emerging centres at a local level become connected to the citywide level over time. The constitution of spatial centrality works through its spatial configuration and the route choices of people within a street network in line with Hillier's theory of the natural movement economic process.

3   The Case Study of Vienna in Austria

Vienna was selected as a case study because, according to the annual Mercer study that evaluates over 450 cities worldwide, Vienna has been ranked as the most liveable city in the world several times [13]. The evaluation defines 10 criteria which encompass different aspects of the spatial, social, economic, and political context. From a socio-spatial and socio-economic perspective, walkability is evaluated according to accessibility to functions, green areas, and the quality of the built environment.

Vienna is a historic European city characterised by a radial-concentric spatial design. As of 2021, the population was around 2 million growing steadily since a drop in numbers during the two world wars. Spatially, Yamu [9] (p.522) notes that according to Marshall's classification, Vienna has four distinct urban structures: (1) an "Altstadt" or A-type, which is the core of historic cities, particularly walled cities, with an angularity combined with a variety of directions resulting in a rudimentary radiality; (2) a "Bilateral" or B-type, which is typical in recently built settlements in which the four-way perpendicular junctions result in bilateral directionality; (3) a "Characteristic/ Conjoint" or C-Type, which is descriptive of arterial roads, whether they serve as the heart of a hamlet, an entire settlement, or a suburban extension; and (4) a "Distributory" or D-type, a contemporary hierarchical structure comparable to distribution. Marshall [14] asserts that the ABCD types may manifest individually or in mixed mode. The spatial hierarchy of cities is often influenced by street centrality, as a symbol of accessibility and connectivity. This kind of centrality-based structure is characteristic of traditional European towns and cities [9].

From the citywide and local configurational analysis, six neighbourhoods with different characteristics connected to Marshall's classification were chosen: (1) the historic city core 'Innenstadt', a tourist attraction with high levels of pedestrian movement; (2) 'Mariahilf–Spittelberg', a shopping and hospitality destination for locals and tourists with a shared street concept as its main shopping street; (3) 'Favoriten' with its street markets and multi-cultural background of its residents including the area of the main train station; (4) 'Hietzing', a former village in Vienna adjacent to the Vienna Woods with villas; (5) 'Am Spitz' in Floridsdorf, a former agricultural area; and (6) 'Kaisermühlen' lying in close proximity to the leisure area 'Danube island', a popular destination for locals. The neighbourhood boundaries do not follow administrative borders, but mental boundaries as perceived by locals.

4   Method and Data

The authors used a mixed-method approach combining qualitative and quantitative analysis to evaluate the 15-min city of Vienna as a case study. This approach entails three steps (1) configurational analysis using the space syntax approach; (2) statistical analysis; and (3) photographic survey.

4.1 Computational Analysis with Space Syntax

The street network configuration is analysed using a graph-theory based approach that shows the relationship between one street and the other streets in the spatial system [15, 16]. It is based on the principle of centrality, which is symbolised through accessibility. Using an axial line approach allows for the computation of the same spatial model with topological direction change (axial integration) and angular analysis with metric radii (angular segment integration and angular segment choice).Van Nes and Yamu [9] (p. 140f) explain that the term 'integration' refers to the process of determining how spatially integrated a street is in relation to all other streets in a town or city; the fewer direction changes, the higher the integration value for a street, and the more integrated the street. This is a connectivity-based measure. Additionally, angular segment integration is referred to as 'to-movement'. For the measure of choice, Conroy Dalton proved that the angular relationship of streets has a significant effect on how people orient themselves. Thus, angles affect how people choose their routes at road junctions [17]. Angular choice demonstrates the through-movement potential and is also hierarchically organizing the city in terms of movement. Economic centres gravitate toward areas with a high correlation between integration and choice values to catch to-movement and through-movement. In this paper, the authors applied normalised angular choice (NACH) and normalised angular integration (NAIN) [12], by considering the well-established normalisation approach for data visualisation:

$$NACH = log(Choice(r) + 2) \tag{1}$$

$$NAIN = log(Angular\ Int(r) + 2) \tag{2}$$

Table 1. Calculation of space syntax centralities and comparison to related fields using the primal and dual graph approach [18] (p. 49)

Dual graph – space syntax	Primal graph	Formula	Concept	References
Integration (int.)	Closeness centrality	$C(x) = \frac{1}{\sum_y d(x,y)}$	Measure the distance between elements in a network; in space syntax, denotes the relative accessibility or movement potential of a road-element, as it informs how close – in topological terms – a road-element is in relation to the others	Bavelas, 1950; Sabidussi, 1966

(continued)

Table 1. (*continued*)

Dual graph – space syntax	Primal graph	Formula	Concept	References
Choice (ch.)	Betweenness centrality	$C_B(v) = \sum_{s \neq v \neq t \in V} \frac{\sigma_{st}(v)}{\sigma_{st}}$	Measures the number of times a certain network element is traversed when moving through the shortest paths from all origin-destination pairs of elements within the network. In space syntax, it denotes the hierarchy of preferential routes throughout the system	Freeman, 1977; 1978 Freeman et al.,1979
Connectivity (C)	Degree centrality	$C_D(v) = \deg(v)$	Measures the number of links that are incident upon a node or the number of ties such a node has. In space syntax, it indicates the number of connections between road-elements	Euler (1736)

4.2 Data

To gain a better understanding of Vienna's urban fabric, an axial map was generated using a geographic information system (GIS). The 2014 axial map was modelled in GIS using Google Maps as a base map. For the space syntax analysis, measures with a city-wide radius r = n, a local syntactic radius r = 3, and a metric radius r = 1200 m (which equals a 15-min walk) were applied. The radii allowed for the depiction of city-wide and neighbourhood structures and were connected to the concept of a 15-min city through the potential of the centrality of street segments and accessibility. Further, the natural boundaries of the urban fabric were considered, rather than the administrative boundaries, allowing for an inclusive analysis and taking into consideration the edge effect. This decision was taken as it more accurately reflects the current spatial and functional reality of Vienna. In addition, the neighbourhoods were computed independently as contained networks.

4.3 Statistical Analysis

Firstly, the authors summarise and categorise the properties of the different data sets of the spatial analysis. Secondly, the four-pointed star diagram is demonstrated, by illustrating the relationship between the foreground and the background network in comparison to fifty cities in the world [19]. The four-pointed star diagram of this paper is based on standard deviations and is based on Hillier's study of fifty cities with different spatial patterns. Third, a linear correlation of the measures' connectivity and global integration is used to understand the neighbourhoods' degree of intelligibility. A high degree of intelligibility is indicated by a significant linear correlation between both measures (variables) and vice versa. Intelligibility refers to the area's ease of orientation and navigation, which is vital. A weak correlation between the two variables implies a segregated area in relation to the city.

For the four-pointed star diagram, we use the following formulae for calculating the Z-scores for NACH and NAIN, as stated by van Nes and Yamu [12] (p. 79). Hillier et al. [19] provide the values for the fifty analysed cities:

$$\overline{X}_{max} = \frac{\sum_{i=1}^{50} X_{max}(i)}{50} \tag{3}$$

$$Z_{max}(i) = \frac{X_{max}(i) - \overline{X}_{max}}{\overline{S}_{max}(i)} \tag{4}$$

where $X_{max}(i)$ denotes the maximum value of the city i.

$$\overline{X}_{mean} = \frac{\sum_{i=1}^{50} X_{mean}(i)}{50} \tag{5}$$

$$Z_{mean}(i) = \frac{X_{mean}(i) - \overline{X}_{mean}}{\overline{S}_{mean}(i)} \tag{6}$$

where $X_{mean}(i)$ denotes the mean value of the city i.

4.4 Visual Analysis

Visual analysis enables the assessment of the public domain on a qualitative level. It allows an understanding of streets and squares at a micro-scale, revealing factors that contribute to enhancing or hindering walkability. Thus, the micro-scale is important to understand how the walking potential from the normative space syntax analysis is realised. For this study, a personal photographic database and Google Street View are used to visually analyse streets with significant results from the spatial analysis.

5 Results and Discussion

5.1 Mathematical Street Network Analysis of Vienna

The city-wide through-movement analysis (NACH r = n) reveals a deformed wheel structure for Vienna. The deformed wheel pattern consists of radial and orbital main routes. This deformed wheel connects the understanding of Hillier that cities have a dual nature that consists of a foreground and background street network. The foreground network (streets with high centrality indicated in red in Fig. 1) links urban centres at all scales and levels [10]. These highly central streets form the main routes in Vienna. These main routes form the urban through-movement hierarchy and are the main "arteries" of the city. Important to note is that a street network is highly efficient for movement when the spokes of the deformed wheel structure go through neighbourhoods. Yet, the spokes run through and between neighbourhoods from the inner part of the city to its outskirts, which allows efficient inbound and outbound movement. Thus, it connects city-wide movement with local movement. Many historically grown neighbourhoods, such as Vienna, entail this logic as well as neighbourhoods with planning interventions of the twentieth century. For Transdanubia, the areas across the Danube, the deformed wheel spikes no longer follow a strict deformed wheel logic. This is also the case in those areas that did not play a major role in the formation of Vienna until the nineteenth and twentieth centuries. Recent urban developments and the property price landscape have given Transdanubia more prominence. However, they are an extension of the city's urban core and traditional urban areas.

In contrast, the city-wide to-movement (NAIN r = n) analysis shows a strong central cluster covering the historically evolved structures and major urban planning interventions implemented as a grid structure. Given that to-movement is strongly correlated with connectivity, the grid structure is co-present in its dominance. This is known as the Manhattan Problem [20], which refers to space syntax axial models where it is difficult to distinguish centrality patterns from regular grids, especially in terms of betweenness centralities. However, what is true about the orthogonal grids on a neighbourhood scale for Vienna is that they are highly accessible and in recent years, have become, popular destinations for a culturally diverse local population.

Both through- and to-movement analyses highlight the identification of a well recognisable overlap of the same central streets and roads and is thus indicative of vitality across economic locations. Streets that catch both through- and to-movement allow for a vital economy.

The through-movement analysis with a radius of 1200 m shows highly centralised street segments within a 15-min walking radius (Fig. 2). At the same time, it also shows the spatial mediator between neighbourhoods and urban quarters. From the spatial analytical results, the authors can identify that those areas with a particularly strong city-wide through- and to-movement have a spatial cluster with strong local street centralities. These clusters resemble distinct Viennese neighbourhoods – as a local would consider them independent of their administrative boundaries, but mentally composed by the centrality cohesion of their street network. The local axial integration analysis, for the most part, follows the through-movement logic for Vienna. In addition, more prominent foreground streets are captured in the local to-movement analysis. This can be observed

(a) Vienna: NACH radius n

Normalised angular choice/
Accessibilty
≡ high
≡ low

(b) Vienna: NAIN radius n

Normalised angular integration/
Accessibilty
≡ high
≡ low

0   2,5   5km

Fig. 1. City-wide configurational analysis of Vienna's street network: (a) NACH radius n, (b) NAIN radius n [6] (p. 526), [12] (p.77). (Color figure online)

Fig. 2. Local configurational analysis of Vienna's street network: (a) NACH radius 1200 m, (b) Integration radius 3 (axial map credited to Sebastian Zeddel; model computed by the authors)

especially in urban areas that do not have a distinct background network and are mainly automobile-dependent, as in the urban south, southeast towards the urban fringe and in Transdanubia. In cases where the city's main roads run through neighbourhoods with a central street background network, the movement for the neighbourhood is highly efficient as it gives accessibility for the neighbourhood across scales and establishes vital socio-economic activity across scales. Overall, Vienna's well-established and balanced foreground and background network support a lively city (Fig. 3). In addition, Table 2 shows the topological system size through a number of axial lines and street segments, and the mean values of key measures.

Table 2. Means of syntactic measures

	Number of axial lines	Number of segments	Connectivity	NAIN r = n	NACH r = n	NACH r = 1200 m	Int r = 3
Vienna	18,082	52,716	4.23	0.26	4.97	2.83	1.71

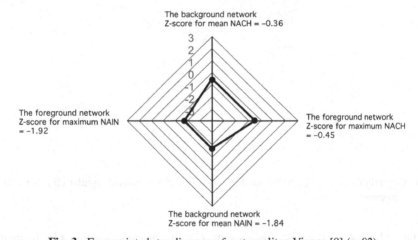

Fig. 3. Four-pointed star diagram of metropolitan Vienna [9] (p. 82)

The four-pointed star diagram reveals how the street network is constituted and enables or hinders the socio-economic success of a city. As the anchor for socio-economic activities, this is represented *inter alia* by centrality, accessibility, and land use. Where the foreground's network centrality correlates well with the background network, a high potential for socio-economic vitality exists (see Figs. 1 and 2; Sect. 2.2). Vienna's foreground and background network in relation to other cities is well balanced and therefore enables the movement of different modes of transport.

5.2 Spatial Centralities of Neighbourhoods

To understand the potential for pedestrian movement six neighbourhoods are isolated and computed using through- and to-movement measures (Fig. 4 and 5).

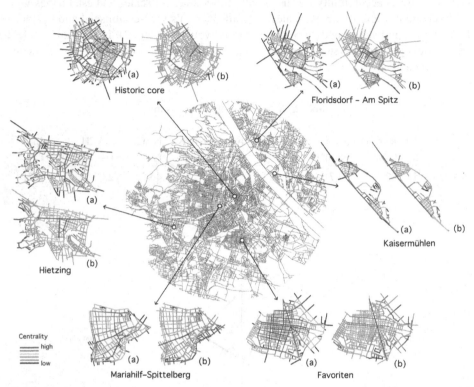

Fig. 4. Centralities for six neighbourhoods in Vienna: (a) Normalised angular choice r = n and (b) Axial integration r = n

The findings show the following aspects. (1) The through-movement in the historic core depicts a dense and fine-grained street network with a route hierarchy while the to-movement results show highly central streets for both car-based and pedestrian-based movement including one of the main shopping streets. (2) In Hietzing, the through-movement has a circular logic with high to-movement centrality for the main shopping street and important connectors to other districts and neighbourhoods, including the historically developed area of this neighbourhood. To- and through-movement correlate well for the local shopping street. (3) In Mariahilf-Spittelberg, the through-movement potential follows a deformed grid logic of the city including all the main strategic streets of this area and the main shopping street. Amerling Street (highlighted in red in both analyses) runs through the high street and enables both through- and to-movement with secondary connectors to other neighbourhoods. Notably, Amerling Street was a strategic location during WWII and has a flak tower, an anti-aircraft gun blockhouse, which is still located there. (4) In Favoriten, the through-movement is influenced by the grid pattern of this neighbourhood making most areas highly accessible. Regarding the to-movement, the main shopping street with public transport hubs is the most central; this area has a long tradition of being home to those from a migrant background. This neighbourhood also has high proximity and accessibility to other neighbourhoods. (5) Kaisermühlen is the location of the United Nations, Vienna, and is also very much car-based. This can be seen from the through- and to-movement analyses as they are congruent in areas where there is high independent motorized traffic. The main through-road is the centre of this neighbourhood. (6) In Floridsdorf, like Kaisermühlen, the route hierarchy is fragmented although the to-movement indicates the potential for establishing a local economic centre. However, in most of these areas, the built environment contributes to a car-based culture.

5.3 Intelligibility

For the six chosen neighbourhoods, the correlation between global integration and connectivity values refers to the concept of "intelligibility" of neighbourhoods and cities. Intelligibility is an important measure to predict wayfinding and environmental cognition, concepts developed by Kevin Lynch [12]. Table 3 shows the correlation coefficient as derived from the space syntax models for each neighbourhood.

Table 3. Linear correlation values (R^2) for six neighbourhoods in Vienna: Intelligibility

Neighbourhood/City	Number of axial lines	Correlation value R^2
Greater vienna	26,359	0.15
Historic core	405	0.51
Mariahilf–Spittelberg	209	0.38
Favoriten – main train station	275	0.53
Hietzing	416	0.30
Floridsdorf – Am Spitz	376	0.26
Kaisermühlen	143	0.23

Favoriten has the highest correlation value at $R^2 = 0.53$ followed by the historic core with $R^2 = 0.51$. For Favoriten, this high value derives from the almost orthogonal street grid of the neighbourhood which establishes high connectivity of streets and therefore high integration values. However, orientation and navigation in this area are easy for visitors and residents. The historic core has high intelligibility given its historically grown structure and optimisation over time. Mariahilf, also a popular neighbourhood in which to live and shop has good intelligibility with a correlation value of $R^2 = 0.38$. The intelligibility linear correlation value of $R^2 = 0.30$ for Hietzing is a mixture of a historically developed structure with intermediate block sizes and large leisure areas like Roter Berg (red mountain) and Lainzer Tiergarten, a wildlife preservation area, adjacent to and part of the Vienna Woods. It means that the historic core is easy to navigate by visitors whereas the more residential areas with their local leisure areas are not a common destination for visitors. This results from the, on average, bigger block sizes with a few very large blocks which were established as functions for the Royal Court, such as the former stables and military functions, which include the National Defence Academy. The lower intelligibility values for Floridsdorf $R^2 = 0.26$ and Kaisermühlen at $R^2 = 0.23$ arrive from the partly fragmented network and fragmented connectivity. For Kaisermühlen the spatial pattern is constituted by large blocks like the United Nations with its restricted access for visitors and locals. Given the large blocks, this neighbourhood is prioritizing in large parts car-based movement. For Floridsdorf, the local centre "Am Spitz" is dominated by its establishment between two supra-regional historic trading and through routes which are mainly car-dominated nowadays. One of these streets, the Brünner Straße, was originally designed as a bypass road, deviating from local centres in proximity. This further influences the intelligibility of the area given its overall lower connectivity.

5.4 Photographic Illustration

The photographic illustrations highlight the difference in the quality of the built environment for the different neighbourhoods. As is the case with the majority of traditional European cities, the historic core has been carefully preserved as a tourist and retail attraction, and the buildings often exhibit several historical features (Fig. 5(a)). Mariahilf's (Fig. 5(c)) highly integrated main shopping street on a local and city-wide scale has been transformed into a shared space in line with the late Hans Monderman's notion [21]. The shared space concept slows down through-movement as traffic users must negotiate the available space since the street belongs to all users – including pedestrians, cyclists, and motorised traffic. However, this concept allows for a lively mixture of stationary activities with both through-movement and to-movement, which also makes this shopping street socio-economically vibrant. Hietzing (Fig. 5(b)) is a residential neighbourhood and district with its villas, single-detached dwellings, and later social housing alongside Schönbrunn Castle. Formerly, it was a village lying close to Vienna with vineyards and gravel pits that were used for building the castle. Nowadays, it is a popular neighbourhood and centre for locals.

In contrast, Favoriten (Fig. 5(d)) is highly efficient when it comes to through-movement, to-movement, and functions. Its built environment is not always very appealing. Long established Viennese economic functions moved out of this area. However, this area is popular for international food and restaurants, especially from the East, and for its local market. This neighbourhood is a heavily populated urban area with residential buildings and intermediate industry, including a business park and the Vienna skyscrapers, the 'Vienna Twin Towers', which are a typical representation of modernism. Many streets in this area are car-based with pavements on either side, but quite inconvenient for walking. Further, Kaisermühlen's (Fig. 5(e)) major landmark is the UNO-city with is Vienna International Centre and the Austria Centre Vienna, a modernistic ensemble. Added to this is the Donau City, a collection of skyscrapers built in the mid-1990s for living and working. This neighbourhood is a traditionally working-class area and is close enough to appreciate the leisure areas along the Danube. Since the 1960s, the neighbourhood has seen significant expansion, in the Zeitgeist of automobile-dependent urban development.

Fig. 5. Photographic illustrations of the six neighbourhoods in Vienna

Furthermore, Floridsdorf (Fig. 5(f)) is a collection of former villages. Because the local centre 'Am Spitz' was a flood plain, its urban development came relatively late. However, settlements can be dated back to the New Stone Age. In the twentieth century, this neighbourhood aimed to become independent from Vienna, which explains the oversized administrative building for this local centre (Fig. 5(f)) and its prominent location in the urban fabric. Today this area is continuously under development.

6 Conclusions

The foreground and background of Vienna's network are well-balanced. This is mostly due to infill developments which contribute to the city's pedestrian-friendly nature. However, the spatial studies suggest that Transdanubia, with the chosen neighbourhoods of Kaisermühlen and Am Spitz, deviates from the efficient spatial logic. This is mostly due to the fact that parts of these areas were flood plains for the Danube River and, hence, remained mostly undeveloped until the late nineteenth century. This changed dramatically during the twentieth century. Nevertheless, Vienna's spatial fabric contributes to a well-balanced socio-spatial and socio-economic context through its mesh/high spatial coverage of citywide and local centres, accessibility to many functions, and public transport network. This contributes to Vienna's overall quality of life [13].

Centrality is an indicator of people's potential movement and socio-economic activities. This can be connected to Hillier's theory of natural movement and economic process, as well as his future thoughts about the foreground and network, to understand and forecast the economic effects and flow of movements caused by the configuration of the urban fabric [9, 12]. The emergence, transformation, and decline of urban centres work through the configuration of a street network. The layout of urban street patterns and their centralities affect land use and social processes. According to Hillier, each location has both a smaller and a much bigger centre nearby with overlapping neighbourhoods based on proximity [22].

Understanding the centrality of individual streets and how local centres function from both a city-wide and neighbourhood perspective, enables understanding not only of how a city is spatially constituted but also where interventions are needed to establish a city of short distances, i.e., the 15-min city. Thus, centrality and accessibility are key to a well-functioning future city and are more socially equitable. To conclude, Vienna is composed of well-functioning central spaces that overlap with local centres, and that are in close proximity to city-wide centres. This is vital for establishing a 15-min city within the framework of walking and cycling. However, there also exist a number of spatially ineffective areas impacting the socio-economic context that need to be transformed in order to provide a base to establish the 15-min city.

Using a targeted approach and analysis of the city of 15-min integrated with a space syntax analysis, this paper has shown Vienna's existing normative potential and challenge for walkability. We further made a link to vitality of neighbourhoods and intelligibility for orientation and wayfinding of pedestrians. The authors intend to develop this study by amplifying the concept of vitality in light of the findings of this research, integrating it with other elements, to enable analysis of the potential for walkability from a more holistic perspective [23–25].

Author Contribution. This paper is the result of the joint work of the authors. In particular, 'Method and data', 'Theoretical framework' and 'Case study of Vienna in Austria' were written jointly by the authors. C.Y. wrote 'Results and discussion' and 'Conclusions' and C.G. wrote the 'Introduction'.

Disclosure Statement. No potential conflict of interest was reported by the authors.

References

1. Duarte, S.P., de Sousa, J.P., de Sousa, J.F.: Designing urban mobility policies in a socio-technical transition context. Transp. Res. Procedia **62**, 17–24 (2022)
2. Pinna, F., Masala, F., Garau, C.: Urban policies and mobility trends in Italian smart cities. Sustainability **9**(4), 494 (2017)
3. Garau, C., Annunziata, A., Coni, M.: A methodological framework for assessing practicability of the urban space: the survey on conditions of practicable environments (SCOPE) procedure applied in the case study of Cagliari (Italy). Sustainability **10**(11), 4189 (2018)

4. Campisi, T., et al.: Anxiety, fear and stress feelings of road users during daily walking in COVID-19 pandemic: Sicilian cities. Transp. Res. Procedia **62**, 107–114 (2022)
5. Finucane, M.L., Beckman, R., Ghosh-Dastidar, M., Dubowitz, T., Collins, R.L., Troxel, W.: Do social isolation and neighborhood walkability influence relationships between COVID-19 experiences and wellbeing in predominantly Black urban areas? Land-scape Urban Plan. **217**, 104264 (2022)
6. Gaglione, F., Gargiulo, C., Zucaro, F., Cottrill, C.: 15-minute neighbourhood accessibility: a comparison between Naples and London. In: European Transport\Trasporti Europei Issue 85, Paper no. 5 (2021). ISSN 1825–3997. https://doi.org/10.48295/ET.2021.85.5
7. Hillier, B.: Space is the Machine. A Configurational Theory of Architecture. Cambridge University Press, Cam-bridge, UK (1996)
8. Hillier, B., Penn, A., Hanson, J.: Natural movement: or configuration and attraction in urban pedestrian movement. Environ. Plann. Plann. Des. **20**, 29–66 (1993)
9. Yamu, C.: Emerging and shifting centralities: evidence from vienna. In: Dillinger, T., Getzner, M., Kanonier, A., Zech, S. (eds.) 50 Jahre Raumplanung an der TU Wien studieren – lehren – forschen. Jahrbuch des Instituts für Raumplanung der TU Wien 2020, Band 8, Neuer Wissenschaftlicher Verlag, Wien, pp. 542–559 (2020)
10. Yamu, C., Van Nes, A., Garau, C.: Bill Hillier's legacy: space syntax—a syn-opsis of basic concepts, measures, and empirical application. Sustainability **13**(6), 3394, pp.1–25 (2021)
11. Garau, C., Annunziata, A.: A method for assessing the vitality potential of urban areas. The case study of the metropolitan city of Cagliari, Italy. City, Territory Arch. **9**(1), 1–23 (2022)
12. Van Nes, A., Yamu, C.: Introduction to Space Syntax in Urban Studies. Cham, Springer (2021)
13. www.wien.gv.at; mobilityexchange.mercer.com. Accessed 1 May 2022
14. Marshall, S.: Streets and Patterns. Spon Press, Oxon (2005)
15. Batty, M.: A New Theory of Space Syntax. UCL Working Papers Series, paper, vol. 75, p. 34 (2004)
16. Van Nes, A., Yamu, C.: Space syntax: a method to measure urban space related to social, economic and cognitive factors. In: Yamu, C., Poplin, A., Devisch, O., De Roo, G. (eds.) The Virtual and the Real in Planning and Urban Design, pp. 136–150. Routledge, Oxon (2018)
17. Conroy Dalton, R.: The secret is to follow your nose: route path selection and angularity. Environ. Dev. **35**(1), 107–131 (2003)
18. Altafini, D.: Spatial-economic models to evaluate industrial agglomerations: novel instruments for urban-regional analysis, unpublished doctoral dissertation, University of Pisa (2022)
19. Hiller, B., Yang, T., Turner, A.: Normalising least angle choice in Depthmap and how it opens new perspectives on the global and local analysis of city space. J. Space Syntax **3**(2), 55–293 (2012)
20. Dalton, N.: Fractional configurational analysis and a solution to the Manhattan problem. In: Van Nes, A. (ed), Proceedings, 5th International Space Syntax Symposium, Delft, p. 26.1–26.13 (2001)
21. Yamu, C., De Roo, G., Frankhauser, P.: Assuming it is all about conditions. Framing a simulation model for complex, adaptive urban space. Environ. Plann. Plann. Des. **43**(6), 1019–1039 (2016)
22. Hillier, B.: The genetic code of cities: is it simpler that we think? In: Portugali, J., Meyer, H., Stolk, E., Tan, E. (eds.) Complexity Theories of Cities Have Come of Age. An Overview with Implications to Urban Planning and Design, Berlin-Heidelberg, Springer, pp. 129–152 (2012). https://doi.org/10.1007/978-3-642-24544-2_8
23. Pinna, F., Garau, C., Annunziata, A.: A literature review on urban usability and accessibility to investigate the related criteria for equality in the city. In: Gervasi, O., et al. (eds.) ICCSA 2021. LNCS, vol. 12958, pp. 525–541. Springer, Cham (2021). https://doi.org/10.1007/978-3-030-87016-4_38

24. Annunziata, A., Garau, C.: A literature review on walkability and its theoretical framework. emerging perspectives for research developments. In: Gervasi, O., et al. (eds.) ICCSA 2020. LNCS, vol. 12255, pp. 422–437. Springer, Cham (2020). https://doi.org/10.1007/978-3-030-58820-5_32

25. Annunziata, A., Garau, C.: A literature review on the assessment of vitality and its theoretical framework. emerging perspectives for geodesign in the urban context. In: Gervasi, O., et al. (eds.) ICCSA 2021. LNCS, vol. 12958, pp. 305–322. Springer, Cham (2021). https://doi.org/10.1007/978-3-030-87016-4_23

International Workshop
on Computational and Applied
Mathematics (CAM 2022)

A Modified Quaternionic Weierstrass Method

Maria Irene Falcão[1] (ID), Fernando Miranda[1](✉)(ID), Ricardo Severino[1](ID),
and Maria Joana Soares[2](ID)

[1] CMAT and Departamento de Matemática, Universidade do Minho, Braga, Portugal
{mif,fmiranda,ricardo}@math.uminho.pt
[2] NIPE, Universidade do Minho, Braga, Portugal
jsoares@math.uminho.pt

Abstract. In this paper we focus on the study of monic polynomials whose coefficients are quaternions located on the left-hand side of the powers, by addressing three fundamental polynomial problems: factor, evaluate and deflate. An algorithm combining a deflaction procedure with a Weierstrass-like quaternionic method is presented. Several examples illustrate the proposed approach.

Keywords: Quaternions · Polynomial computation · Zeros

1 Introduction

In 1941, Niven [16] proved that any polynomial whose coefficients are quaternions located only on the left-hand side of the powers (one-sided polynomials) must have at least one quaternionic root. Since then, there has been a growing interest in studying the problem of characterizing and computing the zeros of these special polynomials, from the theoretical as well as from the applications point of view [7,17,18]. In particular, in the last decade several authors proposed algorithms for computing the zeros of one-sided polynomials. Most of these root-finding methods rely on the connection between the zeros of a quaternionic polynomial and the zeros of a certain real polynomial, usually with multiple zeros, and as such, they face the usual difficulties associated with the computation of multiple zeros or clusters of zeros [2,13,20,21]. One of the few exceptions is the work [4], where a quaternionic version of the well-known Weierstrass iterative root-finding method [23], relying on quaternionic arithmetic is proposed.

Real or complex polynomials have received a lot of attention over the years and classical problems such as factor, evaluate and deflate are well studied. In this paper we consider quaternionic versions of these classical problems. In particular, we revisit the factor problem by recalling a recently proposed quaternionic Weierstrass method [4] and take a fresh look to the problem of evaluating quaternionic polynomials [3]. The main result of the paper is a deflation algorithm to be used together with the Weierstrass method which allows to reestablished its quadratic convergence without requiring higher precision.

© The Author(s), under exclusive license to Springer Nature Switzerland AG 2022
O. Gervasi et al. (Eds.): ICCSA 2022 Workshops, LNCS 13377, pp. 407–419, 2022.
https://doi.org/10.1007/978-3-031-10536-4_27

2   Preliminary Results

We introduce the basic definitions and results needed in the sequel; we refer to [12,15,24] for recalling the main aspects of the quaternion algebra.

Let $\{1, \mathbf{i}, \mathbf{j}, \mathbf{k}\}$ be an orthonormal basis of the Euclidean vector space $\mathbb{R}^4$ with a product given according to the multiplication rules

$$\mathbf{i}^2 = \mathbf{j}^2 = \mathbf{k}^2 = -1, \quad \mathbf{ij} = -\mathbf{ji} = \mathbf{k}.$$

This non-commutative product generates the algebra of real quaternions $\mathbb{H}$. For a quaternion $x = x_0 + \mathbf{i}x_1 + \mathbf{j}x_2 + \mathbf{k}x_3$, $x_i \in \mathbb{R}$, we can define the real part of x, $\operatorname{Re}(x) := x_0$, the vector part of x, $\underline{x} := \mathbf{i}x_1 + \mathbf{j}x_2 + \mathbf{k}x_3$ and the conjugate of x, $\bar{x} := x_0 - \mathbf{i}x_1 - \mathbf{j}x_2 - \mathbf{k}x_3$. The norm of x is given by $|x| := \sqrt{x\bar{x}} = \sqrt{\bar{x}x}$. It immediately follows that each non-zero $x \in \mathbb{H}$ has an inverse given by $x^{-1} = \frac{\bar{x}}{|x|^2}$ and therefore $\mathbb{H}$ is a non-commutative division ring or a skew field.

Two quaternions q and q' are called *similar*, $q \sim q'$, if $\operatorname{Re} q = \operatorname{Re} q'$ and $|q| = |q'|$. Similarity is an equivalence relation in $\mathbb{H}$, partitioning $\mathbb{H}$ in the so-called *similarity class* of q, which we denote by $[q]$. The similarity class of a non-real quaternion $q = q_0 + \mathbf{i}q_1 + \mathbf{j}q_2 + \mathbf{k}q_3$ can be identified with the three-dimensional sphere in the hyperplane $\{(x_0, x, y, z) \in \mathbb{R}^4 : x_0 = q_0\}$, with center $(q_0, 0, 0, 0)$ and radius $\sqrt{q_1^2 + q_2^2 + q_3^2}$.

We consider now polynomials P in one formal variable x of the form

$$P(x) = a_n x^n + a_{n-1} x^{n-1} + \cdots + a_1 x + a_0, \ a_n \neq 0, \tag{1}$$

i.e. polynomials whose coefficients $a_k \in \mathbb{H}$ are located only on the left-hand side of the powers. The set of polynomials of the form (1), with the addition and multiplication defined as in the commutative case, is a ring, referred to as the ring of (left) one-sided polynomials and usually denoted by $\mathbb{H}[x]$.

The evaluation of P at q is defined as $P(q) = a_n q^n + a_{n-1} q^{n-1} + \cdots + a_1 q + a_0$. Moreover, a quaternion q is a zero of P, if $P(q) = 0$. A zero q is called an isolated zero of P, if $[q]$ contains no other zeros of P. A zero q is called a *spherical zero* of P, if q is not an isolated zero; $[q]$ is referred to as a sphere of zeros.

We define now two important polynomials: the conjugate of P, denoted by $\bar{P}$ and defined by conjugating the coefficients of P and the characteristic polynomial of a quaternion q, defined as

$$\Psi_q(x) := (x - q)(x - \bar{q}) = x^2 - 2\operatorname{Re}(q)\, x + |q|^2. \tag{2}$$

Properties concerning these two polynomials, can be seen in e.g. [6].

We end this section by recalling some results concerning the zero-structure and the factorization of polynomials in $\mathbb{H}[x]$. For the proofs and other details we refer to [1,9,15,16]. Besides Niven's Fundamental Theorem of Algebra, stating that any non-constant polynomial in $\mathbb{H}[x]$ always has a zero in $\mathbb{H}$, the following results are essential for the sequel.

Theorem 1. *Consider a polynomial $P \in \mathbb{H}[x]$ of the form* (1).

1. *A quaternion q is a zero of P if and only if there exists $Q \in \mathbb{H}[x]$ such that*

$$P(x) = Q(x)(x - q).$$

2. *A non-real zero q is a spherical zero of P if and only if there exists a polynomial $Q \in \mathbb{H}[x]$ such that*

$$P(x) = Q(x)\Psi_q(x),$$

where Ψ_q is the characteristic polynomial of q given by (2).

3   Polynomial Problems over $\mathbb{H}$

3.1   The Factor Problem

As an immediate consequence of the Fundamental Theorem of Algebra for quaternions and Theorem 1 we conclude that it is always possible, as in the classical case, to write a quaternionic polynomial P as a product of linear factors, i.e. there exist $x_1, \ldots, x_n \in \mathbb{H}$, such that

$$P(x) = (x - x_n)(x - x_{n-1}) \cdots (x - x_1). \tag{3}$$

The quaternions $x_1, \ldots, x_n$ in the factorization (3) are called factor-terms of P and the n-uple $(x_1, \ldots, x_n)$ is called a chain of P.

The link between these factor-terms and the corresponding zeros is not straightforward. In fact if $(x_1, \ldots, x_n)$ is a chain of a polynomial P then any zero of P is similar to some factor-term x_k in the chain and reciprocally every factor-term x_k is similar to some zero of P [15,21]. The next results clarify the link between zeros and factor-terms (we mostly follow [5] and references therein).

Theorem 2 (Zeros from factors). *Consider a chain $(x_1, \ldots, x_n)$ of a polynomial P. If the similarity classes $[x_k]$ are distinct, then P has exactly n zeros ζ_k which are related to the factor-terms x_k as follows:*

$$\zeta_k = \overline{\mathcal{P}}_k(x_k)\, x_k\, \left(\overline{\mathcal{P}}_k(x_k)\right)^{-1}; \quad k = 1, \ldots, n, \tag{4}$$

where

$$\mathcal{P}_1(x) := 1 \quad and \quad \mathcal{P}_k(x) := (x - x_{k-1}) \ldots (x - x_1), \ k = 2, \ldots, n \tag{5}$$

Theorem 3 (Factors from zeros). *If $\zeta_1, \ldots, \zeta_n$ are quaternions such that the similarity classes $[\zeta_k]$ are distinct, then there is a unique polynomial P of degree n with zeros $\zeta_1, \ldots, \zeta_n$, which can be constructed from the chain $(x_1, \ldots, x_n)$, where*

$$x_k = \mathcal{P}_k(\zeta_k)\, \zeta_k\, \left(\mathcal{P}_k(\zeta_k)\right)^{-1}; \quad k = 1, \ldots, n \tag{6}$$

and $\mathcal{P}_k$ is the polynomial (5).

Following the idea of the Weierstrass method in its sequential version [23], a quaternion version was proposed in [4] where it was also shown how to obtain sequences converging, at a quadratic rate, to the factor terms $x_1, \ldots, x_n$ (cf. (3)) of a given polynomial P and with some additional little effort, how these sequences can be used to estimate the zeros $\zeta_1, \ldots, \zeta_n$ of P.

Theorem 4. *Let P be a polynomial of degree n in $\mathbb{H}[x]$ with simple[1] zeros and consider, for $i = 1, \ldots, n$, the iterative schemes*

$$z_i^{(k+1)} = z_i^{(k)} - \left(\mathcal{L}_i^{(k)} P \mathcal{R}_i^{(k)} \right) (z_i^{(k)}) \left(\Psi_i^{(k)}(z_i^{(k)}) \right)^{-1}, \quad k = 0, 1, 2, \ldots \quad (7)$$

where

$$\mathcal{L}_i^{(k)}(x) := \prod_{j=i+1}^{n} \left(x - \overline{z_j^{(k)}} \right), \qquad \mathcal{R}_i^{(k)}(x) := \prod_{j=1}^{i-1} \left(x - \overline{z_j^{(k+1)}} \right) \quad (8)$$

and

$$\Psi_i^{(k)}(x) := \prod_{j=1}^{i-1} \Psi_{z_j^{(k+1)}}(x) \prod_{j=i+1}^{n} \Psi_{z_j^{(k)}}(x), \quad (9)$$

with Ψ_q denoting the characteristic polynomial of q. If the initial approximations $z_i^{(0)}$ are sufficiently close to the factor terms x_i in a factorization of P in the form (3), then the sequences $\{z_i^{(k)}\}$ converge quadratically to x_i. Moreover, the sequences $\{\zeta_i^{(k)}\}$ defined by

$$\zeta_i^{(k+1)} := \overline{\mathcal{R}_i^{(k)}}(z_i^{(k+1)}) \, z_i^{(k+1)} \left(\overline{\mathcal{R}_i^{(k)}}(z_i^{(k+1)}) \right)^{-1}; \, k = 0, 1, 2, \ldots, \quad (10)$$

converge quadratically to the roots of P.

Remark 1. We recall that the evaluation map at a quaternion q is not an algebra homomorphism (see e.g. [15]). This means that if $P(x) = L(x)R(x)$ and $R(q) \neq 0$, then $P(q) = (LR)(q) = L(\tilde{q}) R(q)$, where $\tilde{q} = R(q) \, q \, (R(q))^{-1} \in [q]$.

Remark 2. The proof of Theorem 4 was obtained under the assumption that all the zeros of P are isolated. Several numerical experiments show that the quaternionic Weierstrass method (7)–(9) also works for spherical roots. However, this requires to higher the precision. For example, in [4] the numerical computations have been carried out with the Mathematica system and with the precision increased to 512 significant digits. If this is not performed, then the method produces approximations to the spherical roots with much less precision than those approximating the isolated roots. As expected, for the case of the spherical root, we obtain convergence to two distinct members of the sphere of zeros.

---

[1] A polynomial P of degree n has only simple roots if it has n distinct isolated roots.

3.2   The Evaluating Problem

In [3] the problem of evaluating a polynomial, i.e., given a polynomial P, find its value at a given argument α was addressed. Several polynomial evaluation schemes were considered, which depend on the particular form of the polynomial. The paper mainly focus on two algorithms: the Horner's rule for quaternions and a generalization to $\mathbb{H}$ of the well-known algorithm of Goertzel [8]. The Goertzel's algorithm to obtain $P(\alpha)$ is based on the following result (see [15] for more general Euclidean division results).

Theorem 5. *Consider a quaternionic one-sided polynomial P of degree $n \geq 2$ and the characteristic polynomial Ψ_α of a quaternion α. Then there exists a unique polynomial Q of degree $n - 2$ such that*

$$P(x) = Q(x)\Psi_\alpha(x) + c_1 x + c_0, \tag{11}$$

with $c_1, c_0 \in \mathbb{H}$.

Observe that the form (11) corresponds to the division of P by Ψ_α and can be presented in a compact form by the use of an expanded synthetic division as follows.

Quaternionic Goertzel's algorithm

INPUT: Coefficients a_k of P and α
OUTPUT: Coefficients c_k of Q and $p = P(\alpha)$

- Obtain $r = 2\mathrm{Re}(\alpha)$; $s = |\alpha|^2$;
- Let $c_{n+1} = 0$; $c_n = a_n$;
- **for** $k = n - 1 : -1 : 1$ **do**
    $c_k = a_k + r\,c_{k+1} - s\,c_{k+2}$;
- **end for**
- Compute $c_0 = a_0 - s\,c_2$;
- Compute $p = c_1\alpha + c_0$;

The algorithm produces not only the value $P(\alpha)$, but also the coefficients of the quotient polynomial Q, i.e.

$$p_n(x) = (c_n x^{n-2} + c_{n-1} x^{n-3} + \cdots + c_3 x + c_2)\Psi_\alpha(x) + c_1 x + c_0. \tag{12}$$

We point out that when P is a polynomial with real (or complex) coefficients, this quaternionic algorithm coincides with the classical Goertzel's algorithm for computing $P(\alpha)$, $\alpha \in \mathbb{C}$. This algorithm has advantages, from the complexity of the algorithm point of view, over the well-known Horner's method [5,14]. The Goertzel?s algorithm for computing $P(\alpha)$ is componentwise backward stable both in the complex case [22] and in the quaternionic case [5].

3.3 The Deflate Problem

Given a real polynomial P and one of its roots α, deflating a polynomial means
to find a polynomial Q such that

$$P(x) = Q(x)(x - \alpha);$$

being the additional roots of P exactly the roots of Q. In the case $\alpha \in \mathbb{C}$, one
can deflate by a quadratic factor

$$P(x) = Q(x)(x - \alpha)(x - \bar{\alpha}).$$

In both cases, the polynomial Q can be obtained by synthetic long division
through Goertzel's algorithm (see Sect. 3.2).

In this section we propose a method to deflate a given polynomial so that
the deflating polynomial has no spherical zeros.

The motivation for considering this problem comes from the fact that the
proof of the quadratic convergence to the factor-terms (or equivalently to the
roots) of the Weierstrass method, relies on the assumption that all the roots are
simple (cf. Theorem 4). Several numerical experiments show that it is possible
to reach quadratic convergent to spherical roots at the expense of increasing
the accuracy of calculations, something that is not accessible to all numerical
systems.

We are looking for a factorization of a quaternionic polynomial P of degree
n, of the form

$$P(x) = Q(x)S(x) = S(x)Q(x) \tag{13}$$

such that all the zeros of Q are isolated and all the zeros of S are spherical.
Assuming that P has the spherical roots $\zeta_1, \ldots, \zeta_k$, $(2k \leq n)$ and recalling Theorem 1, we can write S as

$$S(x) = \Psi_{\zeta_1}(x) \ldots \Psi_{\zeta_k}(x), \tag{14}$$

where $\Psi_{\zeta_i}(x)$ is the characteristic polynomial of ζ_i. Since P can be written as

$$P(x) = P_1(x) + P_{\mathbf{i}}(x)\mathbf{i} + P_{\mathbf{j}}(x)\mathbf{j} + P_{\mathbf{k}}(x)\mathbf{k}, \tag{15}$$

where $P_1, P_{\mathbf{i}}, P_{\mathbf{j}}, P_{\mathbf{k}}$ are real polynomials, it is immediate to conclude that Ψ_{ζ} is
a divisor of P if and only if it is a common divisor of $P_1, P_{\mathbf{i}}, P_{\mathbf{j}}, P_{\mathbf{k}}$.

The starting point to obtain the factorization (13) is to compute the set Z
of all the $2k$ common complex zeros of $P_1, P_{\mathbf{i}}, P_{\mathbf{j}}, P_{\mathbf{k}}$, i.e. to construct

$$Z = \{\zeta_1, \bar{\zeta}_1, \ldots, \zeta_k, \bar{\zeta}_k\}.$$

The polynomial Q in (13) is obtained by dividing the polynomial P successively by Ψ_{ζ_i}, $i = 1, \ldots, k$.

4   A Modified Weierstrass Method

In this section we combine the deflation technique described in Sect. 3.3 with the Weierstrass method of Sect. 3.1.

Consider the representation (15) of the monic polynomial P. It is clear that the polynomial P_1 has degree n and the other polynomials $P_\mathbf{i}$, $P_\mathbf{j}$, $P_\mathbf{k}$ have lower degree.

Denoting by P_4, P_3, P_2, P_1 a non-descending sorting of the polynomials P_1, $P_\mathbf{i}$, $P_\mathbf{j}$, $P_\mathbf{k}$ by their degree, we start the process by constructing a list ℓ_C of the complex zeros with positive imaginary part of the real polynomial P_4 and selecting first the one that has the smallest module (see remark at the end of the section), say ζ.

Using the Goertzel's algorithm (in the complex case) to evaluate $P_i(\zeta)$, $i = 1, 2, 3$, we compute simultaneously the (real) coefficients of Q_i such that

$$P_i(x) = Q_i(x)\Psi_\zeta(x) + c_1^i x + c_0^i \tag{16}$$

as in (11)–(12). If ζ is a common zero to all the four polynomials, then we replace the polynomials P_i by the polynomials Q_i (applying in that case the Goertzel's algorithm also to polynomial P_4) and we jump to the next element of the list ℓ_C.

At the end of the procedure, the polynomial $Q(x)$ in (13) is the polynomial

$$Q(x) = P_1(x) + P_\mathbf{i}(x)\mathbf{i} + P_\mathbf{j}(x)\mathbf{j} + P_\mathbf{k}(x)\mathbf{k}, \tag{17}$$

where $P_1, P_\mathbf{i}, P_\mathbf{j}, P_\mathbf{k}$ are the updated polynomials P_1, P_2, P_3, P_4, after a convenient reordering, that comes out of the process.

Once all the spherical roots of P are identified and the deflating polynomial Q is constructed, the isolated zeros of P are computed by applying the Weierstrass method proposed in [4] to Q. The overall process can be summarized as follows:

Modified Weierstrass Algorithm

INPUT: Polynomial P and a tolerance tol.
OUTPUT: Lists ℓ_S and ℓ_I with the spherical and isolated roots of P

- Compute the polynomials P_i, $i = 1, 2, 3, 4$ resulting from sorting the real polynomials in (15) in decreasing order of their degree
- Construct the list ℓ_C of the complex roots with positive imaginary part of P_4 sorted in increasing order of the absolute value of its elements
- **for** each $\zeta_l \in \ell_C$ **do**
    - **for** i=3:-1:1 **do**
        Compute the coefficients c_k^i of P_i as in (16)   % Division of P_i by Ψ_{ζ_l}
        if $|c_1^i \zeta_l + c_0^i|$ >tol **then**
            break   % jump to the next ζ_l; ζ_l is not a root of P_i
        end if
    end for

- Add ζ_l to the list ℓ_S
- Compute the coefficients c_k^4 of P_4 as in (16)
- Update P_i % $P_i(x) = Q_i(x)$
- **end for**
- Construct the polynomial Q from (17)
- Apply Weierstrass method to Q to obtain ℓ_I

Remark 3. In practice, deflation should be used with care, since the use of floating point arithmetic leads to non-exact coefficients in Q. The modified Weierstrass method computes the coefficient of Q in the order from highest power down to the constant term (forward deflation). This turns out to be stable if the roots of smallest absolute value are computed first ([19]). Example 2 illustrates this situation.

5   Numerical Experiments

In this section we illustrate how the deflation technique introduced in the previous section can be combined together with the Weierstrass method to produce accurate approximations to the zeros of a polynomial.

In all the computation, we have used the Matlab system with double floating point arithmetic. For details on the Weierstrass method, in particular, the stopping criteria and the choice of the initial approximations we refer the readers to [4].

Our first example was borrowed from the aforementioned paper, where the results were obtained by the use of the Mathematica system with the precision extended to 512 significant digits. Without using this strategy, it is clear that the approximations to the spherical roots cannot reach the same accuracy as the one exhibited by isolated roots.

Example 1. The polynomial

$$P(x) = x^4 + (-1 + \mathbf{i})x^3 + (2 - \mathbf{i} + \mathbf{j} + \mathbf{k})x^2 + (-1 + \mathbf{i})x + 1 - \mathbf{i} + \mathbf{j} + \mathbf{k},$$

has, apart from the isolated zeros $-\mathbf{i} + \mathbf{k}$ and $1 - \mathbf{j}$, a whole sphere of zeros, $[\mathbf{i}]$.

Starting with the initial guess $z^{(0)} = (1, -2, 0.5\mathbf{i}, 1 + \mathbf{i})$, we obtained, after 14 iterations, the results presented in Table 1.

Observe that P can be written in the form

$$P(x) = P_1(x) + P_2(x)\mathbf{i} + P_3(x)\mathbf{j} + P_4(x)\mathbf{k},$$

where

$$P_1(x) = x^4 - x^3 + 2x^2 - x + 1, \; P_2(x) = x^3 - x^2 + x - 1, \; P_3(x) = P_4(x) = x^2 + 1.$$

Table 1. Weierstrass method for Example 1

Roots	Type	Error
$1 - \mathbf{j}$	Isolated	3×10^{-16}
$-\mathbf{i} + \mathbf{k}$	Isolated	2×10^{-15}
$[\,\mathbf{i}\,]$	Spherical	8×10^{-9}

In this case, Matlab finds exactly the roots $\pm\mathbf{i}$ of P_4 and the use of Goerstzel's algorithm shows that these roots are also roots of P_2 and P_1 and that the division of P by $\Psi_\mathbf{i}$ produces the polynomial

$$Q(x) = -x^3 + 2x - 1 + (-x + 1)\mathbf{i} + \mathbf{j} + \mathbf{k}.$$

Applying now the Weierstrass algorithm to Q with the initial approximation $z^{(0)} = (1, 1 + \mathbf{i})$, we obtain, after 11 iterations, the results presented in Table 2.

Table 2. Modified Weierstrass method for Example 1

Roots	Method	Type	Error
$1 - \mathbf{j}$	Weierstrass	Isolated	7×10^{-17}
$-\mathbf{i} + \mathbf{k}$	Weierstrass	Isolated	2×10^{-18}
$[\,\mathbf{i}\,]$	Deflation	Spherical	0

Example 2. The polynomial

$$P(x) = x^6 + (-1 + \mathbf{i})x^5 + (6 - \mathbf{i} + \mathbf{j} + \mathbf{k})x^4 + (-5 + 5\mathbf{i})x^3$$
$$+ (9 - 5\mathbf{i} + 5\mathbf{j} + 5\mathbf{k})x^2 + (-4 + 4\mathbf{i})x + 4 - 4\mathbf{i} + 4\mathbf{j} + 4\mathbf{k}$$

has the same zeros as the polynomial P in Example 1 and the additional spherical zero $[\,2\mathbf{i}\,]$.

The results of the Weierstrass and Modified Weierstrass methods are presented in Table 3 and 4, respectively, where the advantage of the modified method is already evident.

Table 3. Weierstrass method for Example 2

Roots	Type	Error
$1-j$	Isolated	3×10^{-12}
$-i+k$	Isolated	1×10^{-14}
$[i]$	Spherical	5×10^{-9}
$[2i]$	Spherical	8×10^{-10}

Table 4. Modified Weierstrass method for Example 2

Roots	Method	Type	Error
$1-j$	Weierstrass	Isolated	7×10^{-16}
$-i+k$	Weierstrass	Isolated	8×10^{-16}
$[i]$	Deflation	Spherical	3×10^{-16}
$[2i]$	Deflation	Spherical	5×10^{-16}

Example 3. In the last example we apply both methods to the 8th degree polynomial

$$P(x) = x^8 + (-7+i)x^7 + (37 - 7i + j + k)x^6$$
$$+ (-66 + 36i - 6j - 6k)x^5 + (189 - 60i + 30j + 30k)x^4$$
$$+ (-183 + 159i - 30j - 30k)x^3 + (253 - 153i + 129j + 129k)x^2$$
$$+ (-124 + 124i - 24j - 24k)x + 100 - 100i + 100j + 100k.$$

This polynomial shares all its roots with the polynomial P of Example 2 and has also the extra spherical root $[3 + 4i]$.

It is visible in Table 5 that the difficulties of the Weierstrass in dealing with spherical roots increases with the number of spheres. Moreover these problems are also deteriorating the quality of the approximations for the isolated roots. On the other hand, the Modified Weierstrass method produces very good approximations for both isolated and spherical roots: see Table 6.

Table 5. Weierstrass method for Example 3

Roots	Type	Error
$1-j$	Isolated	9×10^{-6}
$-i+k$	Isolated	1×10^{-5}
$[i]$	Spherical	1×10^{-5}
$[2i]$	Spherical	2×10^{-6}
$[3+4i]$	Spherical	9×10^{-7}

Table 6. Modified Weierstrass method for Example 3

Roots	Method	Type	Error
$1 - \mathbf{j}$	Weierstrass	Isolated	1×10^{-14}
$-\mathbf{i} + \mathbf{k}$	Weierstrass	Isolated	9×10^{-15}
$[\,\mathbf{i}\,]$	Deflation	Spherical	3×10^{-16}
$[\,2\mathbf{i}\,]$	Deflation	Spherical	3×10^{-16}
$[\,3 + 4\mathbf{i}\,]$	Deflation	Spherical	2×10^{-15}

6   Conclusions

We have proposed an algorithm to compute simultaneously all the roots of an one-sided quaternionic polynomial. This algorithm combines a deflation technique, based on the Goertzel's method with the quaternionic Weierstrass method. Several examples specially designed to include spherical roots show the substantial increase of precision of the corresponding approximations.

Given a polynomial P of the form (1), the Goertzel's method produces accurate approximations to the value of $P(\alpha)$, as far as the condition number for the evaluation of the polynomial P at α, i.e.

$$\text{cond } (P, \alpha) := \frac{\sum_{k=0}^{n} |a_k| |\alpha|^k}{|\sum_{k=0}^{n} a_k \alpha^k|}$$

is not large.

For large values of the condition number, the method (in the classical and quaternionic cases) suffers from instability, producing a computed value with few exact digits, which in turn can lead the modified Weierstrass method to failure in the identification of ζ as a spherical root of P. In the classical case, several techniques to overcome such difficulties are known ([10, 11, 22]); we believe they are worth considering in our future work.

Acknowledgments. Research at CMAT was partially financed by Portuguese funds through FCT - Fundação para a Ciência e a Tecnologia, within the Projects UIDB/00013/2020 and UIDP/00013/2020. Research at NIPE has been financed by FCT, within the Project UIDB/03182/2020.

References

1. Beck, B.: Sur les équations polynomiales dans les quaternions. Enseign. Math. **25**, 193–201 (1979)
2. De Leo, S., Ducati, G., Leonardi, V.: Zeros of unilateral quaternionic polynomials. Electron. J. Linear Algebra **15**, 297–313 (2006)

3. Falcão, M.I., Miranda, F., Severino, R., Soares, M.J.: Evaluation schemes in the ring of quaternionic polynomials. BIT Num. Math. **58**(1), 51–72 (2017). https://doi.org/10.1007/s10543-017-0667-8

4. Falcão, M.I., Miranda, F., Severino, R., Soares, M.J.: Weierstrass method for quaternionic polynomial root-finding. Math. Meth. Appl. Sci. **41**(1), 423–437 (2018)

5. Falcão, M.I., Miranda, F., Severino, R., Soares, M.J.: Mathematica tools for quaternionic polynomials. Lecture Notes in Computer Science, vol. 10405, pp. 394–408 (2017)

6. Falcão, M.I., Miranda, F., Severino, R., Soares, M.J.: Polynomials over quaternions and coquaternions: a unified approach. Lecture Notes in Computer Science, vol. 10405, pp. 379–393 (2017)

7. Farouki, R.T., Gentili, G., Giannelli, C., Sestini, A., Stoppato, C.: A comprehensive characterization of the set of polynomial curves with rational rotation-minimizing frames. Adv. Comput. Math. **43**(1), 1–24 (2016). https://doi.org/10.1007/s10444-016-9473-0

8. Goertzel, G.: An algorithm for the evaluation of finite trigonometric series. Amer. Math. Monthly **65**, 34–35 (1958)

9. Gordon, B., Motzkin, T.: On the zeros of polynomials over division rings I. Trans. Amer. Math. Soc. **116**, 218–226 (1965)

10. Graillat, S., Langlois, P., Louvet, N.: Algorithms for accurate, validated and fast polynomial evaluation. Japan J. Indust. Appl. Math. **26**(2–3), 191–214 (2009)

11. Graillat, S., Ménissier-Morain, V.: Accurate summation, dot product and polynomial evaluation in complex floating point arithmetic. Inf. Comput. **216**, 57–71 (2012)

12. Gürlebeck, K., Sprößig, W.: Quaternionic and Clifford Calculus for Physicists and Engineers. John Wiley and Sons (1997)

13. Janovská, D., Opfer, G.: A note on the computation of all zeros of simple quaternionic polynomials. SIAM J. Numer. Anal. **48**(1), 244–256 (2010)

14. Knuth, D.E.: Seminumerical Algorithms, The Art of Computer Programming, vol. 2. Addison-Wesley, second edn. (1981)

15. Lam, T.Y.: A first course in noncommutative rings. Graduate Texts in Mathematics. Springer-Verlag, New York (1991). https://doi.org/10.1007/978-1-4419-8616-0

16. Niven, I.: Equations in quaternions. Amer. Math. Monthly **48**, 654–661 (1941)

17. Pereira, R., Rocha, P.: On the determinant of quaternionic polynomial matrices and its application to system stability. Math. Methods Appl. Sci. **31**(1), 99–122 (2008)

18. Pereira, R., Rocha, P., Vettori, P.: Algebraic tools for the study of quaternionic behavioral systems. Linear Algebra Appl. **400**(1–3), 121–140 (2005)

19. Press, W.H., Teukolsky, S.A., Vetterling, W.T., Flannery, B.P.: Numerical Recipes 3rd Edition: The Art of Scientific Computing, 3rd edn. Cambridge University Press, USA (2007)

20. Serôdio, R., Pereira, E., Vitória, J.: Computing the zeros of quaternion polynomials. Comput. Math. Appl. **42**(8–9), 1229–1237 (2001)

21. Serôdio, R., Siu, L.S.: Zeros of quaternion polynomials. Appl. Math. Lett. **14**(2), 237–239 (2001)

22. Smoktunowicz, A., Wróbel, I.: On improving the accuracy of Horner's and Goertzel's algorithms. Numer. Algorithms **38**(4), 243–258 (2005)

23. Weierstrass, K.: Neuer Beweis des Satzes, dass jede ganze rationale Function einer Veränderlichen dargestellt werden kann als ein Product aus linearen Functionen derselben Veränderlichen. In: Sitzungsberichte der Königlich Preussischen Akademie der Wissenschaften zu Berlin, vol. II. S. 1085–1101. Berlin (1891)
24. Zhang, F.: Quaternions and matrices of quaternions. Linear Algebra Appl. **251**, 21–57 (1997)

Non-symmetric Number Triangles Arising from Hypercomplex Function Theory in $\mathbb{R}^{n+1}$

Isabel Cação[1], M. Irene Falcão[2], Helmuth R. Malonek[1], and Graça Tomaz[1,3]($\boxtimes$)

[1] CIDMA, Universidade de Aveiro, Aveiro, Portugal
{isabel.cacao,hrmalon}@ua.pt
[2] CMAT, Universidade do Minho, Braga, Portugal
mif@math.uminho.pt
[3] Instituto Politécnico da Guarda, Guarda, Portugal
gtomaz@ipg.pt

Abstract. The paper is focused on *intrinsic properties* of a one-parameter family of non-symmetric number triangles $\mathcal{T}(n)$, $n \geq 2$, which arises in the construction of *hyperholomorphic Appell polynomials*.

Keywords: Non-symmetric Pascal triangle · Clifford algebra · Recurrence relation

1 Introduction

A one-parameter family of non-symmetric Pascal triangles was considered in [8] and a set of its basic properties was proved. Such family arises from studies on generalized Appell polynomials in the framework of Hypercomplex Function Theory in $\mathbb{R}^{n+1}, n \geq 1$, (cf. [7]). If $n \geq 2$, it is given by the infinite triangular array, $\mathcal{T}(n)$, of rational numbers

$$T_s^k(n) = \binom{k}{s} \frac{(\frac{n+1}{2})_{k-s}(\frac{n-1}{2})_s}{(n)_k}, \quad k = 1, 2, \ldots, ; s = 0, 1, \ldots, k, \qquad (1)$$

where $(a)_r := a(a+1)\ldots(a+r-1)$, for any integer $r \geq 1$, is the Pochhammer symbol with $(a)_0 := 1, a \geq 0$. If $n = 1$, then the triangle degenerates to a unique column because $T_0^k(1) \equiv 1$ and, as usual $T_s^k(1) := 0$, $s > 0$.

The non-symmetric structure of this triangle $\mathcal{T}(n)$ is a consequence of the peculiarities of a non-commutative Clifford algebra $\mathcal{Cl}_{0,n}$ frequently used in problems of higher dimensional Harmonic Analysis, like the solution of spinor systems as n-dimensional generalization of Dirac equations and their application in Quantum Mechanics and Quantum-Field Theory [6].

Hypercomplex Function Theory in $\mathbb{R}^{n+1}$ is a natural generalization of the classical function theory of one complex variable in the framework of Clifford Algebras. The case $n > 1$ extends the complex case to paravector valued functions

O. Gervasi et al. (Eds.): ICCSA 2022 Workshops, LNCS 13377, pp. 420–434, 2022.
https://doi.org/10.1007/978-3-031-10536-4_28

of n hypercomplex non-commutative variables or, by duality, of one paravector valued variable. For more details we refer to the articles [6,8,9,11].

Important to notice that the use of non-commutative Clifford algebras $\mathcal{C}\ell_{0,n}$ causes interesting challenges for dealing with polynomials in the hypercomplex setting. In particular, this concerns a hypercomplex counterpart of the *Binomial Theorem* and, naturally, some type of a hypercomplex Pascal triangle. In fact, the non-symmetric $\mathcal{T}(n)$, $n \geq 2$, plays just the role of the array of coefficients in a sequence of generalized hypercomplex Appell polynomials as binomial coefficients are playing in the binomial expansion of $(x + iy)^k$ (cf. [8]).

From the other side, the definition of hypercomplex Appell polynomials as adequate generalization of $z^k = (x + iy)^k$ together with the characteristic property

$$(z^k)' = kz^{k-1}, \ k = 1, \ldots, \ \text{and} \ z^0 = 1,$$

formally allows to construct an analogue of the geometric series in hypercomplex setting. Naturally, for a full analogy to the complex case, this raises the question, if the kernel of the hypercomplex Cauchy integral theorem derived from Greens formula in $\mathbb{R}^{n+1}$ (see [6]) could be expanded in form of that hypercomplex geometric series. The answer is affirmative as it has been shown by methods of Hypercomplex Function Theory in [3], where the alternating sums of the k-th row's entries in $\mathcal{T}(n)$, i.e. the one-parameter family of rational numbers

$$c_k(n) := \sum_{s=0}^{k} (-1)^s T_s^k(n), \ k = 0, 1, \ldots, \tag{2}$$

plays an important role. Moreover, in [3] it has been shown that the $c_k(2)$ coincide exactly with numbers, for the first time used by Vietoris in [14] and playing an important role in the theory of orthogonal polynomials as well as questions of positivity of trigonometric sums (see [1]). Consequently, based on a suggestive closed representation of (2) the authors introduced in [4] the sequence of generalized Vietoris numbers as follows

Definition 1. *Let $n \in \mathbb{N}$. The generalized Vietoris number sequence is defined by $\mathcal{V}(n) := (c_k(n))_{k \geq 0}$ with*

$$c_k(n) := \frac{\left(\frac{1}{2}\right)_{\lfloor \frac{k+1}{2} \rfloor}}{\left(\frac{n}{2}\right)_{\lfloor \frac{k+1}{2} \rfloor}}. \tag{3}$$

Remark 1. A general analysis of the coefficients in the sequence $\mathcal{V}(n)$ reveals the following picture. For $n = 1$ all elements are identically equal to 1 for all $k \geq 0$. For a fixed $n > 1$ the floor function in the representation of the coefficients (3) implies a repetition of the coefficient with an even index $k = 2m$ following after that with an odd index, i.e. $c_{2m-1}(n) = c_{2m}(n)$. The value of the next following odd-indexed coefficient is decreasing by a variable factor given by the formula

$$c_{2m+1}(n) = \frac{2m+1}{2m+n} c_{2m}(n). \tag{4}$$

For readers, not so much interested in the hypercomplex origins of $\mathcal{T}(n)$ or $\mathcal{V}(n)$, we finish our introduction recalling some formulas from [4]. They show the specific interrelationship of $\mathcal{V}(n)$ with the dimension of the space of homogeneous polynomials in n variables of degree k. This became evident in [4] where Vietoris numbers (3), contrary to [1], have been studied by real methods without directly relying on Jacobi polynomials $P_k^{(\alpha,\beta)}$. In fact, we found that the Taylor series expansion of the rational function

$$\frac{1}{(1-t)^\gamma (1+t)^\delta}$$

in the open unit interval with the special values

$$\gamma = \frac{n+1}{2} \text{ and } \delta = \frac{n-1}{2}$$

implies the following series development

$$\frac{1}{(1-t)^{\frac{n+1}{2}}(1+t)^{\frac{n-1}{2}}} = \sum_{k=0}^{\infty} \frac{(n)_k}{k!} c_k(n) t^k. \tag{5}$$

Formula (5) shows that generalized Vietoris numbers (3) appear also in coefficients of a special power series multiplied by a term that characterizes the space of homogeneous polynomials in higher dimension. Indeed,

$$\frac{(n)_k}{k!} = \binom{n+k-1}{k} = \dim \mathcal{H}_k(\mathbb{R}^n),$$

where $\mathcal{H}_k(\mathbb{R}^n)$ is the space of homogeneous polynomials in n variables of degree k.

As mentioned before,

$$T_0^k(1) \equiv 1 \text{ and } T_s^k(1) = 0, \text{ if } 0 < s \le k.$$

and for $n = 1$ formula (5) is the sum of the ordinary geometric series due to the special values of γ and δ. Since the geometric series in one real respectively one complex variable coincide (in the latter case (5) has to be considered as a Taylor series expansion in the unit complex disc) our hypercomplex approach contains the complex case as particular case $\mathbb{R}^{1+1} \cong \mathbb{C}$.

The important role of ordinary Vietoris numbers, corresponding to $n = 2$ in (3), in the theory of orthogonal polynomials is discussed in [1]. The paper of Ruschewey and Salinas [12] shows the relevance of the celebrated result of Vietoris for a complex function theoretic result in the context of subordination of analytic functions.

In this paper we deal with interesting properties of $\mathcal{T}(n)$. In particular, in Sect. 2 we present results concerning sums over the entries of the rows of $\mathcal{T}(n)$.

The consideration of the main diagonal, in Sect. 3, includes results on series over its entries and also a recurrence relation which has a certain counterpart with the ordinary Pascal triangle in the limit case $n \to \infty$. Additionally, in Sect. 4 some relations to *Jacobsthal numbers* have been found.

2   Sums over Entries of the Rows in the Non-symmetric Number Triangles

The general structure of the triangle in Fig. 1 can easily be recognized by using the relations between its entries indicated by the arrows in different directions (see [8, Theorems 3.1–3.3]). In this section we want to complete and extend some other properties.

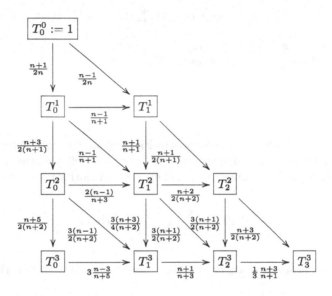

Fig. 1. Relations between the first triangle elements

The first results that we mention in this section are relations between (1) and the corresponding binomial coefficients. We start by listing a set of properties already presented and proved in [8], but which will be useful to prove new results.

I. Relation between adjacent elements in the $s-$th column ([8], Theorem 3.1):

$$T_s^{k+1}(n) = \frac{(k+1)(n+2k-2s+1)}{2(k-s+1)(n+k)}\, T_s^k(n),\qquad (6)$$

for $k = 0, 1, \ldots$; $s = 0, \ldots, k$;

II. Relation between adjacent "diagonal" elements ([8], Theorem 3.2):

$$T_{s+1}^{k+1}(n) = \frac{(k+1)(n+2s-1)}{2(s+1)(n+k)}\, T_s^k(n),\qquad (7)$$

for $k = 0, 1, \ldots$; $s = 0, \ldots, k$;

III. Relation between adjacent elements in the k–th row ([8], Theorem 3.3):

$$T_{s+1}^k(n) = \frac{(k-s)(n+2s-1)}{(s+1)(n+2k-2s-1)} T_s^k(n), \tag{8}$$

for $k = 0, 1, \ldots$; $s = 0, \ldots, k-1$;

IV. Relation between adjacent elements in the k–th row and an element in the $(k-1)$–th row ([8], Theorem 3.5):

$$(k-s)T_s^k(n) + (s+1)T_{s+1}^k(n) = kT_s^{k-1}(n), \tag{9}$$

for $k = 1, 2, \ldots$; $s = 0, \ldots, k-1$;

V. Partition of the unit ([8], Theorem 3.7):

$$\sum_{s=0}^k T_s^k(n) = 1. \tag{10}$$

Following the accompanying factors in Fig. 1 along the corresponding paths, the identity (10) does not come as a surprise. Its proof relies on the definition (1) and the well known Chu-Vandermonde convolution identity for the Pochhammer symbols

$$(x+y)_m = \sum_{r=0}^m \binom{m}{r} (x)_r (y)_{m-r}. \tag{11}$$

Remark 2. We observe that, considering $n \to \infty$ in (1), the entries of $\mathcal{T}(n)$ converge to

$$T_s^k(\infty) = 2^{-k} \binom{k}{s}. \tag{12}$$

Because the sum of all binomial coefficients in row k of the ordinary Pascal triangle equals 2^k, (12) relates the limit case of the triangle in Fig. 1 with an *ordinary normalized* Pascal triangle whose row sum is constantly 1. The next formula [5, Theorem 1], is an analogue of a property of binomial coefficients multiplied by the counting index s in their sum which can be obtained by simply differentiation of the corresponding binomial formula.

Proposition 1. *For $k = 0, 1, 2, \ldots$*

$$\sum_{s=0}^k sT_s^k(n) = \frac{k(n-1)}{2n}.$$

We prove now some new properties of the triangle $\mathcal{T}(n)$. The next is another analogue of a property of binomial coefficients that can also be obtained by differentiation of the corresponding binomial formula. In this case, the proof uses some not so trivial relations between binomial coefficients and the Pochhammer symbol.

Proposition 2. *For $k = 0, 1, 2, \ldots$*

$$\sum_{s=0}^{k} s^2 T_s^k(n) = \frac{k(k+1)(n-1)}{4n}.$$

Proof. Recalling that $s\binom{k}{s} = k\binom{k-1}{s-1}$ and $\left(\frac{n-1}{2}\right)_s = \frac{n-1}{2}\left(\frac{n+1}{2}\right)_{s-1}$, from (1) we can write

$$\sum_{s=0}^{k} s^2 T_s^k(n) = \sum_{s=0}^{k} s^2 \binom{k}{s} \frac{\left(\frac{n+1}{2}\right)_{k-s}\left(\frac{n-1}{2}\right)_s}{(n)_k}$$

$$= \frac{k(n-1)}{2(n)_k} \sum_{s=1}^{k} s\binom{k-1}{s-1}\left(\frac{n+1}{2}\right)_{k-s}\left(\frac{n+1}{2}\right)_{s-1}.$$

From $s\left(\frac{n+1}{2}\right)_{s-1} = \left(\frac{n+1}{2}\right)_s - \left(\frac{n-1}{2}\right)_s$, we obtain

$$\sum_{s=0}^{k} s^2 T_s^k(n) = \frac{k(n-1)}{2(n)_k} \sum_{s=1}^{k} \binom{k-1}{s-1}\left[\left(\frac{n+1}{2}\right)_{k-s}\left(\frac{n+1}{2}\right)_s - \left(\frac{n+1}{2}\right)_{k-s}\left(\frac{n-1}{2}\right)_s\right]$$

$$= \frac{k(n-1)}{2(n)_k}\left[\frac{n+1}{2}\alpha_s^k(n) - \frac{n-1}{2}\beta_s^k(n)\right],$$

with

$$\alpha_s^k(n) = \sum_{s=1}^{k} \binom{k-1}{s-1}\left(\frac{n+1}{2}\right)_{k-s}\left(\frac{n+3}{2}\right)_{s-1} \tag{13}$$

and

$$\beta_s^k(n) = \sum_{s=1}^{k} \binom{k-1}{s-1}\left(\frac{n+1}{2}\right)_{k-s}\left(\frac{n+1}{2}\right)_{s-1}. \tag{14}$$

Using in (13) and (14) the Chu-Vandermonde convolution identity (11) with $x = \frac{n+3}{2}, y = \frac{n+1}{2}$ and $x = y = \frac{n+1}{2}$, respectively, we get

$$\alpha_s^k(n) = (n+2)_{k-1} \text{ and } \beta_s^k(n) = (n+1)_{k-1}.$$

Therefore

$$\sum_{s=0}^{k} s^2 T_s^k(n) = \frac{k(n-1)}{4(n)_k}\left[(n+1)(n+2)_{k-1} - (n-1)(n+1)_{k-1}\right]$$

$$= \frac{k(n-1)}{4(n)_k}(n+1)_{k-1}(k+1) = \frac{k(k+1)(n-1)}{4n}.$$

$\square$

Remark 3. In the limit case $n \to \infty$, the equalities of the Proposition 1 and Proposition 2 become the well known identities $\sum_{s=0}^{k} s\binom{k}{s} = 2^{k-1}k$ and $\sum_{s=0}^{k} s^2\binom{k}{s} = 2^{k-2}k(k+1)$, respectively ([2, p. 14]) .

Alternating sums involving (1) can be connected to the Vietoris sequence introduced in Definition 1, as follows:

Proposition 3. *For* $k = 0, 1, 2, \ldots,$

$$\sum_{s=0}^{k} (-1)^s s T_s^k(n) = \begin{cases} \frac{1-n}{2} c_k(n), & \text{if } k \text{ is odd} \\ 0, & \text{if } k \text{ is even.} \end{cases}$$

Proof. Noting that

$$\sum_{s=0}^{k} (-1)^s s T_s^k(n) = \sum_{s=0}^{k-1} (-1)^{s+1}(s+1) T_{s+1}^k(n),$$

the result follows from

$$\sum_{s=0}^{k-1} (-1)^s (s+1) T_{s+1}^k(n) = \begin{cases} \frac{1}{2} \frac{k(n-1)}{n+k-1} c_{k-1}(n), & \text{if } k \text{ is odd} \\ 0, & \text{if } k \text{ is even} \end{cases}$$

(cf. [[8], Theorem 3.9]), and (4). $\square$

The following proposition shows again the connection with the Pascal triangle, this time with the central binomial coefficients. The result follows immediately from (6).

Proposition 4.
$$T_k^{2k}(n) = T_k^{2k-1}(n).$$

Remark 4. We note that, letting $n \to \infty$ in the assertion of Proposition 4, the identity $\binom{2k}{k} = 2\binom{2k-1}{k}$ is obtained.

3   Recurrences and Series over the Entries in the Main Diagonal

The richness and beauty of the Pascal triangle and the already mentioned connections with the triangle $T(n)$ motivated the search for new structures and patterns within $T(n)$.

The family of sequences we are going to consider contains the main diagonal elements of the triangle (see Fig. 2), where we use the abbreviation

$$\mathcal{T}_k(n) := T_k^k(n) = \frac{\left(\frac{n-1}{2}\right)_k}{(n)_k}, \quad k = 0, 1, 2, \ldots; n = 2, 3, \ldots. \tag{15}$$

Observe that this sequence can be written in terms of the generalized Vietoris sequence (3), as

$$\mathcal{T}_k(n) = \frac{c_{2k}(2n)}{c_{2k}(n-1)} = \frac{c_{2k-1}(2n)}{c_{2k-1}(n-1)}.$$

The next property shows how an element in the main diagonal can be obtained by simply subtracting two consecutive elements in the first column.

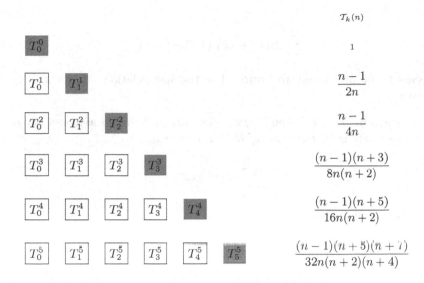

$$\mathcal{T}_k(n)$$

T_0^0 1

T_0^1 T_1^1 $\dfrac{n-1}{2n}$

T_0^2 T_1^2 T_2^2 $\dfrac{n-1}{4n}$

T_0^3 T_1^3 T_2^3 T_3^3 $\dfrac{(n-1)(n+3)}{8n(n+2)}$

T_0^4 T_1^4 T_2^4 T_3^4 T_4^4 $\dfrac{(n-1)(n+5)}{16n(n+2)}$

T_0^5 T_1^5 T_2^5 T_3^5 T_4^5 T_5^5 $\dfrac{(n-1)(n+5)(n+7)}{32n(n+2)(n+4)}$

Fig. 2. The sequence $(\mathcal{T}_k(n))_{k\geq 0}$ as main diagonal in $\mathcal{T}(n)$

Proposition 5.
$$\mathcal{T}_k(n) = T_0^{k-1}(n) - T_0^k(n).$$

Proof. The repeated use of (8), relating consecutive elements in the same row, allows to write
$$\mathcal{T}_k(n) = \frac{n-1}{n+2k-1}T_0^k(n),$$
while (6) gives
$$T_0^k(n) = \frac{n+2k-1}{2n+2k-2}T_0^{k-1}(n).$$
The result follows at once, by combining these two last identities. $\square$

Considering now some series built of elements of the main diagonal, we use (15) and connect this representation formula with special values of the hypergeometric function $_2F_1\,(a,b;c;z)$. Gauss' hypergeometric series is defined by

$$_2F_1\,(a,b;c;z) = \sum_{k=0}^{\infty} \frac{(a)_k(b)_k}{(c)_k}\frac{z^k}{k!}$$

on the disk $|z| < 1$ and by analytic continuation elsewhere. In particular on the circle $|z| = 1$, Gauss' series converges absolutely when $\mathrm{Re}(c - a - b) > 0$. Therefore, choosing $a = 1$, $b = \frac{n-1}{2}$, $c = n$ (we recall that $n \geq 2$) and $z = \pm 1$, it follows immediately from (15)

$$\sum_{k=0}^{\infty}(-1)^k\mathcal{T}_k(n) = {}_2F_1\left(1, \tfrac{n-1}{2}; n; -1\right) \tag{16}$$

and

$$\sum_{k=0}^{\infty} \mathcal{T}_k(n) =_2 F_1\left(1, \tfrac{n-1}{2}; n; 1\right). \tag{17}$$

It seems to be of interest to notice that the last relation admits an explicit evaluation.

Proposition 6. *The series built of all elements of the main diagonal is convergent and its sum is independent of the parameter n, i.e.*

$$\sum_{k=0}^{\infty} \mathcal{T}_k(n) = 2.$$

Proof. We recall Gauss' identity

$$_2F_1(a, b; c; 1) = \frac{\Gamma(c)\Gamma(c-a-b)}{\Gamma(c-a)\Gamma(c-b)}, \quad \mathrm{Re}(c-a-b) > 0,$$

and rewrite result (17) in the form

$$\sum_{k=0}^{\infty} \mathcal{T}_k(n) = \frac{\Gamma(n)\Gamma(\tfrac{n-1}{2})}{\Gamma(n-1)\Gamma(\tfrac{n+1}{2})}.$$

Then the sum of the considered series can simply be read off by using the basic properties of the Gamma function, $\Gamma(z+1) = z\Gamma(z)$ and $\Gamma(n) = (n-1)!$. $\square$

The next result about the evaluation of the alternating series (16) for $n = 2$, uses the relation of $\mathcal{T}_k(2)$ to the celebrated Catalan numbers $\mathcal{C}_k = \frac{1}{k+1}\binom{2k}{k}$, which already was mentioned in [5].

Proposition 7. *For the particular case of $\mathcal{T}_k(2)$, the alternating series (16) converges and its sum is given by*

$$\sum_{k=0}^{\infty} (-1)^k \mathcal{T}_k(2) = 2(\sqrt{2} - 1).$$

Proof. According to (15), we have

$$\mathcal{T}_k(2) = \frac{1}{2^{2k}} \mathcal{C}_k. \tag{18}$$

Applying the Catalan identity

$$\sum_{k=0}^{\infty} \frac{(-1)^k \mathcal{C}_k}{4^k} = 2(\sqrt{2} - 1),$$

which follows from the generating function of Catalan numbers $g(x) = \frac{1-\sqrt{1-4x}}{2x}$, with $x = -\frac{1}{4}$ (see e.g. [13]), we recognize the result as identical with the Catalan identity. $\square$

It is worth noting that all the elements of the triangle $\mathcal{T}(2)$ are related to Catalan numbers. It is enough to use (18) together with the relation (9) in order to obtain any element of the triangle as a linear combination of Catalan numbers.

Before arriving to another group of general but more intrinsic properties of the sequence $\mathcal{T}_k(n)$ we prove an auxiliary relation of the entries in a row of the triangle $\mathcal{T}(n)$ which culminates in a binomial transform between $\mathcal{T}_k(n)$ and the sequence of the first column. For arbitrary integers $n \geq 2$, an element $T_s^k(n)$ of the triangle $\mathcal{T}(n)$ is related to the numbers in the main diagonal $\mathcal{T}_m(n)$, $m = s, s+1, \ldots, k$ in the following particular way.

Proposition 8. *For* $k = 0, 1, 2, \ldots$ *and* $r = 0, \ldots, k$, *we have*

$$T_{k-r}^k(n) = (-1)^r \binom{k}{r} \sum_{s=0}^{r} \binom{r}{s}(-1)^s T_{k-s}(n).$$

Proof. If $r = 0$, the statement is obvious.

Assume the statement is true for $r = i$, i.e.,

$$T_{k-i}^k(n) = (-1)^i \binom{k}{i} \sum_{s=0}^{i} \binom{i}{s}(-1)^s T_{k-s}(n). \tag{19}$$

Using $s = k - (i+1)$ in the relation (9), we obtain

$$(i+1)T_{k-(i+1)}^k(n) + (k-i)T_{k-i}^k(n) = kT_{k-1-i}^{k-1}(n).$$

Combining this relation with the induction hypothesis (19), we get

$$T_{k-(i+1)}^k(n) = -\frac{k-i}{i+1}\binom{k}{i}(-1)^i \sum_{s=0}^{i}\binom{i}{s}(-1)^s T_{k-s}(n)$$

$$+ \frac{k}{i+1}\binom{k-1}{i}(-1)^i \sum_{s=0}^{i}\binom{i}{s}(-1)^s T_{k-1-s}(n)$$

$$= (-1)^{i+1}\binom{k}{i+1}\left[\binom{i}{0}T_k(n) + \binom{i}{i}(-1)^{i+1}T_{k-(i+1)}(n)\right]$$

$$+ (-1)^{i+1}\binom{k}{i+1}\left[\sum_{s=1}^{i}\left(\binom{i}{s} + \binom{i}{s-1}\right)(-1)^s T_{k-s}(n)\right]$$

$$= (-1)^{i+1}\binom{k}{i+1}\sum_{s=0}^{i+1}(-1)^s\binom{i+1}{s}T_{k-s}(n).$$

That is, the statement also holds for $r = i + 1$. Hence, by induction, the result is achieved. $\quad\square$

Remark 5. For the case $r = k$, the equality of Proposition 8 is equivalent to

$$T_0^k(n) = \sum_{s=0}^{k}(-1)^s \binom{k}{s} \mathcal{T}_s(n), \tag{20}$$

showing that the sequence $\left(T_0^k(n)\right)_{k\geq 0}$, formed by the elements of the first column of the triangle $\mathcal{T}(n)$ is the binomial transform of the main diagonal sequence $(\mathcal{T}_k(n))_{k\geq 0}$. For completeness, we mention also the corresponding inverse binomial transform given by

$$\mathcal{T}_k(n) = \sum_{s=0}^{k}(-1)^s \binom{k}{s} T_0^s(n).$$

The binomial transform (20) in some sense completes another relation between both partial sequences of entries of $\mathcal{T}(n)$, namely Proposition 5, where one element of the main diagonal is expressed as a difference of two elements of the first column.

The next property is of another type and could be considered as an intrinsic property of $\mathcal{T}_k(n)$. The proof relies on both, Proposition 5 and relation (20).

Proposition 9. *For $k = 0, 1, 2, \ldots$*

$$\sum_{s=0}^{k}(-1)^s \binom{k+1}{s} \mathcal{T}_{s+1}(n) = \begin{cases} 2\mathcal{T}_{k+2}(n), & \text{if } k \text{ is even,} \\ 0, & \text{if } k \text{ is odd.} \end{cases}$$

Proof. Observe that

$$\sum_{s=0}^{k}(-1)^s \binom{k+1}{s} \mathcal{T}_{s+1}(n) = \sum_{s=0}^{k}(-1)^s \left(\binom{k+2}{s+1} - \binom{k+1}{s+1}\right) \mathcal{T}_{s+1}(n)$$

$$= \sum_{s=1}^{k+1}(-1)^{s-1} \binom{k+2}{s} \mathcal{T}_s(n) + \sum_{s=1}^{k+1}(-1)^s \binom{k+1}{s} \mathcal{T}_s(n)$$

$$= -\sum_{s=0}^{k+2}(-1)^s \binom{k+2}{s} \mathcal{T}_s(n) + \mathcal{T}_0(n) + (-1)^{k+2}\mathcal{T}_{k+2}(n)$$

$$+ \sum_{s=0}^{k+1}(-1)^{s-1} \binom{k+1}{s} \mathcal{T}_s(n) - \mathcal{T}_0(n).$$

Combining this with (20) we obtain

$$\sum_{s=0}^{k}(-1)^s \binom{k+1}{s} \mathcal{T}_{s+1}(n) = -T_0^{k+2} + (-1)^{k+2}\mathcal{T}_{k+2}(n) + T_0^{k+1}.$$

Finally, the use of Proposition 5 allows to write

$$\sum_{s=0}^{k}(-1)^s \binom{k+1}{s} \mathcal{T}_{s+1}(n) = (1 + (-1)^k)\mathcal{T}_{k+2}(n)$$

and the result is proved. $\square$

Proposition 10. *For any integer* $n \geq 2$, $\mathcal{T}_k(n)$ *is a positive decreasing sequence convergent to zero.*

Proof. From (7), we obtain

$$\mathcal{T}_{k+1}(n) = \frac{2k+n-1}{2k+2n}\mathcal{T}_k(n) < \mathcal{T}_k(n)$$

and

$$\mathcal{T}_k(n) = \frac{\Gamma(n)}{\Gamma(\frac{n-1}{2})} \frac{\Gamma(k+\frac{n-1}{2})}{\Gamma(k+n)} \xrightarrow[k\to\infty]{} 0.$$

$\square$

Let $(D_k(n))_{k\geq 0}$ be the sequence consisting of alternating partial sums of the main diagonal elements, i.e.

$$D_k(n) := \sum_{s=0}^{k}(-1)^s \mathcal{T}_s(n).$$

Proposition 11. *The sequence* $(D_k(n))_{k\geq 0}$, *satisfies the recurrence relation*

$$(n+1)D_{k+1}(n) - 2(k+n+1)D_{k+2}(n) + (2k+n+1)D_k(n) = 0$$

with initial conditions

$$D_0(n) = 1; \quad D_1(n) = \frac{n+1}{2n}.$$

Proof. First we note that, for each $n \in \mathbb{N}$,

$$(-1)^k \mathcal{T}_{k+1}(n) = D_k(n) - D_{k+1}(n) \tag{21}$$

and

$$D_{k+2}(n) = D_k(n) + (-1)^{k+1}\mathcal{T}_{k+1}(n) + (-1)^{k+2}\mathcal{T}_{k+2}(n). \tag{22}$$

Applying (21) and (7) to (22), we obtain

$$D_{k+2}(n) = D_{k+1}(n) + \frac{n+2k+1}{2(n+k+1)}(D_k(n) - D_{k+1}(n)),$$

which leads to the result. $\square$

The first elements of the sequences $(D_k(n))_{k\geq 0}$, for some values of n, are shown in Fig. 3.

n	$D_k(n)$
2	$1, \frac{3}{4}, \frac{7}{8}, \frac{51}{64}, \frac{109}{128}, \frac{415}{512} \cdots$
3	$1, \frac{2}{3}, \frac{5}{6}, \frac{11}{15}, \frac{4}{5}, \frac{79}{105} \cdots$
4	$1, \frac{5}{8}, \frac{13}{16}, \frac{45}{64}, \frac{99}{128}, \frac{1485}{2048} \cdots$
$\cdots$	$\cdots$
r	$1, \frac{r+1}{2r}, \frac{3r+1}{4r}, \frac{(r+1)(5r+7)}{8r(r+2)}, \frac{11r^2+28r+9}{16r(r+2)}, \frac{(1+r)(107+112r+21r^2)}{32r(2+r)(4+r)}, \cdots$
$\cdots$	$\cdots$
∞	$1, \frac{1}{2}, \frac{3}{4}, \frac{5}{8}, \frac{11}{16}, \frac{21}{32} \cdots$

Fig. 3. First elements of $(D_k(n))_{k\geq 0};\ n = 2, 3, 4, r, \infty.$

4   A Relation to the Sequence of Jacobsthal Numbers

In the limit case $n \to \infty$, $\mathcal{T}_k(\infty) = 2^{-k}$ and the rational numbers $D_k(\infty)$ are *weighted* terms of the Jacobsthal sequence $(J_k)_{k\geq 0}$ given explicitly by

$$0, 1, 1, 3, 5, 11, 21, 43, 85, 171, 341, \ldots$$

or generated by its Binet form

$$J_k = \frac{1}{3}\left(2^k - (-1)^k\right), \quad k = 0, 1, 2, \ldots$$

(cf. [10, page 447]). Next result shows the relation between $D_k(\infty)$ and the sequence of Jacobsthal numbers.

Proposition 12. *Consider the Jacobsthal sequence* $(J_k)_{k\geq 0}$. *Then*

$$D_k(\infty) = \frac{1}{2^k} J_{k+1}, \quad k = 0, 1, 2, \ldots.$$

Proof. The result follows by observing that

$$D_k(\infty) = \sum_{s=0}^{k}(-1)^s \mathcal{T}_s(\infty) = \sum_{s=0}^{k}(-2)^{-s}$$

$$= \frac{2}{3}\left(1 - (-2)^{-(k+1)}\right) = \frac{1}{2^k}\frac{1}{3}\left(2^{k+1} - (-1)^{k+1}\right)$$

$$= \frac{1}{2^k} J_{k+1}, \quad k = 0, 1, 2, \ldots.$$

$\square$

Considering Proposition 12, the recurrence satisfied by the Jacobsthal sequence,

$$J_k = J_{k-1} + 2J_{k-2}, \quad k = 2, 3, \ldots$$
$$J_0 = 0; \quad J_1 = 1,$$

is transformed into a simple recurrence of order 2 with constant coefficients for the elements $D_k(\infty)$. Indeed, it holds

$$D_k(\infty) = \frac{1}{2}\left(D_{k-1}(\infty) + D_{k-2}(\infty)\right), \quad k = 2, 3, \ldots$$
$$D_0(\infty) = 1; \quad D_1(\infty) = \frac{1}{2}.$$

Acknowledgement. This work was supported by Portuguese funds through the CMAT – Research Centre of Mathematics of University of Minho – and through the CIDMA – Center of Research and Development in Mathematics and Applications (University of Aveiro) – and the Portuguese Foundation for Science and Technology ("FCT – Fundação para a Ciência e Tecnologia"), within projects UIDB/00013/2020, UIDP/00013/2020, UIDB/04106/2020, and UIDP/04106/2020.

References

1. Askey, R.: Vietoris's inequalities and hypergeometric series. In: Milovanović, G.V. (ed.) Recent Progress in Inequalities, pp. 63–76. Kluwer Academic Publishers, Dordrecht (1998)
2. Boros, C., Moll, V.: Irresistible Integrals: Symbolics. Analysis and Experiments in the Evaluation of Integrals. Cambridge University Press, Cambridge, England (2004)
3. Cação, I., Falcão, M.I., Malonek, H.R.: Hypercomplex polynomials, Vietoris' rational numbers and a related integer numbers sequence. Complex Anal. Oper. Theory **11**, 1059–1076 (2017)
4. Cação, I., Falcão, M.I., Malonek, H.R.: On generalized Vietoris' number sequences. Discrete App. Math. **269**, 77–85 (2019)
5. Cação, I., Falcão, M.I., Malonek, H.R., Tomaz, G.: Some remarkable combinatorial relations based on methods of hypercomplex function theory. In: Simsek, Y., et al. (eds.) Proceedings Book of the 2nd Mediterranean International Conference of Pure & Applied Mathematics and Related Areas (MICOPAM2019), pp. 72–77. Université d'Evry/Université Paris-Saclay, Evry, Paris (2019)
6. Delanghe, R., Sommen, F., Souček, V.: Clifford Algebra and Spinor-Valued Functions: A Function Theory for the Dirac Operator. Mathematics and its Applications, vol. 53, Kluwer Academic Publishers, Dordrecht (1992)
7. Falcão, M.I., Cruz, J., Malonek, H.R.: Remarks on the generation of monogenic functions. In: 17th International Conference on the Appl. of Computer Science and Mathematics on Architecture and Civil Engineering. Weimar (2006)
8. Falcão, M.I., Malonek, H.R.: A note on a one-parameter family of non-symmetric number triangles. Opuscula Math. **32**(4), 661–673 (2012)
9. Gürlebeck, K., Habetha, K., Sprößig, W.: Application of Holomorphic Functions in Two or Higher Dimensions. Birkhäuser Verlag, Basel (2016)

10. Koshy, T.: Fibonacci and Lucas Numbers with Applications, Volume 2 (Pure and Applied Mathematics: A Wiley Series of Texts, Monographs, and Tracts). Wiley, USA (2019)
11. Malonek, H.R., Cação, I., Falcão, M.I., Tomaz, G.: Harmonic analysis and hyper-complex function theory in co-dimension one. In: Karapetyants, A., Kravchenko, V., Liflyand, E. (eds.) OTHA 2018. SPMS, vol. 291, pp. 93–115. Springer, Cham (2019). https://doi.org/10.1007/978-3-030-26748-3_7
12. Ruscheweyh, S., Salinas, L.: Stable functions and Vietoris' theorem. J. Math. Anal. Appl. **291**, 596–604 (2004)
13. Stanley, R.P.: Catalan Numbers. Cambridge University Press, USA (2015)
14. Vietoris, L.: Über das Vorzeichen gewisser trigonometrischer Summen. Sitzungsber. Österr. Akad. Wiss. **167**, 125–135 (1958). (in German)

A Sixth-Order CEV Option Valuation Algorithm on Non-uniform Spatial Grids

Nawdha Thakoor[✉][iD]

Department of Mathematics, University of Mauritius, Moka, Mauritius
n.thakoor@uom.ac.mu

Abstract. Due to its ability to fit skew implied volatility profiles of market option prices, the constant elasticity of variance (CEV) model overcomes a short-coming of the constant volatility assumption used by the Black-Scholes lognormal model. Although the CEV model has an analytical formula for European options, the presence of the non-central Chi-square distribution in the formula brings instability in the computation of European option prices for certain parameter ranges. For efficient valuation of the option prices for all realistic option parameters, a sixth-order finite difference method is proposed in this work. The computational procedure employs a seven-point discretisation of the space derivatives on non-uniform grids together with a mesh-refinement technique around the option's strike price. This new technique is very fast and is shown to achieve sixth-order numerical convergence ratios. The stability of the finite difference method is demonstrated through its capability to generate accurate prices for strongly negative elasticity factors. The numerical method is thus a superior technique to existing methods for numerical computations of CEV option prices.

Keywords: Option valuation · Constant elasticity of variance model · Finite difference algorithm · Non-uniform grids

1 Introduction

Implied volatilities of market option prices across strike prices are not consistent with the assumption of constant volatility in the lognormal dynamics of stock prices. In the CEV model, the constant volatility in the geometric Brownian motion is replaced by a deterministic price-dependent volatility function and the discounted expected payoff of a European style option under the risk-neutral CEV density results in a pricing formula which is in terms of complementary non-central shi-square distribution. When the elasticity parameter in the CEV model is close to a value of one, the computation of option prices becomes very slow [16]. Many authors have considered the efficient computation of the CEV option pricing formula and a comparison of different methods is given in [7].

An alternative to the use of analytical techniques is the computation of option prices by finite difference methods. A fourth-order compact scheme for European options is described in [12] and the methodology of high-order compact discretisation has been

O. Gervasi et al. (Eds.): ICCSA 2022 Workshops, LNCS 13377, pp. 435–449, 2022.
https://doi.org/10.1007/978-3-031-10536-4_29

extended to the pricing of different types of barrier options under the CEV dynamics in [13]. An accurate and fast algorithm for CEV American options is described in [14] and localised radial basis functions finite difference (RBF-FD) methods are considered for the pricing of both European and American options in [15]. All these numerical schemes are implicit finite difference methods on uniform grids.

This work proposes a different approach based on explicit finite difference discretisations on non-uniform grids. The method is designed to give significant increases in accuracy over an existing fourth-order accurate method [12] since it achieves sixth-order accuracy, which is two-orders of accuracy higher. The significant gain in accuracy is obtained by employing a non-uniform mesh with grid stretching at the strike price of the European option. The finite difference approximations of the space derivatives in the pricing equations are obtained by interpolation on the non-uniform grid. Analytical formulas for determinants of Vandermonde matrices lead to analytical expressions for the coefficients for approximating the first and second space derivatives. An exponential time stepping scheme [13] leads to fast convergence in time.

Numerical results confirm the sixth-order convergence for options under the Constant Elasticity of Variance (CEV) model. An advantage is that the numerical method remains stable for highly negative values for the parameter of elasticity. This is an important property of the new technique since it is known that, in such cases, low-order computational methods yield inaccurate prices for negative values of the elasticity parameter.

An outline of this work is as follows. The CEV dynamics and the option pricing equation is described in Sect. 2 and explicit finite differences for approximations of the space derivatives in the equation are derived in Sect. 3.

2   The CEV Option Pricing Model

Under the CEV model [2], the stock price dynamics S_t at time $t \geq 0$ follows the stochastic differential equation

$$dS_t = rS_t \, dt + \delta S_t^\beta \, dW_t^{\mathbb{Q}}, \tag{1}$$

where β represents the elasticity parameter for the instantaneous local volatility function $\tilde{\sigma}(S) = \delta S^{\beta-1}$ with δ being a positive scale parameter, r is the expected instantaneous return of the stock and W_t, $t \geq 0$ is the standard Brownian motion under $\mathbb{Q}$, the risk-neutral probability measure.

When β is negative, the model (1) produces implied volatility surfaces which are similar to those observed in index options and empirical observations [6] showed that β can become as low as -3 in markets for index options.

The CEV model nests several well-known models as special cases. When $\beta = 1$, the problem reduces to the Black-Scholes model while for $\beta = 1/2$, we obtain the square root diffusion model. Closed form expression for $\beta < 1$ for a European put option with stock price S having maturity T years and strike E are given by

$$V^{\text{exact}} = Ee^{-rT}[1 - \chi^2(d, c, b)] - S\chi^2(b, c+2, d), \tag{2}$$

where

$$b = \frac{[Ee^{-rT}]^{2(1-\beta)}}{(1-\beta)^2 f}, \quad c = \frac{1}{1-\beta}, \quad d = \frac{S^{2(1-\beta)}}{(1-\beta^2)f}, \quad f = \frac{\delta^2[e^{2r(\beta-1)T} - 1]}{2r(\beta-1)},$$

and $\chi^2(z, k, l)$ represents the cumulative distribution function (cdf) of a non-central chi-squared random distribution with $k \in \mathbb{N}$ degrees of freedom and $l > 0$ is the non-centrality parameter. It is well know that the evaluation of the non-central χ^2 distribution can become slow as β approaches one, for low volatility problems or small time to maturity and this motivates the use of numerical methods for such options under the CEV model. Fourth-order numerical methods on uniform grids with local mesh refinement have been proposed in [12, 13]. In this work, we propose higher-order numerical methods up to order six.

2.1 The CEV PDE

Using no-arbitrage principle, it can be shown that the European option price solves the partial differential equation

$$\frac{\partial V}{\partial t} + \frac{1}{2}\delta^2 S^{2\beta}\frac{\partial^2 V}{\partial S^2} + rS\frac{\partial V}{\partial S} - rV = 0, \quad t \in [0, T], \quad S \geq 0, \tag{3}$$

Pricing a European put option requires (3) using the terminal payoff function $V(S, T) = \max(E - S, 0)$ with left boundary condition as $V(0, t) = Ee^{-rt}$ and right boundary condition given by $V(S, t) = 0$ as $S \to +\infty$.

Let the time to maturity be denoted by $\tau = T - t$, then the European put price can be obtained by solving the problem

$$\frac{\partial V}{\partial \tau} = \frac{1}{2}\delta^2 S^{2\beta}\frac{\partial^2 V}{\partial S^2} + rS\frac{\partial V}{\partial S} - rV, \quad S \geq 0, \quad \tau \in [0, T], \tag{4}$$
$$V(S, 0) = \max(E - S, 0), \quad S \geq 0,$$
$$V(0, \tau) = Ee^{-r\tau}, \quad \tau \in [0, T],$$
$$V(S, \tau) = 0 \text{ as } S \to +\infty, \quad \tau \in [0, T].$$

3 High-Order Non-uniform Scheme

High-order approximations based on a non-uniform spatial grid is derived using the technique described in [1]

3.1 N^{th}-Order Scheme

Let M be the number of spatial grid nodes and $S_1, S_2, \ldots, S_M$ be the set of distinct non-uniformly spaced grid points. Let $D_{n_p}^{(d)}V(S_m)$ denote the n_p-point approximation for the dth derivative $V^{(d)}(S_m)$ of V at the reference node x_m for $m = 0, 1, \ldots, M$.

Suppose that we require finite difference approximations, $D_{n_p}^{(d)}[V]$, the derivatives of order $(n_p - 1)$ at a given reference node S_m in the form [1]

$$D_{n_p}^{(d)}[V] = \sum_{i=1}^{n_p} w_i V(S_m), \quad 0 \le d \le n_p - 1.$$

Using a Taylor series expansion about S_m, we have

$$V(S_m) = \sum_{j=0}^{\infty} \frac{\alpha_{m+k}^j}{j!} \frac{\partial^j V}{\partial S^j}(S_m),$$

where $\alpha_{m+k} = (S_{m+k} - S_m)$ is the displacement of any node S_{m+k} to the reference node S_m where

$$-q \le k \le q, \quad \text{with} \quad q = \left\lfloor \frac{n_p}{2} \right\rfloor.$$

Truncating the Taylor series expansion up to order $(n_p - 1)$ gives

$$D_{n_p}^{(d)}[V] = \sum_{k=-q}^{q} w_{m+k}^{(n_p, d)} \left(\sum_{j=0}^{n_p-1} \frac{\alpha_{m+k}^j}{j!} \frac{\partial^j f}{\partial S^j}(S_m) \right).$$

Since the above is a finite sum, interchanging the summations we obtain,

$$D_{n_p}^{(d)}[V] = \sum_{j=0}^{n_p-1} \left(\sum_{k=-q}^{q} w_{m+k}^{(n_p, d)} \frac{\alpha_{m+k}^j}{j!} \right) \frac{\partial^j V}{\partial S^j}(S_m).$$

For every d, $0 \le d \le n_p - 1$, we obtain n_p equations

$$\sum_{k=-q}^{q} \alpha_{m+q}^j w_{m+k}^{(n_p, d)} = j! \delta_{d,j}, \quad 0 \le j \le n_p - 1.$$

Let $\mathbf{A}$ be the Vandermonde matrix given by

$$\mathbf{A} = \begin{pmatrix} 1 & 1 & 1 & \cdots & 1 \\ \alpha_{m-q} & \alpha_{m-q+1} & \alpha_{m-q+2} & \cdots & \alpha_{m+q} \\ \alpha_{m-q}^2 & \alpha_{m-q+1}^2 & \alpha_{m-q+2}^2 & \cdots & \alpha_{m+q}^2 \\ \vdots & \vdots & \vdots & \ddots & \vdots \\ \alpha_{m-q}^{n_p-1} & \alpha_{m-q+1}^{n_p-1} & \alpha_{m-q+2}^{n_p-1} & \cdots & \alpha_{m+q}^{n_p-1} \end{pmatrix}.$$

Thus for every d, $0 \le d \le n_p - 1$, we have to solve the matrix equation

$$\mathbf{A} \mathbf{w}^{(n_p, d)} = \mathbf{b}_d,$$

where

$$\mathbf{w}^{(n_p, d)} = \left[w_{m-q}^{(n_p, d)}, w_{m-q+1}^{(n_p, d)}, \dots, w_{m+q}^{(n_p, d)} \right]^T,$$

$$\mathbf{b}_d = \left[\delta_{d,0},\ \delta_{d,1},\ 2!\delta_{d,2},\ 3!\delta_{d,3},\ \ldots,\ (n_p - 1)!\delta_{d,n_p-1} \right]^T,$$

and the Kronecker delta is defined as

$$\delta_{i,j} = \begin{cases} 1,\ i = j; \\ 0,\ i \neq j. \end{cases}$$

Since

$$\det \mathbf{A} = \prod_{1 \le i < j \le n_p} (\alpha_i - \alpha_j),$$

using Cramer's rule, we find that

$$w_{m+k}^{(n_p, d)} = \frac{-\det \begin{pmatrix} \mathbf{A} & \mathbf{b}_d \\ \mathbf{c}(k) & 0 \end{pmatrix}}{\det \mathbf{A}}, \quad -q \le k \le q,$$

where

$$\mathbf{c}(k) = \left[\delta_{m-q, m+k},\ \delta_{m-q+1, m+k},\ \cdots,\ \delta_{m, m+k},\ \delta_{m+1, m+k},\ \cdots,\ \delta_{m+q, m+k} \right].$$

Second-Order Approximations. For an $n_p = 3$-point stencil approximation centered at the reference node S_m, we can obtain second-order approximate results and we require the solution of

$$w_{m+k}^{(3,d)} = \frac{-\det \begin{pmatrix} 1 & 1 & 1 & \delta_{d,0} \\ \alpha_{m-1} & \alpha_m & \alpha_{m+1} & \delta_{d,1} \\ \alpha_{m-1}^2 & \alpha_m^2 & \alpha_{m+1}^2 & 2!\delta_{d,2} \\ \delta_{m-1, m+k} & \delta_{m, m+k} & \delta_{m+1, m+k} & 0 \end{pmatrix}}{\det \begin{pmatrix} 1 & 1 & 1 \\ \alpha_{m-1} & \alpha_m & \alpha_{m+1} \\ \alpha_{m-1}^2 & \alpha_m^2 & \alpha_{m+1}^2 \end{pmatrix}}, \quad k = -1, 0, 1.$$

The weights for the first derivative $(d = 1)$ and the second derivative $(d = 2)$ are given in the Table 1.

Table 1. Weights for $n_p = 3$ points

weights for first derivative $(d = 1)$	weights for second Derivative $(d = 2)$
$w_{m-1}^{(3,1)} = -\dfrac{\alpha_m + \alpha_{m+1}}{(\alpha_{m-1} - \alpha_m)(\alpha_{m-1} - \alpha_{m+1})}$	$w_{m-1}^{(3,2)} = \dfrac{2}{(\alpha_{m-1} - \alpha_{m+1})(\alpha_{m-1} - \alpha_m)}$
$w_m^{(3,1)} = \dfrac{\alpha_{m-1} + \alpha_{m+1}}{(\alpha_{m-1} - \alpha_m)(\alpha_m - \alpha_{m+1})}$	$w_m^{(3,2)} = \dfrac{2}{(\alpha_m - \alpha_{m+1})(\alpha_m - \alpha_{m-1})}$
$w_{m+1}^{(3,1)} = \dfrac{\alpha_{m-1} + \alpha_m}{(\alpha_{m-1} - \alpha_{m+1})(\alpha_{m+1} - \alpha_m)}$	$w_{m+1}^{(3,2)} = \dfrac{2}{(\alpha_{m+1} - \alpha_m)(\alpha_{m+1} - \alpha_{m-1})}$

The matrices for the derivatives of order one and two for $D_{n_p}^{(d)}[V]$ are then constructed as

$$
D_3^{(1)} = \begin{pmatrix} \tilde{\omega}_{1+}^{(3,\,1)} & \tilde{\omega}_{2+}^{(3,\,1)} & \tilde{\omega}_{3+}^{(3,\,1)} & & & \\ w_0^{(3,\,1)} & w_1^{(3,\,1)} & w_2^{(3,\,1)} & & & \\ & \ddots & \ddots & \ddots & & \\ & & w_{M-2}^{(3,\,1)} & w_{M-1}^{(3,\,1)} & w_M^{(3,\,1)} \\ & & \tilde{\omega}_{-3}^{(3,\,1)} & \tilde{\omega}_2^{(3,\,1)} & \tilde{\omega}_{-1}^{(3,\,1)} \end{pmatrix}, \quad D_3^{(2)} = \begin{pmatrix} \tilde{\omega}_{1+}^{(3,\,2)} & \tilde{\omega}_{2+}^{(3,\,2)} & \tilde{\omega}_{3+}^{(3,\,2)} & \tilde{\omega}_{4+}^{(3,\,2)} & & \\ w_0^{(3,\,2)} & w_1^{(3,\,2)} & w_2^{(3,\,2)} & & & \\ & \ddots & \ddots & \ddots & & \\ & & w_{M-2}^{(3,\,2)} & w_{M-1}^{(3,\,2)} & w_M^{(3,\,2)} \\ & \tilde{\omega}_{-4}^{(3,\,2)} & \tilde{\omega}_{-3}^{(3,\,2)} & \tilde{\omega}_{-2}^{(3,\,2)} & \tilde{\omega}_{-1}^{(3,\,2)} \end{pmatrix}. \quad (5)
$$

Note that at the left boundary S_0, instead of using central approximations, we use one-sided approximations and we expand at the reference node S_0 where $\alpha_i = S_i - S_0$, $i = 0, 1, 2$, which gives

$$
\left[\tilde{\omega}_{1+}^{(3,\,1)}, \, \tilde{\omega}_{2+}^{(3,\,1)}, \, \tilde{\omega}_{3+}^{(3,\,1)} \right] = \left[\frac{\alpha_2 - \alpha_1}{\alpha_1 \alpha_2}, \, \frac{\alpha_2}{\alpha_1 (\alpha_2 - \alpha_1)}, \, \frac{\alpha_1}{\alpha_2 (\alpha_1 - \alpha_2)} \right].
$$

Similarly at the right boundary, we approximate at the reference node S_M where $\alpha_i = S_i - S_M$, $i = M - 2, M - 1, M$, with $\alpha_M = 0$, which gives

$$
\left[\tilde{\omega}_{-3}^{(3,\,1)}, \, \tilde{\omega}_{-2}^{(3,\,1)}, \, \tilde{\omega}_{-1}^{(3,\,1)} \right] = \left[-\frac{\alpha_{M-1}}{\alpha_{M-2}(\alpha_{M-2}\alpha_{M-1})}, \, \frac{\alpha_{M-2} - \alpha_{M-1}}{\alpha_{M-1}(\alpha_{M-1}\alpha_{M-2})}, \, -\frac{\alpha_{M-2} + \alpha_{M-1}}{\alpha_{M-2}\alpha_{M-1}} \right].
$$

The same procedure with 4 points instead of 3, is adopted for weights corresponding to the second derivatives and the one-sided coefficients at the nodes S_0 and S_M are given by

$$
\left[\tilde{\omega}_{1+}^{(3,\,2)}, \, \tilde{\omega}_{2+}^{(3,\,2)}, \, \tilde{\omega}_{3+}^{(3,\,2)}, \, \tilde{\omega}_{4+}^{(3,\,2)} \right] =
$$
$$
\left[\frac{2(\alpha_1 + \alpha_2 + \alpha_3)}{\alpha_1 \alpha_2 \alpha_3}, \, \frac{-2(\alpha_2 + \alpha_3)}{\alpha_1(\alpha_1 - \alpha_3)(\alpha_1 - \alpha_2)}, \, \frac{-2(\alpha_1 + \alpha_3)}{\alpha_2(\alpha_2 - \alpha_3)(\alpha_2 - \alpha_1)}, \, \frac{-2(\alpha_1 + \alpha_2)}{\alpha_3(\alpha_3 - \alpha_1)(\alpha_3 - \alpha_2)}, \right]
$$

and

$$
\tilde{\omega}_{-4}^{(3,\,2)} = \frac{-2(\alpha_{M-2} + \alpha_{M-1})}{\alpha_{M-3}(\alpha_{M-3} - \alpha_{M-2})(\alpha_{M-3} - \alpha_{M-1})}, \quad \tilde{\omega}_{-3}^{(3,\,2)} = \frac{-2(\alpha_{M-3} + \alpha_{M-1})}{\alpha_{M-2}(\alpha_{M-2} - \alpha_{M-3})(\alpha_{M-2} - \alpha_{M-1})}
$$

$$
\tilde{\omega}_{-2}^{(3,\,2)} = \frac{-2(\alpha_{M-3} + \alpha_{M-2})}{\alpha_{M-1}(\alpha_{M-1} - \alpha_{M-3})(\alpha_{M-1} - \alpha_{M-2})}, \quad \tilde{\omega}_{-1}^{(3,\,2)} = \frac{2(\alpha_{M-3} + \alpha_{M-2} + \alpha_{M-1})}{\alpha_{M-3}\alpha_{M-2}\alpha_{M-1}}.
$$

Fourth-Order Approximations. With an $n_p = 5$-point stencil approximation centered at the reference node S_m and taking a fourth-order Taylor series expansion of V gives the approximation for the dth derivative as

$$
D_5^{(d)}[V] = \sum_{k=-2}^{2} \left(w_{m+k}^{(5,\,d)} \left(\sum_{j=0}^{\infty} \frac{\alpha_{m+k}^j}{j!} \frac{\partial^j V}{\partial S^j}(S_m) \right) \right).
$$

The weights are then obtained by solving

$$
w_{m+k}^{(5,d)} = \frac{-\det \begin{pmatrix}
1 & 1 & 1 & 1 & 1 & \delta_{d,0} \\
\alpha_{m-2} & \alpha_{m-1} & \alpha_m & \alpha_{m+1} & \alpha_{m+2} & \delta_{d,1} \\
\alpha_{m-2}^2 & \alpha_{m-1}^2 & \alpha_m^2 & \alpha_{m+1}^2 & \alpha_{m+2}^2 & 2!\delta_{d,2} \\
\alpha_{m-2}^3 & \alpha_{m-1}^3 & \alpha_m^3 & \alpha_{m+1}^3 & \alpha_{m+2}^3 & 3!\delta_{d,3} \\
\alpha_{m-2}^4 & \alpha_{m-1}^4 & \alpha_m^4 & \alpha_{m+1}^4 & \alpha_{m+2}^4 & 4!\delta_{d,4} \\
\delta_{m-2,\,m+k} & \delta_{m-1,\,m+k} & \delta_{m,\,m+k} & \delta_{m+1,\,m+k} & \delta_{m+2,\,m+k} & 0
\end{pmatrix}}{|\mathbf{A}_5|},
$$

for $k = -2, -1, 0, 1, 2$, where $|\mathbf{A}_5|$ is the determinant of the toeplitz matrix corresponding to $n_p = 5$ points. The weights for the first derivative are then given by

$$
w_{m-2}^{(5,1)} = -\frac{\alpha_m\alpha_{m+1}\alpha_{m+2} + \alpha_{m-1}\left(\alpha_{m+1}\alpha_{m+2} + \alpha_m\left(\alpha_{m+1} + \alpha_{m+2}\right)\right)}{\left(\alpha_{m-2} - \alpha_{m-1}\right)\left(\alpha_{m-2} - \alpha_m\right)\left(\alpha_{m-2} - \alpha_{m+1}\right)\left(\alpha_{m-2} - \alpha_{m+2}\right)},
$$

$$
w_{m-1}^{(5,1)} = \frac{\alpha_m\alpha_{m+1}\alpha_{m+2} + \alpha_{m-2}\left(\alpha_{m+1}\alpha_{m+2} + \alpha_m\left(\alpha_{m+1} + \alpha_{m+2}\right)\right)}{\left(\alpha_{m-2} - \alpha_{m-1}\right)\left(\alpha_{m-1} - \alpha_m\right)\left(\alpha_{m-1} - \alpha_{m+1}\right)\left(\alpha_{m-1} - \alpha_{m+2}\right)},
$$

$$
w_m^{(5,1)} = \frac{\alpha_{m-1}\alpha_{m+1}\alpha_{m+2} + \alpha_{m-2}\left(\alpha_{m+1}\alpha_{m+2} + \alpha_{m-1}\left(\alpha_{m+1} + \alpha_{m+2}\right)\right)}{\left(\alpha_{m-2} - \alpha_m\right)\left(\alpha_m - \alpha_{m-1}\right)\left(\alpha_m - \alpha_{m+1}\right)\left(\alpha_m - \alpha_{m+2}\right)}
$$

$$
w_{m+1}^{(5,1)} = \frac{\alpha_{m-1}\alpha_m\alpha_{m+2} + \alpha_{m-2}\left(\alpha_m\alpha_{m+2} + \alpha_{m-1}\left(\alpha_m + \alpha_{m+2}\right)\right)}{\left(\alpha_{m-2} - \alpha_{m+1}\right)\left(\alpha_{m+1} - \alpha_{m-1}\right)\left(\alpha_{m+1} - \alpha_m\right)\left(\alpha_{m+1} - \alpha_{m+2}\right)},
$$

$$
w_{m+2}^{(5,1)} = \frac{\alpha_{m-1}\alpha_m\alpha_{m+1} + \alpha_{m-2}\left(\alpha_m\alpha_{m+1} + \alpha_{m-1}\left(\alpha_m + \alpha_{m+1}\right)\right)}{\left(\alpha_{m-2} - \alpha_{m+2}\right)\left(\alpha_{m+2} - \alpha_{m-1}\right)\left(\alpha_{m+2} - \alpha_m\right)\left(\alpha_{m+2} - \alpha_{m+1}\right)},
$$

and those for the second derivatives are given by

$$
w_{m-2}^{(5,2)} = \frac{2\left(\alpha_{m+1}\alpha_{m+2} + \alpha_m\left(\alpha_{m+1} + \alpha_{m+2}\right) + \alpha_{m-1}\left(\alpha_m + \alpha_{m+1} + \alpha_{m+2}\right)\right)}{\left(\alpha_{m-2} - \alpha_{m-1}\right)\left(\alpha_{m-2} - \alpha_m\right)\left(\alpha_{m-2} - \alpha_{m+1}\right)\left(\alpha_{m-2} - \alpha_{m+2}\right)},
$$

$$
w_{m-1}^{(5,2)} = \frac{2\left(\alpha_{m+1}\alpha_{m+2} + \alpha_m\left(\alpha_{m+1} + \alpha_{m+2}\right) + \alpha_{m-2}\left(\alpha_m + \alpha_{m+1} + \alpha_{m+2}\right)\right)}{\left(\alpha_{m-1} - \alpha_{m-2}\right)\left(\alpha_{m-1} - \alpha_m\right)\left(\alpha_{m-1} - \alpha_{m+2}\right)\left(\alpha_{m-1} - \alpha_{m+1}\right)},
$$

$$
w_m^{(5,2)} = -\frac{2\left(\alpha_{m+1}\alpha_{m+2} + \alpha_{m-1}\left(\alpha_{m+1} + \alpha_{m+2}\right) + \alpha_{m-2}\left(\alpha_{m-1} + \alpha_{m+1} + \alpha_{m+2}\right)\right)}{\left(\alpha_{m-2} - \alpha_m\right)\left(\alpha_m - \alpha_{m-1}\right)\left(\alpha_m - \alpha_{m+1}\right)\left(\alpha_m - \alpha_{m+2}\right)},
$$

$$
w_{m+1}^{(5,2)} = -\frac{2\left(\alpha_m\alpha_{m+2} + \alpha_{m-1}\left(\alpha_m + \alpha_{m+2}\right) + \alpha_{m-2}\left(\alpha_{m-1} + \alpha_m + \alpha_{m+2}\right)\right)}{\left(\alpha_{m-2} - \alpha_{m+1}\right)\left(\alpha_{m+1} - \alpha_{m-1}\right)\left(\alpha_{m+1} - \alpha_m\right)\left(\alpha_{m+1} - \alpha_{m+2}\right)},
$$

$$
w_{m+2}^{(5,2)} = -\frac{2\left(\alpha_m\alpha_{m+1} + \alpha_{m-1}\left(\alpha_m + \alpha_{m+1}\right) + \alpha_{m-2}\left(\alpha_{m-1} + \alpha_m + \alpha_{m+1}\right)\right)}{\left(\alpha_{m-2} - \alpha_{m+2}\right)\left(\alpha_{m+2} - \alpha_{m-1}\right)\left(\alpha_{m+2} - \alpha_m\right)\left(\alpha_{m+2} - \alpha_{m+1}\right)}.
$$

The derivatives matrices for $D_{n_p}^{(d)}[V]$ using the 5-point stencil are then constructed as in (5) in the form

$$
D_5^{(1)} = \operatorname{diag}\left[w_{m-2}^{(3,1)}, \, w_{m-1}^{(3,1)}, \, w_m^{(3,1)}, \, w_{m+1}^{(3,1)}, \, w_{m+2}^{(3,1)}\right],
$$

$$
D_5^{(2)} = \operatorname{diag}\left[w_{m-2}^{(3,1)}, \, w_{m-1}^{(3,2)}, \, w_m^{(3,2)}, \, w_{m+1}^{(3,2)}, \, w_{m+2}^{(3,2)}\right],
$$

for $2 \leq m \leq M - 2$ and $D_5^{(d)} \in \mathbb{R}^{(M+1)\times(M+1)}$.

For the 5-point scheme, one sided approximations are required at left ends S_0, S_1 and the right ends S_{M-1}, S_M of the computational domain. The coefficients can be determined using a similar way as above using the displacements $\alpha_i = S_i - S_j$ for $j = 0, 1, M - 2, M - 1$. For instance, for the first row of $D_5^{(1)}$ which corresponds to grid node S_0, the displacements is given by

$$\{\alpha_0, \alpha_1, \alpha_2, \alpha_3, \alpha_4\} = \{0, S_1 - S_0, S_2 - S_0, S_3 - S_0, S_4 - S_0\},$$

and the weights are calculated accordingly. Similarly the entries of the second row of $D_5^{(1)}$ evaluated at S_1 are obtained by calculating the weights corresponding to the displacements

$$\{\alpha_0, \alpha_1, \alpha_2, \alpha_3, \alpha_4\} = \{S_0 - S_1, 0, S_2 - S_1, S_3 - S_1, S_4 - S_1\}.$$

The one-sided approximations for the 5-point second derivative matrix is calculated in a similar way.

Sixth-Order Approximations. To obtain sixth order approximations, we use an $n_p = 7$-point stencil approximation centered at the reference node S_m and proceeding in the same way we obtain the weights for the first derivative as

$$w_{m-3}^{(7,1)} = -\frac{\begin{array}{c}\alpha_{m-1}\alpha_m\alpha_{m+1}\alpha_{m+2}\alpha_{m+3} + \alpha_{m-2}(\alpha_m\alpha_{m+1}\alpha_{m+2}\alpha_{m+3} \\ + \alpha_{m-1}(\alpha_{m+1}\alpha_{m+2}\alpha_{m+3} + \alpha_m(\alpha_{m+2}\alpha_{m+3} + \alpha_{m+1}(\alpha_{m+3} + \alpha_{m+2}))))\end{array}}{\begin{array}{c}(\alpha_{m-3} - \alpha_{m-2})(\alpha_{m-3} - \alpha_{m-1})(\alpha_{m-3} - \alpha_m) \\ (\alpha_{m-3} - \alpha_{m+1})(\alpha_{m-3} - \alpha_{m+3})(\alpha_{m-3} - \alpha_{m+2})\end{array}},$$

$$w_{m-2}^{(7,1)} = \frac{\begin{array}{c}\alpha_{m-1}\alpha_m\alpha_{m+1}\alpha_{m+2}\alpha_{m+3} + \alpha_{m-3}(\alpha_m\alpha_{m+1}\alpha_{m+2}\alpha_{m+3} \\ + \alpha_{m-1}(\alpha_{m+1}\alpha_{m+2}\alpha_{m+3} + \alpha_m(\alpha_{m+2}\alpha_{m+3} + \alpha_{m+1}(\alpha_{m+3} + \alpha_{m+2}))))\end{array}}{\begin{array}{c}(\alpha_{m-3} - \alpha_{m-2})(\alpha_{m-2} - \alpha_{m-1})(\alpha_{m-2} - \alpha_m) \\ (\alpha_{m-2} - \alpha_{m+2})(\alpha_{m-2} - \alpha_{m+1})(\alpha_{m-2} - \alpha_{m+3})\end{array}},$$

$$w_{m-1}^{(7,1)} = -\frac{\begin{array}{c}\alpha_{m-2}\alpha_m\alpha_{m+1}\alpha_{m+2}\alpha_{m+3} + \alpha_{m-3}(\alpha_m\alpha_{m+1}\alpha_{m+2}\alpha_{m+3} \\ + \alpha_{m-2}(\alpha_{m+1}\alpha_{m+2}\alpha_{m+3} + \alpha_m(\alpha_{m+2}\alpha_{m+3} + \alpha_{m+1}(\alpha_{m+2} + \alpha_{m+3}))))\end{array}}{\begin{array}{c}(\alpha_{m-1} - \alpha_{m-2})(\alpha_{m-1} - \alpha_{m-3})(\alpha_{m-1} - \alpha_m) \\ (\alpha_{m-1} - \alpha_{m+1})(\alpha_{m-1} - \alpha_{m+3})(\alpha_{m-1} - \alpha_{m+2})\end{array}},$$

$$w_m^{(7,1)} = \frac{\begin{array}{c}\alpha_{m-2}\alpha_{m-1}\alpha_{m+1}\alpha_{m+2}\alpha_{m+3} + \alpha_{m-3}(\alpha_{m-1}\alpha_{m+1}\alpha_{m+2}\alpha_{m+3} \\ + \alpha_{m-2}(\alpha_{m+1}\alpha_{m+2}\alpha_{m+3} + \alpha_{m-1}(\alpha_{m+2}\alpha_{m+3} + \alpha_{m+1}(\alpha_{m+3} + \alpha_{m+2}))))\end{array}}{\begin{array}{c}(\alpha_m - \alpha_{m+1})(\alpha_{m-3} - \alpha_m)(\alpha_m - \alpha_{m-2})(\alpha_m - \alpha_{m+3}) \\ (\alpha_m - \alpha_{m+2})(\alpha_m - \alpha_{m-1})\end{array}},$$

$$w_{m+1}^{(7,1)} = \frac{\begin{array}{c}\alpha_{m-2}\alpha_{m-1}\alpha_m\alpha_{m+2}\alpha_{m+3} + \alpha_{m-3}(\alpha_{m-1}\alpha_m\alpha_{m+2}\alpha_{m+3} \\ + \alpha_{m-2}(\alpha_m\alpha_{m+2}\alpha_{m+3} + \alpha_{m-1}(\alpha_{m+2}\alpha_{m+3} + \alpha_m(\alpha_{m+2} + \alpha_{m+3}))))\end{array}}{\begin{array}{c}(\alpha_{m-3} - \alpha_{m+1})(\alpha_{m+1} - \alpha_{m-2})(\alpha_{m+1} - \alpha_{m-1}) \\ (\alpha_{m+1} - \alpha_m)(\alpha_{m+1} - \alpha_{m+3})(\alpha_{m+1} - \alpha_{m+2})\end{array}},$$

$$w_{m+2}^{(7,1)} = \frac{\begin{array}{c}\alpha_{m-2}\alpha_{m-1}\alpha_m\alpha_{m+1}\alpha_{m+3} + \alpha_{m-3}(\alpha_{m-1}\alpha_m\alpha_{m+1}\alpha_{m+3} \\ + \alpha_{m-2}(\alpha_m\alpha_{m+1}\alpha_{m+3} + \alpha_{m-1}(\alpha_{m+1}\alpha_{m+3} + \alpha_m(\alpha_{m+1} + \alpha_{m+3}))))\end{array}}{\begin{array}{c}(\alpha_{m+2} - \alpha_m)(\alpha_{m+2} - \alpha_{m-2})(\alpha_{m+2} - \alpha_{m-1}) \\ (\alpha_{m-3} - \alpha_{m+2})(\alpha_{m+2} - \alpha_{m+1})(\alpha_{m+2} - \alpha_{m+3})\end{array}},$$

$$w_{m+3}^{(7,1)} = \frac{\begin{aligned}&\alpha_{m-2}\alpha_{m-1}\alpha_m\alpha_{m+1}\alpha_{m+2} + \alpha_{m-3}(\alpha_{m-1}\alpha_m\alpha_{m+1}\alpha_{m+2}\\&+ \alpha_{m-2}(\alpha_m\alpha_{m+1}\alpha_{m+2} + \alpha_{m-1}(\alpha_{m+1}\alpha_{m+2} + \alpha_m(\alpha_{m+2} + \alpha_{m+1}))))\end{aligned}}{\begin{aligned}(\alpha_{m+3} - \alpha_{m+2})\,(\alpha_{m-3} - \alpha_{m+3})\,(\alpha_{m+3} - \alpha_{m-2})\,(\alpha_{m+3} - \alpha_{m-1})\\(\alpha_{m+3} - \alpha_{m+1})\,(\alpha_{m+3} - \alpha_m)\end{aligned}}.$$

The weights for the second derivative are given by

$$w_{m-3}^{(7,2)} = \frac{\begin{aligned}&2(\alpha_m\alpha_{m+1}\alpha_{m+2}\alpha_{m+3} + \alpha_{m-1}(\alpha_{m+1}\alpha_{m+2}\alpha_{m+3} + \alpha_m(\alpha_{m+2}\alpha_{m+3}\\&+ \alpha_{m+1}(\alpha_{m+2} + \alpha_{m+3}))) + \alpha_{m-2}(\alpha_{m+1}\alpha_{m+2}\alpha_{m+3} + \alpha_m(\alpha_{m+2}\alpha_{m+3}\\&+ \alpha_{m+1}(\alpha_{m+2} + \alpha_{m+3})) + \alpha_{m-1}(\alpha_{m+2}\alpha_{m+3} + \alpha_{m+1}(\alpha_{m+2} + \alpha_{m+3})\\&+ \alpha_m(\alpha_{m+1} + \alpha_{m+2} + \alpha_{m+3}))))\end{aligned}}{\begin{aligned}(\alpha_{m-3} - \alpha_{m-2})(\alpha_{m-3} - \alpha_{m-1})(\alpha_{m-3} - \alpha_m)\\(\alpha_{m-3} - \alpha_{m+1})(\alpha_{m-3} - \alpha_{m+2})(\alpha_{m-3} - \alpha_{m+3})\end{aligned}}$$

$$w_{m-2}^{(7,2)} = -\frac{\begin{aligned}&2(\alpha_m\alpha_{m+1}\alpha_{m+2}\alpha_{m+3} + \alpha_{m-1}(\alpha_m\,\alpha_{m+1}\alpha_{m+3} + \alpha_m(\alpha_{m+2}\alpha_{m+3}\\&+ \alpha_{m+1}(\alpha_{m+2} + \alpha_{m+3}))) + \alpha_{m-3}(\alpha_{m+1}\alpha_{m+2}\alpha_{m+3} + \alpha_m(\alpha_{m+2}\alpha_{m+3}\\&+ \alpha_{m+1}(\alpha_{m+2} + \alpha_{m+3})) + \alpha_{m-1}(\alpha_{m+2}\alpha_{m+3} + \alpha_{m+1}(\alpha_{m+2} + \alpha_{m+3})\\&+ \alpha_m(\alpha_{m+1} + \alpha_{m+2} + \alpha_{m+3}))))\end{aligned}}{\begin{aligned}(\alpha_{m-2} - \alpha_{m-1})(\alpha_{m-2} - \alpha_m)(\alpha_{m-3} - \alpha_{m-2})(\alpha_{m-2} - \alpha_{m+1})\\(\alpha_{m-2} - \alpha_{m+3})(\alpha_{m-2} - \alpha_{m+2})\end{aligned}}$$

$$w_{m-1}^{(7,2)} = -\frac{\begin{aligned}&2(\alpha_m\alpha_{m+1}\alpha_{m+2}\alpha_{m+3} + \alpha_{m-2}(\alpha_{m+3}\alpha_{m+1}\alpha_{m+2} + \alpha_m(\alpha_{m+2}\alpha_{m+3}\\&+ \alpha_{m+1}(\alpha_{m+2} + \alpha_{m+3}))) + \alpha_{m-3}(\alpha_{m+1}\alpha_{m+2}\alpha_{m+3} + \alpha_m(\alpha_{m+2}\alpha_{m+3}\\&+ \alpha_{m+1}(\alpha_{m+2} + \alpha_{m+3})) + \alpha_{m-2}(\alpha_{m+2}\alpha_{m+3} + \alpha_{m+1}(\alpha_{m+2} + \alpha_{m+3})\\&+ \alpha_m(\alpha_{m+1} + \alpha_{m+2} + \alpha_{m+3}))))\end{aligned}}{\begin{aligned}(\alpha_{m-3} - \alpha_{m-1})(\alpha_{m-1} - \alpha_{m-2})(\alpha_{m-1} - \alpha_m)\\(\alpha_{m-1} - \alpha_{m+1})(\alpha_{m-1} - \alpha_{m+2})(\alpha_{m-1} - \alpha_{m+3})\end{aligned}}$$

$$w_{m}^{(7,2)} = -\frac{\begin{aligned}&2(\alpha_{m-1}\alpha_{m+1}\alpha_{m+2}\alpha_{m+3} + \alpha_{m-2}(\alpha_{m+1}\alpha_{m+2}\alpha_{m+3} + \alpha_{m-1}(\alpha_{m+2}\alpha_{m+3}\\&+ \alpha_{m+1}(\alpha_{m+2} + \alpha_{m+3}))) + \alpha_{m-3}(\alpha_{m+1}\alpha_{m+2}\alpha_{m+3} + \alpha_{m-1}(\alpha_{m+2}\alpha_{m+3}\\&+ \alpha_{m+1}(\alpha_{m+2} + \alpha_{m+3})) + \alpha_{m-2}(\alpha_{m+2}\alpha_{m+3} + \alpha_{m+1}(\alpha_{m+2} + \alpha_{m+3})\\&+ \alpha_{m-1}(\alpha_{m+1} + \alpha_{m+2} + \alpha_{m+3}))))\end{aligned}}{\begin{aligned}(\alpha_m - \alpha_{m-2})(\alpha_m - \alpha_{m-1})(\alpha_m - \alpha_{m+1})\\(\alpha_m - \alpha_{m+2})(\alpha_{m-3} - \alpha_m)(\alpha_m - \alpha_{m+3})\end{aligned}}$$

$$w_{m+1}^{(7,2)} = -\frac{\begin{aligned}&2(\alpha_{m-1}\alpha_m\alpha_{m+2}\alpha_{m+3} + \alpha_{m-2}(\alpha_m\alpha_{m+2}\alpha_{m+3} + \alpha_{m-1}(\alpha_{m+2}\alpha_{m+3}\\&+ \alpha_m(\alpha_{m+2} + \alpha_{m+3}))) + \alpha_{m-3}(\alpha_m\alpha_{m+2}\alpha_{m+3} + \alpha_{m-1}(\alpha_{m+2}\alpha_{m+3}\\&+ \alpha_m(\alpha_{m+2} + \alpha_{m+3})) + \alpha_{m-2}(\alpha_{m+2}\alpha_{m+3} + \alpha_m(\alpha_{m+2} + \alpha_{m+3})\\&+ \alpha_{m-1}(\alpha_m + \alpha_{m+2} + \alpha_{m+3}))))\end{aligned}}{\begin{aligned}(\alpha_{m-3} - \alpha_{m+1})(\alpha_{m+1} - \alpha_{m-2})(\alpha_{m+1} - \alpha_{m-1})\\(\alpha_{m+1} - \alpha_m)(\alpha_{m+1} - \alpha_{m+2})(\alpha_{m+1} - \alpha_{m+3})\end{aligned}}$$

$$2(\alpha_{m-1}\alpha_m\alpha_{m+1}\alpha_{m+3} + \alpha_{m-2}(\alpha_m\alpha_{m+1}\alpha_{m+3} + \alpha_{m-1}(\alpha_{m+1}\alpha_{m+3}$$
$$+ \alpha_m(\alpha_{m+1} + \alpha_{m+3}))) + \alpha_{m-3}(\alpha_m\alpha_{m+1}\alpha_{m+3} + \alpha_{m-1}(\alpha_{m+1}\alpha_{m+3}$$
$$+ \alpha_m(\alpha_{m+1} + \alpha_{m+3})) + \alpha_{m-2}(\alpha_{m+1}\alpha_{m+3} + \alpha_m(\alpha_{m+1} + \alpha_{m+3})$$

$$w_{m+2}^{(7,2)} = -\frac{+ \alpha_{m-1}(\alpha_m + \alpha_{m+1} + \alpha_{m+3}))))}{(\alpha_{m+2} - \alpha_{m-1})(\alpha_{m-3} - \alpha_{m+2})(\alpha_{m+2} - \alpha_{m-2})}$$
$$(\alpha_{m+2} - \alpha_m)(\alpha_{m+2} - \alpha_{m+1})(\alpha_{m+2} - \alpha_{m+3})$$

$$2(\alpha_{m-1}\alpha_m\alpha_{m+1}\alpha_{m+2} + \alpha_{m-2}(\alpha_m\alpha_{m+1}\alpha_{m+2} + \alpha_{m-1}(\alpha_{m+1}\alpha_{m+2}$$
$$+ \alpha_m(\alpha_{m+1} + \alpha_{m+2}))) + \alpha_{m-3}(\alpha_m\alpha_{m+1}\alpha_{m+2} + \alpha_{m-1}(\alpha_{m+1}\alpha_{m+2}$$
$$+ \alpha_m(\alpha_{m+1} + \alpha_{m+2})) + \alpha_{m-2}(\alpha_{m+1}\alpha_{m+2} + \alpha_m(\alpha_{m+1} + \alpha_{m+2})$$

$$w_{m+3}^{(7,2)} = -\frac{+ \alpha_{m-1}(\alpha_m + \alpha_{m+1} + \alpha_{m+2}))))}{(\alpha_{m-3} - \alpha_{m+3})(\alpha_{m+3} - \alpha_{m-2})(\alpha_{m+3} - \alpha_{m-1})}$$
$$(\alpha_{m+3} - \alpha_m)(\alpha_{m+3} - \alpha_{m+1})(\alpha_{m+3} - \alpha_{m+2})$$

At the left and right boundaries, the weights are calculated as described earlier. The Mathematica code used to obtain the weights is given in Fig. 1.

```
(* Input Parameters *)
np = 7; d = 1;
(* Construction of the VanderMonde Matrix *)
q = Floor[np / 2];
list = Table[α_k, {k, m - q, m + q}];
vandermonde[a_] := Transpose[Outer[Power, a, Range[0, Length[a] - 1]]]
A = vandermonde[list];
(* Obtaining the weights for the derivative matrix of order d *)
DetA = Simplify[Det[A]];
b = ConstantArray[0, np]; b[[d + 1]] = d!;
row[v_] := {v}; col[v_] := {#} & /@ v; sca[x_] := {{x}}
i = 0;
For[k = -q, k <= q, k++,
  i++;
  c = ConstantArray[0, np]; c[[i]] = 1;
  AugA_i = ArrayFlatten[{{A, col[b]}, {row[c], sca[0]}}];
  w_i = Simplify[ 1/DetA * -Simplify[Det[AugA_i]]]; Print[w_{m+k}, "=", w_i]]
```

Fig. 1. Mathematica code to derive the weights for the derivative matrices using n_p-point stencil.

4 Applications to Option Pricing

We next consider an application of the high-order method in §3 to option pricing when the asset price follows a CEV process.

4.1 Numerical Discretisation of the CEV PDE

We localise the problem (4) to a finite computational domain $\Omega = [S_{\min}, S_{\max}] \times [0, T]$. The non-uniform spatial grid is constructed as in Sect. 4.2. Let $V_m(\tau) = V(S_m, \tau)$ and let $\mathbf{V}(\tau) = [V_0(\tau), V_1(\tau), \ldots, V_M(\tau)]^T$. The pde (4) becomes

$$\mathbf{V}'(\tau) = \mathbf{L}\mathbf{V}(\tau), \tag{6}$$

where $\mathbf{L} \in \mathbb{R}^{(M+1)\times(M+1)}$ is given by

$$\mathbf{L} = \frac{1}{2}\delta^2 \mathbf{S}_I^{2\beta} \mathbf{D}_{n_p}^{(2)} + r\mathbf{S}_I \mathbf{D}_{n_p}^{(1)} - r\mathbf{I},$$

where the first order and second order derivative matrices $\mathbf{D}_{n_p}^{(1)}$ and $\mathbf{D}_{n_p}^{(2)}$ are constructed using the weights derived in Sect. 3.1 for $n_p \in \{3, 5, 7\}$, $\mathbf{I}$ represents the $(M+1) \times (M+1)$ identity matrix and

$$\mathbf{S}_I = \text{diag}[S_0, S_1, \ldots, S_M] \quad \in \mathbb{R}^{(M+1)\times(M+1)}.$$

An exponential time integration [9] of (6) between 0 and T gives

$$\mathbf{V}(T) = e^{\mathbf{L}T}\mathbf{V}(0), \tag{7}$$

where $\mathbf{V}(0) = [(E - S_0)^+, (E - S_1)^+, \ldots, (E - S_M)^+]$ with $(E - S_m)^+ = \max(E - S_m, 0)$. The evaluation of the exponential matrix in (7) can be efficiently performed by the Carathéodory-Fejér approximation and contour integrals [8].

For the pricing of the more complex American options, we employ an operator splitting strategy [5] for solving the linear complementarity problem [11] as employed in the case of a 5-point stencil approximation using a localised radial point interpolation method [10].

4.2 Grid-Spacing

Consider the finite computational domain $[S_{\min}, S_{\max}] \times [0, T]$. Due to the non-smooth payoff function for option pricing problems which hampers the rate of convergence of high-order methods, a grid stretching strategy near the payoff's kink E is required to restore numerical solutions exhibiting high-order convergence rates. We therefore employ a grid stretching strategy to concentrate more grid nodes at E which restores the expected high-order rate of convergence with the effect of decreasing the error at the point of discontinuity. Let $y \in [0, 1]$ be the transformed grid with $y_m = mh$ where $h = 1/M$, then

$$S_m = E + \frac{1}{\xi}\sinh\left(c_1 + (c_2 - c_1)y_m\right),$$

where

$$c_1 = \sinh^{-1}\left(\xi(S_{\min} - E)\right), \quad c_2 = \sinh^{-1}\left(\xi(S_{\max} - E)\right),$$

and ξ is a stretching parameter.

5   Numerical Experiments

We present some numerical examples for pricing options using the high-order non-uniform methods under CEV model which also nests the popular lognormal Black-Scholes model for $\beta = 1$. All computations have been carried out using MATLAB R2020 on a Core i5 laptop with 8 GB RAM and speed 2.60 GHZ.

Our first example prices a $T = 1$ year European put option when the stock has an initial price $S^0 = 100$. The other parameters are $\tilde{\sigma} = 0.1$, strike price $E = 100$ and $r = 0.05$. The corresponding results are shown in Table 2.

The errors over the whole computational domain are computed as

$$\|e\|_{\ell_2} = \sqrt{\frac{\sum_{j=0}^{M} |V_j^{\text{approx}}(T) - V_j^{\text{exact}}(T)|^2}{M+1}},$$

and the rate of convergence is obtained from

$$\text{Order} = \log_2 \left(\frac{\|e(M)\|_{\ell_2}}{\|e(2M)\|_{\ell_2}} \right).$$

Table 2. Errors and convergence in the ℓ_2-norm under the lognormal Black-Scholes model

$\beta = 1, S^0 = 100, E = 100, \tilde{\sigma} = 0.1, r = 0.05, T = 1, \xi = 80$								
	3-point			5-point			7-point		
M	$\|e\|_{\ell_2}$	Order	Cpu(s)	$\|e\|_{\ell_2}$	Order	Cpu(s)	$\|e\|_{\ell_2}$	Order	Cpu(s)
20	2.1e−1	–	0.009	1.5e−1	–	0.006	8.0e−1	–	0.005
40	5.3e−2	1.998	0.012	1.1e−2	3.790	0.012	8.1e−3	6.626	0.011
80	1.3e−2	1.989	0.014	7.6e−4	3.832	0.016	1.3e−4	5.997	0.013
160	3.3e−3	1.997	0.018	4.9e−5	3.956	0.019	2.2e−6	5.863	0.016
320	8.4e−4	1.999	0.024	3.1e−6	3.989	0.023	3.7e−8	5.883	0.018
640	2.1e−4	2.000	0.031	1.9e−7	3.994	0.035	3.5e−10	6.717	0.022
Exact price = 6.80474876423									

It is observed that the expected convergence rates of order 2, 4 and 6 with the 3, 5 and 7 point stencil schemes are achieved respectively. While the 3-point and 5-point schemes yield a numerical solution having an error of magnitude 10^{-4} and 10^{-6} in around 22 ms, the 7-point scheme leads to an error of magnitude 10^{-10} in the same computational time.

We next consider the pricing of a one-year European put option where the stock price follows the CEV dynamics. The exact price is obtained using (2) and the errors are calculated at the spot price $S^0 = 100$. We choose $\beta = -2$ and other parameters are listed in Table 3. The option prices for varying M, errors, convergence rates and the computational times are given in Table 3. It can be observed that highly accurate prices are obtained in little computational time.

Table 3. Price, errors and convergence rates under CEV model.

$\beta = -2$, $E = 100$, $S^0 = 100$, $\tilde{\sigma} = 0.1$, $\xi = 70$, $r = 0.05$, $T = 1$

M	3-point				5-point				7-point			
	Price	Error	Order	Cpu(s)	Price	Error	Order	Cpu(s)	Price	Error	Order	Cpu(s)
20	6.581204	2.2e−1	–	0.006	6.940188	1.3e−1	–	0.005	6.548769	2.6e−1	–	0.006
40	6.754252	5.8e−2	1.995	0.009	6.822525	1.0e−2	3.629	0.009	6.807916	4.3e−3	5.950	0.008
80	6.797551	1.5e−2	1.986	0.013	6.812904	7.3e−4	3.827	0.014	6.812094	8.1e−5	5.711	0.011
160	6.808510	3.7e−3	1.996	0.016	6.812222	4.7e−5	3.955	0.017	6.812174	1.4e−6	5.859	0.013
320	6.811258	9.2e−4	1.999	0.021	6.812178	3.0e−6	3.989	0.021	6.812175	2.4e−8	5.841	0.018
640	6.811946	2.3e−4	2.000	0.029	6.812175	1.9e7	3.994	0.029	6.812175	3.8e−10	5.989	0.020

Exact price = 6.81217523240787

In Table 4, we show that the proposed technique also yields accurate results for highly negative values of the elasticity parameter. The prices and errors for different values of β with different strike prices are reported in the Table 4.

Table 4. Highly negative values of the elasticity parameter under CEV model.

$S^0 = 100$, $T = 1$, $\xi = 70$, $M = 320$, $\tilde{\sigma} = 0.1$, $r = 0.05$					
	$E = 90$		$E = 100$		$E = 110$	
β	Price	Error	Price	Error	Price	Error
−3	14.851632	2.7e−8	6.821461	2.3e−8	1.703848	4.0e−7
−4	14.952419	2.8e−8	6.835034	2.4e−8	1.568522	3.9e−7
−5	15.073118	3.1e−8	6.853756	3.1e−8	1.442271	3.9e−7
−6	15.218544	3.7e−8	6.879111	4.3e−8	1.324391	3.8e−7
−7	15.383637	4.0e−8	6.912053	5.7e−8	1.214294	4.4e−7

Finally the last numerical example illustrate the effectiveness of the proposed method for pricing American options for which no simple closed-form formula exists. Comparisons is carried out against the Han-Wu algorithm [4] and a RBF-FD method [3]. The results obtained using the 5-point scheme, interpolated at the initial stock price $S^0 = 100$ are shown in Table 5. It is observed that the results obtained using 5-point scheme agree well with the well-known benchmark prices which are available in the literature.

Table 5. American options using the 5-point scheme with $M = 1000$.

S_0	Han Wu [4]		RBF-FD [3]		5-point		Benchmark
	Price	Error	Price	Error	Price	Error	
80	20.00000	2.0e−7	20.00000	1.2e−6	20.00000	4.1e−7	20.00000
90	10.66603	3.0e−6	10.66009	5.9e−3	10.66605	4.4e−5	10.66610
100	4.65552	1.0e −4	4.65167	4.0e−3	4.65563	4.2e−5	4.65568
110	1.66797	4.7e−6	1.66622	1.8e−3	1.66798	7.7e−6	1.66799
120	0.49758	2.1e−5	0.49714	4.2e−4	0.49756	1.3e−5	0.49756

$\beta = 1$, $r = 0.05$, $E = 100$, $T = 0.5$, $\tilde{\sigma} = 0.2$

6 Conclusion

In this work, we proposed a new sixth-order method for pricing options under the stock price dynamics with heteroscedasticity. The capability to compute accurate prices for strongly negative elasticity parameters shows the merit of the new method.

Acknowledgement. The author gratefully acknowledges the funding support for a high-performance laptop under the award number ID-2019-14 from the Higher Education Commission, Mauritius, which was used for the symbolic derivations in Mathematica and numerical computations in Matlab.

References

1. Bowen, M.K., Smith, R.: Derivative formulae and errors for non-uniformly spaced points. Math. Phys. Eng. Sci. **461**, 1975–1997 (2005)
2. Cox, J.: The constant elasticity of variance option pricing model. J. Portf. Manag. **22**, 16–17 (1996)
3. Golbabai, A., Mohebianfar, E.: A new stable local radial basis function approach for option pricing. Comput. Econ. **49**, 271–288 (2017)
4. Han, H., Wu, X.: A fast numerical method for the Black-Scholes equation of American options. SIAM J. Numer. Anal. **41**, 2081–2095 (2003)
5. Ikonen, S., Toivanen, J.: Operator splitting methods for American option pricing. Appl. Math. Lett. **17**, 809–814 (2004)
6. Jackwerth, J., Rubinstein, M.: Recovering stochastic processes from option prices. Working Paper, University of California, Berkeley, CA (2001)
7. Larguinho, M., Dias, J.C., Braumann, C.A.: On the computation of option prices and Greeks under the CEV model. Quant. Finan. **13**, 907–917 (2013)
8. Schmelzer, T., Trefethen, L.N.: Evaluating matrix functions for exponential integrators via Carathéodory-Fejér approximation and contour integrals. Electron. T Numer. Ana. **29**, 1–18 (2007)
9. Tangman, D.Y., Gopaul, A., Bhuruth, M.: Exponential time integration and Chebychev discretisation schemes for fast pricing of options. Appl. Numer. Math. **58**, 1309–1319 (2008)

10. Thakoor, N.: Analytical shape functions and derivatives approximation formulas in local radial point interpolation methods with applications to financial option pricing problems. Comput. Math. Appl. **78**, 3770–3789 (2019)
11. Thakoor, N., Behera, D.K., Tangman, D.Y., Bhuruth, M.: A new Howard-Crandall-Douglas algorithm for the American option problem in computational finance. In: Behera, H., Nayak, J., Naik, B., Abraham, A. (eds.) Computational Intelligence in Data Mining, vol. 711, pp. 5–13. Springer, Singapore (2018). https://doi.org/10.1007/978-981-10-8055-5_13
12. Thakoor, N., Tangman, D.Y., Bhuruth, M.: A new fourth-order scheme for option pricing under the CEV model. Appl. Math. Lett. **26**, 160–164 (2013)
13. Thakoor, N., Tangman, D.Y., Bhuruth, M.: Efficient and high accuracy pricing of barrier options under the CEV diffusion. J. Comput. Appl. Math. **259**, 182–193 (2014)
14. Thakoor, N., Tangman, D.Y., Bhuruth, M.: Fast valuation of CEV American options. Wilmott Mag. **2015**, 54–61 (2015)
15. Thakoor, N., Tangman, D.Y., Bhuruth, M.: RBF-FD schemes for option valuation under models with price-dependent and stochastic volatility. Eng. Anal. Boundary Elem. **92**, 207–217 (2018)
16. Wong, H.Y., Zhao, J.: An artificial boundary method for American option pricing under the CEV model. SIAM J. Numer. Anal. **46**, 2183–2209 (2008)

Fixed Points for Cubic Coquaternionic Maps

Maria Irene Falcão[1] (ID), Fernando Miranda[1] (ID), Ricardo Severino[1(✉)] (ID),
and Maria Joana Soares[2] (ID)

[1] CMAT and Departamento de Matemática, Universidade do Minho, Braga, Portugal
{mif,fmiranda,ricardo}@math.uminho.pt
[2] NIPE, Universidade do Minho, Braga, Portugal
jsoares@math.uminho.pt

Abstract. This paper deals with the dynamics of a special two-parameter family of coquaternionic cubic maps. By making use of recent results for the zeros of one-sided coquaternionic polynomials, we analytically determine the fixed points of these maps. Some numerical examples illustrating the theory are also presented. The results obtained show an unexpected richness for the dynamics of cubic coquaternionic maps when compared to the already studied dynamics of quadratic maps.

Keywords: Iteration of cubic maps · Fixed points · Coquaternions · Coquaternionic polynomials

1 Introduction

The four dimensional algebra of coquaternions, also known in the literature as split quaternions, was introduced by Sir James Cockle (1819–1895) at about the same time that Sir William Hamilton (1805–1865) discovered the algebra of quaternions.

Although never as popular as their famous "cousins" quaternions, coquaternions have recently been attracting the attention of mathematicians and physicists who recognize the potential of applications of these hypercomplex numbers numbers [1–3,9–16].

In a previous study [4] the authors discussed the dynamics of the family of coquaternionic quadratic maps of the form $x^2 + c$ and, more recently, they considered quadratic maps of the form $x^2 + bx$ [7]. The present paper can be seen as continuation of the studies initiated in [4] and [7] and is a first step to deal with the – naturally much more interesting, but also much more demanding – problem of the dynamics of cubic coquaternionic maps.

The remaining of the paper is organized as follows: Sect. 2 contains a brief revision of the main definitions and results on the algebra of coquaternions and on unilateral coquaternionic polynomials; Sect. 3 contains the main results of the paper. Finally, Sect. 4 contains carefully chosen examples illustrating some of the conclusions contained in Sect. 3.

O. Gervasi et al. (Eds.): ICCSA 2022 Workshops, LNCS 13377, pp. 450–465, 2022.
https://doi.org/10.1007/978-3-031-10536-4_30

2   Preliminary Results

In this section, we present a summary of the results on coquaternions and coquaternionic polynomials which are essential to the understanding of the rest of the paper. For more details, we refer the reader to [4–7].

2.1   The Algebra $\mathbb{H}_{coq}$

Let $\{1, i, j, k\}$ be an orthonormal basis of the Euclidean vector space $\mathbb{R}^4$ with a product given according to the multiplication rules

$$i^2 = -1, \ j^2 = k^2 = 1, \ ij = -ji = k.$$

This non-commutative product generates the algebra of real coquaternions, which we will denote by $\mathbb{H}_{coq}$. We will identify the space $\mathbb{R}^4$ with $\mathbb{H}_{coq}$ by associating the element $(q_0, q_1, q_2, q_3) \in \mathbb{R}^4$ with the coquaternion $q = q_0 + q_1 i + q_2 j + q_3 k$. Given $q = q_0 + q_1 i + q_2 j + q_3 k \in \mathbb{H}_{coq}$, its *conjugate* $\bar{q}$ is defined as $\bar{q} = q_0 - q_1 i - q_2 j - q_3 k$; the number q_0 is called the *real part* of q and is denoted by $\mathrm{re}\, q$ and the *vector part* of q, denoted by $\mathrm{vec}\, q$, is $\mathrm{vec}\, q = q_1 i + q_2 j + q_3 k$. We will identify the set of coquaternions whose vector part is zero with the set $\mathbb{R}$ of real numbers. We call *determinant* of q and denote by $\det q$ the quantity given by $\det q = q\, \bar{q} = q_0^2 + q_1^2 - q_2^2 - q_3^2$. Not all non-zero coquaternions are invertible. It can be shown that a coquaternion q is invertible (also referred to as nonsingular) if and only if $\det q \neq 0$. In that case, we have, $q^{-1} = \frac{\bar{q}}{\det q}$.

We identify three particularly important subspaces of dimension two of $\mathbb{H}_{coq}$, usually called the *canonical planes* or *cycle planes*. The first is simply the complex plane $\mathbb{C}$; the second, which we denote by $\mathbb{P}$ and whose elements are usually called *perplex numbers* is given by $\mathbb{P} = \mathrm{span}_{\mathbb{R}}(1, j)$ and corresponds to the classical *Minkowski plane*; the third, denoted by $\mathbb{D}$, is the subspace of the so-called *dual numbers*, $\mathbb{D} = \mathrm{span}_{\mathbb{R}}(1, i+j)$ and can be identified with the classical *Laguerre plane*.

A concept which will play an important role in this paper is the concept of *quasi-similarity* of coquaternions. We say that two elements $p, q \in \mathbb{H}_{coq}$ are *quasi-similar* if and only if they satisfy $\mathrm{re}\, p = \mathrm{re}\, q$ and $\det p = \det q$ (or, equivalently, if $\mathrm{re}\, p = \mathrm{re}\, q$ and $\det(\mathrm{vec}\, p) = \det(\mathrm{vec}\, q)$). This is easily seen to be an equivalence relation in $\mathbb{H}_{coq}$; the class of an element $q \in \mathbb{H}_{coq}$ with respect to this relation is denoted by $[\![q]\!]$ and referred to as the *quasi-similarity class* of q. Observe that the quasi-similarity class of a coquaternion q is given by

$$[\![q]\!] = \left\{ x_0 + x_1 i + x_2 j + x_3 k : x_0 = q_0 \text{ and } x_1^2 - x_2^2 - x_3^2 = \det(\mathrm{vec}\, q) \right\}$$

which we can identify with a hyperboloid in the hyperplane $x_0 = q_0$: a hyperboloid of two sheets if $\det(\mathrm{vec}\, q) > 0$, a hyperboloid of one sheet if $\det(\mathrm{vec}\, q) < 0$ and a degenerate hyperboloid, i.e. a cone, if $\det(\mathrm{vec}\, q) = 0$.

2.2   Unilateral Coquaternionic Polynomials

We now summarize some results on the zeros of coquaternionic polynomials [6]. We deal only with monic unilateral left polynomials, i.e. polynomials of the form

$$P(x) = x^n + a_{n-1}x^{n-1} + \cdots + a_1 x + a_0, \ a_i \in \mathbb{H}_{coq}, \tag{1}$$

with addition and multiplication of such polynomials defined as in the commutative case, where the variable is allowed to commute with the coefficients.

Given a quasi-similarity class $[\![q]\!] = [\![q_0 + \text{vec}\,q]\!]$, the *characteristic polynomial* of $[\![q]\!]$, denoted by $\Psi_{[\![q]\!]}$, is the polynomial given by

$$\Psi_{[\![q]\!]}(x) = x^2 - 2q_0\,x + \det q.$$

This is a second degree monic polynomial with real coefficients with discriminant $\Delta = -4\det(\text{vec}\,q)$. Hence, $\Psi_{[\![q]\!]}$ has two complex conjugate roots, if $\det(\text{vec}\,q) > 0$, and is a polynomial of the form $(x - r_1)(x - r_2)$, with $r_1, r_2 \in \mathbb{R}$, if $\det(\text{vec}\,q) \leq 0$. Reciprocally, any second degree monic polynomial $S(x)$ with real coefficients is the characteristic polynomial of a uniquely defined quasi-similarity class; if $S(x)$ is irreducible with two complex conjugate roots α and $\overline{\alpha}$, then $S = \Psi_{[\![\alpha]\!]}$; if S has real roots r_1 and r_2 (with, eventually, $r_1 = r_2$), then $S = \Psi_{[\![q]\!]}$ with $q = \frac{r_1 + r_2}{2} + \frac{r_1 - r_2}{2}j$.

We say that $z \in \mathbb{H}_{coq}$ is a *zero* of the polynomial P if $P(z) = 0$ and we denote by $Z(P)$ the *zero set* of P, i.e. the set of all the zeros of P.

Given a polynomial P of the form (1), its *conjugate polynomial* is the polynomial defined by $\overline{P}(x) = x^n + \overline{a}_{n-1}x^{n-1} + \cdots + \overline{a}_1 x + \overline{a}_0$ and its *companion polynomial* is the polynomial given by $\mathcal{C}_P(x) = P(x)\overline{P}(x)$.

The following theorem contains an important result relating the characteristic polynomials of the quasi-similarity classes of zeros of a given polynomial P and the companion polynomial of P [6].

Theorem 1. *Let P be a polynomial of the form* (1). *If $z \in \mathbb{H}_{coq}$ is a zero of P, then $\Psi_{[\![z]\!]}$ is a divisor of $\mathcal{C}_P$.*

It can be shown easily that $\mathcal{C}_P$ is a polynomial of degree $2n$ with real coefficients and, as such, considered as a polynomial in $\mathbb{C}$, has $2n$ roots. If these roots are $\alpha_1, \overline{\alpha}_1, \ldots, \alpha_m, \overline{\alpha}_m \in \mathbb{C} \setminus \mathbb{R}$ and $r_1, r_2, \ldots, r_\ell \in \mathbb{R}$, where $\ell = 2(n - m)$, $(0 \leq m \leq n)$, then it is easy to conclude that the characteristic polynomials which divide $\mathcal{C}_P$ are the ones associated with the following quasi-similarity classes:

$$[\![\alpha_k]\!]; \ k = 1, \ldots, m, \tag{2a}$$

$$[\![r_{ij}]\!]; \ i = 1, \ldots, \ell - 1, j = i + 1, \ldots, \ell, \tag{2b}$$

with

$$r_{ij} = \frac{r_i + r_j}{2} + \frac{r_i - r_j}{2}j. \tag{2c}$$

We thus have the following result concerning the zero set of P.

Theorem 2. *Let P be a polynomial of the form* (1)*. Then:*

$$Z(P) \subseteq \bigcup_k [\![\alpha_k]\!] \bigcup_{i,j} [\![r_{ij}]\!],$$

where $[\![\alpha_k]\!]$ and $[\![r_{ij}]\!]$ are the quasi-similarity classes defined by (2)*.*

We call the classes given by (2) the *admissible classes* of the polynomial P.

The results given in the following theorem show how to find the set of zeros of P belonging to a given admissible class [6].

Theorem 3. *Let $P(x)$ be a polynomial of the form* (1) *and let $[\![q]\!] = [\![q_0 + \text{vec}\,q]\!]$ be a given admissible class of $P(x)$. Also, let $\mathsf{A} + \mathsf{B}x$, with $\mathsf{B} = B_0 + B_1 i + B_2 j + B_3 k$, be the remainder of the division of $P(x)$ by the characteristic polynomial of $[\![q]\!]$.*

1. *If $\det \mathsf{B} \neq 0$, then $[\![q]\!]$ contains only one zero of P, given by $\mathsf{z} = -\mathsf{B}^{-1}\mathsf{A}$.*
2. *If $\mathsf{A} - \mathsf{B} = 0$, then $[\![q]\!] \subseteq Z(P)$.*
3. *If $\mathsf{B} \neq 0, \det \mathsf{B} = 0, \det(\text{vec}\,q) \leq 0$ and $\mathsf{A} = -\gamma_0 \mathsf{B}$ with*

$$\gamma_0 = q_0 \pm \sqrt{-\det(\text{vec}\,q)} \tag{3}$$

then the zeros of P in $[\![q]\!]$ form the following line in the hyperplane $x_0 = q_0$,

$$\mathcal{L} = \left\{ q_0 + \alpha i + (k_2\alpha + k_1(q_0 - \gamma_0))j + (k_2(q_0 - \gamma_0) - k_1\alpha+)k : \alpha \in \mathbb{R} \right\}, \tag{4a}$$

with k_1 and k_2 given by

$$k_1 = -\frac{B_0 B_2 + B_1 B_3}{B_0^2 + B_1^2} \quad and \quad k_2 = \frac{B_1 B_2 - B_0 B_3}{B_0^2 + B_1^2}. \tag{4b}$$

4. *If $\mathsf{B} \neq 0, \det \mathsf{B} = 0$ and $\mathsf{A} = -\mathsf{B}(\gamma_0 + \gamma_1 i)$ $(\gamma_1 \neq 0)$, then the class $[\![q]\!]$ contains only one zero of P, given by*

$$\mathsf{z} = q_0 + (\beta + \gamma_1)i + (k_2\beta + k_1(q_0 - \gamma_0))j + (-k_1\beta + k_2(q_0 - \gamma_0))k,$$

where

$$\beta = \frac{\det(\text{vec}\,q) + (q_0 - \gamma_0)^2 - \gamma_1^2}{2\gamma_1}$$

and k_1 and k_2 are given by (4b)*.*
5. *If none of the above conditions holds, then there are no zeros of P in $[\![q]\!]$.*

In cases (1) and (4), we say that the zero z is an *isolated zero* of P; in case (2), we say that the class $[\![q]\!]$ (or any of its elements) is a *hyperboloidal zero* of P and in case (3) we call the line $\mathcal{L}$ (or any of its elements) a *linear zero* of P.

3   Fixed Points for Cubic Coquaternionic Maps

We consider the following two-parameter family of cubic coquaternionic maps

$$f_{a,b}(x) = x^3 - (a + b)x^2 + abx + x, \quad x \in \mathbb{H}_{coq} \tag{5}$$

with $a, b \in \mathbb{H}_{coq}$ and seek to determine its fixed points, i.e. the points $x \in \mathbb{H}_{coq}$ such that $f_{a,b}(x) = x$.

The reason for choosing this rather peculiar family of maps has to do with the fact that its fixed points turn out to be the zeros of the simple factorized polynomial

$$P(x) = f_{a,b}(x) - x = (x - a)x(x - b). \tag{6}$$

Since $x(x - b)$ is a right factor of $P(x)$, its zeros are always zeros of $P(x)$; this means that the fixed points of the quadratic $g_b(x) = x^2 - (b + 1)x$ – which is a kind of family studied in detail by the authors in [7] – are always fixed points of $f_{a,b}$. This will enable us to highlight the richness of the dynamics of cubic coquaternionic maps when compared to the dynamics of quadratic coquaternionic maps.

This paper deals only with the case where the parameter b is a non-real perplex number, i.e. is of the form

$$b = b_0 + b_2 j, \ b_2 \neq 0. \tag{7}$$

Other type of values for the parameter b will be object of future studies. We note that this choice of b is the one for which the quadratic $g_b(x)$ shows the most interesting dynamics; see [7] for details.

To determine the fixed points of the cubic map (5), or, in other words, to find the zeros of the polynomial P given by (6), we proceed as follows: we first compute the roots of the companion polynomial C_P of P and identify all the admissible classes; then, to discuss the zeros in each class $[\![q]\!] = [\![q_0 + \operatorname{vec} q]\!]$ we determine the remainder of the division of P by the polynomial $x^2 - 2q_0x + \det q$ and make use of Theorem 3.

This remainder is easily seen to be the polynomial $Bx + A$, where

$$\begin{aligned} A &= K_2(K_1 - a - b) \\ B &= K_1(K_1 - a - b) + ab - K_2 \end{aligned} \tag{8}$$

with $K_1 = 2q_0$ and $K_2 = \det q$.

In what follows, for the sake of simplicity, we refer to a quadratic or cubic with i isolated fixed points, ℓ lines of fixed points and h hyperboloids of fixed points as a (i, ℓ, h) map.

3.1   Case $a \in \mathbb{P}$

We start by discussing with detail the case where the parameter a is a (non-real) perplex number

$$a = a_0 + a_2 j, \ a_2 \neq 0. \tag{9}$$

In this case, the zeros of the companion polynomial $\mathcal{C}_P$ of P are

$$r_1 = r_2 = 0, \quad r_3 = a_0 - a_2, \quad r_4 = a_0 + a_2, \quad r_5 = b_0 - b_2, \quad r_6 = b_0 + b_2,$$

and so there are, at most, 11 admissible classes

$$\mathcal{C}_1 = [\![0]\!], \quad \mathcal{C}_2 = [\![\tfrac{a_0-a_2}{2} + \tfrac{a_0-a_2}{2}\mathsf{j}]\!], \quad \mathcal{C}_3 = [\![\tfrac{a_0+a_2}{2} + \tfrac{a_0+a_2}{2}\mathsf{j}]\!]$$

$$\mathcal{C}_4 = [\![\tfrac{b_0-b_2}{2} + \tfrac{b_0-b_2}{2}\mathsf{j}]\!], \quad \mathcal{C}_5 = [\![\tfrac{b_0+b_2}{2} + \tfrac{b_0+b_2}{2}\mathsf{j}]\!]$$

$$\mathcal{C}_6 = [\![a_0 + a_2\mathsf{j}]\!] = [\![\mathsf{a}]\!], \quad \mathcal{C}_7 = [\![\tfrac{a_0 \ a_2+b_0-b_2}{2} + \tfrac{a_0-a_2-b_0+b_2}{2}\mathsf{j}]\!],$$

$$\mathcal{C}_8 = [\![\tfrac{a_0-a_2+b_0+b_2}{2} + \tfrac{a_0-a_2-b_0-b_2}{2}\mathsf{j}]\!], \quad \mathcal{C}_9 = [\![\tfrac{a_0+a_2+b_0-b_2}{2} + \tfrac{a_0+a_2-b_0+b_2}{2}\mathsf{j}]\!],$$

$$\mathcal{C}_{10} = [\![\tfrac{a_0+a_2+b_0+b_2}{2} + \tfrac{a_0+a_2-b_0-b_2}{2}\mathsf{j}]\!], \quad \mathcal{C}_{11} = [\![b_0 + b_2\mathsf{j}]\!] = [\![\mathsf{b}]\!]$$

It is important to remark that, for a of the form (9) and b of the form (7), one has $\mathsf{ab} = \mathsf{ba}$ and so the polynomials $x(x-\mathsf{a})(x-\mathsf{b})$ and $x(x-\mathsf{b})(x-\mathsf{a})$ coincide. This means, in particular, that the results concerning the classes $\mathcal{C}_4, \mathcal{C}_5, \mathcal{C}_9$ and $\mathcal{C}_{11}$ may be obtained easily from the ones for the classes $\mathcal{C}_2, \mathcal{C}_3, \mathcal{C}_8$ and $\mathcal{C}_6$, respectively, by simply swapping a with b; this also implies that, in addition to 0 and b, we always have a as a zero of P.

We first consider the case where the classes are all distinct i.e. we assume that none of the following conditions holds:

$$\mathsf{C}_{1,1} : a_2 = a_0, \quad \mathsf{C}_{1,2} : a_2 = -a_0, \quad \mathsf{C}_{1,3} : b_2 = b_0, \quad \mathsf{C}_{1,4} : b_2 = -b_0,$$

$$\mathsf{C}_{1,5} : b_2 = a_0 + a_2 - b_0, \quad \mathsf{C}_{1,6} : b_2 = -a_0 - a_2 + b_0, \tag{10}$$

$$\mathsf{C}_{1,7} : b_2 = a_0 - a_2 - b_0, \quad \mathsf{C}_{1,8} : b_2 = -a_0 + a_2.$$

Zeros in class $\mathcal{C}_1$
This corresponds to $K_1 = K_2 = 0$, and so we have

$$\mathsf{A} = 0$$
$$\mathsf{B} = a_0 b_0 + a_2 b_2 + (a_2 b_0 + a_0 b_2)\mathsf{j} \tag{11}$$
$$\det \mathsf{B} = (a_0^2 - a_2^2)(b_0^2 - b_2^2).$$

Conditions (10) guarantee that $\det \mathsf{B} \neq 0$ and hence the class contains only the zero $\mathsf{z} = 0$.

Zeros in class $\mathcal{C}_2$
This corresponds to $K_1 = a_0 - a_2$ and $K_2 = 0$, leading to

$$\mathsf{A} = 0$$
$$\mathsf{B} = a_2(a_2 - a_0 + b_2 + b_0) + a_2(a_2 - a_0 + b_2 + b_0)\mathsf{j} \tag{12}$$
$$\det \mathsf{B} = 0$$

We thus have $B \neq 0$ and, since we are dealing with a class $[\![q]\!]$ with q of the form $q = q_0 + q_0 j$, we have $\det(\text{vec}\, q) = -q_0^2 < 0$ and the condition $\gamma_0 B = -A$ is trivially satisfied for $\gamma_0 = q_0 - \sqrt{-\det(\text{vec}\, q)} = 0$; hence we are in case (3) of Theorem 3; moreover, we have, with the notations of that theorem, $B_0 = B_2$ and $B_1 = B_3 = 0$ and so we get $k_1 = 1$ and $k_2 = 0$, leading us to conclude that the class contains the following line of zeros

$$\mathcal{L} = \left\{ \tfrac{a_0 - a_2}{2} + \alpha i - \tfrac{a_0 - a_2}{2} j + \alpha k : \alpha \in \mathbb{R} \right\} \tag{13}$$

Zeros in class $\mathscr{C}_3$
The study of the zeros in this class is very similar to the study of the previous class. In this case, we obtain

$$A = 0$$
$$B = a_2(a_0 + a_2 - b_0 + b_2) - (a_2(a_0 + a_2 - b_0 + b_2))j \tag{14}$$
$$\det B = 0$$

and it will follow that the zeros in the class will form the following line

$$\mathcal{L} = \left\{ \tfrac{a_0 + a_2}{2} + \alpha i + \tfrac{a_0 + a_2}{2} j - \alpha k : \alpha \in \mathbb{R} \right\} \tag{15}$$

Zeros in class $\mathscr{C}_4$
The expression for the zeros in this class is obtained by simply replacing a_0 and a_2 with b_0 and b_2, respectively, in the expression of the zeros of class $\mathscr{C}_2$; we thus conclude that the zeros form the line

$$\mathcal{L} = \left\{ \tfrac{b_0 - b_2}{2} + \alpha i - \tfrac{b_0 - b_2}{2} + \alpha k : \alpha \in \mathbb{R} \right\}.$$

Zeros in class $\mathscr{C}_5$
The zeros in this class form the line

$$\mathcal{L} = \left\{ \tfrac{b_0 + b_2}{2} + \alpha i - \tfrac{b_0 + b_2}{2} + \alpha k : \alpha \in \mathbb{R} \right\}.$$

Zeros in class $\mathscr{C}_6$
This corresponds to $K_1 = 2a_0$ and $K_2 = a_0^2 - a_2^2$, from which we obtain

$$A = (a_0^2 - a_2^2)(a_0 - b_0 - (a_2 + b_2)j)$$
$$B = a_0(a_0 - b_0) + a_2(a_2 + b_2) + (a_2 b_0 - a_0(2a_2 + b_2))j \tag{16}$$
$$\det B = (a_0^2 - a_2^2)(a_0 - a_2 - b_0 - b_2)(a_0 + a_2 - b_0 + b_2).$$

Conditions (10) guarantee that $\det B \neq 0$, leading us to conclude that this class contains only the isolated zero $z = a$.

Zeros in class $\mathscr{C}_7$
Here, we have $K_1 = a_0 - a_2 + b_0 - b_2$ and $K_2 = (a_0 - a_2)(b_0 - b_2)$ and we get

$$A = (a_0 - a_2)(b_0 - b_2)(a_2 + b_2) + (a_0 - a_2)(b_0 - b_2)(a_2 + b_2)j$$
$$B = a_2(a_2 - a_0) + b_2(2a_2 - b_0 + b_2) + (a_2(a_2 - a_0) + b_2(2a_2 - b_0 + b_2))j \tag{17}$$
$$\det B = 0$$

We now show that, when none of the condition (10) holds, this class contains no zeros of P. First, we note that we cannot have $A = B = 0$, since

$$a_2 + b_2 = 0 \wedge 2a_2 - b_0 + b_2 = 0 \Rightarrow b_2 = b_0.$$

Hence we are not in case 1 of Theorem 3. Since $A = A_0 + A_0 j$ and $B = B_0 + Bj$, we cannot be in case (4); it remains to verify that we cannot be in case (3). For $\gamma_0 = q_0 + \sqrt{-\det(\text{vec } q)} = a_0 - a_2$, we have

$$B\gamma_0 = -A \Rightarrow a_2(a_2 - a_0) + b_2(2a_2 - b_0 + b_2) = -(b_0 - b_2)(a_2 + b_2)$$
$$\Rightarrow a_2(a_2 - a_0 + b_0 + b_2) = 0$$

which contradicts the hypothesis that $C_{1,8}$ does not hold. The case $\gamma_0 = q_0 - \sqrt{-\det(\text{vec } q)} = b_0 - b_2$ is analogous.

Zeros in class $\mathscr{C}_8$

In this case, $K_1 = a_0 - a_2 + b_0 + b_2$ and $K_2 = (a_0 - a_2)(b_0 + b_2)$ and we get

$$A = (a_0 - a_2)(a_2 - b_2)(b_0 + b_2) + (a_0 - a_2)(a_2 + b_2)(b_0 + b_2)j$$
$$B = a_2(a_2 - a_0) + b_2(b_0 + b_2) + (a_2(a_2 - a_0) - b_2(b_0 + b_2))j \qquad (18)$$
$$\det B = -4a_2 b_2(a_0 - a_2)(b_0 + b_2).$$

Since none of the conditions (10) is satisfied, we have $\det B \neq 0$, and we may conclude that there is only one zero in this class, given by

$$z = -\frac{B}{\det B}A = \frac{a_0 - a_2 + b_0 + b_2}{2} + \frac{a_2 - a_0 + b_0 + b_2}{2}j.$$

Zeros in class $\mathscr{C}_9$

This class contains only the zero

$$z = \frac{a_0 + a_2 + b_0 - b_2}{2} + \frac{a_0 + a_2 - b_0 + b_2}{2}j.$$

Zeros in class $\mathscr{C}_{10}$

The study of this case is trivial adaptation of the study conducted for the class $\mathscr{C}_7$; in this case, we obtain

$$A = -(a_0 + a_2)(b_0 + b_2)(a_2 + b_2) + (a_0 + a_2)(b_0 + b_2)(a_2 + b_2)j$$
$$B = a_2(a_2 + a_0) + b_2(2a_2 + b_0 + b_2) - (a_2(a_2 + a_0) + b_2(2a_2 + b_0 + b_2))j \quad (19)$$
$$\det B = 0$$

and we can conclude that there are no zeros of P in this class.

Zeros in class $\mathscr{C}_{11}$

This class contains only the zero $z = b$.

From the previous discussion, it is clear that, if none of conditions $C_{1,1} - C_{1,8}$ given in (10) holds, then the cubic (5) has the following five isolated fixed points

$$z_1 = 0, \quad z_2 = a, \quad z_3 = b$$
$$z_4 = \frac{a_0 - a_2 + b_0 + b_2}{2} + \frac{a_2 - a_0 + b_0 + b_2}{2}j \quad z_5 = \frac{a_0 + a_2 + b_0 - b_2}{2} + \frac{a_0 + a_2 + b_2 - b_0}{2}j \qquad (20)$$

and the following four lines of fixed points

$$\mathcal{L}_1 = \left\{ \tfrac{a_0 - a_2}{2} + \alpha i - \tfrac{a_0 - a_2}{2}j + \alpha k : \alpha \in \mathbb{R} \right\}$$
$$\mathcal{L}_2 = \left\{ \tfrac{a_0 + a_2}{2} + \alpha i + \tfrac{a_0 + a_2}{2}j - \alpha k : \alpha \in \mathbb{R} \right\}$$
$$\mathcal{L}_3 = \left\{ \tfrac{b_0 - b_2}{2} + \alpha i - \tfrac{b_0 - b_2}{2}j + \alpha k : \alpha \in \mathbb{R} \right\} \tag{21}$$
$$\mathcal{L}_4 = \left\{ \tfrac{b_0 + b_2}{2} + \alpha i + \tfrac{b_0 + b_2}{2}j - \alpha k : \alpha \in \mathbb{R} \right\}$$

i.e. is (5,4,0) map.

Naturally, when some of the conditions (10) hold, the situation is different. Consider, for example, the case where condition $C_{1,1} : a_0 = a_2$ is satisfied, but none of the other conditions $C_{1,2}$ – $C_{1,8}$ holds. In this case, we have $\mathscr{C}_2 \equiv \mathscr{C}_1$, $\mathscr{C}_6 \equiv \mathscr{C}_3$, $\mathscr{C}_7 \equiv \mathscr{C}_4$ and $\mathscr{C}_8 \equiv \mathscr{C}_5$, i.e., there are only 7 admissible classes. Let us see what modifications occur in the zeros contained in these classes due to the fact that $a_2 = a_0$.

Zeros in class $\mathscr{C}_1$ when $a_2 = a_0$
In this case, we have $A = 0$, $B = a_0(b_0 + b_2) + a_0(b_0 + b_2)j$ and $\det B = 0$; see (11). Since $B \neq 0$ and $\exists \gamma_0 = 0$ such that $B\gamma_0 = -A$, we are in case 3.2 (i) of Therorem 3 and we conclude that the zeros of P in this class form the line

$$\mathcal{L} = \{\alpha i + \alpha k : k \in \mathbb{R}\}.$$

Zeros in class $\mathscr{C}_3$ when $a_2 = a_0$
It is simple to verify that the zeros in this class will still form the line (15) which, for $a_0 = a_2$, takes the simpler form

$$\mathcal{L} = \{a_0 + \alpha i + a_0 j - \alpha k : \alpha \in \mathbb{R}\}.$$

Zeros in class $\mathscr{C}_7$ when $a_2 = a_0$
In this case, we have $A = 0$, $B = b_2(2a_2 - b_0 + b_2) + b_2(2a_2 - b_0 + b_2)j$ and $\det B = 0$; see (17). Since condition $C_{1,5}$ does not hold, we conclude that $B \neq 0$ and hence it is simple to see that the zeros in this class form the line

$$\mathcal{L} = \left\{ \tfrac{b_0 - b_2}{2} + \alpha i - \tfrac{b_0 - b_2}{2}j + \alpha k : \alpha \in \mathbb{R} \right\}.$$

Zeros in class $\mathscr{C}_8$ when $a_2 = a_0$
In this case, $A = 0$, $B = b_2(b_0 + b_2) - b_2(b_0 + b_2)j$ and $\det B = 0$; see (18). Since condition $C_{1,4}$ does not hold, we have $B \neq 0$ and we may conclude that the zeros in this class form the following line

$$\mathcal{L} = \left\{ \tfrac{b_0 + b_2}{2} + \alpha i + \tfrac{b_0 + b_2}{2}j - \alpha k : \alpha \in \mathbb{R} \right\}.$$

Zeros in class $\mathscr{C}_{10}$ when $a_2 = a_0$
The situation concerning the zeros in class $\mathscr{C}_{10}$ previously described does not change when $a_2 = a_0$, i.e. the class has no zeros.

In summary, we conclude that when $a_2 = a_0$ is the unique of conditions (10) holding, the cubic is a $(2, 4, 0)$ map.

A similar study was conducted for all the different situations that occur due to the fulfillment of one or more of the conditions (10) and the corresponding results are summarized in Table 1.

Table 1. Case $a = a_0 + a_2j$ and $b = b_0 + b_2j$

a	b	Type of map
$a_0 + a_2j$	$b_0 + b_2j$	$(5,4,0)$
$a_0 + a_2j$	$b_0 + (a_0 + a_2 - b_0)j$	$(3,3,0)$
$a_0 + a_2j$	$b_0 - (a_0 + a_2 - b_0)j$	$(3,4,1)$
$a_0 + a_2j$	$b_0 + (-a_0 + a_2 + b_0)j$	$(3,3,0)$
$a_0 + a_2j$	$a_0 + a_2j$	$(2,2,0)$
$a_0 + a_2j$	$a_0 - a_2j$	$(3,0,3)$
$a_0 \pm a_0j$	$b_0 + b_2j$	$(2,4,0)$
$a_0 + a_0j$	$b_0 + b_0j$	$(0,3,0)$
$a_0 + a_0j$	$b_0 - b_0j$	$(1,2,1)$
$a_0 + a_0j$	$a_0 + a_0j$	$(0,2,0)$
$a_0 + a_0j$	$a_0 - a_0j$	$(1,0,2)$
$a_0 + a_0j$	$b_0 + (2a_0 - b_0)j$	$(1,3,0)$
$a_0 + a_0j$	$b_0 - (2a_0 - b_0)j$	$(1,3,1)$
$a_0 - a_0j$	$b_0 - b_0j$	$(0,3,0)$
$a_0 - a_0j$	$b_0 \pm (2a_0 - b_0)j$	$(1,3,0)$
$a_0 - a_0j$	$a_0 - a_0j$	$(0,2,0)$

A little explanation of how the table must be read is due. When, for example, we write $a = a_0 + a_0j$ and $b = b_0 + b_2j$, this must be interpreted as meaning that a satisfies condition $C_{1,1}$, but b_2 does not have any of the special forms given by conditions $C_{1,3} - C_{1,8}$. For completeness, the first line of the table gives the situation where none of the conditions (10) is verified. Finally, we point out that we do not include in the table the cases which can be obtained by simply replacing the roles of a and b.

3.2   Case $a \in \mathbb{R}$

When $a = a_0 \in \mathbb{R}, a_0 \neq 0$, the zeros of the companion polynomial C_P of P are

$$r_1 = r_2 = 0, \quad r_3 = r_4 = a_0, \quad r_5 = b_0 - b_2, \quad r_6 = b_0 + b_2$$

and so there are, at most, 8 admissible classes

$$\mathscr{C}_1 = [\![0]\!], \quad \mathscr{C}_2 = [\![\tfrac{a_0}{2} + \tfrac{a_0}{2}j]\!],$$

$$\mathscr{C}_3 = [\![\tfrac{b_0-b_2}{2} + \tfrac{b_0-b_2}{2}j]\!], \quad \mathscr{C}_4 = [\![\tfrac{b_0+b_2}{2} + \tfrac{b_0+b_2}{2}j]\!],$$

$$\mathscr{C}_5 = [\![a_0]\!] = [\![a]\!], \quad \mathscr{C}_6 = [\![\tfrac{a_0+b_0-b_2}{2} + \tfrac{a_0-b_0+b_2}{2}j]\!],$$

$$\mathscr{C}_7 = [\![\tfrac{a_0+b_0+b_2}{2} + \tfrac{a_0-b_0-b_2}{2}j]\!], \quad \mathscr{C}_8 = [\![b_0 + b_2j]\!] = [\![b]\!]$$

Corresponding to conditions (10), in this case we have to consider the following conditions

$$C_{2,1} : b_2 = b_0, \quad C_{2,2} : b_2 = -b_0, \quad C_{2,3} : b_2 = b_0 - a_0, \quad C_{2,4} : b_2 = a_0 - b_0 \quad (22)$$

When none of these conditions holds, the cubic has the isolated fixed points $z_1 = 0$, $z_2 = a$ and $z_3 = b$, four lines of fixed points

$$\mathcal{L}_1 = \left\{ \tfrac{b_0-b_2}{2} + \alpha i - \tfrac{b_0-b_2}{2}j + \alpha k : \alpha \in \mathbb{R} \right\}$$

$$\mathcal{L}_2 = \left\{ \tfrac{b_0+b_2}{2} + \alpha i + \tfrac{b_0+b_2}{2}j - \alpha k : \alpha \in \mathbb{R} \right\}$$

$$\mathcal{L}_3 = \left\{ \tfrac{b_0-b_2+a_0}{2} + \alpha i - \tfrac{b_0-b_2-a_0}{2}j + \alpha k : \alpha \in \mathbb{R} \right\}$$

$$\mathcal{L}_4 = \left\{ \tfrac{b_0+b_2+a_0}{2} + \alpha i + \tfrac{b_0+b_2-a_0}{2}j - \alpha k : \alpha \in \mathbb{R} \right\}$$

and also the hyperboloid of fixed points $\mathcal{H} = [\![\tfrac{a_0}{2} + \tfrac{a_0}{2}j]\!]$, i.e. is a $(3,4,1)$ map.

Table 2 gives a full description of the types of maps that are obtained when one or more of the conditions (22) are satisfied.

Table 2. Case $a = a_0$ and $b = b_0 + b_2j$

b	Type of map
$b_0 + b_2j$	$(3,4,1)$
$b_0 \pm b_0j$	$(1,3,1)$
$b_0 \pm (a_0 - b_0)j$	$(1,3,1)$
$\tfrac{a_0}{2} \pm \tfrac{a_0}{2}j$	$(0,2,1)$

We observe that in this case, we always have a hyperboloid of fixed points coexisting with lines of fixed points, a situation that never occurs with the quadratic map.

3.3   Case $a \in \mathbb{C}$

We now discuss the case where $a = a_0 + a_1i$, with $a_1 \neq 0$. In this case, the zeros of the companion polynomial $\mathcal{C}_P$ of P are

$$r_1 = r_2 = 0, \ r_3 = a_0 + a_1i, \ r_4 = a_0 - a_1i, \ r_5 = b_0 - b_2, \ r_6 = b_0 + b_2,$$

and so there are, at most, 5 admissible classes

$$\mathscr{C}_1 = [\![0]\!], \quad \mathscr{C}_2 = [\![a_0 + a_1 \mathsf{i}]\!] = [\![\mathsf{a}]\!],$$

$$\mathscr{C}_3 = [\![\tfrac{b_0 - b_2}{2} + \tfrac{b_0 - b_2}{2}\mathsf{j}]\!], \quad \mathscr{C}_4 = [\![\tfrac{b_0 + b_2}{2} + \tfrac{b_0 + b_2}{2}\mathsf{j}]\!]$$

$$\mathscr{C}_5 = [\![b_0 + b_2 \mathsf{j}]\!] = [\![\mathsf{b}]\!]$$

In this case we have to consider the conditions

$$C_{3,1} : b_2 = b_0, \quad C_{3,2} : b_2 = -b_0, \quad C_{3,3} : b_2^2 = (a_0 - b_0)^2 + a_1^2 \tag{23}$$

When none of these conditions holds, the cubic has the isolated fixed points

$$\mathsf{z}_1 = 0, \quad \mathsf{z}_2 = \mathsf{b},$$
$$\mathsf{z}_3 = a_0 + \frac{a_1\big((a_0 - b_0)^2 + a_1^2 + b_2^2\big)}{(a_0 - b_0)^2 + a_1^2 - b_2^2}\mathsf{i} + \frac{2a_1^2 b_2}{(a_0 - b_0)^2 + a_1^2 - b_2^2}\mathsf{j} + \frac{2a_1(-a_0 + b_0)b_2}{(a_0 - b_0)^2 + a_1^2 - b_2^2}\mathsf{k} \tag{24}$$

and the two lines of fixed points

$$\mathcal{L}_1 = \big\{ \tfrac{b_0 + b_2}{2} + \alpha \mathsf{i} + \tfrac{b_0 + b_2}{2}\mathsf{j} - \alpha \mathsf{k} : \alpha \in \mathbb{R} \big\}$$
$$\mathcal{L}_2 = \big\{ \tfrac{b_0 - b_2}{2} + \alpha \mathsf{i} - \tfrac{b_0 - b_2}{2}\mathsf{j} + \alpha \mathsf{k} : \alpha \in \mathbb{R} \big\}. \tag{25}$$

Table 3 gives a full description of the types of maps that are obtained when one or more of the conditions (23) are satisfied. Since conditions (23) do not impose any restriction on a, the table only contains the special forms of b that influence the type of map we obtain.

Table 3. Case $\mathsf{a} = a_0 + a_1 \mathsf{i}$ and $\mathsf{b} = b_0 + b_2 \mathsf{j}$

b	Type of map
$b_0 + b_2 \mathsf{j}$	$(3, 2, 0)$
$b_0 \pm b_0 \mathsf{j}$	$(1, 2, 0)$
$b_0 \pm \sqrt{a_1^2 + (a_0 - b_0)^2}\,\mathsf{j}$	$(2, 2, 0)$
$\frac{a_0^2 + a_1^2}{2a_0} \pm \frac{a_0^2 + a_1^2}{2a_0}\mathsf{j}$ $(a_0 \neq 0)$	$(0, 2, 0)$

3.4   Case $\mathsf{a} \in \mathbb{D}$

Finally, we consider the case where a is a dual number $\mathsf{a} = a_0 + \mathsf{i} + \mathsf{j}$. In this case the zeros of the companion polynomial $\mathcal{C}_P$ of P are

$$r_1 = r_2 = 0, \; r_3 = r_4 = a_0, \; r_5 = b_0 - b_2, \; r_6 = b_0 + b_2,$$

and so there are, at most, 6 admissible classes

$$\mathscr{C}_1 = [\![0]\!], \quad \mathscr{C}_2 = [\![\tfrac{a_0}{2} + \tfrac{a_0}{2}\mathbf{j}]\!], \quad \mathscr{C}_3 = [\![a_0]\!] = [\![\mathbf{a}]\!],$$

$$\mathscr{C}_4 = [\![\tfrac{b_0-b_2}{2} + \tfrac{b_0-b_2}{2}\mathbf{j}]\!], \quad \mathscr{C}_5 = [\![\tfrac{b_0+b_2}{2} + \tfrac{b_0+b_2}{2}\mathbf{j}]\!]$$

$$\mathscr{C}_6 = [\![b_0 + b_2\mathbf{j}]\!] = [\![\mathbf{b}]\!]$$

In this case, we must consider the conditions

$$\begin{aligned}
&\mathsf{C}_{4,1} : a_0 = 0, \quad \mathsf{C}_{4,2} : b_2 = b_0, \quad \mathsf{C}_{4,3} : b_2 = -b_0, \\
&\mathsf{C}_{4,4} : b_2 = a_0 - b_0, \quad \mathsf{C}_{4,5} : b_2 = -a_0 + b_0, \\
&\mathsf{C}_{4,6} : (a_0 - b_0)^2 = b_2(2 + b_2)
\end{aligned} \tag{26}$$

When none of the above conditions holds, the fixed points of the cubic are

$$\mathbf{z}_1 = 0, \qquad \mathbf{z}_2 = \mathbf{b},$$

$$\mathbf{z}_3 = \tfrac{b_0+b_2+a_0}{2} + \tfrac{b_0-b_2-a_0}{2}\mathbf{i} + \tfrac{b_0+b_2-a_0}{2}\mathbf{j} - \tfrac{b_0-b_2-a_0}{2}\mathbf{k},$$

$$\mathbf{z}_4 = \tfrac{b_0-b_2+a_0}{2} - \tfrac{b_0+b_2-a_0}{2}\mathbf{i} - \tfrac{b_0-b_2-a_0}{2}\mathbf{j} - \tfrac{b_0+b_2-a_0}{2}\mathbf{k},$$

$$\mathbf{z}_5 = a_0 + \tfrac{(a_0-b_0)^2+b_2^2}{(a_0-b_0)^2-b_2(2+b_2)}\mathbf{i} + \tfrac{(a_0-b_0)^2-b_2^2}{(a_0-b_0)^2-b_2(2+b_2)}\mathbf{j} + \tfrac{2(-a_0+b_0)b_2}{(a_0-b_0)^2-b_2(2+b_2)}\mathbf{k}$$

and

$$\mathcal{L}_1 = \left\{ \tfrac{b_0+b_2}{2} + \alpha\mathbf{i} + \tfrac{b_0+b_2}{2}\mathbf{j} - \alpha\mathbf{k} : \alpha \in \mathbb{R} \right\},$$

$$\mathcal{L}_2 = \left\{ \tfrac{b_0-b_2}{2} + \alpha\mathbf{i} - \tfrac{b_0-b_2}{2}\mathbf{j} + \alpha\mathbf{k} : \alpha \in \mathbb{R} \right\},$$

$$\mathcal{L}_3 = \left\{ \tfrac{a_0}{2} + \alpha\mathbf{i} + \tfrac{a_0 b_2(a_0-b_0)+\alpha((a_0-b_0)^2-b_2^2)}{(a_0-b_0)^2+b_2^2}\mathbf{j} + \tfrac{a_0((a_0-b_0)^2-b_2^2)+4b_2\alpha(b_0-a_0)}{2((a_0-b_0)^2+b_2^2)}\mathbf{k} : \alpha \in \mathbb{R} \right\},$$

i.e. we have a $(5, 3, 0)$ map.

In Table 4, one can see the types of maps occurring when one or more of the conditions (26) are satisfied.

Table 4. Case $a = a_0 + i + j$ and $b = b_0 + b_2 j$

a	b	Type of map
$a_0 + i + j$	$b_0 + b_2 j$	$(5,3,0)$
$a_0 + i + j$	$b_0 \pm b_0 j$	$(2,3,0)$
$a_0 + i + j$	$b_0 \pm (a_0 - b_0)j$	$(3,2,0)$
$a_0 + i + j$	$b_0 + (-1 \pm \sqrt{1 + (a_0 - b_0)^2})j$	$(4,3,0)$
$a_0 + i + j$	$\frac{a_0}{2} \pm \frac{a_0}{2}j$	$(1,2,0)$
$a_0 + i + j$ $(a_0 \neq -1)$	$\frac{a_0^2}{2(1+a_0)} + \frac{a_0^2}{2(1+a_0)}j$	$(1,3,0)$
$a_0 + i + j$ $(a_0 \neq 1)$	$\frac{a_0^2}{2(1-a_0)} - \frac{a_0^2}{2(1-a_0)}j$	$(1,3,0)$
$i + j$	$b_0 + b_2 j$	$(1,3,0)$
$i + j$	$b_0 \pm b_0 j$	$(0,2,0)$
$i + j$	$b_0 + (-1 \pm \sqrt{1 + b_0^2})j$	$(1,3,0)$

4   Examples

We now present some examples illustrating the theoretical results obtained in the previous section. In the determination of the zeros of the polynomials considered in the examples, we made use of a set of Mathematica functions – the package `CoqPolynomial` – which were specially designed to deal with coquaternionic polynomials [8].

Example 1. For the choice of parameters $a = 12 - 4j$ and $b = 10 + 8j$, the cubic map $f_{a,b}$ has the following five isolated fixed points:

$$z_1 = 0, \quad z_2 = 12 - 4j, \quad z_3 = 10 + 8j, \quad z_4 = 17 + j, \quad z_5 = 5 + 3j$$

and the following four lines of fixed points:

$$\mathcal{L}_1 = \{8 + \alpha i - 8j + \alpha k : \alpha \in \mathbb{R}\}, \quad \mathcal{L}_2 = \{4 + \alpha i + 4j - \alpha k : \alpha \in \mathbb{R}\},$$
$$\mathcal{L}_3 = \{1 + \alpha i - j + \alpha k : \alpha \in \mathbb{R}\}, \quad \mathcal{L}_4 = \{9 + \alpha i + 9j - \alpha k : \alpha \in \mathbb{R}\}.$$

The results of [7] show that the quadratic g_b has z_1, z_3, $\mathcal{L}_3$ and $\mathcal{L}_4$ as fixed points and we would like to remark how the simple introduction of a new linear factor made us move form a $(2,2,0)$ map to a $(5,4,0)$ map.

Example 2. For the choice of parameters $a = 11 + j$ and $b = 7 - 5j$, the cubic map $f_{a,b}$ has the three isolated fixed points

$$z_1' = 0, \quad z_2' = 6 - 4j, \quad z_3' = 12,$$

the four lines of fixed points

$$\mathcal{L}_1' = \{5 + \alpha i - 5j + \alpha k : \alpha \in \mathbb{R}\}, \quad \mathcal{L}_2' = \{1 + \alpha i + j - \alpha k : \alpha \in \mathbb{R}\},$$
$$\mathcal{L}_3' = \{7 + \alpha i - 5j - \alpha k : \alpha \in \mathbb{R}\}, \quad \mathcal{L}_4' = \{11 + \alpha i + j + \alpha k : \alpha \in \mathbb{R}\}$$

and the hyperboloid of fixed points

$$\mathcal{H} = [\![6 + 6j]\!].$$

Thus we have a $(3, 4, 1)$ map, as predicted by the theory, since we are in the case where b has the special form $b = b_0 + (-a_0 - a_2 + b_0)j$; see Table 1.

We would like to observe that all the fixed points listed in (20) and (21) are still fixed points of the cubic, but $z_2 = a$ and $z_3 = b$ are no longer isolated: $z_2 \in \mathcal{L}'_4$ and $z_3 \in \mathcal{L}'_3$. But, more interesting is the fact that the lines $\mathcal{L}_2$ and $\mathcal{L}_3$ given in (21) are both contained in the hyperboloid $\mathcal{H}$.

Example 3. In this example we consider the parameters $a = -4 + i + j$ and $b = -4 - 2j$. The corresponding cubic map $f_{a,b}$ has the four isolated fixed points

$$z_1 = 0, \quad z_2 = -4 - 2j, \quad z_3 = -5 + i - j - k, \quad z_4 = -3 + i - j + k,$$

and the three lines of fixed points

$$\mathcal{L}_1 = \{-3 + \alpha i - 3j - \alpha k : \alpha \in \mathbb{R}\},$$
$$\mathcal{L}_2 = \{-1 + \alpha i + j + \alpha k : \alpha \in \mathbb{R}\},$$
$$\mathcal{L}_3 = \{-2 + \alpha i - \alpha j + 2k : \alpha \in \mathbb{R}\}.$$

Note that we are in the case where b has the special form $b = b_0 + (-1 - \sqrt{1 + (a_0 - b_0)^2})j$ and that the type of map obtained is as predicted by the theory; see Table 4.

This is an interesting example in the sense that neither a nor any of the elements in its class are fixed points of the map.

Acknowledgment. Research at CMAT was partially financed by Portuguese funds through FCT - Fundação para a Ciência e a Tecnologia, within the Projects UIDB/00013/2020 and UIDP/00013/2020. Research at NIPE has been financed by FCT, within the Project UIDB/03182/2020.

References

1. Ata, E., Yayli, Y.: Split quaternions and semi-Euclidean projective spaces. Chaos, Solitons Fractals **41**(4), 1910–1915 (2009)
2. Bekar, M., Yayli, Y.: Involutions of complexified quaternions and split quaternions. Adv. Appl. Clifford Algebras **23**, 283–29 (2013)
3. Brody, D., Graefe, E.M.: On complexified mechanics and coquaternions. J. Phys. A: Math. Theory **44**, 1–9 (2011)
4. Falcão, M.I., Miranda, F., Severino, R., Soares, M.J.: Iteration of quadratic maps on coquaternions. Int. J. Bifurcation Chaos **25**, 1730039 (2017)
5. Falcão, M.I., Miranda, F., Severino, R., Soares, M.J.: Polynomials over quaternions and coquaternions: a unified approach. Lecture Notes in Computer Science, vol. 10405, pp. 379–393 (2017)
6. Falcão, M.I., Miranda, F., Severino, R., Soares, M.J.: The number of zeros of unilateral polynomials over coquaternions revisited. Linear Multilinear Algebra **67**(6), 1231–1249 (2019)

7. Falcão, M.I., Miranda, F., Severino, R., Soares, M.J.: Dynamics of the coquaternionic maps $x^2 + bx$. Rendiconti del Circolo Matematico di Palermo Series 2 (2022)
8. Falcão, M.I., Miranda, F., Severino, R., Soares, M.J.: Mathematica tools for coquaternions. In: Gervasi, O., et al. (eds.) ICCSA 2021. LNCS, vol. 12952, pp. 449–464. Springer, Cham (2021). https://doi.org/10.1007/978-3-030-86973-1_32
9. Gao, C., Chen, X., Shen, Y.-G.: Quintessence and phantom emerging from the split-complex field and the split-quaternion field. Gen. Relativ. Gravit. **48**(1), 1–23 (2015). https://doi.org/10.1007/s10714-015-2006-1
10. Gogberashvili, M.: Split quaternions and particles in (2+1)-space. Eur. Phys. J. C **74**(12), 1–9 (2014). https://doi.org/10.1140/epjc/s10052-014-3200-0
11. Jiang, T., Zhang, Z., Jiang, Z.: Algebraic techniques for Schrödinger equations in split quaternionic mechanics. Comput. Math. Appl. **75**, 2217–2222 (2018)
12. Kula, L., Yayli, Y.: Split quaternions and rotations in semi Euclidean space e_2^4. J. Korean Math. Soc. **44**(6), 1313–1327 (2007)
13. Ni, Q.Y., Ding, J.K., Cheng, X.H., Jiao, Y.N.: 2×2 matrix representation forms and inner relationships of split quaternions. Adv. Appl. Clifford Algebras **29**(34) (2019). https://doi.org/10.1007/s00006-019-0951-6
14. Özdemir, M., Ergin, A.: Some geometric applications of split quaternions. Proceedings of the 16th International Conference of the Jangjeon Mathematical Society, vol. 16, pp. 108–115 (2005)
15. Özdemir, M., Ergin, A.: Rotations with unit timelike quaternions in Minkowski 3-space. J. Geometry Phys. **56**(2), 322–336 (2006)
16. Özdemir, M., Simsek, H.: Rotations on a lightcone in Minkowski 3-space. Adv. Appl. Clifford Algebras **27**, 2841–2853 (2017)

Remarks on the Zeros of Quadratic Coquaternionic Polynomials

Maria Irene Falcão[1]([⊠])(iD), Fernando Miranda[1](iD), Ricardo Severino[1](iD), and Maria Joana Soares[2](iD)

[1] CMAT and Departamento de Matemática, Universidade do Minho, Braga, Portugal
{mif,fmiranda,ricardo}@math.uminho.pt
[2] NIPE, Universidade do Minho, Braga, Portugal
jsoares@math.uminho.pt

Abstract. In this paper we focus on the study of monic quadratic polynomials whose coefficients are coquaternions and present several new results concerning the number and nature of its zeros. Examples specially constructed to illustrate the diversity of cases that can occur are also presented.

Keywords: Coquaternions · Polynomial computation · Zeros

1 Introduction

Coquaternions, also known in the literature as split quaternions, were introduced in 1849 by the English mathematician Sir James Cockle [4]. This four dimensional hypercomplex real algebra generalizes complex numbers and recent years have witnessed an increased interest among mathematicians and physicists on applications of these numbers [1–3,11–18,20].

One can find also in recent literature results concerning polynomials whose coefficients are coquaternions [7,8,19]. In particular, in [8], the structure of the zero-set of such polynomials was described, revealing the existence of non-isolated zeros of two different natures, namely the so-called hyperboloidal and linear zeros.

These results motivated the authors of this paper to start studying the dynamics of the quadratic map in the coquaternionic setting [5,6,10] leading to preliminary results which can be considered as even richer than the ones obtained in the well known complex case. A complete understanding of the dynamics requires a deep knowledge of the quadratic equation: number of zeros; coexistence of zeros of different nature, etc. For this reason we study, in this paper, the zeros of the equation $x^2 + bx + c$, where b and c are coquaternions.

The paper is organized as follows: Sects. 2 and 3 contain some background on the algebra of coquaternions and the basic results concerning the ring of polynomials with coquaternionic coefficients. Section 3 describes the zero-set of monic quadratic polynomials by adapting the results of [8, Theorem 3.14] to the present context. Some aspects concerning the existence/coexistence of hyperboloidal zeros and linear zeros are also clarified. The last section details all the possible situations that may occur concerning the number and nature of the zeros together with several examples clearly illustrating each case.

2 Basic Results and Notations

Let $\{1, \mathbf{i}, \mathbf{j}, \mathbf{k}\}$ be an orthonormal basis of the Euclidean vector space $\mathbb{R}^4$. The algebra of real coquaternions, which we denote by $\mathbb{H}_{\mathrm{coq}}$, is generated by the product given according to the following rules

$$\mathbf{i}^2 = -1, \ \mathbf{j}^2 = \mathbf{k}^2 = 1, \ \mathbf{ij} = -\mathbf{ji} = \mathbf{k}.$$

In analogy with the complex and quaternionic case, the *conjugate* $\overline{q}$ of a coquaternion $q = q_0 + q_1\mathbf{i} + q_2\mathbf{j} + q_3\mathbf{k}$ is defined as $\overline{q} = q_0 - q_1\mathbf{i} - q_2\mathbf{j} - q_3\mathbf{k}$; the number q_0 is called the *real part* of q and denoted by $\mathrm{Re}\,q$ and the *vector part* of q, denoted by $\underline{q}$, is given by $\underline{q} = q_1\mathbf{i} + q_2\mathbf{j} + q_3\mathbf{k}$. We identify the set of elements in $\mathbb{H}_{\mathrm{coq}}$ whose vector part is zero with the set $\mathbb{R}$ of real numbers. The quantities $\mathrm{tr}\,q = q - \underline{q} = 2\mathrm{Re}\,q$ and $\det q = q\overline{q} = q_0^2 + q_1^2 - q_2^2 - q_3^2$ are called the *trace* and *determinant* of q, respectively. Finally, it can be shown that a coquaternion q is invertible or nonsingular if and only if $\det q \neq 0$. In that case, we have, $q^{-1} = \frac{\overline{q}}{\det q}$.

The notion of quasi-similarity for two coquaternions will play an important role in this paper. We say that two coquaternions p and q are *quasi-similiar* if $\mathrm{Re}\,p = \mathrm{Re}\,q$ and $\det \underline{p} = \det \underline{q}$. Naturally, quasi-similarity is an equivalence relation in $\mathbb{H}_{\mathrm{coq}}$ and the corresponding equivalence class of q is called the *quasi-similarity class* of q and denoted by $[\![q]\!]$. We can identify

$$[\![q]\!] = \left\{ x_0 + x_1\mathbf{i} + x_2\mathbf{j} + x_3\mathbf{k} : x_0 = q_0 \text{ and } x_1^2 - x_2^2 - x_3^2 = q_1^2 - q_2^2 - q_3^2 \right\}$$

with a hyperboloid in the hyperplane $x_0 = q_0$, which will be a hyperboloid of two sheets if $\det \underline{q} > 0$, a hyperboloid of one sheet if $\det \underline{q} < 0$ and a cone, if $\det \underline{q} = 0$.

Given a quasi-similarity class $[\![q]\!] = [\![q_0 + \underline{q}]\!]$, its *characteristic polynomial* is the polynomial $\Psi_{[\![q]\!]}$ defined as

$$\Psi_{[\![q]\!]}(x) = x^2 - 2q_0\,x + \det q. \tag{1}$$

Since $\Psi_{[\![q]\!]}$ is a second degree monic polynomial with real coefficients, it can be written as

$$\Psi_{[\![q]\!]} = \begin{cases} (x - \alpha)(x - \overline{\alpha}), \ \alpha \in \mathbb{C} \setminus \mathbb{R}, & \text{if } \det \underline{q} > 0 \\ (x - r_1)(x - r_2), \ r_1, r_2 \in \mathbb{R}, & \text{if } \det \underline{q} \leq 0 \end{cases} \tag{2}$$

Reciprocally, if Q is a second degree monic polynomial with real coefficients, it is easy to see that it is the characteristic polynomial of a uniquely defined quasi-similarity class, namely

$$Q = \begin{cases} \Psi_{[\![\alpha]\!]}, & \text{if the roots of } Q \text{ are } \alpha, \overline{\alpha} \in \mathbb{C} \setminus \mathbb{R} \\ \Psi_{[\![\frac{r_1+r_2}{2} + \frac{r_1-r_2}{2}\mathbf{j}]\!]}, & \text{if the roots of } Q \text{ are } r_1, r_2 \in \mathbb{R} \end{cases} \tag{3}$$

3 Polynomials in $\mathbb{H}_{coq}[x]$

We denote by $\mathbb{H}_{coq}[x]$ the set of polynomials P whose coefficients are only located on the left of the variable, i.e. P is of the form

$$P(x) = c_n x^n + c_{n-1} x^{n-1} + \cdots + c_1 x + c_0, \ c_i \in \mathbb{H}_{coq}. \tag{4}$$

The addition and multiplication of such polynomials are defined as in the commutative case, where the variable is assumed to commute with the coefficients. This is a ring, referred to as the ring of (left) *one-sided* polynomials in $\mathbb{H}_{coq}$.

Given a polynomial P of the form (4), its *conjugate polynomial* is the polynomial defined by $\overline{P}(x) = \overline{c}_n x^n + \overline{c}_{n-1} x^{n-1} + \cdots + \overline{c}_1 x + \overline{c}_0$, and its *companion polynomial* is the polynomial (with real coefficients) given by

$$\mathcal{C}_P(x) = P(x)\overline{P}(x).$$

If $P(z) = 0$, we say that z is a *zero* (or a root) of the polynomial P and we denote by $Z(P)$ the *zero-set* of P.

In a previous work [8] we gave a complete characterization of the zero-set $Z(P)$ of a given coquaternionic polynomial P, distinguishing between three types of zeros z:

1. *isolated zero*, if $[\![z]\!]$ contains no other zeros of P;
2. *hyperboloidal zero*, if $[\![z]\!] \subseteq Z(P)$;
3. *linear zero*, if z is neither an isolated zero nor a hyperboloidal zero of P.

We also proved that the zeros of any nth degree polynomial belong to, at most, $n(2n-1)$ similarity classes. In what follows, we will treat all the zeros belonging to the same quasi-similarity class as forming a single zero, i.e., we will refer to a whole hyperboloid of zeros or a line of zeros simply as a hyperboloidal zero or a linear zero, respectively. We end this section by presenting two important results in the context of the present work. Full details and proofs can be found in [8].

Theorem 1. *If $z \in \mathbb{H}_{coq}$ is a zero of a polynomial P of the form* (4), *then $\Psi_{[\![z]\!]}$ is a divisor of $\mathcal{C}_P$.*

Denote by $\alpha_1, \overline{\alpha}_1, \ldots, \alpha_m, \overline{\alpha}_m \in \mathbb{C} \backslash \mathbb{R}$ and $r_1, r_2, \ldots, r_\ell \in \mathbb{R}$, where $\ell = 2(n-m)$, $(0 \le m \le n)$, the $2n$ roots of $\mathcal{C}_P$. It is easy to see (cf. (3)) that the characteristic polynomials which divide $\mathcal{C}_P$ are the ones associated with the classes:

$$[\![\alpha_k]\!]; \ k = 1, \ldots, m, \tag{5}$$

$$[\![r_{ij}]\!]; \ i = 1, \ldots, \ell - 1, \ j = i+1, \ldots, \ell, \tag{6}$$

with

$$r_{ij} = \frac{r_i + r_j}{2} + \frac{r_i - r_j}{2}\mathrm{j}. \tag{7}$$

This leads to the next result concerning the zero-set of P.

Theorem 2. *Let P be a polynomial of the form* (4). *Then:*

$$Z(P) \subseteq \bigcup_k [\![\alpha_k]\!] \bigcup_{i,j} [\![r_{ij}]\!],$$

where $[\![\alpha_k]\!]$ *and* $[\![r_{ij}]\!]$ *are the quasi-similarity classes defined by* (5)–(7).

Last result underpins the use of the designation *admissible classes* (with respect to the zeros) of the polynomial P, for classes given by (5)–(7).

4   The Zero Structure of Quadratic Polynomials in $\mathbb{H}_{\mathrm{coq}}[x]$

In what follows we consider the quadratic equation

$$x^2 + bx + c = 0, \ b, c \in \mathbb{H}_{\mathrm{coq}}. \tag{8}$$

It is already known that equations of this form can have at most 6 zeros; what remains to be seen is how many zeros of each type can they have. For our purpose here we rewrite Theorem 3.14 of [8] for a quadratic polynomial in the following form:

Theorem 3. *Consider a quadratic polynomial P of the form* (8). *For each admissible class* $[\![q]\!] = [\![q_0 + \underline{q}]\!]$ *of P, denote by $A + Bx$ the polynomial*

$$A + Bx = P(x) - \Psi_{[\![q]\!]},$$

with $A, B \in \mathbb{H}_{\mathrm{coq}}$. *The nature of the zero of P in* $[\![q]\!]$ *(if any) is the following:*

1. *If* $\det B \neq 0$, *then* $[\![q]\!]$ *contains only the **isolated zero** $-B^{-1}A$;*
2. *If* $A = B = 0$, *then* $[\![q]\!]$ *is a **hyperboloidal zero** of P;*
3. *If* $B \neq 0, \det B = 0, \det \underline{q} \leq 0$ *and* $A = -(q_0 \pm \sqrt{-\det \underline{q}})B$, *then* $[\![q]\!]$ *contains a **linear zero** of P;*
4. *If* $B \neq 0$, $\det B = 0$ *and* $A = -B\gamma$, *for some* $\gamma \in \mathbb{C} \setminus \mathbb{R}$, *then the class* $[\![q]\!]$ *contains only one **isolated zero** of P;*
5. *If none of the above conditions holds, then there are **no zeros** of P in* $[\![q]\!]$.

We point out that the result in [8] is more complete since it also provides the expression for the zeros. Since we are interested only in the number of zeros of each type, we chose to present a simplified version of the result.

The following result clarify some aspects concerning the zeros of quadratic polynomials in $\mathbb{H}_{\mathrm{coq}}[x]$.

Theorem 4. *Consider a quadratic polynomial P of the form* (8).

1. *If* $[\![z]\!]$ *is a hyperboloidal zero of P, then $\mathcal{C}_P$ has two double roots or one real root with multiplicity 4, if* $\det \underline{z} \neq 0$ *or* $\det \underline{z} = 0$, *respectively.*

2. If $[\![z]\!]$ contains a linear zero, then the roots of $\mathcal{C}_P$ are all reals and at least one of them is also a root of P.

3. P cannot have both linear and hyperboloidal zeros.

Proof. It is clear from Theorem 3 that $[\![z]\!]$ is a hyperboloidal zero of a quadratic polynomial P if and only if $\Psi_{[\![z]\!]} = P$. Taking into account relation (3), we conclude that

$$[\![z]\!] = [\![\alpha]\!],\ \alpha \in \mathbb{C} \setminus \mathbb{R}\ \text{or}\ [\![z]\!] = [\![\tfrac{r_1+r_2}{2} + \tfrac{r_1-r_2}{2}\mathbf{j}]\!],\ r_1, r_2 \in \mathbb{R},$$

i.e. P is of one of the forms

$$P(x) = (x - \alpha)(x - \bar{\alpha})\ \text{or}\ P(x) = (x - r_1)(x - r_2). \tag{9}$$

This implies that

$$\mathcal{C}_P(x) = (x - \alpha)^2(x - \bar{\alpha})^2\ \text{or}\ \mathcal{C}_P(x) = (x - r_1)^2(x - r_2)^2.$$

Observing that $\tfrac{r_1+r_2}{2} + \tfrac{r_1-r_2}{2}\mathbf{j}$ has singular vector part if and only if $r_1 = r_2$, the result 1. follows.

From Theorem 3 (3.) it also follows that a class of the type (5) will never contains a linear zero, since $\det \underline{\alpha} > 0$, for all $\alpha \in \mathbb{C} \setminus \mathbb{R}$.

Consider now a class $[\![\tfrac{r_i+r_j}{2} + \tfrac{r_i-r_j}{2}\mathbf{j}]\!]$ of the form (6)–(7). If such class contains a linear zero, then by Theorem 3 (3.), P can be written as

$$P(x) = (x - r_i)(x - r_j) + Bx + A,$$

with $B \neq 0$, $\det B = 0$ and $A = -\left(\tfrac{r_i+r_j}{2} \pm \tfrac{r_i-r_j}{2}\right)B$, i.e. P has one of the forms

$$P(x) = (x - r_i)(x - r_j) + B(x - r_i)\ \text{or}\ P(x) = (x - r_i)(x - r_j) + B(x - r_j), \tag{10}$$

for some singular coquaternion $B \neq 0$. Therefore either r_i or r_j is a zero of P. This proves part 2.

Finally, assume that P has one hyperboloidal zero $[\![z_1]\!]$ and one linear zero in $[\![z_2]\!]$. The use of 1. and 2. allows to conclude that $[\![z_1]\!] = [\![\tfrac{r_1+r_2}{2} + \tfrac{r_1-r_2}{2}\mathbf{j}]\!]$ and, from (9),

$$\mathcal{C}_P(x) = (x - r_1)^2(x - r_2)^2,$$

with $r_1 \neq r_2$ (otherwise P would have just one zero). The admissible classes that can contain linear zeros are $[\![r_1]\!]$ and $[\![r_2]\!]$. Assume first that $[\![z_2]\!] = [\![r_1]\!]$. The use of Theorem 3 gives

$$P(x) = (x - r_1)(x - r_2) = \Psi_{[\![r_1]\!]}(x) + Bx + A = (x - r_1)^2 + Bx + A,$$

which implies that $B = r_1 - r_2$. Since $r_1 \neq r_2$, it follows that the necessary condition $\det B = 0$ for the existence of linear zeros does not hold. The same reasoning leads to the conclusion that $[\![r_2]\!]$ is not also a linear zero. $\qquad\square$

5   The Number and Nature of the Zeros

We now discuss in detail all the cases that may occur concerning the zeros of the companion polynomial of the quadratic polynomial P – a 4th degree polynomial with real coefficients – having in mind the correspondence between these zeros and the admissible classes of P, which we know already are at most 6 (cf. Sect. 3).

To illustrate each case, we construct polynomials, by using a set of Mathematica functions – CoqPolynomial – specially design to deal with coquaternionic polynomials [9].

Case 1: $\mathcal{C}_P(x) = (x - \alpha)(x - \bar{\alpha})(x - \beta)(x - \bar{\beta})$, $\alpha, \beta \in \mathbb{C} \setminus \mathbb{R}$;

In this case, the number of admissible classes is 1 ($[\![\alpha]\!]$, if $\alpha = \beta$) or 2 ($[\![\alpha]\!]$ and $[\![\beta]\!]$, if $\alpha \neq \beta$). From Theorem 4, it follows that there are no linear zeros, but P can have: one hyperboloidal zero $[\![\alpha]\!]$, if $\alpha = \beta$; or at most two isolated zeros.

Example 1. Consider the polynomials

$$P_1(x) = x^2 - 2x + 4 \qquad\qquad P_2(x) = x^2 - 3ix - 3 + i$$
$$P_3(x) = x^2 + (2 - 4i)x - 3 - 4i \qquad P_4(x) = x^2 + 1 - i - j.$$

The details about the zero-sets of each polynomial and its companion polynomial are as follows:

1. $Z(\mathcal{C}_{P_1})$: $1 \pm \sqrt{3}i$, $1 \pm \sqrt{3}i$
   $Z(P_1)$: **one** hyperboloidal zero $[\![1 + \sqrt{3}i]\!]$
2. $Z(\mathcal{C}_{P_2})$: $-1 \pm 2i$, $1 \pm i$
   $Z(P_2)$: **two** isolated zeros $-1 + 2i$ and $1 + i$
3. $Z(\mathcal{C}_{P_3})$: $-1 \pm 2i$, $-1 \pm 2i$
   $Z(P_3)$: **one** isolated zero $-1 + 2i$
4. $Z(\mathcal{C}_{P_4})$: $\pm i$, $\pm i$
   $Z(P_4)$: **no** zeros

Case 2: $\mathcal{C}_P(x) = (x - \alpha)(x - \bar{\alpha})(x - r_1)(x - r_2)$, $\alpha \in \mathbb{C} \setminus \mathbb{R}, r_1, r_2 \in \mathbb{R}$

In this situation it follows at once from Theorem 4 that there are only (if any) isolated roots. Since there are two admissible classes $[\![\alpha]\!]$ and $[\![\frac{r_1+r_2}{2} + \frac{r_1-r_2}{2}j]\!]$, the polynomial P has at most 2 isolated zeros.

Example 2. The following polynomials illustrate Case 2.

$$P_1(x) = x^2 + (1 + i + k)x + 1 + i - j - k$$
$$P_2(x) = x^2 + (1 + i + k)x + 1 - i - j - k$$
$$P_3(x) = x^2 + (1 + i + j + k)x + 1 + i + j + k$$

1. $Z(\mathcal{C}_{P_1})$: $\pm\sqrt{3}i$, 0, -2
   $Z(P_1)$: **two** isolated zeros $-4i + 3j - 2k$ and $-1 + i + j - k$
2. $Z(\mathcal{C}_{P_2})$: $-1 \pm \sqrt{7}i$, 0, -1
   $Z(P_2)$: **one** isolated zero $\frac{1}{2}(-1 + 3i + 3j + k)$

3. $Z(cal\,C_{P_3})$: $-1 \pm 2\mathbf{i}, 0, 0$
   $Z(P_3)$: **no** zeros

Case 3: $C_P(x) = (x - r_1)(x - r_2)(x - r_3)(x - r_4)$, $r_1, r_2, r_3, r_4 \in \mathbb{R}$

In this case, we have to distinguish between 5 different cases.

Case 3.1: $r_1 = r_2 = r_3 = r_4$

In this case there is just one admissible class $[\![r_1]\!]$, which means that there is at most one zero of P. In case of existence, such zero can be of any of the three different natures, as it is shown in Example 3 (cf. [8, Example 4.5]).

Example 3. The companion polynomial of the following quadratic polynomials

$$P_1(x) = x^2 - 2x + 1$$
$$P_2(x) = x^2 - (2 + \mathbf{i} + \mathbf{j})x + 1 + \mathbf{i} + \mathbf{j}$$
$$P_3(x) = x^2 - (2 + 6\mathbf{i} + 5\mathbf{j} + 3\mathbf{k})x + 3\mathbf{i} + 2\mathbf{j} + 2\mathbf{k}$$
$$P_4(x) = x^2 - 2x + 1 + 5\mathbf{i} + 4\mathbf{j} + 3\mathbf{k}.$$

has 1 as a zero of multiplicity 4. However the situation concerning the zeros of the correspondent polynomials is quite different.

1. $Z(P_1)$: **one** hyperboloidal zero $[\![1]\!]$
2. $Z(P_2)$: **one** linear zero $\{1 + \lambda(\mathbf{i} + \mathbf{j}) : \lambda \in \mathbb{R}\}$
3. $Z(P_3)$: **one** isolated zero $\frac{1}{2}(1 + 5\mathbf{i} + 4\mathbf{j} + 3\mathbf{k})$
4. $Z(P_4)$: **no** zeros

Case 3.2: $r_1 = r_2 = r_3 \neq r_4$.

The admissible classes are $\mathcal{C}_1 = [\![r_1]\!]$ and $\mathcal{C}_2 = [\![\frac{r_1+r_4}{2} + \frac{r_1-r_4}{2}\mathbf{j}]\!]$. Since there are no hyperboloidal zeros, the possiblities for the zeros of P are: 2 linear zeros, 1 linear zero and/or 1 isolated zero or only isolated zeros (at most 2).

We are going to show that $\mathcal{C}_1$ contains a linear zero if and only if $\mathcal{C}_2$ contains a linear zero.

Assume first that $\mathcal{C}_1$ contains a linear zero. From (10) we know that r_1 itself is a zero of P. Following Theorem 3 for the class $\mathcal{C}_2$, we obtain

$$P(x) = (x - r_1)(x - r_4) + Bx + A$$

and since $P(r_1) = 0$, it follows that $A = -r_1 B$. Observe that for any $q = q_0 + \underline{q} \in \mathcal{C}_2$ we have that $q_0 = r_1$ and $\det \underline{q} = 0$. To conclude that $\mathcal{C}_2$ contains a linear zero it remains to prove that $\det \bar{B} = 0$. But, if B is nonsingular, then the first part of Teorem 3 gives that the only zero of P in $\mathcal{C}_2$ is r_1 which clearly is not possible ($r_1 \in \mathcal{C}_2 \Leftrightarrow r_1 = r_4$).

We prove now that the converse is also true. If $\mathcal{C}_2$ contains a linear zero, then either r_1 or r_4 is a zero of P (see Theorem 4). Clearly r_4 can not be a zero of P, because it is not (at least) a double zero of its companion polynomial. To classify the zero (if any) in the class $\mathcal{C}_1$, we write

$$P(x) = (x - r_1)^2 + Bx + A.$$

Since r_1 is a zero of P, then $A = -r_1 B$. We argue now that B is singular. If B is nonsingular, then the first part of Theorem 3 gives that the only zero of P in $\mathcal{C}_1$ is r_1. But

$$P(x) = (x - r_1)(x - r_1 + B)$$

which means that $r_1 - B$ is a zero of P, which in turn implies that $r_1 - B \in \mathcal{C}_1$ or $r_1 - B \in \mathcal{C}_2$. In the first case we get $\det B = 0$, while in the second one we obtain $\operatorname{Re} B = \frac{r_1 - r_4}{2}$ and $\det \underline{B} = \frac{(r_1 - r_4)^2}{4}$. This also leads to $\det B = 0$.

In conclusion, the possibilities for the zeros of P are: 2 linear zeros or only isolated zeros (at most 2), as is illustrated in Example 4.

Example 4. Consider the polynomials:

$$P_1(x) = x^2 + (1 + 5\mathbf{i} + 3\mathbf{j} + 5\mathbf{k})x - 2 + 10\mathbf{i} + 6\mathbf{j} + 10\mathbf{k}$$
$$P_2(x) = x^2 + (1 + \mathbf{i} + 2\mathbf{k})x + 1 + \mathbf{j} + \mathbf{k}$$
$$P_3(x) = x^2 + (-5 + \mathbf{i} + \mathbf{j} + \mathbf{k})x + 6 + \mathbf{i} - 3\mathbf{j} + \mathbf{k}$$

The details about the zero-set of each polynomial and its companion polynomial are as follows:

1. $Z(\mathcal{C}_{P_1})$: $-2, -2, -2, 4$

   $Z(P_1)$: **two** linear zeros
   $\{-2 + \lambda(17\mathbf{i} + 15\mathbf{j} + 8\mathbf{k}) : \lambda \in \mathbb{R}\}$ and $\{1 - 3\mathbf{j} + \lambda(\mathbf{i} + \mathbf{k}) : \lambda \in \mathbb{R}\}$
2. $Z(\mathcal{C}_{P_2})$: $-1, -1, -1, 1$
   $Z(P_2)$: **two** isolated zeros $-1 - \mathbf{i} - \mathbf{k}$ and $-2\mathbf{i} + \mathbf{j} - 2\mathbf{k}$
3. $Z(\mathcal{C}_{P_3})$: $1, 3, 3, 3$
   $Z(P_3)$: **one** isolated zero $1 + 5\mathbf{i} + 4\mathbf{j} + 3\mathbf{k}$

Case 3.3: $r_1 = r_2 \neq r_3 = r_4$

The admissible classes are $\mathcal{C}_1 = [\![r_1]\!]$, $\mathcal{C}_2 = [\![r_3]\!]$ and $\mathcal{C}_3 = [\![\frac{r_1 + r_3}{2} + \frac{r_1 - r_3}{2}\mathbf{j}]\!]$. It is clear that, in case of existence, the only hyperboloidal zero would be $\mathcal{C}_3$; in this case the polynomial is $P(x) = (x - r_1)(x - r_3)$ which means that there are also two isolated zeros: r_1 and r_3.

Concerning the linear zeros we prove now that neither $\mathcal{C}_1$ nor $\mathcal{C}_2$ can contain such kind of zeros. In fact, if $\mathcal{C}_1$ contains a linear zero, then

$$P(x) = (x - r_1)^2 + B(x - r_1) = (x - r_1)(x - r_1 + B),$$

for some singular B. Therefore

$$\mathcal{C}_P(x) = (x - r_1)^3(x - r_1 + 2\operatorname{Re} B),$$

and r_1 would be a zero of $\mathcal{C}_P$ with multiplicity 3. The same reasoning leads to the conclusion that $\mathcal{C}_2$ can not contain a linear zero. This means that linear zeros, if any, are in $\mathcal{C}_3$. If such kind of zeros exists, then

$$P(x) = (x - r_1)(x - r_3 + B) \quad \text{or} \quad P(x) = (x - r_3)(x - r_1 + B),$$

for some singular B, which also shows that there is one isolated zero in C_1 and another one in C_2. In fact, if P is of the first form, then it has the roots $r_1 \in C_1$ and $r_3 - B$. Moreover

$$\mathcal{C}_P(x) = (x - r_1)^2 (x - r_3)(x - r_3 + 2\operatorname{Re} B),$$

which leads to the conclusion that $\operatorname{Re} B = 0$ and the zero $r_3 - B \in C_2$. If P is of the second form, we use similar arguments to prove that $r_1 - B \in C_1$.

In conclusion, the possibilities in the case under consideration are: one hyperboloidal zero and 2 isolated zeros; one linear zero and 2 isolated zeros or only isolated zeros (at most 3).

Example 5. To illustrate Case 3.3, we have chosen the following polynomials:

$$P_1(x) = x^2 + 4x + 1$$
$$P_2(x) = x^2 + (3 + 5i + 3j + 4k)x + 2 + 10i + 6j + 8k$$
$$P_3(x) = x^2 + (1 + i + j + k)x - \tfrac{1}{6}(9 + 10i + j + 6k)$$
$$P_4(x) = x^2 + (-1 + \tfrac{1}{2}i + j + \tfrac{1}{2}k)x + \tfrac{1}{2} + i + \tfrac{1}{2}j - k$$
$$P_5(x) = x^2 + (1 - 3i - 3j - k)x + \tfrac{1}{2}(1 - 3i - 3j - k)$$

1. $Z(\mathcal{C}_{P_1})$: $-2 \pm \sqrt{3}$, $-2 \pm \sqrt{3}$
   $Z(P_1)$: **one** hyperboloidal zero $[\![-2 + \sqrt{3}j]\!]$
       two isolated zeros $-2 + \sqrt{3}$ and $-2 - \sqrt{3}$

2. $Z(\mathcal{C}_{P_2})$: $-2, -2, -1, -1$
   $Z(P_2)$: **one** linear zero $\{-\tfrac{3}{2} - \tfrac{2}{5}j + \tfrac{3}{10}k + \lambda(5i + 3j + 4k) : \lambda \in \mathbb{R}\}$
       two isolated zeros -2 and $-\tfrac{3}{2} + \tfrac{1}{2}j$

3. $Z(\mathcal{C}_{P_3})$: $-2, -2, 1, 1$
   $Z(P_3)$: **three** isolated zeros $-2 - \tfrac{29}{24}i - \tfrac{5}{6}j - \tfrac{7}{8}k$, $-\tfrac{1}{2} - \tfrac{4}{3}i + \tfrac{1}{6}j - 2k$ and
       $1 + \tfrac{5}{12}i - \tfrac{1}{3}j + \tfrac{1}{4}k$

4. $Z(\mathcal{C}_{P_4})$: $0, 0, 1, 1$
   $Z(P_4)$: **two** isolated zeros $\tfrac{1}{2} - \tfrac{3}{2}i - \tfrac{3}{2}j + \tfrac{1}{2}k$ and $1 - i - j$

5. $Z(\mathcal{C}_{P_5})$: $-1, -1, 0, 0$
   $Z(P_5)$: **one** isolated zero $-\tfrac{1}{2} + \tfrac{3}{2}i + \tfrac{3}{2}j + \tfrac{1}{2}k$

Case 3.4: $r_1 = r_2 \neq r_3 \neq r_4$

The admissible classes are $C_1 = [\![r_1]\!]$, $C_2 = [\![\frac{r_1 + r_3}{2} + \frac{r_1 - r_3}{2}j]\!]$, $C_3 = [\![\frac{r_1 + r_4}{2} + \frac{r_1 - r_4}{2}j]\!]$ and $C_4 = [\![\frac{r_3 + r_4}{2} + \frac{r_3 - r_4}{2}j]\!]$. It follows at once that there are no hyperboloidal zeros and arguments similar to those used in Case 3.3 lead to the conclusion that, in case of existence, the linear zeros are contained in C_2 and C_3 and in this case there are also two isolated zeros, one in each of classes C_1 and C_4.

Finally, the polynomial P can have only isolated zeros (up to 4). It is easy to see that when P has an isolated zero in the class C_2, then there is also an isolated zero of P in C_3, being the converse also true.

Example 6. To illustrate this situation, we use the polynomials:

$$P_1(x) = x^2 + (-\tfrac{7}{2} + i + \tfrac{1}{2}j + k)x + \tfrac{5}{2} - i - \tfrac{1}{2}j - k$$
$$P_2(x) = x^2 + (-1 + j + 2k)x - 2 + 6i + 6j - 2k$$
$$P_3(x) = x^2 + (1 - 2i - j + 2k)x - 2 - 2j$$
$$P_4(x) = x^2 + 2x + 2i - 2j - k$$

The corresponding details are as follows:

1. $Z(\mathcal{C}_{P_1})$: 1, 1, 2, 3
   $Z(P_1)$: **two** linear zeros

   $$\{\tfrac{3}{2} - \tfrac{3}{10}j + \tfrac{2}{5}k + \lambda(5i + 4j + 3k)\} \text{ and } \{2 - k + \lambda(i + k)\} \ (\lambda \in \mathbb{R})$$

   two isolated zeros 1 and $\tfrac{5}{2} - i - \tfrac{1}{2}j - k$
2. $Z(\mathcal{C}_{P_2})$: -2, 0, 0, 4

   $Z(P_2)$: **four** isolated zeros $-1 + 8i + 7j - 4k$, $-5i - 4j + 3k$, $1 - 2i - 3j - 2k$
   and $2 - i - 2j - k$
3. $Z(\mathcal{C}_{P_3})$: -2, -2, 0, 2
   $Z(P_3)$: **three** isolated zeros $-2 + i - k$, $-1 - j$ and $1 + j$
4. $Z(\mathcal{C}_{P_4})$: -1, -1, $-1 \pm \sqrt{2}$
   $Z(P_4)$: **two** isolated zeros $-1 - \tfrac{1}{\sqrt{2}} + \sqrt{2}i - \sqrt{2}j - \tfrac{1}{\sqrt{2}}k$ and

   $$-1 + \tfrac{1}{\sqrt{2}} - \sqrt{2}i + \sqrt{2}j + \tfrac{1}{\sqrt{2}}k$$

Case 3.5: $r_1 < r_2 < r_3 < r_4$

In this last situation, there are 6 admissible classes and all the zeros are isolated.

Example 7. The zeros of the following polynomials are all isolated.

$$P_1(x) = x^2 + (-2 + i - 2j - 2k)x - 2 + 3i + 2j - 3k$$
$$P_2(x) = x^2 + (-i - 3j - k)x + 1 + i - j + k$$
$$P_3(x) = x^2 + 3kx + 1 + k$$

1. $Z(\mathcal{C}_{P_1})$: -2, 0, 1, 5
   $Z(P_1)$: **six** isolated zeros $-1 + j$, $\tfrac{1}{2}(-1 - i + 3j - k)$, $\tfrac{1}{2}(1 + 3i - j - 3k)$,
   $\tfrac{1}{6}(9 + 5i + 21j + 5k)$, $\tfrac{1}{2}(5 - 21i - 5j + 21k)$ and $\tfrac{1}{9}(27 - 29i + 3j + 34k)$
2. $Z(\mathcal{C}_{P_2})$: -2, -1, 0, 3
   $Z(P_2)$: **five** isolated zeros $-1 - i + j - k$, $\tfrac{1}{2}(-1 - i + j - k)$, $\tfrac{1}{2}(1 + i + 5j + 2k)$,
   $\tfrac{1}{5}(5 + 2i + 10j + 2k)$ and $\tfrac{1}{2}(3 - 2i + 2j + 3k)$
3. $Z(\mathcal{C}_{P_3})$: -2, -1, 0, 3
   $Z(P_3)$: **four** isolated zeros $-1 - k$, $1 - 2k$, $\tfrac{1}{2}(-1 - k)$, $\tfrac{1}{2}(1 - 5k)$,

Table 1. Summary of the results

Case	Number of zeros (max)
1	1 HZ or 2 IZ
2	2 IZ
3.1	1 HZ or 1 LZ or 1 IZ
3.2	2 LZ or 2 IZ
3.3	1 HZ + 2 IZ or 1 LZ + 2 IZ or 3 IZ
3.4	2 LZ + 2 IZ or 4 IZ
3.5	6 IZ

6   Conclusions

Table 1 summarizes the main contributions of this paper concerning the maximum number of isolated (IZ), linear (LZ) and hyperboloidal zeros a quadratic coquaternionic polynomial may have. We believe that the results obtained are interesting from a theoretical point of view, but may also be useful for applications.

Acknowledgments. Research at CMAT was partially financed by Portuguese funds through FCT - Fundação para a Ciência e a Tecnologia, within the Projects UIDB/00013/2020 and UIDP/00013/2020. Research at NIPE has been financed by FCT, within the Project UIDB/03182/2020.

References

1. Ata, E., Yayli, Y.: Split quaternions and semi-Euclidean projective spaces. Chaos, Solitons Fractals **41**(4), 1910–1915 (2009)
2. Bekar, M., Yayli, Y.: Involutions of complexified quaternions and split quaternions. Adv. Appl. Clifford Algebras **23**, 283–29 (2013)
3. Brody, D., Graefe, E.M.: On complexified mechanics and coquaternions. J. Phys. A: Math. Theory **44**, 1–9 (2011)
4. Cockle, J.: On systems of algebra involving more than one imaginary; and on equations of the fifth degree. Phil. Mag. **35**(3), 434–435 (1849)
5. Falcão, M.I., Miranda, F., Severino, R., Soares, M.J.: Basins of attraction for a quadratic coquaternionic map. Chaos, Solitons Fractals **104**, 716–724 (2017)
6. Falcão, M.I., Miranda, F., Severino, R., Soares, M.J.: Iteration of quadratic maps on coquaternions. Int. J. Bifurcation Chaos **25**, 1730039 (2017)
7. Falcão, M.I., Miranda, F., Severino, R., Soares, M.J.: Polynomials over quaternions and coquaternions: a unified approach. In: Gervasi, O., et al. (eds.) ICCSA 2017. LNCS, vol. 10405, pp. 379–393. Springer, Cham (2017). https://doi.org/10.1007/978-3-319-62395-5_26
8. Falcão, M.I., Miranda, F., Severino, R., Soares, M.J.: The number of zeros of unilateral polynomials over coquaternions revisited. Linear Multilinear Algebra **67**(6), 1231–1249 (2019)

9. Falcão, M.I., Miranda, F., Severino, R., Soares, M.J.: Mathematica tools for coquaternions. In: Gervasi, O., et al. (eds.) ICCSA 2021. LNCS, vol. 12952, pp. 449–464. Springer, Cham (2021). https://doi.org/10.1007/978-3-030-86973-1_32
10. Falcão, M.I., Miranda, F., Severino, R., Soares, M.J.: Dynamics of the coquaternionic maps $x^2 + bx$. Rendiconti del Circolo Matematico di Palermo (Article in Press) (2022)
11. Gao, C., Chen, X., Shen, Y.-G.: Quintessence and phantom emerging from the split-complex field and the split-quaternion field. Gen. Relativ. Gravit. **48**(1), 1–23 (2015). https://doi.org/10.1007/s10714-015-2006-1
12. Gogberashvili, M.: Split quaternions and particles in (2+1)-space. Eur. hys. J. C **74**(12), 1–9 (2014). https://doi.org/10.1140/epjc/s10052-014-3200-0
13. Jiang, T., Zhang, Z., Jiang, Z.: Algebraic techniques for Schrödinger equations in split quaternionic mechanics. Comput. Math. Appl. **75**, 2217–2222 (2018)
14. Kula, L., Yayli, Y.: Split quaternions and rotations in semi Euclidean space E_2^4. J. Korean Math. Soc. **44**(6), 1313–1327 (2007)
15. Ni, Q.-Y., Ding, J.-K., Cheng, X.-H., Jiao, Y.-N.: 2 × 2 matrix representation forms and inner relationships of split quaternions. Adv. Appl. Clifford Algebras **29**(2), 1–12 (2019). https://doi.org/10.1007/s00006-019-0951-6
16. Özdemir, M., Ergin, A.: Some geometric applications of split quaternions. In: Proceedings of the 16th International Conference on Jangjeon Mathematical Society, vol. 16, pp. 108–115 (2005)
17. Özdemir, M., Ergin, A.: Rotations with unit timelike quaternions in Minkowski 3-space. J. Geometry Phys. **56**(2), 322–336 (2006)
18. Özdemir, M., Simsek, H.: Rotations on a lightcone in Minkowski 3-space. Adv. Appl. Clifford Algebras **27**, 2841–2853 (2017)
19. Scharler, D.F., Siegele, J., Schröcker, H.-P.: Quadratic split quaternion polynomials: factorization and geometry. Adv. Appl. Clifford Algebras **30**(1), 1–23 (2019). https://doi.org/10.1007/s00006-019-1037-1
20. Serôdio, R., Beites, P., Vitória, J.: Intersection of a double cone and a line in the split-quaternions context. Adv. Appl. Clifford Algebras **27**(3), 2795–2803 (2017)

International Workshop
on Computational and Applied Statistics
(CAS 2022)

A Note on Kendall's Tau Coefficient for Gap Times in Presence of Right Censoring

Cecilia Castro[(✉)] [iD] and Ana Paula Amorim[iD]

Centre of Mathematics, University of Minho, Braga, Portugal
{cecilia,apamorim}@math.uminho.pt

Abstract. In several clinical and epidemiology studies, data from events that occur successively in time in the same individual, are frequently reported. Among these, the most common are recurrent events where each subject may experience a number of failures over the course of follow-up. Examples include repeated hospitalization of patients, recurrences of tumor, recurrent infections, among others. In this work, the interest is to study the correlation between successive recurrent events, gap times, in the presence of right censoring. To measure the association between two gap times we use the Kendall's τ correlation coefficient, by incorporating suitable bivariate estimators of the joint distribution function of the gap times and of the marginal distribution function of the second gap time, into the integrals that define the probability of concordant pairs and the probability of discordant pairs. Two of the estimators of the joint distribution function of the gap times considered in this work are already known, but we consider also estimators with Kaplan-Meier weights defined by using decision trees and random forests methodology. We conclude that all the estimators perform better in a scenario of negative association. When the association is moderately negative, the performance of the estimator with smoothed weights using random forests is superior. In the case of strong positive association, the best estimator is the presmoothed nonparametric but, in the case of moderate positive association, this estimator has identical performance as the estimator with presmoothed weights using random forests.

Keywords: Right censoring · Decision trees · Kendall's Tau · Random forests

1 Introduction

Recurrent events that occur in the same subject successively in time, are frequently reported in clinical studies. Examples include repeated hospitalizations of patients, tumor recurrences, recurrent infections, among others.

Supported by Portuguese funds through Centre of Mathematics, University of Minho.

In this work, the interest is to study the correlation between gap times, that is, times between two successive recurrent events.

Correlations between gap times are of interest in themselves, when investigating whether the first gap time is predictive of the occurrence of the second event. To measure the possible association between two gap times, it is usual to use the nonparametric estimator of the correlation coefficient Kendall's τ, because it has good properties, like invariance to monotone transformations and robustness in the presence of outliers [12].

Measuring correlation can be challenging in the presence of right censoring where some data values are not observed due to an upper detection limit, dropout or due to the end of the study.

Right censoring is present in a wide range of survival data, so it is natural that one or both of the gap times may not be observed.

Several different methods have been proposed to measure and test the correlation between two right-censored time-to-event variables [5,8,10,11].

In this paper we define estimators of τ that accounts for joint information of the random pair of gap times in the presence of right censoring. In fact, a natural way to estimate τ is to incorporate a suitable bivariate estimator of the joint distribution function into the integrals that define the probability of concordant pairs and the probability of discordant pairs in the context of Kendall's tau definition. This is not the usual approach in the papers that have been published on this topic. In general, the authors use a compact formula for the estimator, considering the complementarity of concordant and discordant events.

When looking to a single subject, the censoring time distribution may be the same for time to the first failure and for time to the second failure. However, the censoring time for the second gap time depends on the time to the first failure and on the censoring time for the total time.

Two of the estimators of the joint distribution function of the gap times used in this work are already known (see [1,2]), but we propose another estimators for the Kaplan-Meier weights, defined with the same reasoning used in the definition of the known semiparametric estimator of the bivariate distribution function (see [2]), but using decision trees and random forests to define the weights used in the Kaplan-Meier estimator for the joint distribution function of the gap times. The study presented is supported by simulations.

This paper is divided into 6 sections. In the first section we present an introduction to the topic, a brief bibliographical review and we establish the notation. In the Sect. 2 we present estimators of the joint distribution function of gap times and justifications for using decision trees and random forests methodologies to define the Kaplan-Meier weights. In the Sect. 3 we define Kendall's tau estimators based on the probability of concordance and probability of discordance of pairs of gap times, and we justify this approach based on theoretical results. This section also presents a detailed description of the numerical procedure for obtaining estimates of the probabilities of concordance and probabilities of discordance. The Sect. 4 is dedicated to the simulation procedure and the main results. In Sect. 5 is presented an application example of the proposed methodology with real data. Finally, in the last section, are the main conclusions of the work.

1.1 Notations and Definitions

Let T_1 be the time from the begining of the study to the first occurrence of the event of interest or *failure* (first gap time) and T_2 be the time between the first *failure* and the second *failure* (second gap time). The random times T_1 and T_2 are possibly correlated. Let (T_{1i}, T_{2i}) and (T_{1j}, T_{2j}), $i \neq j$, be independent realizations from (T_1, T_2).

Definition 1. *The pair (i, j) is said to be concordant if $(T_{1i}-T_{1j})(T_{2i}-T_{2j}) > 0$ and discordant if $(T_{1i} - T_{1j})(T_{2i} - T_{2j}) < 0$. If T_1 and T_2 are continuous, the Kendall's correlation between T_1 and T_2 is given by*

$$\tau = P\left((T_{1i} - T_{1j})(T_{2i} - T_{2j}) > 0\right) - P\left((T_{1i} - T_{1j})(T_{2i} - T_{2j}) < 0\right) \quad (1)$$

The correlation coefficient, τ, is such that $-1 \leq \tau \leq 1$ and $\tau = 0$ if (T_1, T_2) are independent.

Denoting marginal and joint cumulative distribution functions of T_1 and T_2 as $F_1(x) = P(T_1 \leq x)$, $F_2(y) = P(T_2 \leq y)$ and $F_{12}(x, y) = P(T_1 \leq x, T_2 \leq y)$, respectively, and defining $F.(x^-) = \lim_{t \uparrow x} F.(t)$, we have

$$p_c = P\left((T_{1i} - T_{1j})(T_{2i} - T_{2j}) > 0\right) = 2 \int_0^{+\infty} \int_0^{+\infty} F_{12}(x^-, y^-) F_{12}(dx, dy) \tag{2}$$

and

$$p_d = P\left((T_{1i} - T_{1j})(T_{2i} - T_{2j}) < 0\right) = 2 \int_0^{+\infty} \int_0^{+\infty} U(x^-, y^-) F_{12}(dx, dy) \quad (3)$$

where

$$U(x, y) = P(T_1 > x, T_2 < y) = F_{12}(\infty, y^-) - F_{12}(x, y^-)$$

Now the tau Kendall's coefficient is given by:

$$\tau = p_c - p_d \tag{4}$$

2 Estimators of the Bivariate Distribution Function for Censored Gap Times

Let C be the right censoring time. This censoring time is the minimum between the time from the start of study to the end of the study, and the time from the start of study to dropout. So, the support of C is bounded.

We made the standard assumption that the first gap time, T_1, and the total time, $Y = T_1 + T_2$, are subject to independent right censoring. As T_1 and Y are observed in a single subject, the distribution function of the censoring time C, say $G(.)$, may be the same for both T_1 and Y. So, the marginal distribution of the first gap time F_1, can be consistently estimated by the Kaplan and Meier estimator, based on the observable pair $(\tilde{T}_1, \delta_1)$ where $\tilde{T}_1 = \min\{T_1, C\}$ and the distribution of the total time, Y, say F, can also be estimated by the Kaplan and Meier estimator based on $(\tilde{Y}, \delta_2)$ where $\tilde{Y} = \min\{Y, C\}$ [9]. The indicator variables $\delta_j, j = 1, 2$ are defined by $\delta_j = 1$, if $T_i \leq C$, and equal to 0, otherwise. However, the second gap time, T_2, and the censoring time, $C_2 = (C - T_1)\delta_1$, are in general dependent. Let $\tilde{T}_2 = \min\{T_2, C_2\}$ and the marginal distributions of $\tilde{T}_1$ and $\tilde{T}_2$ are $H_1(x) = P(\tilde{T}_1 \leq x)$ and $H_2(y) = P(\tilde{T}_2 \leq y)$ and the joint distribution of $\left(\tilde{T}_1, \tilde{T}_2\right)$ is $H(x, y) = P(\tilde{T}_1 \leq x, \tilde{T}_2 \leq y)$.

The estimators for the bivariate distribution function of gap times (T_1, T_2), $F_{12}(x, y)$, are weighted Kaplan-Meier estimators with the same weights used in the definition of the estimator of the total time distribution function $\hat{F}(y)$ (see [1,2,8]), based on the ranks of $\tilde{Y}_i$, $R_i = Rank(\tilde{Y}_i)$, where, in the case of ties, the ranks of the censored observations $\tilde{Y}_i$'s are higher than the ranks of the uncensored observations.

$$\hat{F}_{12}(x, y) = \sum_{i=1}^{n} W_i \, \mathrm{I} \left(\tilde{T}_{1i} \leq x, \tilde{T}_{2i} \leq y\right) \tag{5}$$

with $\mathrm{I}(A)$ the usual indicator function of the event A.

The second gap time distribution function estimator is easily obtained from Eq. (5). In fact, we have

$$\hat{F}_2(y) = \hat{F}_{12}(\infty, y) = \sum_{i=1}^{n} W_i \, \mathrm{I} \left(\tilde{T}_{2i} \leq y\right) \tag{6}$$

The weights W_i in Eq. (5) presented in the expressions (7) and (9) are already known and the corresponding estimators have already been studied (see [1,2]).

$$W_i = \frac{\delta_{2i}}{n - R_i + 1} \prod_{j=1}^{i-1} \left(1 - \frac{\delta_{2j}}{n - R_j + 1}\right) \tag{7}$$

With the weights defined in (7), the estimator (5) only assigns positive mass to pairs of gap times with both components uncensored.

In order to assign positive mass to pairs of gap times in which only the second gap time T_2 is censored, while the weight assigned to pairs with the first gap time censored remains zero, a binary classification model $m(x, y)$ can be used, which, based on the observed values of the first gap time and the total time, assigns a non-zero probability to the event $\delta_2 = 1$.

$$m(x, y) = P \left(\delta_2 = 1 | \tilde{T}_1 = x, \tilde{Y} = y\right), \, x \leq y \tag{8}$$

$$W_i = W_i(m) = \frac{m(\tilde{T}_{1i}, \tilde{Y}_i)}{n - R_i + 1} \prod_{j=1}^{i-1} \left(1 - \frac{m(\tilde{T}_{1i}, \tilde{Y}_i)}{n - R_j + 1}\right) \tag{9}$$

When the model m is parametric, like the logistic model, we must estimate the model parameters, typically computed by maximizing the conditional likelihood of the δ_2's given $(\widetilde{T}_1, \widetilde{T}_2)$ for those cases with $\delta_1 = 1$ (see [6,7]).

An alternative way for the definition of the Kaplan-Meier weigths, is to consider the probability $m(x, y)$ in Eq. (8) given by decision trees or random forests methodologies. The incorporation of smoothed Kaplan-Meier weigths in the estimation of the bivariate function aims to reduce the bias imposed by right censoring. When estimating the probabilities of the second gap time observations being censored, knowing the values of the first gap time and the total time, the objective is not to explain but to predict. So it might make sense to use decisions trees or random forests to get these probabilities. In fact, in general terms, if the focus is mainly on explanation, logistic regression tends to perform better than random forests, but this in not completely true if the focus is on prediction rather than explanation [4]. On the other hand, logistic regression requires there to be little or no multicollinearity among the independent variables. This means that the independent variables should not be too highly correlated with each other which, in the case under analysis, is not verified since the first gap time x and the total time y can be strongly associated.

3   Estimators of the Kendall's Tau Coefficient for Censored Gap Times

With the definition and notations of Subsect. 1.1, to estimate the correlation τ between two gap times, T_1 and T_2, we use the definition for Kendall's tau coefficient as the difference between the concordance probability, p_c, and discordance probability of T_1 and T_2, p_d, given by expressions (2) and (3), respectively. These probabilities depend only on the joint distribution function of the interval times, F_{12}, since the marginal distribution of the second interval time, T_2, can be obtained from the joint distribution function F_{12}. Under right censoring, the estimator of p_c, $\widehat{p}_c$, obtained from the distribution function estimator $\widehat{F}_{12}$, only converges to p_c in a restricted domain, and the same goes for the estimator $\widehat{p}_d$ of p_d. In general we have $\widehat{p}_c + \widehat{p}_d \leq 1$, therefore we will calculate these estimates separately. In fact, denoting by τ_H the upper bound of the support of the distribution function of $\widetilde{Y}$, say H_y, variable assumed to be continuous, and defining

$$F_{12}^0 = P(T_1 \leq x, T_2 \leq y, T_1 + T_2 \leq \tau_H) \tag{10}$$

it was proved that the estimators of F_{12}, defined on Sect. 2, converges to F_{12}^0, as $n \to \infty$, and not to F_{12} (see [2] for detailed explanation). The same situation occurs for the estimator of the marginal distribution function of T_2, $\widehat{F}_2$, which is given by

$$\widehat{F}_2(y) = \widehat{F}_{1,2}(\infty, y) = \sum_{i=1}^{n} W_i(m) I(\widetilde{T}_{2i} \leq y) \tag{11}$$

In fact,

$$\lim_{n \to \infty} \widehat{F}_2(y) = P(T_2 \leq y, T_1 + T_2 \leq \tau_H) \equiv F_2^0(y) \neq F_2(y) \tag{12}$$

3.1   Procedure for Obtaining Kendall's Tau Estimates

In this subsection we present the numerical procedure for obtaining estimates of Kendall's tau coefficient. A data matrix with 4 columns and n rows is given, $M \equiv M[i,j]$, $i = 1, \ldots, n$; $j = 1, \ldots, 4$. Each line i corresponds to one case.

- $M[,1]$ – time until the first event occurs;
- $M[,2]$ – total time until the second event occurs;
- $M[,3]$ – boolean variable: 1 if the time until the occurrence of the first event is observed, 0 if it is censored;
- $M[,4]$ – boolean variable: 1 if the time until the occurrence of the second event is observed, 0 if it is censored.

Step 1. The values of the columns of M are sorted in such a way that the uncensored observations relative to the first time and relative to the total time appear first.

Step 2. Assign a weight to each observation in such a way that the observations with the highest rank have a greater weight. In the case of the estimator proposed by J. de Uñã-Álvarez and L. Meira-Machado [1], the censored observations both in the first time and in the total time have a weight of 0.

In the remaining estimators, the weight assigned to observation i is a function of the probability of this observation being censored in the second time, knowing that it was not censored in the first time.

Example of the R code for this procedure:

```
R <- rank(M[, 2], ties.method="first")
n <- nrow(M)

  Pkm <- rep(1,n)
  for (i in 1:n){
    for (j in 1:n){
      if (R[j] < R[i])
        Pkm[i] <- Pkm[i]*(1 - M2[j,4]/(n-R[j]+1))
      }
    Wkm[i,1] <- Pkm[i]*M2[i,4]/(n-R[i]+1)
  }

  n1 <- sum(M[,3])

  glm.fitted <- fitted (glm(M[1:n1, 4] ~ M[1:n1,1] + M2[1:n1, 2],
    family=binomial))

  Mlogit <- c(glm.fitted, rep(0, n-n1))

  P1 <- rep(1,n)
  for (i in 1:n){
```

```
    for (j in 1:n){
     if (R[j]<R[i])
      P1[i] <- P1[i]*(1-Mlogit[j]/(n-R[j]+1))
       }
     W1[i,1]<-P1[i]*Mlogit[i]/(n-R[i]+1)
     }
}
```

Step 3 :: Define two indicator matrices I1 and I2 to indicate, respectively, the concordant and discordant pairs in the data set.

R code for this procedure:

```
t2 <- M [ , 2] - M [ , 1]
for (i in 1:n) {
  for (j in 1:n) {
    if((M[j,1]<M[i,1]  &  t2[j]<t2[i])|(M[j,1]>M[i,1]
         & t2[j] > t2[i])) I1[i j] <- 1 elseI I1[i,j] <- 0
    if((M[j,1] > M[i,1] & t2[j] < t2[i])|(M[j,1]<M[i,1]
         & t2[j] > t2[i])) I2[i,j] <- 1 elseI I2[i,j] <- 0
  }
  }
```

Step 4 :: Calculate the estimates of probability of concordance, probability of discordance and the estimate of Kendall's tau coefficient.

R code for this procedure:

```
hatpc1 <- t(as.matrix(W1))%*%I1%*%(as.matrix(W1))
hatpckm <- t(as.matrix(Wkm))%*%I1%*%(as.matrix(Wkm))
hatpd1 <- t(as.matrix(W1))%*%I2%*%(as.matrix(W1))
hatpdkm <- t(as.matrix(Wkm))%*%I2%*%(as.matrix(Wkm))
tau1 <- hatpc1-hatpd1
tau_km <- hatpckm-hatpdkm
```

4   Simulation Study

We can simulate correlated gap times by using copulas. In this work, we simulated gap times with unitary exponential marginal distribution, obtained from the Frank copula. The motivation for using the Frank copula is justified because it allows to obtain positive or negative, strong or moderate, correlations. Furthermore, this copula does not have any tail dependence, so the dependencies are relatively similar for all values of the marginals.

The Frank copula is an archimedean copula, with association parameter $\alpha \in \mathbb{R} - \{0\}$, with generator ϕ given by

$$\phi(t) = -\log\left(\frac{e^{-\alpha t} - 1)}{e^{-\alpha} - 1}\right), t \in [0, 1]$$

For this copula, the Kendall's tau coefficient is given by

$$\tau = 1 + \frac{4(D(\alpha) - 1)}{\alpha}, \quad \text{with} \quad D(\alpha) = \frac{1}{\alpha} \int_0^\alpha \frac{t}{e^t - 1} dt$$

Samples of dimensions 50, 100, 150, 200 and 250 were considered. To implement random censoring, for both the first gap time and the total time, we independently generated uniform times on the interval $[0, N]$, where N was selected to achieve a given proportion of censoring. Assuming independence between the random variables $C \sim U[0, N]$ with distribution function G (density g) and $Y \sim Exp(1)$ with density f_y, we have

$$P(C < Y) = \int_0^\infty \int_0^y f_y(y) g(c) dc dy = \int_0^N \frac{1 - e^{-y}}{N} dy = \frac{N - \sinh(b) + \cosh(b) - 1}{N}$$

In the present work we take $N = 4$ to reach about 25% censoring for the first gap time and a little more than 48% censoring for the total time.

```
#t1 first gap time; y total time
  cens[,1] = runif(n,0,N)
  for (i in 1:n){
    ytilde[i,1] = min(y[i,1],cens[i,1])
    d[i,1]=1
    d1[i,1]=1
  }
  for (i in 1:n){
    if (ytilde[i,1] < y[i,1]) d[i,1]=0
  }
  for (i in 1:n){
    t1tilde[i,1] = min(t1[i,1],cens[i,1])
  }
   for (i in 1:n){
    if (t1tilde[i,1] < t1[i,1]) d1[i,1]=0
  }
```

We considered 10,000 repetitions of each procedure for generate the estimates of Kendall's tau coefficient. The final estimate was the mean of the estimates produced in the simulation process. The standard deviation, the bias and the Mean Squared Error of the estimate were also calculated.

4.1   Simulation Results

The tables presented in this section contain the results of the simulations, namely the estimates for τ and the corresponding bias, standard deviation (SD) and the Mean Squared Error (MSE) of the estimator. The different methods are identified as WKM for the weights given by expression (7), WSP for the weights in the semiparametric estimator (9), WTree and WRF have the same expression for the weights as the latter, but the estimated probabilities for the weights based on the model m (see (8)) are calculated with decision trees and random forests methodologies, respectively.

In all cases, the values of standard deviation and MSE decrease as the sample size increases, implying the consistency of the estimates. In what concerns to bias it gets smaller and smaller with increasing sample size in all cases except for low negative association in WSP estimator (Table 2).

Low Positive Association. The Table 1 show the performance for all estimators for gap times with low positive association. In this case, WSP performs better with lower SD and MSE for all sample sizes considered.

Table 1. True tau 0.1100

n	$Method$	$\hat{\tau}$	$\hat{\tau}-\tau$	$SD(\hat{\tau})$	$MSE(\hat{\tau})$
50	WSP	0.0270	−0.0830	**0.0983**	**0.0165**
	WKM	0.0241	−0.0860	0.1269	0.0235
	WTree	0.0223	−0.0878	0.1065	0.0190
	WRF	0.0215	−0.0885	0.1087	0.0197
100	WSP	0.0348	−0.0753	**0.0737**	**0.0111**
	WKM	0.0272	−0.0828	0.0952	0.0159
	WTree	0.0293	−0.0807	0.0818	0.0132
	WRF	0.0272	−0.0828	0.0822	0.0136
150	WSP	0.0367	−0.0733	**0.0623**	**0.0093**
	WKM	0.0277	−0.0823	0.0805	0.0132
	WTree	0.0291	−0.0810	0.0698	0.0114
	WRF	0.0285	−0.0816	0.0702	0.0116
200	WSP	0.0381	−0.0719	**0.0557**	**0.0083**
	WKM	0.0277	−0.0823	0.0719	0.0119
	WTree	0.0292	−0.0809	0.0625	0.0104
	WRF	0.0289	−0.0812	0.0629	0.0105
250	WSP	0.0402	−0.0698	**0.0513**	**0.0075**
	WKM	0.0280	−0.0820	0.0659	0.0111
	WTree	0.0292	−0.0808	0.0581	0.0099
	WRF	0.0297	−0.0803	0.0579	0.0098

Low Negative Association. In what concerns to data with low negative association, the results present in Table 2, reveal that WSP estimator is again the best estimator, but as the sample size grows, there is a change in the sign of the bias of this estimator. The smallest values of bias are achieved for moderately sized samples ($n = 100, 150$).

Table 2. True tau -0.1100

n	$Method$	$\hat{\tau}$	$\hat{\tau} - \tau$	$SD(\hat{\tau})$	$MSE(\hat{\tau})$
50	WSP	**−0.1052**	**0.0048**	**0.1097**	**0.0121**
	WKM	−0.1211	−0.0111	0.1286	0.0166
	WTree	−0.1163	−0.0063	0.1148	0.0132
	WRF	−0.1209	−0.0109	0.1136	0.0130
100	WSP	**−0.1099**	**0.0002**	**0.0841**	**0.0071**
	WKM	−0.1260	−0.0161	0.0986	0.0100
	WTree	−0.1192	−0.0092	0.0872	0.0077
	WRF	−0.1246	−0.0146	0.0874	0.0078
150	WSP	**−0.1109**	**−0.0009**	**0.0704**	**0.0050**
	WKM	−0.1272	−0.0171	0.0827	0.0071
	WTree	−0.1214	−0.0114	0.0730	0.0054
	WRF	−0.1254	−0.0154	0.0737	0.0057
200	WSP	**−0.1127**	**−0.0027**	**0.0631**	**0.0040**
	WKM	−0.1286	−0.0186	0.0728	0.0056
	WTree	−0.1231	−0.0130	0.0650	0.0044
	WRF	−0.1270	−0.0170	0.0650	0.0045
250	WSP	**−0.1131**	**−0.0031**	**0.0586**	**0.0034**
	WKM	−0.1294	−0.0194	0.0664	0.0048
	WTree	−0.1248	−0.0147	0.0595	0.0038
	WRF	−0.1276	−0.0176	0.0597	0.0039

Moderate Positive Association. In case of moderate positive association, the results presented in Table 3 show that although the estimative of τ is closer to WKM than the other estimates, this one has greater variability. In terms of consistency, both WSP and WRF perform better with a lower MSE, the latter being slightly better because of its lower bias.

Table 3. True tau 0.3881

n	$Method$	$\hat{\tau}$	$\hat{\tau} - \tau$	$SD(\hat{\tau})$	$MSE(\hat{\tau})$
50	WSP	0.1922	−0.1959	0.0966	0.0477
	WKM	0.2070	−0.1811	0.1249	0.0484
	WTree	0.1890	−0.1992	0.0981	0.0492
	WRF	0.1958	−0.1923	0.1028	**0.0476**
100	WSP	0.2093	−0.1788	0.0722	**0.0372**
	WKM	0.2188	−0.1694	0.0944	0.0376
	WTree	0.2048	−0.1833	0.0765	0.0395
	WRF	0.2122	−0.1759	0.0788	**0.0372**
150	WSP	0.2153	−0.1729	0.0615	0.0337
	WKM	0.2222	−0.1659	0.0816	0.0342
	WTree	0.2124	−0.1758	0.0679	0.0355
	WRF	0.2184	−0.1697	0.0689	**0.0335**
200	WSP	0.2208	−0.1673	0.0553	**0.0311**
	WKM	0.2256	−0.1626	0.0732	0.0318
	WTree	0.2180	−0.1701	0.0627	0.0329
	WRF	0.2231	−0.1650	0.0621	**0.0311**
250	WSP	0.2242	−0.1639	0.0506	**0.0294**
	WKM	0.2269	−0.1613	0.0676	0.0306
	WTree	0.2209	−0.1673	0.0587	0.0314
	WRF	0.2256	−0.1625	0.0573	0.0297

Moderate Negative Association. In the case of moderate negative association, the results presented in the Table 4 show a better performance for all estimators, with the bias being considerably reduced compared to the corresponding values in the case of moderate positive association. However, as in the previous case, the estimator WKM exhibits greater variability and a higher value for the MSE than any of the estimators WSP and WRF. In this case WRF performs better.

Table 4. True tau -0.3881

n	Method	$\hat{\tau}$	$\hat{\tau} - \tau$	$SD(\hat{\tau})$	$MSE(\hat{\tau})$
50	WSP	-0.3056	0.0826	0.1152	0.0201
	WKM	-0.3167	0.0714	0.1261	0.0210
	WTree	-0.3130	0.0751	0.1137	0.0186
	WRF	-0.3154	0.0727	0.1128	**0.0180**
100	WSP	-0.3234	0.0648	0.0855	0.0115
	WKM	-0.3309	0.0572	0.0939	0.0121
	WTree	-0.3307	0.0575	0.0863	0.0107
	WRF	-0.3298	0.0583	0.0843	**0.0105**
150	WSP	-0.3311	0.0570	0.0720	0.0084
	WKM	-0.3380	0.0502	0.0796	0.0088
	WTree	-0.3374	0.0508	0.0730	0.0079
	WRF	-0.3372	0.0510	0.0715	**0.0077**
200	WSP	-0.3364	0.0517	0.0634	0.0067
	WKM	-0.3408	0.0474	0.0709	0.0073
	WTree	-0.3411	0.0470	0.0652	0.0065
	WRF	-0.3405	0.0476	0.0638	**0.0063**
250	WSP	-0.3392	0.0488	0.0582	0.0057
	WKM	-0.3435	0.0446	0.0644	0.0061
	WTree	-0.3435	0.0446	0.0596	0.0055
	WRF	-0.3433	0.0448	0.0582	**0.0054**

High Positive Association. In relation to high positive association, according to the results shown in the Table 5, all estimators present worse performance when compared to the corresponding ones in the case of moderate positive association. Both the bias, the standard deviation and the MSE present higher values in all estimators. For strong positive association, the estimator WSP presents a smaller MSE and the estimator WTree has lower SD.

Table 5. True tau 0.7626

n	$Method$	$\hat{\tau}$	$\hat{\tau} - \tau$	$SD(\hat{\tau})$	$MSE(\hat{\tau})$
50	WSP	0.4849	−0.2778	0.1226	**0.0921**
	WKM	0.4856	−0.2770	0.1368	0.0954
	WTree	0.4136	−0.3489	**0.1058**	0.1329
	WRF	0.4465	−0.3160	0.1153	0.1132
100	WSP	0.5212	−0.2414	0.0995	**0.0681**
	WKM	0.5079	−0.2547	0.1088	0.0767
	WTree	0.4410	−0.3216	**0.0790**	0.1096
	WRF	0.4776	−0.2850	0.0922	0.0897
150	WSP	0.5363	−0.2263	0.0889	**0.0591**
	WKM	0.5128	−0.2498	0.0937	0.0712
	WTree	0.4593	−0.3033	**0.0705**	0.0970
	WRF	0.4888	−0.2738	0.0799	0.0813
200	WSP	0.5485	−0.2140	0.0814	**0.0524**
	WKM	0.5205	−0.2421	0.0847	0.0658
	WTree	0.4748	−0.2878	**0.0663**	0.0872
	WRF	0.5006	−0.2619	0.0730	0.0739
250	WSP	0.5538	−0.2088	0.0786	**0.0498**
	WKM	0.5219	−0.2407	0.0809	0.0645
	WTree	0.4840	−0.2785	**0.0638**	0.0816
	WRF	0.5053	−0.2573	0.0694	0.0710

High Negative Association. The results in the Table 6 are in line with what happens in moderate negative association. There is a considerable reduction in the bias, standard deviation and MSE of the estimators in a scenario of strong negative association. There is also a better performance of the estimator WSP in relation to the others.

Table 6. True tau −0.7626

n	Method	$\hat{\tau}$	$\hat{\tau} - \tau$	$SD(\hat{\tau})$	$MSE(\hat{\tau})$
50	WSP	−0.6310	0.1315	0.0862	**0.0247**
	WKM	−0.6268	0.1358	0.1094	0.0304
	WTree	−0.6047	0.1578	0.1021	0.0353
	WRF	−0.6171	0.1455	0.0970	0.0306
100	WSP	−0.6609	0.1017	0.0569	**0.0136**
	WKM	−0.6530	0.1096	0.0819	0.0187
	WTree	−0.6507	0.1119	0.0716	0.0176
	WRF	−0.6494	0.1132	0.0717	0.0179
150	WSP	−0.6729	0.0897	0.0457	**0.0101**
	WKM	−0.6656	0.0970	0.0700	0.0143
	WTree	−0.6654	0.0972	0.0592	0.0130
	WRF	−0.6638	0.0988	0.0615	0.0135
200	WSP	−0.6796	0.0830	0.0386	**0.0084**
	WKM	−0.6717	0.0908	0.0628	0.0122
	WTree	−0.6741	0.0885	0.0522	0.0106
	WRF	−0.6717	0.0909	0.0548	0.0113
250	WSP	−0.6834	0.0792	0.0343	**0.0074**
	WKM	−0.6753	0.0873	0.0573	0.0109
	WTree	−0.6786	0.0839	0.0471	0.0093
	WRF	−0.6760	0.0866	0.0494	0.0099

5   Example of Application with Real Data

In this section, the methods described in Sect. 3 are applied to data from a bladder cancer study in which patients had superficial bladder tumors that were removed. Some patients had multiple recurrences of tumors during the study [3]. The R survival package contains data from 85 subjects in the placebo and thiotepa treatment groups. Considering the first two recurrences times (in months) and the corresponding gap times, T1 and T2 we have, of the total of 85 patients, 47 relapsed at least once and 29 of these had a new recurrence. This data contain a high percentage of total censored time. In fact 66% of total observations is censored and 44.7% of the observations on first gap time are censored (see Fig. 1).

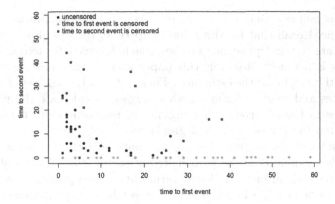

Fig. 1. Bladder data with censored observations

In this example, the estimates obtained with the presmoothing estimator, WSP, and with the estimator with weights obtained using the random forests methodology, WRF, show less variability, according with the results of a nonparametric bootstrap approach to calculate the confidence intervals of Kendall's τ (see Table 7). Table 7 also contains the value of the point estimate of τ, using the various estimators, as well as the mean and standard deviation calculated from 200 bootstrap samples. If we consider the results of simulation presented in this study, WSP is the best estimator in this case, so there is no evidence of association of the two gap times in this study (bootstrap quantiles in Table 7).

Table 7. Tau estimatives and bootstrap CI: bladder data

Method	$\hat{\tau}$	Mean	SD	$\chi_{.025}$	$\chi_{.975}$
WSP	**−0.0614**	−0.0619	**0.0345**	**−0.1253**	**0.0047**
WKM	−0.0915	−0.0915	0.0366	−0.1701	−0.0268
WTree	−0.0979	−0.0979	0.0449	−0.1542	0.0186
WRF	−0.0857	−0.0857	**0.0350**	−0.1513	−0.0175

6 Conclusions

In this paper we estimate Kendall's tau coefficient from the estimates of the probability of concordance and discordance of right-censored gap times pairs. This is not the usual approach in the papers that have been published on this topic. In general, the authors use a compact formula for the estimator, considering the complementarity of concordant and discordant events. Both for estimating the probability of concordance and for estimating the probability of discordance, we used estimators of the joint distribution function of the gap times under right censoring, as well as estimators for the marginal distribution function of the second gap time. Recall that for the second gap time, the distributions of T_2 and censorship are not independent. The approach followed to accommodate this dependency is not new. However, this paper presents two new alternatives for smoothing the weights of the estimator. These alternatives consist of considering decision trees and random forests methodologies, to calculate the probabilities associated with the occurrence of censoring in the second gap time, given the total time and the values of the first gap time.

The results of the simulations are compatible with the behavior already known of the estimators of the joint distribution function of pairs of gap times previously studied. In fact, the lower variability of the presmoothed semiparametric estimator (see [2]) in relation to the weighted Kaplan-Meier is also presented in the corresponding Kendall's tau estimators. Regarding the estimator with smoothed weights using random forests, the simulation results are compatible with the best performance of this one in relation to both the weighted Kaplan-Meier and the smoothed weight estimator using decision trees.

Estimators generally perform better in a scenario of negative association of gap times. Furthermore, if the association is strongly negative, there is a very marked reduction in bias, standard deviation and MSE of all estimators, even in a context of small or moderate samples. When the association is moderately negative, the performance of estimator with smoothed weights using random forests is superior to the other estimators.

In the case of positive association, the best performing estimator is the presmoothed nonparametric, if the association is strong and, in the case of moderate positive association, this estimador and the estimator with smoothed weights using random forests perform identically.

Acknowledgements. This work was supported by Portuguese funds through the CMAT - Research Centre of Mathematics of University of Minho - within projects UIDB/00013/2020 and UIDP/00013/2020.

Authors thank to referees for their careful reading and for their constructive suggestions.

References

1. Uñã-Álvarez, J., Meira-Machado, L.: A simple estimator of the bivariate distribution function for censored gap times. Stat. Probab. Lett. **78**, 2440–2445 (2008). https://doi.org/10.1002/bimj.201000063
2. Uñã-Álvarez, J., Amorim, A.: A simple semiparametric estimator of the bivariate distribution function for censored gap times. Biometr. J. **53**(1), 113–127 (2011). https://doi.org/10.1002/bimj.201000063
3. Byar, D.P.: The Veterans administration study of chemoprophylaxis for recurrent stage I bladder tumours: comparisons of placebo, pyridoxine and topical thiotepa. In: Pavone-Macaluso, M., Smith, P.H., Edsmyr, F. (eds) Bladder Tumors and other Topics in Urological Oncology. Ettore Majorana International Science Series, vol. 1. Springer, Boston (1980). https://doi.org/10.1007/978-1-4613-3030-1_74

4. Couronné, R., Probst, P., Boulesteix, A.L.: Random forest versus logistic regression: a large-scale benchmark experiment. BMC Bioinform. **19**, 270 (2018). https://doi.org/10.1186/s12859-018-2264-5

5. Dabrowska, D.M.: Kaplan-Meier estimate on the plane: weak convergence, LIL, and the bootstrap. J. Multivar. Anal. **29**(2), 308–325 (1989). https://doi.org/10.1016/0047-259X(89)90030-4

6. Dikta, D.: On semiparametric random censorship models. J. Stat. Plann. Inference **66**, 253–279 (1998). https://doi.org/10.1016/S0378-3758(97)00091-8

7. Dikta, D.: The strong law under semiparametric random censorship models. J. Stat. Plann. Inference **83**, 1–10 (2000). https://doi.org/10.1016/S0378-3758(99)00086-5

8. Fan, J., Hsu, L., Prentice, R.L.: Dependence estimation over a finite bivariate failure time region. Lifetime Data Anal. **6**(4), 343–355 (2000). https://doi.org/10.1023/a:1026557315306

9. Kaplan, E.L., Meier, P.: Nonparametric estimation from incomplete observations. J. Am. Stat. Assoc. **53**(282), 457–481 (1958)

10. Oakes, D.: A model for association in bivariate survival data. J. Roy. Stat. Soc.: Ser. B (Methodol.) **44**(3), 414–422 (1982)

11. Oakes, D.: Bivariate survival models induced by frailties. J. Am. Stat. Assoc. **84**(406), 487–493 (1989). https://doi.org/10.2307/2289934

12. Oakes, D.: On consistency of Kendall's tau under censoring. Technical report. Department of Biostatistics and Computational Biology, University of Rochester, Rochester, NY (2006)

A Bootstrap-Surrogate Approach for Sequential Experimental Design for Simulation Models

Rommel G. Regis[✉][iD]

Saint Joseph's University, Philadelphia, PA 19131, USA
rregis@sju.edu

Abstract. The bootstrap method is a widely used tool for quantifying the uncertainty associated with a given statistical estimator or machine learning method. This paper proposes a novel approach for sequential experimental design that uses the bootstrap in conjunction with an interpolating surrogate model. Consider the problem of fitting a surrogate to a computationally expensive simulation model that yields a numerical output given the values of a set of continuous input variables. To fit a surrogate, initial data points are obtained by running the simulations at a set of space-filling design points. The proposed Bootstrap-Surrogate method improves on this experimental design by sequentially identifying points where the surrogate prediction uncertainty is high and then evaluating the simulation at those points. The surrogate prediction uncertainty at a candidate simulation point is estimated using a weighted combination of two criteria, one based on the bootstrap standard error of the surrogate predictions at the candidate point and the other based on the minimum distance of the candidate point from previous design points. The method is implemented using a radial basis function (RBF) surrogate and tested on groundwater bioremediation models and several test problems. The results show that the Bootstrap-RBF approach generally yields better experimental design points for surrogate modeling (as measured by RMSE on a large test set) than those obtained by an optimum Latin hypercube sample or a sequential experimental design based on a maximin criterion on the groundwater bioremediation models and on the test problems with similar structures.

Keywords: Experimental design · Simulation model · Surrogate model · Bootstrap method · Radial basis functions

1 Introduction

This paper examines the problem of identifying a set of experimental design points that can be used to build a surrogate for a computationally expensive simulation model. Specifically, suppose we have a deterministic simulation model represented by $y = f(x)$ where $x \in [\ell, u] \subset \mathbb{R}^d$ and the functional relationship f

© The Author(s), under exclusive license to Springer Nature Switzerland AG 2022
O. Gervasi et al. (Eds.): ICCSA 2022 Workshops, LNCS 13377, pp. 498–513, 2022.
https://doi.org/10.1007/978-3-031-10536-4_33

is a black box. That is, the mathematical form of f is not explicitly available and all we have is a simulator that yields a single numerical output y given an input vector $x \in \mathbb{R}^d$. Deterministic simulation models are found in many engineering applications involving finite element or computational fluid dynamics simulations. Our goal is to identify a set of design points in the domain $[\ell, u]$ where the simulation can be run thereby producing data points that can be used to build a surrogate model for $f(x)$. Here, a surrogate model is just an inexpensive approximation of the expensive function $f(x)$. In many cases, the goal is not simply to build a surrogate, but to also to find a global optimum of the expensive function. However, in this paper, the focus is simply on building a surrogate that is as accurate as possible given a limited budget on function evaluations. Once such a surrogate is available along with the corresponding experimental design points, one can then perform optimization on the surrogate, or if additional computational budget is available, use a surrogate-based optimization method to further improve the model in promising regions while searching for the global optimum. Examples of widely used surrogates for simulation and optimization models in the literature include Kriging or Gaussian Process models (e.g., see [3,13,15]), and Radial Basis Function (RBF) models (e.g., see [4,23]).

There is a substantial body of literature on surrogate-based approaches that find an approximate global or local minimum of an expensive simulation-based function (e.g., [24,30]). Among the most popular approaches include Bayesian optimization methods (e.g., [2,22]) and radial basis function methods (e.g., [7,27,31]). These surrogate-based approaches begin with a space-filling experimental design such as a Latin hypercube design that is used to build the initial surrogate for the sequential optimization process. In the context of expensive black-box optimization, the main goal is optimization and expending computational effort to build an accurate global model of $f(x)$ is not always the best approach as has been observed with the success of local surrogate-based approaches in comparison with global surrogate-based methods (e.g., [27]).

There is also a large body of work on experimental designs for black-box simulation-based models along with some optimality criteria for these designs (e.g., see [14,18,28]). Experimental designs can be static/one-shot or adaptive/sequential. A static or one-shot approach tends to be space-filling since the goal is to cover as much of the domain as possible without taking into account any information about the black-box function. In many applications, particularly those involving expensive simulation models, the adaptive or sequential approach is preferred since it incorporates information obtained from previous design points to perform a trade-off between exploration (improving coverage) and exploitation (sampling interesting regions) in selecting the next design point where the simulation will take place [8]. The interesting regions are those where the black-box function is highly nonlinear or those where the uncertainty of the surrogate approximation is high. Sequential experimental design approaches are also referred to as active learning methods in the field of machine learning. Several approaches have been proposed for sequential or adaptive experimental design, including the LOLA (Local Linear Approximation) algorithm with Voronoi approximation [9], ASRSM (Adaptive Sequential Response Surface Methodology) [1] and Bayesian approaches [20,21]. A review of some of these sequential experimental design approaches can be found in [8] and [16].

This paper presents a novel sequential experimental design approach that uses the bootstrap method [11,12] in conjunction with an interpolating surrogate model. The bootstrap is widely used for quantifying the uncertainty of a statistical estimator or machine learning method. Moreover, the parametric bootstrap and distribution-free bootstrap have been used to estimate the Kriging predictor variance in the context of simulation-optimization [19]. However, it does not appear to have been used solely for sequential experimental design and with other types of surrogates. The proposed Bootstrap-Surrogate experimental design approach is very general and flexible in that it can be used with any surrogate including multivariable polynomials from traditional response surface methodology, Kriging or Gaussian process models, radial basis functions, regression splines, neural networks or support vector regression models. The proposed method begins by running the simulations at a set of space-filling design points. Then, it improves on this experimental design by sequentially identifying candidate points where the surrogate prediction uncertainty is high and then evaluating the simulation at those points. The surrogate prediction uncertainty at a candidate simulation point is estimated using a weighted combination of two criteria, one based on the bootstrap standard error of the surrogate predictions at the candidate point and the other based on the minimum distance of the candidate point from previous design points. The proposed method is implemented using a radial basis function (RBF) surrogate and tested on groundwater bioremediation models and on 17 synthetic test problems. The results show that the Bootstrap-RBF approach generally yields better experimental design points for surrogate modeling (as measured by RMSE on a large test set) than those obtained by an optimum Latin hypercube sample or a sequential experimental design based on a maximin criterion on the groundwater bioremediation models and on the test problems with similar structures.

2   Algorithm Description

This section presents the *Bootstrap-Surrogate* method for sequentially generating experimental design points that are needed to build an accurate surrogate model for an expensive black box function. For simplicity, assume that the domain $[\ell, u] \subset \mathbb{R}^d$ of the black-box function $f(x)$ is simply the unit hypercube $[0, 1]^d$. This assumption is not restrictive since any function defined over a hyperrectangle in $\mathbb{R}^d$ can be easily transformed to a function whose domain is the unit hypercube $[0, 1]^d$. Moreover, in this paper, we focus only on using interpolating surrogate models such as radial basis functions and Kriging (or Gaussian Process) models since these are widely used in expensive simulation-based optimization. However, some of the ideas here can be used for non-interpolating surrogate models such as multivariable polynomial regression models, regression splines and support vector regression models.

The Bootstrap-Surrogate method begins by performing simulations to obtain the actual function values at an initial set of space-filling design points in the domain $[0, 1]^d$ such as a Latin hypercube sample [6]. Next, while the computational budget has not been exhausted, the algorithm sequentially adds a new experimental design point as it goes through a loop. To select the next design point where the simulation will be run, generate trial points uniformly at random throughout the domain. Then, generate b bootstrap samples from the set of previous simulation points. Then, for each bootstrap sample, fit a surrogate using the actual function values from the chosen simulation points, and use this surrogate to predict the function value at each of the trial points. One measure of uncertainty of the surrogate prediction at each trial point is then the standard error of the surrogate predictions from the bootstrap samples. This bootstrap approach is similar to that used in [17] in estimating the standard error of a regression coefficient except that, here, we are estimating the standard error of the prediction. Next, for each trial point, calculate its distance to each of the previous simulation points, and determine the smallest of these distances.

The next step is to calculate a measure of uncertainty of the surrogate prediction at each trial point that incorporates two criteria: (i) the standard error of the surrogate predictions from the bootstrap samples; and (ii) the minimum distance from previous simulation points. A minimum distance criterion is incorporated because the bootstrap standard error criterion alone might not yield the best strategy since it is possible to obtain a high bootstrap standard error at trial points that are very close to previous simulation points. However, since we are using an interpolating surrogate model, the prediction error of the surrogate at each of the previous simulations is zero, and for twice continuously differentiable surrogates, the prediction errors at trial points in small neighborhoods of the any previous simulation point are expected to be small. This combined measure of uncertainty is calculated as follows. For each trial point, calculate a continuous ranking between 0 and 1 of the bootstrap standard error criterion, where a rank of 0 is given to the trial point with the largest value of the bootstrap standard error of the surrogate predictions and a rank of 1 is given to the trial point with the smallest value of this bootstrap standard error criterion. Similarly, for each trial point, calculate a continuous ranking between 0 and 1 of the minimum distance criterion, where a rank of 0 is given to the trial point with the maximum value of the minimum distance to the previous simulation points among all trial points, and a rank of 1 is given to the trial point with the smallest value of this minimum distance criterion. Next, for each trial point, calculate a weighted ranking of the standard error criterion and the minimum distance criterion using a weight $0 < w_B < 1$ for the former. We require the weight w_B of the bootstrap standard error criterion to be strictly positive and strictly less than 1, so that both criteria are always incorporated. The next simulation point is then chosen to be the trial point with the best (minimum) weighted ranking of the bootstrap standard error and the minimum distance criteria. Then, the simulator is run at the selected trial point, and then the algorithm iterates until the computational budget in terms of number of simulations is reached. Finally, the algorithm returns the sequential experimental design points obtained together with the function values and the surrogate approximation to the expensive function.

Below is a pseudo-code of the proposed Bootstrap-Surrogate method for sequential experimental design. Here, n is the counter for the number of simulations, x_n is the nth simulation point, $\mathcal{P}_n$ is the set of data points after n simulations, and $\mathcal{T}_n$ is the set of uniform random trial points where the $(n+1)$st simulation point will be selected. Moreover, $\widehat{\mathrm{SE}}_n^B(x)$ is the standard error of the surrogate predictions at $x \in \mathcal{T}_n$ from the bootstrap samples and $\Delta_n(x)$ is the minimum distance of $x \in \mathcal{T}_n$ from previous simulation points $\{x_1, \ldots, x_n\}$.

Bootstrap-Surrogate Algorithm

Inputs:

- Black box function $f(x)$ defined for all $x \in [0,1]^d$ (e.g., a computationally expensive simulator).
- Size of the experimental design to build, denoted by N.
- Initial space-filling experimental design $\mathcal{I}_0 = \{x_1, \ldots, x_{n_0}\}$ such that $n_0 < N$ (e.g., an optimum Latin hypercube sample).
- An interpolating surrogate model to approximate the black box function (e.g., radial basis functions or Gaussian Process models).
- Number of uniform random trial points to generate on $[0,1]^d$ in each iteration, denoted by t_{rand}.
- Number of bootstrap samples, denoted by b.
- Weight for the bootstrap standard error criterion: $0 < w_B < 1$.

Outputs: An extension of the initial experimental design $\mathcal{I}_0$ together with the function values at the design points and the surrogate approximation to $f(x)$.

(1) *(Initial Experimental Design Simulations)* Perform simulations to obtain $f(x)$ at all $x \in \mathcal{I}_0$. Set the simulation counter $n \leftarrow |\mathcal{I}_0| = n_0$ and the simulation data points $\mathcal{P}_{n_0} = \{(x_1, f(x_1)), \ldots, (x_{n_0}, f(x_{n_0}))\}$.
(2) *(Perform Iterations)* While $n < N$, do:
  (a) *(Generate Random Trial Points)* Generate t_{rand} trial points $\mathcal{T}_n$ uniformly at random throughout $[0,1]^d$.
  (b) *(Estimate Uncertainty of Surrogate Prediction at Each Trial Point)* Generate b bootstrap samples from the current set of simulation data points $\mathcal{P}_n$. For each bootstrap sample, fit a surrogate using the data points in the bootstrap sample and use this surrogate to predict $f(x)$ for all $x \in \mathcal{T}_n$. Calculate the standard error of the surrogate predicted values, denoted by $\widehat{\mathrm{SE}}_n^B(x)$, which is the bootstrap estimate of the standard error of the surrogate prediction at x.
  (c) *(Calculate Minimum and Maximum Standard Error of Surrogate Prediction Among Trial Points)* Calculate $\widehat{\mathrm{SE}}_n^{B,\min} = \min\{\widehat{\mathrm{SE}}_n^B(x) \mid x \in \mathcal{T}_n\}$ and $\widehat{\mathrm{SE}}_n^{B,\max} = \max\{\widehat{\mathrm{SE}}_n^B(x) \mid x \in \mathcal{T}_n\}$.

(d) *(Calculate Minimum Distance of Each Trial Point from Previous Simulation Points)* For each $x \in \mathcal{T}_n$, calculate $\Delta_n(x) = \min_{1 \leq i \leq n} \|x - x_i\|$, where $\|\cdot\|$ is the 2-norm.

(e) *(Calculate Minimum and Maximum of the Minimum Distances from Previous Simulation Points)* Calculate $\Delta_n^{\min} = \min\{\Delta_n(x) \mid x \in \mathcal{T}_n\}$ and $\Delta_n^{\max} = \max\{\Delta_n(x) \mid x \in \mathcal{T}_n\}$.

(f) *(Calculate Standard Error Rank for Each Trial Point)* For each $x \in \mathcal{T}_n$, calculate

$$\mathcal{R}_n^B(x) = \frac{\widehat{\mathrm{SE}}_n^{B,\max} - \widehat{\mathrm{SE}}_n^{B}(x)}{\widehat{\mathrm{SE}}_n^{B,\max} - \widehat{\mathrm{SE}}_n^{B,\min}}$$

provided $\widehat{\mathrm{SE}}_n^{B,\min} \neq \widehat{\mathrm{SE}}_n^{B,\max}$; otherwise, set $\mathcal{R}_n^B(x) = 1$.

(g) *(Calculate Minimum Distance Rank for Each Trial Point)* For each $x \in \mathcal{T}_n$, calculate

$$\mathcal{R}_n^\Delta(x) = \frac{\Delta_n^{\max} - \Delta_n(x)}{\Delta_n^{\max} - \Delta_n^{\min}}$$

provided $\Delta_n^{\min} \neq \Delta_n^{\max}$; otherwise, set $\mathcal{R}_n^\Delta(x) = 1$.

(h) *(Calculate Weighted Rank for Each Trial Point)* For each $x \in \mathcal{T}_n$, calculate $\mathcal{R}_n(x) = w_B \mathcal{R}_n^B(x) + (1 - w_B)\mathcal{R}_n^\Delta(x)$.

(i) *(Select Next Simulation Point)* Set $x_{n+1} = \mathrm{argmin}\ \{\mathcal{R}_n(x) \mid x \in \mathcal{T}_n\}$.

(j) *(Evaluate Function at Simulation Point and Update Data Points)* Run the simulator to get the value of $f(x_{n+1})$. Then, set $\mathcal{P}_{n+1} = \mathcal{P}_n \cup \{(x_{n+1}, f(x_{n+1}))\}$ and reset $n \leftarrow n+1$.

(3) *(Return the Experimental Design Points Found)* Return the experimental design points and function values given by $\mathcal{P}_n$ and the corresponding surrogate approximation to the black box function.

2.1 Radial Basis Function Interpolation

The Bootstrap-Surrogate algorithm for sequential experimental design is implemented using the interpolating RBF model in Powell [23] and the resulting experimental design method is called *Bootstrap-RBF*. In this interpolating RBF model, each data point is a center and the basis functions are not necessarily Gaussian. This type of RBF model has been successfully used in expensive black-box optimization (e.g., see [7,25,27,31]).

Given n distinct design points $x_1, \ldots, x_n \in \mathbb{R}^d$ with their function values $f(x_1), \ldots, f(x_n)$. We use an interpolating RBF model of the form:

$$s_n(x) = \sum_{i=1}^n \lambda_i \phi(\|x - x_i\|) + c^T x + c_0, \ x \in \mathbb{R}^d,$$

where $\|\cdot\|$ is the 2-norm, $\lambda_i \in \mathbb{R}$ for $i = 1, \ldots, n$, $\phi(r) = r^3$ (cubic form), $c \in \mathbb{R}^d$ and $c_0 \in \mathbb{R}$. Here, $c^T x + c_0$ represents a linear polynomial tail in d variables. There are other options for the radial function $\phi(r)$ including $\phi(r) = r^2 \log r$ (thin plate spline) and $\phi(r) = \exp(-\gamma r^2)$ (Gaussian), where γ is a hyperparameter. This model is fit by solving a linear system that is described in [23].

Fig. 1. 3-D surface plots of GWB2A and GWB2B

3   Computational Experiments

3.1   Test Problems

The proposed Bootstrap-RBF method for sequential experimental design is applied to three simulation-based models involving the management of groundwater bioremediation [32] and on 17 synthetic test problems. Groundwater bioremediation is the process by which microorganisms are used to break down harmful chemicals in the groundwater. Groundwater bioremediation simulation models are typically computationally expensive since they often involve numerical solutions of partial differential equations. The synthetic test problems are not simulation-based and are inexpensive to evaluate, but we include them in this study and pretend that each function evaluation is costly by limiting the number of function evaluations allowed. The performance of the proposed method on these synthetic problems will most likely be similar to its performance on simulation-based problems that have similar structure.

The groundwater bioremediation problems, labeled as GWB2A, GWB2B and GWB3, are 2-D and 3-D versions of the simulation-based problem used in [27] where some of the variables have been fixed. Figure 1 shows the 3-D surface plots of the GWB2A and GWB2B problems. The plots reveal that the highly nonlinear part of the surfaces in these problems are mostly limited to a corner or one side of the domain $[0, 1]^2$.

Next, the synthetic problems Skewed Multimodal1 (SKMM1), Skewed Multimodal2 (SKMM2) and the Modified Shekel problems (ModShekel2A, ModShekel2B up to ModShekel3C) have characteristics similar to that of the groundwater bioremediation problems where the highly nonlinear part is confined to a corner or side of the domain. In particular,

$$\text{SKMM1}(x^{(1)}, x^{(2)}) = -3x^{(1)}x^{(2)} \exp\left(-(x^{(1)})^2 - (x^{(2)})^2\right), \quad -2 \le x^{(1)}, x^{(2)} \le 5,$$

and

$$\text{SKMM2}(x^{(1)}, x^{(2)}) = \frac{x^{(1)} + x^{(2)}}{2((x^{(1)})^2 + (x^{(2)})^2 + 16)}, \quad -20 \le x^{(1)}, x^{(2)} \le 40.$$

Moreover, the Modified Shekel problems are a variation of the 2-D and 3-D Shekel problems in [26] and have mathematical forms similar to that of the well-known Shekel test problems for global optimization (e.g., see [29]). The nine remaining synthetic test problems are well-known problems from the optimization literature such as the Ackley, Beale, Branin, Goldstein-Price, Hartman3 whose domains were rescaled to the unit hypercube. The R codes for these test functions can be obtained from [29].

The GWB3, ModShekel3A, ModShekel3B, ModShekel3C and Hartman3 are all 3-D problems while the rest are 2-D problems. Future work will include extending the capability of the Bootstrap-RBF approach to higher dimensional problems. In particular, since the bootstrap is a computationally intensive procedure, the method could benefit from the use of high-performance computing techniques.

3.2   Experimental Setup

All numerical experiments are conducted using the R software via the RStudio platform on an Intel(R) Core(TM) i7-7700T CPU @ 2.90GHz, 2904 Mhz, 4 Core(s), 8 Logical Processor(s) Windows-based machine. Moreover, the *boot* [5, 10] and *lhs* [6] R packages are used to implement the proposed method. Two instances of the Bootstrap-Surrogate method with the weights for the bootstrap standard error criterion set to $w_B = 0.50$ and $w_B = 0.25$ are implemented using interpolating RBF surrogates with the cubic form. These methods are labeled as Bootstrap-RBF ($w_B = 0.50$) and Bootstrap-RBF ($w_B = 0.25$). Each Bootstrap-RBF algorithm starts with an optimum Latin hypercube sample (LHS) of size $10(d + 1)$ and is extended to an experimental design of size up to $15(d + 1)$. Factors of $d+1$ are used since $d+1$ is the minimum number of points needed to fit a linear model, which is the simplest surrogate that can be used. Moreover, the number of uniform random trial points generated in each iteration is $t_{\text{rand}} = \min(500d, 1000)$ and the number of bootstrap replicates is $b = 1000$.

The Bootstrap-RBF algorithms are compared with two alternative approaches for constructing the experimental design given various computational budgets starting with $10(d + 1) + 1 = 10d + 11$ (one more than the initial space-filling design used by Bootstrap-RBF) up to $15(d+1)$. One approach is simply an optimum Latin hypercube sample that uses up the entire computational budget. This method is labeled as *Optimum LHS*. The other approach is a sequential experimental design method that begins with the same space-filling design of size $10(d+1)$ as the Bootstrap-RBF method and then sequentially adds a new experimental design point that is far from all previous design points. This approach, labeled *Sequential Maximin Design*, has a similar algorithmic structure as the Bootstrap-Surrogate method except it only uses the Minimum Distance criterion in selecting the random trial point where the simulator will be evaluated.

Both the Optimum LHS and the Sequential Maximin Design approaches attempt to spread out the simulation points so they can explore the entire domain. They generally perform well in terms of obtaining good surrogate models on many well-known test problems that are highly nonlinear. In fact, optimal Latin hypercube designs are widely used as starting points for many sequential surrogate-based optimization methods (e.g., [30]). However, these approaches do not use any information about the function values. Hence, they are not expected to perform as well as the Bootstrap-RBF approach on problems where the highly nonlinear part of the actual surface, which corresponds to a region of high uncertainty for a surrogate, is limited to a small region of the domain such as that of the groundwater bioremediation problems.

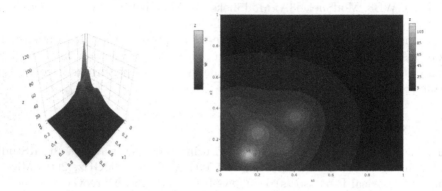

Fig. 2. 3-D surface and contour plots of ModShekel2A

3.3   Results and Discussion

First, we demonstrate the Bootstrap-RBF ($w_B = 0.50$) method on the Mod-Shekel2A test function. Figure 2 shows the 3-D surface plot and contour plot of this function. Next, the top left of Fig. 3 shows the contour plot of the RBF approximation after the $10(d + 1) = 30$ initial experimental design points were evaluated. The top right of the figure shows the corresponding contour plot of the bootstrap estimate of the standard error of the RBF prediction. The bottom left of Fig. 3 shows the contour plot of the RBF approximation after an additional $2(d+1) = 6$ evaluations while the bottom right shows the corresponding contour plot of the bootstrap estimate of the standard error of the RBF prediction. The newly added points (colored red) in the bottom figures tended to be in regions where the uncertainty is high in the top figures.

Each method is run for 30 trials on each of the 20 test problems (3 groundwater models and 17 synthetic problems). To get a fair and more accurate comparison of performance, the same initial optimum LHS of size $10(d+1)$ is used by the Bootstrap-RBF and Sequential Maximin Design methods, though the optimum LHS varies from trial to trial. The experimental design points obtained by the various methods are compared in terms of the Root Mean Square Error (RMSE) on an independent test set of $1000d$ uniform random points on $[0, 1]^d$ of the final interpolating RBF surrogate on the design points. Tables 1 and 2 show the mean and standard error (over 30 trials) of the RMSE of the final RBF surrogate for

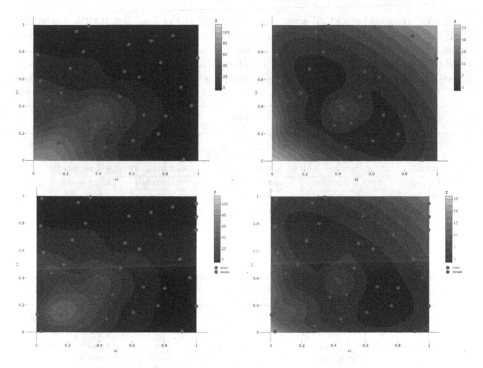

Fig. 3. Contour Plots of RBF approximation (left) and bootstrap estimate of standard error of RBF prediction (right) for ModShekel2A after the initial optimum LHS of $10(d + 1) = 30$ points (top) and after $12(d + 1) = 36$ simulations (bottom). (Color figure online)

the given function constructed from the experimental design points obtained by Bootstrap-RBF and the alternative methods. The test problems are arranged in the table so that the groundwater bioremediation remediation models are given first, followed by the synthetic test problems whose structures resemble those of the groundwater problems, and finally the well-known synthetic test problems. Moreover, Figs. 4, 5, 6 and 7 show the mean RMSE on the test set for various computational budgets (function evaluations or simulations) beginning with the initial optimum LHS of size $10(d + 1)$ up to $15(d + 1)$ for some of the problems.

The results show that the Bootstrap-RBF methods are generally better than the Sequential Maximin Design (SeqMaximin) and the Optimum LHS (OptLHS) on the GWB problems and on the synthetic test problems, especially those whose characteristics are similar to the GWB problems. In particular, from Table 2, Bootstrap-RBF ($w_B = 0.25$) is consistently better than OptLHS on all 20 problems, including the three GWB application problems, after $15(d+1)$ simulations. From Table 1, Bootstrap-RBF ($w_B = 0.25$) is also better than OptLHS on 19 of the 20 problems (all except on ModShekel3B) even after a smaller computational budget of only $12(d + 1)$ simulations. Moreover, from Table 2, Bootstrap-RBF ($w_B = 0.25$) is better or comparable with SeqMaximin on 16 of the test

Table 1. Mean and standard error (over 30 trials) of the Test Set RMSE of the final RBF surrogate for the given function obtained by various experimental design methods after $12(d+1)$ simulations, where d is the dimension of the problem. Each test set consists of $1000d$ random points from a uniform distribution on $[0,1]^d$. The best result is indicated by a solid blue box and the second best is given by a dashed magenta box.

Test Function	Bootstrap-RBF ($w_B = 0.50$)	Bootstrap-RBF ($w_B = 0.25$)	Sequential Maximin	Optimum LHS
GWB2A	136.5235 (7.7458)	137.2738 (8.1856)	148.381 (9.7442)	163.7199 (10.8559)
GWB2B	3759.2088 (199.0513)	3666.2356 (227.9467)	3851.3788 (213.9667)	4135.8759 (260.661)
GWB3A	6373.6969 (322.7452)	6390.9581 (237.9389)	6206.3263 (321.2515)	6832.68 (391.6532)
SKMM1	0.0992 (0.0052)	0.0994 (0.0053)	0.0989 (0.0054)	0.1054 (0.0075)
SKMM2	0.0076 (6e-04)	0.0082 (5e-04)	0.0082 (6e-04)	0.0084 (5e-04)
ModShekel2A	5.9227 (0.3344)	6.084 (0.4019)	6.0727 (0.3812)	8.3211 (1.2786)
ModShekel2B	4.1322 (0.2522)	4.3843 (0.2955)	4.6127 (0.3063)	5.993 (0.7565)
ModShekel2C	13.3697 (0.8508)	13.4286 (0.8645)	13.6476 (0.8431)	16.2502 (1.5902)
ModShekel3A	1.8575 (0.123)	1.9106 (0.1444)	2.0392 (0.1607)	1.9734 (0.1798)
ModShekel3B	5.3532 (0.9234)	5.4139 (1.0309)	6 (1.3251)	5.4089 (0.5817)
ModShekel3C	3.0242 (0.1967)	3.1252 (0.2139)	3.2585 (0.2252)	3.1983 (0.358)
Ackley	1.0734 (0.036)	1.0453 (0.0324)	1.0334 (0.0302)	1.0635 (0.0393)
Beale	5.30e+06 (2.61e+05)	4.41e+06 (2.27e+05)	4.46e+06 (2.32e+05)	6.30e+06 (2.79e+05)
Scaled Branin	5.9358 (0.5776)	5.0214 (0.3256)	4.796 (0.2539)	6.1424 (0.2908)
Camel6	270.7728 (13.5849)	245.9454 (11.3749)	247.0293 (8.9303)	281.6692 (9.0757)
Scaled Goldstein-Price	2.61e+04 (2.70e+03)	2.11e+04 (1.75e+03)	2.19e+04 (1.75e+03)	3.25e+04 (2.97e+03)
Hartman3	0.3139 (0.0103)	0.3022 (0.0112)	0.301 (0.0102)	0.3132 (0.0113)
Shubert	38.791 (1.6439)	38.6717 (1.6446)	38.7257 (1.5927)	40.4656 (1.7946)
Styblinski-Tang	11.8467 (0.6124)	10.6934 (0.5807)	10.4657 (0.3535)	13.4364 (0.4631)
Zakharov	873.2725 (128.4875)	572.1549 (66.469)	667.718 (65.9827)	1156.8956 (103.4355)

problems (all except on the Branin, Goldstein-Price, Hartman3 and Shubert) after $15(d+1)$ simulations. Also, from Table 1, Bootstrap-RBF ($w_B = 0.25$) is better than or comparable with SeqMaximin on 13 of the test problems, including on GWB2A and GWB2B, after $12(d+1)$ simulations. In addition, on most of the problems where the mean RMSE for Bootstrap-RBF ($w_B = 0.25$) is worse than that for SeqMaximin after either $12(d+1)$ or $15(d+1)$ simulations, the performance of the latter is close to that of the former.

Next, from Tables 1 and 2, Bootstrap-RBF ($w_B = 0.50$) is better than OptLHS on 18 of the 20 problems (all except on Ackley and Hartman3) after $12(d+1)$ simulations and also after $15(d+1)$ simulations. Moreover, from Table 2, Bootstrap-RBF ($w_B = 0.50$) has better mean RMSE values than SeqMaximin after $15(d+1)$ simulations on 11 of the 20 problems, including on GWB2A and GWB3 and on all eight synthetic problems whose characteristics are similar to that of the GWB problems. Also, from Table 1, Bootstrap-RBF ($w_B = 0.50$) is better than SeqMaximin after $12(d+1)$ simulations on only 9 of the 20 problems. However, Bootstrap-RBF ($w_B = 0.50$) did better on GWB2A and GWB2B and on 7 of the 8 synthetic problems that have similar structure to the GWB problems.

Table 2. Mean and standard error (over 30 trials) of the Test Set RMSE of the final RBF surrogate for the given function obtained by various experimental design methods after $15(d+1)$ simulations. Each test set consists of $1000d$ random points from a uniform distribution on $[0,1]^d$. The best result is indicated by a solid blue box and the second best is given by a dashed magenta box.

Test Function	Bootstrap-RBF ($w_B = 0.50$)	Bootstrap-RBF ($w_B = 0.25$)	Sequential Maximin	Optimum LHS
GWB2A	93.893 (7.4832)	110.8165 (6.1768)	125.8128 (6.8813)	152.0495 (7.7863)
GWB2B	3318.0344 (197.6043)	2859.8088 (163.5086)	3011.8386 (176.9743)	3823.7482 (259.4735)
GWB3A	5111.4867 (291.8695)	4984.2276 (260.509)	5165.1892 (199.5755)	6212.3128 (388.0434)
SKMM1	0.0668 (0.006)	0.0663 (0.0055)	0.0788 (0.0057)	0.0766 (0.0056)
SKMM2	0.0037 (3e-04)	0.0058 (4e-04)	0.0068 (5e-04)	0.007 (4e-04)
ModShekel2A	5.1081 (0.2705)	5.0901 (0.3025)	5.417 (0.2943)	6.1908 (0.6207)
ModShekel2B	3.9863 (0.3345)	3.9713 (0.2306)	4.0883 (0.2421)	4.5961 (0.3219)
ModShekel2C	11.3725 (0.5673)	11.6233 (0.826)	12.6408 (0.8945)	13.1401 (1.1904)
ModShekel3A	1.6439 (0.1146)	1.7217 (0.1138)	1.8564 (0.1223)	1.7974 (0.1074)
ModShekel3B	4.8914 (0.7565)	5.0113 (0.8666)	5.1751 (0.8841)	5.5127 (1.2035)
ModShekel3C	2.7259 (0.1712)	2.8662 (0.1474)	2.935 (0.1579)	3.1398 (0.331)
Ackley	1.0372 (0.0323)	0.967 (0.0326)	0.9757 (0.0303)	1.0331 (0.0341)
Beale	4.44e+06 (2.90e+05)	3.12e+06 (1.56e+05)	3.26e+06 (1.45e+05)	5.20e+06 (2.29e+05)
Scaled Branin	4.6224 (0.3067)	3.3324 (0.2032)	2.8131 (0.1425)	4.9123 (0.3683)
Camel6	227.5138 (12.7108)	180.504 (6.9274)	181.3427 (5.9533)	229.1421 (8.591)
Scaled Goldstein-Price	1.88e+04 (1.81e+03)	1.53e+04 (1.03e+03)	1.52e+04 (1.14e+03)	2.49e+04 (2.60e+03)
Hartman3	0.2771 (0.0077)	0.2584 (0.0084)	0.2569 (0.0092)	0.2601 (0.0083)
Shubert	37.7721 (1.2746)	38.5864 (1.4775)	38.2659 (1.3992)	39.4475 (1.5612)
Styblinski-Tang	9.313 (0.5173)	6.9234 (0.2679)	7.0488 (0.2591)	9.8954 (0.3673)
Zakharov	405.3347 (59.2295)	325.3212 (30.0241)	395.5428 (36.162)	811.1953 (87.3768)

Overall, it is worth noting that on the GWB application problems and on the 8 synthetic problems with characteristics that are similar to those of the GWB problems, the Bootstrap-RBF methods consistently obtained better mean RMSEs than those for the alternatives. On the remaining 9 synthetic test problems, the Bootstrap-RBF methods also did better than OptLHS. Moreover, Bootstrap-RBF ($w_B = 0.25$) has comparable performance with SeqMaximin on these test problems. However, SeqMaximin obtained better mean RMSEs than Bootstrap-RBF ($w_B = 0.50$) on these test problems though the mean RMSEs are not too far apart. A reasonable explanation is that since the nonlinearity of the surface is spread throughout the domain on the well-known test problems, having a measure of uncertainty through the bootstrap standard error does not provide much of an advantage over an approach that spreads out the design points. In any case, the performance of the Bootstrap-RBF approach does not seem to significantly deteriorate on the other synthetic test problems.

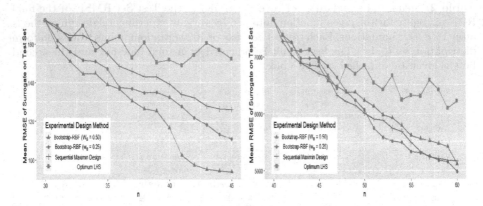

Fig. 4. Results on GWB2A (left) and GWB3 (right)

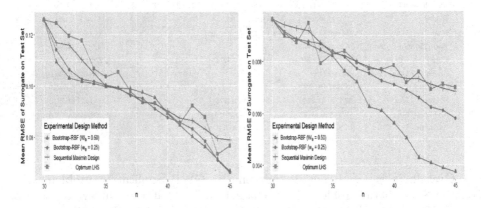

Fig. 5. Results on SKMM1 (left) and SKMM2 (right)

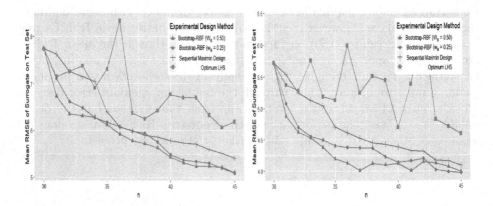

Fig. 6. Results on Modified Shekel2A (left) and Modified Shekel2B (right)

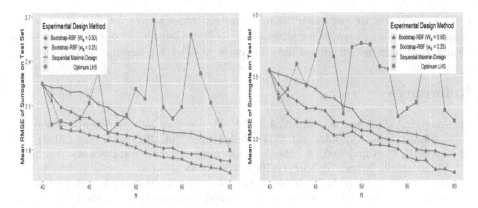

Fig. 7. Results on Modified Shekel3A (left) and Modified Shekel3C (right)

4   Summary and Conclusions

This paper proposed the Bootstrap-Surrogate approach for sequential experimental design for simulation-based functions where a bootstrap standard error criterion and a minimum distance criterion are used to quantify the uncertainty of a surrogate model prediction at a given point. It begins by evaluating the simulation-based function at the points of a space-filling experimental design and then successively identifies the next simulation point as a point where the aggregate uncertainty measure is high. The method is implemented using a radial basis function (RBF) surrogate and using two different weights for the bootstrap standard error criterion. The resulting Bootstrap-RBF methods are compared with an Optimum Latin Hypercube Sample (LHS) and a Sequential Maximin Design (SeqMaximin) on three groundwater bioremediation (GWB) problems and on a series of synthetic test problems. The methods are compared in terms of the RMSE of the final surrogate built using the experimental design points obtained on an independent test set on each of the test problems. The results show that the Bootstrap-RBF methods consistently performed better than OptLHS and SeqMaximin on the three GWB problems and on eight synthetic test problems similar to the GWB problems when given a computational budget of up to $15(d+1)$ simulations. Moreover, the Bootstrap-RBF methods also performed better than OptLHS and are generally competitive with SeqMaximin on another nine widely used test problems. The results suggest that the advantage of the Bootstrap-RBF approach is on problems where the nonlinearity of the function is limited to a smaller subregion of the domain, which is a characteristic of the simulation-based problems involving groundwater bioremediation. However, it also works reasonably well in comparison to a more static approach of using a fixed optimum space-filling design on other test problems where the nonlinearity is spread throughout the entire domain.

Future work will consider adapting the method to work well on higher dimensional problems and on other practical simulation-based problems. Moreover, the

Bootstrap-Surrogate approach has great potential for sequential surrogate-based optimization and provides an alternative to Bayesian global optimization techniques that also use an uncertainty measure in selecting simulation points.

References

1. Alaeddini, A., Yang, K., Murat, A.: ASRSM: a sequential experimental design for response surface optimization. Qual. Reliab. Eng. Int. **29**(2), 241–258 (2013)
2. Archetti, F., Candelieri, A.: Bayesian Optimization and Data Science. Springer, Cham (2019). https://doi.org/10.1007/978-3-030-24494-1
3. Bouhlel, M.A., Bartoli, N., Regis, R.G., Otsmane, A., Morlier, J.: Efficient global optimization for high-dimensional constrained problems by using the kriging models combined with the partial least squares method. Eng. Optim. **50**(12), 2038–2053 (2018)
4. Buhmann, M.: Radial Basis Functions: Theory and Implementations (Cambridge Monographs on Applied and Computational Mathematics). Cambridge University Press, Cambridge (2003)
5. Canty, A., Ripley, B.: boot: Bootstrap R (S-Plus) Functions. R package version 1.3-28 (2021). https://CRAN.R-project.org/package=boot
6. Carnell, R.: lhs: Latin Hypercube Samples. R package version 1.1.3 (2021). https://CRAN.R-project.org/package=lhs
7. Costa, A., Nannicini, G.: RBFOpt: an open-source library for black-box optimization with costly function evaluations. Math. Program. Comput. **10**(4), 597–629 (2018). https://doi.org/10.1007/s12532-018-0144-7
8. Crombecq, K.: Surrogate Modelling of Computer Experiments with Sequential Experimental Design. Ph.D. thesis. Ghent University (2011)
9. Crombecq, K., Gorissen, D., Deschrijver, D., Dhaene, T.: A novel hybrid sequential design strategy for global surrogate modeling of computer experiments. SIAM J. Sci. Comput. **33**(4), 1948–1974 (2011)
10. Davison, A.C., Hinkley, D.V.: Bootstrap Methods and Their Applications. Cambridge University Press, Cambridge (1997). ISBN 0-521-57391-2
11. Efron, B.: Bootstrap methods: another look at the jackknife. Ann. Stat. **7**, 1–26 (1979)
12. Efron, B., Tibshirani, R.: An Introduction to the Bootstrap. Chapman & Hall/CRC, Boca Raton (1993)
13. Forrester, A.I.J., Sobester, A., Keane, A.J.: Engineering Design via Surrogate Modelling: A Practical Guide. Wiley, Hoboken (2008)
14. Garud, S.S., Karimi, I.A., Kraft, M.: Design of computer experiments: a review. Comput. Chem. Eng. **106**, 71–95 (2017)
15. Gramacy, R.B.: Surrogates: Gaussian Process Modeling, Design, and Optimization for the Applied Sciences. Chapman and Hall/CRC, New York (2020)
16. Greenhill, S., Rana, S., Gupta, S., Vellanki, P., Venkatesh, S.: Bayesian optimization for adaptive experimental design: a review. IEEE Access **8**, 13937–13948 (2020)
17. James, G., Witten, D., Hastie, T., Tibshirani, R.: An Introduction to Statistical Learning with Applications in R. Springer, New York (2013). https://doi.org/10.1007/978-1-4614-7138-7
18. Joseph, V.R.: Space-filling designs for computer experiments: a review. Qual. Eng. **28**(1), 28–35 (2016)

19. Kleijnen, J.P.C.: Simulation-optimization via Kriging and bootstrapping: a survey. J. Simul. **8**(4), 241–250 (2014)
20. Kleinegesse, S., Drovandi, C., Gutmann, M.U.: Sequential Bayesian experimental design for implicit models via mutual information. Bayesian Anal. **16**(3), 773–802 (2021)
21. Pandita, P., Tsilifis, P., Awalgaonkar, N.M., Bilionis, I., Panchal, J.: Surrogate-based sequential Bayesian experimental design using non-stationary Gaussian Processes. Comput. Methods Appl. Mech. Eng. **385**, 114007 (2021)
22. Pourmohamad, T., Lee, H.K.H.: Bayesian Optimization with Application to Computer Experiments. Springer, Cham (2021). https://doi.org/10.1007/978-3-030-82458-7
23. Powell, M.J.D.: The theory of radial basis function approximation in 1990. In: Light, W. (ed.) Advances in Numerical Analysis, Volume 2: Wavelets, Subdivision Algorithms and Radial Basis Functions, pp. 105–210. Oxford University Press, Oxford (1992)
24. Regis, R.G.: A survey of surrogate approaches for expensive constrained black-box optimization. In: Le Thi, H.A., Le, H.M., Pham Dinh, T. (eds.) WCGO 2019. AISC, vol. 991, pp. 37–47. Springer, Cham (2020). https://doi.org/10.1007/978-3-030-21803-4_4
25. Regis, R.G.: Constrained optimization by radial basis function interpolation for high-dimensional expensive black-box problems with infeasible initial points. Eng. Optim. **46**(2), 218–243 (2014)
26. Regis, R.G.: Trust regions in Kriging-based optimization with expected improvement. Eng. Optim. **48**(6), 1037–1059 (2016)
27. Regis, R.G., Shoemaker, C.A.: A stochastic radial basis function method for the global optimization of expensive functions. Informs J. Comput. **19**(4), 497–509 (2007)
28. Santner, T.J., Williams, B.J., Notz, W.I.: Space-filling designs for computer experiments. In: The Design and Analysis of Computer Experiments. SSS, pp. 145–200. Springer, New York (2018). https://doi.org/10.1007/978-1-4939-8847-1_5
29. Surjanovic, S., Bingham, D.: Virtual Library of Simulation Experiments: Test Functions and Datasets (2013). http://www.sfu.ca/~ssurjano. Accessed 12 Apr 2022
30. Vu, K.K., D'Ambrosio, C., Hamadi, Y., Liberti, L.: Surrogate-based methods for black-box optimization. Int. Trans. Oper. Res. **24**, 393–424 (2017)
31. Wild, S.M., Regis, R.G., Shoemaker, C.A.: ORBIT: optimization by radial basis function interpolation in trust-regions. SIAM J. Sci. Comput. **30**(6), 3197–3219 (2008)
32. Yoon, J.-H., Shoemaker, C.A.: Comparison of optimization methods for groundwater bioremediation. J. Water Resour. Plan. Manag. **125**(1), 54–63 (1999)

Forecasting Models: An Application to Home Insurance

Luís Filipe Pires[1,3], A. Manuela Gonçalves[1,2]([✉]) [ID], Luís Filipe Ferreira[3], and Luís Maranhão[3]

[1] Department of Mathematics, University of Minho, Guimarães, Portugal
mneves@math.uminho.pt
[2] Centre of Mathematics, University of Minho, Guimarães, Portugal
[3] International Insurance Group, Guimarães, Portugal

Abstract. Forecasting in time series is one of the main purposes for applying time series models. The choice of the forecasting model depends on data structure and the objectives of the study. This study presents a comparison of Box Jenkins SARIMA and Holt-Winters exponential smoothing approaches to time series forecasting to increase the likelihood of capturing different patterns in the data (in this specific case, home insurance data) and thus improve forecasting performance. These methods are chosen due to their ability to model seasonal fluctuations present in insurance data. The forecasting performance is demonstrated by a case study of home insurance monthly time series: total and frequency rate time series. In order to assess the predictive and forecasting performance of the two methodologies adopted, several evaluation measures are used, namely MSE, RMSE, MAPE, and Theil's U-statistics. A comparison is made and discussed, and the results obtained demonstrate the superiority of the SARIMA model over the other forecasting approach. Holt-Winters also produces accurate forecasts, so it is considered a viable alternative to SARIMA.

Keywords: Home insurance · Time series · Forecasting · SARIMA · Holt-winters

1 Introduction

A time series is a set of observations usually ordered in equally spaced intervals. Time series forecasting is an important area in which past observations of the same variable are collected and analyzed to develop a model describing the underlying relationship. The model is then used to extrapolate the time series into the future. Forecasting methods are a key tool in decision-making processes in many areas, such as economics, insurance, management or environment. There are several approaches to modeling time series, but we decided to study and compare the accuracy of the Box Jenkins SARIMA and Holt-Winters exponential smoothing models for forecasting home insurance time series, because both models can increase the chance of capturing the proprieties and the dynamics of the

O. Gervasi et al. (Eds.): ICCSA 2022 Workshops, LNCS 13377, pp. 514–529, 2022.
https://doi.org/10.1007/978-3-031-10536-4_34

data and thus improve forecast accuracy. Both methods have the ability to deal with time series seasonality. The time series analysis of both processes was carried out using the statistical software R programming language and specialized packages for modeling and forecasting.

The problem proposed by the International Insurance Group, Portugal, was to find the models that best fit and forecast (the focus will be on forecasting) the monthly time series of total home insurance, including storm damage and claims, contents damage, leaking or escape of water in the home, accidental damage, damage to fridge/freezer food in the home, building damage, theft or robbery, fire and others, in order to use them to forecast future values. For example, see the importance of this type of insurance in economic terms: at least 85% of homeowners in the U.S. have homeowners insurance, and policies cost on average $1,445 per year. While it's not a required form of coverage by the government, home insurance is typically required as a condition for applying for a mortgage and it is very valuable because of the protection it provides homeowners. Home insurance policies generally provide coverage for damage to a home's structure, damage to personal property and liability coverage in case the policy holder is considered at fault for property damage or bodily injury to another party. There is a growing number of accidents taking place, either caused by humans actions or by nature. Population growth at a national level certainly entails increasing numbers of accidents (recorded by insurance companies). Another major factor with tremendous weight in these records is climate change. Contrary to what one might assume at first glance, this phenomenon not only contributes to hotter summers, but also to colder winters, i.e., climate change increases the volatility of Earth' s temperature. This results in more intense and more frequent storms, which are ultimately reflected in insurance markets. In these markets, a claim is defined as an event that results in material loss to an insured individual.

In this study the claims data regard home insurance (total home insurance as defined above). Our data source are the records of the claims registered in the period from January 2015 to June 2021 on a monthly basis (data from Portugal). The main goal is to forecast these claims in monthly time series. Two time series are considered: the total home insurance (number of claims registered in the month) and a monthly frequency rate. This monthly frequency rate is defined as follows

$$\frac{\text{number of claims registered in the month}}{\text{number of people exposed to risk in the month}} \qquad (1)$$

which varies between 0 and 1, where the number of people exposed to risk in a given month is equal to the number of portfolios open. It should be stressed that the main focus of this study is to establish accurate forecasting models to support managerial performance the decision-making process to improve the services provided to policyholders.

2 Methodologies

2.1 SARIMA Model

The Box Jenkins SARIMA$(p, d, q)(P, D, Q)_s$ is a short memory model and a very flexible model, given that it accounts for stochastic seasonality, and is one of the most versatile models for forecasting seasonal time series. Such seasonality is present when the seasonal pattern of a time series changes over time. The theory of SARIMA models has been developed by many researchers and its wide application results from the work by Box et al. [1], who developed a systematic and practical model-building method. Through an iterative three-step model-building process, model identification, parameter estimation and model diagnosis, the Box-Jenkins methodology has proven to be an effective practical time series modeling approach.

The SARIMA model has the following form

$$\Phi_p(B)N_P(B^s)(1 - B)^d(1 - B^s)^D Y_t = \Theta_q(B)H_Q(B^s)\epsilon_t, \tag{2}$$

where Y_t is the time series, with

$$\Phi_p(B) = 1 - \phi_1 B - \cdots - \phi_p B^p,$$
$$N_P(B^s) = 1 - \nu_1 B^s - \cdots - \nu_P P_s,$$
$$\Theta_q(B) = 1 + \theta_1 B + \cdots + \theta_q B^q,$$
$$H_Q(B^s) = 1 + \eta_1 B^s + \cdots + \eta_Q Q_s,$$

where s is the seasonal length, B is the backshift operator defined by $B^k Y_t = Y_{t-k}$, $\Phi_p(B)$ and $\Theta_q(B)$ are the regular autoregressive and moving average polynomials of orders p and q, respectively, $N_P(B^s)$ and $H_Q(B^s)$ are the seasonal autoregressive and moving average polynomials of orders P and Q, respectively, and ϵ_t is a sequence of white noises with zero mean and constant variance σ^2. $(1 - B)^d$ and $(1 - B^s)^D$ are the nonseasonal and seasonal differencing operators, respectively.

The model with the minimum AIC (Akaike's Information Criterion) value and the minimum BIC (Bayesian's Information Criterion) value is often the best model for forecasting [2]. We investigated the required transformations for variance stabilization and decided to apply logarithms to the time series under study.

Once the model has been specified, its autoregressive, moving average, and seasonal parameters (SARIMA model) need to be estimated. The parameters of SARIMA models are usually estimated by maximizing the likelihood of the model.

2.2 Holt-Winters Model

The Holt-Winters method is an extension of the Holt method, and is applied whenever the data behavior is trendy and is seasonal. The seasonal type can be additive or multiplicative, depending on the oscillatory movement over the time period. In both versions, the forecasts will depend on the following three components of a seasonal time series: level, trend and seasonal coefficient. In addition, both are implemented in the Holt-Winters function of the *forecast* package in R. The additive version ought to be considered whenever the seasonal pattern of a series has constant amplitude over time [3]. In such case, the series can be written by $Y_t = T_t + S_t + \varepsilon_t$, where T_t represents the trend (the sum of the level and the slope of the series at time t), S_t is the seasonal component, and ε_t are error terms with mean 0 and constant variance. When a series displays a seasonal pattern characterized by amplitude that varies with the series level, the multiplicative version is a better choice. In such case, the series can be represented by $Y_t = T_t \times S_t + \varepsilon_t$. The multiplicative and additive Holt-Winters methods have the recursive equations presented in the Table 1. The exploratory analysis of all eight time series indicated the presence of a seasonal pattern.

Table 1. The recursive equations of the Holt-Winters methods.

Multiplicative H-W	$F_t = \alpha \frac{Y_t}{f_{t-s}} + (1-\alpha)(F_{t-1} + b_{t-1}),\ 0 \le \alpha \le 1$
	$b_t = \beta(F_t - F_{t-1}) + (1-\beta)b_{t-1},\ 0 \le \beta \le 1$
	$f_t = \gamma \frac{Y_t}{F_t} + (1-\gamma)f_{t-s},\ 0 \le \gamma \le 1$
	$\hat{Y}_{t+k} = (F_t + kb_t)f_{t+k-ms},\ m=1, 1 \le k \le s, m=2, s < k \le 2s,$ etc.
Additive H-W	$F_t = \alpha(Y_t - f_{t-s}) + (1-\alpha)(F_{t-1} + b_{t-1}),\ 0 \le \alpha \le 1$
	$b_t = \beta(F_t - F_{t-1}) + (1-\beta)b_{t-1},\ 0 \le \beta \le 1$
	$f_t = \gamma(Y_t - F_t) + (1-\gamma)f_{t-s},\ 0 \le \gamma \le 1$
	$\hat{Y}_{t+k} = F_t + kb_t + f_{t+k-ms},\ m=1, 1 \le k \le s, m=2, s < k \le 2s,$ etc.

The Bootstrap method introduced in [4] provides a way to estimate parameters, approximate a sampling distribution or derive confidence intervals when we have data but do not know the underlying distribution. If the population represented through a probability distribution and its parameters are unknown, the Bootstrap idea is to take (re-)samples $(y_1^*, y_2^*, \ldots, y_n^*)$, drawn with replacement from the original sample $(y_1, y_2, \ldots, y_n)$. Computing prediction intervals are an important part of the forecasting process and aim to indicate the likely uncertainty in point forecasts. The prediction intervals are usually based on the Mean Square Error (MSE), which denotes the variance of the one-step-ahead forecast errors [5]. Prediction intervals (whenever a normality assumption is verified) for both at one-step-ahead and at m-steps-ahead are given by the following expression:

$$\left[\hat{Y}_{k+m} - z_{1-\alpha/2}\sqrt{MSE_m}, \hat{Y}_{k+m} + z_{1-\alpha/2}\sqrt{MSE_m}\right]$$

where z is the quantile of probabilty $1 - \alpha/2$ of the standard Normal distribution and $MSE_m = \frac{1}{k-m}\sum_{t=m+1}^{k}(\epsilon_t^{(m)})^2$ denote the variance of the m-steps-ahead errors. The idea is to look at the bootstrap percentiles rather than the sampling distribution percentiles, and the confidence interval is based on the

Bootstrap distribution (i.e., on the percentiles). Different methods are available for the construction of Bootstrap confidence intervals: the percentile method, the percentile-t method, the bias-corrected method [4] and the accelerated bias-corrected method [4]. The Bootstrap percentile confidence interval is based on the quantiles of the Bootstrap estimates distribution and is obtained as follows: suppose F_k is the empirical cumulative distribution function $\{\hat{y}_{n+k}^b, b = 1, \ldots, B\}$, then the prediction interval is given by $\left[F_k^{-1}(\alpha/2), F_k^{-1}(1 - \alpha/2)\right]$, where for an interval with 95% confidence and B replicates the limits of the intervals are the percentiles $F_k^{-1}(0.025)$ and $F_k^{-1}(0.975)$.

2.3 Forecasting Models Evaluation

Let's denote the actual observation for time period t by Y_t and the estimated or forecasted value for the same period by $\hat{Y}_t$ and n is the total number of observations. The most commonly used forecast error measures are the mean squared error (MSE), the root mean squared error (RMSE), the mean absolute percentage error (MAPE), and Theil's U-statistics [2]. MSE, RMSE, and MAPE are defined by the following formulas, respectively:

$$\text{MSE} = \frac{1}{n}\sum_{t=1}^{n} e_t^2 = \frac{1}{n}\sum_{t=1}^{n}(Y_t - \hat{Y}_t)^2, \text{RMSE} = \sqrt{\frac{1}{n}\sum_{t=1}^{n} e_t^2}, \tag{3}$$

$$\text{MAPE} = \frac{1}{n}\sum_{t=1}^{n}\left|\frac{Y_t - \hat{Y}_t}{Y_t}\right| \times 100 \quad (\%). \tag{4}$$

Theil's U-statistics allows a relative comparison of forecasting methods with naïve approaches and also squares the errors involved so that large errors are given much more weight than small errors. It is defined as

$$\text{U-Theil} = \sqrt{\frac{\sum_{t=1}^{n-1}\left(\frac{\hat{Y}_{t+1}-Y_{t+1}}{Y_t}\right)^2}{\sum_{t=1}^{n-1}\left(\frac{Y_{t+1}-Y_t}{Y_t}\right)^2}}. \tag{5}$$

Since there is no universally agreed-upon performance measure that can be applied to every forecasting situation, multiple criteria are often required to enable a comprehensive assessment of forecasting models [2]. When comparing forecasting methods, the method with the lowest MSE, RMSE, MAPE or Theil's U-statistics is the preferred one. Often, different accuracy measures will lead to different results as to the best forecast method.

3 Dataset

The study started with exhaustive comprehensive description of the data to understand their behavior over time but also globally. The first step in the analysis of any time series is the description of the historic series. It includes the graphical representation of the data. When a time series is plotted, common patterns are frequently found. These patterns might be explained by many possible cause-and-effect relationships. Common components are the trend, seasonal effect, cyclic changes and randomness. A more interesting and ambitious task is to forecast future values of a series based on its recorded past, and more specifically to calculate forecasting intervals. Therefore, identifying these components is important when selecting a forecasting model.

Table 2 presents descriptive statistics for the total monthly time series. As expected, standard deviation is higher and indicates a larger variability during the observed period. The mean and median are around 1466 and 1400 claims by month, respectively.

Table 2. Descriptive statistics of the total monthly time series.

Beginning	01/2015
End	06/2021
Dimension	78
Range	1013–2707
$Q_{0.25}$	1250
Median	1400
$Q_{0.75}$	1623
Mean	1466.13
Standard deviation	340.97
Variance	116258.6
Variation coefficient	0.23
Number of outliers	4

The years 2020 and 2021, in particular 2021, show a different behaviour from the previous years: 2021 presents a huge variability and higher values. This is due to COVID-19 pandemic context (Fig. 1). There are four outlier observations: January 2015 (1669 claims), March 2018 (2707 claims), January 2020 (2138 claims), and December 2020 (2131 claims).

Before implementing the modeling processes, it was decided to transform the data regarding the total home insurance (number of claims registered in the month) with values greater than 2000 claims per month (a threshold of 2000 claims). Thus, if the value observed (y_o) in a given month was greater than 2000 claims the following transformation is applied $y_o = \frac{y_{o-12} + y_{o+12}}{2}$ with regard to the annual seasonality ($s = 12$ months) inherent in the data (an increase at the end of each year, followed by a decrease at the beginning of the following year), which the graphic representations of the FAC and FACP indicate (see Fig. 2). Therefore, six values were transformed (Fig. 3).

Table 3 presents the values above the 2000 threshold and the transformed values.

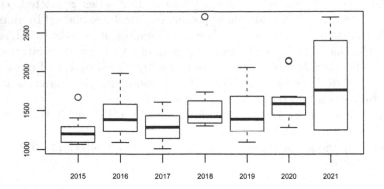

Fig. 1. Boxplots of the total time series from 2015 to 2021.

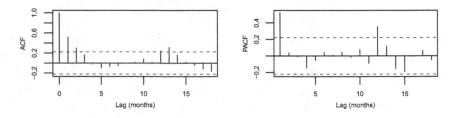

Fig. 2. ACF and PACF of the total monthly time series.

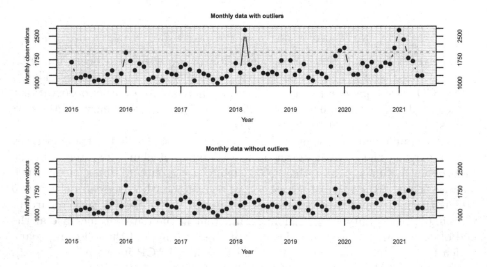

Fig. 3. Effect of the threshold smoothing in the total monthly time series.

Table 3. Values before and after transformation.

Date	Before	After
03/2018	2707	1428
12/2019	2051	1410
01/2020	2138	1694
12/2020	2131	1406
01/2021	2700	1716
02/2021	2396	1604

It should be noted that this transformation was not applied to the monthly frequency rate time series (a ratio ranging between 0 and 1). In the same context, the frequency rate time series also presents 12 month seasonality (Fig. 4).

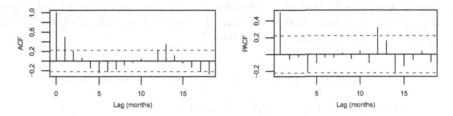

Fig. 4. ACF and PACF of the total monthly frequency rate time series.

Also, the graphical representation of the two time series clearly shows that time series exhibit seasonal behavior (Fig. 5 and Fig. 6), as expected due to the nature of the data. The monthly data exhibits a strong monthly seasonality (a period of 12 months).

4   Results

The results obtained from the application of the SARIMA and Holt-Winters methods are reported in this section. The methods considered in this study are applied to two data sets: training data (in-sample data) and testing data (out-of-sample data) in order to test the accuracy of the proposed forecasting models. This process is implemented regarding both time series: the total home insurance (number of claims registered in the month) and the monthly frequency rate. The selected training period was from January 2015 to December 2020 (first 72 observations/months) and was used to fit the models to the data, and the test period included the last 6 months, i.e., the period from January 2021 to June 2021 was used to forecast. This approach allows comparing the effectiveness of different methods of prediction.

Note that the final results that will be presented always refer to the number of claims registered per month, i.e., the rates time series are modeled and forecasted but the final results presented in this paper are transformed back to the initial values: the total home insurance (number of claims registered in the month).

4.1   SARIMA Model

The ADF (Augmented Dickey-Fuller) and KPSS (Kwiatkowski, Phillips, Schmidt, and Shin) tests (with a 5% significance level) were applied to the total home insurance time series to test series's stationarity and nonstationarity. A Box-Cox transformation was applied to the data, deciding on a $\lambda = -0.184$. Therefore, the SARIMA model will be fitted to this time series for the observations with Box-Cox transformation. The main task in SARIMA forecasting is to select an appropriate model order, i.e., the p, d, q, P, D, Q and s values ($s = 12$).

Tables 4 and 5 show the five models with lower AIC and BIC fitted to the training time series for both cases: the total home insurance (number of claims registered in the month) and a monthly frequency rate. All combinations of parameters p, d, q, P, D, and Q were tested.

Table 4. Adjustment of SARIMA models for the total monthly time series.

Model	AIC	Model	BIC
SARIMA$(1,0,2)(0,1,1)_{12}$	862.62	SARIMA$(1,0,0)(0,1,1)_{12}$	870.01
SARIMA$(2,0,1)(0,1,1)_{12}$	863.26	SARIMA$(0,0,1)(0,1,1)_{12}$	870.04
SARIMA$(1,0,0)(0,1,1)_{12}$	863.73	SARIMA$(0,0,0)(0,1,1)_{12}$	871.92
SARIMA$(0,0,1)(0,1,1)_{12}$	863.76	SARIMA$(1,0,0)(0,1,2)_{12}$	872.54
SARIMA$(1,0,2)(0,1,2)_{12}$	863.82	SARIMA$(1,0,0)(1,1,1)_{12}$	872.85

Table 5. Adjustment of SARIMA models for the total frequency rate time series.

Model	AIC	Model	BIC
SARIMA$(2,0,2)(1,0,2)_{12}$	−487.91	SARIMA$(1,0,0)(0,0,0)_{12}$	−478.95
SARIMA$(2,0,1)(0,0,0)_{12}$	−487.51	SARIMA$(0,0,1)(0,0,0)_{12}$	−478.45
SARIMA$(2,0,1)(0,0,1)_{12}$	−486.79	SARIMA$(1,0,0)(0,0,1)_{12}$	−477.05
SARIMA$(2,0,2)(0,0,2)_{12}$	−486.27	SARIMA$(0,0,1)(0,0,1)_{12}$	−476.61
SARIMA$(1,0,0)(0,0,1)_{12}$	−486.16	SARIMA$(1,0,0)(1,0,0)_{12}$	−476.54

On the bases of the AICs e BICs criteria, it is preferred the SARIMA$(1,0,0)(0,1,1)_{12}$ model for total monthly time series, and the SARIMA$(1,0,0)(0,0,1)_{12}$ model for total frequency rate time series.

The estimation results of these two models can be consulted in more detail in Table 6.

Table 6. Characteristics of the SARIMA models.

Monthly time series	AIC = 863.73	BIC = 870.01	$\hat{\sigma} \approx 0.0216$
SARIMA$(1,0,0)(0,1,1)_{12}$	Parameter	ϕ_1	η_1
	Estimate	0.3788	-0.6851
	Standard deviation	0.1238	0.2027
Frequency rate	AIC $= -486.16$	BIC $= -477.05$	$\hat{\sigma} \approx 0.008$
SARIMA$(1,0,0)(0,0,1)_{12}$	Parameter	ϕ_1	η_1
	Estimate	0.3601	0.2101
	Standard deviation	0.1124	0.1300

Figures. 5 and 6 present the original values of the two time series, as well as the estimates in the modeling period (training period).

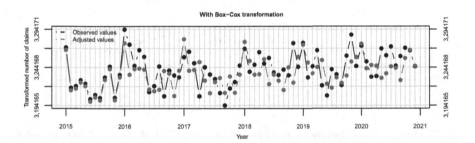

Fig. 5. Adjustment of the SARIMA model for the monthly total time series.

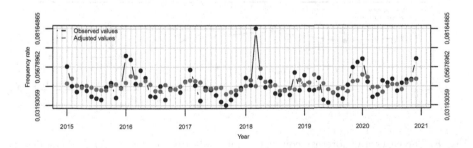

Fig. 6. Adjustment of the SARIMA model for the total frequency rate time series.

Once the forecasts' accuracy (punctual) is evaluated, it is essential to understand the effectiveness of the forecast intervals.

Theoretically, the forecast intervals are calculated at 95% confidence level, which means that 95% of the intervals must include the real observation. That is, it is considered that the most effective interval forecasts are those whose effective coverage rate is closer to 95%. Note that the forecast intervals are obtained based on the testing series for each distinct series where (in this study) they contain only 6 observations (6 months) and, therefore, the analysis of coverage rates must be taken to consideration. Also the testing period is from January 2021 to June 2021, corresponding to half a year of COVID-19 pandemic, which had a tremendous impact on society as a whole, including on human behavior and consequently on the number of claims on home insurance which clearly behaved differently from previous periods. In the two time series under study, total monthly time series and total frequency rate, with coverage rates of 100% and 67%, respectively, are calculated. It should be noted that the 100% coverage rate is due to a greater amplitude of the forecasting interval. It is noteworthy that the model formulated for the time series corresponding to the total claims monthly presents better results (Figs. 7 and 8).

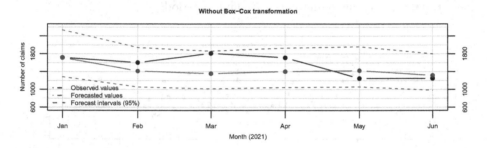

Fig. 7. Forecasts and forecast confidence intervals (95%) of the SARIMA model for the total monthly time series.

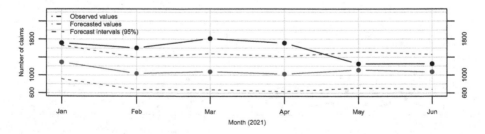

Fig. 8. Forecasts and forecast confidence intervals (95%) of the SARIMA model for the total frequency rate time series.

The models validation was assessed by means of the residuals analysis. The independency assumptions were assessed by estimating the autocorrelation and the partial autocorrelation functions of residuals and the assumption that the residuals are identically normally distributed were also verified (by performing the Kolmogorov-Smirnov test).

4.2 Holt-Winters Model

We applied the additive and multiplicative Holt-Winters to the first k observations (we considered the period from January 2015 to June 2015, the first semester), and we obtained the initial values for the smoothing parameters. We obtained the residuals and we calculated the MSE to compare the forecasting accuracy. The additive Holt-Winters models proved to have the best predictive performance. So, for all times series, we considered the models obtained by the additive Holt-Winters method. Tables 7 and 8 show the smoothing constants estimates of the two additive models for the training time series for both cases: the total home insurance (number of claims registered in the month) and a monthly frequency rate.

Table 7. Holt-Winters additive model parameters estimates for the monthly counts.

$\widehat{\alpha} \approx 0.1603$	$\widehat{\beta} \approx 0.0212$	$\widehat{\gamma} \approx 0.5974$	$\widehat{l}_1 \approx 1644.5000$	$\widehat{b}_1 \approx 8.4710$
$\widehat{s}_1 \approx 154.2854$	$\widehat{s}_2 \approx -112.3845$	$\widehat{s}_3 \approx -175.0366$	$\widehat{s}_4 \approx -87.0292$	$\widehat{s}_5 \approx -1.2906$
$\widehat{s}_6 \approx -110.3108$	$\widehat{s}_7 \approx -15.5516$	$\widehat{s}_8 \approx -200.5818$	$\widehat{s}_9 \approx -177.1819$	$\widehat{s}_{10} \approx -35.7976$
$\widehat{s}_{11} \approx 54.6681$	$\widehat{s}_{12} \approx -206.0083$			

Table 8. Estimates for the frequency rate Holt-Winters additive model's parameters.

$\widehat{\alpha} \approx 0.0839$	$\widehat{\beta} \approx 0.0128$	$\widehat{\gamma} \approx 0.3795$	$\widehat{l}_1 \approx 0.0526$	$\widehat{b}_1 \approx 0.0002$
$\widehat{s}_1 \approx 0.0081$	$\widehat{s}_2 \approx 0.0002$	$\widehat{s}_3 \approx -0.0012$	$\widehat{s}_4 \approx 0.0027$	$\widehat{s}_5 \approx -0.0034$
$\widehat{s}_6 \approx -0.006$	$\widehat{s}_7 \approx -0.0052$	$\widehat{s}_8 \approx -0.0091$	$\widehat{s}_9 \approx -0.0074$	$\widehat{s}_{10} \approx 0.0043$
$\widehat{s}_{11} \approx -0.0005$	$\widehat{s}_{12} \approx 0.0037$			

In Fig. 9 and Fig. 10 are represented the original values of the claims time series, the total home insurance (number of claims registered in the month) and a monthly frequency rate, respectively, and the estimates in the modeling period (training period).

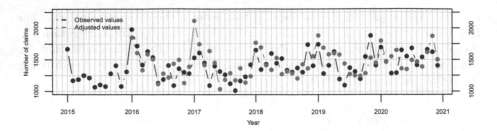

Fig. 9. Adjustment of the Holt-Winters model for the total monthly time series.

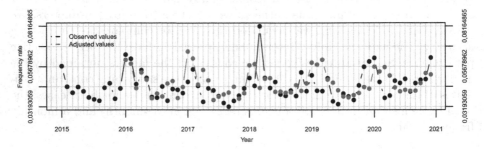

Fig. 10. Adjustment of the Holt-Winters model for the total frequency rate time series.

The Holt-Winters procedure associated to the Bootstrap resampling method was programmed in the R software by taking $B = 2000$ replicates in the residuals resampling process. Thus, the Bootstrap percentile confidence interval obtained is based on the quantiles of the Bootstrap estimates distribution. The forecasts from January 2021 to June 2021 for both time series processes were computed to assess the performance of the methodologies, namely by the forecast 95% confidence intervals range.

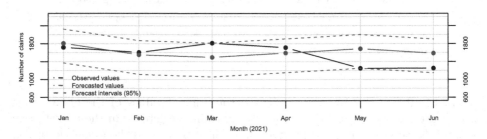

Fig. 11. Forecasts and forecast Bootstrap percentile confidence interval (95%) of the Holt-Winters model for the total monthly time series.

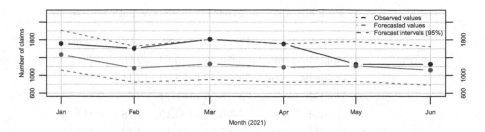

Fig. 12. Forecasts and forecast Bootstrap percentile confidence interval (95%) of the Holt-Winters model for the total frequency rate time series.

Figure 11 and Fig. 12 present the original values, the forecasts in the forecasting period (testing period) and the Bootstrap forecast confidence intervals for a 95% confidence level for the two Holt-Winters models. The coverage rate of empirical confidence of corrected forecasts is 83% and 100% (this happens because the amplitude of the forecast interval is larger), for the total monthly time series and total frequency rate time series, respectively, of the confidence intervals with a 95% confidence level (5 and 6 observations of the testing series belong to the confidence interval).

4.3 Models Performance

Tables 9 and 10 show the results of the accuracy measures calculated for the entire observation period (a total period of observation of 78 months), training and testing periods for the two methods applied to the time series under study. The performance comparisons of the competing models (SARIMA and Holt-Winters) were evaluated using MSE, RMSE, MAPE, and Theil's U- statistics. The results obtained showed that the SARIMA, which requires fewer parameters to be estimated, is (predominantly) more accurate than Holt-Winters and performs better for all period times (total, training and test periods). From the two models performed, we selected the most adequate model which has the lowest forecast error when comparing predicted data using a suitable test set: SARIMA. Therefore, the SARIMA models can more efficiently capture the dynamic behavior of the total monthly time series and total frequency rate time series compared to Holt-Winters.

Table 9. Evaluation metrics of the SARIMA models of both time series.

	Time series	MSE	RMSE	MAPE	U-Theil
Total	Monthly counts	189950.30	435.83	9.90	0.78
	Frequency rate	39239.89	198.09	12.11	0.83
Training set	Monthly counts	33028.16	181.74	9.69	0.80
	Frequency rate	37320.45	193.19	11.78	0.81
Testing set	Monthly counts	62092.11	249.18	12.40	1.18
	Frequency rate	62273.19	249.55	16.00	1.23

Table 10. Evaluation metrics of the Holt-Winter models of both time series.

	Time series	MSE	RMSE	MAPE	U-Theil
Total	Monthly counts	48410.05	220.02	12.68	0.98
	Frequency rate	331902.60	576.11	36.70	2.52
Training set	Monthly counts	46119.56	214.75	12.36	0.97
	Frequency rate	350710.00	592.21	38.41	2.60
Testing set	Monthly counts	71315.00	267.05	15.81	1.36
	Frequency rate	143828.40	379.25	19.53	1.71

5   Conclusions

The main objective of this study was to establish accurate forecasting models to enable the Insurance Company level to (monthly) forecast the number of housing claims with good accuracy to optimize costs at the managerial level. The SARIMA models provided superior point forecasts over the remaining methodology, with the Holt-Winters model proving to be a viable alternative. The lowest observed value was 249 claims (root mean squared error) per month for the forecasting with the total monthly time series modeling process (see Table 9). Contrary to expectations, claims modeling via monthly rate did not result in better estimates or better forecasts for the process of obtaining accurate claims numbers. Thus, future research should only consider the forecasting process of the time series via the original data (number of claims by month). In fact, for the total home insurance, both model processes in terms of accuracy forecasting and coverage rates have performed well regarding the number of claims registered by month.

Acknowledgements. A. Manuela Gonçalves was partially financed by Portuguese Funds through FCT (Fundação para a Ciência e a Tecnologia) within the Projects UIDB/00013/2020 and UIDP/00013/2020 of CMAT-UM.

References

1. Box, G., Jenkins, G., Reinsel, G.: Time Series Analysis, 4th edn. Wiley, Hoboken (2008)
2. Hyndman, R.J., Athanasopoulos, G.: Forecasting: Principles and Practice. Online Open-Acess Texbooks. http://otexts.com/fpp. Accessed 5 Oct 2020
3. Kalekar, P.S.: Time series forecasting using holt-winters exponential smoothing. Kanwal Rekhi School Inf. Technol. **4329008**, 1–13 (2004)
4. Efron, B., Tibshirani, R.: Bootstrap methods for standard errors, confidence intervals, and another measures of statistical accuracy. Stat. Sci. **1**(1), 54–77 (1986)
5. Cordeiro, C., Neves, M.M.: Séries Temporais e Modelos de Previsão. Aplicação da Metodologia Bootstrap. Actas do XI Congresso Anual da SPE, Lisboa, pp. 153–164 (2003)

A New Approach on Density-Based Algorithm for Clustering Dense Areas

Paola Perchinunno[⊠] and Samuela L'Abbate

Department of Economics, Management and Business Law, University of Bari "Aldo Moro", Bari, Italy
{paola.perchinunno,samuela.labbate}@uniba.it

Abstract. This paper presents a new approach to density-based clustering for the identification of dense areas. In particular, the focus is on identification of breast masses in the X-ray imaging of a mammography. The idea was to apply cluster analysis by identifying breast masses as clusters, understood as dense regions of space separated by areas of lower density. Attention was focused on a particular method of clustering based on density, the DBSCAN, proposing a new approach by applying it to a real dataset: a supervised approach, based on ROC curves and a weighted distance, for the choice of input parameters.

Keywords: Cluster analysis · DBSCAN · ROC curves

1 Introduction

The rapid developments in the availability and access to spatially referenced information in a variety of areas, has induced the need for better analysis techniques to understand the various phenomena. Spatial clustering algorithms, which groups similar spatial objects into classes, can be used for the identification of areas sharing common characteristics. DBSCAN is the first density-based algorithm. In fact, these algorithms identify clusters as dense regions of space, separated by areas of lower density (noise). These algorithms therefore possess the ability to detect clusters of arbitrary shape as concave zones. The aim of this paper is to presents a new approach to density-based clustering for the identification of dense areas. Special attention was paid to the identification of breast masses in the X-ray imaging of a mammography.

2 DBSCAN Method

2.1 Description of Algorithm

DBSCAN (Density Based Spatial Clustering of Application with Noise) [1] is the first density-based algorithm. The key idea of this algorithm lies in the concept of proximity

---

The contribution is the result of joint reflections by the authors, with the following contributions attributed to S. L'Abbate (chapter 2, 3, 4) and to P. Perchinunno (chapter 1, 5).

O. Gervasi et al. (Eds.): ICCSA 2022 Workshops, LNCS 13377, pp. 530–542, 2022.
https://doi.org/10.1007/978-3-031-10536-4_35

between patterns. A pattern of a cluster must have other patterns in its vicinity, that is, in the vicinity of a pattern the density of the points must exceed a certain threshold. Conversely, the density calculated in the noise zones does not exceed a certain threshold. So each point, to belong to a cluster, must have, within a certain radius, at least a certain number of other patterns. This intuitive idea was formalized with the DBSCAN algorithm.

DBSCAN is one of the cluster analysis algorithms that allows to identify clusters of different shapes from the ellipsoidal one. In fact, the shape around the pattern depends on the type of distance function chosen for two patterns p and q denoted by dist(p; q). There is no predetermined distance function to use, but it can be chosen according to the application.

The algorithm needs two input parameters ε and *MinPts* with which to distinguish the points present in the dataset into core points, border points and noise points.

The formal description of the algorithm proposed in [2] and reformulated in [3–5], requires the following definitions:

Definition 1: (ε-neighborhood)
Fixed a point p of the dataset and a parameter ε, the ε -neighborhood, that is, the $\varepsilon-$ neighborhood of p with respect to ε, is the set of points of the dataset with distance from p less than ε:

$$N_\varepsilon(p) = \{x | dist(x, p) \le \varepsilon\}$$

Indicated *MinPts* the minimum number of points around the point p it is possible to define a core point that differs from a border point and a noise point.

A point p is called a core point or inner point if there are at least *MinPts* points in its ε radius circle: $|N_\varepsilon(p)| \ge MinPts$.

A point p is called a border point if there are fewer than *MinPts* points in its ε radius circle: $|N_\varepsilon(p)| < MinPts$, that is, if it is not a core point, but is within a neighborhood of radius ε and q center for some core point q.

A point p is called a noise point if it is not a core neither a border point. See Fig. 1.

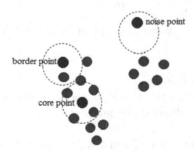

Fig. 1. Core point, border point and noise, with $\varepsilon = 1$ and *MinPts* $= 5$

Definition 2: (directly density-reachable)
A point *p* is *directly density-reachable* from point *q* with respect to ε and *MinPts* in a set of points *D* if.

1) $N_\varepsilon(q)$, where $N_\varepsilon(q)$ is the subset of D contained in the ε-neighborhood of q, i.e.
   $N_\varepsilon(q) = \{p \in D | dist(p, q) \le \varepsilon\}$.
2) $|N_\varepsilon(q)| \ge MinPts$.

The second condition means that q is a *core point*. Only from core points, other points can be directly density-reachable. (See Fig. 2a).

Definition 3: (density-reachable)
A point p is *density-reachable* from a point q with respect to ε and *MinPts* in the set of points D if there is a chain of objects $p_1, \ldots, p_n$ with $p_1 = q$ and $p_n = p$, such that $p_i \in D$ and p_{i+1} is directly density-reachable from p_i with respect to ε and *MinPts*.

Density-reachability is the transitive hull of direct density reachability and this relation is not symmetric in general; only core points can be mutually density-reachable. (See Fig. 2 b).

Definition 4: (density-connected)
A point p is *density-connected* to point q with respect to ε and *MinPts* in the set of points D if there is a point $o \in D$ such that both p and q are density-reachable from o. (See Figure c).

A density-based *cluster* is now defined as a set of density-connected points which is maximal with respect to density-reachability and the *noise* is the set of points not contained in any cluster.

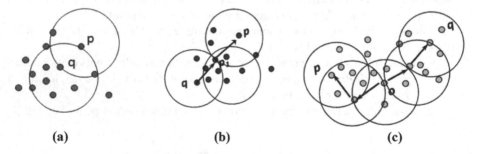

(a)   (b)   (c)

Fig. 2. a) Directly density-reachable, b) Density-reachable, c) Density connected

Definition 5: (cluster and noise)
Let D be a set of points. A *cluster* C with respect to ε and *MinPts* in D is a non-empty subset of D satisfying the following conditions:

1) Maximality: $\forall p, q \in D$: if $p \in C$ and q is density-reachable from p with respect to ε and *MinPts*, then also $q \in C$.
2) Connectivity: $\forall p, q \in C$: p is density-connected to q with respect to ε and *MinPts* in D then.

Every point not contained in any cluster is *noise*. Note that a cluster contains not only core points but also points that do not satisfy the core point condition: border points.

These points of the cluster are, however, directly density-reachable from at least one core point of the cluster (in contrast to noise points).

The algorithm DBSCAN [1], which discovers the clusters and the noise in a database according to the above definitions, is based on the fact that a cluster is equivalent to the set of all points in D which are density-reachable from an arbitrary core point in the cluster. The retrieval of density-reachable points is performed by iteratively collecting directly density-reachable points. DBSCAN checks the ε -neighborhood of each point in the database. If the ε -neighborhood $N_\varepsilon(p)$ of a point p has more than *MinPts* points, a new cluster C containing the objects in $N_\varepsilon(p)$ is created. Then, the ε -neighborhood of all points q in C which have not yet been processed is checked. If $N_\varepsilon(q)$ contains more than *MinPts* points, the neighbors of q which are not already contained in C are added to the cluster and their ε-neighborhood is checked in the next step. This procedure is repeated until no new point can be added to the current cluster C.

2.2   DBSCAN: Advantages and Disadvantages

The DBSCAN algorithm has several advantages: it detects clusters of arbitrary size and shape; it does not require a priori the number of clusters to be searched for and the initial patterns with which to start the algorithm; automatically determines noise points; is applicable to any metric space.

The greatest advantages of DBSCAN are that it can follow the shape of the clusters and that it requires only one distance function and two input parameters. Their choice is crucial because they determine whether a group is a cluster of points or a simple noise.

In [2] the authors provide a heuristic that they consider sufficiently valid for the determination of ε and to choose as a threshold (ε) the point at the first depression that can be noticed in the trend of the graph; and as a graph they recommend choosing the sorted k-dist graph for k = 4 as experimental results have shown a very similar trend for values above 4, instead of a considerable increase in time required for the construction of the graph itself. However, this determination of ε has ambiguities within it since the graph does not have a net depression but often oscillations are evident so the choice of the ε is reduced to a choice of attempts of the most appropriate.

2.3   Supervised Approach to Choosing MinPts

ROC curves were obtained by plotting the fraction of true positives (sensitivity) along the y axis and the fraction of false positives (1 − specificity) along the x axis. The area A_z under the ROC curve was obtained to serve as a measure of the diagnostic accuracy of the feature.

R.O.C.- Receiver Operating Characteristic curves are used to evaluate the validity of a diagnostic test (see [6–9]). A ROC curve is drawn by placing on the ordinate axis the values of sensitivity (the fraction of true-positive):

$$Se = \frac{TP}{TP + FN}$$

where TP means true positive, FN means false negatives; and on that of abscissa the values of 1-specificity (the fraction of false-positives):

$$Sp = \frac{TN}{FP + TN}$$

where TN means true negative.

The A_z area under the ROC curve is a measure of accuracy (performance) of a diagnostic test, [10, 11]. The value of A_z is between 0 and 1; the greater the better the method is, that is, the more correct the classification. In this work the DBSCAN algorithm was modified for the choice of the optimal value to be assigned to *MinPts* with a supervised approach that uses ROC curves to measure the effectiveness of the classification obtained with respect to a reference ideal. Calculating the sensitivity and specificity, for different values of *MinPts*, we have chosen as the optimal value to be assigned to *MinPts* the one corresponding to the curve with the highest area under the curve (AUC-area under curve), see Fig. 3.

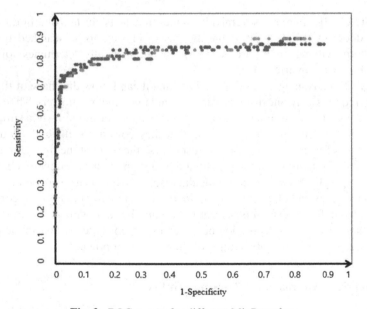

Fig. 3. ROC curves for different MinPts values

2.4 Choice of Epsilon

Being able to attribute a certain value to ε is functional to limit the arbitrariness of its choice and thus reduce the time of formation of clusters. For each dataset, the distribution of ε, is considered, and for a fixed value of *MinPts* a histogram is constructed. The first relative minimum of the histogram is then chosen as the value of ε optimal, as shown in Fig. 4.

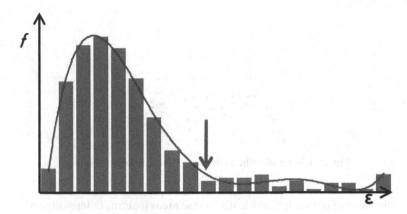

Fig. 4. Graphical representation of the distribution of ε

2.5   Choosing the Distance Function

In general, the function chosen as distance for the DBSCAN method depends on the application studied and must satisfy the typical properties of a distance.

In the epidemiological or environmental field, the analysis of clusters using a density-based approach aims to identify areas where a given phenomenon assumes values significantly higher than those recorded in other parts of the territory.

In the case study examined, starting from an X-ray image, a map was created by matching each pixel of the X-ray image with a color value based on a grayscale. Therefore it is necessary that the variable that describes the phenomenon is decisive in discriminating the neighboring points in the sense as well as topographical also under the analyzed aspect.

The presence of the phenomenon is understood as a weight that makes two points closer with high intensity of the phenomenon and two points distant spatially close but with low intensity of the phenomenon analyzed. For example, it is possible that two pairs of points: $(A; B)$ and $(C; D)$ are such that $d(A; B) = d(C; D)$, they are pairs of points close spatially, indicated by F the weight that evaluates the measure of the phenomenon for each point, we have that:

$$d(A; B) \cdot F(A; B) > d(C; D) \cdot F(C; D)$$

that is, the spatial distance is altered by this weight. The weighted distance can be extended to the case of n variables in which the weights can also be represented by several variables.

If the Euclidean distance were used, the DBSCAN would identify the clusters only on the basis of the geographical proximity of the points, see Fig. 5, without considering the intensity index represented by the third variable.

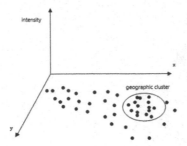

Fig. 5. Cluster identified with respect to Euclidean distance

The objective of our study is to identify dense areas in terms of intensity so instead of the Euclidean distance a function was chosen that deforms the geometric space in such a way that the geographically close points and that have similar intensities are even closer while geographically close points but with different intensities become more distant. The function that binds in the above terms two points:$A(x_A; y_A; w_A)$ and $B(x_B; y_B; w_B)$ is a weighted distance obtained by relating the Euclidean distance to the average power with negative exponent between the points under examination:

$$d(A, B) = \frac{\sqrt{(x_A - x_B)^2 + (y_A - y_B)^2}}{\sqrt[-t]{\frac{w_A^{-t} + w_B^{-t}}{2}}}$$

This function satisfies the first three axioms of distance but does not verify the triangular inequality. In general, it is precisely the fourth and last property of distance that is discriminating and the fact that it is satisfied or not distinguishes metric measurements from so-called semimetric ones. Therefore the weighted distance that we propose is semimetric, however this restriction does not affect the Definitions 3 and 4 of Sect. 2.1 respectively of reachability and connection for which the properties of reflexivity and symmetry are necessary which remain satisfied. With this function at pairs of points with low intensity value the distance increases so that these are penalized in the formation of clusters, see Fig. 6. Empirically it has been verified that the most appropriate value of t is 5.

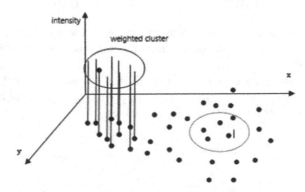

Fig. 6. Cluster detected with respect to weighted distance

3   Application

Database concerns digital X-ray images of mammograms related to benign and malignant lesions. Of each breast mass we know the diagnostic classification by biopsy and the outline drawn by hand by a radiologist specialized in mammograms, Fig. 7.

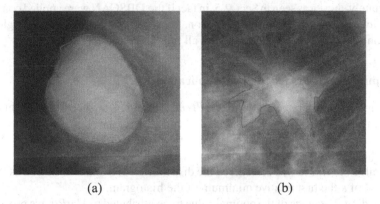

(a)   (b)

Fig. 7. a) benign lesion, b) malignant lesion

Several maps were generated from the scanned X-ray images by matching each pixel of the X-ray image with a color value established based on a grayscale as shown in Fig. 8.

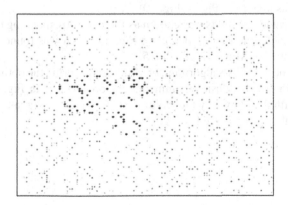

Fig. 8. Example of a map generated from an X-ray image

It was decided to apply, for the generated maps, the DBSCAN described in Sect. 2.1 because it allows to identify clusters as dense regions of space, separated by areas with lower density (noise) and can detect clusters of arbitrary shape as concave zones (the spicules in breast masses). In the application under consideration, therefore, dense areas are those areas whose points in addition to being spatially close have a high intensity of color, therefore a presence of the phenomenon. First of all, a distance function was appropriately chosen as seen in Sect. 2.5, in fact if the DBSCAN were applied considering the Euclidean distance function as a function, the algorithm would detect a single cluster corresponding to the rectangle containing all the points.

3.1 Input Parameters for Method Application

Regarding the input parameters ε and *MinPts* that the algorithm needs, the optimal values have been obtained as illustrated in Sects. 2.3 and 2.4. For the choice of ε, proceeding by trial and error would produce a high waste of time, see Fig. 3.3; as described in Sect. 2.4 to limit the arbitrariness of your choice and thus reduce training time of the clusters, for a fixed value of *MinPts* was considered the distribution of ε and was chosen as the value of optimal of ε the first relative minimum of the histogram.

Regarding the choice of the optimal value to be attributed to *MinPts*, we proceeded as described in Sect. 2.4 with a supervised approach. The sensitivities and specificities were calculated, for different *MinPts* values, comparing the contour drawn by the radiologist with the elaborated curve, meaning with true positives: the points of the cluster correctly classified, with true negatives: the correctly classified noise points, with false positives: the noise points classified as points of the cluster and finally with false negatives: cluster points classified as noise, see Fig. 9 (Fig. 10).

The optimal value of MinPts was chosen as the one corresponding to the curve with the highest area under the curve (AUC), see Fig. 11 and it was found that the optimal value to be attributed to MinPts is equal to 5.

By applying the DBSCAN algorithm, modified considering the optimal input parameters, the detection of the cluster is immediately obtained as in Fig. 3.6 whose contour coincides with that drawn by the radiologist also returning greater precision in the identification of the spicules, see Fig. 12.

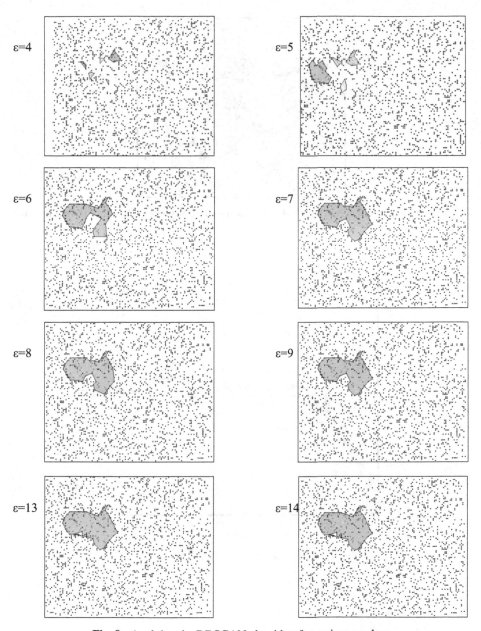

Fig. 9. Applying the DBSCAN algorithm for various ε values

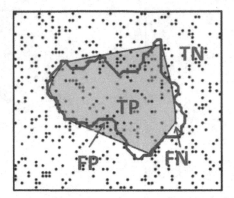

Fig. 10. Comparison between the radiologist's contour and the processed curve: TP: True Positive, TN: True Negative, FP: False Positive and FN: False Negative

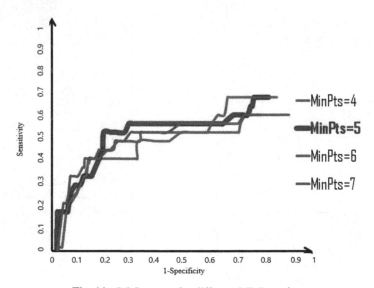

Fig. 11. ROC curves for different MinPts values

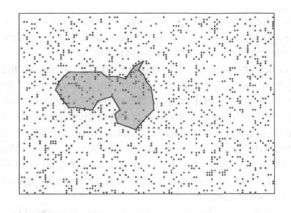

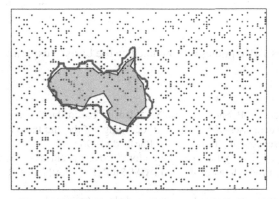

Fig. 12. Application of the DBSCAN algorithm with $\varepsilon = 8$ and MinPts $= 5$ and overlapping the contour extracted by the radiologist to the obtained cluster applying the DBSCAN algorithm with $\varepsilon = 8$ and MinPts $= 5$

4 Conclusions and Future Advancements

The basic idea that guided this work was to be able to apply a density-based clustering algorithm, DBSCAN, for the detection of dense areas such as breast masses.

The intuition that led to propose an optimization of the algorithm was to see the breast masses as 'spots'; therefore, clusters understood as dense regions of space, separated by areas with lower density. Hence the need to introduce an appropriate distance function that would identify the areas where the phenomenon examined assumed significantly higher values than in other areas.

The goal was to speed up the clustering algorithm, developing new methodologies to overcome the limits of typical clustering algorithms based on density, i.e. the arbitrariness of input parameters.

The ability of DBSCAN to detect clusters of arbitrary shape and in particular the concave areas has motivated the research to recognize also the spiculated breast masses. The results obtained were very satisfactory, the algorithm also identified clusters with particular concave or spicule areas. The comparison with the contour drawn by the radiologist showed the high reliability in the recognition of the cluster that represented the breast masses. Automating the density-based clustering algorithm can support the radiologist in extracting the contour of breast masses.

In addition, being able to classify according to the shape of the contour means having information on the very nature of the pathology, because the morphology of the lesion is linked to its degree of malignancy. The shape is a fundamental characteristic to distinguish benign and malignant masses, so a correct clustering leads to the recognition of the actual form and therefore to a more likely exact distinction between malignant and benign mass. One of the future developments is in fact to define indices related to the shape of the cluster that based on the degree of irregularity can establish the pathology of the breast mass of which the contour is extracted, in order to provide a valid support to the verdict of the radiologist.

A next step will be to delve the cluster validity indices for data clustering with respect to internal and external criteria proposing a new inferential approach.

The future perspectives are many and are both methodological and applicative and demonstrate how statistics can also represent a valid investigative tool to quantify and rationalize notions and hypotheses formulated on the basis of experimental observations.

References

1. Ester, M., Kriegel, H.-P., Sander, J., Xu, X.: A density-based algorithm for discovering clusters in large spatial databases with noise. In: Proceedings of the 2nd International Conference on Knowledge Discovery and Data Mining, Portland (1996)
2. Ester, M., et al.: A density-based algorithm for discovering clusters in large spatial databases with noise. In: Proceedings of the 2nd ACM SIGKDD, Portland, OR, USA, pp. 226–231 (1996)
3. Montrone, S., et al.: A modified density-based algorithm for clustering. In: Supplemento ai Rendiconti del Circolo Matematico di Palermo. II 84, Palermo, Italy, pp. 231–239 (2012)
4. Montrone, S., et al.: Comparing SaTScan and DBSCAN methods inspatial phenomena. In: SPATIAL2, Spatial Data Methods for Environmental and Ecological Processes, 2nd edn. Baia delle Zagare, Foggia, Italy, pp. 116–119 (2011)
5. Montrone, S., et al.: Statistical methods for detecting geographical clustering of housing poverty. In: Rivista Italiana di Economia, Demografia e Statistica, vol. LXV. 3/4. SIEDS, Roma, Italy, pp. 157–164 (2011)
6. Metz, C.E.: Basic principles of ROC analysis. Seminars Nucl. Med. **VIII**(4), 283–298 (1978)
7. Metz, C.E.: ROC Methodology in radiologic imaging. Invest. Radiol. **21**, 720–733 (1986)
8. Pepe, M.S.: The Statistical Evaluation of Medical Tests for Classification and Prediction. Oxford University Press, New York (2003)
9. Zou, K.H.: Receiver operating characteristic (ROC) literature research (2002). http://splweb.bwh.harvard.edu:8000/pages/ppl/zou/roc.html
10. Hanley, J.A., McNeil, B.I.: A method of comparing the areas under receiver operating characteristic curves derived from the same cases. Radiology **148**(3), 839–843 (1983)
11. Hanley, J.A., McNeil, B.I.: Statistical approaches to the analysis of receiver operating characteristic (ROC) curves. Med. Decis. Making **4**, 137–150 (1984)
12. Montrone, S., Massari, A., Perchinunno, P., Ligorio, C., L'Abbate, S.: Statistical Methods for Detecting Geographical Clustering of Housing poverty. In: Rivista Italiana di Economia, Demografia e Statistica, vol. LXV, no. 3/4 (2011). ISSN: 0035-6832
13. Efron, B.: Bootstrap methods: another look at the jackknife. In: The Annals of Statistics, vol. 7, pp. 1–26. Institute of Mathematical Statistics (1979)

Percentile Growth Curves for Placenta Measures: A Dynamic Shiny Application

Samuel Alves[1]([✉]) [iD], Ana Cristina Braga[2] [iD], and Rosete Nogueira[3,4] [iD]

[1] University of Minho, 4710-057 Braga, Portugal
samuelcnalves@gmail.com
[2] ALGORITMI Centre, University of Minho, 4800-058 Guimarães, Portugal
acb@dps.uminho.pt
[3] School of Medicine and Life and Health Sciences Research Institute (ICVS) and ICVS/3B's -
PT Government Associate Laboratory, University of Minho, Braga, Portugal
[4] Embryo & Fetal and Placental Pathology Laboratory, CGC, Unilabs, Porto, Portugal

Abstract. For decades, researchers and health professionals have been using fetal and newborns measurements to evaluate its development. In recent years, there have been new studies suggesting that the placenta's measurements and its evolutions are capable of reflecting changes in the fetus's development and even newborn and adult diseases.

Most of these analyses are done using growth curves that use linear regression methodologies such as previous studies done. To account for errors associated with this regression and use a more robust method, quantile regression is used to create the placenta's growth curves. The dataset used for this study was collected on Portuguese CGC Genetics and involves the Portuguese parturient population from different regions.

It is also an objective of this study to create a dynamic application that allows the researcher or health professional to enter placental growth values and compare them to the created growth curves to evaluate the evolution of the placenta. This application uses a CSV file with the information gathered from the placenta and is uploaded to the application which then plots the values on the created growth curves. The application also allows the user to edit the values. This application was created on Shiny and can be accessed at https://samuelalves.shinyapps.io/APP2/.

Keywords: Placenta · Growth curves · Quantile regression · Shiny

1 Introduction

The placenta is one of the largest and first organs to develop during pregnancy, it is considered by some experts as one of the most important organs due to its crucial role in the normal development of the baby. As such the placenta is considered highly regulated and coordinated to allow highly efficient exchange of different products and nutrients between the mother and the fetus.

This work has been supported by FCT – Fundação para a Ciência e Tecnologia within the R&D Units Project Scope: UIDB/00319/2020

O. Gervasi et al. (Eds.): ICCSA 2022 Workshops, LNCS 13377, pp. 543–554, 2022.
https://doi.org/10.1007/978-3-031-10536-4_36

The xenobiotic protector effect of the placenta is also highly important just as is the effect on hormone regulation and its ability to react to the different changes in the circulatory and nutritional environment to allow different proportions of nutrients to be supplied to the fetus.

There have been different studies relating the measurements of the placenta to different problems during the pregnancy, the newborn and the health later in life (Asgharnia et al. 2008; Barker et al. 1990; Hindmarsh et al. 2001).

In the most recent years, there has been an increase in interest in studying this organ although there are some gaps in the knowledge about it and its biological significance due to the lack of interest from researchers to study it compared to the fetus.

Additionally, there is a problem associated with the fact that it is difficult to get the placenta's measurements and standardise them. Moreover, there is still a lack of the placenta measurements data and the problem is that the values change according to the different races and the available data is considered old.

To improve the knowledge about the placenta, a work is previously done by Doctor Rosete Nogueira (Nogueira et al. 2019), which made possible the creation of percentile curves of the Portuguese population's placenta.

Considering this, the goal of this study was to create growth charts with placenta dimensions of the Portuguese population and create an application that allows the user (either a health professional or researcher) to enter the placental values and compare them with the previously created on this study growth charts. This will allow the clinician to assess the growth of the placenta in different stages of the pregnancy process.

This paper is structured as follows. Section 2 presents a state of the art, where some works related to the models and statistical methods used, as well as the software are briefly reported. The theoretical methodology of quantile regression is presented in Sect. 3. The exploratory results of the dataset used as well as the growth curves for the measures and the development of an application, are in Sect. 4 and Sect. 5, respectively. Finally, the main conclusions and the proposed future work are described in Sect. 6.

2   State of the Art

2.1   Models and Statistical Methods

Since the beginning of the creation of growth charts, there have been several different ways to do it. It started with fitting smoothing curves on sample quantiles of the segmented age groups. The problem associated with these methods comes from the fact that these are not robust (robustness is considered the resilience of statistical procedures to deviations from the assumptions of hypothetical models (Koenker and Bassett 1978)) to outliers and a large sample is needed to estimate the percentiles with good precision (Chen 2005).

Another problem associated with the usual growth charts created is that they are built on the assumption that the measurements are normally distributed which is not true since for example, if adult heights from a relatively homogenous population are considered close to normal, children's heights are usually non-normally distributed and this problem can be even bigger in other measurements such as weight.

To solve these problems, the majority of the studies about growth charts use regression models.

Regression is a statistical method that allows the user to study the relationships between variables. Of the many regression methods available, quantile regression is a method that is used to estimate functional relations between variables for all portions of a probability distribution (Cade and Noon 2003).

Quantile regression is a nonparametric method that due to the increase in computing power is becoming more frequently used. It is independent of any distribution or transformation to normality since it estimates distribution directly and as such, it is more robust against outliers (Kiserud et al. 2018).

2.2 Shiny Applications

Shiny is a package used in R, that allows the user to easily create dynamic web applications using R code.

With Shiny we can make the Back End and Front End of an application, interact with languages external to R, such as CSS, HTML and JavaScript and also host an app on a cloud.

A great disadvantage of shiny is that it requires timely updates, i.e., as the functions used in the app get outdated sometimes with newer package versions, it becomes necessary to update the shiny app from time to time.

Several authors have already shown its usefulness and how it may revolutionize the way models' simulations are shared. It has also been shown by authors different ways that these applications can be shared such as ShinyApps.io, Shiny Server and Shiny Server Pro which allows the sharing of these applications to a wider audience due to being hosted on a web server instead of locally (Wojciechowski et al. 2015).

3   Quantile Regression

Quantile regression was proposed by Koenker and Bassat and is a method used to estimate functional relations between variables for all portions of a probability distribution which allows the studying of the conditional distribution of Y on X at a different location, offering a global view of the interrelations of X and Y (Cade and Noon, 2003).

An important note has to be made that this work is done on a non-normal distributed sample. The distribution can also be different about the mean or a specific quantile. For example, modelling using only the mean (which happens when using linear regression) can lead to missing important aspects of the association between the outcome and its predictors (Beyerlein 2014).

As such the quantile regression method was chosen to allow to fill gaps created by other methods and allow the creation of a better solution for the researchers.

According to Buhai 2004, considering the ordinary quantile, which has a real value random variable Y, with the following distribution:

$$F(y) = \Pr(Y \leq y) \tag{1}$$

Thus for any $\tau \in (0, 1)$, the τ-*th* quantile of Y is defined as

$$Q(\tau) = inf\{y : F(y) \geq \tau\} \tag{2}$$

The median is $Q(1/2)$, the first quartile $Q(1/4)$ and the first decile $Q(1/10)$. The quantile function allows the user to create a complete characterization of Y, like the distribution of function F. The quantiles can be written as solutions to this optimization:

$$\rho_\tau(u) = u(\tau - I(i < 0)), \quad \tau \in (0, 1) \tag{3}$$

where $I(.)$ is the usual indicator function. Thus, the solution to the minimization is

$$\hat{\alpha}(\tau) = \arg min_{\xi \in \mathbb{R}} E[\rho_\tau(Y - \xi)] \tag{4}$$

The sampled analogue of $Q(\tau)$ is based on a random sample $\{y_1, \ldots, y_n\}$ of Y. The τ-*th* quantile can be identified as any solution to:

$$\hat{a}_\tau = \arg \min_{\xi \in \mathbb{R}} \sum_{i=1}^{n} \rho_\tau(Y - \xi) \tag{5}$$

Let $x_i, i = \overline{1 \ldots n}$, a $K \times 1$ vector of regressors. It can be written the equivalent to the first expression as

$$F_{u_\tau}\left(\tau - \mathbf{x}_i^T \boldsymbol{\beta}_\tau | \mathbf{x_i}\right) = \Pr(y_i \leq \tau | \mathbf{x_i}) \tag{6}$$

Which is a different form of:

$$y_i = \mathbf{x}_i^T \boldsymbol{\beta}_\tau + u_{\tau_i} \tag{7}$$

considering the distribution of the error term, u_{τ_i} is left unspecified, the only constraint being the quantile restriction $Q_\tau\left(u_{\tau_i} | \mathbf{x_i}\right) = 0$.

Using an analogy, the estimation of conditional mean functions as in

$$\hat{\beta} = \arg min_{\beta \in \mathbb{R}^K} \sum_{i=1}^{n} (y_i - \mathbf{x}_i^T \beta)^2 \tag{8}$$

The linear conditional quantile function,

$$Q_Y(\tau | \mathbf{X} = \mathbf{x}) = \mathbf{x}_i^T \boldsymbol{\beta}_\tau \tag{9}$$

Can be estimated by solving the equivalent of expression 8:

$$\hat{\beta}_\tau = \arg min_{\beta \in \mathbb{R}^K} \sum_{i=1}^{n} \rho_\tau(y_i - \mathbf{x}_i^T \beta)^2 \tag{10}$$

According to Yu *et al.* (2003) to discuss model estimation we need to take in mind the principles of the least-squares estimation.

Considering the regression model that is the simplest, the β is estimated through the quadratic loss function $r(u) = u^2$ and given a data set with observations $\{x_i, y_i\}_{i=1}^{n}$, its estimation is done by minimizing:

$$\sum_{i=1}^{n} r\left(y_i - x_i^T \beta\right) = \sum_{i=1}^{n} r\left(y_i - x_i^T \beta\right)^2 \tag{11}$$

As such, modelling using only the mean which is what happens in linear regression can lead to missing important aspects of the association between the outcome and its predictors (Beyerlein 2014).

Thus, the quantile regression allows for the examination of changes in distribution and provides more specific information than linear regression, allowing for a better understanding of how pertinent variables affect the entire distribution of an outcome variable rather than just the mean of the distribution (Hajovsky et al. 2020).

4 Case of Study

4.1 Dataset

The dataset used for this study was previously collected on CGC Genetics and is composed of placentas collected from 12 to 41 gestational ages of singleton pregnancies. Of the 2248 entries only 1951 had the available information for this study and as such only these were used. To not allow the direct identification of the patient, the name and information of the patient were changed to a process number.

Table 1 presents a brief description of the variables available in the dataset for this study. As a note, since the placenta is not a perfect circle, two diameters were measured: Diameter1 which is the biggest diameter and Diameter2 which is the smallest.

Table 1. Description of variables available on the dataset.

Variable name	Description	Scale of measurement	Values
MaternalAge	Maternal age	Proportional	Years
GA	Gestational age	Proportional	From 12 to 41
Fetusgender	Fetus gender	Nominal	Levels: M - Male, F - Female, A - Ambigous, 9 - Missing Information
Fetalweight	Birthweight	Proportional	Grams, g
Placentalshape	Placental shape	Nominal	Levels: Normal, Bilobate, Circunvalate, Membranous
Placentalweight	Placental weight	Proportional	Centimetre, cm

(continued)

Table 1. (*continued*)

Variable name	Description	Scale of measurement	Values
Diameter1	Diameter 1 - the smallest value of placental diameter	Proportional	Centimetre, cm
Diametre2	Diameter 2 - the highest value of placental diameter	Proportional	Centimetre, cm
Placentalthickness	Placental thickness	Proportional	Centimetre, cm
Placental_vol	Placental volume	Proportional	Cubic Centimetre, cm^3

Table 2 presents some of the summary statistics for the quantitative metrics. We can see that the gestational age varies between 12 and 41 weeks, and the fetal weight has a minimum of 5.4 g and a maximum of 4880 g. The mean was 1248.7 g and 50% of the fetus presents a weight less than 766 g. Concerning the placenta weight, it was observed a minimum of 6 g and a maximum of 995.0 g. The mean placenta weight observed in this sample was 233. 2 g, and the median was 195 g.

Table 2. Descriptive statistics for the quantitative measures.

	GA	Fetalweight	Placentalweight	Diameter1	Diameter2
Min.	12.0	5.4	6.0	1.7	1.50
1st Q	19.0	235.5	101.0	10.0	8.0
Median	26.0	766.0	195.0	13.0	11.0
Mean	26.71	1248.7	233.2	14.48	12.8
3rd Q	35.0	2220.0	345.5	17.0	14.6
Max.	41.0	4880.0	995.0	32.0	30.0

4.2 Growth Curves

Using the previously described dataset the growth charts were made. These charts were created using the package *quantregGrowth* (which uses the package *quantreg*) and *ggplot2*, both are R's packages.

The plots created are illustrated on graphs in Figs. 1, 2, 3 and 4. The values used are not differentiating the genders since splitting the data would lead to a less robust chart and there were no observable differences between the genders that would justify the separation. The choice of percentiles is in line with those that are most common in the medical community.

The 97th percentile in both Fig. 1 and Fig. 2 show a decrease in the slope between the intervals of 35 to 40 weeks of gestational age. Even though we are still not sure about what is happening to cause this, we have two hypotheses: from a statistical point of view, there could be the need for more data to allow to create of a better curve. From a biological point of view, this could show alterations in the placenta in the late stages of the pregnancy.

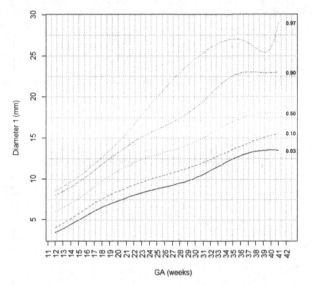

Fig. 1. Growth curve for diameter1 vs GA.

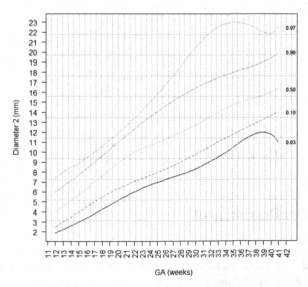

Fig. 2. Growth curve for diameter2 vs GA.

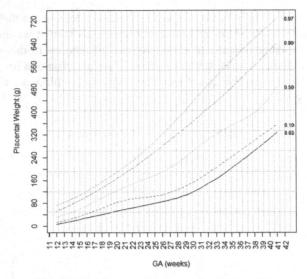

Fig. 3. Growth curve for placental weight vs GA.

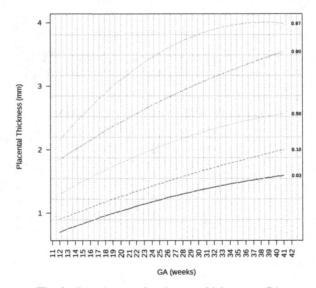

Fig. 4. Growth curve for placenta thickness vs GA.

5   Application Development

5.1   System Architecture

Packages Used. The main package used to create the application is the RStudio's with package Shiny. Another package used is *ggplot2* to show the charts and *rhandsontable* for the tables.

Application. To illustrate how the application works we design the workflow presented in Fig. 5.

The user starts by uploading the files that will create the charts. The User Interface is composed of 4 tabs: 1 tab for the plot and the other for the table for both diameters. It has also a sidebar composed of 2 forms to allow the user to upload the d1 and d2.csv files containing their values. It also has a button that allows the user to save the changes made to the files.

The files uploaded by the user are uploaded on a reactive function to allow the data to be dynamically changeable while the application is executed. After that, two reactive objects are created to store the values that the user changes. Another function is to when the button is pressed, save the CSV file with the changes made by the user by allowing the user to download it.

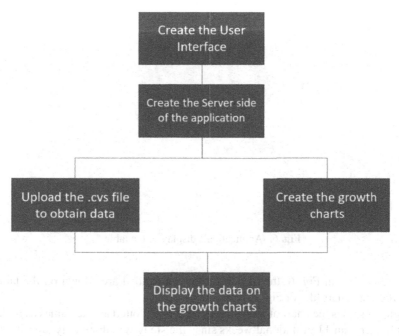

Fig. 5. Workflow for the application.

5.2 Instruction's Manual to Use the Application

The way the application works is by the user uploading a.csv with the different values gathered from the analysis of the placenta. The file has the value 0 for all the gestational ages at the beginning. The user will then change them with the values gathered. After all the changes are made the user can save the CSV file. All the values will also be plotted on the chart allowing the user to see the progression of those values.

Fig. 6. Application's display of the table.

As illustrated in Fig. 6. the files after being uploaded are shown on the table and updated on the chart like in Fig. 7.

Figure 7 shows the chart of the uploaded file. It is plotted all the values as points (all values higher than 11 gestational weeks since the study was done only after it) and the growth curves each with a different colour.

The user can then edit the values on the app. At the moment, to see the changes on the chart the user has to save the file and then upload it again.

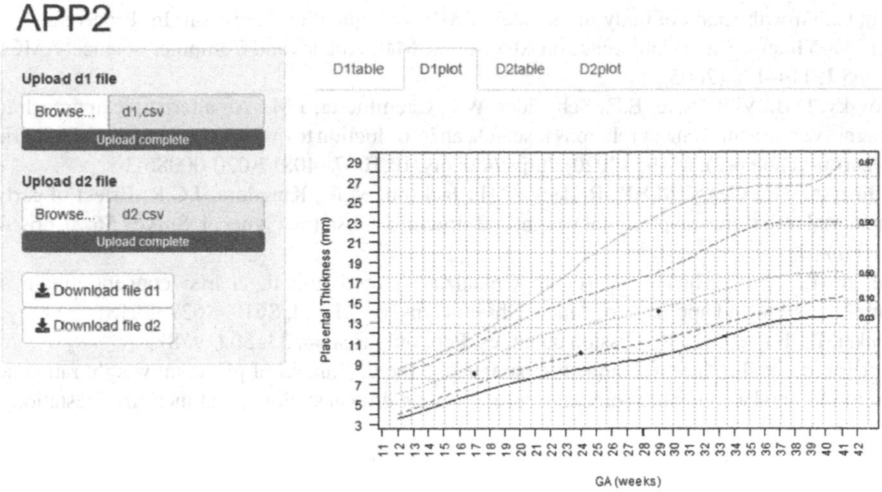

APP2

Fig. 7. Application's display of the chart.

6 Conclusion and Future Work

The newly created placenta's growth curves were generated using a more robust regression method consolidating the Portuguese population's placenta growth curves allowing the researchers and doctors to start using these in their studies and patient appointments to better evaluate the fetus's current and future health.

The created application allows the user (a researcher or a clinician) a way to see the evolution of the placenta's dimensions using a simple and robust graph.

Regarding future works, the UI could be improved, allowing the user to change the values and see the changes immediately on the plots without needing to re-upload the file. An interesting idea would be to set up the applications in a real-world situation and be used by many researchers and medical professionals and hear their opinions about the applications and start improving based on their insights.

References

Asgharnia, M., Esmailpour, N., Poorghorban, M., Atrkar-Roshan, Z.: Placental weight and its association with maternal and neonatal characteristics. Acta Medica Iranica 46(6), 467–472 (2008)

Barker, D.J.P., Bull, A.R., Osmond, C., Simmonds, S.J.: Fetal and placental size and risk of hypertension in adult life. BMJ 301(6746), 259–262 (1990). https://doi.org/10.1136/bmj.301.6746.259

Beyerlein, A.: Quantile regression - Opportunities and challenges from a user's perspective. Am. J. Epidemiol. 180(3), 330–331 (2014)

Buhai, S.: Quantile regression: overview and selected applications. Ad-Astra-The Young Rom. Sci. J. 1–20 (2004)

Cade, B.S., Noon, B.R.: A gentle introduction to quantile regression for ecologists. Front. Ecol. Environ. 1(8), 412–420 (2003)

Chen, C.: Growth charts of body mass index (BMI) with quantile regression. In: Proceedings of the 2005 International Conference on Algorithmic Mathematics and Computer Science, AMCS 2005 **1**, 114–120 (2005)

Hajovsky, D.B., Villeneuve, E.F., Schneider, W.J., Caemmerer, J.M.: An alternative approach to cognitive and achievement relations research: an introduction to quantile regression. J. Pediatric Neuropsychol. **6**(2), 83–95 (2020). https://doi.org/10.1007/s40817-020-00086-3

Hindmarsh, P.C., Geary, M.P.P., Rodeck, C.H., Jackson, M.R., Kingdom, J.C.P.: Effect of early maternal iron stores on placental weight and structure. Obstetric Gynecol. Survey **56**(2), 66–67 (2001)

Kiserud, T., et al.: The World Health Organization fetal growth charts: concept, findings, interpretation, and application. Am. J. Obstet. Gynecol. **218**(2), S619–S629 (2018)

Koenker, R., Bassett, G.: Regression quantiles. Econometrica **46**, 33–50 (1978)

Nogueira, R., et al.: Placental biometric parameters: the usefulness of placental weight ratio and birth/placental weight ratio percentile curves for singleton gestations as a function of gestational age. Jcap **4**, 1–3 (2019)

Wojciechowski, J., Hopkins, A.M., Upton, R.N.: Interactive pharmacometric applications using R and the Shiny package. CPT: Pharmacomet. Syst. Pharmacol. **4**(3), 146–159 (2015)

Yu, K., Lu, Z., Stander, J.: Quantile regression: applications and current research areas. J. Royal Stat. Soc. Ser. D: Stat. **52**(3), 331–350 (2003)

Early Delirium Detection Using Machine Learning Algorithms

Célia Figueiredo[1]([✉]) [iD], Ana Cristina Braga[1] [iD], and José Mariz[2] [iD]

[1] ALGORITMI Centre, University of Minho, 4800-058 Guimarães, Portugal
`celianlfg@hotmail.com`, `acb@dps.uminho.pt`
[2] ICVS - Life and Health Sciences Research Institute, 4700-057 Braga, Portugal

Abstract. Delirium is a common manifestation of severe acute neuropsychiatric dysfunction prevalent in hospital settings, which due to the complex multi-factorial causes is often under-diagnosed and neglected. Early detection of delirium is a critical concern that can be effectively addressed using machine learning (ML) techniques. As such, some methods to improve the accuracy of ML classification models for the detection of delirium are covered in this document. The aim of this paper is to develop and validate a tool for use in a hospital setting to accurately identify delirium during the admission of a patient.

A database collected at a Portuguese hospital between 2014 and 2016 was used to conduct this experimental research. Available data comprised 511 records and 124 variables, including patient demographics, medications administered, admission category, urgent admission, hospitalization period, history of alcohol abuse and laboratory results.

The methodologies used included data pre-processing, data imbalance processing, feature selection, train and test model with different ML classifiers, evaluating model performance and development of a Python web-based application.

The model achieved consists of 26 predictors assessed during admission to a healthcare facility. This model combines the *SelectFromModel* method with the logistic regression algorithm, resulting in an area under the receiver operating characteristic curve of 0.833 and an area under the precision-recall curve of 0.582.

Although the prediction model can be enhanced, this approach could be a useful support tool to identify patients at increased risk for delirium in healthcare settings. The application developed is available on: https://bit.ly/3waT3T7.

Keywords: Delirium · Logistic regression · Machine learning · Random forest

---

This work has been supported by FCT - Fundação para a Ciência e Tecnologia within the R&D Units Project Scope: UIDB/00319/2020.

1   Introduction

Over the past few years, the average life expectancy has increased. But along with the ageing population, chronic diseases have increased significantly [9]. These are characterized by high levels of disability and are often responsible for causing pressure on the healthcare system. The biological ageing which an individual is exposed to has a variable course. In this natural degradation, many alterations can occur in the normal functioning of the body. Emphasizing here the deterioration that occurs at the cognitive level, which is a very common impairment in the elderly. A slight impairment in the person caused by a change in the condition of the disease, medication, hospitalization, recent physical deficit, or a combination of these may lead to confused and disoriented states. Delirium is a frequent manifestation of severe acute neuropsychiatric dysfunction, and is widespread in hospital settings. Due to its clinical presentation and variability, it is often under-diagnosed and neglected [21].

Delirium can affect people of all ages, but predominantly affects hospitalized older adults. This geriatric syndrome leads not only to an increase in morbidity and mortality, but also to an increase in the period of hospitalization and a deterioration of the physical and mental state of the individual. The ability to assess delirium is an essential component of the patient assessment strategy for the prevention or treatment of delirium. Some studies suggest that early diagnosis and an appropriate approach are associated with decreased rates of morbidity and mortality associated with delirium [13, 21].

In recent years, several clinical assessment tools for delirium have been developed, which represents an important methodological advance in the study and diagnosis of this disorder. Since delirium can easily go unnoticed by healthcare professionals, especially in the intensive care unit (ICU) and emergency departments, it is indispensable to use screening tools that make it possible to detect this disorder faster. Not only to improve the quality of life of patients, but also to reduce patient care costs [23]. Based on this need, screening tools for this disorder have been developed and validated for use in daily clinical practice [8]. Currently, there are several validated instruments to support the diagnosis of delirium that have been adapted according to patients involved [17]. Consequently, there are already more than 30 instruments developed and tested for the assessment of delirium [1, 31]. However, in a hospital setting where time is often short and answers must be obtained quickly, it is likely that this type of syndrome goes unnoticed by many medical professionals. Hence, the need has arisen to investigate tools to make diagnosis more quickly and accurately than usual. And, since we already had data collected between 2014 and 2016 in a Portuguese hospital regarding this topic, it was decided to develop a web application that would determine the risk of a patient developing delirium in a hospital setting using ML algorithms.

In this paper, we seek to provide a survey of the current understanding of the delirium problem and to propose a possible solution to aid diagnosis. We will first review the state-of-the-art solutions based on ML to address this problem in Sect. 2. We then describe the data and data techniques used in data preparation, as well as the ML algorithms used and the metrics for evaluating classifier performance. In Sect. 4 are displayed the experimental results, the best model achieved and the application developed. Finally, a conclusion is provided in Sect. 5.

2 Related Work

The rapid development of artificial intelligence has increasingly allowed the application of ML to fulfil the needs of human life [32]. A study conducted in 2020 by Vellido indicates that the current conjecture of technological development has triggered the idea that the use of ML would be the way forward to solve health-related problems, as well as being an asset to improve the quality of health services [27]. Similarly, another study highlights the potential of ML implementation in healthcare by promoting an improvement in the quality of medicine and allowing to accelerate the pace of evolution of complex diagnostic techniques [14].

The PREdiction of DELIRium for Intensive Care patients (PRE-DELIRIC), was a delirium prediction model created in 2012 for use in adult intensive care patients. The model was developed using data from 1613 consecutive intensive care patients in one hospital and was temporally validated using 549 patients from the same hospital. This model predicts the development of delirium throughout the hospital stay by 10 risk factors (age, Acute Physiology and Chronic Health Evaluation-II (APACHE-II) score, admission group, coma, infection, metabolic acidosis, use of sedatives and morphine, urea concentration, and urgent admission) accessible 24 h after patient admission. The model produced an area under the receiver operating characteristic curve (AUC-ROC) of 0.87 (95% confidence interval: 0.85 to 0.89) and 0.86 after bootstrapping. Temporal and external validation resulted in an AUC-ROC of 0.89 (95% confidence interval: 0.86 to 0.92) and 0.84 (95% confidence interval: 0.82 to 0.87), respectively [26]. According to Liang et al., the PRE-DELIRIC has a high predictive value and the authors suggested that this model can be adopted in ICU to detect delirium in high-risk patients, as it contributes to improving the management of resources, as well as improving patient lives [18].

In 2015, an alternative model for early detection of delirium in intensive care, called Early PREdiction of DELIRium for Intensive Care patient (E-PRE-DELIRIC), was validated. The E-PRE-DELIRIC model uses the data available at ICU admission to predict the development of delirium during the patient's hospital stay. It is composed of nine predictors: age, history of cognitive impairment, history of alcohol abuse, blood urea nitrogen, admission category, urgent admission, mean arterial blood pressure, use of corticosteroids, and respiratory failure. This study emerged as a need to fill the gap in the previous model where predictors are required from the first 24 h after admission to the ICU. Data from 2914 patients was included. The AUC-ROC obtained was 0.76 (95 % confidence interval: 0.73 to 0.77) in the development dataset and 0.75 (95% confidence interval: 0.71 to 0.79) in the validation dataset. An AUC-ROC of 0.70 (95% confidence interval: 0.67 to 0.74) was obtained in the case of delirium that developed until two days and 0.81 (95% confidence interval: 0.78 to 0.84) for delirium that developed after six days [30]. In order to understand which of the two models would be better prepared for clinical use, the study "Delirium prediction in the intensive care unit: comparison of two delirium prediction models" was conducted in the year 2017. This study concluded that the PRE-DELIRIC model predicts delirium better, however, ICU physicians prefer E-PRE-DELIRIC because it is more convenient to use than PRE-DELIRIC [29].

In 2018, a study was conducted to evaluate the prediction of delirium using the random forest (RF) algorithm. For this purpose, a data collection was previously performed, which involved screening for delirium using Confusion Assessment Method (CAM), and collecting the electronic health data from 64038 patients. The data used included demographic data, comorbidities, medications, procedures, and physiological measures. These data were randomly divided into 80% for training and 20% for testing and applied to the RF algorithm. This predictive model produced an AUC-ROC of 0.909, which demonstrated that this algorithm is highly accurate and has the potential to provide a clinically useful predictive model [7].

More recently, in 2021, a retrospective cohort study was published that developed and validated ML algorithms to detect delirium. To conduct this study, data were collected over 5 years period and the Delirium Observation Screening Scale (DOSS) was applied to inpatients and the Confusion Assessment Method for the Intensive Care Unit (CAM-ICU) for ventilated patients. The information collected included medical history, medications administered, physiological measurements, and laboratory results. The algorithms investigated included RL, Decision Tree, RF, Gradient Boosting Machine, Gaussian Naïve Bayes, Support Vector Machine, and K Nearest Neighbour. This study concluded that RF, gradient-boosted machine, and logistic regression (LR) models demonstrated the best predictive ability with respective AUCs of 0.85 to 0.86 [16].

3   Materials and Methods

3.1   Data

This study used data from a Portuguese hospital that was extracted between 2014 and 2016. The study population comprised patients admitted in the emergency department (ED), patients were aged between 18 and 100 years old. The outcome measure of this study was a positive delirium diagnosis determined by Richmond Agitation Sedation Scale (RASS). The data available included patient demographics, patient origin, admission category, urgent admission, length of stay in the ED, alcohol dependence, date of death, SIRS criteria, medications administered, and lab results. In total, the data provided contained information about 511 individuals admitted to the ED and 124 variables. This data, although a few years old, are still suitable since they correspond to a sample of the ED patient population that has remained constant: many comorbidities and advanced age. This is due to the Portuguese demography which has remained stable and without major differences due to migratory flows or population fluctuations. Moreover, ED admissions during this period are similar to the current post-pandemic period.

Data Preparation. Consists of raw data analysis techniques to produce quality data, such as data collection, handling missing data, cleaning, transformation and data reduction [33].

ML analysis can frequently be complicated by missing data values. Missing values can occur because values are missing at random or for unknown reasons, and values that, when absent, provide useful information about the task to be performed. Due to the lack of almost 50% of data, the first step was to collect missing data from the hospital's computer system. During collection, it was noted that information on 77 patients was no longer available. As a result, these data set rows were excluded. The next step was to analyse variables, which included the elimination of columns with repeated information and the exclusion of columns with a single value (zero variation). Thus, after collecting missing data, excluding irrelevant variables and deleting rows where information was unavailable, the resulting database comprises information from 434 individuals and 53 independent variables.

The next step was to apply dimensionality reduction, wherein the redundancy of input data was explored. A small set of new variables was created, each being a combination of input variables with essentially the same information. This dimensional reduction consisted of clustering drugs variables and allowed a better organization of the data, as well as a reduction of the dimensionality without loss of relevant information. In this sense, research was conducted to group the drugs by their respective pharmacological group. As a result of this approach, there was a decrease from 53 to 28 independent variables.

The final step involved data transformation. Since ML algorithms at their core operate on numerical data, it was necessary to execute a data transformation to satisfy this requirement. This means that there was a need for categorical variable encoding techniques in this database. In addition, a normalization of the data was also performed because the database consists of 13 numerical variables which comprise different measurement scales and are therefore difficult to compare.

Imbalanced Data. A common roadblock in many ML applications to healthcare is the significant imbalance relation between classes. For example, it is more common to obtain more data on healthy people than on people with an illness. In total, this dataset included 96 positive and 338 negative examples. After splitting data into test and train sets, were obtained 73 positive and 204 negative examples in the training set and the remaining for testing set. Without data balancing, the overall accuracy of the predictions (percentage of predictions that were correct) was 74%. Although this appears reasonable, accuracy is not an appropriate measure to evaluate performance in this context because a null classifier that simply predicts all the samples without delirium achieves nearly the same accuracy. In this context, it is more appropriate to evaluate separately sensitivity (fraction of delirium detected) and precision (percentage of predicted delirium that is truly delirium).

Ordinarily to address this problem is to apply data balancing techniques to the training data, which can be classified into two major approaches: under-sampling and oversampling. The first approach involves reducing the number of examples of the majority class, and the second generates synthetic records of the minority class. In this study, due to the small amount of data, an oversampling technique was considered, namely Adaptive Synthetic Sampling (ADASYN). The main idea behind the ADASYN algorithm is to use a systematic method to create an adaptive way, different amounts of synthetic data according to their distributions [28]. With this approach, new samples of the minority class were synthetically created and a balance of the proportion of the categories was achieved.

In general, the most appropriate performance measure is dependent on the intended application of the classifier. For problems such as identifying health issues, it may be equally important to identify delirium or not. A wide variety of performance measures are used in practice, and in this paper were included the F_1, the AUC-ROC and area under the precision-recall curve (AUC-PR).

Feature Selection - Most of the time, the dataset is made up of numerous variables, some of which may not be relevant or redundant to the classification model. For this reason, prior to constructing the model, it is important to select the best set of independent variables to be included in the predictive model. For this purpose, statistical and exploratory techniques were studied to select and delete variables that contribute less to the model. The main objective is to find a subset of variables that best correlates with the response variable, without eliminating relevant information, allowing a reduction in computational costs and an increase in the predictive power of the classifier. There are three types of algorithms for feature selection: filter methods, wrapper methods, embedded methods [15]. In this project was used a wrapper approach to select features.

In the wrapper approach, the learning algorithm is used to determine the optimal feature subset. Different combinations of subsets are defined, and their performance is evaluated using a classification algorithm. The classification model is first constructed using a subset of samples for training, and then the model is evaluated by the rest of the samples to test the model. The resulting classifier is evaluated according to evaluation metrics such as accuracy, precision, recall, F_1, AUC-ROC, AUC-PR, among others. The subset with the highest outcomes is the subset used to construct the final model. This method is quite suitable for the selection of relevant variables, but implies a high computation cost and can be prone to overfitting [5,25].

Sequential forward selection, sequential backward selection and bidirectional selection are examples of wrapper methods which behave quite similar. All belong to the same group, sequential search, where the method selects only one variable per loop among all successors. The *scikit-learn* [22] presents the *SequentialFeatureSelector* (SFS) function that contains two configurable parameters that allow to change between methods. The forward strategy begins with no variables in the model, then adds variables to the model one by one. At each step, each remaining variable is tested in order to be included in the model. In each subsequent iteration, the most significant variable is added first. When the newly added variable does not improve model performance, the method ends. In the backward model, on the other hand, the procedure is initiated with all the predictors to be included in the model and in each iteration the least significant variable that allows for an improvement in model performance is eliminated. This process is repeated until no improvement in model performance is observed. The two-way model combines the two techniques mentioned above, and can be combined so that at each step, the procedure selects the best attribute and removes the worst one from among the remaining attributes. It is considered less greedy than the two previous procedures, since it reconsiders the addition of predictors in the model that were removed and vice-versa [6]. The *SelectFromModel* is also a wrapper technique, which extracts the best features of a given dataset according to the importance of weights. The *SelectFromModel* is a meta-estimator that determines the weight importance by comparing to the given threshold value. This function requires an estimator, like RF or LR, which must have attributes to provide the indexes of selected data. Recursive feature elimination (RFE) is another wrapper approach that fits a model and recursively eliminates the least important features based on specific attributes taken by the estimator, until the specified number of features is reached. Finally, the Recursive Feature Elimination with Cross-Validation (RFECV) is an algorithm that eliminates irrelevant features based on validation scores. First, the estimator is trained on the initial set of variables and the importance of each variable is obtained through a specific attribute. Then, the less important variables are pruned from the current set of variables. This procedure is repeated recursively on the pruned set until the desired number of features to be selected is reached [22].

3.2 Machine Learning Algorithms

Random Forest, as its name suggests, is a combination of tree classifiers where each tree depending on a set of random variables, that combines the performance of a wide range of decision tree algorithms to classify or predict the value of a variable [4]. The RF classifier consists of randomly selected features or a combination of features at each node to grow a tree. Instead of searching for the most important feature while splitting a node, it searches for the best feature among a random subset of features. This results in a wide diversity that generally results in a better model. The outcome is classified by taking the most popular voted class from all the tree predictors in the forest [4].

There are several approaches to the selection of attributes used for decision tree induction and most approaches assign a quality measure directly to the attribute. The most frequently used attribute selection measures in decision tree induction are the Information Gain Ratio criterion and the Gini Index [11]. However, *scikit-learn* provides a tool that measures feature importance, also known as the Gini index, by looking at how much the tree nodes that use that feature reduces impurity across all trees in the forest. The greater the increase in leaf purity, the more important the variable is. The score is automatically computed for each feature after training, and the results are scaled so the sum of all importance is equal to one.

One of the biggest advantages of RF is its versatility. It can be used for both regression and classification tasks [4]. The main limitation of RF is that a large number of trees can make the algorithm too slow and ineffective for real-time predictions.

Logistic Regression is a statistical technique designed to generate observations based on a set of observations, a model that allows the prediction of values taken by a categorical variable, based on one or several continuous and/or binary independent variables. This technique uses similar general principles used in linear regression, the difference is in the response variable which in LR is binary (dichotomous) whereas in the linear regression model it is continuous [12]. The intention behind using LR is to find the best fitting model to describe the relationship between the dependent and the independent variable. LR uses the sigmoid function to map predicted values to probabilities. This function is useful to map any value into another value between 0 and 1. *Scikit-learn* provides a tool that measures the coefficient value of each variable. In general, methods used to find coefficients of a logistic function follow an iterative process of selection of a candidate variable and calculate the logarithm of the probability. This process is repeated until convergence is achieved, and the maximum likelihood is found. Therefore, to interpret the coefficient values we need to calculate the odds ratio (OR).

According to Stoltzfus (2011), regression techniques are versatile when applied to medical research because of their ability to predict outcomes and control variables. He also argues that LR is an effective and powerful way to analyse the impact of a group of independent variables on a binary outcome, quantifying the contribution of each variable [24].

3.3 Metrics for Evaluating Classifier Performance

Classification models should be evaluated before adoption in a real-life setting, because if the classifier is not properly calibrated, it may mislead healthcare professionals and consequently cause harm to the target population. Therefore, in order to minimize such occurrences, it is imperative to evaluate the quality of the resulting forecasts. In order to generate evaluation metrics, the different types of successes or errors must first be represented. This was done using the terms summarized in the confusion matrix: false positive (FP), true negative (TN), true positive (TP) and false negative (FN) [11]. According to previous four outcomes from the confusion matrix, several evaluation measures can be described as follows:

Recall: This may be defined as the probability that the model correctly classifies a person with the delirium syndrome, given that the individual carries the syndrome. This measure is also known as true positive rate (TPR), in other words, this measure assesses the ability of the test to detect delirium when it is indeed present, and its value can be estimated using the following formula [11]:

$$Recall = Sensitivity = TPR = \frac{TP}{TP + FN} \tag{1}$$

Precision: It can be considered as a measure of 'exactness' [11], i.e., it measures the probability of the classifier labelled a person with delirium, given that the person does not have delirium. Its value can be estimated according to the following formula.

$$Precision = \frac{TP}{TP + FP} \tag{2}$$

F_1: This metric is the harmonic mean of precision and recall, giving equal weight to both. It evaluates models by considering both FP and FN, and is usually more useful than accuracy if the data have an imbalanced distribution [11].

$$F_1 = \frac{2 * precision * recall}{precision + recall} \tag{3}$$

ROC Curve: One way to evaluate the ability of a diagnostic test to discriminate between two populations is by receiver operating characteristic (ROC) analysis [10]. This analysis is based on signal detection theory and was developed during World War II, where it was used to analyse radar images [3,19]. The science of signal detection theory was later extended to other scientific domains, including diagnostic medicine [20]. Being a commonly used tool in medical diagnostics due to its discriminative capacity [3].

In general, the ROC curve can show the performance of an ML model for binary classification. It is a two-dimensional graphical representation, plotting sensitivity (true positive rate) on the y-axis against 1-specificity (false positive rate) on the x-axis. Whether the test can be affirmed as having the ability to discriminate between individuals with and without delirium is directly linked to a measure of ROC curve accuracy, called the AUC-ROC. Using this measure, it was possible to transform the ROC performance into a scalar value, which allowed to evaluate the discriminant ability of the ROC curve. A closer curve in the upper left corner presents a higher discriminating capacity and the AUC can reach the maximum value of 1, meaning perfect discrimination. On the other hand, if the curve approaches the diagonal, the discriminant capability of the model is null. In summary, the ROC analysis provides important information about diagnostic test performance, and the closer the curve approaches the upper left corner, the greater discriminatory capability of the test.

Precision-Recall Curve: This measure is useful to evaluate the quality classifier's results in cases involving imbalanced datasets, which is an alternative to the ROC curve. The Precision-Recall (PR) curve indicates the balance between precision and recall for different thresholds. There is a great difference between the visual representation of between the ROC curve and the PR curve, because the objective of the ROC space is in the upper left corner while the objective of the PR space is in the upper right corner. Thus, a high AUC-PR represents both high recall and high precision, where high precision is associated with a low false positive rate and high recall is associated with a low false negative rate.

4   Results

This section presents and discusses different models derived from the application of RF (Table 1) and LR (Table 2) classification algorithms and the multiple combinations of feature selection methods. The dataset used was previously transformed by the methods described in Sect. 3.1. The result was a dataset with 343 instances and 38 variables (including features created by one-hot encoding). For testing different algorithms, the dataset was divided: 36% for test and 74% for train.

In Table 1, the results obtained for the feature selection with the RF classification algorithm are shown. Model 0 displays the results obtained without using a feature selection method. This model is used as the control model, i.e., the default model for comparisons between models.

The values selected for the threshold of the *SelectFromModel* method ranged between 0.01 and 0.05 (Model 1 to 5). As the threshold value increases, the number of selected variables decreases. Particularly, a slight variation in the

Table 1. Results obtained by the RF algorithm for feature selection

	Method	Selected variables	Accuracy	Recall	Precision	F_1	AUC-PR	AUC-ROC
Random Forest								
0	–	38	78.34	37.14	52	43.33	0.42	0.789
1	*SelectFromModel* (threshold = 0.01)	37	82.8	45.71	66.67	54.24	0.47	0.808
2	*SelectFromModel* (threshold = 0.015)	17	75.16	31.43	42.31	36.07	0.417	0.765
3	*SelectFromModel* (threshold = 0.02)	14	78.34	31.43	52.38	39.29	0.425	0.796
4	*SelectFromModel* (threshold = 0.03)	13	76.43	34.14	46.43	41.27	0.43	0.76
5	*SelectFromModel* (threshold = 0.05)	9	78.34	42.86	51.72	46.88	0.428	0.748
6	RFECV	31	78.98	40	53.85	45.9	0.508	0.789
7	SFS (forward)	33	78.98	42.86	53.57	45.62	0.445	0.786
8	SFS (backward)	35	80.25	37.14	59.08	45.61	0.457	0.796
9	SFS (both backward)	34	77.71	37.14	50	42.62	0.485	0.785
10	SFS (both forward)	32	77.07	40	48.28	43.75	0.463	0.786

threshold from 0.01 to 0.015 resulted in a decrease of 20 variables. In general, models 1 and 3 show a slight improvement of AUC-ROC in comparison with Model 0. For the remaining thresholds, there was no significant improvement in the AUC-ROC and AUC-PR. An alternative method tested was the RFECV, which corresponding to model 6 (Table 1) was the one that obtained the best results when comparing the AUC-PR. The number of variables decreased from 38 to 31 and the AUC-PR increased by 0.088. Finally, the SFS was tested. The models corresponding to this method (Table 1) are 7, 8, 9 and 10, and only Model 8 showed a slight improvement and the remaining models did not show any significant improvement compared to model 0 when comparing the AUC-ROC. After observing the AUC-PR column, it was found that only model 6 had a value slightly higher than 0.50. These findings suggest that none of the tested models is capable of making quality predictions, since this metric is widely used in the evaluation of forecasting models with imbalanced data.

Table 2. Results of feature selection with LR algorithm (**bold** denotes best model)

Logistic Regression								
Model	Method	Selected variables	Accuracy	Recall	Precision	F_1	AUC-PR	AUC-ROC
0	–	38	83.44	60	63.64	61.76	0.579	0.8320
1	SFS (forward)	23	80.25	48.57	56.67	52.31	0.506	0.766
2	SFS (backward)	26	78.98	57.14	52.63	54.79	0.500	0.802
3	SFS (both forward)	27	70.06	54.529	38	44.71	0.4590	0.755
4	SFS (both backward)	19	78.98	57.14	52.63	54.79	0.5260	0.788
5	RFE	19	80.25	60	55.26	57.53	0.565	0.7827
6	RFECV	18	78.34	51.43	51.43	51.43	0.543	0.755
7	*SelectFromModel* (threshold = 0.02)	38	83.44	60	63.64	61.76	0.579	0.8320
8	***SelectFromModel*** **(threshold = 0.09)**	**36**	**84.71**	**60**	**67.74**	**63.64**	**0.582**	**0.8333**
9	*SelectFromModel* (threshold = 0.1)	35	84.08	60	65.62	62.69	0.578	0.8311
10	*SelectFromModel* (threshold = 0.2)	33	84.08	60	65.62	62.69	0.575	0.8278
11	*SelectFromModel* (threshold = 0.3)	27	82.17	60	60	60	0.563	0.8290
12	*SelectFromModel* (threshold = 0.5)	24	80.89	60	50.76	58.33	0.542	0.8208
13	*SelectFromModel* (threshold = 1)	14	77.71	40	50	44.44	0.499	0.7250
14	*SelectFromModel* (threshold = 1.5)	7	70.7	54.29	38.78	45.24	0.509	0.7207

Table 2 shows the results achieved by the different feature selection methods with the LR classification method. Similar to the previous classification model,

Model 0 was also registered, which corresponds to the results achieved without the feature selection technique. Models 1 to 4 are related to the SFS algorithm, and none of them improved the evaluation metrics obtained in Model 0.

The models RFE and RFECV reduced the number of variables to 19 and 18 respectively, and the AUC-PR values although slightly lower, are close to AUC-PR value obtained by Model 0. Finally, models 7 to 14 depict results obtained by the *SelectFromModel* function. It is possible to verify that Model 8 performed best by comparing the AUC-ROC and AUC-PR metrics with the other models. Models 7, 9, 10 and 11 also provide reasonable results for this project, with the AUC-PR showing results of almost 0.57 and the AUC-ROC near 0.83. Of these models mentioned, the one that presents the best results in terms of model dimensionality is Model 11, as it selects 27 variables allowing for a significant decrease in model dimensionality. However, Model 8 with 36 variables was chosen, since the best value obtained by the evaluation metrics was prioritized. Models 12 to 14 were dismissed, because they presented AUC-PR and AUC-ROC values below 0.55 and 0.83, respectively.

The variables selected by Model 8 and the respective coefficients are shown in Table 3. The results show that the coefficient values vary between negative and positive scores. This means coefficients with positive values indicate the variable predicts class delirium. On the other hand, coefficients with negative values determine the absence of delirium.

Table 3. Variables selected by Model 8 with respective coefficients and OR

Variable	Coef	OR	Variable	Coef	OR
Age	2.763	15.852	pH	−40.338	0.713
Other medications	1.589	4.901	Urgent admission	−40.547	0.579
Antipsychotics	1.089	2.974	HCO3	−40.665	0.514
Glucose	0.661	1.937	Intra-Hospital	−40.692	0.500
Urea	0.605	1.831	Home	−0.717	0.488
CO2	0.565	1.759	Analgesics	−0.778	0.459
Length of stay	0.560	1.751	Gender	−0.919	0.399
Creatinine	0.356	1.428	Hemato-Oncology	−1.187	0.305
CRP	0.301	1.351	Neurology	−1.268	0.281
Anticoagulants	0.287	1.332	Respiratory	−1.312	0.269
SIRS criteria	0.268	1.307	Nursing home	−1.316	0.268
Alcohol dependence	0.250	1.284	Other admission category	−1.334	0.264
Corticosteroids	0.230	1.258	Inter-Hospital	−1.481	0.227
Antidepressants	0.093	1.098	Cardiovascular	−1.829	0.160
Digitalis	−0.140	0.869	O2	−1.844	0.158
Sodium	−0.184	0.832	Musculoskeletal	−2.006	0.134
Ionized calcium	−0.199	0.819	Genitourinary	−2.079	0.125
Antidyslipidemics	−0.303	0.738	Gastrointestinal	−2.221	0.108

The variables most contributive to the prediction of delirium are age, other medications and antipsychotics. The 'Antipsychotic' variable is composed of the medicines Haloperidol, Quetiapine, Risperidone, Paliperidone and Iloperidone. The variable related to other drugs present includes drugs such as Ranitidine, Scopolamine, Desloratadine, Hydroxyzine, Trihexyphenidyl and Throspium. The inclusion of this variable as one of the most influential in delirium prediction caused some uncertainty, because this group included drugs from several pharmacological groups, which make it impossible to draw any conclusion about which group of drugs has a real effect on the development of delirium. In addition, there are only 18 records in this group, of which 16 (88.89%) are classified as delirium. Based on these statistics, we may consider that this variable may effectively have a significant importance on delirium prediction, since the probability of getting a case of delirium when any of these drugs is present is high. In the case of the variable 'Age', the result shows that for a change of one unit in age, the probability of developing delirium increases 15.8 times. As regards categorical variables, such as the variables 'Other Med' and 'Antipsychotics', the individuals who take this group of drugs are, respectively, 4.9 times and 2.97 times more likely to develop delirium than those who do not take this group of drugs. On the other hand, individuals whose pharmacological therapy contains analgesics or antidyslipidemic drugs are 0.45 times (54%) or 0.73 times (26%) less likely to develop delirium, respectively.

To facilitate the use of this predictive model, a web application was built. This type of format allows easy viewing of the prediction results in real time and on any platform. The purpose of this tool is to easily and quickly calculate the probability of occurrence or absence of delirium in individuals admitted to healthcare settings. The construction of this application implied the use of the prediction model previously selected and Python language. The prediction is performed by filling in all the requested fields in the application form, corresponding to the 26 variables selected by the wrapper method (Fig. 1).

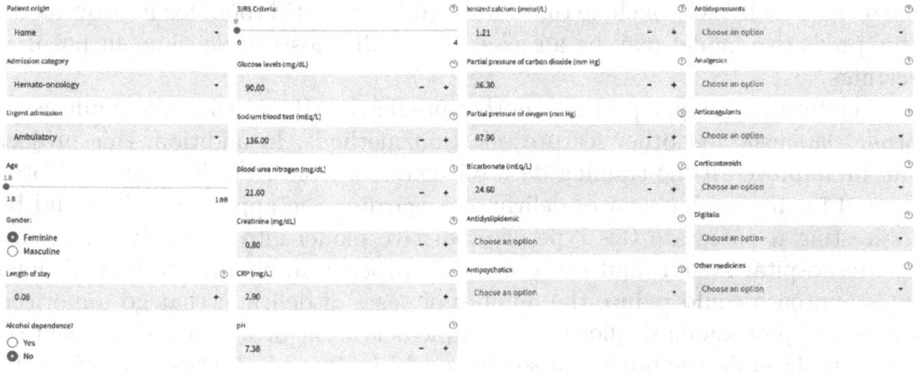

Fig. 1. Screenshot of delirium application developed

The application was developed with *streamlit* and is available through the link: https://bit.ly/3waT3T7. The variables asked on the application form are: patient origin (home, nursing home, intra-hospital, inter-hospital), admission category, urgent admission, age, gender, length of stay, alcohol dependence, SIRS criteria, glucose levels, sodium blood test, blood urea nitrogen, creatinine, C-reactive protein, pH, ionized calcium, partial pressure of carbon dioxide (pCO_2), partial pressure of oxygen (pO_2), bicarbonate (HCO_3), antidyslipidemic (Rosuvastatine, Atorvastatine, Pravastatine, Sinvastatine, Fluvastatine), antipsychotics (Haloperidol, Quetiapine, Risperidone, Paliperidone, Iloperidone), antidepressant (Fluvoxamine, Paroxetine, Sertraline, Venlafaxine, Trazodone, Amitriptyline), analgesics (Nifedipine, Captopril, Clonidine), anticoagulants (Warfarin, Dipyridamole), corticosteroids (Hydrocortisone, Prednisone), digitalis (Digoxin)and other medicines (Ranitidine, Scopolamine, Desloratadine, Hydroxyzine, Trihexyphenidyl, Trospium).

After filling in the application fields, the delirium prediction is calculated. The result is composed of a message generated according to the prediction result.

5   Conclusion

This study demonstrated the importance of data preparation in an ML project to obtain accurate predictions.

The model developed allows the prediction of delirium with an AUC-ROC of 0.833 and an AUC-PR of 0.582. The application developed might be a useful support tool for early delirium detection in healthcare settings. In addition, it is simple to use and adjustable to different types of devices. Although the model obtained has a reasonable predictive capacity, it is postulated that if the set of data collected contained a higher number of records, the predictive model could get a higher hit rate. This assumption is based on the fact that the model was constructed with a reduced number of records and a considerable number of variables. As a consequence, ML algorithms may encounter difficulties to detect patterns. Finally, we conclude that although there is still room for improvement, this predictive model may be an asset in the diagnosis of delirium in hospital settings.

In a future work perspective, another predictive ML model can be built using other classifiers and other feature selection methods. In addition, this project can be improved if the training data set contains more records, namely records related to the development of delirium. Regarding the application, it would be interesting to integrate this type of predictive model into an electronic record of the hospital system and carry out this process automatically in real-time. This approach could reduce the number of cases of delirium that go unnoticed by health professionals, allowing an implementation of a delirium prevention program. Overall, the quality of service could be improved, thus improving the quality of life of hospitalised individuals.

References

1. Adamis, D., Sharma, N., Whelan, P.J.P., MacDonald, A.J.D.: Delirium scales: a review of current evidence. Aging Ment. Health **14**(5), 543–555 (2010). https://doi.org/10.1080/13607860903421011
2. American Psychiatric Association, Diagnostic and statistical manual of mental disorders (5th ed.). Washington DC (2013)
3. Braga, A.C., Oliveira, P.: Diagnostic analysis based on ROC curves: theory and applications in medicine. Int. J. Health Care Qual. Assurance (2003)
4. Breiman, L.: Random forests. Mach. Learn. **45**(1), 5–32 (2001)
5. Cherrington, M., Thabtah, F., Lu, J., Xu, Q.: Feature selection: filter methods performance challenges. In: 2019 International Conference on Computer and Information Sciences (ICCIS), pp. 1–4. IEEE (2019). https://doi.org/10.1109/ICCISci.2019.8716478
6. Chowdhury, M.Z.I., Turin, T.C.: Variable selection strategies and its importance in clinical prediction modelling. Family Med. Commun. Health **8**(1), e000262 (2020). https://doi.org/10.1136/fmch-2019-000262
7. Corradi, J.P., Thompson, S., Mather, J.F., Waszynski, C.M., Dicks, R.S.: Prediction of incident delirium using a random forest classifier. J. Med. Syst. **42**(12), 1–10 (2018). https://doi.org/10.1007/s10916-018-1109-0
8. De, J., Wand, A.P.F.: Delirium screening: a systematic review of delirium screening tools in hospitalized patients. Gerontologist **55**(6), 1079–1099 (2015). https://doi.org/10.1093/geront/gnv100
9. DuGoff, E.H., Canudas-Romo, V., Buttorff, C., Leff, B., Anderson, G.F.: Multiple chronic conditions and life expectancy. Med. Care **52**(8), 688–694 (2014). https://doi.org/10.1097/MLR.0000000000000166
10. Fawcett, T.: An introduction to ROC analysis. Pattern Recogn. Lett. **27**(8), 861–874 (2006). https://doi.org/10.1016/j.patrec.2005.10.010
11. Han, J., Kamber, M., Pei, J.: Data mining: Concepts and Techniques. Elsevier, Morgan Kaufmann (2012)
12. Hosmer, D.W., Lemeshow, S., Sturdivant, R.X.: Applied Logistic Regression. Wiley Series in Probability and Statistics (2013)
13. Inouye, S.K., Westendorp, R.G.J., Saczynski, J.S.: Delirium in elderly people. Lancet **383**(9920), 911–922 (2014). https://doi.org/10.1016/S0140-6736(13)60688-1
14. Kareemi, H., Vaillancourt, C., Rosenberg, H., Fournier, K., Yadav, K.: Machine learning versus usual care for diagnostic and prognostic prediction in the emergency department: a systematic review. Acad. Emerg. Med. **28**(2), 184–196 (2021). https://doi.org/10.1111/acem.14190
15. Kumar, V.: Feature selection: a literature review. Smart Comput. Rev. **4**(3) (2014). https://doi.org/10.6029/smartcr.2014.03.007
16. Lee, S., Mueller, B., Nick Street, W., Carnahan, R.M.: Machine learning algorithm to predict delirium from emergency department data. BMJ (2021). https://doi.org/10.1101/2021.02.19.21251956
17. Leonard, M.M., et al.: Practical assessment of delirium in palliative care. J. Pain Symptom Manage. **48**(2), 176–190 (2014). https://doi.org/10.1016/j.jpainsymman.2013.10.024
18. Liang, S., Chau, J.P.C., Lo, S.H.S., Bai, L., Yao, L., Choi, K.C.: Validation of PREdiction of DELIRium in ICu patients (PRE-DELIRIC) among patients in intensive care units: a retrospective cohort study. Nursing in Critical Care, (August), 1–7 (2020). https://doi.org/10.1111/nicc.12550

19. Lloyd, M.A., Appel, J.B.: Signal Detection theory and the psychophysics of pain: an introduction and review. Psychosom. Med. **38**(2), 79–94 (1976). https://doi.org/10.1097/00006842-197603000-00002

20. Lusted, L.B.: Decision-making studies in patient management. N. Engl. J. Med. **284**(8), 416–424 (1971). https://doi.org/10.1056/NEJM197102252840805

21. Mittal, V., et al.: Delirium in the elderly: a comprehensive review. Am. J. Alzheimers Dis. Other Demen. **26**(2), 97–109 (2011). https://doi.org/10.1177/1533317510397331

22. Pedregosa, F., et al.: Scikit-learn: machine learning in python. J. Mach. Learn. Res. **12**(2014), 2825–2830 (2012). http://arxiv.org/abs/1201.0490

23. Shintani, A.K., et al.: Costs associated with delirium in mechanically ventilated patients. Crit. Care Med. **32**(4), 955–962 (2004). https://doi.org/10.1097/01.ccm.0000119429.16055.92

24. Stoltzfus, J.C.: Logistic regression: a brief primer. Acad. Emerg. Med. **18**(10), 1099–1104 (2011). https://doi.org/10.1111/j.1553-2712.2011.01185.x

25. Suppers, A., van Gool, A., Wessels, H.: Integrated chemometrics and statistics to drive successful proteomics biomarker discovery. Proteomes **6**(2), 20 (2018). https://doi.org/10.3390/proteomes6020020

26. Van Den Boogaard, M., et al.: Development and validation of PRE-DELIRIC (PREdiction of DELIRium in ICu patients) delirium prediction model for intensive care patients: Observational multicentre study. BMJ (Online), **344**(7845), 17 (2012). https://doi.org/10.1136/bmj.e420

27. Vellido, A.: The importance of interpretability and visualization in machine learning for applications in medicine and health care. Neural Comput. Appl. **32**(24), 18069–18083 (2019). https://doi.org/10.1007/s00521-019-04051-w

28. Vluymans, S.: Learning from imbalanced data. In: Dealing with Imbalanced and Weakly Labelled Data in Machine Learning using Fuzzy and Rough Set Methods. SCI, vol. 807, pp. 81–110. Springer, Cham (2019). https://doi.org/10.1007/978-3-030-04663-7_4

29. Wassenaar, A., et al.: Delirium prediction in the intensive care unit: comparison of two delirium prediction models. Crit. Care **22**(1), 114 (2018). https://doi.org/10.1186/s13054-018-2037-6

30. Wassenaar, A., et al.: Multinational development and validation of an early prediction model for delirium in ICU patients. Intensive Care Med. **41**(6), 1048–1056 (2015). https://doi.org/10.1007/s00134-015-3777-2

31. Wong, C.L., Holroyd-Leduc, J., Simel, D.L., Straus, S.E.: Does this patient have delirium?: value of bedside instruments. JAMA **304**(7), 779–786 (2010)

32. Xia, H., Wang, C., Yan, L., Dong, X., Wang, Y.: Machine learning based medicine distribution system. In: Proceedings of the 2019 10th IEEE International Conference on Intelligent Data Acquisition and Advanced Computing Systems: Technology and Applications, IDAACS 2019, vol. 2, pp. 912–915. IEEE (2019). https://doi.org/10.1109/IDAACS.2019.8924236

33. Zhang, S., Zhang, C., Yang, Q.: Data preparation for data mining. Appl. Artif. Intell. **17**(5–6), 375–381 (2003). https://doi.org/10.1080/713827180

Drowsiness Detection Using Multivariate Statistical Process Control

Ana Rita Antunes[1,2]([✉])[ID], Ana Cristina Braga[2][ID], and Joaquim Gonçalves[1][ID]

[1] 2Ai, Polytechnic Institute of Cávado and Ave, 4750-810 Barcelos, Portugal
{arantunes,jgoncalves}@ipca.pt
[2] ALGORITMI Center, University of Minho, 4710-057 Braga, Portugal
acb@dps.uminho.pt

Abstract. Drowsiness at the wheel has been studied for different countries since it is important for road safety and its prevention. Since it is considered a public health problem, solutions must be found to avoid worse scenarios and to identify a low-cost system.

Therefore, this work aims to detect the drowsy state, without labeling it manually, considering the heart rate variability. To make this possible, driving simulations were performed, using a wearable device. In terms of methodology, multivariate statistical process control, considering principal component analysis, was implemented, and compared with a similar study. Three principal components were computed taking into consideration time, frequency, and non-linear domain, every two minutes. Thereafter, Hotelling T^2 and squared prediction error statistics were estimated. These statistics were estimated considering each principal component, individually. Thereby, the results achieved seemed to be promising to identify drowsiness peaks. However, the study developed has limitations, like the identification of points out-of-control occurred due to signal noise and it does not identify all the drowsiness peaks. Conversely, it was not used information from the participants' awake states as a reference. Therewith, new simulations must be done, and new information must be added to avoid noise and to detect more drowsiness peaks.

Keywords: Drowsy · Driving · Simulation · Heart rate variability · Multivariate statistical process control · Principal component analysis

1 Introduction

Sleep is essential for the physical and psychological well-being and longevity of a human being, where it is crucial for cognitive processes, emotional regulation,

This paper was funded by the project "NORTE-01-0247-FEDER-0039720", supported by Northern Portugal Regional Operational Programme (Norte2020), under the Portugal 2020 Partnership Agreement, through the European Regional Development Fund (ERDF)".

O. Gervasi et al. (Eds.): ICCSA 2022 Workshops, LNCS 13377, pp. 571–585, 2022.
https://doi.org/10.1007/978-3-031-10536-4_38

executives, and attention. These processes are very important for memory, learning, productivity, and concentration [1,2]. Consequently, sleep deprivation can have serious problems in security, health, and quality of life that can lead to a decrease in the individual's productivity, as well as an increase in work accidents, such as driving [1,3,4]. Sleep disorders are a public health problem and have been associated with increased risk of hypertension, depression, obesity, heart attack, and stroke [5]. In Portugal, 22.3% of drivers confirmed that fell asleep while they were driving and 1.7% had an accident for falling asleep [6].

The devices available use moves sensors at the wheel and/or cameras located in the rearview mirror and the system recognize the driver fatigue and send an alert. These technologies are expensive and are only available in major brands. Therefore, these technologies are available for those who have purchase power [7]. It is necessary to replace the detection systems with a forecasting one and detection of disturbance problems or sleep deprivation.

Thus, drowsiness at the wheel has been studied over the years and there are still aspects to be improved. Most of the studies found intended to classify the sleepy state, using different machine learning algorithms. Even thought Multivariate Statistical Process Control (MSPC) is widely used in industry area, this methodology has been applied in the healthcare area, in recent years, considering the Heart Rate Variability (HRV). For example, this approach was developed for epileptic seizure prediction and to detect driver drowsiness [8–10].

In this work, MSPC based on Principal Component Analysis (MSPC-PCA) is performed to identify a drowsy state using biometric data, from driving simulator experiments. The work is carried out by the comparison of the work [10], where the methodology was implemented differently in an attempt to obtain more out-of-control points that are related to the detection of sleepiness.

This article is structured as follows. Section 2 presents a literature review, where some concepts about drowsy detection methods, questionnaires to evaluate sleep disorders and MSPC-PCA concepts are briefly explained. Materials and Methods are presented in Sect. 3, where it is explained the proposed drowsiness detection procedure, variables description and the implementation details. In Sect. 4 there are the information of the results achieved. Firstly, it is introduced the participants description, then the HRV analysis is performed and the discussion of results. Finally, the main conclusions and the proposed of future work are described in Sect. 5

2   Literature Review

In this section, it will be firstly introduced the existing methods for detecting sleepiness, than the questionnaires to identify sleep disorders. Therefore, the MSPC-PCA concepts are presented.

2.1   Methods for Detecting Sleepiness

For the detection of sleepiness, there are different types of methods, that can be divided into subjective, vehicle, behavioral and physiological measures.

Subjective Measures. Subjective measures are used to assess the level of sleepiness considering the drivers' opinion. Where the Karolinska sleepiness scale [11,12] is widely implemented and has nine situations: (1) extremely alert, (2) very alert, (3) alert, (4) fairly alert, (5) neither alert nor sleepy, (6) some signs of sleepiness, (7) sleepy, but no effort to keep alert, (8) sleepy, some effort to keep alert, (9) very sleepy, great effort to keep alert, fighting sleep. This measure is not practical in real driving situations and is based on opinions. Note that the driver is not always aware that he/she is showing signs of sleepiness [13].

Vehicle-Based Measures. The vehicle-based measures use the information available in the cars' intelligent systems. Thus, it can extract information about driving speed, and standard deviation of lane position, this is the variability of lane position, steering wheel movement, and driving duration [14]. This type of measure can be easily collected but, in some situations, is very limited since it depends on external factors like the road's geometric characteristics. For example, road marking, climatic, and lighting conditions. On the other hand, when the alert of sleepiness is sent to the driver it means that the driver presents already signs of sleepiness. This can be a problem since it may not prevent road accidents due to late detection [13,15].

Behavioral Measures. Behavioral measures aim to evaluate the driver behavior in order to detect the drive fatigue. Thus, it can be acquired the number and duration of blinks, frequent yawning, head position, and, a well-known metric, the percentage of eyelid closure over the pupil over time [16,17]. These metrics are non-intrusive for the driver activity, but the illumination and the use of glasses can be a problem, even though there are cameras with better performance during the day and others during the night [13,18].

Physiological Measures. The physiological measures are the most reliable metrics to detect sleepiness since it can alert the driver beforehand. Thus, electroencephalogram (EEG), electrocardiogram (ECG), electrooculogram (EOG), electromyogram (EMG), and photoplethysmograph (PPG) are the most known signs. Where these signs take into consideration brain activity, heart rate, eye movement, muscles activity, and blood volume changes, respectively [19–21]. Note that the EEG, EOG, and EMG are the signs used to identify the respective sleep phases [22]. Even though these metrics are the most reliable, they can be extracted wrong information and it is very intrusive to drivers' activity. Moreover, it is important to rectify this disadvantage, where non-intrusive solutions have been developed using wearable devices to measure these signs [13].

2.2   Questionnaires

The Epworth sleepiness scale [23] is widely used to measure the level of daytime sleepiness. There are eight questions based on different situations, where the subject has to rate on a scale of 0 to 3 how likely they would fall asleep, considering their recently routine. So, the final score can be between 0 and 24. If the final score is greater than 10, the subject has hypersomnia.

In contrast, the STOP-Bang questionnaire [24] is applied to identify the risk of developing obstructive sleep apnea. This one takes into consideration the snoring, tiredness, observed apnea, high blood pressure, body mass index, age, neck circumference, and male gender. Thus, there are eight dichotomous questions and the final score is between 0 and 8. Those with scores equal to or greater than 5 have a high risk of developing moderate to severe obstructive sleep apnea.

Another questionnaire available and commonly used is the Pittsburgh sleep quality [25] that assesses the sleep quality in the previous month. This one has 19 questions that are divided into seven components: subjective sleep quality, sleep latency, sleep duration, habitual sleep efficiency, sleep disturbances, use of sleeping medications, and daytime dysfunction. Each component has a score of 0 to 3 and, the final score (0 to 21) is the sum of the scores of each component. The subjects with a final score greater than 5 have a bad sleep quality.

The circadian rhythm, our twenty-four-hour rhythm, is another aspect to analyze, when sleepiness is being studied since it is possible to identify when the subject wants to be awake or asleep. For example, a diurnal person has a preference to stay awake during the day and sleep at night [26]. Thus, the Morning-Eveningness questionnaire [27] consists of 19 questions and the final score is between 16 to 86. The subjects with classification between 16 to 30 is a definitely evening type, 31 to 41 moderately evening type, 42 to 58 neither type, 59 to 69 moderately morning type and 70 to 86 definitely morning type.

2.3   Multivariate Statistical Process Control Based on Principal Component Analysis

Statistical process control is used to monitor the process performance to verify if it is working like should be and to detect when an anomaly occurs. Control charts are a very practical visual method for understanding the operation of a given process, where it is possible to do a univariate or multivariate analysis. This is, evaluate one variable individually or all variables in simultaneously [28].

However, some analyses can be misleading and difficult to interpret due to the highly correlated between variables. Thus, there are some difficulties when multivariate process data is being analyzed, like the dimensionality, colinearity, the presence of noise, and missing data [29].

Principal Component Analysis (PCA) is an alternative method capable to simplify the analysis and the process of monitoring faults since it projects the data into low dimensional spaces. Thus, in order to eliminate colinearity and dimensionality, PCA computes a set of orthogonal and linearly uncorrelated variables capable to explain the original information, call as principal components [28].

Considering the matrix $\mathbf{X} \in \mathbb{R}^{N \times M}$, where N and M are the number of observations and the number of variables, respectively. Where the firsts components explain most of the variability, in the original data, and R ($\leq M$) is the number of components retained. Note that the values in $\mathbf{X}$ are scaled to zero mean and unit variance. The principal components can be expressed as Eq. 1,

$$\mathbf{T} = \mathbf{XP} + \mathbf{E} \tag{1}$$

where $\mathbf{T} \in \mathbb{R}^{N \times R}$ is called the scores matrix, $\mathbf{P} \in \mathbb{R}^{M \times R}$ is the loading matrix and $\mathbf{E} \in \mathbb{R}^{N \times M}$ is the residuals, in other words, is the information that is not explained by the PCA model. Furthermore, the estimation of $\mathbf{X}$ can be made considering Eq. 2 and, consequently, the errors can be written as Eq. 3 [28,30,31].

$$\hat{\mathbf{X}} = \mathbf{TP^T} \tag{2}$$

$$\mathbf{E} = \mathbf{X} - \hat{\mathbf{X}} \tag{3}$$

Considering this information, the Squared Prediction Error (SPE), also known as the Q statistic, can be expressed like in Eq. 4. This statistic is used to measure the difference between the original information and the R dimensional subspace.

$$SPE = \sum_{i=1}^{M}(\mathbf{x}_i - \hat{\mathbf{x}}_i)^2 \tag{4}$$

Another statistic widely used to monitoring the process stability is the Hotelling's T^2. The expression is given by Eq. 5,

$$T_i^2 = \mathbf{t_i^T}\mathbf{\Lambda}^{-1}\mathbf{t_i} = \sum_{r=1}^{R}\frac{t_r^2}{\lambda_r} \tag{5}$$

where $\Lambda \in \mathbb{R}^{R \times R}$ is the covariance matrix of $\mathbf{T}$, $\mathbf{t_i^T} = \{t_{i1}, t_{i2}, \ldots, t_{iR}\}$ is the score vector for the ith observation and λ_r is the eigenvalues of the R component.

Hence, the upper limit control (ULC) for Hotelling's T^2 (Eq. 6) can be compute considering the F-distribution, considering the $100(1 - \alpha)\%$ confidence.

$$ULC(T^2) = \frac{R(N^2 - 1)}{N(N - R)} \times F_{R,(N-R),\alpha} \tag{6}$$

However, the SPE control limit, considering the significant level α, is express like in Eq. 7,

$$UCL(SPE) = \frac{v}{2b}\chi^2_{\left(\frac{2b^2}{v},\alpha\right)} \tag{7}$$

where b and v are the sample mean and variance values.

3   Materials and Methods

This section addresses the drowsiness detection procedure, where all the steps are explained. Besides that, a brief explanation of the variables, in the study, and the implementation details is also presented.

3.1   Drowsiness Detection Procedure

The drowsiness detection procedure developed requires several steps. Figure 1 shows a summary of the required steps to implement the proposed methodology.

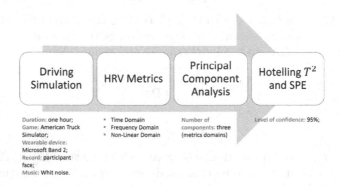

Fig. 1. Work flowchart.

Thus, in order to identify the participants' awake and drowsy state, a strategy was designed to distinguish these different states. For the achievement of this a driving simulation was conducted, between July 5 and August 3, 2021. All the participants agreed to be part of the study and the anonymity was guaranteed.

Thus, the participants had to fill out four questionnaires about daytime sleepiness, the risk of obstructive sleep apnea, sleep quality, and the circadian rhythm [23–25, 27]. Therefore, during the simulation, the participant used a wearable device, Microsoft Band 2, to collect physiological information. With this device, there is information about the heart rate and R-R intervals. Note that the simulation room was completely empty to not compromise the participant's condition with noise and the lights were off.

In terms of the game, it was used for the `American Truck Simulator` since there are highways with long kilometers and it is possible to define a single route for all participants. The simulation duration was about one hour [32,33]. When the participant is driving within a city, the maximum speed is 30 km/h and on a highway is 55 km/h. It was asked to each participant to not exceed the speed limits to make it more real and to induce sleepiness. Another way to induce more sleepiness was to play a monotonous music [1] along the route and with the sound of the truck working.

The next step was to extract the HRV metrics, known as time, frequency and non-linear domains. This information it will be used to detect the drowsy state. Where the implementation of PCA is the next step to take into consideration, which aims to divide the variables by their respective domains as they are properly validated.

---

[1] Available in: https://www.youtube.com/watch?v=wzjWIxXBs_s. Acceded between July 5 and August 3, 2021.

Lastly, the identification of the Hotelling T^2 and SPE statistics and control limits are the final step. This information was estimated for each principal component, individually, to identify the maximum number of observation out-of-control and verify if there are signs of drowsiness using the video recording.

3.2 Variables Description

Heart Rate Variability (HRV) is the time between consecutive heartbeats, which gives rise to the R-R intervals or Inter-beat interval (IBI) [34,35]. It is an essential tool for characterizing and understanding the regulation of the cardiovascular system through the autonomic nervous system (ANS) [36]. In Fig. 2 it is presented the ECG signal, where the time between two adjacent highest peaks, known as R-peak, is the R-R interval [34].

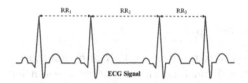

Fig. 2. RR-Intervals for ECG signals (from [34]).

Furthermore, there are time domain, frequency and non-linear metrics. Time domain measures quantify the amount of HRV over a given period of time. However, frequency metrics compute absolute or relative signal power and, conversely, the non-linear metrics measure the unpredictability and complexity [35]. The time [T], frequency [F] and non-linear [NL] variables were extracted using the python open-source package *HRV-analysis*, every two minutes, and the follow descriptions [37].

T mean$_{nni}$: R-R intervals mean;

T sdnn: R-R standard deviation;

T sdsd: The standard deviation of differences between adjacent R-R intervals;

T rmssd: The square root of the mean of the sum of the squares of differences between adjacent N-N intervals;

T median$_{nni}$: Median Absolute values of the successive differences between the R-R intervals;

T nni$_{50}$: Number of interval differences of successive R-R intervals greater than 50 ms;

T pnni$_{50}$: The proportion derived by dividing nni_50 by the total number of R-R intervals;

T nni$_{20}$: Number of interval differences of successive R-R intervals greater than 20 ms;

T pnni$_{20}$: The proportion derived by dividing nni_20 by the total number of RR-intervals;

T range$_{nni}$: Difference between the maximum and minimum nn_interval;
T cvsd: Coefficient of variation of successive differences equal to the rmssd divided by mean$_{nni}$;
T cvnni: Coefficient of variation equal to the ratio of sdnn divided by mean_nni;
T mean$_{hr}$: The mean Heart Rate;
T max$_{hr}$: Maximum heart rate;
T min$_{hr}$: Minimum heart rate;
T std$_{hr}$: Standard deviation of heart rate;
F total power: Total power density spectral;
F vlf: variance in HRV in the very low frequency;
F lf : variance in HRV in the low frequency;
F hf: variance in HRV in the high frequency;
F lf_hf_ratio: lf/hf ratio;
NL csi: Cardiac Sympathetic Index.
NL cvi: Cadiac Vagal Index.
NL Modified csi: Modified CSI;
NL sampen: sample entropy.

Before the variables extraction, the R-R intervals must be resample at equal intervals and afterward must be clean, this is, the outliers and ectopic beats must be treated. In terms of outliers, the values below 300 and above 2000 were considered. The package *HRV-analysis* has two functions to remove the outliers and ectopic beats, *remove_outliers* and *remove_ectopic_beats*. The next step was to interpolate the missing values, considering the cubic method and the function *interpolate_nan_values* [37]. Figure 3 presents a summary of what was done to extract the variables through a flowchart.

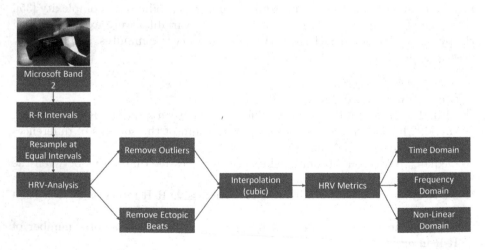

Fig. 3. Flowchart for the variables extraction.

3.3   Implementation Details

In order to produce the HRV analysis, the software Python (version 3.8.5) was used [38]. Firstly, the csv file was imported using the library pandas considering the function read_csv [39]. In a second instance, the library matplotlib was employed to graphically visualize the biometric data collected and the questionnaire results using the pyplot function [40].

Then, after the variables extraction, the standardization of data was performed using the mean() and std() pandas functions [39]. Moreover, PCA was conducted considering the library pca, the functions pca, and fit_transform to identify the scores of the three principal components and the loading's values [41].

Thereafter, the identification of the Hotelling T^2 and SPE statistics and control limits were assessed with the numpy and SciPy libraries [42,43]. The covariance matrix was computed with the fuction cov and its inverse value by the function linalg.inv. Then, matrix multiplication was performed with the dot function. In the case of the SPE statistic, the sum of the errors was done with the sum function. Finally, the distributions were calculated by the functions f.ppf and chi2.ppf.

4   Results

In this section, the participants information is provided and the questionnaires results are shown. Moreover, the HRV analysis is conducted by applying MSPC-PCA, and finally, it is made a discussion of the results.

4.1   Participants Description

The simulation was conducted during one month, where the number of participants was twelve. Each volunteer performed at least two simulations, one in the morning and one in the afternoon. Thus, thirty-one simulations were carried out with voluntary participation, at the Polytechnic Institute of Cávado and Ave.

The age range of the participants varies from 22 to 53 years old. Although, 50% are under the age of 28. According to Fig. 4, most of the participants are male (83.3%), with normal weight (50%), 41.7% have overweight and 8.3% have class I obesity.

In terms of sleep disorders, the questionnaires results are present in Fig. 5. There are 33.3% of participants that are a morning type, 41.7% neither type, 8.3% as definitively morning and 16.7% evening type. Nonetheless, 25% has excessive daytime sleep and risk of developed obstructive sleep apnea, and 8.3% has bad sleep quality.

4.2   Heart Rate Variability

In this subsection, only the results of two participant will be presented. The chosen participants had different experiences, where Participant 1 did not experience drowsiness, unlike Participant 2, according to their opinions.

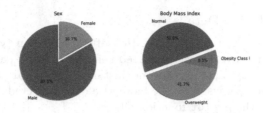

Fig. 4. Sex and body mass index for the participants.

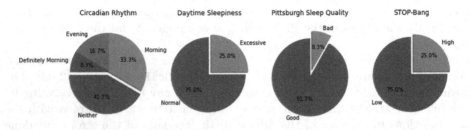

Fig. 5. Questionnaires results.

Moreover, the heart rate descriptive statistics are shown in Table 1. According to the results presented, Participant 1 has a lower mean heart rate than Participant 2. However, Participant 2 has a greater variability when comparing the minimum and maximum heart rate values. Although, the standard deviation and the coefficient of variation (CV) are smaller for Participant 2.

Table 1. Heart rate descriptive statistics for Participant 1 and 2.

Participant	Mean	Std	CV	Minimum	Q1	Median	Q3	Maximum	Range
1	63.16	3.53	5.59	5 2.64	60.87	62.80	65.20	77.61	24.97
2	77.86	3.46	4.44	63.96	75.83	78.17	79.94	91.41	27.45

Therefore, in order to detect drowsy state, considering the HRV, three principal components were firstly estimated. Since the HRV metrics are divided into time, frequency, and non-linear domains, the principal components were divided considering this separation.

After this estimation, the Hotelling T^2 and SPE statistic were assessed considering each principal component, using 95% confidence level. Figure 6 presents the results achieved for the Participant 1 (Fig. 6a) and Participant 2 (Fig. 6b). With this visualization, it is possible to identify that there are five and eight points out-of-control, for Participant 1 and Participant 2, respectively.

The next step was to identify when the out-of-control points occurred, in terms of time, and visualize the video to identify if there are clear signs of drowsiness.

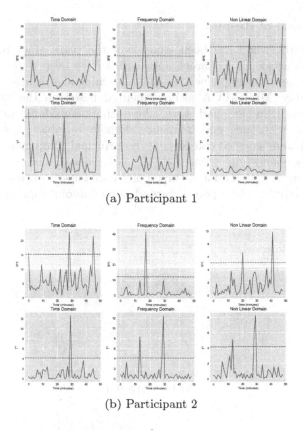

(a) Participant 1

(b) Participant 2

Fig. 6. Hotelling T^2 and SPE statistic.

In the case of Participant 1, the first two points occurred at the beginning of the wearable device placement, where there was more movement. On the remaining points, there is more frequent blinking and, in some cases, slightly slower blinking and deeper breathing.

In terms of Participant 2, the first point is noise since there was more movements. Moreover, it was identified as slower blinking, arms movement, difficulty keeping eyes open, more frequent blinking, yawning, head landing and closes eyes for a few seconds. The fifth and sixth out-of-control points are followed, where in the first one there are clear signs of drowsiness and since the participant closed his eyes for a few seconds, when he opened his eyes he had to control the truck. Therefore, the participant needed to be more attentive and concentrated. In the last point out-of-control, the participant seemed to be more concentrated.

Furthermore, the same analysis was replicated for the remaining participants and it was possible to identify signs of drowsiness, in some participants. Although, in some cases, it was difficult to understand or identify the drowsy state.

4.3   Discussion of Results

Drowsiness at the wheel has been study over the years, since it is one of the causes of road accidents. Different approaches have been developed to detect signs of drowsiness and implement machine learning algorithms.

In this study, MSPC-PCA is implemented based on the work developed by [10]. Although, in the cited work, the authors considered only one principal component with time and frequency domain variables. Hotelling T^2 and SPE statistics were assessed considering the principal component.

If the methodology implemented at [10] is considered, the results achieved are presented in Fig. 7. Only two and three points are out-of-control for Participant 1 and 2, respectively. These points were identified in our approach.

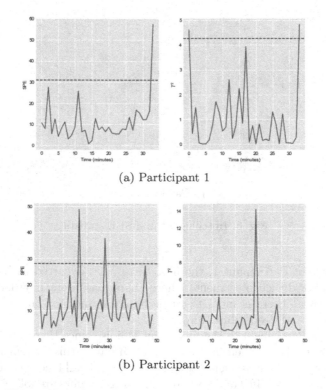

(a) Participant 1

(b) Participant 2

Fig. 7. SPE statistic considering one principal component.

In our proposed methodology, three principal components were implemented take into consideration the different HRV domains, this is, time, frequency, and non-linear. SPE and Hotelling T^2 statistics were computed for the three principal components, individually. Using this approach it was possible to identify five and eight points out-of-control, for Participant 1 and Participant 2, respectively.

The Participant 2 was the one that showed the most signs of drowsiness, to the point of falling asleep briefly. However, there were more peaks of drowsiness that were not identified using the proposed methodology. The same analysis was made for the others participants, where our approach detects more points out-of-control. Thus, the proposed methodology achieved promising results to detect more peaks of drowsiness, although it does not yet detect all the drowsiness peaks. Besides that, some points out-of-control were due to greater movement of the arms, for example, when it is necessary to turn left or right, in the city, or at freeway exits.

5 Conclusions and Future Works

The present work propose a new approach to detect signs of drowsiness, without labelling it manually, taking into consideration the HRV. A driving simulation was conducted, for one hour, where the participants used a wearable device, and their face was recorded to help identify signs of sleepiness. Four questionnaires were answered to identify possible sleep disorders, where most of the participants are healthy.

Using the R-R intervals, time, frequency, and non-linear domain variables were extracted, every two minutes. After this, three principal components were evaluated taking into account the division of the variables. Moreover, the Hotelling T^2 and SPE statistic for each principal component, separately, were computed, considering 95% confidence level. The proposed methodology presented promising results when compared with a similar study since it identified more signs of drowsiness.

Although, this study has some limitations. Some points out-of-control occurred due to major movements and caused noise in the signal. Moreover, there are signs of sleepiness that were not identified considering the proposed approach. Another limitation is that information from the participants' awake state was not used as a reference.

As future work, a new principal component can be added with the accelerometer information to identify the points caused by noise. Besides that, it is important to consider awake information and then apply the proposed methodology. Wherefore, it is essential to perform more simulations and add more measures to detect drowsiness. Moreover, the contribution plots must be performed and assessed to identify which features contribute to the out-of-control points.

References

1. Samouco, A.I., et al.: A Ciência do Sono - Da Fisiologia à (Psico)patologia. 1 ed. (2020)
2. Kortelainen, J.M., Mendez, M.O., Bianchi, A.M., Matteucci, M., Cerutti, S.: Sleep staging based on signals acquired through bed sensor. IEEE Trans. Inf Technol. Biomed. **14**(3), 776–785 (2010)
3. Higgins, J.S., et al.: Asleep at the wheel-the road to addressing drowsy driving. Sleep **40**(2) (2017)
4. Strine, T.W., Chapman, D.P.: Associations of frequent sleep insufficiency with health-related quality of life and health behaviors. Sleep Med. **6**(1), 23–27 (2005)

5. Altevogt, B.M., Colten, H.R., et al.: Sleep disorders and sleep deprivation: an unmet public health problem (2006)
6. Gonçalves, M., et al.: Sleepiness at the wheel across Europe: a survey of 19 countries. J. Sleep Res. **24**(3), 242–253 (2015)
7. Spurnỳ, P., Andrš, J., Bouchner, P., Pučelík, J., Rokyta, R.: Testing a system for predicting microsleep. Lékař a technika-Clinician and Technology **46**(2), 51–54 (2016)
8. Braga, A.C., et al.: Multivariate statistical process control based on principal component analysis: implementation of framework in R. In: Gervasi, O., et al. (eds.) ICCSA 2018. LNCS, vol. 10961, pp. 366–381. Springer, Cham (2018). https://doi.org/10.1007/978-3-319-95165-2_26
9. Fujiwara, K., et al.: Epileptic seizure prediction based on multivariate statistical process control of heart rate variability features. IEEE Trans. Biomed. Eng. **63**(6), 1321–1332 (2015)
10. Abe, E., Fujiwara, K., Hiraoka, T., Yamakawa, T., Kano, M.: Development of drowsiness detection method by integrating heart rate variability analysis and multivariate statistical process control. SICE J. Control, Measur. Syst. Integr. **9**(1), 10–17 (2016)
11. Åkerstedt, T., Gillberg, M.: Subjective and objective sleepiness in the active individual. Int. J. Neurosci. **52**(1–2), 29–37 (1990)
12. Åkerstedt, T., Anund, A., Axelsson, J., Kecklund, G.: Subjective sleepiness is a sensitive indicator of insufficient sleep and impaired waking function. J. Sleep Res. **23**(3), 242–254 (2014)
13. Sahayadhas, A., Sundaraj, K., Murugappan, M.: Detecting driver drowsiness based on sensors: a review (2012)
14. Liu, C.C., Hosking, S.G., Lenné, M.G.: Predicting driver drowsiness using vehicle measures: recent insights and future challenges. J. Saf. Res. **4**, 239–245 (2009)
15. Choudhary, P., Sharma, R., Singh, G., Das, S., et al.: A survey paper on drowsiness detection & alarm system for drivers. Int. Res. J. Eng. Technol. (IRJET) **3**(12), 1433–1437 (2016)
16. Fan, X., Yin, B.C., Sun, Y.F.: Yawning detection based on Gabor wavelets and LDA. Beijing Gongye Daxue Xuebao / J. Beijing Univ. Technol. (2009)
17. Yin, B.C., Fan, X., Sun, Y.F.: Multiscale dynamic features based driver fatigue detection. Int. J. Pattern Recogn. Artifi. Intell. **23**, 575–589 (2009)
18. Salles, A.F., et al.: Detecção automática de sonolência em condutores de veículos utilizando redes neurais artificiais (2018)
19. Khushaba, R.N., Kodagoda, S., Lal, S., Dissanayake, G.: Driver drowsiness classification using fuzzy wavelet-packet-based feature-extraction algorithm. IEEE Trans. Biomed. Eng. **58**, 121–131 (2011)
20. Kurt, M.B., Sezgin, N., Akin, M., Kirbas, G., Bayram, M.: The ANN-based computing of drowsy level. Expert Syst. Appl. **36**, 2534–2542 (2009)
21. Allen, J.: Photoplethysmography and its application in clinical physiological measurement. Physiol. Meas. **28**, 1–39 (2007)
22. Rundo, J.V., Downey, R.: Polysomnography. In: Handbook of Clinical Neurology, vol. 160 (2019)
23. Johns, M.W.: A new method for measuring daytime sleepiness: the Epworth sleepiness scale. Sleep **14**(6), 540–545 (1991)
24. Chung, F., Abdullah, H.R., Liao, P.: Stop-bang questionnaire: a practical approach to screen for obstructive sleep apnea. Chest **149**(3), 631–638 (2016)

25. Buysse, D.J., Reynolds, C.F., III., Monk, T.H., Berman, S.R., Kupfer, D.J.: The Pittsburgh sleep quality index: a new instrument for psychiatric practice and research. Psychiatry Res. **28**(2), 193–213 (1989)
26. Walker, M.: Why we sleep: unlocking the power of sleep and dreams (2017)
27. Horne, J.A., Östberg, O.: Individual differences in human circadian rhythms. Biol. Psychol. **5**(3), 179–190 (1977)
28. Ferrer, A.: Multivariate statistical process control based on principal component analysis (MSPC-PCA): some reflections and a case study in an autobody assembly process. Qual. Eng. **19**(4), 311–325 (2007)
29. MacGregor, J.F.: Using on-line process data to improve quality: challenges for statisticians. Int. Stat. Rev. **65**(3), 309–323 (1997)
30. Jackson, J.E., Mudholkar, G.S.: Control procedures for residuals associated with principal component analysis. Technometrics **21**(3), 341–349 (1979)
31. Alcala, C.F., Qin, S.J.: Analysis and generalization of fault diagnosis methods for process monitoring. J. Process Control **21**(3), 322–330 (2011)
32. Li, G., Chung, W.-Y.: A context-aware EEG headset system for early detection of driver drowsiness. Sensors **15**(8), 20873–20893 (2015)
33. Leng, L.B., Giin, L.B., Chung, W.-Y.: Wearable driver drowsiness detection system based on biomedical and motion sensors. In: 2015 IEEE SENSORS, pp. 1–4. IEEE (2015)
34. Akhter, N., Tharewal, S., Gite, H., Kale, K.: Microcontroller based RR-interval measurement using PPG signals for heart rate variability based biometric application. In: 2015 International Conference on Advances in Computing, Communications and Informatics (ICACCI), pp. 588–593. IEEE (2015)
35. Shaffer, F., Ginsberg, J.P.: An overview of heart rate variability metrics and norms. Frontiers in public health **5**, 258 (2017)
36. Pinheiro, N., et al.: Can PPG be used for HRV analysis? In: 2016 38th Annual International Conference of the IEEE Engineering in Medicine and Biology Society (EMBC), pp. 2945–2949. IEEE (2016)
37. Champseix, R., Ribiere, L., Le Couedic, C.: A python package for heart rate variability analysis and signal preprocessing. J. Open Res. Software **9**(1) (2021)
38. Van Rossum, G., Drake, F.L.: Python 3 Reference Manual. CreateSpace, Scotts Valley (2009)
39. McKinney, W., et al.: pandas: a foundational python library for data analysis and statistics. Python High Perform. Sci. Comput. **14**(9), 1–9 (2011)
40. Ari, N., Ustazhanov, M.: Matplotlib in python. In: 2014 11th International Conference on Electronics, Computer and Computation (ICECCO), pp. 1–6. IEEE (2014)
41. pca's documentation!. https://erdogant.github.io/pca/pages/html/index.html. Accessed 28 Mar 2022
42. Harris, C.R., et al.: Array programming with Numpy. Nature **585**(7825), 357–362 (2020)
43. Virtanen, P., et al.: Scipy 1.0: fundamental algorithms for scientific computing in python. Nat. Methods **17**(3), 261–272 (2020)

International Workshop
on Computational Approaches
for Smart, Conscious Cities (CASCC
2022)

Concepts and Challenges for 4D Point Clouds as a Foundation of Conscious, Smart City Systems

Ole Wegen[✉][iD], Jürgen Döllner, and Rico Richter

Hasso Plattner Institute, Prof.-Dr.-Helmert-Straße 2-3, 14482 Potsdam, Germany
{ole.wegen,juergen.doellner,rico.richter}@hpi.uni-potsdam.de
https://www.hpi.de

Abstract. Point clouds represent the as-is geometry of indoor and outdoor environments by sets of 3D points. They allow for constructing 3D models of objects, sites, cities, and landscapes and, hence, form the base data for almost any conscious, smart city system and application. For implementing such systems, we need a spatio-temporal data structure that enables efficient storage and access to 4D point clouds. In particular, the data structure should allow continuous updates, change tracking, and support for spatial and spatio-temporal analysis. This paper discusses challenges and approaches for a 4D point cloud data structure. In particular, the challenges arise from repeated scanning of environments in terms of sparsity, data redundancy, and geometric blurring of the corresponding point clouds. We outline a scheme for incremental storage of 4D point clouds via signed distance fields using a sparse, voxel-based representation. To efficiently implement analysis operations, we discuss how the data structure supports access based on both spatial and temporal criteria. In particular, we outline how machine learning-based interpretations used to classify point clouds and derive object-based information can work with the data structure.

Keywords: Point clouds · Spatio-temporal data · Smart city database

1 Introduction

The concept of smart city has been studied extensively in the last decades, but gained popularity recently due to the increase in inexpensive Internet of Things (IoT) devices. Smart cities build on the idea that "[...] cities are systems of systems, and that there are emerging opportunities to introduce digital nervous systems, intelligent responsiveness, and optimization at every level of system integration - from that of individual devices and appliances [...] to that of buildings, and ultimately to that of complete cities and urban regions" [20].

In this context, digital twins, as virtual representation of real-world objects, have been perceived as the "ultimate technological apparatus for 'smartening' cities" [35]. Such digital twins are tied together with their physical counterpart by means of data connections [8], enabling the monitoring, analysis, and control

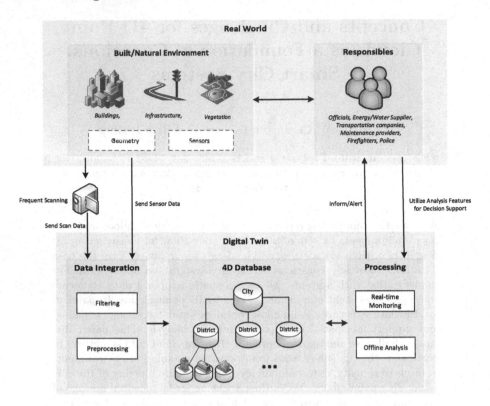

Fig. 1. Real-world data obtained by fixed sensors or frequent scanning of the environment is used to update the spatial data base. It reflects the state of the city in a hierarchical, object-structured manner. Real-time monitoring of the current state can inform responsible parties (e.g., if the breakout of a fire is detected, an unexpected increase in energy or water usage emerges, or failure of devices occur). Additionally, analysis features can operate on top of the database (e.g., for traffic flow monitoring or vegetation analysis).

of the corresponding object in the real world. Therefore, digital twins fulfill a key role in enabling future smart cities. Figure 1 depicts the integration of a digital twin into the city environment and existing responsibility structures.

The spatial representation of the geometric realities of physical objects is an important feature of the digital twin. Brilaikis *et al.* perceive this geometric information "as a starting point for a comprehensive digital twin" [3]. For constructing such virtual, spatial representation of cities and environments, 3D point clouds can serve as the base data, as they are a common artifact of as-is environment capturing of both indoor and outdoor scenes and there exist cost-efficient methods for acquiring them [21]. In general, 3D point clouds are unorganized, unstructured, but geo-referenced sets of points. Multiple 3D point clouds that share a common geographic extent, but were captured at different points in time (i.e., spatio-temporal datasets), are denoted 4D point clouds. The increasing degree of automation regarding the data acquisition and integration processes enables nowadays the capturing of such 4D point clouds by means of frequent environment scanning (e.g., using devices equipped with Light Detection and Ranging (LiDAR)-sensors or camera systems used to capture image data for photogrammetric point cloud creation). As 4D point clouds capture the history (i.e., changes over time) of the environment and provide the data used to derive object-related and structure-related information, they are the key component for constructing and maintaining a digital twin and operating conscious, smart city systems, services, or applications.

However, the question arises, how to store this massive, city-scale, spatio-temporal data, while at the same time enabling access for a broad range of analysis features, such as object or change detection, required for operating a smart city system. This work outlines the requirements and challenges for constructing a suitable data structure and proposes a first concept.

Section 2 reviews related work for smart cities, digital twins, and 4D point clouds. We then outline the key requirements and challenges for a spatio-temporal data structure in the context of smart cities in Sect. 3. Subsequently, we propose a scheme for storing 4D point cloud data via signed distance fields (Sect. 4) and describe the support for spatial and spatio-temporal access. Additionally, we outline how machine learning-based analysis approaches can work with the data structure. Finally, we conclude this work in Sect. 5.

2   Related Work

To understand the requirements for a spatio-temporal data structure in the context of smart cities, the application scenarios for smart cities, the use-cases and characteristics of digital twins, and the challenges connected to 4D point clouds are outlined in the following.

2.1   Smart Cities

The application scenarios for smart cities include real-time monitoring, process optimization, as well as intelligent responsiveness and control, across the whole city hierarchy from single buildings, over infrastructure networks, to whole urban areas. Key application areas of smart cities include energy, water, mobility, buildings, vegetation, and government [19] with use cases such as "enhanced street lighting controls, infrastructure monitoring, public safety and surveillance, physical security, gunshot detection, meter reading, and transportation analysis and optimization systems [...] on a city-wide scale". Ulusoy and Mundy describe "urban growth analysis, construction site monitoring, natural resource management, surveillance and event analysis" as common applications for 4D real-world data [34]. The direct relation of these applications to the smart city concept shows the importance of 4D data in this context. Daniel and Doran stress the importance of geomatics for smart cities. They state that "location is [...] core information" and the "geographical characteristics [...] and spatial understanding capabilities participate significantly in the design and operation of Smart

City service and management infrastructures" [6]. This emphasizes the need for geometric digital twins as key components of smart city systems.

2.2 Digital Twins

Table 1. Overview of use-cases and characteristics of digital twins, according to previous work in this area.

Publication	Characteristics	Use-cases
M. Grieves, 2014 [8]	Virtual objects linked to physical objects through data connections	Comprehension through conceptualization; Comparison of as-is and should-be; Collaboration
A. El Saddik, 2018 [7]	Seamless data transmission between physical and virtual world; Unique identifier for communication; Sensors and actuators on the real-world object; AI for intelligent decisions; Virtual representation	Monitor, understand, and optimize the functions of all physical entities to improve health and well-being
Qi *et al.* , 2018 [25]	Virtualization of physical entities; Ability to guide/optimize the phyiscal process	Virtual verification; Simulation; High-fidelity real-time monitoring; Predicting and diagnosing problems; Optimizing and improving processes
Brilakis *et al.* , 2019 [3]	Representation of current asset condition; Visualization of information and simulation results; Regular updates	Asset condition monitoring; Facility management and operation; Decision making; Sustainable developement
Wan *et al.* , 2019 [35]	Progressive developement; Machine learning techniques; Spatial/temporal resolution corresponding to use-case	Planning, constructing and managing national infrastructure; Optimising use of resources; Reducing service disruption; Increasing resilience; Boosting quality of life for citizens
Minerva *et al.* , 2020 [18]	Mirror the physical object; Register status changes; Store historic status changes; Simulate behaviour over time	Enabling virtual objects and smart cities

Grieves describes a concept of a digital twin for manufacturing, defining a digital twin as a three-part entity comprising the physical objects of the real world, the virtual objects in virtual space, and the data connections that links these two together [8]. Three use-cases for digital twins are presented: Comprehension is improved by eliminating inefficient mental steps through conceptualization, comparison between the as-is and the should-be state is facilitated, and collaboration becomes feasible due to a shared conceptualization. In smart manufacturing, the digital twin is described as "the virtualization of physical entities", guiding "the physical process to perform the optimized solution" [25]. In particular, the seamless data transmission between physical and virtual world is core feature of the digital twin concept, which El-Saddik extends to living beings with the goal to improve health and well-being [7]. In contrast, Khajavi et al. study the application of the digital twin concept to buildings [12]. Perceiving the developments in the area of IoT as the driving factor that enables the creation of digital twins, sensoric parts are considered as key components for operating a digital twin. For digital twin construction, geometric and structural information from a Building Information Model (BIM) is combined with a wireless sensor network and data analytics; for visualization, information extracted from the BIM or a custom 3D model is used. However, this is based on the assumption that the as-is geometry of the model still corresponds to the real-world situation; the changes over time are not considered. With respect to this, Brilakis et al. state that a digital twin "should be updated regularly in order to represent the current condition of the physical asset", enabling real-time monitoring [3]. Challenges for updating, maintaining, and operating geometric digital twins include occlusion during environment capturing, effective visualization of complex information and simulation results, and finding a lightweight, scalable, stable, and exchangeable geometric representation.

Several publications describe the applications and required characteristics of digital twins. Table 1 gives an overview of these, as described in literature. Especially the tight data connection between physical and virtual object is emphasized. Regular updates of the digital twin are required to mirror the state of the real world and to enable real-time asset monitoring. Process optimization and prediction/simulation for supporting decision making are also commonly stated use-cases.

Minerva et al. discuss basic properties of digital twins, including [18]:

- **Reflection:** A digital twin mirrors behaviour and status of the physical object.
- **Entanglement:** A digital twin is connected to the physical object to register status changes.
- **Memorization:** A digital twin stores all the historical status changes that occurred to the physical object.
- **Predictability:** A digital twin has the ability to simulate behaviour over time.

As spatial and georeferenced digital twins operate over time, underlying spatio-temporal data structures are essential system components for reflecting and memorizing changes, integrating continuous updates, and enabling simulation and analysis.

Regarding the boundary conditions for building city-level digital twins, "the spatial/temporal resolution of the digital twin should be informed by the purpose it serves" [35]. As digital twins serve multiple purposes, they require different spatial and temporal resolutions. To this end, spatio-temporal data structures should support Level-of-Detail (LoD).

2.3   4D Point Clouds

3D point clouds have become one of the most prominent geospatial data formats. Stojanovic *et al.* present a workflow for data acquisition to generate as-is BIM datasets, using regular 3D point cloud capturing to represent structural and spatial features of the environment [30]. However, "although the 3D point cloud is very practical, the huge data volume of a 3D point cloud limits its extensive applications" [15], that is, 3D point clouds always require post processing to be handled by applications or systems (e.g., compression or LoD).

The extension of 3D point clouds to the temporal domain, i.e., the capturing and reconstruction of the environment at different points in time, increases the data volume further. Thus, 4D point clouds are faced by massive storage requirements, in particular due to the high degree of redundancy leading to inefficient use of storage capacity, e.g., in scenarios where the environment changes only slightly between two points in time. Ulusoy *et al.* argue similarly that storing a 3D model in every timestamp "does not scale well in dealing with thousands of frames of data" [33] and Milani *et al.* state that dynamic point clouds are "highly inefficient in terms of storage space" [16]; This unanimous view of 4D point clouds in literature shows that storage and access issues become crucial for such data and a suitable data structure is urgently required. Additionally, visualizing such massive amounts of data is challenging and requires out-of-core approaches, as presented by Richter *et al.* for massive (city-scale) point clouds [27].

Apart from the storage issue, point clouds pose several other issues concerning noise levels (due to illumination, motion, and sensor noise), sparsity, and uneven distribution [4]. These issues can lead to inconsistent reconstruction of the same object at different timestamps and therefore impede 4D analysis, as the differentiation "between actual changes in the scene from false alarms caused by inconsistent reconstructions" is complicated [34].

To summarize, 4D point clouds as supposed to be the data basis for conscious, smart city models, are faced by a number of challenges:

- The huge overall data volume complicates efficient storage. Redundancy in the spatial and temporal domain is one part of this problem.
- The sparsity and uneven distribution of 3D points in each sample makes direct comparison of point clouds difficult, complicating analysis. Additionally, the implementation of incremental storage schemes for a more compact memory representation are also complicated.
- Inconsistencies due to error-prone acquisition and reconstruction processes as well as random noise hinder the analysis.
- The inability to control the LoD of a 4D point cloud meaningfully stands contrary to the fact that different analysis approaches require different LoD in the spatial or temporal domain. Storing multiple LoDs for point clouds

directly by removing high frequencies per level either involves a decrease in point cloud density, or an increase in memory consumption (e.g., smoothing the point cloud with different strength at each level and storing the results multiplies the required memory by the number of LoDs).

3 Challenges for Spatio-Temporal Data Structures

Based on the observations in Sect. 2, we now derive requirements and challenges for a 4D data structure in the context of smart cities. While some of the requirements complement each other, other requirements conflict. In practice, an appropriate trade-off between the different requirements has to be found, considering the concrete application scenario and use-cases.

3.1 Requirements and Challenges for a 4D Data Structure

Compact Memory Representation. A 4D data structure for smart city applications should be able to represent the current state, as well as past states, of physical objects. The spatial and temporal redundancy should be exploited for enabling a compact memory representation and reducing storage requirements. Incremental storage approaches are, however, faced with the challenge of geometric fuzziness and inconsistencies in the data.

High Spatial Scale and Sufficient Detail. As we are considering whole buildings, roads, and even cities, a data structure should be able to handle this high spatial scale. At the same time, sufficient detail is required, for the data to be useful for representing and analyzing the real world. This requirement stands in contrast to the compact memory representation. Out-of-core streaming approaches may be required to realize digital twin construction and operation on a city-wide scale. A corresponding data structure therefore has to be able to support this.

Fast Access. A data structure has to provide fast access in the spatial and temporal domain for real-time visualization, continuous monitoring, and efficient spatio-temporal analysis. Especially the task of change detection is one of the core tasks in the context of digital twins for smart city applications. Fast access often conflicts with a compact memory representation.

LoD Support. A data structure should support LoD approaches for access, as "the spatial/temporal resolution of the digital twin should be informed by the purpose it serves. [...] not all digital twins have to aim at real-time, nor the finest spatial unit of analysis. For city and infrastructure planning, the resolution of a digital twin model should be informed by the scale/rate of change of the policy question" [35]. Additionally, the hierarchical nature of the smart city has to be considered: buildings forming a site, sites forming a district, districts forming a city. Depending on the use-case, a different hierarchy level may be required.

Support for Offline Analysis. Tasks such as measuring key figures or optimizing processes through simulation and prediction build on (offline) analysis methods. For 4D point clouds, a broad range of analysis methods is already available. A data structure should support interoperability with these existing and well-working analysis approaches.

Fast Construction and Data Integration. A data structure should be able to integrate new data that is recorded from the real world on a regular basis in a fast manner. As near real-time monitoring is one of the use-cases for digital twins in smart city applications, the speed for integration of new data should be suitable for this task. The initial construction of the data structure does not necessarily need to be very fast, but it would be a beneficial trait.

Compression. If data is archived or should be transmitted over a network, the size of the data needs to be as small as possible; fast access is not required in these scenarios. For these use-cases, a data structure should support compression methods for reducing the size of the data.

Semantics. The data structure should be able to store point-specific attributes in addition to the geometric properties (i.e., point coordinates). These attributes could result from analysis and classification operations and can be used to access subsets of the point cloud belonging to a defined surface category (e.g., ground, building, vegetation, road). Further, such semantic classification can be used to separate dynamic objects, such as pedestrians or cars, from the static scene, which is an important task for meaningful change detection.

Graphics Processing Unit (GPU) Support. To enable efficient analysis on the data structure and real-time visualization of the data, GPU-based approaches are necessary. These require that the data structure is manageable on the GPU and that efficient streaming methods exist for loading the currently relevant parts of the data.

3.2   Existing Spatio-temporal Storage Approaches

Section 2 made clear that a huge problem of 4D point clouds, which are the common artifact of as-is environment capturing, is the high memory footprint. To reduce the storage requirements, compression methods have been proposed, which exploit the redundancy in the temporal domain. Most approaches use an octree, containing the voxelized point cloud, as intermediate representation for compression.

Thanou et al. present a compression scheme for dynamic point clouds, based on interpreting leaf nodes of an octree as graphs and position and color attributes as signals on the graph [32]. Queiroz and Chou present a lossy compression for dynamic point clouds using block-wise motion compensation [26]. A voxelized point cloud is split into blocks and each "block is either encoded in intra-frame mode or is replaced by a motion-compensated version of a block in the previous frame". Milani *et al.* presented a 4D point cloud compression scheme based on a voxelization and cellular automata transforms, tailored to the statistics of the data [16]. The MPEG have launched the standardization of point cloud compression in 2017. Liu *et al.* evaluate the proposed point cloud compression approaches in extensive experiments [15]. The results show that point cloud encoding can take several seconds or even minutes (for dynamic point clouds).

These compression methods have in common that a point cloud has to be decompressed again in order to access the single points. Therefore, while point cloud compression provides a solution to the high storage requirements, other challenges, such as fast data integration or fast data access, are not solved. Additionally, most of the compression methods were tested on scenes with low spatial extent.

With respect to the challenges of high spatial scale and sufficient detail, Blaha *et al.* proposed a hierarchical scheme for reconstruction of large scale scenes (whole cities). An implicit volumetric representation is used that supports variable volumetric resolution, refining the reconstruction adaptively only near surfaces in order to save memory while maintaining sufficient detail [1].

Regarding compact memory representation with fast data integration and access, Miller *et al.* presented an approach to reconstruct and dynamically update a 3D model from images [17]. They use a hybrid representation consisting of a regular grid and a shallow octree per grid cell. This data structure stores a probabilistic, volumetric representation of the 3D model, i.e., each cell stores the probability of being a surface "to represent the ambiguity in reconstruction of surface from images".

Based on the work of Miller *et al.* , Ulusoy and Mundy present an image-based method to update a reconstructed 3D model of a real-world object only when a change is detected in images at a later time [34]. "The resulting 4-d models allow visualization of the full history of the scene from novel viewpoints[...], as well as spatio-temporal analysis for applications such as tracking and event detection". They use the data structure proposed in their previous work [33]: a grid of octrees for spatial decomposition, and binary trees for modeling temporal variation per cell of the volumetric model. "This representation is shown to achieve compression of 4-d data and provide efficient spatio-temporal processing". The proposed data structure seems to fulfill many of the challenges described in Sect. 3.1. It provides a compact memory representation, fast spatio-temporal access, easy change detection, GPU support, and possibly efficient compression. Nevertheless, some challenges remain. Interoperability with existing approaches is not given and chunking the data along the temporal dimension (for out-of-core or LoD approaches) is difficult due to the nested structure. The scalability to city-level scenes and long timespans is also in question, as in their approach the tree depth is limited to enable fast GPU-based processing.

4   Concept for an Incremental Spatio-temporal Data Structure

In the following we describe the concept for a spatio-temporal data structure to be used for smart city applications. To provide a compact memory representation, the temporal redundancy has to be eliminated. Therefore, the basic idea is to store a base geometry G_0 for a timestamp t_0, while for each subsequent timestamp $t_i, i > 0$, only the changes C_i compared to the previous timestamp t_{i-1} are stored (similar to Laplacian pyramids for images). As change detection is an important task in the context of smart cities, storing the changes explicitly is advantageous for monitoring and analysis.

4.1   The Problem of Using Point Clouds

As described in Sect. 1, 4D point clouds serve as the key component for applications in the area of smart cities. However, using a point cloud as base representation for the proposed data structure is problematic, as calculating changes is not trivial for two point clouds due to missing point-to-point correspondences. Lague *et al.* describe three basic approaches for point cloud change detection [13]: Grid-based approaches, approaches based on intermediate representations (e.g., a local plane or a mesh), or direct pointcloud-to-pointcloud comparison. Additionally, they proposed the nowadays well-known M3C2 algorithm for change detection, which is based on measuring the mean surface change along the surface normal for a number of representative core points. Nevertheless, point cloud change detection is still an active field of research. In addition to the problem of computing changes for point clouds, the question arises, how to store these changes, especially if the number of points varies between point clouds from different timestamps.

In summary, 4D point clouds, while easy to acquire, may not be the most efficient way to store spatio-temporal data. This has been underlined as well by other research in this area [17,33]. We therefore propose, to use a voxel-based Signed Distance Function (SDF) representation that provides an interface for access similar to a point cloud and can also be converted back to a point cloud for faster processing, if necessary.

4.2   Voxel-Based, Signed Distance Field Representation

Point clouds are usually derived from LiDAR scans or RGB-D data. Using Truncated Signed Distance Field (TSDF) fusion, such data can also be used to reconstruct a voxel volume containing the signed distance to the surface for every voxel in vicinity to this surface [5,10]. These signed distance fields have some desirable properties.

In contrast to point clouds, they provide an implicit, continuous surface, mitigating problems that are related to the sparsity of point clouds (e.g., rendering closed surfaces or performing spatial scaling). Further, their regularity makes them easy to process, e.g., in the context of compression. Due to their regular nature, the distance values can be directly interpreted as signals on a 3D grid. Based on this, Jones presents a lossless compression method for distance fields [11]. Point clouds, on the other hand, have to construct intermediate data structures (e.g., octrees [15,16] or graphs [32]). The advantage of the regularity of distance fields, e.g., for compression purposes, is also underlined by the fact that Laney et al. use a distance field as intermediate representation for mesh compression [14]. Additionally, the regularity of distance fields leads to the fact that they can be subtracted from each other, which is a useful property for incremental storage approaches that exploit the temporal redundancy of the data.

We therefore propose to use a TSDF volume as base representation in our data structure. However, storing the full voxel grid is memory inefficient, especially in light of the fact that a change C_i might only contains few relevant voxel cells. A sparse representation of the TSDF is therefore key to a compact storage format. Niessner et al. presented a spatial hashing approach for TSDFs, with a special focus on GPU-based, real-time reconstruction from depth data [22]. Their approach is well suited for sparse voxel grids that have to be updated very often. This hash-based approach seems to be suitable as a base data structure in the context of smart cities. It was developed for GPU-based processing, providing a compact memory representation through a sparse voxel structure, without the overhead of hierarchical structures. Fast access is achieved by means of a hash table, scalability in the spatial domain is ensured by out-of-core streaming.

We therefore propose to use such a hash-based approach for storing TSDFs, representing the base geometry implicitly as a sparse field of distances. The changes can also be stored in the form of TSDFs, understood as distance fields in the temporal domain. Attributes, such as the color or semantic class, can also be derived from RGB-D images or point clouds and stored in the data structure for each voxel (in addition to the signed distance). Figure 2 gives an overview of our proposed data structure.

4.3   Concept for Data Integration

We now describe how new scan data can be integrated, using the proposed data structure. Given a base geometry G_0 and changes up to this point $C_1, ..., C_i$, all of them represented as TSDFs. Data recorded for timestamp t_{i+1} can be integrated in the following way:

1. **Calculate TSDF for timestamp** t_{i+1}: Calculate G_{i+1} directly from LiDAR or RGB-D data for best results. Alternatively, a TSDF can be deducted from a point cloud, e.g., using Jump Flooding [28] or neural approaches [23].
2. **Retrieve TSDF for** t_i: To retrieve TSDF G_i, accumulate the changes up to timestamp t_i:

$$G_i = G_0 + \sum_{n=1}^{i} C_n. \tag{1}$$

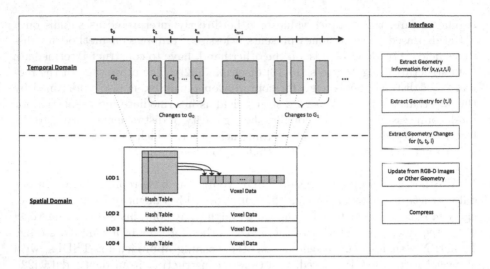

Fig. 2. Conceptual overview of the proposed spatio-temporal data structure. In the temporal domain, only changes to a base geometry are stored. For faster access, full geometry representations are stored in regular intervals. Each geometry or change is represented as a TSDF with different resolutions (LoDs), stored using a hashing approach for compact memory representation. The geometry can be updated using RGB-D images or other geometry representations (e.g., point clouds). This data structure enables the access of single points at any timepoint and LoD, as well as the export of the geometry at any timestamp t_i. Additionally, the changes at different LoDs can be inspected for analysis purposes. The TSDFs can be compressed easily (e.g., using wavelet transforms).

3. **Compute changes for** t_{i+1} : $C_{i+1} = G_{i+1} - G_i$. It has to be ensured that the spatial extent of both geometries is equal. Cases have to be handled, where voxels contain distance values in G_{i+1} but not in G_i or vice versa.

As two scans are never exactly the same, even if nothing has changed in the scene, approaches have to be developed to avoid storing "changes" that are none. A (local) threshold-based approach could be used, where the amount of change is measured and the change is only stored if it exceeds the threshold. However, it has to be considered that some things change slowly over time, e.g., plants.

To facilitate LoD approaches, the base geometry and the changes $C_1 \ldots C_n$ can also be stored in different granularity levels (TSDF resolutions). Similar to storing only the changes to the previous timestamp in the temporal domain, we store in the spatial domain for each LoD the change to the previous LoD. To obtain a representation for a specific LoD, the different levels have to be summed. The memory impact and the access times (especially for higher LoDs) for such an approach would have to be investigated.

4.4 Concept for Spatio-temporal Access

Access in the spatial domain is achieved by means of a hash table, as described in [22]. Access in the temporal domain, requires accumulation of changes up to a certain timestamp. To access the distance value stored at a voxel $v_i = (x, y, z, t_i)$, the changes to this voxel have to be accumulated:

$$v_i = v_0 + \sum_{n=1}^{i} v_n. \tag{2}$$

The performance of this accumulation of changes is dependent on the access performance of the underlying spatial data structure that is used for storing the TSDFs.

A high resolution in the temporal domain could lead to decreased access performance, as possibly a lot of changes have to be accumulated. This problem can be mitigated by storing a full representation every x timestamps and calculating v_i as:

$$v_i = v_a + \sum_{n=a+1}^{i} v_n, \text{ with } a = \left\lfloor \frac{i}{x} \right\rfloor * x. \tag{3}$$

Alternatively, multiple changes could be squashed into one change representation after a certain valid-time for the recorded data has been exceeded.

4.5 Support for Machine Learning

Machine learning is a fundamental building block for smart cities. "The advancement of data science, particularly the machine learning techniques, will complement existing theories of cities and infrastructure and jointly contribute to the essential knowledge for developing digital twins" [35]. Thus, a data structure has to support existing machine learning approaches.

Camuffo et al. give a comprehensive overview of deep learning approaches for point clouds in the areas of semantic scene understanding, compression, and completion. Additionally, they introduce typical data structures, acquisition approaches, and common point cloud data sets [4]. "When dealing with deep learning algorithms, point clouds are usually not the most suitable data structure to process. Thus, the input data are frequently subject to transformations that allow them to satisfy the specific needs of the architecture" [4]. Deep learning approaches either operate

- **Discretization-based:** The point cloud is transformed into a discrete structure, such as a voxel grid or an octree (e.g., SEGCloud [31], LatticeNet [29]).
- **Projection-based:** The point cloud is remapped to a simpler structure, such as multiview images, a sphere, or a cylinder (e.g., SnapNet [2], SqueezeSeg [36]).
- **Point cloud-based:** The neural net directly processes the points (e.g., PointNet [24], RandLA-Net [9]).

Using the proposed TSDF-based storage format, all of these deep learning input formats can be derived. A point cloud can be computed in a preprocessing step by retrieving the distance value for each surface voxel for a timestamp, computing the surface normals using central differences, and deriving the corresponding surface points. If no preprocessing should take place, the points can also be directly accessed without prior conversion to the full geometry. This involves, however, distance value accesses and normal calculation, every time a point is accessed. The ability to convert from TSDFs to point clouds and vice versa ensures the interoperability with existing analysis approaches. While the derived point cloud can then be converted to the other input formats, it is also possible to directly use the TSDF-based representation. As the proposed data structure is already regular and discrete it can be used directly for discretization-based approaches. However, for some deep learning approaches it might be required to convert the distances to occupancies and arrange the voxels in a hierarchical data structure. The TSDF-based data structure can also be used for projection, using ray marching methods. As a TSDF provides a continuous surface, the problem of holes, when using point clouds, is mitigated.

5   Conclusions

This work presented the digital twin as one of the key components for smart city applications. Such digital twin is the basis for real-time monitoring and offline analysis of the physical world. Therefore, it has to reflect the current status of the physical object, memorize the state changes, and offer functionality for simulation and prediction.

We focused on exploring the boundary conditions, requirements, and challenges of a data structure for spatio-temporal data in this context. We derived these requirements and challenges from the applications and characteristics of digital twins for use in smart city systems. Providing a high spatial scale and sufficient detail, while maintaining a compact memory representation is one of the main challenges for such a data structure. Further, fast access and LoD support for GPU-based analysis approaches is required. New data has to be integrated efficiently and existing analysis methods should be able to operate on the data structure. Compression approaches are useful for archiving and transmission of data.

These requirements should be considered, when searching for a data structure that is suited for the spatio-temporal data that we have to store and process for enabling smart cities.

While 4D point clouds are commonly used in the context of digital twins, as they are a typical artifact of environment scanning, they come with high storage requirements and deficiencies regarding LoD approaches. We therefore proposed to use a TSDF-based data structure, using an incremental storage scheme for exploiting redundancy in the temporal domain. The data structure has the following advantages:

– In comparison to storing single point clouds for each timestamp, the memory requirements are reduced by only storing changes to a base geometry.

This base geometry is represented as a TSDF using a hash-based approach, facilitating further compression.

- High spatial scale and high detail is supported by using a sparse distance field and disentangling the spatial and temporal domain, facilitating out-of-core approaches.
- Fast access is facilitated by avoiding deep hierarchical data structures.
- Interoperability with existing approaches is ensured as direct access to point data or conversion to other geometry representations is possible.
- LoD approaches for adapting to different resolution requirements are enabled by decomposing the geometry into different spatial granularities.
- Explicitly storing the changes over time, enables efficient change detection, which is one of the main tasks for a digital twin in the context of smart cities.

The presented data structure is to be understood as a first proposal and conceptual step towards developing a base data structure for smart city applications. In the future, it has to be tested thoroughly and the performance with respect to the presented requirements, different data acquisition techniques, and different application domains has to be studied in more detail.

Acknowledgements. We thank the anonymous reviewers for their valuable feedback. This work was partially supported by the Federal Ministry of Education and Research (BMBF), Germany (PunctumTube, 01IS18090) and by the Federal Ministry for Digital and Transport (BMDV), Germany (TWIN4ROAD, 19F2210).

References

1. Blaha, M., Vogel, C., Richard, A., Wegner, J.D., Pock, T., Schindler, K.: Large-scale semantic 3d reconstruction: An adaptive multi-resolution model for multi-class volumetric labeling. In: 2016 IEEE Conference on Computer Vision and Pattern Recognition, pp. 3176–3184. IEEE Computer Society (2016). https://doi.org/10.1109/CVPR.2016.346
2. Boulch, A., Guerry, J., Saux, B.L., Audebert, N.: Snapnet: 3d point cloud semantic labeling with 2d deep segmentation networks. Comput. Graph. **71**, 189–198 (2018). https://doi.org/10.1016/j.cag.2017.11.010
3. Brilakis, I., et al.: Built environment digtial twinning. Technical report, International Workshop on Built Environment Digital Twinning presented by TUM Institute for Advanced Study and Siemens AG (2019)
4. Camuffo, E., Mari, D., Milani, S.: Recent advancements in learning algorithms for point clouds: an updated overview. Sensors **22**(4) (2022). https://doi.org/10.3390/s22041357
5. Curless, B., Levoy, M.: A volumetric method for building complex models from range images. In: Proceedings of the 23rd Annual Conference on Computer Graphics and Interactive Techniques, SIGGRAPH 1996, pp. 303–312. Association for Computing Machinery (1996). https://doi.org/10.1145/237170.237269
6. Daniel, S., Doran, M.A.: Geosmartcity: geomatics contribution to the smart city. In: Proceedings of the 14th Annual International Conference on Digital Government Research, dg.o '13, pp. 65–71. Association for Computing Machinery (2013). https://doi.org/10.1145/2479724.2479738

7. El-Saddik, A.: Digital twins: the convergence of multimedia technologies. IEEE Multim. **25**(2), 87–92 (2018). https://doi.org/10.1109/MMUL.2018.023121167
8. Grieves, M.: Digital twin: manufacturing excellence through virtual factory replication. White paper **1**, 1–7 (2014)
9. Hu, Q., et al.: Randla-net: Efficient semantic segmentation of large-scale point clouds. In: 2020 IEEE/CVF Conference on Computer Vision and Pattern Recognition, CVPR 2020, pp. 11105–11114. Computer Vision Foundation/IEEE (2020). https://doi.org/10.1109/CVPR42600.2020.01112
10. Izadi, S., et al.: Kinectfusion: real-time 3d reconstruction and interaction using a moving depth camera. In: Pierce, J.S., Agrawala, M., Klemmer, S.R. (eds.) Proceedings of the 24th Annual ACM Symposium on User Interface Software and Technology, pp. 559–568. ACM (2011). https://doi.org/10.1145/2047196.2047270
11. Jones, M.W.: Distance field compression. In: The 12-th International Conference in Central Europe on Computer Graphics, Visualization and Computer Vision'2004, WSCG 2004, pp. 199–204 (2004)
12. Khajavi, S.H., Motlagh, N.H., Jaribion, A., Werner, L.C., Holmström, J.: Digital twin: vision, benefits, boundaries, and creation for buildings. IEEE Access **7**, 147406–147419 (2019). https://doi.org/10.1109/ACCESS.2019.2946515
13. Lague, D., Brodu, N., Leroux, J.: Accurate 3d comparison of complex topography with terrestrial laser scanner: Application to the rangitikei canyon (n-z). ISPRS J. Photogramm. Remote. Sens. **82**, 10–26 (2013). https://doi.org/10.1016/j.isprsjprs.2013.04.009
14. Laney, D.E., Bertram, M., Duchaineau, M.A., Max, N.L.: Multiresolution distance volumes for progressive surface compression. In: 1st International Symposium on 3D Data Processing Visualization and Transmission (3DPVT 2002), pp. 470–479. IEEE Computer Society (2002). https://doi.org/10.1109/TDPVT.2002.1024102
15. Liu, H., Yuan, H., Liu, Q., Hou, J., Liu, J.: A comprehensive study and comparison of core technologies for MPEG 3-d point cloud compression. IEEE Trans. Broadcast. **66**(3), 701–717 (2020). https://doi.org/10.1109/TBC.2019.2957652
16. Milani, S., Polo, E., Limuti, S.: A transform coding strategy for dynamic point clouds. IEEE Trans. Image Process. **29**, 8213–8225 (2020). https://doi.org/10.1109/TIP.2020.3011811
17. Miller, A., Jain, V., Mundy, J.L.: Real-time rendering and dynamic updating of 3-d volumetric data. GPGPU-4. Association for Computing Machinery (2011). https://doi.org/10.1145/1964179.1964190
18. Minerva, R., Crespi, N.: Digital twins: properties, software frameworks, and application scenarios. IT Prof. **23**(1), 51–55 (2021). https://doi.org/10.1109/MITP.2020.2982896
19. Minoli, D., Sohraby, K., Occhiogrosso, B.: Iot considerations, requirements, and architectures for smart buildings - energy optimization and next-generation building management systems. IEEE Internet Things J. **4**(1), 269–283 (2017). https://doi.org/10.1109/JIOT.2017.2647881
20. Mitchell, W.J.: Smart cities: Vision. https://smartcities.media.mit.edu/frameset.html. Accessed 11 May 2022
21. Nebiker, S., Bleisch, S., Christen, M.: Rich point clouds in virtual globes - a new paradigm in city modeling? Comput. Environ. Urban Syst. **34**(6), 508–517 (2010). https://doi.org/10.1016/j.compenvurbsys.2010.05.002
22. Nießner, M., Zollhöfer, M., Izadi, S., Stamminger, M.: Real-time 3d reconstruction at scale using voxel hashing. ACM Trans. Graph. **32**(6), 169:1–169:11 (2013). https://doi.org/10.1145/2508363.2508374

23. Park, J.J., Florence, P., Straub, J., Newcombe, R.A., Lovegrove, S.: Deepsdf: Learning continuous signed distance functions for shape representation. In: IEEE Conference on Computer Vision and Pattern Recognition, CVPR 2019, pp. 165–174. Computer Vision Foundation/IEEE (2019). https://doi.org/10.1109/CVPR.2019.00025

24. Qi, C.R., Su, H., Mo, K., Guibas, L.J.: Pointnet: deep learning on point sets for 3d classification and segmentation. In: 2017 IEEE Conference on Computer Vision and Pattern Recognition, CVPR 2017. pp. 77–85. IEEE Computer Society (2017). https://doi.org/10.1109/CVPR.2017.16

25. Qi, Q., Tao, F.: Digital twin and big data towards smart manufacturing and industry 4.0: 360 degree comparison. IEEE Access 6, 3585–3593 (2018). https://doi.org/10.1109/ACCESS.2018.2793265

26. de Queiroz, R.L., Chou, P.A.: Motion-compensated compression of dynamic voxelized point clouds. IEEE Trans. Image Process. 26(8), 3886–3895 (2017). https://doi.org/10.1109/TIP.2017.2707807

27. Richter, R., Discher, S., Döllner, J.: Out-of-Core Visualization of Classified 3D Point Clouds, pp. 227–242. Springer International Publishing, Cham (2015). https://doi.org/10.1007/978-3-319-12181-9_14

28. Rong, G., Tan, T.S.: Jump flooding in gpu with applications to voronoi diagram and distance transform, vol. 2006, pp. 109–116, January 2006. https://doi.org/10.1145/1111411.1111431

29. Rosu, R.A., Schütt, P., Quenzel, J., Behnke, S.: Latticenet: fast point cloud segmentation using permutohedral lattices. In: Toussaint, M., Bicchi, A., Hermans, T. (eds.) Robotics: Science and Systems XVI, Virtual Event (2020). https://doi.org/10.15607/RSS.2020.XVI.006

30. Stojanovic, V., Trapp, M., Richter, R., Hagedorn, B., Döllner, J.: Towards the generation of digital twins for facility management based on 3d point clouds. In: 34th Annual ARCOM Conference, pp. 270–279 (2018)

31. Tchapmi, L.P., Choy, C.B., Armeni, I., Gwak, J., Savarese, S.: Segcloud: Semantic segmentation of 3d point clouds. In: 2017 International Conference on 3D Vision, 3DV 2017, pp. 537–547. IEEE Computer Society (2017). https://doi.org/10.1109/3DV.2017.00067

32. Thanou, D., Chou, P.A., Frossard, P.: Graph-based compression of dynamic 3d point cloud sequences. Trans. Img. Proc. 25(4), 1765–1778 (2016). https://doi.org/10.1109/TIP.2016.2529506

33. Ulusoy, A.O., Biris, O., Mundy, J.L.: Dynamic probabilistic volumetric models. In: IEEE International Conference on Computer Vision, ICCV 2013, pp. 505–512. IEEE Computer Society (2013). https://doi.org/10.1109/ICCV.2013.68

34. Ulusoy, A.O., Mundy, J.L.: Image-based 4-d reconstruction using 3-d change detection. In: Fleet, D., Pajdla, T., Schiele, B., Tuytelaars, T. (eds.) ECCV 2014. LNCS, vol. 8691, pp. 31–45. Springer, Cham (2014). https://doi.org/10.1007/978-3-319-10578-9_3

35. Wan, L., Nochta, T., Schooling, J.: Developing a city-level digital twin - propositions and a case study. In: International Conference on Smart Infrastructure and Construction 2019, ICSIC 2019: Driving Data-Informed Decision-Making, pp. 187–193 (01 2019). https://doi.org/10.1680/icsic.64669.187

36. Wu, B., Wan, A., Yue, X., Keutzer, K.: Squeezeseg: Convolutional neural nets with recurrent CRF for real-time road-object segmentation from 3d lidar point cloud. In: 2018 IEEE International Conference on Robotics and Automation, ICRA 2018, pp. 1887–1893. IEEE (2018). https://doi.org/10.1109/ICRA.2018.8462926

A Conscious, Smart Site Model
for a Solar-Water Energy System

S. Merino[1]([⊠]) [ID], F. Guzmán[2] [ID], J. Martínez[1] [ID], R. Guzmán[3] [ID], J. Lara[2] [ID],
and J. Döllner[4]

[1] Department of Applied Mathematics, University of Málaga, 29071 Málaga, Spain
smerino@uma.es
[2] Department of Electrical Engineering, University of Málaga, 29071 Málaga, Spain
[3] Department of Design and Projects, University of Málaga, 29071 Málaga, Spain
[4] Hasso Plattner Institute, Prof.-Dr.-Helmert-Straße 2-3, 14482 Potsdam, Germany

Abstract. This paper proposes a global model of sustainable desalination in the hydrological context of any river with a reservoir close to the sea. For this purpose, a desalination plant is installed, located on the coast, which transports the pumped water using the course of the river itself and discharges it directly into the reservoir. The concept of sustainability lies in the fact that the energy required to provide for the entire process is obtained by means of a floating photovoltaic park located in the reservoir. The electrical energy generated by this park provides a self-consumption solution for both the desalination plant and the pumping stations, either by injecting and balancing its energy into the electrical grid or directly to the desalination plant. In addition, as a remarkable product in the desalination process, various derivatives are obtained and the project becomes a source of green hydrogen.

Keywords: Sustainable desalination system · Floating photovoltaic park ·
Circular economy · Green hydrogen

1 Water+S Project

1.1 Introduction

This paper proposes the application of a sustainable desalination cycle in the hydrological context of the Vélez river and the Viñuela reservoir in the municipality of Vélez-Málaga.

The first part of the project requires obtaining desalinated water from the sea. For this purpose, a desalination plant is installed at the mouth of the Vélez river, which discharges the pumped water, using the course of the same river, directly into the reservoir of the Viñuela.

The concept of sustainability lies in the fact that the energy needed to power the entire process would be obtained by means of a floating photovoltaic park located in the reservoir itself (taking into account all the biological parameters necessary for it to have no ecological impact). The electrical energy generated in this park would be justified by the self-consumption of the desalination plant and the pumping stations, but it would inject energy into the electricity supply network which would provide energy to users in the area and could even be sized for greater production. In practice, both the desalination plant and the pumping stations would be directly supplied from the general electricity grid, but free of charge, as the same energy would be injected into the system from the photovoltaic plant.

Currently, there are numerous examples of separate installations that follow the presented design, but it has never been considered to combine these models in a joint way, in a way that works with the sustainability concept of the desalination system. Therefore, this proposal would be pioneering at world level, from the technological point of view, and totally replicable in any of the river basins that have a reservoir, close to the coast, from which drinking water is distributed for both irrigation and human consumption.

1.2 Project Advantages

This project is proposed because it is of great benefit to all stakeholders involved in the project:

a. Firstly, it will ensure the supply of water to the Viñuela rteservoir, regardless of the rainfall contribution in the area.
b. It will make possible to generate a significant amount of electricity (up to 500 MWh), using renewable energy and without the need to occupy land that can be used for other purposes. In practice, much more energy will be generated globally than is necessary for the operation of the system, making it a very attractive project for the provision of electricity to the general grid.
c. As it has been designed as a modular project, starting from a base corresponding to the production of 10 Hm^3 of water per year, it can be expanded according to the needs that are observed and does not require a gigantic dimensioning from the beginning.
d. At no time is private land used to locate any of the facilities, so no land expropriation would be necessary.
e. The water brought into the reservoir basin will be mixed with the water collected there, so it will not be necessary to mineralise it and, furthermore, it will be channelled through the existing distribution network, so there will be no need to install additional pipelines.
f. Control of the quantity of water stored in the reservoir will ensure the supply to the irrigation network in the area, thus enabling the agro-industrial development of the area without the problem of restrictions that could endanger it.
g. The desalination process under evaluation will allow the production of brine by-products (such as hydrogen, hydrochloric acid and sodium hydroxide).

1.3 Current Situation

Over the last few decades, the agricultural development of the Axarquía region (Málaga) has been exponential. The introduction of subtropical fruits and their confluence with a climate and land adapted to them, has meant the creation of an economic growth pole for Spain. Today, tens of thousands of jobs have been generated and many hectares of productive land that make up a strategic value chain, which has turned this area into one of the richest in Europe. But like all wealth it has its own Achilles' heel, which is the scarcity of water in the area.

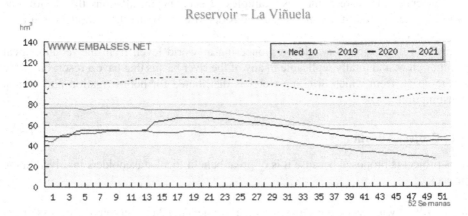

It is hard to believe that a place bathed by the Mediterranean Sea would have water problems on such a scale as those suffered by Axarquía today. Certainly, the solution is a rainfall increase, but humans are not yet capable of generating the rainfall they want to recharge the Viñuela reservoir:

Dammed Water (14-12-2021)	28 hm³	16.97 %
Change previous week	-1 hm³	-0.61 %
Capacity:	165 hm³	
Same Week (2020):	45 hm³	27.27 %
Same Week (Med. 10 Years):	90 hm³	54.55 %

Therefore, more imagination is required in these scarcity moments and that is why the team formed by the **Agrarian Society of Transformation "Trops"** and the **Andalusian Institute of Domotic and Energy Efficiency** propose a solution that is firmly in line with the requirements of the European projects.

1.4 Previous Technical Data Assessed on the Proposed Project

Characteristics of the Viñuela reservoir:

- Area: 565 Ha (5,565,000 m²)
- Water capacity: 170 Hm³
- Current water consumption for irrigation: 20 Hm³/annual

- Volume of storage water (as of 10/12/2021): 28,60 Hm^3
- Daily flow required: 54,794 m^3

The use of the reservoir area should not exceed 30% in order not to influence the food chain. Therefore, the total surface area of photovoltaic panels to be installed could be around 1,669,500 m^2.

It has been demonstrated that floating photovoltaic installations [5] have a 20% higher yield than those located on land. Therefore, considering an output of 350 W/m^2, the potential generation of electrical energy that could be obtained in case of maximum use (which is not our case) in the installation would be of

$$1.669.500 \times 350 = 584.325.000 \, \text{KWh} = 584,325 \, \text{MWh}$$

the daily light cycle will of course have to be considered.
Total current water needs would amount to some

$$54.794 * 365 = 19.999.810 \, \text{m}^3 \cong 20 \, Hm^3$$

According to studies and internationally collected data in desalination plants already in operation, it is estimated that between 3 and 6 KWh are required per m^3 desalinated and pumped. Therefore, we consider that the following are required

$$54.794 \, \text{m}^3 * 6 \, \text{KWh} = 328.764 \, KWh/day$$

Given that the proposed operation involves the continuous pumping of water 24 h a day (the system is supplied from the general electricity grid), the desalination plant will be dimensioned in the most efficient and energy-efficient way so that it can generate a flow capable of covering the proposed needs.

The electrical power to be installed in the photovoltaic plant can be estimated according to the specifications to be supplied into the grid, but it must always be sized to exceed 328.764 MWh/day during the hours of sunshine.

1.5 Proposed Solution

This solution proposes the establishment of three coordinated infrastructures:

1. Floating Solar Photovoltaic Plant: the richness of the agricultural land in the area provides this innovative solution for supplying the energy required for desalination. The floating plants already existing in various places on our planet allow high quality electricity generation on the water, given the permanent stability of both its liquid surface and its average temperature. On the other hand, they protect the reservoir itself from the proliferation of algae that must be removed for human consumption and from atmospheric pollution that may fall on its surface.

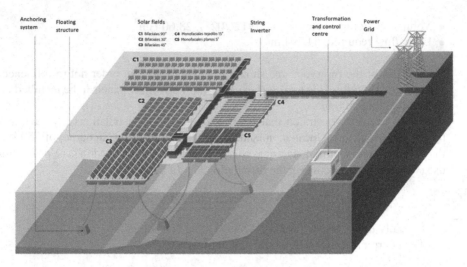

2. Pumping stations network: necessary to pump the desalinated water through the course of the Vélez River until it is discharged into the reservoir. This network is sized according to the quantity of water to be pumped, the density it has according to its desalination quality and the distance it travels.

3. Desalination Plant: located near the sea, it would be responsible for desalinating the amount of water necessary to recharge the Viñuela reservoir, this water finally being mixed with water from peripheral rivers and streams. This plant would generate a quantity of brine that would allow a parallel industry for the creation of hydrogen, salt, chlorine and other chemical derivatives of commercial interest.

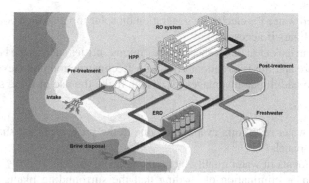

The development of such a project meets several of the most important indicators for European projects:

1. The solar energy production and the citizens' consumption are synchronous, i.e. both coincide in the peak hours of electricity consumption in our industries and cities. Therefore, this production is the most favourable for the economic interests of all citizens, by providing sources that can reduce the energy price.
2. Solar energy production and desalinated water generation are asynchronous, i.e. desalination can be contracted during the hours of lowest energy prices, thus minimizing operating costs.
3. The energy generation and water desalination system matches to the circular economy [8], generating a zero consumption loop and maintaining the electricity grids and the global energy balance stability.
4. Brine generation would be incorporated into the actions proposed by the European Sea4Value project, which analyses the maximum industrial use of the by-products generated. On the other hand, and thanks to the advances made in recent months in the field of seawater hydrolysis, we are faced with a great source of hydrogen production [9], compatible with the Spanish and European objectives for this energy source.

2 Floating Photovoltaic Plant

2.1 Introduction

Open floating photovoltaic systems offer new possibilities for expanding the capacity to generate electricity using the solar energy. They have many advantages over land-based installations, both economically and in terms of infrastructure, as they have shown up to 20% higher energy yields compared with them (thanks to the dust absence, solar reflection on the water surface and the cooling of the panels due to the water effect), and it is possible to use existing electricity transmission networks in hydroelectric environments (very close to the demand centres) as a means of evacuating the energy generated [4].

This system was initially proposed to reinforce the existing hydroelectric power plants production, normally at the reservoirs foot, to boost their energy yield and help to manage low water availability periods, and even to use this input to condition the need to use stored water for electricity generation on solar input (which could be restricted to night-time hours if necessary).

Work carried out in this respect by prestigious entities such as the National University of Singapore and the International Bank for Reconstruction and Development in 2019, have shown additional advantages [7], which make the use of these systems advisable, such as:

- reduced water reservoirs evaporation due to the protection and shading provided by the solar panels
- improvements in water quality by reducing algae growth
- reduction or elimination of shading that the surrounding plants and terrain could produce on the panels
- elimination of the significant site preparation need (ground levelling, foundations, etc.) compared to land-based installation
- easiness of installation and deployment at sites with low anchoring and mooring requirements as well as a high degree of modularity, leading to faster installations.

The capital costs of floating systems are like those of onshore installations, although they are expected to decrease due to greater scale economies. In 2018 they ranged from €0.7 to €1 per Wp installed, depending on project location, reservoir basin depth and system size [6].

2.2   International Benchmarks for the Implementation of These Technologies

The first FPV system was built in 2007 in Aichi (Japan), followed by several other countries including France, Italy, Korea, Spain and the United States. All of these were for research and demonstration purposes. The first commercial installation took place in 2008 in California (USA) with 175 kW capacity, when the FPV market grew worldwide. By 2020 more than 60 countries implemented these power plants, of which 35 were in operation generating around 2.6 GW of global capacity. The fast increase in the number of these installations reinforces their attractiveness.

The World Bank estimates that by using only 5% of the available surface area of water reservoirs in Latin America, it would be possible to install more than 180 GW of floating solar power, equivalent to the total installed generation capacity of hydroelectric power plants.

The Inter-American Development Bank (IDB) is currently supporting the FPV development in Suriname with a Technical Cooperation funded by Japan Special Funds to study the feasibility of integrating these systems into the Afobaka hydroelectric power plant (which generates 50% of the total electricity consumed in the country). Electricity supply in Suriname is critical during the dry seasons' peak periods, coinciding with the hottest and sunniest periods of the year, also the air conditioning consumption in buildings tends to be higher.

This project will help to supply electricity during these peaks and optimize the management of water resources to hold reserves at critical times. The FPV system can be connected to the same transmission line from the hydropower plant, managing both solar and hydroelectric power generation in an integrated and optimal way for the grid.

The Technical Cooperation will also analyse the value chain for the supply, installation, operation and maintenance (O&M) of the project and propose recommendations to increase local content and create new local jobs.

According to Energies Market Research (2019), FPV systems are expected to continue to grow and become established in the market, generating between 4 and 10 GW in the next five years.

If countries are truly interested in accelerating the decarbonisation agenda, all technically and economically feasible options should be considered, and VPPs have the potential in Andalusia for a solid contribution to that common goal.

2.3 National Benchmarks for the Implementation of These Technologies

In Spain, experiences with these technologies can be seen, for example, in the Sierra Brava reservoir (Caceres), which for weeks now has housed 3,000 solar panels on the water with an output of 1.1 MW of electricity. The installation expands for 12,000 m^2 within the more than 1,600 hectares of the reservoir, which represents around 0.08% of its surface area. The plant is divided into five zones in which different inclination degrees of the panels and floating systems on the water are tested. The data collected will be used for future installations.

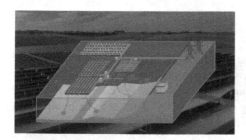 

The platform's anchoring system consists of a network of 74 ropes that anchor the platform to the bottom of the reservoir, attached to concrete blocks. The pandemic paralyzed the installation of the plant, which began at the beginning of the year, and was inaugurated at the end of July with the visit of the president of the Junta de Extremadura, Guillermo Fernández Vara. The plant also has an environmental impact on its surroundings, which is rich in bird species such as the great bustard, little bustard and common kestrel. This is why the project caught the attention of the environmental organization SEO Birdlife, who contacted Acciona to work as an independent body and will monitor it to analyse its compatibility with the birds' habitat. Acciona has undertaken to build nesting supports for the birds and the company claims that it would have a minor impact than on dry land because no excavation or earthworks are required.

In the province of Córdoba, the Aquasol complex will be built at the Urrá hydro-electric power plant. It is the first in the country with an installed capacity of 1.5 MW, which, in compliance with Sustainable Development Goal (SDG) 7, Affordable and clean energy, and SDG 12, Climate action, will occupy 1.7 ha of the reservoir. It will be installed using 5,600 solar panels supported by a floating structure.

In the Canary Islands, although it is not a valid example for our approach as it is located in the sea, the construction of a floating photovoltaic plant has been approved by the Norwegian company Fred Olsen Renewables as part of the European Boost project, with a budget of four million euros [10].

3 Pumping Network

3.1 Introduction

In accordance with the approach taken in the project to discharge the desalinated water into the Viñuela reservoir basin, we must have a network of pumping stations that allow the water to be driven through a pipeline that would run along the course of the Vélez River. This network will be sized according to the quantity of water to be pumped, its density according to its desalination quality and the distance it will travel.

3.2 Location and Distance of the Installation

The distance to be covered from the location of the desalination plant (mouth of the river Vélez) to the Viñuela reservoir is approximately 20 km with a maximum gradient of 285 m at the highest point.

Given the distance, the route unevenness and the losses in the pipeline, it would be advisable to locate a second impulsion block at 12 km from the desalination plant, which is also where the unevenness increases.

3.3   Technical Summary Table for a Desalination Plant of 10 Hm³/Year

As the project has been designed in a modular way, we have evaluated the technical characteristics of the pumping for a production of 10 Hm³/year [3].

Flow rate

Sewater flow rate m³/day	Daily rejection (brine) flow rate m³/day	Waterflow produced m³/day	Theoretical capacity produced per year	Actual production capacity per year
63,000 m³/day	34,000 m³/day	28,000 m³/day	10 Hm³	8 Hm³

Energy Data

Energy power (Kw)	Working voltage	Specific energy consumption
10 MW	6.6 kV	2.8 KWh/m³

Further information

Number of reverse osmosis racks installed, for production of 7000 m³/day (*)	Consumption population benefited	Total built-up area, desalination plant
4 Lines	200.000	3.000 m²

(*) reverse osmosis for seawater.

The new generation of desalination plants developed by Tesacua's engineers feature advanced technological innovations that allow the desalination of seawater by reverse osmosis, with low energy consumption thanks to the energy recovery systems they incorporate, with an energy efficiency of up to 97%.

3.4   Pumping Stages

Three stages are planned for the water pumping:

- Intake pumps, which will be responsible for supplying seawater to the desalination plant.
- High pressure impulsion pumps, which will oversee carrying the water from the desalination plant outlet to the re-impulsion point.
- Booster pump located about 12 km from the previous one and would push the water to the reservoir, (this stage would be like stage 2).

3.5 Technical Characteristics of the Different Stages

Intake Pumps. They will be responsible for carrying the water from the marine deposit to the desalination plant. It will be necessary to take the water by means of several boreholes of a certain diameter and depth, according to the characteristics of the project and the underwater terrain topography.

The seawater will be collected in an underwater pipeline, by means of suction from the collection pumps and boosting it to the desalination plant. In a first estimate, the water captured should be in the order of 63,000 m^3/day for the estimated 10 Hm^3.

A First Proposal Could Be to Use Blocks of 5 Pumps, so that One of them remains in reserve in the event of a breakdown or reduction in production. The power would be around 250 KW Each, with a Total Pumping Capacity of 0.9 m^3/s. The Pumps Adopted Are Horizontal Centrifugal Pumps, with Mechanical Seal and Independent Priming System for Each One. Adequate Protection Will Be Provided to Prevent Water Hammer.

High Pressure Booster Pumps. They will be responsible for carrying the desalinated water to the reservoir basin. Given the characteristics of the installation, we propose those of the manufacturer IDEAL, model APM-100 (see attached catalogue). For high pressure boosting, groups of turbo-pumps have been planned, with a total flow of 2625 m^3/h and 71.2 kg/cm^2.

The most important features of the APM-100 model are:

- Pumps that are intended for large industrial applications such as desalination plants.
- These are **high pressure multistage centrifugal** pumps for transferring clean or slightly contaminated fluids that do not contain abrasive substances.
- They comply with ISO 9906 Gr II and allow for optimum performance and good NPSH (Net Positive Suction Head) values, also known as Net Positive Suction Head (ANPA).
- Standard rotation direction from the coupling in clockwise direction, but other arrangements are possible depending on customer requirements.
- Working temperature range 90–110 °C (gasket or mechanical sealed construction respectively). For higher temperatures, external cooling or special mechanical seals are used.

1. High pressure booster pumps, they should have the same characteristics as those in Sect. 2, as the flow rate is the same (28.000 m^3 /day).

3.6 Pipeline

According to the technical data of the expected flow, the pipe estimated diameter should be about 500 mm. The recommended material for the piping would be polypropylene, "AWADUKT PP SN10" from Rehau, specially designed for piping systems requiring high resistance.

4 Desalination Plant to Supply Water to the la Viñuela Reservoir

4.1 Introduction

According to the Spanish Association of Desalination and Reuse, **Spain is one of the countries in the world that produces the most desalinated water**. It is currently **the fourth** largest country in terms of installed capacity, i.e. the production capacity of all the desalination plants built in our country, behind only **Saudi Arabia, the United States and the United Arab Emirates** [1]. According to the most up-to-date data available to AEDyR, **around 5,000,000 m³/day of desalinated water is currently produced in Spain for supply, irrigation and industrial use.**

To get an idea of this figure magnitude, we can say that if all this water were used for human consumption, estimating an average consumption per person per day of 150 L, which is higher than the estimated average (according to the latest data from the National Institute of Statistics in Spain, we consume 132 L per inhabitant per day), it could supply around 34 million people.

Although the main use of desalinated water is for water supply, industrial and agricultural uses are not negligible. In fact, the use of desalinated water for agricultural irrigation is quite remarkable compared to other countries and has spread much more and earlier than in other parts of the world.

A curious fact is that, while large capacity desalination is the best known and often receives the most political and media attention, **small and medium capacity desalination is of great importance in our country since**, if we consider the number of desalination plants of these sizes, the percentage is considerably higher.

How many desalination plants are there in Spain?

There are currently a total of 765 desalination plants installed in Spain with a production of more than 100 m³/day. Of these, 360 are seawater desalination plants and 405 are brackish water desalination plants.

- In terms of production, 99 are high-capacity plants. Large capacity plants are those with a production of between 10,000 and 250,000 m³/day. Of these, 68 are seawater plants and 31 are brackish water plants.
- Medium capacity plants, i.e. those with a production capacity of between 500 and 10,000 m³/day, total 450 (207 seawater and 243 brackish water).
- Finally, small capacity plants, i.e. those with an output of between 100 and 500 m³/day, total 216, of which 85 are seawater plants and 131 are brackish water plants.

4.2 Existing Problem

The tropical fruit sector in the province of Malaga, and especially in the Axarquía area, has been threatened for years by the lack of water. For example, on 8 October 2021, the regional delegate for Agriculture, Livestock and Fisheries in Malaga, specified that the contribution for agricultural irrigation in the Axarquía region would be reduced by a third, as proposed by the Malaga water resources committee, dependent on the Junta de Andalucia, in view of the extreme drought situation in which the La Viñuela reservoir finds itself. Thus, the irrigation communities' farmers of the Guaro Plan will have from 3,000 to 2,000 m^3 of water per hectare. These irrigation communities have almost 6,300 ha of crops and will have 12.6 hm^3 of water from the reservoir, compared to 18.7 hm^3 in the last hydrological year.

4.3 Followed Objectives

The objective of this proposal is the construction of a scalable seawater desalination system, which can improve water problems that the tropical sector of the Guaro river irrigation community has been experiencing. To this end, a scalable desalination plant will be built in modules of 10 by 10 hm^3.

The construction of this desalination plant will not only ensure the currently cultivated area supply, but with subsequent extensions it will also be able to serve the possible increase in irrigated areas.

On the other hand, we must not lose sight of the service that this reservoir provides for the water supply to the city of Malaga, with which it is interconnected by pipeline.

4.4 Desalination Systems

There are currently a multitude of methods for the separation of water and salt. The following table shows the different technologies and the energy used. Although more than ten types can be seen in the table, not all of them are used to desalinate large quantities of water. The different desalination methods are divided into two groups:

Thermal desalination or phase change, energy input or extraction is needed in order to obtain the phase change.

- Multiple effect distillation (MED)
- Flash Evaporation (MSF)
- Freeze desalination (CO)
- Vapour compression (CV)

Membrane technology.

- Desalination by reverse osmosis (RO)
- Electro dialysis (ED).

Process	Energy	Method	Symbology
Evaporation	Thermal	Flash evaporation	MSF
		Multi-effect distillation	MED
		Thermal vapour compression	TVC
		Solar distillation	DS
Crystallization	Thermal	Freezing	CO
		Carbohydrate formation	FH

(continued)

(continued)

Process	Energy	Method	Symbology
Filtration and evaporation	Thermal	Membrane distillation	DC
Evaporation	Mechanics	Mechanical Vapour Compression	CV
Filtration	Mechanics	Reverse Osmosis	OI
Selective Filtration	Electric	Electro dialysis	ED
Chemistry	Electric	Exchange	ITI

4.5 Some Interesting Facts

a. Investment and operating costs of different reverse osmosis sea water desalination plants (Source: extended table adapted from Cosin, 2019)

Planta	País	Año construcción	Capacidad (m³/día)	Inversión (millones €)	Ratio (€-m³/día instalado)	Tarifa producción (€/m³)	Tipo de contrato
Larnaca	Chipre	2001	52.000	47	904	0,64	EPC
Ashkelon	Israel	2005	396.000	182	460	0,45	BOT
Singspring	Singapur	2005	136.380	100	733	0,42	BOO
Honaine	Argelia	2005	200.000	194	970	0,65	BOT
Perth	Australia	2006	143.000	333	2329	1,01	BOD
Aguilas	España	2008	210.000	290	1381	0,50	EPC+O&M
Skikda	Argelia	2009	100,00	95	950	0,64	DBO
Beni Saf	Argelia	2010	200.000	132	660	0,60	DBO
Chennai	India	2010	100.000	78	780	0,89	BOT
Limassol	Chipre	2012	40.000	47	1175	0,75	BOT
SSDP (Perth II)	Australia	2012	306.000	517	1690	0,35	Alliance
Quingdao	China	2013	100.000	116	1160	0,61	EPC+O&M
Tuaspring	Singapur	2013	318.500	546	1714	0,31	BOOT
Ashdod	Israel	2014	384.000	320	833	0,46	EPC
Torrevieja	España	2014	240.000	341	1420		EPC+O&M
Tenes	Argelia	2015	200.000	199	995	0,51	DBO
Tuas III	Singapur	2018	136.000	187	1375	0,46	DBOO
Shuqaiq 3	Arabia Saudí	2021	450.000	516	1147	0,45	BOT
Rabigh	Arabia Saudí	2022	600.000	559	932	0,47	DBO
Taweelah	EAU	2022	900.000	473-1.032	526-1147	0,42	BOT

It is very difficult to generalize about the investment costs of desalination as each plant can be very different from the others (due to different collection systems, pretreatment, civil works type, tanks, sea distance, pumping, etc.) and the costs are very variable depending on the country [2]. From this table, we can draw some interesting conclusions:

- Long-term concession-type contract formats (BOT, BOD, BOO, DBO, DBOO), normally for 20–25 years, are in an international level, the majority for large desalination plants, although these public-private participation formulas have been rarely used in Spain in the water sector, where EPCs (design and construction with or without subsequent operation) have predominated.
- The construction ratios range from 460 to 2,329 euros per m^3/day installed, with an average value of 1,121.
- In these facilities, there are obviously scale economies, although investment costs are more dependent on the country than on the plant size or its year of construction. In countries with high labour costs, investments are much higher in relative terms (as is clearly the case in Australia) than in countries such as the Middle East, North Africa or China.
- In the last 5 years, there has been strong competition in the sector (mainly from Asian or Middle Eastern companies), with desalinated water prices in concession formats below 0.5 €/m^3, including the amortization of the installation.

b. According to the Directorate General for Infrastructures and Exploitation, in its economic study, the rate for the use of water from the Viñuela reservoir for 2011 was 29.85 euros/1000 m^3, i.e. 0.3 €/m^3.

c. While the use of desalinated water for agriculture is a practically irrelevant activity worldwide, representing no more than 2% of total uses (IDA, 2015), Spain is an uncommonness in this regard, being the country with the highest use for this application, with values above 21% (Zarzo et al. 2013).

   In Spain, the structural water deficit has led the Irrigation Communities and agricultural companies in the Spanish Levante region to rely on desalination as part of their water resources, integrating surface water from water transfers, groundwater, reused water and desalinated water (brackish and seawater), thus obtaining a reasonable price thanks to the mixture of all these inputs. In addition, the high returns on investment in greenhouse crops, which are high-tech with "out of season" products, make the cost of desalinated water affordable within the production costs for this sector of high-quality products.

d. According to Carlos Cosín (IAGUA) "La evolución de las tarifas en desalación (Parte I)" the average price of the investment needed in Spain for reverse osmosis desalination plants ranges from 0.2 to 0.36 USD per m^3.

   https://www.iagua.es/blogs/carlos-cosin/evolucion-tarifas-desalacion-parte-i

e. The following is a comparison of energy consumption in various reverse osmosis desalination plants in Spain:

	Planta A	Planta B	Planta C	Planta D
PARÁMETROS OPERACIÓN				
Presión de trabajo (Atm)	70,0	67,6	70,0	70,0
Índice de Conversión	45%	45%	45%	45%
RENDIMIENTOS				
Motor eléctrico	95,0%	94,0%	94,0%	94,0%
Bombas alta presión	83,0%	84,0%	83,0%	84,0%
Turbina recuperación	88,0%	90,0%	88,0%	90,0%
Rendimiento global calculado	64,3%	65,1%	63,6%	65,5%
CONSUMOS (kWh/m³)				
Consumo físico ideal	1,97	1,90	1,97	1,97
Consumo industrial óptimo	2,74	2,65	2,74	2,74
Consumo industrial calculado	3,06	2,92	3,10	3,01
Consumo real registrado	3,45	3,26	3,53	3,27
Rendimiento global registrado	57,1%	58,3%	55,8%	60,2%
% Incr. Cons. Registrado/Calculado	13%	11%	14%	9%

Energy consumption in reverse osmosis seawater desalination: current situation and prospects (Antonio Estevan and Manuel García Sánchez-Colomer).

a. Economic analysis. Desalination by reverse osmosis (RO)

Percentage of Reverse Osmosis (RO) desalination costs

4.6   Water Flow in the Plant

1st Seawater harvesting.

The most important aspect to clarify, in the case of new desalination plants, is their location and, linked to this, their collection and discharge system, both highly conditioned, not only by their technical and economic aspects, but also, and especially in the Mediterranean, by their possible environmental effects.

The water volume to be produced is the first and most important determining factor in the abstraction, and entails abandoning the idea of abstraction by means of wells or drains. Following an extensive investigation of the aquifers in the area in its double aspect of guaranteeing the necessary flow and the absence of risks derived from abstraction in the aquifer in terms of zero risk of marine intrusion or lowering of piezometric levels in the existing wells in the surrounding area.

Currently, the main seawater harvesting systems for desalination can be classified as follows:

- Open intakes.
- Vertical wells/boreholes
- Horizontal drains.
- Mixed intakes.

In relation to the qualitative aspect, the open intake generates more uncertainties, as it is more vulnerable to all kinds of polluting discharges, has more variability in quality, and is subject to temperature variations. On the other hand, water from wells and drains, is generally, of better quality and more homogeneous.

However, from the point of view of flow guarantee, the advantages are for the open intake, as experience shows the difficulty of guaranteeing the production flow in water from wells and drains. So that, for medium/high production plants, the open intake of seawater is recommended under normal conditions, although it has the disadvantage of greater complexity of execution and in many cases greater investment in the pre-treatment stage.

2nd Physic-chemical pre-treatment.

To guarantee optimum conditions for the water feed to the reverse osmosis system racks, a physicochemical pre-treatment is usually designed, by adding sodium hypochlorite as a disinfectant and to avoid the precipitation of salts on the membranes. In this way, the pH is corrected by injecting sulphuric acid into the feed water, thus also favouring the disinfectant action of the hypochlorite.

To remove suspended solids and present colloids in the seawater, ferric chloride is added, which results in the formation of flocs that are subsequently removed in the sand filters. After this, to reduce the residual chlorine before the water reaches the membranes, sodium metabisulphite is added in-line. Finally, antiscalant is added to prevent the precipitation of salts on the surface of the membranes.

In physical pre-treatment plants, flocs and other particles in the raw water are removed by passing it through sand filters with silica sand layers of different grain sizes.

3rd Reverse osmosis desalination and energy recovery.

The desalination system consists of lines fed by high-pressure and split-chamber pumps, a reverse osmosis membrane mixer and an energy recovery system.

Energy recovery is usually carried out by one of these systems:

- Inverted pumps
- Pelton Turbines
- Turbo chargers (centrifugal hydraulic converters)
- Isobaric chamber systems.
- Two-way isobaric chambers.
- One-way isobaric chamber.
- Revolver cameras

With the energy recovery system using pressure exchangers, the high-pressure pump pressurises 40% to 45% of the seawater. The rest of the water flow is pressurised through the pressure exchangers, where the high-pressure brine flow is transferred from the low-pressure seawater. At this point, booster pumps fitted with frequency converters increase the seawater pressure at the outlet of the pressure exchangers to match the inlet pressure to the reverse osmosis system. The flow rate of these pumps is coupled with the flow rate of the high-pressure pumps before the water reaches the inlet of the RO system mixers. In this way, lower power high-pressure pumps can be used and considerable energy savings can be achieved. This pressure transfer process occurs by momentary contact of both flows in the rotor tubes of the pressure exchanger, which is located inside two ceramic shells with very precise tolerances, creating an almost frictionless hydraulic sliding bearing when filled with high-pressure water.

4th Post treatment by remineralisation.

As the last step of the water treatment line, the Langelier index of the RO permeate water is corrected to achieve a final quality suitable for use as drinking water. For this purpose, a post-treatment is carried out, which consists of a remineralisation using carbon dioxide and calcite and adding sodium hypochlorite. The first two agents increase alkalinity and hardness, while sodium hypochlorite is needed to disinfect the water.

5th Brine removal.

Because of the desalination process, a hypersaline reject water or brine is discharged into the sea. The salinity of this discharge is variable, depending on the origin of the catchment and the treatment process. The dumping methods development, brine management tools, studies on the behaviour of the saline plume, etc., has sought to mitigate these effects on marine ecosystems, in addition to the obtaining of by-products that reduce the environmental impact of dumping and help to reduce the time required to recover the investment through the sale of these products. I.e. Useful Waste System.

References

1. Pérez, M.: Diseño de una planta desalinizadora de 20000 m3/día basada en una tecnología de destilación multiefecto (MED). Universidad de Sevilla (2017)
2. Cosín, C.: LA evolución de las tarifas en desalación. Iagua (2020)
3. González-Herrera, J.M.: Diseño de estación de bombeo de aguas pluviales y fluviales para el abastecimiento de agua potable. Universidad de Cantabria (2013)
4. Fernández, J., Franco, A., Muñoz, A.: Claves para el desarrollo de la fotovoltaica flotante. Infoenergética (2021)
5. Shkaurón, A.E.: Diseño de una instalación fotovoltaica flotante de 1 MW en el embalse superior del complejo hidroeléctrico de bombeo Cortes-La Muela. Universidad Politécnica de Valencia (2021)
6. Alcántara, N.: Estudio técnico-económico de una central fotovoltaica flotante en el embalse de Tavera. Universidad Politécnica de Cartagena (2018)
7. Cienfuegos, B.: estudio ambiental abreviado de la planta solar fotovoltaica flotante de Sierra Brava. Acciona (2019)
8. Gobierno de España: PERTE de energías renovables, hidrógeno renovable y almacenamiento (2021)
9. Gobierno de España: Hoja de ruta del Hidrógeno: Una apuesta por el hidrógeno (2020)
10. Comisión Europea: Plan de recuperación para Europa: NextGenerationEU (2020)

International Workshop
on Computational Mathematics,
Statistics and Information Management
(CMSIM 2022)

A Meta-analysis Approach for Estimating Salary Mean and Its Confidence Interval

Flora Ferreira[1]([✉]), José Soares[1], Fernanda Sousa[2], Filipe Magalhães[2], Isabel Ribeiro[2], Dânia Pinto[1], and Pedro Pacheco[1,2]

[1] BERD - Bridge Engineering Research and Design, Matosinhos, Portugal
{flora.ferreira,jose.soares,dania.pinto,pedro.pacheco}@berd.eu
[2] Faculty of Engineering (FEUP), University of Porto, Porto, Portugal

Abstract. A meta-analysis is the statistical pooling of the summary statistics from several selected studies to estimate the outcome of interest. A job's salary estimate is important information for both job applicants and companies, that is reported on different websites. By combining data from different sources a mean estimate more representative of the target population can be obtained, especially when the data has high variability and dependence on different factors, as in the salary case. However, data are not reported in each source by the same statistics values. Sometimes, the data are summarized by reporting the sample median and one or both of (i) the minimum and maximum values and (ii) the first and third quartiles. Additionally, the sample size is not always reported. In this paper, we aim to provide a step-by-step process to estimate the salary mean and its confidence interval by combining the data from different sources. We illustrate the process with an example dataset of seven job titles. The performance of two different alternatives to estimate the sample mean is evaluated, and the variation in the outcomes between websites is discussed. A high range of other quantitative data could benefit from the proposed process to obtain an estimate representative of the target population.

Keywords: Confidence interval · Meta-analysis · Pool data · Salary estimate

1 Introduction

Meta-analysis is the statistical combination of results from a set of different studies to generate a summary (pooled) estimate. By combining the data from different sources, an outcome estimate more representative of the target population can be provided [3]. Websites like glassdoor.com, salary.com, and payscale.com

This article is a result of the project BEIS (Bridge Engineering Information System), supported by Operational Programme for Competitiveness and Internationalisation (COMPETE 2020), under the PORTUGAL 2020 Partnership Agreement, through the European Regional Development Fund (ERDF).

offer information about salaries, including an estimation of how much a person should be earning based on job title and location. A job's salary estimate is important information for both job applicants and companies [14]. When looking for new job opportunities, the likely salary range helps job seekers understand which professions and locations offer higher average salaries, and on the other hand, helps employers understand what the employee hopes to receive and in making recruitment-related decisions. Getting a salary range estimation by combining the data from different websites will provide a salary estimate more representative of the source population. Ideally, to provide a quantitative estimation of a continuous variable, the sample size, mean, and standard deviation are required [18]. However, sometimes, the statistics reported differs from source to source. Instead, the sample mean and standard deviation, the median, the minimum, and maximum values, and/or the first and third quartiles are reported. In order to pool the results reported in the different sources in a consistent format is important to estimate the sample mean and standard deviation. Different methods have been proposed for estimating the sample mean and the sample standard deviation from the median, range, and/or interquartile range [2,7,9,12,18]. The methods proposed by Luo et al. [9] and Want et al. [18] are the formula-based methods with the best performance in estimating the sample mean and standard deviation, respectively. In these methods, the sample size is used, and higher accuracy for the estimation of the sample mean and standard deviation is achieved compared with other methods, such as proposed in [2,7], where the sample size is not fully used or even ignored. However, in some cases, the sample size is not reported and in these cases, alternative estimators independent of the sample size are useful. The methods proposed in [2,7,9,18] are derived from the assumption that the outcome variable is normally distributed. To overcome the limitation of the normality assumption, in [12], two approaches, Box-Cox (BC) method and Quantile Estimation (QE) method, were proposed to estimate the sample mean and standard deviation when data are suspected to be non-normal. The results presented in [12] show that BC and QE methods often outperformed the methods developed by Luo et al. [9] and Want et al. [18] when applied to non-normal data.

In this paper, with the purpose to obtain a range estimation of a job's salary representative of the reality of the market, we present a step-by-step process to estimate the mean salary and its confidence interval by combining the data from different websites.

In the following section, we introduce the data reported on the websites considered in this study. Taking into account the different sets of summary statistics that are reported on the websites, in Sect. 3, we describe the existing methods for estimating the sample mean and standard deviation. The approaches to meta-analyze the mean and its confidence interval is also introduced in Sect. 3. We describe the proposed process in Sect. 4. The results obtained based on an example dataset of seven job titles are presented and discussed in Sect. 5. The conclusion and future work are presented in Sect. 6.

2   Case Study

Throughout the paper, we use the following notation for sample summary statistics:

a = the minimum value,
q_1 = the first quartile,
$\widetilde{x}$ = the median,
$\overline{x}$ = the mean,
q_3 = the third quartile,
b = the maximum value,
n = the sample size.

In this study, five salary research websites were considered. Table 1 gives a summary of all statistics reported on these websites. On glassdoor.com website the 10th and 90th percentiles as low and high values, respectively, and the sample size are reported. In this study, we assume the low and the high values as minimum and maximum values, respectively, of $n = 0.80\times$ sample size.

Table 1. Summary table of statistics estimates report in each website considered in this study

Website	$\overline{x}$	$\widetilde{x}$	a	q_1	q_3	b	n
averagesalarysurvey.com	X						X
glassdoor.com		X	X			X	X
payscale.com		X		X	X		X
salaryexplorer.com	X	X	X			X	
salaryexplorer.com	X	X	X	X	X	X	

3   Methods

3.1   Sample Mean and Standard Deviation Estimators

Let $\overline{X}$ and S denote estimates of the sample mean and the sample standard deviation, respectively. Based on previous studies [2,7,9,12,18] and the data reported in the different websites (Table 1), we consider the following sets of summary statistics denoted by Scenario 1 ($\mathcal{S}_1$), Scenario 2 ($\mathcal{S}_2$), Scenario 3 ($\mathcal{S}_3$), and Scenario 4 ($\mathcal{S}_4$):

$$\mathcal{S}_1 = \{\widetilde{x}, a, b, n\},$$

$$\mathcal{S}_2 = \{\widetilde{x}, q_1, q_3, n\},$$

$$\mathcal{S}_3 = \{\widetilde{x}, a, b\},$$

$$\mathcal{S}_4 = \{\widetilde{x}, a, q_1, q_3, b\}.$$

In scenarios S_1 and S_2, where the sample size is known, Luo et al. [9] proposed the following sample mean estimators, respectively:

$$\overline{X} = \left(\frac{4}{4 + n^{0.75}}\right)\frac{a + b}{2} + \left(\frac{n^{0.75}}{4 + n^{0.75}}\right)\tilde{x},$$ (1)

$$\overline{X} = \left(0.7 + \frac{0.39}{n}\right)\frac{q_1 + q_3}{2} + \left(0.3 - \frac{0.39}{n}\right)\tilde{x}.$$ (2)

For scenario S_3 where the median, the minimum and maximum are reported, the following estimator for the sample mean proposed by Hozo et al. [7] can be used:

$$\overline{X} = \frac{a + 2\tilde{x} + b}{4}.$$ (3)

For scenarios S_4, following the same idea in Hozo et al. [7], Bland [2] proposed the following estimator for the sample mean:

$$\overline{X} = \frac{a + 2q_1 + 2\tilde{x} + 2q_3 + b}{8}.$$ (4)

The sample standard deviation estimators in scenarios S_1 and S_2 are given by [18]:

$$S = \frac{b - a}{2\Phi^{-1}\left(\frac{n - 0.375}{n + 0.25}\right)},$$ (5)

and

$$S = \frac{q_3 - q_1}{2\Phi^{-1}\left(\frac{0.75n - 0.125}{n + 0.25}\right)},$$ (6)

respectively, where $\Phi^{-1}(z)$ is the inverse function of $\Phi(z) = \int_{-\infty}^{z} \frac{1}{\sqrt{2\pi}}e^{-\frac{z^2}{2}}$, that is, the upper zth percentile of the standard normal distribution.

In scenario S_3, the value of the sample size is unknown. In this case, the following range rule of thumb can be used to estimate the sample standard deviation:

$$S = \frac{b - a}{4}.$$ (7)

Hozo et al. [7] showed that the formula (7) is a good estimator when the sample size range between 15 and 70. For small ($n \leq 15$) and large ($n > 70$) sample sizes Hozo et al. [7] proposed other formulas. However, the lack of knowledge of the value of n makes it not possible to choose the formula based on n.

In the case of scenario S_4, Bland [2] considered the following estimator for the sample standard deviation:

$$S = \left(\tfrac{1}{16}(a^2 + 2q_1^2 + 2\tilde{x}^2 + 2q_3^2 + b^2) + \tfrac{1}{8}(aq_1 + q_1\tilde{x} + \tilde{x}q_3 + q_3b) - \tfrac{1}{64}(a + 2q_1 + 2\tilde{x} + 2q_3 + b)^2\right)^{\frac{1}{2}}.$$ (8)

Summarily, Table 2 presents the proposed estimators under different scenarios based on previous studies [2, 7, 9, 18].

Table 2. Summary table for estimating the sample mean and standard deviation under different scenarios

	$\mathcal{S}_1$	$\mathcal{S}_2$	$\mathcal{S}_3$	$\mathcal{S}_4$
$\overline{X}$	Eq. (1)	Eq. (2)	Eq. (3)	Eq. (4)
S	Eq. (5)	Eq. (6)	Eq. (7)	Eq. (8)

3.2 Box-Cox Transformations

The above estimators perform well when the distribution of the outcome variable is symmetric (normal). McGrath et al. [12] proposed to apply Box-Cox transformations before employing the methods of Luo et al. [9] and Wan et al. [18] to transform a dataset into a more symmetric (normally-distributed) dataset. The proposed method, which McGrath et al. [12] denote by BC method, consists of the following four steps:

1. The power parameter λ is obtained through an optimization algorithm such that the distribution of the transformed data is most likely to be symmetric and therefore most normally distributed.
2. The quantiles of x are converted into the quantiles of $f_\lambda(x)$, where f_λ represent the Box-Cox transformation.
3. The mean and standard deviation of $f_\lambda(x)$ are estimated using the methods Luo et al. [9] and Wan et al. [18], respectively.
4. At last, the mean and standard deviation of $f_\lambda(x)$ are inversely converted into the mean and standard deviation of $x = f_\lambda^{-1}(y)$.

The optimization step consists, specifically, to find a finite value of λ such that:

$$f_\lambda(q_3) - f_\lambda(\tilde{x}) = f_\lambda(\tilde{x}) - f_\lambda(q_1) \tag{9}$$

in $\mathcal{S}_2$,

$$f_\lambda(b) - f_\lambda(\tilde{x}) = f_\lambda(\tilde{x}) - f_\lambda(a) \tag{10}$$

in $\mathcal{S}_3$, and

$$\arg\min_{\lambda} \left[(f_\lambda(q_3) - 2f_\lambda(\tilde{x}) + f_\lambda(q_1))^2 + (f_\lambda(b) - 2f_\lambda(\tilde{x}) + f_\lambda(a))^2 \right] \tag{11}$$

in $\mathcal{S}_4$.

The description of the optimization algorithm used to find λ can be found in Appendix B of [12].

Box-Cox transformation function f_λ and respective inverse Box-Cox transformation function f_λ^{-1} are defined as follows:

$$f_\lambda(x_i) = y_i = \begin{cases} \frac{x_i^\lambda - 1}{\lambda} & \text{if } \lambda \neq 0 \\ \ln(x_i) & \text{if } \lambda = 0 \end{cases}, \tag{12}$$

$$f_\lambda^{-1}(y_i) = x_i = \begin{cases} (\lambda y_i + 1)^{1/\lambda} & \text{if } \lambda \neq 0 \\ e_i^y & \text{if } \lambda = 0 \end{cases}. \tag{13}$$

As in [12], Monte-Carlo simulation was used to compute the mean and standard deviation of $x \sim f_\lambda^{-1}(N'(\mu, \sigma))$, where $N'(\mu, \sigma^2)$ is the symmetrically truncated normal distribution with mean μ and variance σ^2 bounded within support $[f_\lambda(0), 2\mu - f_\lambda(0)]$ (see [12] for more details).

3.3 Measuring Symmetry

To quantify the degree of symmetry of a distribution, different measures of skewness have been proposed [10] based on different statistics measures. Based on the extremes values (maximum and minimum) and the median Galip Altinay [1] proposed the following coefficient of skewness:

$$SK_G = \frac{b + a - 2\tilde{x}}{b - a}. \tag{14}$$

Based on the first and third quartiles and the median, the Bowley's coefficient of skewness is given by:

$$SK_B = \frac{q_3 + q_1 - 2\tilde{x}}{q_3 - q_1}. \tag{15}$$

3.4 Measuring Heterogeneity

Heterogeneity refers to the variation in study outcomes between studies. When the difference in results between studies is higher, the summary estimate may not be representative of individual studies. Then, the heterogeneity among studies considering the similarity of point estimates should be evaluated. The classical measure of heterogeneity/inconsistency is Cochran's Q, which is given by:

$$Q = \sum_{i=1}^{k} w_i \left(\overline{X}_i - \widehat{\mu}\right)^2, \tag{16}$$

where w_i is the weighting factor associated to the study i, $\overline{X}_i$ is the mean of study i, $\widehat{\mu}$ is the global estimated mean, and k the number of studies. The weights w_i are estimated by

$$w_i = \left(S_i^2 + \widehat{\tau}^2\right)^{-1}, \tag{17}$$

where S_i is the estimated standard deviation of ith study and $\widehat{\tau}^2$ is an estimate between-study variation [8]. One commonly used method for estimating is the method of moments estimator by DerSimonian and Laird [4]:

$$\widehat{\tau}_{DL}^2 = \max\left\{0, \frac{\left[\sum_{i=1}^{k}(S_i)^{-2}(\overline{X}_i - \widehat{\mu}_0)^2\right] - (n - 1)}{\sum_{i=1}^{k}(S_i)^{-2} - \sum_{i=1}^{k}(S_i)^{-4}/\sum_{i=1}^{k}(S_i)^{-2}}\right\}, \tag{18}$$

where $\widehat{\mu}_0$ is defined as

$$\widehat{\mu}_0 = \frac{\sum_{i=1}^{k}(S_i)^{-2}\overline{X}_i}{\sum_{i=1}^{k}(S_i)^{-2}}. \tag{19}$$

Statistic I^2 that is calculated from Cochran's Q the corresponding degrees of freedom $(k-1)$ is an intuitive and simple measure of heterogeneity among studies, usually used in meta-analysis [8] and defined by [6]:

$$I^2 = \begin{cases} 0 & \text{if } Q \leq k-1 \\ \frac{Q-(k-1)}{Q} \times 100\% & \text{if } Q > k-1 \end{cases}. \tag{20}$$

If the value of I^2 is between 0% to 40%, 30% to 60%, 50% to 90%, and 75% to 100%, then may represent low, moderate, substantial, and considerable heterogeneity, respectively [3].

3.5 Estimating the Mean and Its Confidence Interval

An estimator for μ is given by:

$$\widehat{\mu} = \frac{\sum_{i=1}^{k} w_i \overline{X}_i}{\sum_{j=1}^{k} w_i} \tag{21}$$

and a $100(1-\alpha)\%$ confidence interval (CI) for the mean, with $\alpha \in (0,1)$, can be calculated as [5]:

$$\left(\widehat{\mu} - z_{1-\frac{\alpha}{2}} \sqrt{\frac{1}{\sum_{j=1}^{k} w_j}}, \widehat{\mu} + z_{1-\frac{\alpha}{2}} \sqrt{\frac{1}{\sum_{j=1}^{k} w_j}} \right), \tag{22}$$

where $z_{1-\frac{\alpha}{2}}$ is the $(1-\frac{\alpha}{2})$th quantile of the standard normal distribution and w_i is given by (17).

In the meta-analysis, there are two statistical procedures: fixed- and random-effects [5]. In the fixed-effects meta-analysis, it is assumed that the between-studies variance is zero ($\tau^2 = 0$), and only the internal sampling variability of each of the studies is considered. By contrast, in random-effects meta-analysis, between-study variance ($\tau^2 > 0$) is considered enabling the modeling of differences between studies. We estimate both a fixed-effect and random-effect pooled mean (and its 95% CI) denoted by $\widehat{\mu}_{FE}(CI_{FE})$ and $\widehat{\mu}_{RE}(CI_{RE})$, respectively. For fixed-effect case we assume $\widehat{\tau}^2 = 0$ and for random-effect case we estimate $\widehat{\tau}^2$ using the formula (18).

4 Proposed Process

The five main steps of the proposed process to estimate the sample mean and its confidence interval are briefly described in Fig. 1. First, a collection of the summary statistics should be collected from different sources (websites). Then, according to the set of summary statistics, the identification of the scenario (S_1, S_2, S_3, S_4 or not defined) must be identified for each source. The relative precision of the estimators depends heavily on the skewness of the data [11,12]. While for symmetry data, the sample mean and standard deviation estimators based on raw quantiles perform best, for skewness data BC method allows to obtain estimates with lower relative error [12]. Therefore, we recommend selecting the estimators' data based on the skewness. Thus, the third step consists of the calculation of the coefficients of skewness. According to the scenario, the sample mean and standard deviation estimates are calculated in the fourth step. The quantiles (raw or BC transformed) associated with the lower coefficient skewness should be used to estimate the two statistics. In the fifth and last step, the mean and its 95% CI as well the heterogeneity measures are obtained.

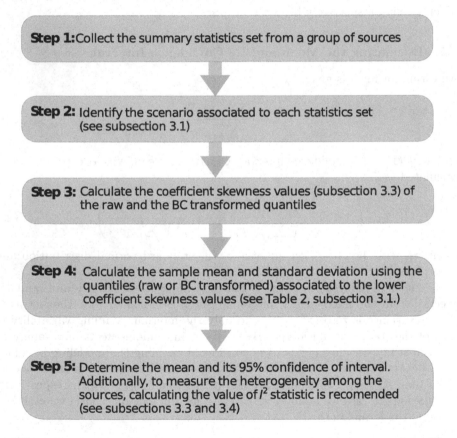

Fig. 1. Recommended steps to obtain the estimating of salary mean and its CI.

5   Results

For this study, a set of seven job titles was randomly chosen to implement the proposed process. The search of the annual salary in euros was done for a selected country on 28 February 2022 (see Table 3). Since in averagesalarysurvey.com just the sample mean and sample size present in Table 3 are available, these data were not used to estimate the mean and the CI. This sample mean was used to verify if the estimated CI includes it (see Subsect. 5.2).

Table 3. Sample mean and sample size of the annual salary in euros reported in averagesalarysurvey.com

j	Job title	Country	$\overline{x}$	n
1	Account Manager	Italy	58437	14
2	Architect	France	37412	20
3	Civil Engineer	Spain	54461	15
4	Financial Analyst	Germany	63414	39
5	Marketing Manager	France	70922	25
6	Project Manager	Spain	51756	27
7	Quality Manager	Germany	57820	3

The Python programming language using open-source software libraries and tools, including Pandas [13], NumPy [15] and SciPy [17] were used to obtain all estimates presented in this section.

5.1   Sample Mean and Standard Deviation Estimation

In the case, of the websites salaryexplorer.com and salaryexplorer.com, as the sample mean value is known, just the standard deviation needs to be estimated. The relative error (RE) of the sample mean was used as a performance measure. The RE is given by:

$$RE(\widehat{x}_j) = \frac{|\overline{X}_j - \overline{x}_j|}{\overline{x}_j}, \tag{23}$$

where j correspond to the job enumerated as $j = 1, ..., 7$.

Table 4 reports the coefficients of skewness (Galip's coefficient, SK_G and/or Bowley's coefficient, SK_B) based on raw and BC transformed quantiles, and the RE values when the sample mean is known. For the data collected from the websites glassdoor.com, payscale.com, and salaryexplorer.com, S_1, S_2, and S_3, the coefficients of skewness values are lower for the BC transformed quantiles, and as expected, in S_3, we can confirm that the relative error for the mean estimated based on BC transformed quantiles (BC method) is lower compared with the mean estimated using directly the raw quantiles. Contrarily, in the case of the data collected from salaryexplorer.com, S_4, the RE is lower when the mean is obtained using the raw quantiles. In fact, while SK_G values are lower for BC transformed quantiles, SK_B values are lower for raw quantiles.

Table 4. Coefficients of skewness based on raw and BC transformed quantiles, and the RE values when the sample mean is known

Website	Job	Raw quantiles			BC transformed quantiles		
(Scenario)	(j)	SK_G	SK_B	$RE(\widehat{x}_j)$	SK_G	SK_B	$RE(\widehat{x}_j)$
glassdoor.com	1	0.43	–	–	0.23	–	–
$(\mathcal{S}_1)$	2	0.13	–	–	<0.01	–	–
	3	0.15	–	–	<0.01	–	–
	4	0.15	–	–	<0.01	–	–
	5	0.24	–	–	0.06	–	–
	6	0.09	–	–	<0.01	–	–
	7	−0.13	–	–	<0.01	–	–
payscale.com	1	–	0.17	–	–	0.07	–
$(\mathcal{S}_2)$	2	–	0.31	–	–	0.21	–
	3	–	0.21	–	–	0.10	–
	4	–	0.28	–	–	0.21	–
	5	–	0.11	–	–	0.03	–
	6	–	−0.08	–	–	<0.01	–
	7	–	−0.08	–	–	<0.01	–
salaryexplorer.com	1	−0.18	–	0.052	<0.01	–	0.035
$(\mathcal{S}_3)$	2	−0.06	–	0.021	<0.01	–	0.017
	3	−0.06	–	0.021	<0.01	–	0.017
	4	−0.05	–	0.020	<0.01	–	0.017
	5	−0.18	–	0.053	<0.01	–	0.035
	6	−0.05	–	0.019	<0.01	–	0.016
	7	−0.06	–	0.021	<0.01	–	0.018
salaryexplorer.com	1	0.13	−0.11	0.039	0.05	−0.16	0.042
$(\mathcal{S}_4)$	2	0.22	−0.14	0.070	−0.22	−0.22	0.075
	3	0.17	−0.13	0.054	0.05	−0.19	0.058
	4	−0.10	−0.04	0.060	−0.01	0.02	0.065
	5	0.17	−0.12	0.053	0.05	−0.18	0.057
	6	−0.03	−0.06	0.027	0.02	−0.03	0.028
	7	−0.10	−0.10	0.060	−0.01	0.02	0.064

5.2 Salary Mean Estimate and Its CI

Table 5 presents the salary mean estimate and its CI obtained by undertaking both a fixed-effect and a random-effects meta-analysis for the seven job titles, as well as the estimated heterogeneity values. In the third case, jobs 2, 3, and 7, the statistics I^2 was 0%, indicating no heterogeneity across the sources. For these

Table 5. Salary mean estimate and its 95%CI

Job(j)	$\bar{x}(n)^a$	$\hat{\mu}_{FE}$	(CI_{FE})	I^2_{FE}	$\hat{\mu}_{RE}$	(CI_{RE})	I^2_{RE}
1	58437(14)	40089	(32179,47999)	31%	42520	(31373,53667)	0%
2	37412(20)	59358	(49269,69448)	0%	59358	(49269,69448)	0%
3	54461(15)	39524	(32138,46910)	0%	39524	(32138,46910)	0%
4	63414(39)	63130	(53311,72948)	11%	63143	(52372,73915)	0%
5	70922(25)	54953	(45314,64592)	51%	60259	(42692,77827)	9%
6	51756(27)	44800	(37541,52059)	2%	44849	(37440,52258)	0%
7	57820(3)	65714	(55494,75934)	0%	65714	(55494,75934)	0%

^aSample mean ($\bar{x}$) and sample size(n) of the annual salary in euros reported in averagesalarysurvey.com (see Table 3).

cases, the obtain mean estimate and respective CI for FE and RE are equal. On the other hand, in the presence of heterogeneity ($I^2 > 0$), jobs 1,4,5, and 6, the confidence intervals CI_{RE} are wider than CI_{FE}, as expected.

Checking if the salary mean reported on averagesalarysurvey.com website (Table 5) that was not used to estimate the confidence of intervals belongs to the corresponding CIs, we can observe that in 3 of the 7 job titles, jobs 1,2, and 3, the salary mean does not belong to both estimated CIs. For job 5, the case with the highest I^2 values, the salary mean reported in averagesalarysurvey.com does not belong to CI_{FE} but belongs to CI_{RE}. In the remaining cases, jobs 4, 6, and 7, the salary mean belongs to both CI_{FE} and CI_{RE}.

6   Discussion and Future Work

In this paper, we proposed a step-by-step process for estimating the salary mean and its confidence interval by pooling means estimated via transformation-based approaches. The pooled salary estimate is more representative of the reality in the market than the salary estimate from an individual source. In our results, the confidence intervals were estimated based on data collected from 4 websites. Checking whether the salary mean reported on another website is not used to determine whether the CIs belongs (or not) to the CIs obtained (Table 5), we can observe that for 4 job titles the salary mean reported on averagesalary-survey.com belongs to at least one of the estimated CI. However, in the remaining 3 job titles, this did not happen. A well-conducted meta-analysis based on data collected from a larger number of sources may provide a more valid and reliable estimate of the outcome of interest [16]. Then, for the salary estimate to be more representative of the salary paid a higher number of websites is recommended.

The salary mean and its confidence interval were obtained both around the random-effects summary estimate and around a fixed-effect summary estimate. When there is no heterogeneity among the studies, the fixed-effect method and the random-effects method will give identical results. When heterogeneity is present, a confidence interval around the random-effects and the fixed effect summary estimate is different, including a wider CI in the case of random-effects. The decision between fixed- and random-effects meta-analyses should not be made on basis of heterogeneity measures, and there is no universal recommendation [3]. A fixed-effect meta-analysis would be preferred if the studies considered are truly identical. However, if the studies differ (e.g. different approaches to acquiring the data) a random-effects meta-analysis is usually more appropriate. In job's salary depends on many factors, including the level of experience, location, possessed skills, and others, we recommend the use of the random-effects analysis. For instance, the salary reported on two websites can represent a salary estimate of the two different groups of workers in terms of location or experience. The salary estimate was obtained based on the sample mean and standard deviation calculated from the median and measures of spread (range and/or interquartile range). Better is the estimate as closer to a symmetric distribution is the data. Following the idea of McGrath et al. [12] the incorporation of Box-Cox transformations into the methods for estimating the sample mean and standard deviation, is a possible solution to overcome the limitation of the assumption of normality when the data is non-normal. For example, in the case of the data collected from salaryexplorer.com, Scenario $\mathcal{S}_3$, the relative errors were all lower when the Box-Cox transformations were incorporated in the process of estimating the sample mean (Table 4). However, if the transformed are not normally distributed, then estimating the mean and standard deviation of the underlying distribution may not be appropriate. In fact, in the case of the data collected from salaryexplorer.com, scenario $\mathcal{S}_4$, the relative error does not decrease with the incorporation of the Box-Cox transformation. In the cases where the studies report medians and heavily skewed data, directly meta-analyzing medians may be better-suited [11]. In future work, we intend to investigate the performance of median-based approaches to estimating a salary range.

In this study, a limited number of sets of summary statistics (4 scenarios) were considered. However, on some sources, a different set of summary statistics including other statistics, such as 10th and 90th percentiles, could be collected. Therefore, in future research, the inclusion of other scenarios should be considered.

Despite some limitations presented, a high range of other quantitative data could benefit from the proposed process to obtain a mean value (and its confidence of interval) representative of the target population.

References

1. Altinay, G.: A simple class of measures of skewness (2016)
2. Bland, M.: Estimating mean and standard deviation from the sample size, three quartiles, minimum, and maximum. Int. J. Stat. Med. Res. **4**(1), 57–64 (2015)
3. Deeks, J.J., Higgins, J.P., Altman, D.G., Group, C.S.M.: Analysing data and undertaking meta-analyses. Cochrane handbook for systematic reviews of interventions, pp. 241–284 (2019)
4. DerSimonian, R., Kacker, R.: Random-effects model for meta-analysis of clinical trials: an update. Contemp. Clin. Trials **28**(2), 105–114 (2007)

5. Hedges, L.V., Vevea, J.L.: Fixed-and random-effects models in meta-analysis. Psychol. Methods **3**(4), 486 (1998)
6. Higgins, J.P., Thompson, S.G., Deeks, J.J., Altman, D.G.: Measuring inconsistency in meta-analyses. Bmj **327**(7414), 557–560 (2003)
7. Hozo, S.P., Djulbegovic, B., Hozo, I.: Estimating the mean and variance from the median, range, and the size of a sample. BMC Med. Res. Methodol. **5**(1), 1–10 (2005)
8. Huedo-Medina, T.B., Sánchez-Meca, J., Marin-Martinez, F., Botella, J.: Assessing heterogeneity in meta-analysis: Q statistic or i^2 index? Psychol. Methods **11**(2), 193 (2006)
9. Luo, D., Wan, X., Liu, J., Tong, T.: Optimally estimating the sample mean from the sample size, median, mid-range, and/or mid-quartile range. Stat. Methods Med. Res. **27**(6), 1785–1805 (2018)
10. Mahmoudi, M.R., Nasirzadeh, R., Baleanu, D., Pho, K.H.: The properties of a decile-based statistic to measure symmetry and asymmetry. Symmetry **12**(2), 296 (2020)
11. McGrath, S., Zhao, X., Qin, Z.Z., Steele, R., Benedetti, A.: One-sample aggregate data meta-analysis of medians. Stat. Med. **38**(6), 969–984 (2019)
12. McGrath, S., Zhao, X., Steele, R., Thombs, B.D., Benedetti, A., Collaboration, D.S.D.D.: Estimating the sample mean and standard deviation from commonly reported quantiles in meta-analysis. Stat. Methods Med. Res. **29**(9), 2520–2537 (2020)
13. McKinney, W., et al.: Data structures for statistical computing in python. In: Proceedings of the 9th Python in Science Conference, vol. 445, pp. 51–56. Austin, TX (2010)
14. Tanwar, K., Kumar, A.: Employer brand, person-organisation fit and employer of choice: Investigating the moderating effect of social media. Personnel Review (2019)
15. Van Der Walt, S., Colbert, S.C., Varoquaux, G.: The numpy array: a structure for efficient numerical computation. Comput. Sci. Eng. **13**(2), 22–30 (2011)
16. Vetter, T.R.: Systematic review and meta-analysis: sometimes bigger is indeed better. Anesthesia Analgesia **128**(3), 575–583 (2019)
17. Virtanen, P., et al.: Scipy 1.0: fundamental algorithms for scientific computing in python. Nature Methods **17**(3), 261–272 (2020)
18. Wan, X., Wang, W., Liu, J., Tong, T.: Estimating the sample mean and standard deviation from the sample size, median, range and/or interquartile range. BMC Med. Res. Methodol. **14**(1), 1–13 (2014)

Mechanical Behavior of the Skin: Men Versus Women, a Preliminary Analysis

M. Filomena Teodoro[1,2](✉) (iD)

[1] CINAV, Center of Naval Research, Naval Academy, Portuguese Navy,
2810-001 Almada, Portugal
[2] CEMAT, Center for Computational and Stochastic Mathematics,
Instituto Superior Técnico, Lisbon University, 1048-001 Lisbon, Portugal
maria.teodoro@tecnico.ulisboa.pt, mteodoro64@gmail.com

Abstract. In order to numerically simulate the contact between equipment and the skin, it is necessary to have equations that satisfactorily reproduce the mechanical behavior of the skin. Taking into account the variability of the mechanical behavior of the skin, it is desirable that the determination of the coefficients of these same equations and the limits of load application are based on experimental results. The mechanical behavior of the skin depends on the place where the contact occurs, the gender and age of the individual, among other factors, as well as the test parameters used, which makes it difficult to obtain these coefficients and limits. The objective of this study is to verify if it is possible to reproduce the mechanical behavior of the skin by performing the ANOVA approach of the experimental data and verify if the limits of load application in safety and comfort remain stable for a group of individuals. Indentation test that allows to obtain the force vs deformation curve in which the maximum reached is when the maximum pain is reached and where the instant where the pain threshold occurs (pain onset) is also recorded. The test was performed at a specific point on the forearm, with a spherical tip indenter, with a diameter of 5 mm, at a speed of 1 mm/s in eighty (80) healthy subjects, aged between 20 and 28 years, 40 women and 40 men.

Keywords: Wearable equipment · Compression test · Soft tissue deformation · Comfort · Statistical analysis · Gender · ANOVA

1 Introduction

Rehabilitation equipment has a high incidence of rejection/discontinuation (30% [1]). One solution to overcome this problem is to use simulation to develop rehabilitation equipment that fits the desired function, but it also takes into account end-user comfort [2]. To do this, it is essential to consider the contact between the user and the device. However, in order to digitally simulate the contact between the device and the skin, it is necessary to create an equation that sufficiently reproduces the mechanical behavior of the skin and to know the application limit of the load for the safety and comfort of the user [3]. Given the changes in the mechanical behavior of the skin, it is desirable to determine the coefficients

© The Author(s), under exclusive license to Springer Nature Switzerland AG 2022
O. Gervasi et al. (Eds.): ICCSA 2022 Workshops, LNCS 13377, pp. 640–652, 2022.
https://doi.org/10.1007/978-3-031-10536-4_42

of these same equations and limit the application of loads based on experimental results. The mechanical behavior of the skin depends, among other things, on the location of contact, the gender and age of the individual, and the test parameters used, making it difficult to obtain these coefficients and limits [4,5].

In this study it is investigated whether the mechanical behavior of the skin can be reproduced by performing ANOVA approach of experimental data, whether the results are consistent for the group of the selected individuals, and whether which are limits to the application of load in safety and comfort. The purpose of this study is as follows: discomfort is one of the main causes for discontinuation of rehabilitation equipment. The compressive forces generated at the interface between the person and the device cause discomfort. Mathematical models are needed to simulate skin contact, such orthosis [4]. Previously it is important to perform a preliminary analysis, to find which are the best explanatory variables to include in models.

In terms of motivation, proper design of portable equipment includes a focus on comfort, imitation of skin contact with the equipment. The preliminary analysis developed in next sections, previously to the proposal of new model, is a practical tool for comfort assessment. There are factors that may trigger or be related to discomfort/pain, namely gender, age, personality, family influence, cultural and hormonal factores [6].

A study presented in [7], based on the indentation method, performed "in vivo", was used as a new method to determine the mechanical properties of the skin. This method also makes possible to determine the properties of the skin surface volume. In addition, the authors of [7] used other mechanical models in order to analyze the effect of the subcutaneous layers during measurements, thus making it possible to know the elastic properties of the skin.

In the present work, the indendation test was performed on 40 women and 40 men, 80 healthy participants aged between $20 - 28$ years, at a speed of 1 mm/s using a spherical tip indenter with a diameter of 5 mm at a specific point on the forearm. This allows to obtain a force-to-deformation curve that records when the maximum pain is reached and when the pain threshold occurs (pain onset).

This article is divided in six sections. An introduction starts the manuscript; in Sect. 2 are presented some theoretical issues about analysis of variance; follows Sect. 3 with a brief description of the used methodology; in Sect. 4 is performed the empirical application; in Sects. 5 the results are detailed and discussed; by last the article ends with the conclusions.

2   Preliminaries

2.1   Analysis of Variance

Experimental Design One Factor. The purpose of these methods is to compare k treatments ($k \geq 2$) [8,9]. Imagine a random selection of k groups of individuals, each with size n_i, $i = 1, \ldots, k$. Each group i supported the treatment i, $i = 1, \ldots, k$. If each group has the same size, the design is considered as balanced. If only two independent random samples are studied ($k = 2$), t-tests are useful to compare the means of each group. The t-tests are adequate to compare two independent samples, but when there exist $k > 2$ independent samples, it is usual to use the analysis of variance technique. The data of k samples is usually written as y_{ij}, with Y the value of the variable under study, for individual j in sample i, $j = 1, \ldots, n_i$, $i = 1, \ldots, k$. To compare simultaneously the means of k groups it is usual to compare simultaneously all groups, for example the parametric methods Scheffé [10] or Tukey are the most used. For a nonparametric approach we can use Jonckheere-Terpstra test [11,12] or even Kruskal Wallis test [13,14]. In [15] the author describes a wide number of nonparametric techniques.

Theoretical Model. Formal inference to compare means of different treatments implies the definition of probabilistic models. It is supposed that the variable under study Y_i associated to the $i - th$ treatment is Gaussian with mean μ_i and variance σ^2. If Y_{ij} is a random variable (rv) associated to the observed value y_{ij} the probabilistic model is given by (1)

$$Y_{ij} = \mu_i + \varepsilon_{ij}, \ (j = 1, \ldots, n_i, \ i = 1, \ldots, k), \tag{1}$$

with ε_{ij} rv's independents and Gaussian

$$\varepsilon_{ij} \cap N(0, \sigma^2). \tag{2}$$

The model can be rewritten as (3)

$$Y_{ij} = \mu + \alpha_i + \varepsilon_{ij}, (i = 1, \ldots, k, \ j = 1, \ldots, n_i). \tag{3}$$

We are able to obtain confidence intervals at $(1 - \alpha) \times 100\%$ for each μ_i. Since $\widehat{\mu}_i = \overline{y}_i$ and from (1) and (2) we can conclude

$$\overline{y}_i \cap N(\mu_i, \sigma^2) \tag{4}$$

following

$$\frac{\overline{y}_i - \mu_i}{\sigma/\sqrt{n_i}} \cap N(0, 1) \tag{5}$$

or, if σ is unknown,

$$\frac{\overline{y}_i - \mu_i}{S/\sqrt{n_i}} \cap t_{[N-k]}. \tag{6}$$

The confidence intervals (CI) considering a confidence level $(1 - \alpha) \times 100\%$ for each μ_i are given by (7)

$$\overline{y}_i - t_{[N-k;1-\alpha/2]}\frac{s}{\sqrt{n_i}} \leq \mu_i \leq \overline{y}_i + t_{[N-k;1-\alpha/2]}\frac{s}{\sqrt{n_i}}. \tag{7}$$

To investigate whether the treatments have identical means or not can be tested the hypothesis (8) using as statistical test the formula (6)

$$H_0 : \mu_1 = \cdots = \mu_k \text{ versus } H_1 : \text{ some } \mu_i \text{ are not equal.} \tag{8}$$

A rejection of H_0 means that there is experiential evidence that treatments differ from each other. In terms of the effect of treatment α_i, the above hypothesis can be described as

$$H_0 : \alpha_1 = \cdots = \alpha_k = 0 \text{ versus } H_1 : \text{ some } \alpha_i \text{ are not null.} \tag{9}$$

To perform the test defined by (9) it is necessary to calculate the total variability of $\widehat{\mu}_i = \overline{y}_i$ around $\widehat{\mu} = \overline{y}$ given by the sum of squares of treatment deviations (16)

$$SS_{TREAT} = \sum_{i=1}^{k} n_i \left(\overline{y}_i - \overline{y} \right)^2. \tag{10}$$

A large SS_{TREAT} suggests that the treatments are distinct. It is necessary to take its average value, dividing by the degrees of freedom (11)

$$MS_{TREAT} = \frac{\sum_{i=1}^{k} n_i \left(\overline{y}_i - \overline{y} \right)^2}{k-1} \tag{11}$$

and compare with the variability of each observation within the sample, i.e., with the mean sum of squared errors defined as (12)

$$MSE = s^2 = \frac{\sum_{i=1}^{k} \sum_{j=1}^{n_i} \left(y_{ij} - \overline{y}_i \right)^2}{N-k} = \frac{SSE}{N-k}. \tag{12}$$

The F test statistic associated to test hypothesis (9) is given by (14)

$$F = \frac{\text{average sum of squares due to treatments}}{\text{mean sum of squares of residuals}} \tag{13}$$

$$= \frac{MS_{TREAT}}{MSE} \cap F(k-1, n-k). \tag{14}$$

The critical region of test (9), for significance level α is given by (15)

$$F_{|H_0} > F_{(k-1, n-k, 1-\alpha)}. \tag{15}$$

The total variability SST (16) is measured by the squared mean of the deviations of each observation from the overall mean

$$SST = \sum_{i=1}^{k} \sum_{j=1}^{n_i} \left(y_{ij} - \overline{y} \right)^2 \tag{16}$$

and can be decomposed by the sum of two terms: the inter-group variability given by SS_{TREAT} and a variability within each group SSE, given by (17)

$$SST = SS_{TREAT} + SSE. \tag{17}$$

3   Methodology

To compute models that estimate the interaction of soft tissues and equipments it is essential to select the participants, collect their individual characteristics and ask them to perform the indentation test of compression/decompression. In Fig. 1 we can find all steps of the present work.

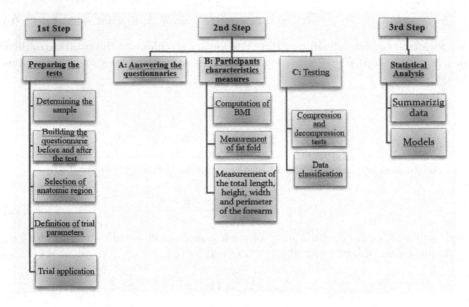

Fig. 1. Methodology summary.

4   Empirical Application

4.1   The Sample

In order to achieve the proposed objectives, indentation tests were performed at a specific point on the harm considering eighty healthy individuals, aged between 20 and 28 years, 40 women and 40 men. The individual physical characteristics can be found in Table 1.

The participants have body mass values between $40kg$ and $110kg$, heights between $1.44m$ and $1.88m$, fat folds between 1.05 mm and 10.7 mm and BMI between 15.56 Kg/m^2 and 34.30 Kg/m^2. The statistical tests of means comparison [8] led us to conclude that the mean and the respective standard deviation referring to the fat fold, body mass, height and BMI are distinct in the different genders. Establishing an analogy between genders, it can be seen that the average of female fat folds is higher than that of males. As for body mass and height, the female gender has lower values than the opposite gender, which leads to a lower BMI value. BMI presents higher levels (pvalue = 0.031) in the male gender compared to the female gender, revealed by the medians of the box-plots. As for the adipose fold, the opposite is verified, also by analyzing the medians (pvalue = 0.045). There is a single strange observation in the male gender, in both variables.

Table 1. Sample means and sample standard deviations corresponding to each measured variable, fat fold, body mass, height and BMI per gender (Males and Females).

	Female				Male			
	Adipose Fold [mm]	Weight [Kg]	Height [m]	BMI [Kg/m^2]	Adipose Fold [mm]	Weight [Kg]	Height [m]	BMI [Kg/m^2]
Sample mean	5,03	59,56	1,625	22,496	3,876	77,42	1,755	25,08
Standart Deviarion	2,872	10,89	0,070	3,572	2,51	12,29	0,057	3,402

4.2 Questionnaires

The implementation of questionnaires were carried out with the aim of analyzing and evaluating the psychological component and physical condition of the individual. Through the pre-questionnaire, parameters such as nervousness, a bad night's sleep, among others, which may or may not interfere with the indentation test to be performed, were evaluated. While the post-questionnaire aims to interpret the individual's feeling before the indentation test to which he was submitted, that is, how the individual himself evaluates the pain and discomfort he felt during it. The questions of interest are found in Table 2. The analysis of results will be performed with detail in a short future.

4.3 Experimental Methods

For the in vivo tests, a single anatomical region was selected, the anterior region of the forearm, due the objective of this study is focused on the feeling of pain associated with discomfort, being necessary to focus only on a single region to avoid disperse results. A precise point of this anatomical region was found, in order to always be the same point tested in all individuals. Initially, the measurement of the total length of the forearm (A1) was performed, and later the point (A2) used in the tests was calculated, which is located at 37% of the distal region of the fist, represented in Fig. 2 [16]. The selection of this region is due to the fact that it promotes less discomfort and has the particularity of being less painful for those undergoing the test. In addition, it is a region that is easily accessible to the indentation equipment and is a region that is less subject to the various natural movements of the body. In this way the working procedure becomes easier [17].

The test equipment used consists of a motor, an indenter and a load cell (see Fig. 3), which joins the motor to the indenter through a wire that allows the reception, by the same, of the applied force and of the felt deformation. It also has a metal platform where the individual will place the forearm. The operator can control various parameters from a portable computer.

Table 2. Per and Post questionnaires questions.

Pre - Questionnaire	Post - Questionnaire
1- Do you feel prepared for the test?	1- Did you feel un-comfortable during the test?
2- Did you sleep well tonight?	2- Did you quickly reach the sensation of pain?
3- How was your physical activity during yesterday?	3- Did you reach yours maximum permissible pain point?
4- Are you tired?	4- Do you have signs of injury?
5- Do you feel nervous?	5- Was it painful to perform the test?
6- Are you sportsman?	-------

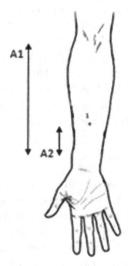

Fig. 2. Selected anatomical point - Anterior region of the forearm. Adapted from [16].

Forces perpendicular to the lower limb surface are applied at a velocity of 1 mm/s [2] until unbearable pain[1] is perceived by the participant (see Fig. 4).

---

[1] Perception of Pain: "Unpleasant emotional and sensory experience associated with tissue damage" [18].

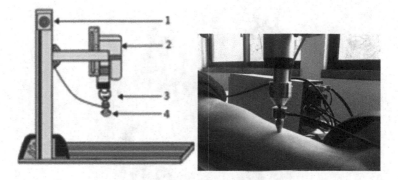

Fig. 3. Left - Equipment of test: Indentation machine 1 - emergency button; 2 - motor; 3 - load cell; 4 - indenter. Rigth - Example how a test is applied. The forearm is supported.

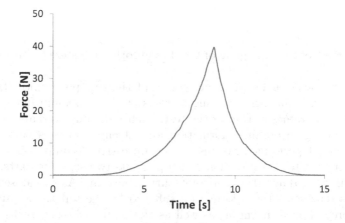

Fig. 4. Forces perpendicular to the upper limb surface are applied at a velocity of 1 mm/s until unbearable pain is perceived by the participant.

The spherical stainless steel indenter with a diameter of 5 mm was applied (see Fig 5). Maximum force and deformation are measured in the specific location (see Fig. 2) that corresponds to the particular point of contact between upper limb and orthosis AFO.

The force is measured by the soft tissues test equipment with a force transducer $(0 - 250N)$ placed in the indenter; a potentiometer transducer (0–50 mm) registers the deformation (see Fig. 3, on left).

The results are obtained at a sampling frequency of 40 Hz. The indenter is positioned perpendicularly to the anatomic test point, approaching the skin and starting the indentation at a constant speed. When the individual feels the maximum pain limit, a controller acts and the indenter turns to its initial position, at the same speed. Five trials are performed for each individual and between each trial there is a two-minute break. During the performance of the

Fig. 5. Spherical stainless steel indenters with 5 mm, 10 mm, 15 mm and 20 mm of diameter. Used indenter: 5 mm of diameter (top left).

same, the value of the beginning of the discomfort is registered (force applied in Newton).

Each test consisted by the compression of the test point until the individual felt the maximum pain, allowing to register the maximum force F_{Max} and the deformation values δ. During the test, each individual verbalized the onset of pain, allowing to obtain deformation and strength for the pain threshold. Each participant performed five tests. A compression-decompression curve was obtained for each test. Notice that Fig. 6 presents two separate parts: the compression curve (top) and decompression curve (bottom). As we can see in Fig. 6, the xx-axis represents the deformation suffered by the soft tissues and the yy-axis the force applied during it, as well as the point referring to the change in mechanical behavior, that is, when the individual reaches the maximum pain, decompression begins. It should be noted that during the compression period the force values obtained are higher than those recorded during decompression, for the same deformation.

5   Results

Summarizing some details about participants, BMI presents higher levels (pvalue = 0.031) in the male gender compared to the female gender, revealed by the medians of the box-plots (see Fig. 7). As for the adipose fold, the opposite is verified, also by analyzing the medians (pvalue = 0.045). There is a single strange observation in the male gender, in both variables.

Force and displacement values for pain threshold and maximum supported pain were recorded. The maximum load limit applied is always the biggest pain and indicates the risk of injury. The pain threshold is the recommended load to keep the device comfortable. These data were statistically processed in two different groups as female and male. The results will be published in a future

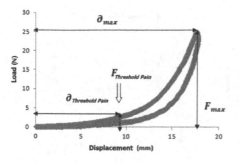
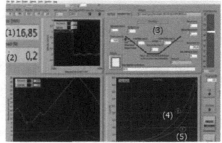

Fig. 6. Left: Representation of typical compression and decompression curves. Right: (1) Value of deformation; (2) Value of cargo;(3) Region where the test is performed, maximum force and rate of indentation; (4) Compression curve; (5) decompression curve.

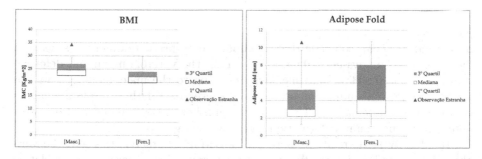

Fig. 7. Left -Box plot for BMI data (male versus women). Rigth - Box plot adipose fold data (male versus women).

article and will present the details of the results, but it can be shown shortly that both the maximum intensity and intensity at pain threshold were generally higher in the male group and also had more variance... 1st and 3rd quartiles are also higher in the male group than in the female group. However, the ratio of the force applied at the pain threshold (maximum pain) is less dispersed in the male group.

Figure 8 left shows the box-plot diagram related to strength for the two groups. These diagrams provide us with a summary of data location and dispersion measures (mean, median, 1st and 3rd quartiles, maximum, minimum, inter-quartile range and extreme observations). The maximum strength and the strength at the pain threshold are, in general, higher in the male group and also present a higher dispersion. In the male group, the dimensions of the 1st and 3rd quartile are also higher in male group than in the female group. However, the ratio between applied force at the pain threshold (maximum pain) has a smaller dispersion for the male group.

Figure 8 right shows the box-plot diagram related to the deformation for the two groups. The maximum deformation and also the deformation in the pain threshold are higher in the male group, and they also present a lower disper-

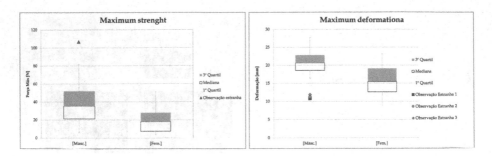

Fig. 8. Left: Box plot for maximum strength data (male versus women). Right: Box plot for maximum deformation data (male versus women).

sion. In the male group, the dimensions of the 1st and 3rd quartile are also lower than in the female group. However, the ratio between deformation in the pain threshold/maximum pain presents a similar dispersion for the two groups. Statistically we can conclude that maximum force presents differences between men and women (pvalue = 0.005), as well as, the variable maximum deformation (pvalue = 0.0035). Both medians, referring to the male gender, as well as the maximum and minimum values, non-discrepant, of the sample are higher compared to the female gender. A greater number of strange observations were detected, at maximum deformation, again in men group.

To identify some relations between individual characteristics and the variables determined during the trials, it was determined the speramann correlation coefficient. The results are summarized in Table 3.

Table 3. Spearman coefficiente between variables.

	GENDER			
	Male		**Female**	
	Adipose Fold	BMI	Adipose Fold	BMI
∂max	-0,103828071	0,228356	-0,024907025	0,272174
Fmax	-0,234153468	-0,05466	0,037853989	0,109998
∂Desconf.	-0,003080148	0,185092	-0,003080148	0,167133
Fdesconf.	-0,089539939	0,010996	-0,114401499	0,029848
Absorved Energy	-0,103828071	0,228356	-0,024907025	0,272174

Between men and women, there is a weak association between the variables under study with BMI and the fat fold, the Spearman correlation coefficient values in Table 3 are not statistically related, (pvalue>0.10).

Finally, using an ANOVA approach in an attempt to associate the studied variables, the F test (see expression 9), for significance level α given by (15) provided a $p - value = 0.003$. This means that men and women have distinct performances. All diagnostic tests, residual analysis and comparison tests under the aim of ANOVA analysis will be described in the extended version of this article.

6   Conclusions

In order to verify if it is possible to reproduce the mechanical behavior of the skin, were performed forearm point indentation tests in 80 participants. In the present manuscript was done a preliminary statistical analysis of the data. Considering the maximum strength, the male gender supports higher strength values and consequently has a higher maximum deformation value in its soft tissues, as well as a higher value of absorbed energy, compared to the female gender. Regarding BMI and adipose fold, although the male gender has a higher BMI than the female, it does not mean that it has a greater adipose fold. Probably it happens because the distribution of fat mass in both genders is different. It was applied the ANOVA technique, the global test F was significant (see expression 9), it is concluded that there are significant differences between men and women in terms of mechanical behavior of the skin. The assessment of psychological behavior and physical condition, through the questionnaires, the male gender practices more physical activity, is more tired and before the test he classified it as more painful compared to the opposite gender but a detailed analysis will be presented later. As future work, to reproduce the mechanical behavior of the skin is still needed an extended effort to characterize both the soft tissues properties and the level of tolerance for applied pressure, deformation and force and hence the ability to design for comfort. We intend to extend the models proposed in [19], taking other explanatory variables just as BMI, adipose fold measure, others and using generally linear models, e.g. logit regression.

Acknowledgements. This work was supported by Portuguese funds through the *Center of Naval Research* (CINAV), Portuguese Naval Academy, Portugal and *The Portuguese Foundation for Science and Technology* (FCT), through the *Center for Computational and Stochastic Mathematics* (CEMAT), University of Lisbon, Portugal, project UID/Multi/04621/2019. The author also aknowledges her colleagues P. Silva and C. Pina by their availability and ideas discussion.

References

1. Mann, W.: Smart Technology For Aging, Disability And Independence: The State Of The Science. Wiley, New York (2005)

2. Rodrigues, M., et al.: Influência da velocidade de penetracão no limiar da dor à compressão. In: Proceedings of 5o Congresso Nacional de Biomecânica, Espinho, Portugal (2013)
3. Sanders, J., Goldstein, B., Leotta, D.: Skin response to mechanical stress: adaptation rather than breakdown - a literature review. J. Rehabil. Res. Dev. **32**, 214–226 (1995)
4. Silva, P.: Computational Modelling of a Wearable Ankle-Foot Orthosis For Locomotion Analysis and Comfort Evaluation. Ph.d. thesis, Instituto Superior Técnico (2011)
5. Silva, P., et al.: Measuring discomfort: from pressure pain threshold to soft tissues deformation. J. Biomech. **45**(S1 S576) (2012)
6. Goonetilleke, R.S.: Designing to minimize discomfort. Ergon. Design **6**(3), 12–19 (1988)
7. Pailler-Mattei, C., Zahouani, H.: In vivo measurements of the elastic mechanical properties of human skin by indentation tests. Med. Eng. Phys. **38**(5), 599–606 (2008)
8. Morgado, L., Teodoro, F., Perdicoulis, T.: Métodos Estatísticos em Ciências Biomédicas. Universidade de Trás-os-Montes e Alto Douro (UTAD), Vila-Real, Portugal (2010)
9. Tamhane, A., Dunlop, D.: Statistics and Data Analysis: from Elementary to Intermediate. Prentice Hall, New Jersey (2001)
10. Scheffé, H.: The Analysis of Variance. Wiley, New York (1959)
11. Jonckheere, A.: A distribution-free k-sample test again ordered alternatives. Biometrika **41**, 133–145 (1954)
12. Terpstra, T.: The asymptotic normality and consistency of kendall's test against trend, when ties are present in one ranking. Indag. Math. **14**(3), 327–333 (1952)
13. Bewick, V., Cheek, L., Ball, J.: Statistics review 9: analysis of variance. Crit. Care **7**, 451–459 (2004)
14. Bewick, V., Cheek, L., Ball, J.: Statistics review 10: further nonparametric method. Crit. Care **8**(3), 196–199 (2004)
15. Sprent, P., Smeeton, N.r.e.: Applied Nonparametric Statistical Methods. Chapman & Hall/CRC, London (2001)
16. Rodrigues, M., Bernardo, V.: Avaliação das propriedades da pele em várias regiões anatómicas. Thesis, Instituto P0litécnico de Setúbal (2012)
17. Seeley, S.: Anatomia e fisiologia. Lda., Loures, LusoCiência - Edições Técnicas e Cientficas (2005)
18. Vitor, A., et al.: The psychology of pain: a literature review. RECIIS - Electron. J. Commun. Inf. Innov. Health **2**(1), 85–94 (2008)
19. Teodoro, M.F.: Modeling the interface between user skin and wearable equipment, a case study. In: Abdel Wahab, M. (ed.) Proceedings of the 4th International Conference on Numerical Modelling in Engineering. Lecture Notes in Mechanical Engineering, vol. 2, pp. 195–207. Springer, Singapore (2022)

Modeling the Forest Fire Occurrence in Some Regions of Portugal. A First Approach

M. Filomena Teodoro[1,2]([✉]) [iD]

[1] CINAV, Center of Naval Research, Naval Academy, Portuguese Navy,
2810-001 Almada, Portugal
mteodoro64@gmail.com
[2] CEMAT, Center for Computational and Stochastic Mathematics,
Instituto Superior Técnico, Lisbon University, 1048-001 Lisbon, Portugal
maria.teodoro@tecnico.ulisboa.pt, maria.alves.teodoro@marinha.pt

Abstract. The forest surveillance carried in Portugal presents some difficulties. To improve and solve some of these problems the use of new technologies such as unmanned aerial vehicle systems (UAVS) can be implemented in an efficient way. To do so we need to determine the risk of occurrence of a forest fires at a certain time in a certain region. With such goal, we have used several statistical techniques, such as ARIMA or GLM approach. We built adequate models in certain regions but for others it was impossible to determine a good quality model. The work is still going on, we expect to enlarge the area where we can get a good quality prevision of risk fire.

Keywords: Forest fire · Risk · Logit · ARIMA

1 Introduction

The Portuguese forest spaces, in addition to harboring, an unquestionable biogenic wealth, it is estimated that they are responsible for generating wealth in the order a thousand million euros/year, adding that they support direct jobs. Fires, according to several studies, are today the phenomenon susceptible to greater destruction that forest areas face. According to data of the National Forestry Authority, statistical data and reports alluding to the burned areas in forest areas, since 1980 some millions of hectares had burned. A more detailed analysis reveals that the greatest number of occurrences occur in the more densely populated districts (Porto and Lisbon). In contrast, the districts with the lowest population density have a lower number of occurrences, although they have substantially larger areas covered by fires. The districts located within the country are a "good" example of this phenomenon. For the same period of time, the districts that have the largest burned area are Guarda, Vise and Caste lo Branco. In Portugal, the Castelo Branco district stands out in terms of forest

© The Author(s), under exclusive license to Springer Nature Switzerland AG 2022
O. Gervasi et al. (Eds.): ICCSA 2022 Workshops, LNCS 13377, pp. 653–666, 2022.
https://doi.org/10.1007/978-3-031-10536-4_43

stands, as they present in the same period a greater burned area. Naturally, the availability of a fire probability map, in the short/medium term, it will be a valuable instrument to support the decision in the election of zones for treatment of fuels, location of certain infrastructures, or the disposition of fire suppression means available in a given territory. The spatial estimate of occurrence of fire derives from a cartographic zoning, in a given territory, with different levels of probability that the phenomenon will occur [1, 2].

The thematic relevance of "forest fire risk" cartography has deserved the greater attention both by the scientific community and the technical community. The definition of the concept of "risk" does not, however, result from unanimous and universally recognized agreement. The concepts of risk and hazardousness have been the subject of attempts at differentiation.

The term hazard, translated in some situations by dangerousness, is usually used to describe the characteristics of forest fuels at a given location and in a certain time period. The term is intended to express above all the potential of fire behavior. The term risk is commonly accepted and derives from the probability occurrence of the phenomenon, in a certain place and at a certain time, considering the nature and incidence of the causative agents. In other words, it is assumed that area has a certain fire potential taking into account the difficulty of determining its ignition probability [3–5].

In addition to the terminological context, the term "risk" has been applied both in the "structural risk" as well as "dynamic risk". By structural risk, or local risk, according with to some authors, it is understood as the interaction of a set of factors with the history of forest fires in a given area and over a period of significant time, such as land occupation and use, fuel load, orography, infrastructures for fire prevention and detection, population density, among others. On the other hand, dynamic risk essentially presupposes the detection of alteration the flammability of forest fuels during the fire season, such as the wind speed and direction or temperature [1, 6, 7]. In the same context, the authors of [8] describe a study about occurrence of wildfires in the Iberian Peninsula based on harmonized data from national forest inventories.

From a conceptual perspective, the implementation of probability methodologies occurrence of forest fires, necessarily presupposes the analysis of factors that explain the appearance, development and impact of fire on populations, material goods and natural resources.

Any fire probability methodology implies the combination of two or more variables, which normally derive from forest fuels, orography and various infrastructures that assume human interaction.

In [9] the author intended the construction of forest fire probability models, with regional specificity, as well as the elaboration of scenarios of spatial probability of occurrence of fires. The considered areas of study were completely different in terms of orography and land occupation and use. The models estimated by logistics regression analysis used as explanatory variables physical parameters, land occupation and location space of certain infrastructures susceptible to human interaction with fire. The two obtained models evidenced regional specific details allowing the construction of probability scenarios of occurrence of fire, which showed spatial agreement levels close both regions, although in different validation periods. In [10], the authors performed a cross regional study in Southern Europe, estimating fire ignition probability using Hurdle models. The authors of [11] used SARIMA models to forecasting the number of hotspots.

The present work focuses its objectives on the development of probabilistic models to estimate the risk of forest fire, using the technique of logistic regression [9,12,13] and ARIMA approach [11,14–16], employing the specificity and regional suitability of the models developed taking into account the importance of the various variables considered.

The manuscript presents a first approach where is done a descriptive statistical analysis considering the data from some regions of Portugal, followed by the estimation of Logit models, taking into consideration the work presented in [9,12].

This article is divided in five sections. An introduction starts the manuscript; in Sect. 2 are presented some details about wildfires occurrence. Follows some theoretical issues about Logit models and ARIMA techniques with a brief description of the used methodology; in Sect. 4 is performed the empirical application; in Sects. 5 are detailed and discussed some remarks.

2   Preliminaries

Vegetation fires occur and spread with the presence of unwanted fires. It swoops over the surface and devours plants no matter the cause artificial (accidental, intentional or negligent) or due to lightning, plant fires are considered natural disasters. Economic and human damage that can destroy property as well as environmental damage endangering material and people's lives. In this sense, it is determinant studying the dynamics of vegetation fire propagation as a study area experimental in nature. It stems from the human need to understand and consequently develop mechanisms to anticipate and control this phenomenon [17]. Fire propagation models are tools that can simulate fire scenarios. The propagation of fire as a function of factors regulating the behavior of fire that much is proposed in [18]. The integration of these models with data from geographic information systems is a qualitative leap forward in the development of computational tools to help create decisions on actions including vegetation fire monitoring, prevention and suppression [18]. Accordingly with [17], the fire behavior is determined by the interaction of three sets of factors: vegetation, atmospheric conditions and topography.

3   Methodology

3.1   ARIMA

The identification of an ARIMA model to model the data can be considered one of the most critical phases when using ARIMA approach. For a stationary time series[1] the selection of the model to be used is mainly based on the estimated auto-correlations and partial auto-correlations, which we will use to compare with the theoretical quantities and identify a possible model for the data.

The auto-regressive models with order p AR(p), the moving average with order q MA(q) and their combination, ARMA(p, q) models have their auto-correlation functions (ACF) with a certain specific feature, similarly to a finger print:

- The ACF of an autoregressive process with order p is infinite in extent that decays according to a damped exponential/sinusoidal;
- The ACF of a moving average with order q process is finite, i.e. presents a cut after the lag q;
- The ACP of ARMA process (p, q) is like a mixture of the processes described in previous items, the ACF has infinite that decays according to expo-nents/damped sinusoidals after the lag $q - p$.

The idea is to identify a pattern that behaves with the same profile that some theoretical model. In particular, the it is useful to identify MA models but it is not so simple to identify other kind of models. As a possible solution, we can compute the partial auto-correlation function (PACF). This function corre-sponds to the correlation of X_t, X_{t-k+1} removing the effect of the observations $X_{t-1}, X_{t-2}, \ldots, X_{t-k-1}$ and is denoted by ϕ_{kk}. In the case a stationary time series we can use the Yule-Walker equations to compute the PACF. Again, the PACF have a specific profile for each process like a proper finger print:

- The PACF of a MA(d) is infinite in extent that decays according to a damped exponential/sinusoidal (similarly to the behaviour of an ACP from a AR(d) process;
- The PACF of AR(p) the process is finite, i.e. presents a cut after the lag q, like the behavior of an ACP from a MA(p) process;
- The PACF of ARMA process (p, q) is similar to an ACF from a MA(q) process.

A general method for finding a.c. for a stationary process with f.a. is using the Yule-Walker equations. This method seems to fail in the case of non-stationary time series (the irregular component is significant). To solve this issue we differ-entiate the non stationary series so many times (d times) as necessary to get a stationary series. After these differences of successive terms of the chain, applied d times, we can apply the same technique: identify which model(s) are identified from ACF and PACF. A model that represents a non-stationary series, differ-enciated d times, with an auto-regressive component with order p and a moving average component with order q is represented as an $ARIMA(p, d, q)$.

ARIMA models are also capable of modeling series that have a seasonal com-ponent, being described as $SARIMA(p, d, q)(P, D, Q)_m$, where the first paren-theses refers to the non-seasonal part of the model $(ARIMA(p, d, q))$ and the second to the seasonal part, with m the number of seasonal periods.

---

[1] A time series that develops in time around a constant mean.

To estimate the best models between several proposals, we usually apply the information criteria AIC, BIC: the best models have the lowest values of AIC and BIC. Also the log of likelihood function is a good statistic to evaluate the quality of the estimated models: the lowest value means a better model.

After selection, the models need to be validated. One of the rules is to analyze the residuals (the ith residual is the difference between the ith obervation and its estimate). Residuals are supposed to be Gaussian and non-correlated. To verify this can be used several testes and other techniques (Llung-Box test, box-Pierce teste, Kolmogorov-Smirnov test, Bera and Jarcke test, some graphics, e.g. boxplots, qq plots.

The estimates precision evaluation is another step to include in all process. For that we can compute the usual measures: MAPE, MADE, etc.

In general the procedure of all process is composed by the following iterates:

1. Models formulation: use of ACF and PACF;
2. Models adjustment: estimation of model parameters, application of suitability measures of estimates;
3. Validation of models: selection of variables, diagnostics, residual analysis and interpretation.
4. Analysis of precision and update the models.

3.2 LOGIT Model

Follows some details about Logistic regression as a particular case of general linear models. In the classical linear model, a vector X with p explanatory variables $X = (X_1, X_2, \ldots, X_p)$ can explain the variability of the variable of interest Y (response variable), where $Y = Z\beta + \epsilon$. Z is a specification matrix with size $n \times p$ (sometimes $Z = X$, considering an unitary vector in first column), β a parameter vector and ϵ a vector of random errors ϵ_i, independent and identical distributed to a reduced Gaussian.

The data are in the form (y_i, x_i), $i = 1, \ldots, n$, as result of observation of (Y, X) n times. The response variable Y has expected value $E[Y|Z] = \mu$.

In GLM, where the model is an extension of classical model, the response variable, following an exponential family distribution [19], does not need to be Gaussian, and a transformation of expected value of response variable is related with explanatory variables. A detailed description of GLM ca be found in [19, 20].

Another extension from the classical model is the fact that the function which relates the expected value and the explanatory variables can be any differentiable function. Each Y_i has expected value $E[Y_i|x_i] = \mu_i = b'(\theta_i)$, $i = 1, \ldots, n$.

Also, it is defined a differentiable and monotone link function g that relates the random component with the systematic component of the response variable.

The expected value μ_i is related with the linear predictor $\eta_i = z_i^T \beta_i$ through the relation

$$\mu_i = h(\eta_i) = h(z_i^T \beta_i), \qquad \eta_i = g(\mu_i) \tag{1}$$

where h is a differentiable function, $g = h^{-1}$ is the link function, β is a vector of parameters with size p (the same size of the number of explanatory variables) and Z is a specification vector with size p.

We can found different link functions in GLM. When the random component of response variable has a Poisson distribution, the link function is logarithmic and the model is log-linear. In particular, when the linear predictor $\eta_i = z_i^T \beta_i$ coincides with the canonical parameter θ_i, $\theta_i = \eta_i$, which implies $\theta_i = z_i^T \beta_i$, the link function is denominated canonical link function.

Usually, in presence of dichotomous data, discrete models are usually estimated by logistic or probit regression [19].

The logistic regression is widely applied in models with dichotomous data and/or proportions. It is supposed that the response variable Y verifies $Y_t \cap Bin(1, \pi_t)$, at time $t = i$ i.e.

$$f(y_i | x_i) = (\pi_i)^{y_i} (1 - \pi_i)^{1 - y_i}, \qquad y_i = 0, 1, \tag{2}$$

where each time i as associated a specification vector z_i which results from p explanatory variables $x = (x_1, x_2, \dots, x_p)$. Knowing that

$$E[Y_i] = \pi_i, \qquad \theta_i = ln\left(\frac{\pi_i}{1 - \pi_i}\right)$$
$$and \qquad \theta_i = \eta_i = z_i^T \beta_i, \tag{3}$$

we conclude that the logistic function is the link function g. The probability of success π_i, the probability of fire occurrence ($P(Y = 1)$) is given by

$$\pi_i = \frac{e^{z_i^T \beta_i}}{1 + e^{z_i^T \beta_i}}. \tag{4}$$

Notice that $E[Y_i] = \pi_i = \mu_i \in [0, 1]$.

Another distribution function can be a good candidate to the link function inverse. One can suppose that the success probability π_i and the covariate vector are related by

$$\pi_i = \Phi(\eta_i) = \Phi(z_i^T \beta_i), \tag{5}$$

where $\phi(.)$ is the Gaussian distribution $N(0, 1)$. In this case, we obtain the link function $g(\mu_i) = \Phi^{-1}(\mu_i)$, the probit function, and the estimated model is named the probit model.

3.3   Extended LOGIT Model

In [21] the authors estimated the forest Fire Probability Mapping in Eastern Serbia using a Logistic regression approach versus a random forest method. The authors of [12] used an extended version of Logit model with spatial and time dependence. The use of a spatio-temporal model is done knowing that if there exist a fire in a certain localization (a,b) at $t = i$ the existent fuel material is burned, the probability of occurrence a new fire at the same point (a, b) in next weeks or months will be low [22]. Also similar topography, weather conditions and vegetation conduce to identical fire risk in distinct positions.

Defining $Y_{iab} = 1$ when there exists a fire at time $t = i$ in position (a, b) and $Y_{iab} = 0$ when there not exists a fire at time $t = i$ in position (a, b) the extended logistic model is based on

$$f(y_{iab}|x_{iab}) = (\pi_{iab})^{y_{iab}} (1 - \pi_{iab})^{1-y_{iab}}, \qquad y_{iab} = 0, 1, \tag{6}$$

where

$$E[Y_{iab}] = \pi_{iab}, \qquad \theta_{iab} = \ln\left(\frac{\pi_{iab}}{1 - \pi_{iab}}\right)$$

$$and \qquad \theta_{iab} = \eta_{iab} = z_{iab}^T \beta_{iab}. \tag{7}$$

The probability of fire occurrence π_{iab} at time $t = i$ in position (a, b) is given by

$$\pi_{iab} = \frac{e^{\theta_{iab}}}{1 + e^{\theta_{iab}}}. \tag{8}$$

4   Empirical Application

4.1   Data

In order to achieve the proposed objectives, it was used the available data during the last 10 years, from 9/2/2011 to 31/12/2021. In Table 1 we can find the variables used in the determined models: year (ano), date and initial hour of the fire occurrence (DHIni), duration of the fire (Dur), burned area (AreaTotal), administrative zone (Concelho), local (Local) and respective latitude (Lat) and longitude (Lon). Some information, considered important in literature, was not available, for example, kind of forest, altitude, declive, humidity level, etc. We expect to complete our data base in a short time.

Summarizing some information, in Fig. 1 is displayed the number of fire occurrences between 2011 and 2020 (in blue) and during 2021 (in orange). We can observe that the districts with bigger density of population have more occurrences (Porto, Lisboa, Aveiro, Braga). We can notice that, in some districts, during 2021 the number of occurrences are almost half of the occurrences in previous 10 years.

Table 1. Available data. Period: from 9/2/2011 to 31/12/2021.

	A	D	E	F	K	L	M	N	O
1	Ano	Tipo	DHIni	Dur	AreaTotal	Concelho	Local	lat	lon
2	2011	Florestal	9/2/2011 16:37	02h18m	0,13	Montemor-o-Novo	Vale Cerejo	38,816	-8,423
3	2011	Florestal	2/4/2011 16:53	01h37m	0,2	Vila Viçosa	MONTE DA ALMAGF	38,726	-7,405
4	2011	Agrícola	14/4/2011 11:38	01h7m	0,174	Montemor-o-Novo	Estrada da Amoreira	38,658	-8,147
5	2011	Agrícola	28/4/2011 15:21	45m	0,46	Portel	Tapada do Serrado	38,312	-7,703
6	2011	Agrícola	5/2/2011 14:25	01h35m	0,055	Crato	Quinta da Nave	39,321	-7,723
7	2011	Florestal	3/3/2011 14:20	02h20m	0,2	Celorico da Beira	Quinta do Gil - Galis	40,594	-7,421
8	2011	Agrícola	4/3/2011 18:00	45m	0,06	Celorico da Beira	Ramisga	40,635	-7,309
9	2011	Florestal	7/4/2011 15:37	02h18m	0,2	Celorico da Beira	Quinta da Carriça-C	40,594	-7,41
10	2011	Florestal	13/4/2011 21:00	35m	1,3	Figueira de Castelo Rodi	Cabreiriças	40,875	6,866
11	2011	Florestal	7/2/2011 14:55	02h50m	3	Celorico da Beira	PRADOS - PNSE (PR/	40,562	-7,378
12	2011	Florestal	8/2/2011 13:57	01h28m	6	Figueira de Castelo Rodi	Rodo de Cebolas	40,869	-6,827
13	2011	Florestal	8/2/2011 19:34	02h56m	0,5	Celorico da Beira	Quinta de São Bent	40,674	-7,3
14	2011	Florestal	28/2/2011 17:26	54m	0,01	Celorico da Beira	IC7 (EN17) Km 121	40,561	-7,479
15	2011	Florestal	6/4/2011 12:48	32h12m	46	Águeda	Lourizela	40,641	-8,318
16	2011	Florestal	5/2/2011 16:45	01h42m	0,73	Felgueiras	CHUQUEIRO (Choqu	41,335	-8,262
17	2011	Florestal	6/2/2011 16:15	55m	0,44	Paredes	Alto da Vila	41,226	-8,381
18	2011	Florestal	7/2/2011 11:20	40m	0,2	Paredes	Penhas Altas	41,233	-8,416
19	2011	Florestal	3/3/2011 17:16	58m	0,395	Paredes	QUINTA DA IGREJA	41,189	-8,378
20	2011	Florestal	3/3/2011 20:04	36m	0,11	Penafiel	LG. RANHA (BUSTÊL	41,23	-8,271
21	2011	Florestal	5/3/2011 9:32	02h8m	0,68	Penafiel	MATO (Matos)	41,228	-8,277
22	2011	Florestal	5/3/2011 13:49	01h11m	0,178	Penafiel	Campo Grande	41,143	-8,351
23	2011	Florestal	5/3/2011 15:00	01h20m	1,087	Paredes	Tourilhe	41,251	-8,362
24	2011	Florestal	7/3/2011 16:51	01h58m	0,8	Felgueiras	L.SARDOAL (Sardoal	41,374	-8,159
25	2011	Florestal	7/3/2011 19:17	01h3m	0,08	Penafiel	L.PEDRANTIL (Pedra	41,22	-8,233
26	2011	Florestal	8/3/2011 12:38	01h42m	0,07	Matosinhos	R. PASSADOURO (Rι	41,24	-8,703
27	2011	Florestal	10/3/2011 13:46	02h14m	1,351	Penafiel	Penoucos	41,226	-8,171
28	2011	Florestal	10/3/2011 15:00	01h25m	0,39	Vila Do Conde	LG. CASAL (Ponte de	41,396	-8,687
29	2011	Florestal	10/3/2011 15:17	02h28m	1,15	Póvoa de Varzim	RUA CRESCENCIOS	41,379	-8,763
30	2011	Florestal	10/3/2011 16:25	04h10m	3,15	Vila Do Conde	RUA NOVA (RIO MA	41,403	-8,679

When we consider the burned area per district (see Fig. 2) between 2011 and 2020 (in blue) and during 2021 (in orange), the major burned area is found in the districts with lower population density (for example, Castelo Branco).

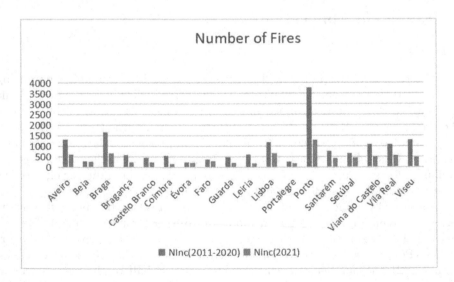

Fig. 1. Number of fire occurrences between 2011 and 2020 (in blue) and during 2021 (in orange). (Color figure online)

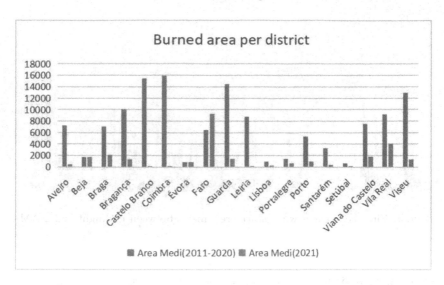

Fig. 2. Burned area per district between 2011 and 2020 (in blue) and during 2021 (in orange). (Color figure online)

We find in Fig. 3 the time at the beginning of fire from 22h to 06h. It suggests a human act due the amount of fires starting during the night period. This fact is also evidenced when we consult Fig. 4, where is displayed a detail from Fig. 3, the occurrences between midnight and 2AM.

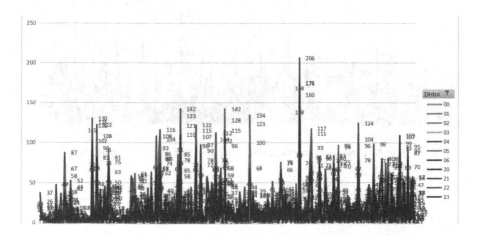

Fig. 3. Fire occurrences when start fire time is during the night period.

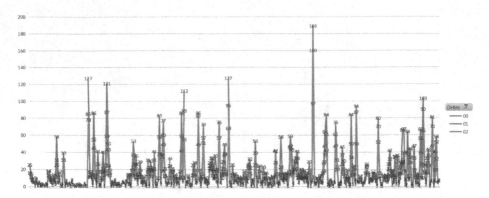

Fig. 4. Fire occurrences when start fire time is between midnight and 2 AM.

We also plot (see Fig. 5) the count of fire occurrences from 07 h to 19 h.

At Figs. 7 and 6 are presented the number of fire occurrences during the day and between midnight and 02 AM in 2021 respectively.

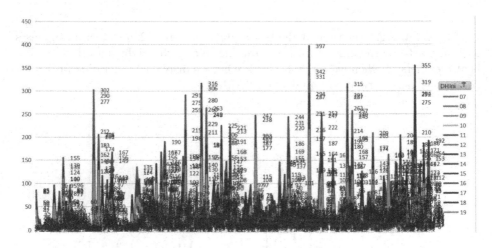

Fig. 5. Fire occurrences when start fire time is during the day.

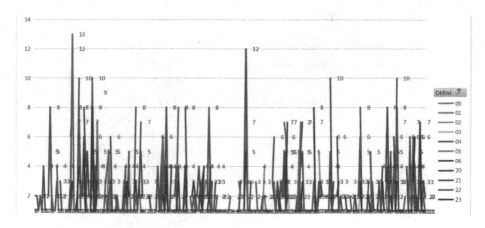

Fig. 6. Fire occurrences when start fire time is during the night period, during 2021.

4.2   Models

Under the aim of building the models, we have codified some variables, namely the duration of fire, and the burned area was classified in intervals, the other variables, latitude, longitude and occurrence time were considered without codification in a first approach.

When one builds a model to estimate the fire risk probability it is necessary to select the region of study. When a certain administrative region is selected to perform the study, several methods are tested to get adequate quality in the pretended forecast. As an initial approach we selected two districts: Castelo Branco and Vila Real. Both districts have a rural profile and a low population density. We have applied a generalized least squares (LOGIT model) and a Sarima app-

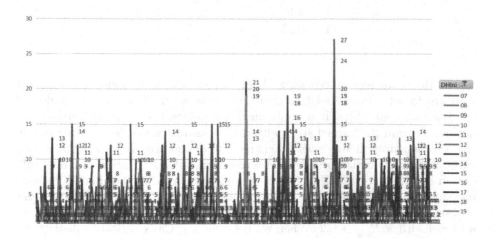

Fig. 7. Fire occurrences when start fire time is during the day in 2021.

Table 2. Codification of variables.

Variables	Description	Codification
Y	Fire occurrence	$1 = $ Yes
		$0 = $ No
x_1	Burned area	$'1'if \leq 0.1$
		$'2'= (]0.1, 0.5])$
		$'3'= (]0.5, 1])$
		$'4'= (]1, 2])$
		$'5'= (]2, 4])$
		$'6'= (]4, 6])$
		$'7'= (]6, 8])$
		$'8'= (]8, 10])$
		$'9'= (]10, 15])$
		$'10'= (]15, 20])$
		$'11'= (]20, 30])$
		$'13'= (]40, 50])$
		$'14'(> 15)$
x_2	Duration	$'1' = (]0, 0.5])$
		$'2' = (]0.5, 1])$
		$'3' = (]1, 2])$
		$'4' = (]2, 4])$
		$'5' = (]4, 6]')$
		$'6' = (]6, 8])$
		$'7' = (]8, 10])$
		$'8' = (]10, 15])$
x_3	Start fire occurrence time	Positive real
x_4	Latitude	
x_5	Longitude	

roach. Here, are reproduced some details about the logit approach. The first step was to get some association measures between the dependent variable and the remaining variables. It was obtained a significant association between the occurrences and the burned area (with delay), also between the occurrences and the duration time. It was considered the date of the occurrence as explanatory variable (in polynomial form or square root form). All usual steps of model validation accordingly with GLM approach were performed. About one of the used measures, the adjusted determination coefficient (R^2_{adj}), we have followed the author of [23], where in this kind of logistic approach, it is considered adequate a model with a $R^2_{adj} > 0.2$. When we consider the Castelo Branco district, we got an adequate logistic model. The best approach to Vila Real district data was obtained by a Sarima approach. The statistical analysis details of the obtained models will be presented in an extended version of this article.

5   Final Remarks

The forest surveillance carried in Portugal presents some difficulties. To improve and solve some of these problems the use of new technologies such as unmanned aerial vehicle systems (UAVS) can be implemented in an efficient way. To do so we need to determine the risk of occurrence of a forest fires at a certain time in a certain region. With such goal, we have used several statistical techniques, such as ARIMA or GLM approach. We were able to get adequate models in some districts, namely Vila Real and Castelo Branco. For some other districts we were enable to get adequate forecasts of the probability of occurrence of a fire. We built adequate models in certain regions but for others it was impossible to determine a good quality model. The work is still at the begining, we expect to enlarge the data base with the details about the kind of tree, accessibility, altimetry, sun exposure, slope, etc., so we can complete our study.

Acknowledgements. This work was supported by Portuguese funds through the *Center of Naval Research* (CINAV), Portuguese Naval Academy, Portugal and *The Portuguese Foundation for Science and Technology* (FCT), through the *Center for Computational and Stochastic Mathematics* (CEMAT), University of Lisbon, Portugal, project UID/Multi/04621/2019. The author also aknowledges her colleagues P. Silva and C. Pina by their availability and ideas discussion.

References

1. Colin, P., Jappiot, M., Mariel, A.: Protection des forêts contre l'incendie : fiches techniques pour les pays du bassin méditerranéen (2001)
2. Vesseron, P., Delarue, F., Rosenberg, P., Sappin, M.: lans de prévention des risques naturels (ppr) - risques d'incendies de forêt, methodogic Guide
3. Chuvieco, E. In: Wildland Fire Danger Estimation and Mapping. The Role of Remote Sensing Data. Series in Remote Sensing, vol. 4. World Scientific, São Carlos, SP (2003)
4. Salinero, E., Isabel, M.: Nuevas tecnologías para la estimación del riesgo de incendios forestales. CSIC, Madrid (2004)
5. Keane, R., et. al.: A method for mapping fire hazard and risk across multiple scales and its application in fire management. Ecological Modelling **221**(1), 2–18 (2010)
6. Freire, S., Carrão, H., Caetano, M.: Produção de cartografia de risco de incêndio florestal com recurso a imagens de satélite e dados auxiliares. IGP, Lisboa (2002)
7. Bergonse, R., Bidarra, J.: Probabilidade bayesiana e regressão logística na avaliação da susceptibilidade de ocorrência de incêndios de grande magnitude. Finisterra **45**(89), 79–104 (2010)
8. Nunes, L., et al.: Analysis of the occurrence of wildfires in the iberian peninsula based on harmonised data from national forest inventories. Ann. For. Sci. **76**(27), 1–17 (2019)

9. Silva, A.S.: Modelação e mapeamento da probabilidade de incêndio florestal. Master thesis, Instituto Politécnico de Castelo Branco (2011)

10. D'Este, M., et. al.: Modeling fire ignition probability and frequency using hurdle models: a cross-regional study in Southern Europe. Ecological Processes **9**(1), 1–14 (2020)

11. Espinosa, M.M., Prado, S.M., Ghellere, M.: Uso do modelo sarima na previsão do número de focos de calor para os meses de junho a outubro no estado de mato grosso. Ciência e Natura, UFSM **32**(2), 7–21 (2010)

12. Preisler, H.K., et. al.: Probability based models for estimation of wildfire risk. Int. J. Wildland Fire **13**(2), 133–142 (2003)

13. Hamilton, J.D.: Time Series Analysis. Princeton University Press, New Jersey (1994)

14. Box, G., Jenkins, G., Reinsel, G.C.: Time Series: Forecasting and Control. Prentice Hall, New Jersey (1994), 3rd edn

15. Chatfield, C.: The Analysis of Time Series: An Introduction. Chapman and Hall/CRC, Boca Raton FL (2004), 6th Edition

16. Cleveland, R.B., Cleveland, W.S., McRae, J.E., Terpenning, I.: Stl: a seasonal-trend decomposition procedure based on loess. J. Official Stat. **6**(1), 3–73 (1990)

17. Pyne, J.S., Andrews, P.L., Laven, R.D.: Introduction to wildland fire. Wiley, New York (1996), 2nd Edition

18. Pastor, E., Zarate, L., Planas, E., Arnaldos, J.: Mathematical models and calculation systems for the study of wildland fire behaviour. Prog. Energy Combust. Sci. **29**(2), 139–153 (2003)

19. Turkman, M.A., Silva, G.: Modelos Lineares Generalizados da teoria a prática. Sociedade Portuguesa de Estatística, Lisboa (2000), 2nd Edition

20. Nelder, J.A., Wedderburn, R.W.M.: Linear models. J. Roy. Stat. Soc. **35**, 370–384 (1972)

21. Milanović, S., et al.: Forest fire probability mapping in eastern serbia: Logistic regression versus random forest method. Forests **2**(5), 1–17 (2021)

22. Ricardo, A.C.: Modelação da Probabilidade de Ocorrência de Incêndio em Povoamentos Florestais de Portugal Continental. Master thesis, Instituto Superior de Agronomia, UTL (2010)

23. Hosmer, D., Lemeshow, S., Sturdivant, R.X.: Applied Logistic Regression. John Wiley, New York (2013), 3rd Edition

Mining Web User Behavior: A Systematic Mapping Study

Nail Taşgetiren[(✉)] and Mehmet S. Aktas

Computer Engineering Department, Yildiz Technical University, Istanbul, Turkey
`nail.tasgetiren@std.yildiz.edu.tr`, `aktas@yildiz.edu.tr`

Abstract. Nowadays, the number of people using the internet online increases day by day. Therefore, there is a growing need to analyze user behavior trends using navigational clickstream data these days. User behavior can be defined as the collection of the user's click sequence and transition movements between pages within site. Application areas of user behavior play an important role in many areas, from e-commerce to the banking sector. User behavior is a good argument for analyzing users' interests. Although there are many research studies in the literature related to user behavior mining, we could not identify a comprehensive literature review on this topic. This paper gives a systematic map of the analysis and mining of web domain users' activity in this research. We give exact user behavior measures, and publications that we anticipate will help other researchers discover study gaps and possibilities in this paper.

Keywords: Web mining · User Behavior Analysis · Clickstream Analysis · Systematic Literature · Literature Review

1 Introduction

The main purpose of mining web user behavior is to analyze and determine which aspects of the user behavior's results are most concerning to the user. Web usage data provides insight into the design of any website in terms of user behavior [9,11]. More efficient content can be suggested by analyzing users' navigation clickstreams and classifying them according to their interests. Therefore, mining web user behavior is an essential task in understanding the behavior of users. Olmezogullari and Aktas describe user behavior as "The navigational webpage patterns exhibited by clickstream sequences can be clustered to identify user activity." [15]. That's why collecting and clustering user behaviors are essential for useful mining results [10].

Over the last few years, for transferring information, the WWW has become increasingly popular and user-friendly [4,21] and the number of people who use the Internet has increased. In December 2021, Internet users were about 5 billion and the In 2022 will about 8 billion. This increase in the use of the Internet makes examining the behavior of users more critical. As a result, clickstream data is frequently noisy, and finding an optimum representation might be difficult.

© The Author(s), under exclusive license to Springer Nature Switzerland AG 2022
O. Gervasi et al. (Eds.): ICCSA 2022 Workshops, LNCS 13377, pp. 667–683, 2022.
https://doi.org/10.1007/978-3-031-10536-4_44

The importance of user behavior defined as "Understanding user behavior can dramatically improve a users' experience, either through better performance, customized user interface features, or better targeted ads." [25]. Therefore, user behavior attracts attention in the academic community and the private sector. Figure 1 shows the distribution of articles related to "web "user behavior" mining for the last five years. As seen in Fig. 1, the number of "Web "User Behavior" Mining" searches increases over time.

We discovered a survey study for web usage mining [17] and another survey for predicting user behavior [2] when searching the literature for secondary studies. Despite the topic's importance and popularity (Fig. 1), we were unable to locate any literature review studies on "Web "User Behavior" Mining" in general.

In this article, by examining the studies on the subject of mining web user behavior, these studies have not been studied before or which subjects have been studied more statistically. In line with this statistical information, we present the results on subject mining web user behavior to facilitate future research directions. These results provide academics with statistical data, enabling them to explore unstudied or understudied areas of mining web user behavior.

Following is the rest of the article: Sect. 2: Systematic Mapping Process explains how we conducted this literature mapping analysis. Section 3 presents synthesis data from primary investigations to answer the research questions. Section 4 analyzes the dangers to the mapping study's validity, and Sect. 5 wraps up the research and looks ahead to future projects.

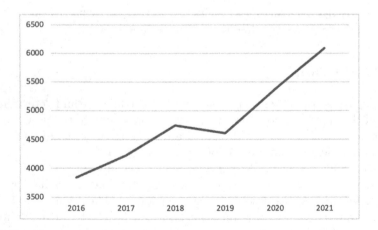

Fig. 1. Number of articles by year for "Web "User Behavior Mining".

2   Systematic Mapping Process

A preliminary study is primary empirical work in a particular field. On the other hand, a secondary study is defined as "a research that analyses all primarily related studies to a certain research issue to integrate/synthesize knowledge related to that research question." [7].

In our secondary investigation, we used a systematic mapping study method [7,19] on Mining Web User Behavior: A Systematic Literature Review.

2.1   Definition of Research Scope

To determine the body of knowledge regarding linked literature, we posed simple questions. The study questions and their preliminary research goals are listed in Table 1.

Table 1. Research questions

Research questions	Main motivation
RQ-1: What is the primary goal, necessity and basic process of mining user or customer behavior?	The main purpose is to analyze the clickstream and behavior of users or customers in the web environment
RQ-2: What research concerns in web user behavior mining are covered, and how many publications are there to cover them all?	Determine which research fields are frequently mentioned in articles about mining web user behavior mining
RQ-3: What are the most common used data types and methods for web user behavior mining?	Provide data and method for the most often studied web user behavior mining
RQ-4: Which embedding methodologies are used in the previous studies?	Determine which research embedding methodologies are frequently mentioned in articles
RQ-5: What is the paper-publication frequency?	Provide a graph with trend analysis
RQ-6: Which journals contain papers on mining web user behavior?	Determine which journals researchers should submit their research to

Figure 2 shows the basic map of the systematic literature review. The main purpose of this SLR is to identify Mining Web User Behavior methods, framework and data types used in Mining Web User Behavior.

Fig. 2. Basic mind map of the SLR

Table 2. Search strings

(Web)
AND
(User or Customer)
AND
(Behavior or Pattern)
AND
(Mining)

2.2   Search for Primary Studies

As part of a literature evaluation, we explored digital databases for preliminary investigations [19]. We chose the keywords web, user, behavior, and mining, and then created search strings using their synonyms (Table 2).

We applied the identical search strings to four digital libraries and gathered the outcomes without time constraints after settling on search strings (Table 3). We did not limit the search by year to track the topic's rise in popularity. As a result, we received the findings, released by February 2022. As a result, studies published after February 2022 were excluded. Downloading, maintaining, and working on a collection of documents are time-consuming operations that cannot be accomplished using spreadsheet apps alone. As a result, we deployed various reference management solutions, including Zotero. We used Zotero to handle all of the research we obtained, integrate them, apply the filter, apply exclusion criteria, and download references automatically from digital databases.

Table 3. Search results in digital libraries

No	Name	Result
1	IEEE	2.316
2	ACM	209
3	Science Direct	417
4	Springer Link	749
	Total	**3.691**

To avoid duplicate research acquired from different digital resources, we gathered search results and consolidated them. To find primary studies, we used three filters (Fig. 3). Table 4 lists the filters we used to narrow the search results (3691 papers). We got 86 primary studies at the end of the filtering procedure.

Table 4. Filters applied to search results

Filters	Definition
First filter	We omitted research from irrelevant journals and conferences
Second filter	To exclude papers that were not relevant, we examined the study title and abstract
Third filter	We read abstracts and titles, and in certain cases, whole papers, to apply our inclusion and exclusion criteria

2.3 Inclusion and Exclusion Criteria

We must choose some papers to answer the research questions in systematic mapping studies. In order to ensure that the research selection criteria is objective, we utilize inclusion and exclusion criteria. These criteria are established at the start of the selection process to eliminate selection bias [3,13].

We used these criteria to restrict two results to select our preliminary studies.

Inclusion Criteria: Studies that conclusively contributed to the mining of web user behavior were included. We considered short papers also traditional study papers. We accepted the new version of a study with multiple versions unless there was an expansion to main study. Therefore, both versions were included.

Exclusion Criteria: We did not include research that was not clearly linked to mining web user behavior or did not look into the matter thoroughly. We also did not include duplicate publications. Book chapters, secondary research, theses, and experimental investigations that did not suggest a solution or method were rejected.

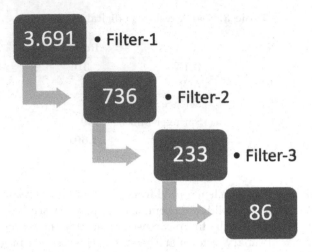

Fig. 3. The change in the number of main papers with the application of the filters in Table 4

2.4   Classification Schema

With a view of mining web user behavior as application level logs, application server logs and web server logs, we gathered 86 studies that we obtained after the filtering procedure. Figure 4 shows how we classified studies.

Web data mining is classified into three groups based on the different data mining objects: Weblog mining, web content mining, and web structure mining [26]. Our interest is Weblog mining. Web Usage Mining uses data mining techniques to find exciting usage patterns in Web content to understand better and satisfy Web-based applications' demands [12]. The practice of discovering browsing trends by studying a user's navigational behavior is known as web usage mining. This information takes as input usage data, which is data stored in web server logs that record user visits to a website [6]. The type of usage data being analyzed might further categorize web usage mining:

Web Server Logs: User information is logged by the Web server. These data can be the User's IP, page reference, and access time to the Web server [8].

Application Server Logs: A critical feature is the ability to track various business events and log them in application server logs.

Application Level Logs: It is the logging of the user's clicks and transitions between pages within the application. These logs can be categorized by dividing them into related categories. It may be necessary to use combinations of these logs in order to obtain more meaningful logs.

Fig. 4. Classification framework

We also classified in Table 5 the research issues as well as the contributions of the researchers.

Table 5. Research issues

User Behavior Analysis	The primary goal of the user's visit record analysis is to determine which aspects of the mining results are most concerning to the user [10]
Web (Usage or Data) Mining	Web usage mining uses data mining techniques to find patterns in Web data to understand better and service the demands of Web-based applications [23]
Clickstream Analysis	The clickstream data are made up of a jumble of misleading navigational URLs with no annotation information about their true identity, making them useless for any analytical activities [16]
Predict and Analysis User Behavior	One can remodel a website, portal, or e-commerce along with the behavior of online users by evaluating and predicting people's navigation patterns and their relationship with web content [22]

2.5   Data Extraction and Mapping of the Literature

Subsequently picking the preliminary study articles, we obtain the essential information from the studies to examine them. Following the creation of the data extraction form in Table 6, we referenced this form for the analysis procedures. If the content of an article is not fully understood or does not contain relevant information for our topic, we have omitted this section in order not to make any assumptions.

The following is our data extraction methodology: We chose a small dataset at random before beginning the data extraction process for 86 studies. Then, using Table 6 as a guide, we extracted data. We double-checked for the same data set. We produced this research to inspect a conflict and determine what created the conflict when we uncovered it. We used the data extraction technique to 86 papers to get the findings after satisfying all of these matters on the dataset.

Table 6. Form for data extraction

No	Data extraction columns
No-1	Study ID (example: S-1)
No-2	Title: Paper's title (example: Mining Web User Behavior: A Systematic Literature)
No-3	Author: Author's name
No-4	Year: Publication year (example: 2021)
No-5	Conference or journal name: Any conference or journal name (ex: IEEE Data Mining 2021)
No-6	Research Issues: User Behavior Analysis, ClickStream Analysis
No-7	Usage of Data Type (Application Level Logs)
No-8	Approach (Semi-supervised approach)
No-9	Research Method: Theory/Survey/Experiment/Own Experience/Review

3   Results

In this chapter, the study's findings are given and discussed the goal. The study's research questions were answered, and the results were given.

3.1   RQ-1: What is the Primary Goal, Necessity and Basic Process of Mining User or Customer Behavior?

User profiles can be used to summarize a user's enormous amount of data and achieve goals like product suggestions and personalized knowledge distribution. Users can contribute explicit information through registration and surveys, which can be included in a user profile [1,20]. Explicit information can also include simple facts about consumers' behaviors or transactions. For instance, such data could comprise;

- the number of times a visitor views a website.
- the average amount paid on each purchase, and
- the product category with the most sales.

The information listed above can process the user's data and prepare a better website usage experience for the user. A user browsing an e-commerce site may be presented with different products that he may need based on the products user's clicks.

One of the most important necessity for mining user behavior is a well-prepared data set. As the variety and range of the data set expands, the experience offered to the user increases.

The Fig. 5 shows that a basic level graph of the web mining flow to analyze user behavior.

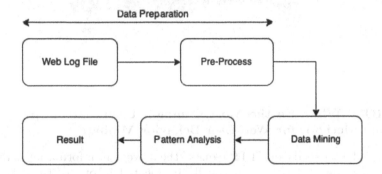

Fig. 5. Basic process of web mining user or customer behavior

3.2 RQ-2: Which Research Issues in Web User Behaviour Mining are Addressed and How Many Papers Cover the Different Research Issues?

We've covered a number of study topics connected to Mining Web User Behavior. The findings of our literature review are shown in Fig. 6. A total of 79 papers are grouped into four (4) different research issues after thorough evaluation and application of inclusion-exclusion criteria.

RQ2 aims to find new ways to address unsolved research problems. According to the findings, the top two topics addressed by the research community are user behavior analysis and web (usage or data) mining. Clickstream analysis and predicting and analyzing user behavior, on the other hand, are the most challenging difficulties. As a result, we consider clickstream analysis and predicting and analyzing user behavior the most promising research areas in the coming years.

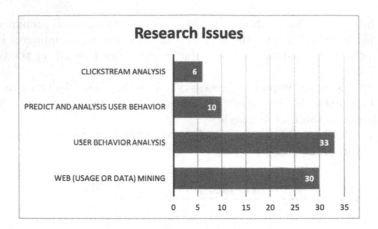

Fig. 6. Publications are distributed according to research topics.

3.3   RQ-3: What are the Most Common Used Data Types and Methods for Web User Behavior Mining?

When a Web user sends an HTTP request, the movement information is recorded in a Weblog file. A log file can usually be located in one of three locations: Application Level Logs, Application Server Logs and Web Server Logs.

The data types from the publications that remained after the most recent extractions were evaluated and classified using the three criteria listed above. The Fig. 7 shows the distribution of papers on the studied data. According to the result obtained from this graph, it has been observed that the Application Level Logs can be used more and more valuable and usable results are obtained through this data type.

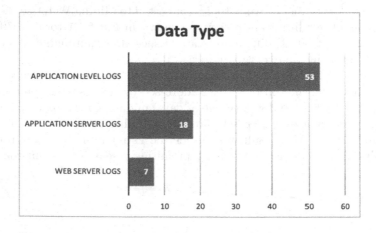

Fig. 7. Data types

The types of methods used in the research literature differ on paper. The methods used to measure user behavior are listed in the Table 7. The diversity of methods indicates that the research perspective is inclusive. This diversity shows that more papers will be added to the literature with different methods.

Hidden Markov Models (HMM) are used by Erdem et al. [5] to map topic-based unseen data sequences to URL sequences.

Uygun et al. [24] used both partitioning-based and hierarchical clustering approaches in the clustering phase of their studies. So they use K-means or Bisecting K-means, respectively.

Table 7. Method types

Support vector machines	DBSCAN&Chameleon
Kohanen Neural Network	Random Forest
LOGSOM (Log Self-Organizing Map)	Visual Attention Map(CNN)
Pattern-tree	SSPRA (Single Scan Pattern Recognition Algorithm)
Ant-Based Clustering	FP-Growth
K-Means	Apriori Algorithm
K Nearest Neighbor	Markov chain model
Matrix Decomposition	Frequent Pattern Analysis
M5 Model Tree	Web Map Service Platforms (WMSPs)
Word2Vec	Unsupervised Approach
Node2Vec	Semisupervised Approach
Fluxicon Disco	Cosine Similarity Measure
Pattern2Vec	Frequent Link and Access Tree (FLaAT)
LDA Model	ID3 algorithm
DBSCAN	Hidden Markov Model (HMM)
UpDown Tree for Finding Contiguous Sequential Patterns (CSP)	SMAP-Mine
ProCrawl (PROcess CRAWLer)	Markov Model with the Pre-Order Linked WAP-Tree Mining (PLWAP) Algorithm
Assoc. Rule Appr. (ARA) vs Cogn. Map Appr. (CMA)	Probabilistic Latent Semantic Analysis (PLSA)

3.4   RQ-4: Which Embedding Methodologies are Used in the Previous Studies?

In this chapter; we discovered that which embedding methodologies are used literature has exploded in recent years. We divided the embedding methodologies into two (2). These are; URL Embedding Methodologies and URL Sequence

Embedding Methodologies. The data in Fig. 8 show the embedding methodologies. Table 8 shows that list of the URL and URL Sequence Embedding Methodologies.

Oguz et al. [14] worked on predicting users' behavior on the e-commerce site based on clickstream sequences data in this study. This study discovered new datasets using a GAN (Generative Adversarial Networks)-based deep learning algorithm. They have developed a new prototype to demonstrate performance tests. They chose URL Sequence Embedding Methodology as their reference.

Oz et al. [18] worked on automating test scripting using LSTM (Long Short Term Memory). As the data set, they chose clickstream sequences data. They chose URL Sequence Embedding Methodology as their reference.

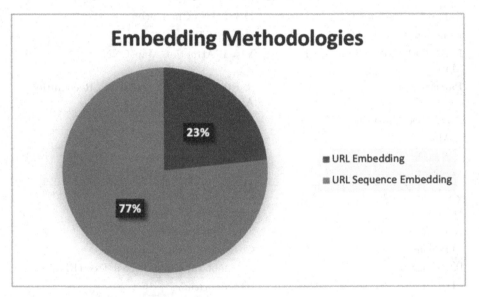

Fig. 8. Embedding methodologies

Table 8. List of embedding methodologies

No	Data extraction columns
URL	word2vec
URL	url2vec
URL Sequence	graph2vec
URL Sequence	DeepWalk
URL Sequence	subgraph2vec
URL Sequence	node2vec
URL Sequence	pattern2vec
URL Sequence	struc2vec

3.5   RQ-5: What is the Paper-Publication Frequency?

In this chapter; we discovered that mining web user behavior literature has exploded in recent years, owing to the widespread use of computers and other mobile phones in everyday (Fig. 9). The data in Fig. 9 show the overall number of publications per year. We believe that there is a relation between the maturity of the topic domain and this.

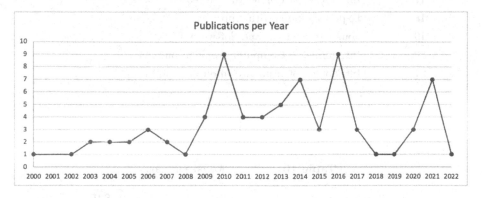

Fig. 9. Yearly publication frequency

3.6   RQ-6: Which Journals Contain Papers on Mining Web User Behavior?

Names of Journals are listed in Table 9.

Table 9. Journal names

Journal no	Names of journals
1	Concurrency and Computation: Practice and Experience
2	Journ. of Retailing and Consumer Services
3	Engineering Applications of Artificial Intelligence
4	Decision Support Systems
5	Materials Today: Proceedings
6	Inf. and Software Tech.
7	International Journ. of Circuits, Systems and Signal Processing
8	ACM Transactions on the Web
9	Procedia Engineering
10	SIGKDD Explor. Newsl.
11	SIGSOFT Softw. Eng. Notes
12	Physical Review E
13	Data in Brief

(*continued*)

Table 9. (*continued*)

Journal no	Names of journals
14	MethodsX
15	Procedia Computer Science
16	Information Processing and Management
17	Int. Journ. of Engineering Research
18	Expert Systems with App
19	Journ. of Systems and Software
20	Int. Journ. of Computer Applications
21	Int. Journ. of Human-Computer Studies

Table 10 shows the Scimago Journal Rank (SJR) values. Journal publications are ordered according to their SJR value.

Table 10. SJR of selected journals

Journal Publications	SJR
Journal of Retailing and Consumer Services	1,57
Decision Support Systems	1,56
Expert Systems with Applications	1,37
Engineering Applications of Artificial Intelligence	1,11
Information Processing and Management	1,06
Physical Review E	0,9
Int. Journ. of Human-Computer Studies	0,73
Journ. of Systems and Software	0,64
Inf. and Software Technology	0,61
ACM Transactions on the Web	0,44
MethodsX	0,36
Materials Today: Proceedings	0,34
Procedia Computer Science	0,33
Procedia Engineering	0,32
Concurrency and Computation: Practice and Experience	0,31
Int. Journ. of Computer Applications	0,29
Int. Journ. of Engineering Research	0,24
Int. Journ. of Circuits, Systems and Signal Processing	0,16
Data in Brief	0,12
SIGKDD Explor. Newsl.	0,00
SIGSOFT Softw. Eng. Notes	0,00

4   Threats to Validity of Research

Generally, some situations threaten the general validity of mapping studies. These; research questions, publication selection, and data extraction in selected publications. We have our suggestions for removing these three risks.

Research Questions: Research questions may not cover all mining web user behavior issues in detail. We searched only a portion of the literature on the mining web user behavior issue at a particular time. As a result, this literature study did not focus on a particular subject.

Publication Selection: Despite searching four big digital databases, we could not apply our criterion to all web user behavior mining topic. While we cannot eliminate the threat, we have attempted to decrease it by including as many publications.

Data Extraction: Because personal perspectives can be significant in the data extraction process, the data were double-checked to mitigate the risk, and the data were analyzed from a subjective standpoint. When an inconsistency was found, the data set was re-evaluated. It was included in the research was related to our topic.

5   Conclusion and Future Work

The literature review aimed to identify and analyze trends, datasets and methods in web mining user behavior. We conducted a literature review covering the years 2000-2021. We found 3691 published papers between these years. After applying the criterias for these papers. Finally, we analyzed and worked 86 papers.

By examining the outcomes in Fig. 6 and Fig. 7, we conclude that web mining user behavior is generally open to new contributions. Especially the studies on clickstream analysis show the lack of research studies in this area. This shortcoming may provide further research opportunities. The results also demonstrate the intensive research needs of clickstream analysis and predict and analyze user behavior research topics using application-level logs datasets. While analyzing the data, we see that prior studies have placed a high value on user behavior analysis.

This study is continued by expanding it to make a systematic literature review on the subject of web mining user behavior. We will also explore how to design a framework for clickstream analysis using application-level logs data in the future.

Acknowledgements. This study was supported by Getir Perakende Lojistik A.ş. company. We would like to thank Getir Perakende Lojistik A.Ş. for providing us with the necessary resources and funding.

References

1. Ahn, J., et al.: Open user profiles for adaptive news systems: help or harm? In: Proceedings of the 16th international conference on World Wide Web, pp. 11–20 (2007)
2. Anitha, V., Isakki, P.: A survey on predicting user behavior based on web server log files in a web usage mining. In: 2016 International Conference on Computing Technologies and Intelligent Data Engineering (ICCTIDE 2016), pp. 1–4. IEEE (2016)
3. Budgen, D., Brereton, P.: Performing systematic literature reviews in software engineering. In: Proceedings of the 28th International Conference on Software Engineering, pp. 1051–1052 (2006)
4. Dixit, V.S., Bhatia, S.K.: Refinement and evaluation of web session cluster quality. Int. J. Syst. Assurance Eng. Manage. 6(4), 373–389 (2014). https://doi.org/10.1007/s13198-014-0266-x
5. Erdem, I., et al.: Test script generation based on hidden markov models learning from user browsing behaviors. In: 2021 IEEE International Conference on Big Data (Big Data), pp. 2998–3005. IEEE (2021)
6. Kalaichelvi, S.: Web mining classification: a survey. Int. J. Eng. Res. Technol. (IJERT) 53(3), 1–15 (2014)
7. Keele, S., et al.: Guidelines for performing systematic literature reviews in software engineering. Technical report, Ver. 2.3 EBSE Technical Report. EBSE (2007)
8. Lei, X.: Modeling and intelligent analysis of web user behavior of web user behavior. In: 2018 International Conference on Engineering Simulation and Intelligent Control (ESAIC), pp. 192–195. IEEE (2018)
9. Liao, Z., et al.: Task trail: an effective segmentation of user search behavior. IEEE Trans. Knowl. Data Eng. 26(12), 3090–3102 (2014)
10. Luo, X., et al.: User behavior analysis based on user interest by web log mining. In: 2017 27th International Telecommunication Networks and Applications Conference (ITNAC), pp. 1–5. IEEE (2017)
11. Mahajan, R., et al.: Usage patterns discovery from a web log in an Indian e-learning site: a case study. Educ. Inf. Technol. 21(1), 123–148 (2016)
12. Nguyen, S.T.: Efficient web usage mining process for sequential patterns. In: Proceedings of the 11th International Conference on Information Integration and Web-based Applications & Services, pp. 465–469 (2009)
13. Novais, R.L., et al.: Software evolution visualization: a systematic mapping study. Inf. Softw. Technol. 55(11), 1860–1883 (2013)
14. Oguz, R., et al.: Extracting information from large scale graph data: Case study on automated ui testing (2021)
15. Olmezogullari, E., Aktas, M.S.: Representation of click-stream datasequences for learning user navigational behavior by using embeddings. In: 2020 IEEE International Conference on Big Data (Big Data), pp. 3173–3179. IEEE (2020)
16. Olmezogullari, E., Aktas, M.S.: Pattern2vec: representation of clickstream data sequences for learning user navigational behavior. Concurrency Comput. Practice Exp. 34(9), e6546 (2022)
17. Omar, R., et al.: Web usage mining: a review of recent works. In: The 5th International Conference on Information and Communication Technology for The Muslim World (ICT4M), pp. 1–5. IEEE (2014)
18. Oz, M., et al.: On the use of generative deep learning approaches for generating hidden test scripts. Int. J. Software Eng. Knowl. Eng. 31(10), 1447–1468 (2021)

19. Petersen, K., et al.: Systematic mapping studies in software engineering. In: 12th International Conference on Evaluation and Assessment in Software Engineering (EASE) 12, pp. 1–10 (2008)
20. Raghu, T., et al.: Dynamic profiling of consumers for customized offerings over the internet: a model and analysis. Decis. Support Syst. **32**(2), 117–134 (2001)
21. Romero, C., et al.: Applying web usage mining for personalizing hyperlinks in web-based adaptive educational systems. Comput. Educ. **53**(3), 828–840 (2009)
22. Sılahtaroğlu, G., Dönertaşli, H.: Analysis and prediction of e-customers' behavior by mining clickstream data. In: 2015 IEEE International Conference on Big Data (Big Data), pp. 1466–1472. Ieee (2015)
23. Srivastava, J., et al.: Web usage mining: discovery and applications of usage patterns from web data. ACM SIGKDD Explorations Newsl. **1**(2), 12–23 (2000)
24. Uygun, Y., et al.: On the large-scale graph data processing for user interface testing in big data science projects. In: 2020 IEEE International Conference on Big Data (Big Data), pp. 2049–2056. IEEE (2020)
25. Wang, G., et al.: Unsupervised clickstream clustering for user behavior analysis. In: Proceedings of the 2016 CHI Conference on Human Factors in Computing Systems, pp. 225–236 (2016)
26. Yin, B., et al.: Research and application of data mining technology used in the analysis of smart home user behavior. In: 2014 Sixth International Conference on Measuring Technology and Mechatronics Automation, pp. 476–479. IEEE (2014)

Numerical Solution of a 3D System of Transient and Nonlinear PDEs Arising from Larvae-Algae-Mussels Interactions

Ramoni Z. S. Azevedo[1], Charles H. X. B. Barbosa[2],
Isaac P. Santos[1,3][(✉)], José C. R. Silva[4], Dayse H. Pastore[4],
Anna R. C. Costa[4], Claudia M. Dias[2], Raquel M. A. Figueira[5],
and Humberto F. M. Fortunato[5]

[1] Federal University of Espírito Santo, Vitória, Espírito Santo, Brazil
`ramoni.sedano@aluno.ufes.br`
[2] Federal Rural University of Rio de Janeiro, Seropédica, Rio de Janeiro, Brazil
`mazza@ufrrj.br`
[3] Federal University of Espírito Santo, São Mateus, Espírito Santo, Brazil
`isaac.santos@ufes.br`
[4] Federal Centers of Technical Education Celso Suckow da Fonseca, Rio de Janeiro,
Rio de Janeiro, Brazil
`{jose.rubianes,dayse.pastore,anna.costa}@cefet-rj.br`
[5] hubz, Rio de Janeiro, Rio de Janeiro, Brazil
`{raquel.figueira,humberto.fortunato}@hubz.com.br`

Abstract. In this work we present a numerical solution of a 3D system of transient and nonlinear partial differential equations. The model arises from larvae, algae and mussel interactions, which takes place in the Pereira Barreto channel, connecting an important Brazilian hydroelectric plant to a river. The mathematical model, proposed in Silva [1] for the two-dimensional case, is composed of three advective-diffusive-reactive equations for species densities coupled with the Navier-Stokes equations to simulate the velocity field of the channel. A numerical discretization of the model is proposed within the framework of the finite element method. Since the problem is advection-dominated, we resort to the well-known stabilization schemes, SUPG and CAU, to obtain oscillations-free solutions. The spatial discretization produces a fully implicit set of nonlinear differential algebraic equations that is integrated numerically in time by the two-step Backward Differentiation Formula of second order, whereas the nonlinear process is solved by a Picard fixed point iteration. The proposed formulation is used to simulate the dynamics of species proliferation and to quantify the golden mussel population in a stretch of the Pereira Barreto channel, with a focus on population control measures. The preliminary results, as well as other considerations related to the problem and the numerical model, are discussed.

Keywords: Larvae-Algae-Mussel model · Numerical method ·
Nonlinear system of PDEs

O. Gervasi et al. (Eds.): ICCSA 2022 Workshops, LNCS 13377, pp. 684–697, 2022.
https://doi.org/10.1007/978-3-031-10536-4_45

1   Introduction

The presence of golden mussel (*Limnoperna fortunei* (Dunker, 1857)) in Brazil is considered an environmental problem of great concern today. The Brazilian Institute for the Environment and Renewable Natural Resources (IBAMA) classifies the golden mussel as one of the three priority invasive species for control, since its overpopulation can cause serious problems for the native fauna [2]. It is a small freshwater bivalve mollusk, commonly known as the golden mussel due to its yellowish shell. This is a filter feeding species with a capacity to filter more than its own weight in microalgae per hour [3]. The animal has external reproduction, releasing gametes in the water which then produce planktonic larvae that can be carried by water currents for up to 10–20 days [4]. After this period, the mussel will go through recruitment in which the larvae will seek a proper substrate for attachment and will form a byssus for permanent fixation on the selected spot. Originating in China with its high tolerance to different environments and counting on human assistance in its transport, this species adapted well to Brazilian rivers, and is a threat even to the Amazonian aquatic ecosystems, which hold the largest and still unknown aquatic biodiversity in the world.

It is known that the areas invaded by the mussel undergo significant modifications [5], especially in environments already affected by human activity such as hydroelectric power plant reservoirs. In these areas, the animals can block the grids, pipes and heat exchangers, a particularly favored spot where the temperature contributes to the reproduction and growth of the bivalve.

Mathematical modeling is a very useful tool in the study of the relationship between biological species and their environment, having the ability to efficiently integrate and evaluate multiple complex processes simultaneously, helping to understand biological phenomena. In [1] is presented a mathematical model combining hydrodynamics and populational dynamics to simulate the distribution of mussels considering a two-dimensional geometry of the reservoir of the Três Irmãos Hydroelectric Power Plant (HPP), in Brazil.

The good results obtained by the model in two-dimensional experiments motivated us to evaluate its behavior in a three-dimensional domain. Thus, in this work we present a 3D numerical formulation, based on the finite element method, for the model described in [1], with the aim of analyze the mussel infestation in a stretch of the Pereira Barreto channel, located in the municipality of the same name in the state of São Paulo. The channel is the second largest artificial freshwater channel in the world, $9,600\,\text{m}$ long, bottom width variable between 50 and $70\,\text{m}$, $12\,\text{m}$ deep at the height upstream and $8\,\text{m}$ at the minimum level and maximum flow of $1,600\,\text{m}^3/\text{s}$. It makes the hydraulic interconnection of the reservoirs of the Três Irmãos and Ilha Solteira HPPs, and enabling the optimization of energy generation electricity in these plants and the navigation between the north and south stretches of the Paraná waterway and the connection to the north stretch of the Paraná waterway with Tietê waterway. In this way, the channel became a propagation medium for the golden mussel between the Tietê and São José dos Dourados rivers.

The mathematical model is composed of two advective-diffusive-reactive equations for larvae and algae densities, one diffusive-reactive equation for mussels density, coupled with the unsteady incompressible Navier-Stokes equations. Since the problem is convection-dominated, we apply the Streamline Upwind Petrov Galerkin (SUPG) method to obtain global oscillations-free solutions [6], and the discontinuity capturing Consistent Approximate Upwind (CAU) scheme which represents boundary layers accurately [7,8]. The spatial discretization produces a fully implicit set of nonlinear differential algebraic equations that are integrated numerically in time by the two-step Backward Differentiation Formula of second order, whereas the nonlinear process is solved using Picard fixed point iteration.

The remainder of this work is organized as follows. The mathematical model is presented in Sect. 2. We present the numerical formulation in Sect. 3. Section 4 is devoted to numerical simulations and Sect. 5 concludes this paper.

2 Mathematical Model

Let $\Omega \subset \mathbb{R}^3$ be a bounded domain with a Lipschitz boundary Γ with an outward unit normal $\boldsymbol{n}$, and $[0, t_F]$ the temporal interval, with $t_F > 0$. Denoting by $L = L(\boldsymbol{x}, t)$, $M = M(\boldsymbol{x}, t)$ and $A = A(\boldsymbol{x}, t)$ the densities of larvae, mussels and algae, respectively, at $(\boldsymbol{x}, t) \in \Omega \times [0, t_F]$, the Larvae-Mussel-Algae model consists of finding L, M and A such that

$$\frac{\partial L}{\partial t} - D_L \Delta L + \boldsymbol{u} \cdot \nabla L = r_1 M \left(1 - \frac{L}{K_L}\right) - (b_1 + \lambda_L)L, \text{ in } \Omega \times [0, t_F], \tag{1}$$

$$\frac{\partial M}{\partial t} - D_M \Delta M = \lambda_M \left(\frac{A^2}{c_1^2 + A^2}\right) L \left(1 - \frac{M}{K_M}\right) - b_2 M, \text{ in } \Omega_M \times [0, t_F], \tag{2}$$

$$\frac{\partial A}{\partial t} - D_A \Delta A + \boldsymbol{u} \cdot \nabla A = r_2 A \left(1 - \frac{A}{K_A}\right) - b_3 \left(\frac{A^2}{c_2^2 + A^2}\right) M, \text{ in } \Omega \times [0, t_F]. \tag{3}$$

The mathematical model (1)–(3), with appropriate boundary and initial conditions, is presented in [1] to solve a two-dimensional problem for quantifying the population of golden mussels in HPP reservoirs. In the equation for larvae, Eq. (1), $D_L > 0$ is the diffusivity coefficient, r_1 is the intrinsic growth rate, K_L is the limiting factor, b_1 is the mortality rate and λ_L is the maturation rate, which represents the larvae that successfully turns into adult golden mussel. In the equation for mussels, Eq. (2), $D_M > 0$ is the diffusivity coefficient, K_M is the the carrying capacity, c_1 is half saturation constant for the adults, b_2 is the mortality rate due to fish predation, and λ_M is the maturation rate. In the equation for algae, Eq. (3), $D_A > 0$ is the diffusivity coefficient, K_A is the the carrying capacity, r_2 is the intrinsic growth rate, b_3 is the mortality rate due to predation by golden mussels, and c_2 is half saturation constant for algae; $\Omega_M \subset \Omega$ is the spatial domain for the mussels, representing a layer close to the boundary walls (solid substrates and side walls). For a better understanding of this model see [1].

Equations (1), (2) and (3) form a system of transient and nonlinear coupled partial differential equations which models advective-diffusive-reactive phenomenons. Advective terms appear in the larvae and algae equations, where the free divergence velocity field, $\boldsymbol{u}$, is obtained from the unsteady incompressible Navier-Stokes equations.

Dirichlet boundary conditions are imposed only for the mussel equation, that is,

$$M(\boldsymbol{x},t) = g_M^D(\boldsymbol{x}), \ \forall \ (\boldsymbol{x},t) \in \Gamma_M^D \times [0,t_F], \tag{4}$$

where Γ_M^D represents the Dirichlet boundary for the mussels and $g_M^D(\cdot)$ is a given function. Homogeneous Neumann boundary conditions are defined for the larvae and algae equations on Γ, that is,

$$D_L \boldsymbol{\nabla} L(\boldsymbol{x},t) \cdot \boldsymbol{n}(\boldsymbol{x}) = 0, \ \forall \ (\boldsymbol{x},t) \in \Gamma^N \times [0,t_F], \tag{5}$$

$$D_A \boldsymbol{\nabla} A(\boldsymbol{x},t) \cdot \boldsymbol{n}(\boldsymbol{x}) = 0, \ \forall \ (\boldsymbol{x},t) \in \Gamma^N \times [0,t_F], \tag{6}$$

where $\Gamma^N \subset \Gamma$ is the part of the boundary with Neumann conditions. The homogeneous Neumann boundary condition means that there is no population movement of larvae and algae across the boundary, Γ. The mathematical model (1)–(3) is completed by assuming the initial conditions,

$$L(\boldsymbol{x},0) = L_0(\boldsymbol{x}), \quad M(\boldsymbol{x},0) = M_0(\boldsymbol{x}), \quad A(\boldsymbol{x},0) = A_0(\boldsymbol{x}), \tag{7}$$

where L_0, M_0, A_0 are given functions representing the initial densities of larvae, mussels and algae, respectively.

In order to describe the variational formulation of this problem we define the following function spaces, $V_L = V_A = H^1(\Omega)$ and

$$V_M = \{w \in H^1(\Omega_M); \ w_h = g_M^D \text{ on } \Gamma_M^D\}, \tag{8}$$

where $H^1(\Omega)$ is the Sobolev space consisting of functions for which all partial derivatives up to order one are square integrables in Ω; V_L, V_M, V_A are function spaces associated with the equations for larvae, mussels and algae, respectively. Thus, for $t \in [0,t_F]$, the variational formulation of (1)–(3) consists of finding $(L,M,A) \in V_L \times V_M \times V_A$ such that

$$\left(\frac{\partial L}{\partial t}, v_L\right) + D_L(\boldsymbol{\nabla} L, \boldsymbol{\nabla} v_L) + (\boldsymbol{u} \cdot \boldsymbol{\nabla} L, v_L) + (\sigma_L L, v_L) = (f_L, v_L), \tag{9}$$

$$\left(\frac{\partial M}{\partial t}, v_M\right) + D_M(\boldsymbol{\nabla} M, \boldsymbol{\nabla} v_M) + (\sigma_M M, v_M) = (f_M, v_M), \tag{10}$$

$$\left(\frac{\partial A}{\partial t}, v_A\right) + D_A(\boldsymbol{\nabla} A, \boldsymbol{\nabla} v_A) + (\boldsymbol{u} \cdot \boldsymbol{\nabla} A, v_A) + (\sigma_A A, v_A) = (f_A, v_A), \tag{11}$$

for all $v_L \in V_L$, $v_A \in V_A$, and $v_M \in V_M^0 = \{w \in H^1(\Omega);\ w_h = 0$ on $\Gamma_M^D\}$, where

$$\sigma_L = \sigma_L(M) = \left(\lambda_L + b_1 + \frac{r_1}{K_L}M\right), \quad f_L = f_L(M) = r_1 M,$$

$$\sigma_M = \sigma_M(A, L) = \left[b_2 + \frac{\lambda_M}{K_M}\left(\frac{A^2}{c_1^2 + A^2}\right)L\right], \quad f_M = f_M(A, L) = \lambda_M\left(\frac{A^2}{c_1^2 + A^2}\right)L,$$

$$\sigma_A = \sigma_A(A, M) = \left[b_3\left(\frac{AM}{c_2^2 + A^2}\right) + \frac{r_2 A}{K_A}\right], \quad f_A = f_A(A) = r_2 A.$$

The velocity field $\boldsymbol{u}$ in the advective terms of (1) and (3) is obtained from the unsteady incompressible Navier-Stokes equations, given by

$$\frac{\partial \boldsymbol{u}}{\partial t} + (\boldsymbol{u} \cdot \boldsymbol{\nabla})\boldsymbol{u} - \nu\Delta\boldsymbol{u} + \boldsymbol{\nabla}p = \boldsymbol{f}, \quad \forall\, (\boldsymbol{x}, t) \in \Omega \times [0, t_F], \tag{12}$$

$$\boldsymbol{\nabla} \cdot \boldsymbol{u} = 0, \quad \forall\, (\boldsymbol{x}, t) \in \Omega \times [0, t_F], \tag{13}$$

$$\boldsymbol{u} = \boldsymbol{0}, \quad \forall\, (\boldsymbol{x}, t) \in \Gamma_u^D \times [0, t_F], \tag{14}$$

$$\boldsymbol{u} = \boldsymbol{g}_u^D, \quad \forall\, (\boldsymbol{x}, t) \in \Gamma_u^{D,in} \times [0, t_F], \tag{15}$$

$$\boldsymbol{u}(\boldsymbol{x}, 0) = \boldsymbol{u}_0(\boldsymbol{x}), \quad \forall\, \boldsymbol{x} \in \Omega, \tag{16}$$

where p is the rate between the pressure and the density, ν is the kinematic viscosity (constant), $\boldsymbol{f}$ is a given external force field per unit mass, $\boldsymbol{u}_0(\cdot)$ is the initial velocity, $\boldsymbol{g}_u^D$ is a known function defined on the Dirichlet inflow boundary, $\Gamma_u^{D,in} = \{\boldsymbol{x} \in \Gamma;\ \boldsymbol{u} \cdot \boldsymbol{n} \leq 0\}$, and $\Gamma_u^D = \Gamma \setminus (\Gamma_u^{D,in} \cup \Gamma_u^{D,out})$. The Navier-Stokes model was solved by the Characteristic Galerkin method [9].

3   Numerical Formulation

In this section we present a numerical formulation for solving the system (1)–(3) based on the finite element method [9–11].

We consider a regular partition $\mathcal{T}_h = \{K\}$ of the domain $\Omega \subset \mathbb{R}^3$ into tetrahedral elements, where h stands for the mesh size. The finite dimensional spaces associated to V_L, V_M, V_A, V_M^0 are denoted by $V_{h,\alpha}$, $\alpha \in \{L, M, A\}$, and $V_{h,M}^0$, respectively, and defined as

$$V_{h,\alpha} = \{w_h \in H^1(\Omega) : w_h|_K \in \mathbb{P}_1(K), \forall K \in \mathcal{T}_h\}, \alpha \in L, A, \tag{17}$$

$$V_{h,M} = \{w_h \in H^1(\Omega_M) : w_h|_K \in \mathbb{P}_1(K), \forall K \in \mathcal{T}_h,\ w_h = g_M^D \text{ on } \Gamma_M^D\}, \tag{18}$$

$$V_{h,M}^0 = \{w_h \in H^1(\Omega) : w_h|_K \in \mathbb{P}_1(K), \forall K \in \mathcal{T}_h,\ w_h = 0 \text{ on } \Gamma_M^D\}, \tag{19}$$

where $\mathbb{P}_1(K)$ is the set of first order polynomials defined in K.

We approximate the time derivatives by the two-step Backward Differentiation Formula of order 2 (BDF2) [12],

$$\tilde{\mathcal{D}}_{\Delta t}^{\alpha, k+1} = \frac{3\alpha^{k+1} - 4\alpha^k + \alpha^{k-1}}{2\Delta t}, \quad \alpha \in \{L, M, A\}. \tag{20}$$

The BDF2 method is one of the most popular time-stepping methods for solving unsteady problems, due to its good stability property [12]. For the sake of presentation simplicity, we omit the subscript h for functions of the finite dimensional spaces. The numerical solution of (9)–(11) at time t_{k+1} consists of finding $(L^{k+1}, M^{k+1}, A^{k+1}) \in V_{h,L} \times V_{h,M} \times V_{h,A}$ such that

$$(\tilde{\mathcal{D}}_{\Delta t}^{L,k+1}, v_L) + D_L(\boldsymbol{\nabla} L, \boldsymbol{\nabla} v_L^{k+1}) + (\boldsymbol{u} \cdot \boldsymbol{\nabla} L^{k+1}, v_L) + (\sigma_L^{k+1} L^{k+1}, v_L) = (f_L^{k+1}, v_L),$$
$$(\tilde{\mathcal{D}}_{\Delta t}^{M,k+1}, v_M) + D_M(\boldsymbol{\nabla} M^{k+1}, \boldsymbol{\nabla} v_M) + (\sigma_M^{k+1} M^{k+1}, v_M) = (f_M^{k+1}, v_M),$$
$$(\tilde{\mathcal{D}}_{\Delta t}^{A,k+1}, v_A) + D_A(\boldsymbol{\nabla} A^{k+1}, \boldsymbol{\nabla} v_A) + (\boldsymbol{u} \cdot \boldsymbol{\nabla} A^{k+1}, v_A) + (\sigma_A^{k+1} A^{k+1}, v_A) = (f_A^{k+1}, v_A),$$

for all $(v_L, v_M, v_A) \in V_{h,L} \times V_{h,M}^0 \times V_{h,A}$.

The resulting system of nonlinear equations is solved by a Picard fixed point iteration. A numerical solution for L^{k+1}, M^{k+1} e A^{k+1} can be obtained by performing several iterations in the following way: for $s = 1, \cdots, s_{max}$, solve the system

$$\frac{3}{2\Delta t}(\tilde{L}^{s+1}, v_L) + D_L(\boldsymbol{\nabla} \tilde{L}^{s+1}, \boldsymbol{\nabla} v_L) + (\boldsymbol{u} \cdot \boldsymbol{\nabla} \tilde{L}^{s+1}, v_L) + (\tilde{\sigma}_L^s \tilde{L}^{s+1}, v_L) = (\tilde{f}_L^s, v_L)$$
$$+ \frac{2}{\Delta t}(L^k, v_L) - \frac{1}{2\Delta t}(L^{k-1}, v_L),$$

$$\frac{3}{2\Delta t}(\tilde{M}^{s+1}, v_M) + D_M(\boldsymbol{\nabla} \tilde{M}^{s+1}, \boldsymbol{\nabla} v_M) + (\tilde{\sigma}_M^s M^{k+1}, v_M) = (\tilde{f}_M^s, v_M) \qquad (21)$$
$$+ \frac{2}{\Delta t}(M^k, v_M) - \frac{1}{2\Delta t}(M^{k-1}, v_L),$$

$$\frac{3}{2\Delta t}(\tilde{A}^{s+1}, v_A) + D_A(\boldsymbol{\nabla} \tilde{A}^{s+1}, \boldsymbol{\nabla} v_A) + (\boldsymbol{u} \cdot \boldsymbol{\nabla} \tilde{A}^{s+1}, v_A) + (\tilde{\sigma}_A^s \tilde{A}^{s+1}, v_A) = (\tilde{f}_A, v_A)$$
$$+ \frac{2}{\Delta t}(A^k, v_A) - \frac{1}{2\Delta t}(A^{k-1}, v_L),$$

where $\tilde{L}^{s+1}, \tilde{M}^{s+1}$ and $\tilde{L}^{s+1}$ are approximations of L^{k+1}, M^{k+1} and L^{k+1}, respectively; $\tilde{\sigma}_L^s = \sigma_L(\tilde{M}^s)$, $\tilde{f}_L = f_L(\tilde{M}^s)$, $\tilde{\sigma}_M^s = \sigma_M(\tilde{A}^s, \tilde{L}^s)$, $\tilde{f}_M^s = f_M(\tilde{A}^s, \tilde{L}^s)$, $\tilde{\sigma}_A^s = \sigma_A(\tilde{A}^s, \tilde{M}^s)$ and $\tilde{f}_A = f_A(\tilde{A}^s)$; s denotes the index of nonlinear iterations for each time (fixed) t_k. We insert in the model (21) two more terms inherent to the SUPG and CAU methods: the term

$$\sum_{K \in \mathcal{T}_h} \left(R_L(\tilde{L}^{s+1}), \tau_{supg}^L \boldsymbol{u} \cdot \boldsymbol{\nabla} v_L \right)_K + \sum_{K \in \mathcal{T}_h} \left(\xi_{cau}^L(\tilde{L}^s) \boldsymbol{\nabla} \tilde{L}^{s+1}, \boldsymbol{\nabla} v_L \right)_K \qquad (22)$$

in the lef hand side of the first equation, and

$$\sum_{K \in \mathcal{T}_h} \left(R_A(\tilde{A}^{s+1}), \tau_{supg}^A \boldsymbol{u} \cdot \boldsymbol{\nabla} v_A \right)_K + \sum_{K \in \mathcal{T}_h} \left(\xi_{cau}^A(\tilde{A}^s) \boldsymbol{\nabla} \tilde{A}^{s+1}, \boldsymbol{\nabla} v_A \right)_K \qquad (23)$$

in the left hand side of the third one, so that the dominant advection property of the model is well represented. In (22) and (23), $R_L(\cdot)$ and $R_A(\cdot)$ are the residuals of the larvae and algae equations, respectively, given by

$$R_L(\tilde{L}^{s+1}) = \frac{3\tilde{L}^{s+1} - 4L^k + L^{k-1}}{2\Delta t} - D_L \Delta \tilde{L}^{s+1} + \boldsymbol{u} \cdot \boldsymbol{\nabla} \tilde{L}^{s+1} + \tilde{\sigma}_L^s \tilde{L}^{s+1} - \tilde{f}_L^s,$$

$$R_A(\tilde{A}^{s+1}) = \frac{3\tilde{A}^{s+1} - 4A^k + A^{k-1}}{2\Delta t} - D_A \Delta \tilde{A}^{s+1} + \boldsymbol{u} \cdot \boldsymbol{\nabla} \tilde{A}^{s+1} + \tilde{\sigma}_A^s \tilde{A}^{s+1} - \tilde{f}_A^s,$$

where τ_{supg}^L and τ_{supg}^A are the stabilization parameters of the SUPG method for the larvae and algae equations, respectively, whereas $\xi_{cau}^L(\cdot)$ and $\xi_{cau}^A(\cdot)$ are the nonlinear artificial diffusion functions of the CAU method for the larvae and algae equations. The definitions of τ_{supg}^L, τ_{supg}^A, $\xi_{cau}^L(\cdot)$ and $\xi_{cau}^A(\cdot)$ are found in [8].

4   Numerical Experiments

In this section we present the numerical experiments of this first approach for the solution of the proposed methodology. Our objective here is to understand if the solution obtained is close to the densities observed in the field. We used the FreeFem++ software [13] to generate the mesh and obtain the velocity field from the transient incompressible Navier-Stokes equations. A code in Matlab ©was developed to solve the system of partial differential equations, given in Eqs. (1)–(3). We considered a period of time of 4 months to evaluate the beginning of the golden mussel infestation. The 3D domain Ω represents a stretch of the Pereira Barreto channel, with 2 km long, close to the Três Irmãos HPP reservoir, located in the Tietê river basin, close to the municipalities of Pereira Barreto (SP) and Andradina (SP), shown in Fig. 1.

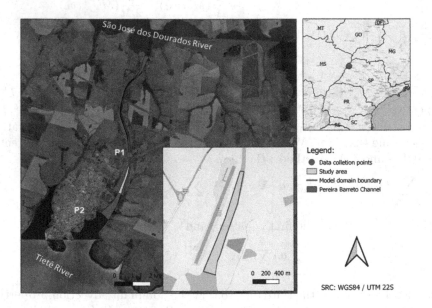

Fig. 1. Pereira barreto channel (adapted from google earth©).

The domain was discretized with 13,290 tetrahedral elements and 3,186 nodes, conforming mesh shown in Fig. 2. The following initial values were used for the populations: $L(\boldsymbol{x},0) = 0.0194115 \; g/l$, $M(\boldsymbol{x},0) = 1 \; g/m^3$ and

$A(x, 0) = 0.001 \ g/l$. First, we obtain the velocity field from the solution of the incompressible transient Navier-Stokes equations, using $u_0 = 0$ in Ω, $g_u^D = 0.13 \ m/s$ in $\Gamma_u^{D,in}$ (channel inlet), and shown in Fig. 3. The parameters used in the simulations are describe in Table 1.

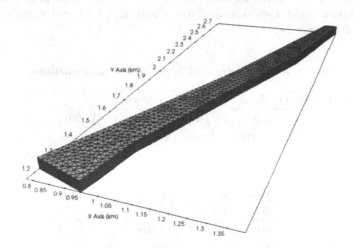

Fig. 2. Mesh used in the numerical experiments.

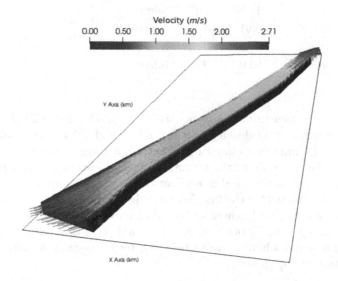

Fig. 3. Velocity field obtained from incompressible transient Navier-Stokes equations.

The solution at the first time step is obtained by the Backward Euler (BDF1) method since the BDF2 is a two-step scheme. Moreover, in each time step the algorithm performed $s_{max} = 20$ nonlinear steps. We carried out numerical simulations with and without the SUPG and CAU stabilized methods, and the importance of these formulations in the model became clear, providing numerical solutions without spurious oscillations and without negative values for the densities of the species.

Table 1. Parameters used in the numerical simulations.

Parameter	Value	Unit	Reference
D_A	1.2	m^2/day	(Cangelosi et al., 2015)
D_M	0.0012	m^2/day	(Montresor, 2014)
D_L	0.012	m^2/day	(Van de Koppel et al. 2005)
b_1	0.015	day^{-1}	Inferred
b_2	0.02	day^{-1}	Inferred
b_3	0.02	day^{-1}	Inferred
λ_M	0.03	day^{-1}	Inferred
λ_L	0.03	day^{-1}	Inferred
r_1	0.07	day^{-1}	Inferred
r_2	0.12	day^{-1}	Inferred
K_L	20	g/l	Inferred
K_M	1,732	g/m^3	Inferred
K_A	0.01	g/l	Inferred
c_1	0.001	g/l	Inferred
c_2	0.001	g/l	Inferred

Recent *in situ* measurements were carried out in December 2020 and August 2021, obtaining a mussel density of $3,936$ g/m^3 and $7,546$ g/m^3, respectively. It is worth mentioning that climatic and anthropic impacts were not included in the model. Below we present the evolution of the infestation over 4 months.

Figure 4 presents a logistical growth for the larvae population homogeneously throughout the channel for the first four months of infestation. As expected, this behavior follows the development of the adult mussel population (Fig. 5). However, we observed that in both cases the growth is slowed after third month. Finally, Fig. 6 shows a homogeneous behavior for the algae population throughout the section of the channel.

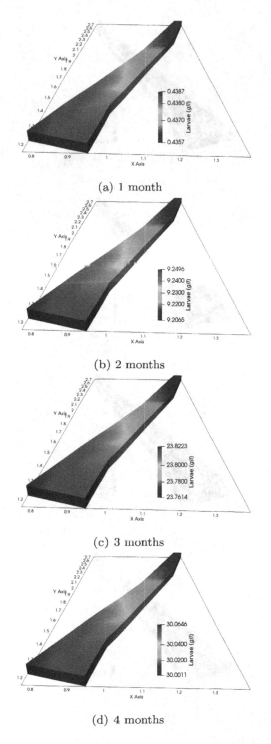

(a) 1 month

(b) 2 months

(c) 3 months

(d) 4 months

Fig. 4. Densities of Larvae after 4 months of infestation.

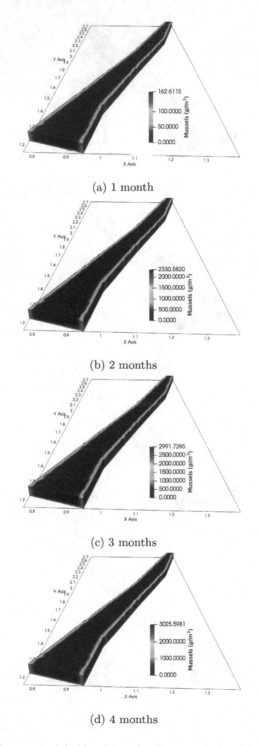

(a) 1 month

(b) 2 months

(c) 3 months

(d) 4 months

Fig. 5. Densities of Golden Mussels after 4 months of infestation.

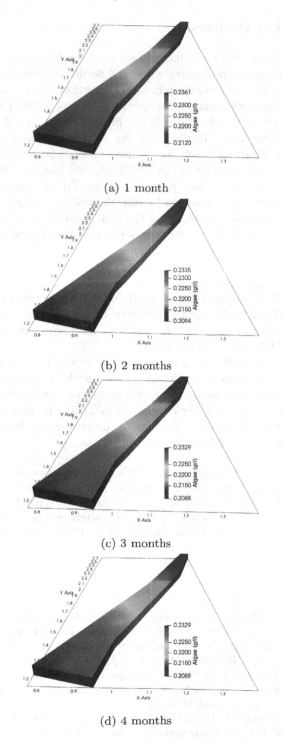

(a) 1 month

(b) 2 months

(c) 3 months

(d) 4 months

Fig. 6. Densities of Algae after 4 months of infestation.

5 Concluding Remarks

We presented a numerical formulation, based on the finite element method, for solving a complex 3D system of transient and nonlinear transport PDEs arising from larvae, algae and mussel interactions. The mathematical model is composed of three scalar transport equations for species densities coupled with the Navier-Stokes equations to simulate the velocity field of the channel. The numerical discretization of the model involves the use of the stabilized methods, SUPG and CAU. The fully implicit set of nonlinear differential algebraic equations is integrated numerically in time by the BDF2 scheme, whereas the nonlinear process is solved by a Picard fixed point iteration. The dynamics of the golden mussel population in their larvae and adult phases, and the algae population in a stretch of the channel, was observed through a preliminary numerical experiment that showed that the model represents well the interaction between the populations in the period of time evaluated. The analysis of the distribution of adult golden mussels corroborates the proposition that the Pereira Barreto channel has been serving as a nursery for the species, and that the infestation of the reservoir at Ilha Solteira HPP is mainly due to the arrival of larvae from the Três Irmãos HPP (already heavily infested), which through the channel, reach the São José dos Dourados river and then the Ilha Solteira HPP, thus forming a route for mussel infestation in the region.

Although this work has presented motivating results, this is a preliminary analysis and the simulations are in accordance with the dynamics recorded in the two-dimensional analysis [1]. A more complex computer simulation is being implemented, evaluating a longer period of time, using more refined meshes and a more extensive spatial domain in order to compare with the *in situ* data, and evaluate the convergence of the numerical process.

Acknowledgements. Research carried out within the scope of the project "Control of the Golden Mussel Infestation by Genetic Induction of Infertility" (PD-10381-0419/2019) with funding from CTG Brasil, SPIC Brasil and Tijoá Energia, within their ANEEL Research & Development Programs. This study was partially financed by the Coordenação de Aperfeiçoamento de Pessoal de Nível Superior - Brasil (CAPES) - Finance Code 001.

References

1. Silva, J.C.R., et al.: Population growth of the golden mussel (L. fortunei) in hydroelectric power plants: a study via mathematical and computational modeling. Braz. J. Water Res. **27** (2022). https://doi.org/10.1590/2318-0331.272220210124
2. IBAMA. Instituto Brasileiro do Meio Ambiente e dos Recursos Naturais Renováveis. Ministério do Meio Ambiente (2019). https://www.ibama.gov.br/especies-exoticas-invasoras/sobre-as-especies-exoticas-invasoras-sobre-especies-exoticas-invasoras. Accessed 31 Mar 2021
3. Sylvester, F., Dorado, J., Boltovskoy, D., Juarez, A., Cataldo, D.: Filtration rates of the invasive pest bivalve Limnoperna fortunei as a function of size and temperature. Hydrobiologia **534**, 71–80 (2005). https://doi.org/10.1007/s10750-004-1322-3

4. Cataldo, D., Boltovskoy, D., Hermosa, J., Canzi, C.: Temperature-dependent rates of larval development in limnoperna fortunei (bivalvia: mytilidae). J. Molluscan Stud. **71**(1), 41–46 (2005). https://doi.org/10.1093/mollus/eyi005
5. Karatayev, A., Burlakova, L., Padilla, D.: The effects of dreissena polymorpha (pallas) invasion on aquatic communities in Eastern Europe. J. Shellfish Res. **16**, 187–203 (1997)
6. Brooks, A.N., Hughes, T.J.R.: Streamline upwind Petrov-Galerkin formulations for convection dominated flows with particular emphasis on the incompressible Navier-Stokes equations. Comput. Methods Appl. Mech. Eng. **32**(1–3), 199–259 (1982)
7. Galeão, A.C., Dutra do Carmo, E.G.: A consistent approximate upwind Petrov-Galerkin method for convection-dominated problems. Comput. Methods Appl. Mech. Eng. **68**(1), 83–95 (1988)
8. Carmo, E.G.D., Alvarez, G.B.: A new stabilized finite element formulation for scalar convection-diffusion problems: the streamline and approximate upwind/Petrov-Galerkin method. Comput. Methods Appl. Mech. Eng. **192**(31–32), 3379–3396 (2003)
9. Donea, J., Huerta, A.: Finite Element Method for Flow Problems. Wiley, Oxford (2003)
10. Hughes, T.J.R.: The Finite Element Method: Linear Static and Dynamic Finite Element Analysis. Prentice-Hall International, Upper Saddle River (1987)
11. Roos, H., Stynes, M., Tobiska, L.: Robust Numerical Methods for Singularly Perturbed Differential Equations: Convection-Diffusion-Reaction and Flow Problems, 2nd edn. Springer, Heidelberg (2008). https://doi.org/10.1007/978-3-540-34467-4
12. Hairer, E., Norsett, S.P., Wanner, G.: Solving Ordinary Differential Equations. Springer Series in Computational Mathematics, 2nd edn. Springer, Heidelberg (2010). https://doi.org/10.1007/978-3-540-78862-1
13. Hecht, F.: New development in FreeFem++. J. Numer. Math. **20**(3–4), 251–266 (2012)

A Novel Sequential Pattern Mining Algorithm for Large Scale Data Sequences

Ali Burak Can[1]([✉]), Meryem Uzun-Per[1,2][iD], and Mehmet S. Aktas[3][iD]

[1] BiletBank Research and Development Center, Akdeniz PE-TUR A.S.,
Istanbul, Turkey
{aliburak.can,meryem.uzunper}@petour.com
[2] Computer Engineering Department, Istanbul Health and Technology University,
Istanbul, Turkey
meryem.uzunper@istun.edu.tr
[3] Computer Engineering Department, Yildiz Technical University, Istanbul, Turkey
aktas@yildiz.edu.tr

Abstract. Sequential pattern mining algorithms are unsupervised machine learning algorithms that allow finding sequential patterns on data sequences that have been put together based on a particular order. These algorithms are mostly optimized for finding sequential data sequences containing more than one element. Hence, we argue that there is a need for algorithms that are particularly optimized for data sequences that contain only one element. Within the scope of this research, we study the design and development of a novel algorithm that is optimized for data sets containing data sequences with single elements and that can detect sequential patterns with high performance. The time and memory requirements of the proposed algorithm are examined experimentally. The results show that the proposed algorithm has low running times, while it has the same accuracy results as the algorithms in the similar category in the literature. The obtained results are promising.

Keywords: Sequential pattern mining · GSP · PrefixSpan · Large scale data sequences · MapReduce programming model

1 Introduction

Due to the increase in e-commerce transaction volume in recent years, the data that must be stored rises exponentially day by day. Therefore, it becomes inevitable to develop both data mining and big data processing methods. One of the main tasks of data mining is to discover useful patterns normally hard to distinguish in data by eye [7,12,24]. Pattern mining have been an active research topic in data mining for years. Apriori [1], ECLAT (Equivalence Class Clustering and bottom-up Lattice Traversal) [33], FP-Growth (Frequent Pattern Growth) [8] algorithms are some example algorithms for association rule mining, while GSP (Generalized Sequential Pattern) [19], SPADE (Sequential PAttern Discovery using Equivalence classes) [32], PrefixSpan (Prefix-projected Sequential

O. Gervasi et al. (Eds.): ICCSA 2022 Workshops, LNCS 13377, pp. 698–708, 2022.
https://doi.org/10.1007/978-3-031-10536-4_46

pattern mining) [13] methods are used for sequential pattern mining applications as both of them are sub-branches of pattern mining. These two different algorithm families differ in their goals. Sequential pattern mining methods consider the order of the items, unlike the association rule mining methods.

As the nature of sequential pattern mining and association rule mining algorithms, they work on different types of datasets. Sequential pattern mining algorithms like PrefixSpan are designed for datasets containing sequential items. On the other hand, association rule mining methods like FP-Growth can be applied for transactional datasets. A transactional dataset consists of unique items corresponding to each Transaction-ID. A symbolic representation could be such as TID-1: A, B, C and TID-2: A, C, D. This example could be interpreted like having two basket records on the dataset of a grocery and product A, product B, and product C in one basket and product A, product C, and product D in another basket. The order of the items is immaterial in this type of dataset. On the contrary, in a dataset containing sequential items corresponding to each Sequence-ID, the items are arranged in order, called Sequential Dataset. It is seen by examining sequences here that there may be more than one element in an itemset. For example, if we consider this symbolic representation SID-1: A, (A, B, C), (A, C), D, (C, F) as the shopping data of a market, in the row corresponding to SID-1; a customer purchases product A on Monday, products A, B, and C on Tuesday, products A and C on Wednesday, product D on Thursday, and product C and F on Friday. Differently, some kinds of datasets like a genome sequence data portrayed in this symbolic representation SID-1: (A), (G), (T) have different characteristics. Even though these datasets are ordered from left to right as the sequential dataset, each itemset has only one element. In other words, each itemset is one-dimensional, or the length of the itemset is 1.

Within the scope of this research, an algorithm is proposed which is designed to detect sequential patterns on big data processing and analysis platforms on sequential datasets (e.g., genome sequence data) containing ordered sequences and containing only one element in each sub-sequence. The algorithm is named $Proposed$-$SPMA$ (Sequential Pattern Mining Algorithm) in this article. In order to demonstrate the success of the proposed algorithm, a prototype implementation has been done.

The algorithm we propose within this study has been compared with the sequential pattern mining methods (PrefixSpan and GSP) in the literature. Apache Spark [11] open source library, which is one of the widely used platforms, is used for the big data processing and analysis platform. While the ready-made function in the Apache Spark MLlib library was used for the PrefixSpan algorithm, the GSP algorithm was developed by using the Apache Spark library.

The rest of this article is organized as follows: Sect. 2 describes the research questions we examined thoroughly in this study in detail. In Sect. 3, sequential pattern mining, and big data processing are examined and also sequential pattern mining studies in big data are summarized. Section 4 gives the pseudocode of the proposed algorithm, its explanation, and its textual explanation through an example. Experimental results and their evaluation are done in Sect. 5. In the last section, a summary of the whole study is given.

2 Research Questions

In this study, it is examined how a high-performance sequential pattern mining algorithm can be created that will allow finding sequential patterns on one-dimensional sequences that are large enough to be stored in a single computer's data storage media (memory and physical disk). We summarize below the research questions that we have been working on within the scope of this research.

1) How a sequential pattern mining algorithm that will work with high performance on datasets with big data characteristics should be to enable finding sequential patterns on single-element itemsets that have come together in a certain order?
2) How can the running time and memory requirements of a sequential pattern mining algorithm be determined experimentally? How is the performance of the proposed sequential pattern mining algorithm in this research, when compared to other algorithms in the same category, in terms of running time and memory requirements?

3 Literature Review

Sequential pattern mining is a subtopic of pattern mining, and it is used to find common patterns in sequential data [7,12,24]. GSP [19] and PrefixSpan [13] algorithms are among the frequently used algorithms for sequential pattern mining, which has many application areas such as bioinformatics [25], market basket analysis [19], and text analysis [14]. Within the scope of this research, a comparative analysis is conducted for the proposed sequential pattern mining algorithm with the GSP and PrefixSpan algorithms.

By inspired by apriori method, GSP algorithm was invented. As Apriori, *support* and *confidence* metrics are also calculated in this algorithm [19]. Support is the probability of a pattern in all of the transactions. Confidence is the probability that a pattern coexists with another pattern. In the GSP algorithm, the dataset is first scanned for candidates for sequential patterns. Then, the candidates that do not meet the predefined minimum support (*minsup*) are removed. Possible candidates of sequential patterns are generated with the remaining candidates. The dataset is scanned again, and the frequencies of the newly generated pattern candidates are calculated. Again, candidates that are below the *minsup* are deleted. Then, potential candidates are generated with patterns that exceed the value of *minsup*, and these processes continue until no new pattern candidates can be created. Similar to the Apriori algorithm, the GSP algorithm has overheads like creating a numerous sequential pattern candidates, dataset scanning several times, and having trouble to find long patterns.

PrefixSpan algorithm does not necessitate the generation of pattern candidates. [13]. In the PrefixSpan algorithm, basically, the projections of the dataset are generated, and sequential patterns are created. Instead of candidates, PrefixSpan uses frequent prefixes in the projections of the dataset. This method diminishes the processing time and boosts the efficiency of the algorithm.

Big data is often characterized by variety, volume, and velocity, and it may be comprised of structured, semi-structured, or unstructured data. One of the most significant aspects of big data processing is the ability to handle data fast [5,16]. Data storage, data processing, and workflow management are the three main categories of the open source big data processing ecosystem. To process big data, there are several system such as Apache Hadoop, Spark, Flink, and Storm. They use HDFS (The Hadoop Distributed File System) for storing technology and YARN (Yet Another Resource Negotiator) for scheduling tasks and managing resources. Compared to Apache Hadoop, Apache Spark [31], an open source platform for distributed big data processing, is faster in terms of iterative transactions because it prevents writing to disk as its capability. In-memory computing and RDDs (Resilient Distributed Datasets) are main attributes of Apache Spark. Hence, it runs 100 times faster in memory and ten times faster on disk than Apache Hadoop. For machine learning applications, Hadoop uses Mahout [2], Spark uses MLlib [11]. Because machine learning algorithms often involve iterative operations, Spark MLlib is faster than Mahout to run these algorithms. The algorithm we propose in this study is designed to work on big data processing and analysis platforms that implement the map-reduce programming model. Apache Spark has been used as the big data processing and analysis platform since it uses the iterative map-reduce programming model, provides high-performance data parallelism, and is easy to use. The Apache Spark MLlib library has been extended, and the proposed algorithm has been implemented on this library.

On Spark and Hadoop, Sequential Pattern Mining methods are implemented. They are also parallelized to avoid the overhead of loading and serialization [10,15,26,29,30]. Yu et al. have proposed a MapReduce-based distributed GSP (DGSP) algorithm on Hadoop [30]. The DGSP method partitions the dataset and assigns tasks to worker nodes, thus optimizing the balance of workload. Li et al. proposed the Ha-GSP algorithm in Hadoop which uses MapReduce's Divide and Conquer functions [10]. Yu et al. also showed an implementation of the GSP algorithm on Apache Spark. [29]. Several database partitioning methods have been proposed for the unbalanced loading problem. To reduce the input-output problem, stored records on HDFS are loaded to Spark RDDs, the database is read from the RDDs, and the intermediate results are stored on the RDDs.

Parallel PrefixSpan algorithms using Hadoop-based MapReduce operations are proposed by Wei et al. [26] and Sabrina et al. [15]. I/O operations on HDFS are necessary for Hadoop, it causes a high I/O issue. Yu et al. [29] proposed a PrefixSpan algorithm on Spark to reduce load by making it scalable, which partitions the projected database, loads them to RDDs to reduce I/O operations, and uses them from RDDs.

Algorithm 1. Proposed-SPMA

Inputs: A sequence database (*database*) which is formed like id-transactions, Minimum Support Value (*minsup*)

Output: *result* (Sequential Patterns and their counts)

1: Count C_1's for each sequence in *database*
2: $F_1 \leftarrow C_1$'s such that its frequency exceeds the *minsup*
3: *database$_k$* $\leftarrow$ Database contains only F_1
4: *result* $\leftarrow F_1$
5: $k \leftarrow 2$
6: **while** $F_k \neq \emptyset$ **do**
7:     Generate candidate sets C_k for each sequence
8:     Count C_k's for each sequence
9:     $F_k \leftarrow C_k$'s such that its frequency exceeds the *minsup*
10:     *result* $\leftarrow$ *result* $+ F_k$
11:     *database$_k$* $\leftarrow$ Database contains only F_k
12:     $k \leftarrow k + 1$
13: **end while**

Another parallel algorithm based on PrefixSpan on Spark has been developed by Kim et al. [9]. PrefixSpan-based methods run faster than GSP-based methods as GSP-based scans database more than one and PrefixSpan-based algorithms scan only the databse which is projected last step. Unlike the studies above, this research proposes an algorithm that can work on big data processing and analysis platforms, optimized to detect sequential patterns on large-scale datasets consisting of single-element, sequential datasets.

We observe a number of studies that focus on big data processing in different studies [3,4,6,17,20–23,27,28]. Different from previous work, in this study, we mainly focus on big data processing techniques for sequential data mining algorithms.

4 Methodology

This study introduces a sequential pattern mining algorithm that can mine sequential patterns on datasets consisting of single-element sequential and large-scale transactions. The pseudocode of the proposed algorithm is given in Algorithm 1.

The algorithm we propose has been designed and developed inspired by the GSP algorithm, which has been presented in Sect. 3. The algorithm first scans the dataset and identifies candidate patterns to find the sequential patterns. Candidate patterns with a frequency less than the minimum support (*minsup*) value are eliminated. The algorithm, unlike the GSP algorithm, aims to reduce the search space in each iteration. In order to reduce the search space, the values below the *minsup* value are deleted from the database, and new candidate patterns are produced based on this cleaned database. While generating the candidate patterns, the IDs are also taken into account. In this way, it enables the search space to be narrowed by clearing the database from elements below the *minsup* value. In the narrowed search space, possible patterns to be examined in the next iteration are created based on the candidates above the *minsup* value.

In Algorithm 1, a step-by-step explanation of the pseudocode of the proposed algorithm is given:

- The inputs are *database*, a sequential dataset consisting of single-element, and *minsup*, a minimum support value.
- The output is *result*, frequent sequential patterns with their corresponding frequencies.

- In line 1, 1-length subsequences in the dataset are counted.
- In line 2, sequences below the *minsup* value are eliminated, and in line 3, these sequences are also deleted from the dataset. Subsequences above the *minsup* value become the initial values of the output *result*, on line 4.
- In line 6, the loop begins and continues until no new candidate can be created.
- The candidate generation part of the algorithm for each sequence is done in the 7th line. While generating the candidate, all other sequences in the dataset are scanned for each sequence. For each sequence, the first element of the first sequence is deleted, and the last element of the sequence is deleted. If the remaining ones are equal, a new candidate is generated. This process may be explained with the following example:
  - For 2-sequence examples, AB and BC, the first element of the first sequence A is deleted, thus remaining is B. The last element of the second sequence C is deleted, therefore remaining is B, the ABC data series candidate can be generated because $B = B$. But, for AB and CB, since $C \neq B$ is, a new candidate cannot be generated from these two.
- Line 8 shows counting generated candidates, and those below the *minsup* value are eliminated in line 9, and these items are also deleted from the dataset as shown on line 11.
- Candidates that meet the *minsup* value requirement in each loop become the sequential patterns that are looked for, and the output is appended to the *result* value in line 10.
- The value k, which specifies the candidate length, is incremented with each iteration.

A textual explanation of the pseudocode given in Algorithm 1 is as follows. The *minsup* value is determined as 2.

The operation of the algorithm is simulated on a dataset consisting of 4 transactions. In each transaction, there are single-element, sequenced data. Their transaction IDs and sequential data in each transaction are as follows: ID-0: B, C, D, F; ID-1:B, D, E, C, F; ID-2: A; ID-3: B, C, D.

The algorithm first calculates the frequency values of single-elements in the dataset. It then eliminates elements with a support value less than 2. It then deletes the eliminated single-elements from the dataset. As a result of this process, in the example given, the next state of the dataset became: ID-0: B, C, D, F; ID-1:B, D, C, F; ID-3: B, C, D.

After this stage, the algorithm performs the following operations on the dataset in a loop.

In the first iteration; As seen in the example, 2-element candidate sequential data arrays were created based on elements. The frequency values of the 2-element candidates on the dataset were calculated. 2-element candidates which are below the support value were eliminated. Using the remaining 2-element frequently recurring sequential data, an updated dataset of 2-element datasets to be used in the next iteration was generated as ID-0: BC, BD, BF, CD, CF, DF; ID-1:BD, BC, BF, DF, CF; ID-3: BC, BD, CD.

In the second iteration, the operations performed in the previous iteration are applied to the dataset consisting of 2-element sequential data. The updated dataset resulting from this iteration is as follows: ID-0: BCD, BCF, BDF; ID-1:BDF, BCF; ID-3: BCD.

In the example, in the third iteration the algorithm exits the loop, since data sequences with a length of 4 elements cannot be created. The output of the algorithm, which shows sequential patterns in the given dataset, are B, C, D, F, BC, BD, BF, CD, CF, DF, BCD, BCF, and BDF.

The time and memory complexity of the proposed algorithm was investigated by experimental tests.

5   Experiments

5.1   Test Design

An Apache Spark cluster was set up to test the proposed algorithm. This setup consisted of 4 worker nodes and 1 master node. Each worker node consisted of 1 CPU core and 2 GB of RAM, while the master node consisted of 1 CPU core and 3 GB of RAM. This Apache Spark environment was built on a virtual machine. Processor speeds within the virtual machine were dynamically adjusted by the hypervisor. The mainframe includes 16 GB of RAM and an Intel Core i7-10510 processor. For comparison, PrefixSpan, GSP, and the proposed algorithm were implemented on Spark. PrefixSpan is readily available in the PySpark library.

During the tests, the execution times and memory usage of these three algorithms were recorded. In order to obtain more consistent results, each test was performed 10 times, and their standard deviations and averages were calculated.

- Execution time: It measures the time between the start and end times of the algorithm for each run.
- Memory usage: Instant memory usage per second is recorded and averaged during operations on a single node.

5.2   Dataset

In the experiments, ChainStore dataset is used. it is a open-source dataset which includes customer purchses from a huge grocery in the United States of America, was used as the dataset. This dataset was obtained from the digital database SPMF [18]. The ChainStore dataset contains 1,112,949 transaction rows, 46,086 unique products, and an average of 7.23 products per transaction.

5.3 Results

Figure 1 shows the execution times for the ChainStore dataset of the three algorithms we ran on Apache Spark. These execution times are also classified according to the total number of worker nodes in the running environment. As seen from the obtained results, the proposed algorithm performs better than the other algorithms in terms of speed.

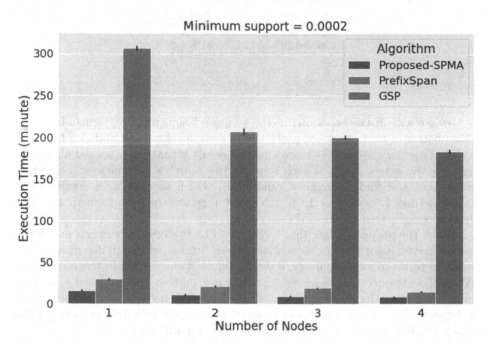

Fig. 1. Execution times of algorithms on different number of worker nodes.

Tables 1 and 2 show the minimum, maximum, and average memory usages of the three algorithms for the master and a worker node. The results show that the proposed algorithm requires less memory than GSP but more memory than PrefixSpan.

Table 1. Memory usage of a worker node

Algorithm	Min.	Max.	Mean
Proposed-SPMA	18%	80%	60%
GSP	20%	85%	74%
PrefixSpan	20%	82%	62%

In this study, a series of tests were conducted for the proposed algorithm in the Apache Spark environment. In the tests carried out to reveal the running time and memory requirements of the proposed algorithm, the proposed algorithm was compared with GSP and PrefixSpan on a different number of worker nodes in terms of speed and memory usage.

Table 2. Memory usage of the master node

Algorithm	Min.	Max.	Mean
Proposed-SPMA	21%	91%	80%
GSP	20%	91%	85%
PrefixSpan	39%	52%	49%

As a result of the experiments, the proposed algorithm performs almost 10 times better in terms of speed performance compared to GSP and also better in terms of memory usage. The reason for this result is that the proposed algorithm narrows the search space at each step. As the search space narrows, candidate generation and finding frequent candidates, which are the most costly parts, take less time. Likewise, as the search space narrows, the average memory usage decreases compared to the GSP.

When the proposed algorithm is compared to PrefixSpan, which is one of the fastest known algorithms of sequential pattern mining, although it is disadvantageous in terms of memory usage, it works almost twice as fast in terms of speed. When the obtained results are evaluated, it is seen that the proposed algorithm runs faster than the PrefixSpan algorithm. Since the dataset used in the tests is a dataset in which the search space can be narrowed easily, this property of the dataset may decrease the running time for our algorithm.

6   Conclusion

In this research, a new sequential pattern mining algorithm is proposed that will work on large-scale datasets containing sequential single-elements. The pseudocode of the proposed algorithm is given, and the working logic of the algorithm is shown in the example.

A prototype application has been developed to demonstrate the success of the proposed algorithm. Using this prototype implementation, the performance of the algorithm in terms of accuracy, running time, run-time memory requirement metrics are compared with the algorithms in similar categories.

The results of the experimental studies show that the proposed algorithm performs very high performance in terms of running time requirements for large-scale datasets.

Our future work will include examining the performance of our proposed sequential pattern mining algorithm on different large datasets. In addition, our future research will include a comparative evaluation of the proposed algorithms with other sequential pattern mining algorithms in the literature.

Acknowledgements. This study was supported by BiletBank R&D Center. We would like to thank BiletBank for providing us with the necessary hardware and access to their datasets.

References

1. Agrawal, R., Srikant, R.: Fast algorithms for mining association rules in large databases. In: Proceedings of the 20th International Conference on Very Large Data Bases, VLDB 1994, pp. 487–499. Morgan Kaufmann Publishers Inc., San Francisco (1994). https://doi.org/10.5555/645920.672836
2. Anil, R., et al.: Apache mahout: machine learning on distributed dataflow systems. J. Mach. Learn. Res. **21**, 1–6 (2020)
3. Bahadır, D., et al.: A big data processing framework for self-healing internet of things applications. In: 12th International Conference on Semantics, Knowledge and Grids (SKG) (2016)
4. Burak, C., et al.: Data feature selection methods on distributed big data processing platforms. In: 3rd International Conference On Computer Science And Engineering (2018)
5. Casado, R., Younas, M.: Emerging trends and technologies in big data processing. Concurr. Comput. Pract. Exp. (CCPE) J. **27**(8), 2078–2091 (2015)
6. Duygu, S., et al.: Implementation of association rule mining algorithms on distributed data processing platforms. In: 4th International Conference on Computer Science and Engineering (UBMK) (2019)
7. Fournier-Viger, P., Lin, J.C.W., Kiran, R.U., Koh, Y.S., Thomas, R.: A survey of sequential pattern mining. Data Sci. Pattern Recogn. **1**(1), 54–77 (2017)
8. Han, J., Pei, J., Yin, Y.: Mining frequent patterns without candidate generation. SIGMOD Rec. **29**(2), 1–12 (2000). https://doi.org/10.1145/335191.335372
9. Kim, B., Yi, G.: Location-based parallel sequential pattern mining algorithm. IEEE Access **7**, 128651–128658 (2019)
10. Li, H., Zhou, X., Pan, C.: Study on GSP algorithm based on hadoop. In: 2015 IEEE 5th International Conference on Electronics Information and Emergency Communication, pp. 321–324 (2015)
11. Meng, X., Bradley, J., Yavuz, B., Sparks, E., Venkataraman, S., Liu, D., Freeman, J., Tsai, D., Amde, M., Owen, S., et al.: Mllib: machine learning in apache spark. J. Mach. Learn. Res. **17**(1), 1235–1241 (2016)
12. Mooney, C.H., Roddick, J.F.: Sequential pattern mining-approaches and algorithms. ACM Comput. Surv. (CSUR) **45**(2), 1–39 (2013)
13. Pei, J., et al.: Mining sequential patterns by pattern-growth: the prefixspan approach. IEEE Trans. Knowl. Data Eng. **16**(11), 1424–1440 (2004). https://doi.org/10.1109/TKDE.2004.77
14. Pokou, Y.J.M., Fournier-Viger, P., Moghrabi, C.: Authorship attribution using small sets of frequent part-of-speech skip-grams. In: The Twenty-Ninth International Flairs Conference (2016)
15. Sabrina, P.N., Saptawati, G.P.: Multiple mapreduce and derivative projected database: new approach for supporting prefixspan scalability. In: 2015 International Conference on Data and Software Engineering (ICoDSE), pp. 148–153. IEEE (2015)
16. Sagiroglu, S., Sinanc, D.: Big data: a review. In: 2013 International Conference on Collaboration Technologies and Systems (CTS), pp. 42–47 (2013)

17. Secil, Y., et al.: On the performance analysis of map-reduce programming model on in-memory nosql storage platforms: a case study. In: International Congress on Big Data, Deep Learning and Fighting Cyber Terrorism (IBIGDELFT) (2018)
18. Spmf an open-source data mining library. http://www.philippe-fournier-viger.com/spmf/index.php?link=datasets.php, Accessed 15 Sept 2021
19. Srikant, R., Agrawal, R.: Mining sequential patterns: generalizations and performance improvements. In: Apers, P., Bouzeghoub, M., Gardarin, G. (eds.) EDBT 1996. LNCS, vol. 1057, pp. 1–17. Springer, Heidelberg (1996). https://doi.org/10.1007/BFb0014140
20. Tas, Y., et al.: An approach to standalone provenance systems for big social provenance data. In: 12th International Conference on Semantics, Knowledge and Grids (SKG) (2016)
21. Tufek, A., et al.: On the provenance extraction techniques from large scale log files. In: Concurrency And Computation-Practice & Experience (Early Access) (2021) https://doi.org/10.1002/cpe.6559
22. Uzun-Per, M., Gürel, A.V., Can, A.B., Aktas, M.S.: An approach to recommendation systems using scalable association mining algorithms on big data processing platforms: A case study in airline industry. In: 2021 International Conference on INnovations in Intelligent SysTems and Applications (INISTA), pp. 1–6. IEEE (2021)
23. Uzun-Per, M., Can, A.B., Gürel, A.V., Aktas, M.S.: Big data testing framework for recommendation systems in e-science and e-commerce domains. In: 2021 IEEE International Conference on Big Data (Big Data), pp. 2353–2361. IEEE (2021)
24. Uzun-Per, M., Gurel, A.V., Can, A.B., Aktas, M.S.: Scalable recommendation systems based on finding similar items and sequences. Concurr. Comput. Pract. Exp., e6841 (2022)
25. Wang, J., Han, J., Li, C.: Frequent closed sequence mining without candidate maintenance. IEEE Trans. Knowl. Data Eng. 19(8), 1042–1056 (2007)
26. Wei, Y.Q., Liu, D., Duan, L.S.: Distributed prefixspan algorithm based on mapreduce. In: 2012 International Symposium on Information Technologies in Medicine and Education, vol. 2, pp. 901–904 (2012)
27. Yasin, U., et al.: Technical analysis on financial time series data based on mapreduce programming model: a case study. In: International Congress on Big Data, Deep Learning and Fighting Cyber Terrorism (IBIGDELFT) (2018)
28. Yasin, U., et al.: On the large-scale graph data processing for user interface testing in big data science projects. In: 8th IEEE International Conference on Big Data (Big Data) (2020)
29. Yu, X., Li, Q., Liu, J.: Scalable and parallel sequential pattern mining using spark. World Wide Web 22(1), 295–324 (2018). https://doi.org/10.1007/s11280-018-0566-1
30. Yu, X., Liu, J., Liu, X., Ma, C., Li, B.: A mapreduce reinforced distributed sequential pattern mining algorithm. In: International Conference on Algorithms and Architectures for Parallel Processing, pp. 183–197 (2015)
31. Zaharia, M., et al.: Apache spark: a unified engine for big data processing. Commun. ACM 59(11), 56–65 (2016). https://doi.org/10.1145/2934664
32. Zaki, M.J.: Spade: an efficient algorithm for mining frequent sequences. Mach. Learn. 42, 31–60 (2004)
33. Zaki, M.J., Parthasarathy, S., Ogihara, M., Li, W.: New algorithms for fast discovery of association rules. In: The Third International Conference on Knowledge Discovery and Data Mining (KDD-97), pp. 283–286. AAAI Press, Newport Beach (1997)

Correction to: Decomposition, Depositing and Committing of Digital Footprint of Complex Composite Objects

Viktor Uglev⬛ and Kirill Zakharin⬛

Correction to:
Chapter "Decomposition, Depositing and Committing
of Digital Footprint of Complex Composite Objects" in:
O. Gervasi et al. (Eds.): *Computational Science and Its*
Applications – ICCSA 2022 Workshops, **LNCS 13377,**
https://doi.org/10.1007/978-3-031-10536-4_17

In an older version of this chapter, the first and last names of the authors were incorrectly ordered. This has been corrected to "Viktor Uglev" and "Kirill Zakharin".

The updated original version of this chapter can be found at
https://doi.org/10.1007/978-3-031-10536-4_17

Author Index